Voters, Parties, and Elections

Voters, Parties, and Elections

Quantitative Essays in the

History of

American Popular Voting Behavior

JOEL H. SILBEY *Cornell University*

SAMUEL T. McSEVENEY *Brooklyn College*

Xerox College Publishing

Lexington, Massachusetts • Toronto

CONSULTING EDITOR: Irwin Unger, *New York University*

To the History Department of the University of Iowa, 1955–1960

Preface

More than twenty years ago the eminent political historian, Roy Franklin Nichols, called for a major reorientation of the study of American political history. Instead of the traditional narrowly focused research with "its exclusive interest in prominent leaders, so-called political issues and the incidents and statistics of campaigning," he wrote, historians should give full attention to "the more intricate causes of mass political behaviour. . . . Politics is but part of a composite pattern of the behaviour of society, and it is closely related to many other forms of behaviour. Consequently, it is essential to be actively interested in social analysis and to secure from the work of those in the other social sciences their ideas and methods. Two are of primary concern: the knowledge of social attitudes and their formation and adjustment, and the capturing and measuring of public opinion. Much progress has been made by psychologists and political scientists in these forms of analysis, but too little of this interest or technique has been much utilized by historians. The result has been contentment with too naive and simple explanations of political thought and action."[1]

In the following introductory essay we discuss the response to Nichols's challenge by a number of American political historians during the past two decades. The findings of their quantitative and behavioral research have been published in several books and many articles. Recently anthologies of this work, emphasizing the methods and concepts of behavioral analysis, have also appeared.[2]

---

[1] Roy F. Nichols, *The Historical Study of Anglo-American Democracy: An Inaugural Lecture* (Cambridge: Cambridge University Press, 1949), pp. 30–32.

[2] Robert P. Swierenga, ed., *Quantification in American History: Theory and Research* (New York: Atheneum Publishers, 1970); Don Karl Rowney and James Q. Graham, Jr., eds., *Quantitative History: Selected Readings in the Quantitative Analysis of Historical Data* (Homewood, Ill.: The Dorsey Press, 1969); and Lee Benson, Allan Bogue, J. Rogers Hollingsworth, Thomas Pressly, and Joel Silbey, eds., *American Political Behavior: Historical Essays and Readings* (New York: Harper & Row, Publishers, forthcoming).
Charles M. Dollar and Richard J. Jensen, *Historian's Guide to Statistics: Quantitative Analysis and Historical Research* (New York: Holt, Rinehart & Winston, 1971) is important on the purpose and methods of quantitative historical research; it also includes a valuable listing of sources and scholarly works in the field.

But one major aspect of recent research — analyses of popular voting behavior over time, studies that taken together offer a major reinterpretation of mass political behavior — has not hitherto been systematically presented in a single volume covering the broad span of American history. It is our hope that the following essays fill this gap.

Many individuals and organizations have contributed to this project. We particularly wish to thank our wives, Rosemary and Sandra; Mrs. Sandra Huttleston; and Professor Irwin Unger of New York University for their assistance.

Contents

Part One / The Historical Structure of American Popular Voting Behavior   1

✓ **1**   Classification of Presidential Elections   *Gerald Pomper*   5

2   Social Determinism and Electoral Decision: The Case of Indiana
V. O. Key, Jr., and Frank Munger   29

3   Analyzing American Voting, 1830–1860: Methods   *Ronald P. Formisano*   46

Part Two / Defining American Popular Voting Behavior, 1800–1860   57

4   Suffrage and Representation in Maryland from 1776 to 1810:
A Statistical Note and Some Reflections   *J. R. Pole*   61

5   Suffrage Classes and Party Alignments: A Study in Voter Behavior
Richard P. McCormick   72

6   Ethnocultural Groups and Political Parties   *Lee Benson*   83

7   The Basis of Alabama's Antebellum Two-Party System
*Thomas B. Alexander, Peggy Duckworth Elmore, Frank M. Lowrey, and
Mary Jane Pickens Skinner*   99

8   The Power of Political Frenzy   *Michael F. Holt*   121

**Part Three / Stability and Realignment: Cultural and Depression Politics,
1860–1896**   139

9   Immigrant Vote in the 1860 Election: The Case of Iowa
George H. Daniels   141

10   Northern Voters and Negro Suffrage: The Case of Iowa, 1868
Robert R. Dykstra and Harlan Hahn   155

11 The Religious and Occupational Roots of Party Identification: Illinois and Indiana in the 1870s   *Richard Jensen*   167

12 The Political Revolution of the 1890s: A Behavioral Interpretation   *Paul Kleppner*   184

13 Voting in the Northeastern States During the Late Nineteenth Century   *Samuel T. McSeveney*   195

Part Four / The Republican Era, 1896–1928   203

14 The Changing Shape of the American Political Universe   *Walter Dean Burnham*   205

15 A Portrait of Ethnic Politics: The Socialists and the 1908 and 1910 Congressional Elections on the East Side   *Arthur Goren*   235

16 The Progressives and the Working Class Vote in California   *John L. Shover*   260

17 Immigrant Ethnicity in a Changing Politics: Chicago from Progressivism to FDR   *John M. Allswang*   274

18 The Cities and the Election of 1928: Partisan Realignment?   *Jerome M. Clubb and Howard W. Allen*   291

Part Five / Recent American Voting Behavior: The New Deal and Beyond, 1932–1970   305

19 The "La Follette Revolution" and the Pittsburgh Vote, 1932   *Bruce Stave*   307

20 The Development and Persistence of Ethnic Voting   *Raymond E. Wolfinger*   313

21 Surge and Decline: A Study of Electoral Change   *Angus Campbell*   332

22 Stability and Change in 1960: A Reinstating Election   *Philip E. Converse, Angus Campbell, Warren E. Miller, and Donald E. Stokes*   349

23 American Voting Behavior and the 1964 Election   *Walter Dean Burnham*   366

24 Continuity and Change in American Politics: Parties and Issues in the 1968 Election   *Philip E. Converse, Warren E. Miller, Jerrold G. Rusk, and Arthur C. Wolfe*   396

Bibliography   429

The Historical Structure of
American Popular Voting Behavior

Part One

In recent years there has been a major revolution in the analysis of contemporary popular voting behavior. Political scientists and political sociologists have adopted modern polling techniques involving systematic surveys of voter attitudes to reveal how the individual voter makes up his mind on election day and the factors affecting his decision. The development of computer technology has made it possible to examine a wide range of social and economic information about voters as well. Data concerning the occupation, income, residence, religion, nativity, and party affiliation of individuals has been correlated with their political choices in order to discern relationships between such demographic characteristics and subsequent behavior at the polls. As a result of the application of these techniques, students of American political behavior have significantly recast their thinking about campaigns, elections, and voters.

The behavioral revolution in the study of voting has affected the study of American political history as well. A number of American historians have borrowed heavily from these new approaches in election research to try to illuminate past patterns of voting behavior. In particular they have adopted the political scientist's commitment to the systematic collection and manipulation of all available electoral and demographic data as the necessary prelude to interpreting voter decisions and campaign outcomes. Of course, political historians have traditionally concerned themselves with how Americans have voted. Studies of individual campaigns and elections, parties and politicians abound. Most historical studies, however, have focused on the strategic plans and operations of the political leadership in particular campaigns rather than on the behavior of the mass of the voters in one election or over time. Such an approach has lent itself to the extensive utilization of readily available surviving newspapers and manuscript collections. Furthermore, although many of these election studies have used statistical data, the amount that could be handled was always limited by its sheer bulk and the lack of any precise method for determining relationships among a mass of such evidence. However, the recent advances in techniques for processing statistical data and the resulting broadening and deepening of research in electoral behavior has provided a means and a model for historical election research, particularly in relation to understanding mass voting behavior over the course of the American past.

The "new political historian," to use Allan Bogue's apt term, closely following the example set by the political scientist, begins his research into past politics by determining the exact amount and location of the electoral support for each party in a given election within a defined set of election units: counties or, where local data are available, precincts, wards, and townships. He then measures changes in each party's support over two or more elections, including in his computations, presidential, congressional, and even off-year state and local contests, since several studies have indicated that significant changes in voting behavior often occur first in nonpresidential elections. The support for each party in particular voting units is also compared with relevant social and economic characteristics of the same electoral units to illuminate relationships between the two. The primary concern at each stage is to incorporate in the analysis as complete a set of election returns and relevant explanatory data as can be located in order to deal with as much of the electoral universe as one can and to assess all possible combinations and permutations in the complex patterns of voter choice.

The importance of these new efforts lies not only in their ability to deal with all voters, of course, but also and primarily in their findings, which have led to the significant restructuring and revising of our knowledge of American voting habits and patterns. The quantitative delimiting of party support over the course of our history has uncovered a strikingly cyclical quality to American electoral behavior. To begin with there have been long periods — during the Jacksonian era, from the Civil War into the 1890s, from the late 1890s until the 1930s and, finally, in the years since the New Deal — in which the support for each party remains steady from election to election as people repeatedly vote for the party with which they identify, despite the pressures of new issues, particular candidates, or intensive and dramatic campaigns. The significant fact about voters in a stable period is that, in the words of one of the outstanding students of current elections, "each election is not a fresh toss of the coin; like all good prejudices, the electorate's basic dispositions have a tremendous capacity to keep people behaving in accustomed ways."

These stable periods are ended by short but intense periods of critical changes in partisan alignments. As the consequence of some violent social or economic experience, a number of groups in the electorate find their traditional voting habits no longer congenial. Many of them permanently change their partisan loyalties, resulting in a new distribution of party support in the electorate and the birth of a new electoral era. Such realignments have occurred three times in our history — in the 1850s, the 1890s, and again in the 1930s — all with significant and long-lasting impact on the American political system.

Our appreciation of these voting cycles has significantly affected our thinking about particular elections. In stable periods, for example, the impact of a particular campaign has to be measured against the massive underlying partisan predisposition of most voters to cast their ballots as they always have. In realigning periods, on the other hand, the questions of which groups shift party allegiance and which remain steadfast and of when and where changes occur are of paramount concern to the analyst. In order to deal with these problems several scholars, building on the massive amounts of voting data we have acquired, have begun to classify every election in American history as to its individual place within the whole pattern of political cycles as the necessary first step prior to dealing with the underlying causes of stability and change in American electoral politics.

This cyclical quality in electoral patterns stems from the nature of individual voting behavior. Recent quantitative studies have carefully identified the different determinants that affect the way people vote in a given election. This research has underscored the primary importance of social and psychological variables such as religious affiliation or party identification in shaping contemporary voting behavior. Historical research has confirmed this for the past as well. Individual voting reflects a complex set of group values and prejudices rather than well-formulated conceptions of the issues currently being discussed. These values originate in the experiences of different groups within American society, the shared values and perspectives toward the world that develop out of these experiences, and, most crucially, the recurring clashes between different groups espousing conflicting norms that have characterized American history.

Analysis of voting data from the different eras of American history, furthermore, has brought into sharp focus the ethnocultural nature of the values that primarily affect voting behavior. Clashing religious and ethnic perspectives more often than anything else shape group attitudes toward politics and lead particular groups to identify with those political institutions that seem either to reflect their specific viewpoints or to serve their specific interests. American mass politics — the conflict between parties, candidates, and issues — has been primarily shaped by the clash of cultural values. Economic differences within the society have occasionally influenced voting behavior but usually have been subordinate to these cultural tensions except in periods of intense economic dislocations such as the 1890s and 1930s. Then some groups found their economic needs the most compelling influence on their political behavior despite the previous importance and continuing presence of cultural determinants. Nevertheless, as we shall see in some of the readings, even in periods of sharp economic conflict in politics, cultural differences strikingly continued to influence much voting behavior.

The political party system is central to the shaping of these group perspectives within the voting universe. As the study by Frank Munger and V. O. Key indicates, it is a simple fact that most voting behavior in any period can be understood and explained primarily in terms of the political party preference of individual voters. What seems to happen is that the various ethnocultural and socioeconomic conflicts shaping political attitudes in the first place become built into the different party coalitions. In a period of party formation or when major realignments of the constituent groups within each party occur, group perspectives are particularly influential in drawing people and different groups into specific parties. Each party, either in reality or symbolically, comes to absorb and reflect in its program and rhetoric major aspects of the norms and values of its constituent groups. In subsequent generations party identification becomes rooted in the habits of the electorate and party labels become the key to individual voting behavior. Despite the rise of new issues and the entry into the electorate of new individuals, these group perspectives and their manifestation in different parties remain potent enough to determine the predominant pattern of popular voting in most elections.

Quantitative analysts have also addressed attention to other properties of the electoral system; for example: (1) the level of voter turnout in specific elections and different eras; (2) the impact of constitutional and institutional changes on voting practices and behavior; and (3) the persistence of a normal system of two-party, rather than multiparty, politics throughout our history. (Third and even fourth and fifth parties have existed in most presidential elections, but usually with little voter appeal or impact on the general patterns of politics.) Some of the results of this research are incorporated in several of the articles included here. But the main significance of quantitative studies lies in their defining of the parameters of the electoral system: the different cycles and determinants of voting behavior.

Of course, historians have had to face some serious methodological and data problems in this research. The contemporary political analyst is fortunate in being able to focus on the individual voter through direct interviewing and polling. But the historian is not as lucky. He has only the aggregate election data to set against the aggregate characteristics of particular voting units. This presents difficulties to the researcher. Some of these stem from the quality of the evidence, others from its nature. Much electoral and demographic information is missing. Often voting and demographic data are not reported from comparable units, posing serious correlation problems. And we can never know from aggregate data just how any individual voter actually behaved. All we can deal with are the tendencies stemming from the apparent relationship between two types of group characteristics: voting behavior and demographic composition. Nevertheless there are many opportunities in this material for the deciphering and understanding of the voting behavior of the American people. The first three articles reprinted introduce some of the methods, problems, and basic findings of recent quantitative analysis of our political history. We have organized the balance of the essays into sections generally corresponding with the periods of stability and realignment that have characterized and defined American popular voting. The articles included in each part illuminate both the overall patterns of each electoral era as well as the specific nature of voting behavior in the different periods.

Classification of Presidential Elections*

Gerald Pomper

1

Gerald Pomper, a political scientist at Rutgers University, critically considers and sorts out the recent research into the structure of voting cycles in the American past. The result is a succinct and very useful description of the electoral history of the American people both across time and by type of election. Pomper's classification scheme, which relies exclusively on election returns from presidential contests, ignores a further refining point: many of the changes within the electoral system can be noted first and most dramatically in off-year elections. Nevertheless, his analysis does effectively illustrate the contribution such measuring devices make to the understanding of the nature of voting behavior throughout our history by providing a foundation for further research into specific eras and particular elections. A number of other definitional studies of the electoral structure are noted in the second footnote in Pomper's article and in the Bibliography.

The accumulation of voting research in the United States[1] has provided a foundation from which we can investigate more than the unique candidates, issues, and events of a specific election. Rather, we can focus on the similarities between different elections, attempt to classify them, and abstract some patterns from the historical realities. This article presents certain methods of classification using aggregate voting statistics, and offers a tentative categorization of presidential elections.

Comparisons between elections can perhaps most usefully be focused on the enduring factors in American politics, the parties, and their sources of support.

SOURCE: Reprinted with permission from *The Journal of Politics*, vol. 29 (August 1967), pp. 535–566.

*I wish to thank the Rutgers University Research Council for financial assistance, Judson James for many helpful comments, Mrs. Doris Paul for programming, I. H. Pomper for mathematical instruction, and Barry Seldes for aid in the calculations. Calculations were performed at the Rutgers Center for Computer Services.

V. O. Key stimulated such study in "A Theory of Critical Elections." Key pointed to "a category of elections . . . in which the decisive results of the voting reveal a sharp alteration of pre-existing cleavages within the electorate. Moreover, and perhaps this is the truly differentiating characteristic of this sort of election, the realignment made manifest in the voting in such elections seems to persist for several succeeding elections."[2]

Building on this concept, the authors of *The American Voter* suggested classifying elections into three categories: Maintaining, Deviating, and Realigning.[3] In the first two types of elections, there is no change in the basic patterns of party loyalty. In a Maintaining election, the "normal" majority party wins its expected victory; in Deviating cases, the minority party wins a short-lived tenure because of temporary factors, such as a popular candidate. In the Realigning election, much as in Key's critical election, the basis of voter cleavage is transformed.[4]

There are three important differences between these approaches: (1) Key's *scope* is narrower, as he is concerned principally with the unusual balloting, while the Michigan researchers attempt a classification of all contests, and tend to emphasize the importance and stability of party loyalty. (2) The *methods* are quite distinct. Key employs electoral data from geographic areas, such as towns in New England or counties or states in the rest of the nation. Campbell and his collaborators use national sample surveys. (3) Because of the last difference, the *historical period* considered differs. While the survey method allows greater precision, reliable data of this kind are lacking for the period before 1936. Electoral data, on the other hand, are available in some usable form for most of American history.[5]

Various methods may be employed in analysis of presidential elections which combine elements of these two schemes. Electoral data for geographic areas, states, are employed here in a four-fold categorization based on that of the Survey Research Center. The SRC classification cannot be used without change. As noted by Irish and Prothro,[6] the Michigan typology is based on two different dimensions which are not clearly distinguished. One of these dimensions is power, i.e., continuity or change in the party controlling the White House. The second dimension is electoral support, i.e., continuity or change in voter cleavages. Four combinations of these factors are possible, but the basic Michigan scheme includes but three.

The deficiency is due to ambiguous use of the Realigning category, applied to elections in which "the basic partisan commitments of a portion of the electorate change, and a new party balance is created."[7] This definition confuses two distinct effects: change in partisan commitments, and change in the party balance. Both results are evident when the former majority is displaced, as was the case in the period around the New Deal. It is also possible, however, that the reshuffling of voters can retain the same majority party, although it is now endorsed by a different electoral coalition. Partisan commitments change, while the party balance continues the same party as the majority.

The election of 1896, perhaps the classical critical contest, illustrates the problem. The Republican party was the majority both before and after this watershed year, winning six of eight presidential elections in each interval. The basis of its support changed significantly in 1896, even though the party balance was not affected. Given the ambiguities of their classification, the Michigan authors find it difficult to deal with this election. At one point, the contest is included in a series of Maintaining elections but, in the space of a few pages, it is discussed as Realigning.[8]

The classification represented in the diagram below [Figure 1.1] separates the two aspects of elections. The horizontal axis is the power of the "normal" majority party. The vertical dimension is continuity or change in electoral cleavages.[9] The terms Maintaining and Deviating are used in a manner similar to that employed by the SRC. Realigning is reserved for elections in which a new majority party comes to power as the electorate substantially revises its loyalties. If the invention of a new label may be excused, Converting is offered as a term for elections in which the majority party retains its position, but there is considerable change in its voter base.

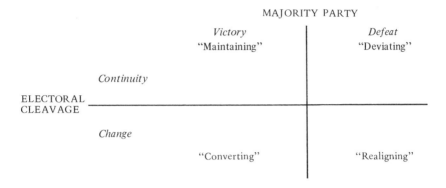

Figure 1.1   *A Classification of Presidential Elections.*

The problem is one of assigning given elections to the proper category. The horizontal dimension presents no difficulties. There are only two possible outcomes, victory or defeat of the majority party, and these are historical facts. Complexities arise in regard to the vertical dimension, in knowing whether a particular result signifies electoral continuity or change. Since both are partially present in every contest, there can be no simple solution. Some reasonable means is needed to locate critical elections, by distinguishing a Maintaining from a Converting victory of the majority party, and discriminating between Deviating and Realigning triumphs of the minority. To deal with these questions, various statistical procedures are applied here to presidential state voting results. If these techniques are valid, they should be applicable to more extensive and detailed studies, using elections for other offices and using data more detailed than the statewide results employed here.

Methods of Classification

A change in the parties' bases of support would be evidenced in various changes in the election returns. The geographical distribution of each party's vote would be different from the past: traditional strongholds would fall, while new areas of strength would become evident. Statistically, the vote in a critical election would not be closely associated with previous results. In individual states, each party's vote would likewise tend to diverge measurably from traditional levels. Taking all states together, each party would experience both gains and losses. The Democratic percentage of the vote, for example, would increase in erstwhile rock-ribbed Republican areas, but would decline in previously Democratic geographical bastions.

Correlation of Successive Elections

The first method employed here is linear correlation of the state-by-state results in paired presidential elections. Linear correlation will indicate the degree to which the results in two elections are similar. The basic data were the Democratic party's percentage of each state's total vote from 1824 to 1964.[10] Each election constituted a variable, and the Democratic percentage in each state was a case of that variable. Each election, or variable, was then paired and correlated with that in every other election. An additional problem is created by the presence of significant third parties in many presidential elections. The possibility exists that these splinter groups are receiving votes which ordinarily would be cast for the Democrats. To deal with this possibility, separate correlations were made. The third party percentage was added to the Democratic share, and the totals for the given year then constituted a new variable, to be correlated with every other election. In all there are forty-seven variables, and a total of 46 +45 ... +1 pairings, or 595 totally.[11] The resulting coefficients provide a measure of the association of the geographical distribution of votes in paired elections.

Correlation analysis will indicate the relative degree of electoral continuity or change. If there is high geographical continuity between two elections, regardless of partisan victory or defeat, the correlation coefficient should be high. If there is change, even if the same party wins both elections considered, we should find a relatively low coefficient.[12] The basic assumption here is that change in the electorate's party preferences will be revealed by changes in the various states' support of the Democrats.[13]

Figure 1.2 pictures the correlation of the Democratic vote in successive elections. The peaks of the diagram indicate that Democratic support in the designated election was highly related to that in the preceding presidential contest. The valleys indicate a change in the sources of support.[14] Significant change in electoral cleavages appear to have occurred five times in American history: (1) Van Buren's victory in 1836; (2) The Civil War and Reconstruction period, with the elections of 1864 and 1872 particularly significant; (3) The Populist and Bryan period of 1892–1896; (4) The time of the Great Depression, particularly in the contests of 1928 and 1932; and (5) The current era, most prominently the Kennedy and Johnson victories of 1960 and 1964. Questions can be raised about each of these, but a fuller discussion can be postponed until the other methods of classification have been presented.

Correlation with Average Democratic Vote

Each election is inevitably unique and will always differ somewhat from its predecessor and its successor. A given election may stand out not because it is truly a critical election, marking the end of one era and the beginning of another, but only because of temporary peculiarities. Thus, MacRae and Meldrum, analyzing shifts in the vote between successive elections, show increased dis-

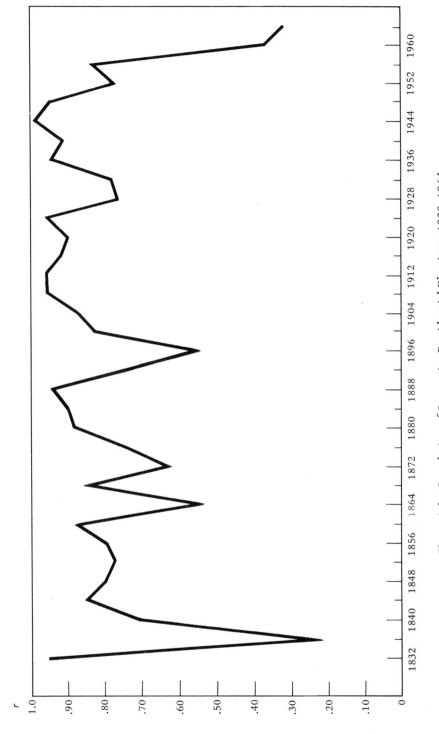

Figure 1.2 Correlation of Successive Presidential Elections, 1828–1964, Graphed at Latter Year.

person in 1920 and 1940, although there is no reason to believe that these elections revealed any basic change in the electorate.[15]

One means of moderating such eccentricities is to average the party's state votes in past elections. The mean Democratic vote in the four preceding elections is taken here to be the "normal" or traditional party vote. Four elections were chosen as sufficient to eliminate influences due solely to particular candidates or similar factors, while avoiding the inclusion of too many elections, and thereby making it difficult to detect significant changes.[16] In a second operation the Democratic state-by-state vote in each election was then correlated with the averages for each state's vote. Separate calculations were again made for those years in which significant third parties existed. Because of the various combinations of third parties possible, an additional ninety-nine correlations result.

Figure 1.3 represents the correlations between the Democratic vote by states in the designated years and the "normal" party vote. The pattern is similar to that in Figure 1.2, with the same dates indicated as critical elections, but there are some refinements. In general, the electoral eras pictured are more distinct from one another. Certain erraticisms are eliminated. The low correlation for 1872 is seen as due largely to the peculiarities of the previously paired contests of 1868 and 1872, rather than any enduring change in the 1872 election itself. In the New Deal period, the election of 1928 stands out as the time of change. In our own time, realignment beginning in 1952 is made more apparent, with the uniqueness of the 1964 election heavily emphasized.

Correlation Matrices

Emphasizing single elections, even critical ones, can be misleading. We cannot assume that all contests between two critical elections are similar, or that no change occurs between them. Instead of focusing on individual results, we can seek to identify periods of voter stability, or electoral eras. These eras are identified by correlations of nonsuccessive elections.[17]

When a stable, persistent voter coalition is established, the vote in nonsuccessive elections will be highly correlated. To identify such eras, the correlation coefficients of the Democratic vote in paired elections over a period of years are placed in a matrix.[18] To be considered in a stable era, the vote in a given year must be related not only to the immediately following or preceding election, but to *every other* consecutive election in that era. Even in a period of change, a large proportion of the voters retain their party loyalty, and spurious correlations may result. Requiring high correlation to a series of elections should avoid inclusion of votes with such meaningless correlations in the designated eras.[19]

Table 1.1, a matrix of the Democratic vote in paired elections from 1924 to 1964, illustrates the method. The core or stable electoral era is the period from 1932 to 1948. Each election in this period is related to every other at a high level, no coefficient being lower than .84. Correlation with the earlier elections of 1924 and 1928 falls below this level, indicating differences in the Democratic party's geographical sources of support from one period to the next. Correlations with the Eisenhower elections are too low to be included in the core period as well, the 1952–1956 votes apparently constituting the postscript to the New Deal Democratic period. A changed basis of support is sharply evident in 1960 and 1964.

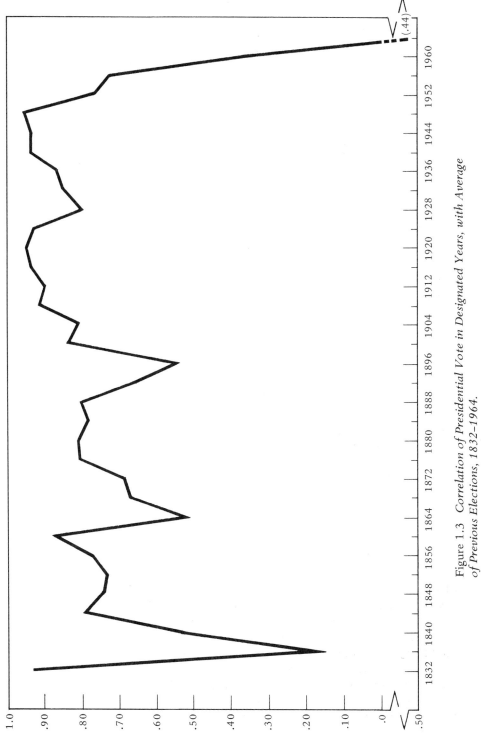

Figure 1.3 *Correlation of Presidential Vote in Designated Years, with Average of Previous Elections, 1832–1964.*

11

	Election Years									
	1928	1932	1936	1940	1944	1948	1952	1956	1960	1964
1924	.77	.79	.78	.88	.86	.88	.72	.54	.18	−.59
	(.79)	(.95)	(.93)	(.87)	(.84)	(.88)	(.57)	(.59)	(.07)	−.73
1928		.78	.76	.80	.82	.85	.58	.43	.22	−.56
1932			.93	.86	.84	.90	.58	.64	.09	−.73
1936				.93	.91	.90	.66	.66	.15	−.74
1940					.98	.94	.78	.64	.27	−.67
1944						.94	.80	.67	.30	−.68
1948							.77	.71	.21	−.68
	(−.43)	(−.29)	(−.32)	(−.36)	(−.41)	(−.33)	(−.16)	(−.08)	(.16)	(.65)
1952								.84	.56	−.39
1956									.38	−.47
1960										.32

*Row figures in parentheses refer to the combined Democratic and Progressive vote in 1924 and the vote of Truman alone in 1948.

Correlation matrices for overlapping earlier periods are presented in reverse chronological order in Tables 1.2, 1.3, and 1.4. The previous stable period seems to be 1900–1920, with the lowest coefficient of any pair of elections .87, a very high degree of association. The coefficients are somewhat lower for 1924, partic-

Table 1.2   Correlation of Democratic Vote in Presidential Elections, 1896-1928[*]

	Election Years								
	1900	1904	1908	1912	1916	1920	1924		1928
1896	.82	.53	.67	.53	.74	.59	.48	(.70)	.47
1900		.87	.93	.88	.93	.89	.83	(.88)	.77
1904			.94	.95	.89	.95	.96	(.81)	.81
1908				.94	.93	.92	.91	(.88)	.79
1912					.92	.93	.93	(.88)	.79
1916						.91	.85	(.90)	.80
1920							.97	(.83)	.76
1924									.77

*Figures in parentheses in 1924 column refer to the combined Democratic and Progressive vote.

ularly if the Progressive vote is added to the Democratic, and lower still in 1928. Another grouping is found in the period 1876–1888, with all paired elections evidencing a coefficient of .70 or better. A similar relationship is found for the elections from 1844–1860. Coefficients for elections in the nineteenth century tend to be lower than in later periods, perhaps partially because of the changing number of states in each contest.[20] However, the median coefficient in the 1876–1888 period is .86 and, in 1844–1860, it is .79.

Of the total of thirty-five presidential elections since the initiation of broad popular participation, we can classify twenty as included within four eras of electoral stability. Critical elections are not usually part of these stable periods, but serve as breaking points, ending one era and leading to the next. Other con-

Table 1.3 Correlation of Democratic Vote in Presidential Elections, 1856-1896*

	Election Years									
	1860	1864	1868	1872	1876	1880	1884	1888	1892	1896
1856	.89	.60	.53	.71	.80	.82	.84	.73	.61	.79
1860		.55	.63	.68	.78	.83	.86	.79	.54	.84
		(−.06)	(−.26)	(.03)	(−.19)	(−.30)	(−.16)	(−.24)	(−.31)	(−.27)
1864			.85	.55	.65	.62	.60	.67	.17	.09
1868				.62	.64	.68	.57	.56	.38	.33
1872					.75	.58	.47	.33	.29	.22
1876						.88	.80	.70	.49	.47
1880							.90	.87	.68	.63
1884								.93	.61	.61
1888									.71	.64
1892										.54
	(.80)	(.31)	(.41)	(.30)	(.58)	(.75)	(.74)	(.80)	(.70)	(.75)

*Row figures in parentheses refer to the Douglas vote alone in 1860 and the combined Democratic and Populist vote in 1892.

Table 1.4 Correlation of Democratic Vote in Presidential Elections, 1828-1864*

	Election Years									
	1832	1836	1840	1844	1848	1852	1856	1860		1864
1828	.93	.05	.38	.68	.60	.67	.82	.79	(−.37)	.39
1832		.22	.50	.77	.65	.74	.77	.77	(−.25)	.08
1836			.71	.62	.46	.48	.24	.17	(.25)	.06
1840				.84	.63	.61	.45	.36	(.14)	−.02
1844					.79	.80	.74	.70	(−.09)	.27
1848						.78	.79	.69	(.15)	.31
1852							.81	.84	(.12)	.46
1856								.89	(−.24)	.60
1860										.55

*Figures in parentheses in 1860 column refer to Douglas vote alone.

[Handwritten note across table: *significant variation within this*]

tests represent transitional elections before and after critical times. The last stable period ended in 1948 with Truman's victory. Since then we have seen four transitional elections significantly different in the geographical distribution of the vote from the preceding period. This last conclusion is seemingly in conflict with the results of voting surveys, which posit considerable stability in the voters' partisan predispositions. We will return to the consideration of this important question after discussing two other methods of analysis and surveying the overall results.

Variations from State Averages

The remaining methods concern the variations in state voters from "normal" Democratic percentages. Even in periods of stability, the state-by-state vote will vary from one election to the next. In periods of substantial alteration in voting cleavages, however, the changes will be larger and more geographically dispersed. For each year, the absolute difference between each state's vote and its "normal" Democratic percentage was calculated. These state differences were then averaged to yield a single national figure. The expectation was that changes from past voting habits would be reflected in a correspondingly higher national mean.[21]

The results of this procedure are charted in Figure 1.4. The regular pattern of the earlier graphs is not evident here, with relatively high means, or apparent voter change, recorded not only in predictable years such as 1896, but also in such unlikely times as the 1916 election.[22] These anomalies indicate the deficiencies of the mean alone as a measurement of change. High means will exist in critical elections, but may also occur even when there is no basic change in the electorate. In a Deviating election, there is likely to be considerable change from past voting habits, although the change does not persist. Thus, in 1916, the peace issue, the reforms of the first Wilson administration, and the remaining Progressive defections induced a crucial marginal group of voters to defect from the normally dominant GOP. This change, however, constituted no essential change in voter loyalties and was short-lived.[23]

The standard deviation provides a means of further distinguishing these two types of elections, by measuring the dispersal of state differences around the national mean. A Deviating election is the result of largely temporary factors, the effect of which is felt generally in the electorate. The shifts of the individual states will therefore tend to be within a relatively narrow range. A low standard deviation will result.[24]

In an election in which cleavages are significantly altered, voters are not equally affected, nor do they tend to be attracted only toward one party. Rather there are movements of unequal degree and in both partisan directions. The shifts of the individual states will therefore vary considerably, and the standard deviation will be relatively high.

Figure 1.5 represents the standard deviation around the national mean of state differences over time. The pattern is pleasantly regular, and there are few anomalies. The standard deviation for 1916, for example, is a low 5.39, substantiating our earlier belief that this was a Deviating rather than a critical election.

Conveniently, the pattern corroborates many of our earlier conclusions. There are peaks in 1836, 1864, 1896, 1924, and 1964, indicating the movement of voters between the parties in these years. However, we find not only isolated critical elections, but periods of assimilation after a decisive vote, indicated by the gradually declining standard deviations, and periods of development before a vital election, with increasing standard deviations. The 1964 increase, for example, was preceded by changes in the four earlier contests.

A Survey of Presidential Elections

We now have five statistical measures available with which to classify elections. To summarize, an ideal Converting or Realigning election would be likely to show a low correlation to the immediately preceding election, to the average of four preceding elections and to the series of individual elections which both precede and follow it. The mean of state differences from the "normal" state votes and the standard deviation would tend to be high. In a Converting election, the majority party would retain its status; in a Realigning con-

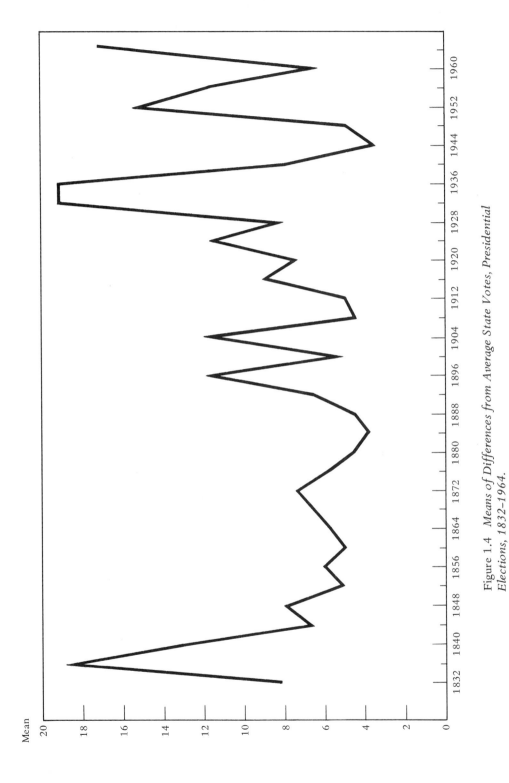

Figure 1.4 Means of Differences from Average State Votes, Presidential Elections, 1832–1964.

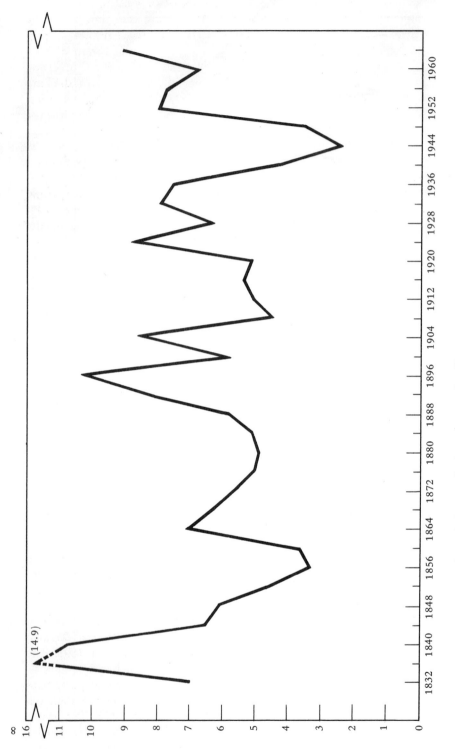

Figure 1.5   *Standard Deviation of Differences from Average State Votes,
Presidential Elections, 1832–1964.*

test, the former minority would become dominant. In the model
Deviating election, the opposite statistical results would be evid
ity party would win the White House in the Maintaining cas
temporarily displaced in a Deviating contest. (Detailed statistic
sented in the Appendix.)

By all indications, the victory of Martin Van Buren in 1836
election. There is a low correlation to the 1828 and 1832 votes, a
increases in the mean of state differences and the standard deviation. Historica
evidence indicates a considerable change in the leadership of both parties, the
center of gravity of the Democratic party moving away from the South toward
the Middle Atlantic states. In the balloting, the basis of party support shifted
strongly in the same direction. The Democrats gained ten or more percentage
points in the six New England states, and lost a similar proportion in ten states,
seven of them slave areas. As McCormick writes of the South in particular,
"Although the new alignments did not become firm in some states until after
1837, the basic outlines of what were to be the Democratic and Whig parties
had been delineated."[25] By 1844 a period of electoral continuity is evident, relatively undisturbed by the plethora of third parties, the admission of new states,
and the substitution of the Republicans as the principal opposition party in 1856.

The second break in electoral continuity resulted from the Civil War. The
1860 vote, in the face of the contemporary upheavals, bears a strong resemblance to the past. If we combine the Douglas and Breckinridge percentages, the
total shows a correlation of .89 with the 1856 results. The party did not change
its geographical support, in other words, but this support had divided into two
opposing factions.

During the War and Reconstruction, changes in party loyalty became evident.
The correlation coefficients tend to be low, whatever figure is used to represent
the Democratic vote of 1860, and the same conclusion results if we compare
later elections or use four-election averages. The net import of these statistics is
a definite break in traditional bases of support. The Republican party became
dominant in the nation, making 1864 a Realigning election. The degree of Republican victory in this year is exaggerated by the absence of the Confederate
states, but the signs of change are evident in the northern states alone, as the
Republicans assimilated former Whigs, Know-Nothings, Constitutional Union-
ists, and even Democrats. The party bore the new name of Union in 1864, and
"it is a much debated question," writes Dennis Brogan, whether it had much "in
common with the agglomeration of 'Anti-Nebraska' men of 1854, or even with
the Republican party of 1856 or 1860."[26] Readjustments in the electorate continued for some time after 1864. Stability returned in 1876, when a considerable
return to antebellum loyalties is evident.[27]

The post-Reconstruction system was not long-lived. Whatever measurement
is used, a transformation of the political order is evident with the Populist
movement of 1892 and the Bryan-McKinley presidential contest of 1896. The
change is evident in both of these years, not only in 1896, which is often classified as the single crucial election of the period.[28] Transformations in party support were geographically widespread. Nineteen states changed more than ten
percentage points from their "normal" Democratic vote in 1896. Ten states
showing Democratic losses were all located in the Northeast. Nine states with
large Democratic gains were all in the South and West. Extensive changes also

red within states and in the leadership of the parties, as evidenced in the centering of each party and in the campaign appeals to social class.[29]

The Populist party was a crucial element in the change. In 1892 Populist votes appear to have come largely from former Democrats; in 1896 many Populists then supported Bryan.[30] The decisive break of 1892–1896, however, did not immediately result in the establishment of a new electoral coalition. Future years saw additional changes, and Republican dominance was scaled more firmly in 1900 than in the more-noticed first contest of McKinley and Bryan. Thus, 1896 was a great watershed, but it did not by itself fix the future contours of American politics.

Another change in the party system took place, as is well-known, in the period 1924–1936. The discontinuity is evident in the measures used here, but it is less dramatic than the revisions of earlier periods. Unlike previous changes, those associated with the time of the depression and New Deal were not principally sectional in character. Realignment occurred in most states, along lines of social class, residence, and ethnicism.[31] Measurements of statewide voting can capture some of these changes, but not in the fine detail of sample surveys.

To the extent that aggregate figures are useful, they point to 1924 as a transitional year, and the Progressive party as a "halfway house" for those leaving their traditional party. Changes in this election are signified by the high mean of differences from "normal" state votes and high standard deviations. The Progressive vote probably came from former adherents of both major parties, but there is some indication that it tended to be more from Republican loyalists.[32]

The transition to a Democratic majority extended over a number of elections, but the most critical appears to be 1928. The correlation coefficients for this election are the lowest for any twentieth-century contest before 1960. Al Smith lost ten percentage points or more from the average Democratic vote in seven states, all of them southern or border. He gained strongly in seven other states, four of them urban and Catholic, the rest largely rural and Progressive. There was sufficient change in 1928 to constitute it a Realigning election, although the new Democratic majority did not become evident until 1932.[33] The new pattern was then continued for the next four contests.[34]

By the methods employed here, the four most recent presidential contests constitute another critical period, culminating in the 1964 conversion of the dominant Democratic majority. Strains in the New Deal coalition were already evident in 1948, when the Dixiecrats temporarily split the party. There was no fundamental alteration in that year, but greater change is evident in 1952, when all of our measures indicate discontinuity from the past. Shifts toward the Republicans occurred in all social groups and in all parts of the nation. Geographical variations were evident within the general trend. Differences from the four-election averages were greatest in sixteen states, all in the South or mountain regions.[35]

The 1964 election represents a radical break from past results, and the statistics strongly suggest that it was a Converting election, retaining the same Democratic party as the majority, but on a new basis of popular support. The correlation coefficients for this election are astoundingly low, given the generally moderate to high figures, even in the case of arbitrarily paired elections. The 1964 Democratic vote is positively related to that of only two years other than 1960, both involving third parties. Johnson's vote is related to Truman's vote alone in 1948 ($r = .65$), and to Douglas's vote alone in 1860 ($r = .40$). In ⟨ these cases the Democratic vote was highly sectional in character, and sever⟨ depressed in the South.

There was large variation from traditional Democratic levels in most states. Of course, the Democratic vote increased substantially, as Johnson gained the largest percentage of the total vote ever achieved by a Democrat. The important point is that the gains were not relatively equal in all states, as would tend to be the case if all areas were reacting only to the temporary oddities of Goldwaterism. The party vote decreased from its four-election average in the five Black Belt states of the South, while it increased over eighteen percentage points in eleven states of the Northeast and five of the Midwest.

The final test of a critical election must remain persistence. In the final analysis, 1968 and 1972 will tell if the pattern of 1964 did constitute a true Converting election. It is possible that the great transfer of voters between the parties was only a temporary reaction to the admittedly unusual circumstances of the time. It would be quite remarkable if such were the case. The events of 1964 left their mark in the control of state legislatures by the Democrats, the passage of "great society" legislation, intensification of the civil rights movement, organizational changes and conflicts in both parties, and the memories of the voters. Republican strength in the South continued to grow in the 1966 elections. Democrats lost considerably last November, but these losses were not simply a return to pre-1964 voting patterns. Democrats were elected in areas of former party weakness, such as Maine and Iowa, but were defeated in traditional bastions such as Illinois and Minnesota. The future impact of "black power" and other developments is now uncertain, but clearly significant. Change, not simple continuity, seems evident.

Limits and Problems

The apparent conversion of the electorate in recent years is generally contrary to the conclusions of sample surveys on the persistence of party identification. After the 1964 election, Stokes found "almost no perceptible shift in the single most important type of response disposition, the electorate's enduring party loyalties." [36] His conclusion both points to the limitations of the methods employed here, and offers an opportunity for discussion of some general problems of electoral analysis.

Geographical units are used here for analysis. We examine the voting patterns of states, not that of individuals, whose behavior must be inferred, rather than directly examined. Evidence of continuity or change in political cleavages is therefore evidence about the persistence of geographical bases of party support, not conclusions about the loyalties of demographic or psychological reference groups.

The use of areal units is partially the simple result of necessity: only these data are historically available. This form of analysis has intellectual validity as well. For much of American history, the important social conflicts have also been geographical, i.e., sectional, conflicts. Party loyalties have been grounded on areal issues, traditions, and leadership. Examination of aggregate voting returns can therefore provide insight into individual behavior. Conclusions based on this data will be made even more confidently as smaller geographical units are analyzed, and as social characteristics are correlated with political material.[37] Moreover, in dealing with the Presidency, we are dealing with a geographical system of selection, the electoral college. Since national parties are centered around the presidential contest, analysis of their support in geographical terms is legitimate.

Areal data are nevertheless subject to certain distortions. As the reapportionment controversy has reminded us, acres or political units are not people. There can be considerable discrepancy between the voting of states, as units, and of the particular voters within them. The likelihood of such discrepancy would appear to be increased when, as above, all states are counted equally regardless of population. To deal with this possibility, a second analysis was performed, using the same techniques, but weighting the vote of each state by its population. Details are provided in the Appendix. The striking conclusion is that there is very little effect on the results: the same elections are located as critical, and the statistics derived do not differ greatly from those obtained previously.

Another possible distortion is the masking of voter changes within a state. Apparent stability in the total state returns might disguise considerable, but countervailing, party shifts by individual voters.[38] When vote shifts are geographically concentrated, the methods employed here will tend to exaggerate the degree of change. In 1948 exclusion or inclusion of the Dixiecrat vote in Truman's total immensely affects all of our statistical indicators, even though the Dixiecrats received less than 3 percent of the national popular vote. The same factor accounts for the extremity of the shifts evidenced in 1960 and 1964, since vote changes have tended to be geographically concentrated, particularly in the South.

Results obtained using aggregate returns will therefore differ from those of surveys of an approximate random sample of individuals. Other differences are to be expected because this study focuses only on presidential voting, while surveys deal with other offices as well. Furthermore, we have been concerned with actual voting, while surveys emphasize "party identification," the voter's basic loyalty to a particular party. These identifications will show considerably less variation than the vote, and a vote for the opposition party will usually precede a change in identification. As Campbell himself suggests, the critical election provides a party with the opportunity, by its actions in office, permanently to win those voters who have given it power, or to regain its lost adherents.[39] Republicans for Johnson and Democrats for Goldwater may have made 1964 a Converting election, but the evidence in changed party identifications will not be fully apparent until later surveys.

These methodological differences are partially responsible for different conclusions about the meaning of recent elections. This analysis of aggregate election returns indicates a shift in electoral cleavages, with the 1964 election altering the geographical basis of support of the majority Democratic party. Reported survey results indicate the continuity of past loyalties. Both conclusions can be right, since they deal with different aspects of the political system.

Even the surveys, however, provide some indications that meaningful change is taking place, although it has not been highlighted by scholarly analysis. Even where identifications have not yet altered, "party images" have been modified. In the South, where the vote change has been greatest, Matthews and Prothro find significant revisions in what the voters "like" and "dislike" about the Democrats and Republicans. Such alterations of traditional images may be the prelude to the further step of changing identifications.[40] Outside the South, results both from the Michigan surveys and from other sources also indicate substantial change in voter perceptions of the parties. Some of the variation may be due to purely temporary factors, but "party images" also include tenacious elements, which directly affect the basic identification.[41]

Most importantly, there is evidence that there has been change in party identifications as well. Belief in their immobility has been an unquestioned, but perhaps unjustified, article of faith. The evidence that party identification has been stable is largely based on aggregate figures from the surveys, not on analysis of individual behavior. We find, for example, that the proportion of Republicans from 1952 to 1964 always remained in the range of 24 to 32 percent of the total electorate.[42] It is therefore assumed that a given 24 percent of the voters were always Republicans, that 68 percent never identified with the GOP, and that only 8 percent ever changed their loyalties. This is a vital error, the same error which is often made in the analysis of aggregate voting data. In both cases, the net change between parties is assumed to be the total change.

The case for stability in party identification is largely based on limited net change. In examining identifications in 1956 and 1960, for example, Converse's data show that 14 percent of southerners and 26 percent of non-southerners changed their loyalties to some degree. Yet, because there is no strong trend in one direction, he devotes little attention to these conversions.[43]

In theory, virtually all voters could have changed their party identifications from 1952–1964, even while the percentage supporting each party remained relatively stable. This is an unlikely situation, but it is also unlikely that the net change and the gross change are the same. Moreover, even marginal shifts can be decisive. An 8 percent change in the vote would usually create a landslide. Similarly, even an 8 percent change in identifications might be indicative of a Converting or Realigning election. In reality, the shifts in party identification are even higher.

The pattern of party loyalties is like a square dance — the important element in the dance is the movement and change of positions. We do not understand the dance by statically noticing that the number of sides to the square is always four or that there are equal numbers of men and women. The action comes when each dancer leaves one partner and takes another. To measure stability in party identifications, it is necessary to examine the behavior of individuals, as the Michigan surveys have indeed done. Ideally, respondents to a previous survey should be reinterviewed, as in the 1960 study. Alternately, persons can be asked to recall past identifications, as was done in the 1956 and 1964 surveys.

The results are interesting. Of the 1956 sample, 18 percent indicated that they had changed their party loyalty at some time in the past. Compare this finding to that obtained upon reinterviewing in 1960. In the intervening four years, using the same categories as in 1956, 11 percent of the total group had changed their identifications. (Changes from Independent *to* either Democratic or Republican, or from strong to weak partisanship are not included, only changes *from* the two parties.) In other words, there was more than half as much change in party loyalty in the four-year period from 1956 to 1960 as in all of the years (perhaps twenty for the average respondent) in which the interviewees had been politically active before 1956.

In 1964 a different sample was interviewed, of which 22 percent indicated some change in party identification in the past. Changes at all elections, not only in the previous four years, are included here. It seems significant that, eight years further away from the realignments induced by the depression and New Deal, stability in party loyalty had actually decreased in comparison to 1956.[44] Fuller analysis of these responses are necessary before any final conclusions are reached, but there does seem sufficient evidence, in the survey results themselves, to support a suspicion that party identification has not been unchanging, but rather that significant numbers of voters have been altering traditional loyalties.[45]

In recent elections, therefore, statistical analysis of state voting indicates considerable shifts in the geographical bases of party support. The extent of change found in sample surveys is less, but there are numerous clues in that material to justify a tentative belief that the 1964 presidential contest was indeed a Converting election.

Conclusions

It is now possible to summarize our findings and to attempt a classification of presidential elections. It is obvious that categorization is not a simple matter, for elections are not always of one type or another. Some convenient simplifications are lacking. For example, change in voter loyalties does not fit any neat cyclical pattern, with change occurring after a fixed number of years.[46] There is a tendency, it is true, for critical elections to occur approximately one in every generation, but the length of time between these contests varies considerably. The party system which became stabilized in 1876 lasted only until 1888, while the different party system which began to appear in 1924 still greatly affects politics today. Electoral change is periodic, but the periods are irregular.

Difficulties also exist in isolating the turning points in these periods, the critical elections. It is apparent that electoral change is neither unheralded nor precipitate. In most cases there is not a single critical election sandwiched between two periods of great stability. Rather there are times of unease preceding the most crucial year, and a period of assimilation after it. Typically the critical election represents a break in electoral continuity, but does not result in the immediate establishment of a new and persistent voter coalition. Thus, the elections identified as critical here do not show high correlations with later ballots, but following contests do demonstrate this stability. Persistence comes after the critical election, and partially as a reaction to its upheavals.

This conclusion is at variance with Key's original definition of a critical election. The disagreement is partially attributable to a difference in method. Key identifies critical elections by focusing on the extreme cases, the areas showing the most change toward or away from the new majority party. The methods used here are based on examination of all areas, and therefore include changes in the middle ranges as well. MacRae and Meldrum, who all also include all areas, show similar results — less precipitous changes coming in the total critical period, rather than in a single election.[47] Key himself recognized the point in his later writings.[48]

Despite the many pitfalls, it may be suggestive to position elections within the categories offered in Figure 1.1. The horizontal dimension clearly represents a nominal classification — the left and right sides are exclusive and exhaustive. The vertical dimension is more in the nature of a continuum — particular elections may not be clearly stable or critical, but may tend to an intermediate position. Therefore, the distinction between a Deviating and Realigning contest, or a Maintaining and Converting election, is somewhat subjective and arbitrary. The change which exists in every election is disguised, as is the existence of critical periods, rather than single crucial ballotings.

On the basis of the data developed here (listed in detail in the Appendix), the elections of 1836, 1896, and 1960–1964 are classified as Converting, and those of 1864 and 1928–1932 as Realigning. The victories of the first Harrison, Taylor, Lincoln in 1860, Cleveland, Wilson, and Eisenhower are considered Deviating, and the others are classified as Maintaining.[49] In order to isolate a small number of critical elections, fairly strict standards have been applied in making this classification. Modified standards would obviously change the designation of individual elections.

The most accurate characterization of our political history would be one of electoral eras. The life cycle of an electoral era typically begins with, or soon follows, a third-party election. The first such era began with the contest of 1836, in which the Democrats faced three opposition Whig candidates. The period came to an end in 1860 with the division of the Democratic party, and the nation. The next period ended with the emergence of the Populists in 1892, and the Republican dominance that began with the victories of McKinley began to disappear with the 1924 appearance of the La Follette Progressives. The end of the New Deal era was heralded by the Democratic split of 1948.

Third parties arise when traditional loyalty seems inadequate to many voters. Often the rise of third parties accompanies or precedes change in these loyalties sufficient to constitute a critical election. This election may continue the same party in power, on the basis of a realigned majority, or result in an overthrow of its power. The changes in the critical year itself, as we have seen, will not necessarily be permanent. Further readjustments are likely in succeeding contests.

After a time, stability is achieved. Stable periods tend to resemble earlier eras. Thus, after the adjustments which result from the critical election, correlations between paired elections of different periods are fairly high. For example, the correlation of the vote in 1876 and 1860 is .78; that in 1900 and 1888, .85; and that in 1932 and 1920, .80. Part of the process of readjustment is an apparent return by the voters in some states to past voting traditions. Even with the transformation of the electoral coalition, a strong degree of continuity is present.

The transition from one electoral era to another, resulting from considerable partisan movement by the voters, is an impressive manifestation of democratic control. Voters intervene decisively to change the political terms of reference. Party support and party programs become more congruent. Old policies and slogans are replaced by new, possibly more appropriate, appeals. The confusions of a waning order give way to the battle cries of an emergent party division. The Eisenhower elections did little to change the content of American politics from the dated themes of the New Deal. The Kennedy-Johnson administration, and the 1960–1964 elections, did present new issues and conflicts. If 1964 did indeed constitute a Converting election, it may have provided the electoral foundation for the governmental resolution of long-standing issues.

Appendix

Since this study is basically one of geographical distribution of party support, no special effort was made to compensate for differences among the states in population or votes. Moreover, past work on this subject, from Key onward, has used unweighted data. A number of readers, however, have suggested the desirability of weighting. To investigate the question, the procedures used were adapted for use with weighted data, leading to a new set of statistics, corresponding to those of Figures 1.3, 1.4, and 1.5.

The weight for each state was its number of representatives in Congress in the designated election year, or in the later of paired years. Although apportionment is not perfectly proportional to population, it is accurate, simple, and a reliable indicator of relative population. The electoral vote, a suggested alternative, was rejected because it is biased toward smaller states. The total vote for each state, another alternative, is more difficult to obtain accurately for distant elections, and harder to use statistically. Weighting by representatives changes the number of cases for each variable, or election. For 1964, illustratively, the number of cases is no longer the fifty states, but is the 435 representatives. Nevada and New York are no longer each a case. Delaware is still one case, but New York is forty-one.

No extended analysis of these results will be offered here; the data are included in the table below. In regard to the location of critical elections, weighted data tend to reinforce the original conclusions. Change in 1836, 1864, 1928, and 1960–1964 is even more marked, although the differences are not great. Weighted data reduce the degree of change evident in 1892–1896, but do not require any modification of these years' designation as a critical period. The general conclusion one would reach is that the additional computational problems occasioned by weighted data do not seem to bring proportionately increased insights. Indeed, in an unusual case, weighted data can cause new problems. The election of 1848, for example, becomes sharply distinguished by this method. The reason does not appear to be that 1848 was a critical election. Rather, the cause is the concentration of votes for the Free Soil party in New York. Van Buren's personal appeal in a state with nearly a sixth of the nation's representatives seriously distorts the weighted results, but his local attraction is not decisive if unweighted votes are used.

The table below [Table 1.5] summarizes all of the data obtained. Included for each year are coefficients of correlation with the previous election and the average of the previous four elections, the mean of state differences, and the standard deviation. The last three statistics for weighted data are also included in the appropriate columns. The number of "associated elections" denotes the number of consecutive elections before and after the given year which are highly correlated with the results of that year. (A high level is defined as a coefficient of .69 or better for the nineteenth century, and .82 for 1900 and later elections.) Each election is also provisionally classified as Maintaining, Deviating, Converting, or Realigning.

Table 1.5 Data for Classification of Presidential Elections[*]

†Year, Category	r: Last Election	r: Four Elections	Mean State Difference	Standard Deviation	Associated Elections Before	After
1832-M	.93	.93, .93	8.34, 5.90	6.83, 5.11	1	0
1836-C	.22	.14, .05	18.81, 15.73	14.89, 14.92	0	1
1840-D	.71	.54, .38	13.27, 12.37	10.56, 10.19	1	1
1844-M	.84	.79, .81	6.82, 6.69	6.22, 6.08	1	4
1848-D	.79	.75, .57	8.12, 10.04	6.02, 8.13	1	3
1852-M	.78	.74, .74	5.02, 4.22	4.53, 3.60	2	2
1856-M	.81	.78, .79	6.33, 6.39	3.35, 3.53	3	1
1860-D	.89	.86, .77	5.06, 5.25	3.55, 3.35	4	0
	(−.24)	(.02, −.29)	(24.33, 23.80)	(18.58, 18.43)	(0	0)
1864-R	.55	.51, .34	5.70, 5.98	6.78, 6.97	0	1
	(−.06)	(.31, .19)	(6.99, 7.43)	(7.69, 7.40)	(0	1)
1868-M	.84	.67, .63	6.43, 5.61	6.09, 5.93	1	0
1872-M	.62	.69, .61	7.41, 6.57	5.58, 5.19	0	1
1876-M	.75	.80, .78	5.94, 5.76	4.99, 4.69	1	3
1880-M	.88	.80, .78	4.50, 3.69	4.89, 4.34	1	2
1884-D	.90	.78, .77	3.88, 3.45	5.08, 4.79	2	1
1888-M	.93	.80, .79	4.38, 3.63	5.81, 5.38	3	1
1892-D	.71	.66, .73	6.55, 5.67	8.05, 5.67	1	0
	(.80)	(.76, .83)	(9.15, 6.87)	(9.95, 7.86)	(3	6)
1896-C	.54	.53, .70	11.53, 7.62	10.21, 6.85	0	1
	(.75)	(.71, .80)	(9.21, 7.02)	(8.49, 5.97)	(1	1)
1900-M	.82	.84, .94	5.16, 3.80	5.59, 3.30	1	6
1904-M	.87	.81, .91	11.68, 9.50	8.70, 6.17	1	5
1908-M	.95	.91, .96	4.47, 3.27	4.48, 3.19	2	4
1912-D	.94	.90, .95	5.02, 3.50	5.04, 3.77	3	3
1916-D	.92	.94, .95	8.96, 7.17	5.34, 4.49	4	2
1920-M	.91	.95, .95	7.30, 8.51	5.15, 5.19	5	1
1924-M	.97	.94, .96	11.69, 10.96	8.81, 8.04	6	0
	(.83)	(.89, .92)	(6.78, 5.48)	(5.71, 5.41)	(4	0)
1928-R	.77	.80, .77	7.94, 9.02	6.19, 6.18	0	0
	(.79)	(.81, .78)	(7.80, 7.97)	(6.12, 6.48)	(0	0)
1932-R	.77	.85, .89	19.21, 18.98	8.02, 6.86	0	4
1936-M	.93	.87, .89	19.20, 19.92	7.50, 6.97	1	3
1940-M	.92	.94, .94	7.78, 7.89	4.16, 4.27	2	2
1944-M	.98	.94, .96	3.35, 2.61	2.38, 2.06	3	1
1948-M	.94	.95, .95	5.01, 5.18	3.45, 3.26	4	0
	(−.33)	(−.35, −.24)	(12.86, 12.21)	(19.68, 18.15)	(0	0)
1952-D	.77	.77, .73	15.31, 13.62	7.98, 8.21	0	1
	(−.16)	(.76, .68)	(13.36, 11.93)	(5.72, 6.18)	(0	1)
1956-D	.83	.73, .71	11.77, 11.44	7.73, 7.31	1	0
1960-C	.37	.36, .28	6.05, 6.05	6.78, 5.83	0	0
1964-C	.31	−.44, −.55	16.82, 16.37	9.00, 7.91	0	0

[*]The second figure listed in columns 3, 4, and 5 are the statistics derived from state election results weighted by the number of congressional representatives.

†The data in parentheses refer: in 1860 and 1864, to the Douglas vote alone in 1860; in 1892 and 1896, to the combined Democratic and Populist vote in 1892; in 1924 and 1928, to the combined Democratic and Progressive vote in 1924; in 1948 and 1952, to the Truman vote alone in 1948. The categories are: M— Maintaining; D— Deviating; C— Converting; and R— Realigning.

NOTES

[1] The most notable works are those of the Survey Research Center, particularly Angus Campbell, et al., *The American Voter* (New York: Wiley, 1960) and *Elections and the Political Order* (New York: Wiley, 1966). A recent important work is V. O. Key, Jr., *The Responsible Electorate* (Cambridge, Mass.: Harvard University Press, 1965).

[2] *Journal of Politics*, vol. 17 (February 1955), p. 4. Key also suggested that critical elections evidenced deep concern and high involvement by voters. However, these characteristics are difficult to establish historially and are not vital to the concept. Further work on the subject includes Key, "Secular Realignment and the Party System," *Journal of Politics*, vol. 21 (May 1959), pp. 198–210; Duncan MacRae, Jr., and James A. Meldrum, "Critical Elections in Illinois: 1888–1958," *American Political Science Review*, vol. 54 (September 1960), pp. 669–683; and Charles Sellers, "The Equilibrium Cycle in Two-Party Politics," *Public Opinion Quarterly*, vol. 29 (Spring 1965), pp. 16–38.

[3] *The American Voter*, pp. 531–538. The additional category, Reinstating, is best understood as a subcategory of Maintaining. Cf. Philip Converse, et al., "Stability and Change in 1960: A Reinstating Election," *American Political Science Review*, vol. 55 (June 1961), pp. 269–280.

[4] Further work by the same authors on this subject is included in chapters 4, 7, and 10 of *Elections and the Political Order*.

[5] The Michigan researchers have resorted to this data when attempting to analyze the more distant past. For imaginative use of this material, see Lee Benson, *The Concept of Jacksonian Democracy* (Princeton: Princeton University Press, 1961). A general discussion of the uses and limits of electoral data is found in Austin Ranney, *Essays on the Behavioral Study of Politics* (Urbana: University of Illinois Press, 1962), chap. 2.

[6] Marian Irish and James Prothro, *The Politics of American Democracy*, 3rd ed. (Englewood Cliffs, N.J.: Prentice-Hall, 1965), pp. 300–301.

[7] *The American Voter*, p. 534; *Elections and the Political Order*, p. 74.

[8] *The American Voter*, p. 531, places Republican victories from the Civil War to the 1920s in the Maintaining category, but on p. 536, the authors write of "the realignment accompanying the election of 1896." In *Elections and the Political Order*, p. 74, the existence of a Republican majority prior to 1896 seems to exclude this election as Realigning, but on p. 76, McKinley is grouped with Lincoln and Franklin Roosevelt as victors in Realigning contests.

[9] The "normal" majority party must be assumed at some point in time for historical evidence. For example, we can make the rather safe assumption that the Democrats were the majority party after 1936. After the initial assumption, the election results will indicate when this majority status began and when other changes have occurred. Emphasizing the success or failure of a given party, rather than change as such, avoids the need for a subcategory such as the SRC's Reinstating election. It also avoids the problems, inherent in Irish and Prothro's scheme, of dealing with two consecutive Deviating elections, as in 1912–1916.

[10] The percentages are from Svend Petersen, *A Statistical History of the American Presidential Elections* (New York: Ungar, 1963); *Congressional Quarterly Weekly Report*, vol. 21 (March 26, 1965), p. 466.

[11] The third-party elections are those of 1848, 1860, 1892, 1904 to 1924, and 1948. It should be noted that the number of states (N for a given variable, or election) is not constant. It increased over time as new states were admitted to the Union and as states began to choose electors by popular vote. It decreased temporarily during the Civil War and Reconstruction, when Confederate states were excluded from the balloting. The correlation of any pair of elections, therefore, is only of those states participating by popular vote in both elections.

[12] For uses of this method using county data, cf. V. O. Key, Jr., and Frank Munger, "Social Determinism and Electoral Decision: The Case of Indiana," in Eugene Burdick and Arthur Brodbeck, *American Voting Behavior* (Glencoe, Ill.: The Free Press, 1959), pp. 281–299; and Thomas A. Flinn, "Continuity and Change in Ohio Politics," *Journal of Politics*, vol. 24 (August 1964), pp. 521–544.

[13] This assumption could prove false if voter realignment occurred within the states, but the net effect of countervailing movements was masked by statewide returns. The Democratic percentage in a given state might then remain stable, but the party's votes would be quite different from those of the past. Political developments affecting social groups differentially should be reflected, however, by unequal vote changes from one state to another. While the divergences of states have lessened greatly in recent decades, considerable diversity remains.

[14] The Democratic percentage of the total vote is used for all years, except 1860, where the Douglas and Breckinridge percentages are combined, and 1948, where the Truman and Thurmond percentages are combined. If the Douglas vote alone is used for 1860, the correlation coefficient drops to —.24. If the Truman vote alone is used, the coefficient decreases to —.41. Since both elections saw a short-lived division of the Democrats, not a real break, it seems appropriate to statistically reunite the factions.

[15] *Op. cit.*, Figure 1, p. 671.

[16] If a state had not participated in all of the four previous elections, its "normal" vote was assumed to be the mean for as many of the four in which it had voted—1, 2, or 3. The "normal" vote figure is therefore less reliable for the period immediately after a state has joined the Union. New states are not included at all for the first election in which they participated. Confederate states are included immediately upon rejoining the Union, their "normal" vote being the pre-war Democratic percentage.

[17] This procedure is suggested by MacRae and Meldrum, p. 670, although they only correlate successive elections. Cf. Benson's discussion, *op. cit.*, pp. 125–131, of "stable phases" and "fluctuation phases."

[18] I have adopted this method from David B. Truman, *The Congressional Party* (New York: Wiley, 1959).

[19] Of the total of 595 correlations of the forty-seven variables, relating elections over 140 years, the mean coefficient of correlation is a reasonably high .54, while the mode and median are .65.

[20] Between 1864 and 1896, the number of states participating in the Presidential election increased from twenty-five to forty-five. During the stable period of 1876–1888, only Colorado entered the electoral college. In 1844–1860, however, coefficients were high even though the number of states increased from twenty-five to thirty-two. Results for the 1824 election are not included because the data are unreliable and because few states then employed popular votes to choose the President.

[21] It is to highlight such changes that absolute differences are used. If signed arithmetical differences were used, negative and positive variations would tend to cancel one another. This method is different from that of MacRae and Meldrum, who measure changes only from one election to the next, *op. cit.*, p. 670, and also different from that of Sellers, *op. cit.*, p. 33f., who concentrates on the differences in the two parties' votes.

[22] It should be noted that this graph and the next are to be interpreted differently from Figures 1.2 and 1.3. Change in the earlier graphs was evidenced by a decline in the curve; in the present cases, change is evidenced by an increase in the vertical values.

[23] Cf. Arthur S. Link, *Wilson: Campaigns for Progressivism and Peace* (Princeton: Princeton University Press, 1965), especially chap. 4.

[24] The cleavages remain, although the partisan breaking-point may change. For a similar analysis of class voting, cf. Robert Alford, *Party and Society* (Chicago: Rand McNally, 1963).

[25] Cf. Richard P. McCormick, *The Second American Party System* (Chapel Hill: University of North Carolina Press, 1966), for an excellent account of the changes in the party system. The quotation is from p. 339.

[26] *Politics in America* (New York: Harper and Row, 1954), p. 55. Cf. David Donald, *The Politics of Reconstruction* (Baton Rouge: Louisiana State University Press, 1965).

[27] Correlation of the 1876 vote with that of Douglas in 1860 is —.19, but it is a high .78 with the combined Douglas and Breckinridge tallies.

[28] Cf. MacRae and Meldrum, *op. cit.*, pp. 678–681. The change in 1892 did not come only in western silver states. Indeed, six of these "radical" states were excluded from the 1892 calculations here, since they were not in the Union in earlier elections.

[29] Cf. Stanley L. Jones, *The Presidential Election of 1896* (Madison: University of Wisconsin Press, 1964).

[30] A statistical indication of the source of Populist votes is the higher correlation of the 1892 vote with that of 1888 (.81) when Populist and Democratic votes are added together than when Democratic votes alone are considered (.71). The correlation of the combined 1892 vote with that of 1896 is .75, higher than the coefficient achieved if comparison is made to the Democratic vote alone, .54.

[31] Cf. *The American Voter*, pp. 153–160; Samuel J. Eldersveld, "The Influence of Metropolitan Party Pluralities in Presidential Elections since 1920," *American Political Science Review*, vol. 43 (December 1949), pp. 1189–1205; Samuel Lubell, *The Future of American Politics* (Garden City: Doubleday, Anchor, 1956); Rutch C. Silva, *Rum, Religion and Votes* (University Park: Pennsylvania State University Press, 1962).

[32] The coefficient for the Democratic vote alone in 1920 and 1924 is extremely high, .97. If the Progressive vote is added to the Democrats' for 1924, however, the correlation falls to .83.

[33] Key, "A Theory of Critical Elections," and MacRae and Meldrum, also find 1928 to be critical. Smith gained votes in Massachusetts, Rhode Island, New York, Illinois, Wisconsin, Minnesota, and North Dakota.

[34] When change takes place over a number of years, classification of individual elections becomes awkward. It might be more precise to classify the 1928 election as a Converting or Deviating election to explain Hoover's victory, but it then becomes even more complicated to correctly appraise the 1932 results.

[35] For indication of change within the South, cf. Donald S. Strong, "The Presidential Election

in the South, 1952," *Journal of Politics*, vol. 17 (August 1955), pp. 343–389.

[36] Donald E. Stokes, "Some Dynamic Elements of Contests for the Presidency," *American Political Science Review*, vol. 60 (March 1966) p. 27.

[37] The Inter-University Consortium for Political Research is still in the process of obtaining and preparing county electoral data and Census material. When this immense task is completed, fuller national analysis will be possible.

[38] See H. Daudt, *Floating Voters and the Floating Vote* (Leiden: Stenfert Kroese, 1961), chap. 2, and the discussion of the New Deal period, pp. 553–554 above.

[39] *The American Voter*, pp. 554–555.

[40] Donald Matthews and James Prothro, *Negroes and the New Southern Politics* (New York: Harcourt, Brace and World, 1966), chap. 13.

[41] "Some Dynamic Elements of Contests for the Presidency," pp. 19–28; *The Harris Survey*, January 11, 1965; Thomas W. Benham, *Public Opinion Trends: Their Meaning for the Republican Party* (Princeton: Opinion Research Corporation, 1965).

[42] *Elections and the Political Order*, p. 13.

[43] *Ibid.*, pp. 224–226.

[44] Percentages are calculated from the data in *The American Voter*, Table 7-2, p. 148; *Elections and the Political Order*, Table 12-2, p. 225; and Inter-University Consortium for Political Research, *1964 Election Study Codebook*, Question 51, Deck 6, col. 11-12. SRC is now preparing further materials on this subject.

[45] In a more recent publication, Angus Campbell writes, "The question which the 1964 vote raises is whether we are entering a period of party realignment. . . . There are indications in our survey data of a movement of this kind." However, this conclusion is also based on analysis of the distribution of party identifications, not on changes in these loyalties. Cf. "Interpreting the Presdential Victory," in Milton C. Cummings, Jr., *The National Election of 1964* (Washington: The Bookings Institution, 1966), especially pp. 275–281.

[46] Cyclical explanations are advanced in Louis Bean, *How to Predict Elections* (New York: Knopf, 1948).

[47] MacRae and Meldrum, *op. cit.*, pp. 681–682.

[48] V. O. Key, Jr., *Politics, Parties, and Pressure Groups*, 5th ed. (New York: Crowell, 1964), p. 537.

[49] Two tests define a critical election: correlation to the last election and to the four-election average of less than .70 (in the nineteenth century) or .80 (twentieth century); and a coefficient of variation greater than .75. The latter measure is the standard deviation divided by the mean, with the result then multiplied by 100. Alternately, low correlation to the previous election alone, combined with a high mean (fifteen or greater) and high standard deviation (eight or greater), would define a critical election.

Social Determinism and Electoral Decision:

The Case of Indiana

V. O. Key, Jr. / Frank Munger

2

The systematic structuring of the patterns of electoral behavior is only a first step in dealing with the nature of popular voting throughout American history. That structure, after all, derives from the way people vote and why they do so. Early studies of contemporary electoral behavior focused on single elections and relied heavily on polling data and individual interviews. They emphasized the importance of an individual's particular social characteristics in determining his voting behavior in a given election. However, the study and comparison of electoral data across a number of elections, the late V. O. Key, Jr., and Frank Munger argue in the following article, reveal a striking historical determinism in the way most people react in specific elections. Put another way, a description that primarily stresses an exclusive relationship between social characteristics and voting decisions ignores too much of the tenacious quality of voting, the traditional attachments of voters to political parties, and their hesitancy to change their political habits despite rapid social changes. Key and Munger's analysis provides a thoughtful methodological demonstration that aggregate data can be fruitfully manipulated to provide crucial insights into the voting process.

The style set in the Erie County study of voting, *The People's Choice*,[1] threatens to take the politics out of the study of electoral behavior. The theoretical heart of *The People's Choice* rests in the contention that "social characteristics determine political preference." Professor Lazarsfeld and his associates, prudent as they are, do not let so bald a statement stand without qualification or exception. Yet almost inevitably from this basic view, which is usually not put so explicitly, there develops a school of analysis that tends to divert attention from critical elements of electoral decision. The focus of analysis under the doctrine of social determinism comes to rest broadly on the capacity of the

SOURCE: Reprinted with permission of The Macmillan Company from *American Voting Behavior*, eds. Eugene Burdick and Arthur Brodbeck, pp. 281–299, 456–459. © by The Free Press of Glencoe, a Corporation, 1959.

"nonpolitical group" to induce conformity to its political standards by the individual voter.

At bottom the tendency of the theory of group or social determinism is to equate the people's choice with individual choice. Perhaps the collective electoral decision, the people's choice, is merely the sum of individual choices. If enough were understood about individual decisions, by addition the collective political decision of the electorate would be comprehended. Yet when attention centers on the individual elector as he is led to decision by the compulsion of his nonpolitical group, the tendency is to lose sight of significant elements that both affect and relate individual decisions to the political aggregate. The study of electoral behavior then becomes only a special case of the more general problem of group inducement of individual behavior in accord with group norms. As such it does not invariably throw much light on the broad nature of electoral decision in the sense of decisions by the electorate as a whole.

The purpose here is not to dissent from *The People's Choice*. It is rather to raise the question whether its fundamental propositions do not provide a base on which, if enough effort were devoted to the matter, a supplementary theoretical structure might be erected that would bring politics into the study of electoral behavior. A few of the possible directions of development are here indicated through questions suggested by an examination of the voting record of Indiana. The simplest of techniques permits the analysis of a variety of types of electoral situations and suggests interpretations not so likely to emerge from the close observation of a single campaign. Parenthetically, it ought to be made explicit that such crude manipulation of aggregate electoral data is not urged as a substitute for the refined techniques of observation and analysis employed in *The People's Choice*.

Traditional Partisan Attachments: A Bench Mark for Analysis

Almost any pioneer inquiry is inevitably beset by the peril of generalization that requires modification after a series of analyses has been made. What seemed a plausible general finding turns out to have been only a characteristic of the peculiar case cast in general terms. Similarly, the inspection of a cross section at a particular moment of a society existing through time may divert attention from characteristics that would be revealed by deliberate attention to the time dimension. Voting decisions made prior to the campaign itself may differ radically from those occurring during the campaign, both in the kinds of voters involved and in the factors associated with decision. Moreover, the factors relevant to decision may differ from time to time.[2]

Explicit attention to the time dimension of electoral decision would probably bring to light a variety of characteristics not readily perceptible by the observation of a single case. Illustrative is the difficulty of obtaining a satisfactory estimate of the nature and significance of traditional or habitual partisan attachments by interviewing a sample at a particular point in time. Often electoral decision is not an action whose outcome is in doubt but a reaffirmation of past decisions, at least for the community as a whole. For generations the Democrats may carry this county and the Republicans may predominate in an adjacent county.

The potency of these traditional attachments may be inferred from the maps in Figure 2.1 which show the distribution of Indiana presidential vote by counties in 1868 and 1900. Although the pattern of 1868 did not move unchanged from election to election to 1900, an astonishing parallelism appears in the county-by-county division of party strength at the two widely separated points in time. Thirty-six of the state's ninety-two counties were over 50 percent Democratic at both elections; forty-five were under 50 percent Democratic at both elections.[3]

Apparently the persistent pattern of party division represented a crystallization of attitudes at the time of the Civil War mainly along lines separating areas with different sources of settlement. The southern half of the state, peopled chiefly from the southern states, contained in 1868 and 1900 most of the Democratic strongholds. Other Democratic areas find a partial explanation in the greater attractiveness of that party to newcomers from abroad. Dearborn, Franklin, Adams, Allen, and Pulaski counties all had large German populations as did Dubois in the south. The Republicanism of certain blocks of counties was related also to the sectional origins of settlers. The block of 1868–1900 Republican counties in east central Indiana was settled by Quakers, whose cultural center was Richmond in Wayne County. Their antislavery sentiments and perhaps other reasons as well made them early converts to Republicanism. Other strongly Republican areas in the northern part of the state had drawn heavily from Federalist and Whig areas of the Northeast. Many of the oddities in detail of the territorial distribution of party strength find explanation in like terms.[4]

From 1868 to 1900 the potency of traditional-party attachments may have been much greater than now, yet such community traits persist as is demonstrated by the scatter-diagram in Figure 2.2. The diagram relates the Republican percentage of the total presidential vote by county in 1920 to the corresponding percentage in 1948. Although most counties were more Democratic in 1948 than in 1920, a substantial correlation, +0.689, existed between the Republican percentages for the two elections. Generally where the Republicans were strong in 1920, they were relatively strong in 1948; where the Democrats were weak in 1920, they were relatively weak in 1948.[5]

The analytical model that centers attention on the campaign as a period of decision obviously obscures a significant dimension of the electoral process. In fact, there tends to be a standing decision by the community, although as a descriptive term *decision* has connotations of deliberate choice that are apt to be misleading. The *decision* may simply represent the balance between two opposing party groups each with striking powers of self-perpetuation. Their original formation may have in some instances represented a simple transplantation of partisan attachments. In others the dominant classes of the community allied themselves with the party whose policies of the moment were most akin to their inclinations. Doubtless great contests and stirring events intensified and renewed partisan loyalties.[6] The clustering of interests, career lines, and community sentiments about the dominant party gives it a powerful capacity for survival.

The relevance of all this to the theoretical problem is that it raises the question whether one needs to supplement the doctrine that "social characteristics determine political preference." May there not also be a political group with to some extent an independence of exterior determinants of membership and attachment? Obviously a simple reconciliation of the persistence of party group-

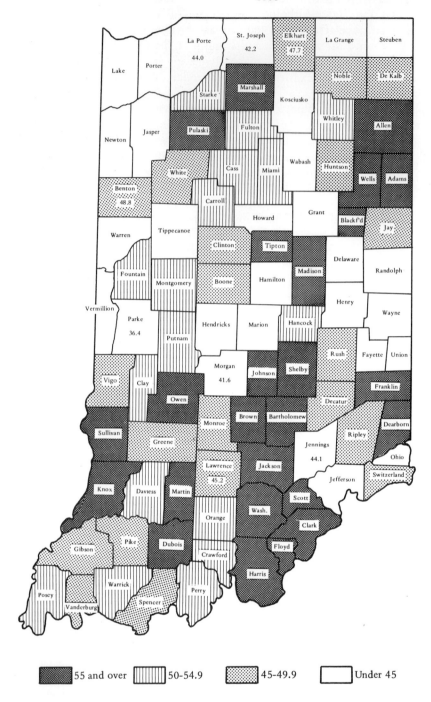

55 and over | | | | | |50-54.9 | 45-49.9 | Under 45

Figure 2.1 *The Traditional Vote: Democratic Percentage of the Two-Party Presidential Vote in Indiana, 1868 and 1900.*

1900

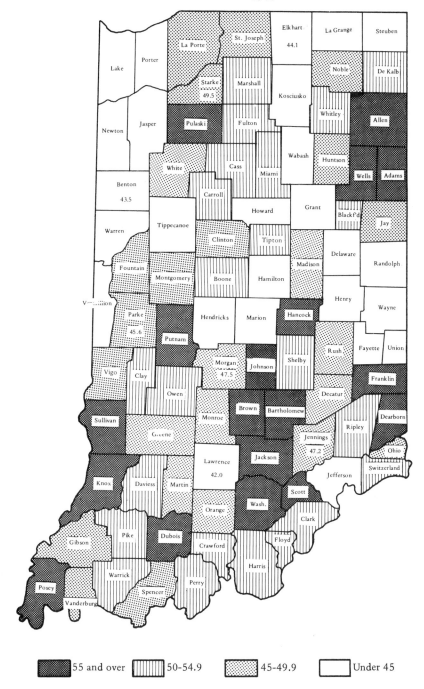

55 and over | 50-54.9 | 45-49.9 | Under 45

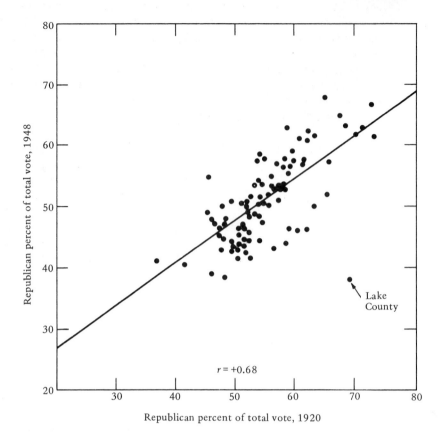

Figure 2.2 *The Traditional Vote: Relation Between Republican Percentage of Total Presidential Vote in 1920 and 1948 by Counties in Indiana.*

ings and the notion of social determinism would be to assert that the stability of "interests" and people associated with geography produces a parallel continuity of partisan attachment. Yet the long persistence of county patterns of party affiliation despite changes in "interest" and the disappearance of issues that created the pattern, and the existence of contrasting partisan patterns in essentially similar counties, point toward a "political" grouping at least to some extent independent of other social groupings.[7] It may be also that the continuity of the life of the party group is not a smooth and uninterrupted flow, as might be inferred from electoral analysis alone. Each election may be accompanied by considerable churning about and crossing of party lines in both directions. From election to election varying proportions of the electorate may be affected by indecision and inner conflict. Yet the net effect over long periods is the maintenance of similar party divisions. Aggregate figures do not, of course, tell us whether this net result is accomplished by stability of individual party attachments or by the power of party groups to maintain their being through a combination of the retention of individual loyalties and the recruitment of new adherents.[8]

Recognition of the time dimension of *decision* suggests the plausibility of an analytical model built on the assumption that political groupings manage to exist, as majorities or minorities, over long periods of time.[9] Their persistence suggests that they may represent, not mere derivatives from other social groupings, but political groups, with a life of their own.[10] To be properly understood these groupings would probably have to be analyzed in their behavior vis-à-vis the institutions of local government as well as in relation to national issues.

Focus on the time dimension of voting behavior compels recognition of the more or less standing nature of electoral decision, at least for a substantial part of the electorate. Yet the traditional vote does not by any means decide all elections nor govern the decisions of all individual voters. The traditional party divisions apparently fix a line of siege which moves to and fro with the fortunes of individual political battles. The balance of electoral strength varies from community to community and is disturbed in varying degrees by the impact of events and of campaigns. In any case the traditional pattern of voting provides a bench mark for the identification and analysis of particular electoral shifts. Electoral decision may be fundamentally a question of whether to depart from preexisting decision. Under what circumstances does the electorate, or parts of it, choose to deviate from old habits of action? Does the nature of these decisions differ from election to election, situation to situation?

Durable Alterations in Partisan Division

Even the most cursory analysis of shifts in party strength from the more or less viscous pattern of traditional behavior suggests that an understanding of the process of electoral decision (and of popular government) must rest on a differentiation of types of electoral decision in the sense of elections as collective decision. It also suggests lines for the supplementation of the theory that "social characteristics determine political preference" to make it a more useful tool for political analysis.

Evidently one type of electoral decision consists in a more or less durable shift in the traditional partisan division within a community. The manner in which such realignments occur should be instructive to advocates of party reconstruction as well as suggestive for speculation about the nature of the party system. This type of alteration is not the work of a moment but may take place in a series of steps spread over a considerable period of time. Or at least such would be the conclusion if the Indiana data mean anything beyond the particular situation.

To identify areas undergoing a secular change in party division one must separate the electoral movements that occur from election to election from those that seem to represent a long-term trend. The long-term tendency of the areas undergoing durable realignment presumably will be retarded or accelerated by those factors peculiar to each election which affect them as well as those areas not touched by the secular trend. A crude separation of short-term movements and long-term trends is accomplished by the arrangement of the data in Figure 2.3. From 1920 to 1948 in fifteen Indiana counties the Democratic proportion of the two-party presidential vote increased by ten percentage points or more.[11] In the chart the average Democratic percentage of these counties is plotted alongside the average Democratic percentage of all counties of the state. Although the fifteen counties evidently felt the election-to-election influences common to all counties, their long-term divergence as a group from the mean of all counties moved them in a sequence of steps over sixteen years from a Republican position to a new and relatively stable pattern of division above the Democratic average for all counties. The shifting counties were more affected by the La-Follette candidacy in 1924 than were the rest of the state's counties.[12] As a

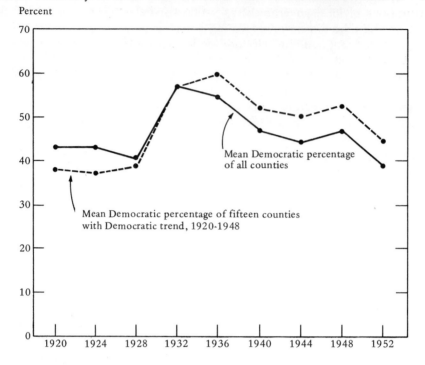

Figure 2.3 *Secular Shift in Partisan Attachment: Mean Democratic Percentage of Two-Party Presidential Vote for All Indiana Counties and for Fifteen Counties with the Most Marked Democratic Growth, 1920–1952.*

group, they withstood the general trend toward Hoover in 1928. In 1932 they moved Democratic as did all other counties but at a slightly higher rate. In 1936 their divergent trend continued and apparently that election fixed a new equilibrium in partisan division. In effect, the analysis segregates out areas undergoing a secular trend that creates a "new traditional" pattern. If the cyclical component of the fifteen-county series in Figure 2.3 were to be removed, the residual secular trend would show a gradual upward movement from 1924 to 1936 after which the series would flatten out.

The phenomenon recorded in the chart has interest purely for its isolation of a secular movement from one party toward the other. Only a panel study over a long period could determine the detailed nature of the secular change, yet from the aggregate statistics some surmises are possible. To the extent that the shift reflected a net change in partisan attachment rather than differentials in accretions to the two parties,[13] it probably occurred by the cumulation of individual shifts. Some persons became disenchanted with the major parties in 1924 and voted for LaFollette. Others were recruited by the Democrats on liquor and religious issues in 1928. The depression made permanent as well as temporary

Democratic converts in 1932. The impact of the New Deal program completed the process in 1936. Party realignment may be accomplished under some circumstances by a series of steps.[14]

If this aggregate analysis identifies a type of electoral shift, can it be brought under the doctrine that "social characteristics determine political preference" or do we need a supplementary theory? If social characteristics determine political preference, it would be supposed that a set of secular social changes occurred in our fifteen counties and guided their political reorientation. Most of the fifteen counties either included within their limits considerable cities or were within the zone of influence of such cities.[15] Yet not all counties containing such cities underwent enough partisan change to be included in the group.[16] Most of the counties enjoyed a continuing growth of urban population and of industry, and in some instances notable additions to the electorate occurred with the coming of age of sons and daughters of immigrants.

It seems most improbable that changes in social characteristics occurred as rapidly as did political change during the period 1924–1936. To fill in one theoretical gap one could posit the existence of a lag in the adjustment of political preference to social characteristics, i.e., that it took some time for political attitude to catch up with urbanization and industrialization. Under some circumstances the process of social determinism may encounter formidable friction in remolding political orientation.

The perspective of time also suggests the utility of taking into account other elements of the field within which the voter acts. Over the period 1920–1948 the political parties and the voter's perceptions of political parties probably changed more than did his social characteristics. The pronouncements of political leadership and alternatives in program tendencies of the parties played upon the voter. Moreover, the group affiliations of the people of our fifteen counties and of the state changed but little in the period 1924–1936, but through the differential effects of depression and party appeals those memberships and characteristics, if they were determinative of political preference, took on a new meaning. Social characteristics do not operate in a political vacuum. It is quite as meaningful, perhaps more, to assert that changes in the structure of political alternatives govern electoral choice as it is to say that social characteristics determine political preference.

All this discussion points, of course, to the proximate relation of group discipline to individual electoral decision. To explain the more or less durable secular shift in partisan loyalty identified here one must go beyond group theory to an analysis of factors that bring particular social characteristics to the level of political consciousness, to changes that alter radically the distribution of the electorate among categories of persons differentiated by politically significant characteristics. Collective electoral decision, at least at times, may be a product of such changes in the aggregate with group determinism functioning more or less as an accessory after the fact.

Short-Term Disturbances of Partisan Patterns: The Relativity of Social Determinism

Another elaboration of the doctrine of social determinism is suggested by observation of the short-term shifts in partisan strength. Evidently at some moments in time these shifts are associated with a particular social characteristic;

at other times that characteristic will be unimportant as a determinant. At one time one social characteristic may seem to fix election results; at another time another will predominate.

Again rough analyses of the Indiana data may illustrate the argument. The charts in Figure 2.4 indicate the movement of the mean of the Republican percentage of the total presidential vote from 1924 to 1928 in four types of coun-

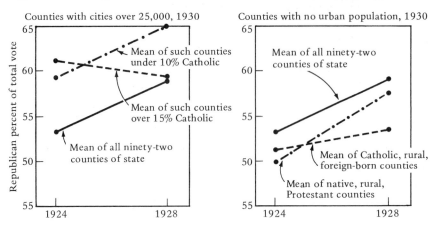

Figure 2.4 *Impact of the 1928 Campaign: Shift from 1924 to 1928 in the Republican Percentage of Total Presidential Vote in Four Types of Indiana Counties.*

ties. In the urban counties with relatively small proportions of their population Roman Catholic, the Republicans gained sharply while their proportion of the vote declined in urban counties with the highest proportions of Roman Catholic population.[17] In the rural counties with the highest proportions of native-born Protestant population, a much sharper Republican gain occurred than in rural counties with relatively high proportions of Catholic and foreign-born.[18]

Obviously these aggregate figures do not establish that Protestants moved from Democratic to Republican ranks from 1924 to 1928. Nevertheless, it is most probable that a shift associated with religion and related factors occurred. To the extent that the data indicate electoral decisions associated with such social attributes, they point toward an additional elaboration of the theory of social determinism. The social characteristics of our contrasting counties changed very little over the period 1924–1928. If these characteristics determined political preference, they acquired a political significance, at least for some people, in 1928 that they lacked in 1924.

The same sorts of propositions find further illustration in the voting behavior of German and non-German counties. Although most Indiana counties from 1936 to 1940 shifted to some degree away from the Democrats, the supposition is that voters of German origin were especially antagonized by Roosevelt's policy toward the Reich.[19] In 1940 Henry Schricker ran as the Democratic candidate for governor. Of German origin, he was reputed to have a potent appeal to voters of that nationality. If the social characteristic of national origin moved in higher degree into the zone of political relevance in 1940, it would be supposed that German voters would support Schricker in higher degree than Roosevelt while the non-German groups would probably give about the same proportion of their vote to both gubernatorial and presidential candidates.

Insofar as election returns give a clue to group voting behavior the graphs in Figure 2.5 support the proposition. The chart compares Dubois County, in high

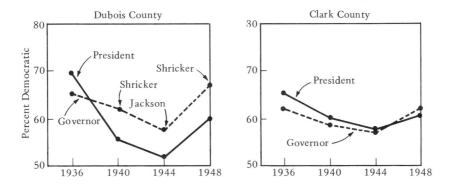

Figure 2.5 *National Origin and the Vote: Democratic Percentage of the Two-Party Vote for President and Governor in Dubois and Clark Counties, Indiana, 1936–1948.*

degree Germanic in origin, with Clark County, an area with relatively fewer citizens of German origin. Dissatisfaction with foreign policy presumably accounted for the especially sharp drop in Dubois in the vote for the Democratic presidential candidate in 1940. The higher vote in that county for Democratic candidates for governor probably reflected primarily a loyalty to the state Democratic ticket unaffected by national policy and perhaps to some extent the special appeal of Henry Schricker, who ran in both 1940 and 1948. On the other hand, in Clark County the Democratic presidential and gubernatorial candidates polled more nearly the same percentages of the vote.

The relativity of social determinism is further illustrated by a type of fluctuation in party strength in which voters are apparently drawn away from their usual party preference by the issue or events of a particular campaign only to return to the fold when the repelling peculiarities of the election disappear.[20] It might be supposed, for example, that in 1928 some persons who usually voted Democratic supported Hoover in preference to Smith yet returned to their party when the commotion subsided. A rough test of the proposition is provided by the data in Figure 2.6, which shows the mean Republican percentage of the total vote for president and for lieutenant-governor of another pair of contrasting groups of counties from 1920 to 1932. Note in particular that the predominantly Protestant rural counties reported about twice as wide a net splitting of tickets to the advantage of Hoover as did otherwise comparable counties with relatively large Catholic populations.[21] In both types of counties the gaps between the state and national votes disappeared in 1932. Such aggregate figures, of course, do not tell us who crossed party lines, whether gross ticket splitting was greater in one set of counties than in the other, or whether ticket splitting was higher at one election than another.[22] Yet the differentials strongly suggest that Protestant Democrats and perhaps Catholic Republicans responded to the situation in 1928 by splitting their tickets. After the religious issue subsided, national

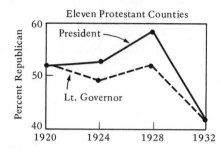
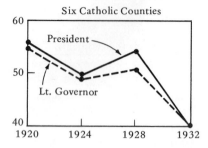

Figure 2.6   *Mean Republican Percentage of the Total Vote for President and Lieutenant-Governor in Selected Protestant and Catholic Counties in Indiana, 1920–1932.*

and local party appeals were more nearly congruent and ticket splitting declined.

The data have an incidental utility in sharper definition of the "independent" voter. Insofar as ticket splitting is regarded as a manifestation of "independence," one type of independence apparently is not a generalized objectivity of judgment but a response of particular classes of voters to the particular issues of the day. The quantity and incidence of this type of voting would be expected to differ from time to time with the issues and personalities of the moment.[23]

All these illustrative analyses in a sense support the doctrine of social determinism of political preference yet they also point to the need for correlative theory. Social characteristics gain a political significance when political alternatives tend to parallel differentials in social attribute. One attribute may be of political significance at one time and another at another. That significance may well be the product of events and actions entirely outside the group concerned. Politicians may, in effect, invest group attributes with political significance. Appeals to group interest, prejudice, and pride are part of the stock-in-trade of the politician who often labors mightily to make the voter conscious of his social characteristics in order that they may determine his political preference.

To gain a broader understanding of electoral choice, it is necessary to account for the circumstances associated with variations in the relevance of social characteristics for electoral decision. That inquiry must lead beyond the nexus of group and individual voter to those factors associated with the political activation of groups or to those factors that bring social characteristics into the zone of political relevance. The data examined suggest such factors as the differentials in impact of market forces on different groups, the changing structure of political alternatives, the interaction of group memories of past and contemporary events. Undoubtedly many types of factors contribute to group tensions and frictions. Their identification permits one to go a step beyond the proximate relations involved in the focus on relationship of group and individual toward a more complete identification of the nature of electoral decision. Unless we can make some such step, we are left more or less with the proposition that those social characteristics that happen to be relevant at a particular time and place determine, or are associated with, political preference.[24]

Unexplained Elements of Decision: The General Drift of Sentiment

While the interaction of the structure of political alternatives and cleavages in social characteristics undoubtedly bears significantly on electoral decision, the preceding analyses implicitly suggest that social determinism may account for only part of the movement of the electorate from party to party over each four-year period. Social groups that move into the zone of political relevance in a particular campaign may transfer their loyalties in a relatively high degree, but it seems not unlikely that in many elections most groups move in the same direction. If this could be demonstrated, it would suggest the existence of some political X factor or factors which may, in most elections, play the determinative role in political decision.

The evidence on the proposition is extremely thin. Obviously the facts differ from election to election, yet it seems fairly plain that in many four-year periods a general drift of sentiment occurs that is shared to some degree by people of all sorts of social characteristics. Some of the charts point in that direction. Some broader possibilities are suggested by the data in Table 2.1, which shows the direction of movement from presidential election to presidential election from 1928 to 1952 of all the counties of Indiana. It will be observed that the more common pattern was for most of the counties to move in the same direction. A sharp deviation from this uniformity occurred in 1936 which was a crucial election in reshaping the traditional composition of the Democratic following, as was indicated by Figure 2.1.

Table 2.1   Number of Indiana Counties with Increasing or Declining Democratic Percentage of Two-Party Presidential Vote, 1928-1952

Period	Increasing Democratic Percentage	Declining Democratic Percentage	No Percentage Change	Total
1928-32	92	0	0	92
1932-36	23	68	1	92
1936-40	0	92	0	92
1940-44	3	89	0	92
1944-48	87	5	0	92
1948-52	0	92	0	92

The figures of Table 2.1 only show, of course, that the people of geographical units as a whole moved in the same direction in most elections. Only insofar as social differentiation is associated with geography do the figures give ground for supposing that various sorts of social groups moved in the same direction. A series of sample surveys covering the same period as the table would be necessary to determine the answer to that question. Yet scattered evidence suggests that it is not uncommon for people of the most diverse social groups to shift their political sentiments in the same direction. Decisions, i.e., to change, may well be conditioned, at least in some elections, by factors more or less independent of social characteristics. It could be that persons of different characteristics shift in the same direction for different reasons, yet that seems inadequate to account for the drastic shifts affecting all types of persons in some elections. Whatever the explanations may be, it seems clear that the search has to extend beyond the tendency of nonpolitical groups to enforce their norms on their members.

Comment

A major burden of the argument has been that the isolation of the electorate from the total governing process and its subjection to microscopic analysis tends to make electoral study a nonpolitical endeavor. That isolation tends, perhaps not of necessity but because of the blinders on perception associated with the method, to divorce the subjects of microscopic examination from their place in the larger political situation. Hence, all the studies of so-called "political behavior" do not add impressively to our comprehension of the awesome process by which the community or nation makes decisions at the ballot box.

It has been suggested that a fruitful avenue of development might be to seek to bridge the gap between microanalysis and macroanalysis, to the improvement of both. Much further refinement of our knowledge of the place of social characteristics in electoral decision, for example, would probably quickly follow once the setting of political alternatives and the matrix of objective conditions within which these determinants operate were brought more specifically into the field of observation. It seems apparent that social characteristics move into and out of the zone of political relevance, that they "explain" the actions of some people and not those of others, and that insofar as social characteristics determine political preference they encounter considerable friction.

Some of the difficulties of theory and analysis will be solved in due course, doubtless in a serendipitous manner, as the number of studies multiplies. New types of election situations will be analyzed; provisional generalizations will be modified to account for new situations; and the process will be repeated. By the observation of a great variety of types of situations it may be possible to tie the study of electoral behavior more directly to the workings of the state. Such a linkage might enable us to talk with a bit more information about the conditions under which an electorate can most effectively perform its decision-making role in the governing process. What are the consequences, for example, of the subjection of differing proportions of the vote to determination by specified social characteristics? Of the existence of a greater or lesser proportion of the electorate loyal to party? Of the intensification of particular types of group loyalties? Of the decay of others? Of the introduction of particular types of issues into the electoral arena? Of integration or atomization of the structure of leadership? Of variations in the range of electoral indifference and in the intensity of electoral involvement?[25]

Another point that recurs is a note of doubt about the doctrine that social characteristics determine political preference. There can be no doubt that there is at times a high degree of association between readily identifiable social characteristics and political preference. At the extreme position it might be argued that political preference is a hitchhiker on social characteristics. Yet there seems to be always a very considerable part of the electorate for which no readily isolable social characteristic "explains" political preference. The query may be raised whether a rather serious void does not exist in the theory. Is there some sort of political order or system of loyalties more or less independent of the identifications of citizens and electors with these nonpolitical groups to which we have an index in their social characteristics? The identification and analysis of the political role of the voter may present considerable difficulty in research design, yet if there is no political community, if citizens, or many of them, have no political role more or less autonomous from their other roles, a good many centuries of political speculation, both hortatory and otherwise, has been beside the point. Some of the considerable variance unaccounted for by social determination might be removed by attempts to analyze the nature of the individual's identification with the community and the nation, the character of his identification with political party, his perception of the political world, his general orientation toward complexes of policy questions, his conception of his role as a voter and as a citizen. There may well be, for a part of the electorate at least, roles, identifications, and preferences of a purely political nature with quite as much reality as his "social characteristics." Perhaps some common denominator ties together the archetype Republican and the Republican unskilled laborer who always turns up in the survey.

In research the answers one gets depend in part on the kinds of questions he asks. If one inquires about social characteristics and political preference, he finds out about social characteristics and politial preference. If one puts other sorts of questions into the research mill, he might well bring out other and more complex characteristics of the process of electoral decision. It might well turn out that the emerging picture would be one of an electorate, or at least of a great many electors, now struggling with great questions, now whipped into a frenzy or into fear by the demagogue, now voting against its own imputed short-term interest, now acting without check or restraint, now weighing as best it may the welfare of the community, all more or less in accord with classical democratic theory.[26]

NOTES

[1] P. F. Lazarsfeld, B. R. Berelson, and Hazel Gaudet, *The People's Choice*, 2nd ed. (New York: Columbia University Press, 1948).

[2] A basic contribution of *The People's Choice* was, of course, its development of a technique for observation of at least short segments of the time dimension of decision, and its authors manifest an awareness of the significance of this factor not common among electoral sociologists.

[3] The similarity between two such maps drawn with the same class intervals in the distribution of counties depends somewhat on the elections chosen for comparison. Since most counties tend to fluctuate in unison, the comparison of elections at which the divison of the entire state's vote is approximately the same maximizes the similarities by the county-by-county pattern.

[4] Thus, the Republican county of Jefferson in the southeast is surrounded by Democratic territory. In the first decades of the nineteenth century the county seat, Madison, was the metropolis of the state and a flourishing river trading center. The county was peopled, the local histories say, by the "educated" and "upper strata of society" from Philadelphia and Baltimore, some of whom built magnificent residences that still stand as monuments to the erstwhile glory of Madison. Long since the river trade virtually disappeared. Dreams of metropolitan grandeur came no longer to haunt the county's declining population. Yet so firmly did the old Whig traders fix the political tradition that the county ranked low in Democratic strength even after 1900.

[5] A word of caution is in order about both the maps and the scatter-diagram. The maps convey an erroneous impression in that they make no allowance for differences in population density. The significance of a metropolitan center in the entire picture is thus minimized. Similary, one dot on the diagram may represent a rural county of small population; another a densely populated metropolitan county. Moreover, differentials in behavior within sub-groups of the population of large counties are concealed by this sort of analysis.

[6] If one plots on the map of Indiana clusters of underground railroad stations and points at which Union authorities had difficulties in drafting troops, he separates, on the whole, Republican and Democratic counties. Whether the sort of animosities associated with such long-past events project themselves far through time in lending strength to political groupings, perhaps unbeknownst to succeeding generations, raises an interesting question.

[7] Some evidence pointing in this direction has been presented by George Belknap and Angus Campbell, "Political Party Identification and Attitudes Toward Foreign Policy," *Public Opinion Quarterly*, vol. 15 (1951–1952), 601–623.

[8] See S. J. Eldersveld, "The Independent Vote: Measurement, Characteristics, and Implications for Party Strategy," *American Political Science Review*, vol. 46 (1952), 732–753.

[9] How one converts this kind of proposition into a problem susceptible of neat empirical testing presents another question.

[10] This factor may partially explain the frustration that almost invariably accompanies attempts to identify party characteristics by correlation of votes with demographic characteristics. One element of the variance unexplained by such analysis may lie in variables in the behavior of "political" man, such as persistence of partisan attachment, which may be quite independent of the so-called determinants.

[11] Obviously the manifestation of a secular trend in particular counties depends to some extent on the terminal points chosen for identifying them. Further it would be erroneous to suppose that all areas moving in a secular manner either begin that movement at the same time or proceed at the same rate.

[12] The mean LaFollette percentage of the total vote in the fifteen counties was 9.0; in all counties the mean was 4.8.

[13] The great upswing in Democratic strength in Indiana from 1920 to 1936 may have represented principally Democratic success in recruiting new voters rather than in the conversion of erstwhile Republicans. With 1920 as 100, the total presidential vote, the Republican vote, and the Democratic vote from 1920 to 1936 were as follows:

	Total	Republican	Democratic
1920	100.0	100.0	100.0
1924	100.8	100.9	96.3
1928	112.5	121.8	110.0
1932	124.7	97.2	168.6
1936	130.7	99.3	182.8

Apart from their temporary expansion in 1928, the Republicans only about held their own from 1920 to 1936, while the Democrats almost doubled their vote. These figures do not prove that the Democrats had greater success in winning new voters. Yet from what is known of the stability of voting attachments, these figures strongly suggest that such an interpretation provides at least a partial explanation.

[14] One should cover himself against the possibility that the apparent secular trend of the fifteen counties is not a secular divergence from the movement of the state but a cyclical fluctuation with a wider amplitude than the cyclical movement of the state as a whole.

[15] The fifteen counties were Blackford (near Muncie), Clark (which falls within the Louisville metropolitan district), Delaware (Muncie), Elkhart (Elkhart), Howard (Kokomo), Knox (Vincennes), Lake (Gary), La Porte (Michigan City), Madison (Anderson), Porter (adjacent to Lake), Starke (in northeastern Indiana, the home of Henry Schricker, important Indiana Democratic leader), St. Joseph (South Bend), Vanderburgh (Evansville), Vermillion (a marginal coal mining county), Vigo (Terre Haute). The range of the 1920 Democratic percentages was from 21.3 (Lake) to 51.0 (Clark). The 1948 range was from 36.7 (Porter) to 61.0 (Clark). Of the fifteen counties, eleven were over 50 percent Democratic in 1948; only one was over 50 percent Democratic in 1920.

[16] For example, Marion (Indianapolis) and Allen (Fort Wayne).

[17] Those counties containing cities of over 25,000 and with less than 10 percent Roman Catholic population were Delaware, Elkhart, Howard, Madison, Marion, Vigo, Wayne. Those with over 15 percent Catholic population were Lake, LaPorte, St. Joseph.

[18] Completely rural counties with under 5 percent Catholic population *and* under 5 percent of their population foreign-born or of foreign or mixed parentage were Brown, Carroll, Crawford, Hendricks, Orange, Owen, Parke, Scott, Switzerland. The other group consisted of rural counties with over 10 percent Catholic population *and* over 10 percent foreign-born or of foreign or mixed parentage. These were Benton, Pulaski, Starke, Franklin, Spencer. It

scarcely need be said that the available census data provide no satisfactory differentiation of counties according to the national origin of their population.

[19] This is the thesis of Louis Bean, *How to Predict Elections* (New York: Alfred A. Knopf, 1948), pp. 93–99.

[20] The possibility should not be excluded that a series of "peculiar" elections may have cumulative effects productive of a secular growth of one party.

[21] The counties compared were drawn from those counties with 20–29.0 percent urban population in 1930 and with no cities of over 10,000. The differentiation of Catholic and non-Catholic counties was based on the percentage of the 1930 total population reported as Roman Catholic by the Census of Religious Bodies of 1936. The counties under 2 percent Catholic were: Boone, Clay, Fulton, Greene, Hamilton, Hancock, Johnson, Kosciusko, Morgan, Putnam, Wells. Those over 12 percent Catholic were Daviess, Decatur, Dubois, Perry, Porter, Warrick. It scarcely need be said that the data on religious composition are not very reliable.

[22] Which, of course, points to one of the great advantages of the sample survey over the analysis of election returns.

[23] The phenomenon of departure and return to party suggests the question whether the pattern of party division among the counties of the state could be regarded as something of an equilibrium which may be disturbed by the impact of particular campaigns yet tends to restore itself when the next campaign comes along. To test the notion the county-by-county Republican percentage in 1916 was regarded as the "normal" pattern. A rank order correlation was made with succeeding elections with the following results: 1920, 0.862; 1924, 0.775; 1928, 0.634; 1932, 0.754. Through 1928 the correlations steadily declined. Each election marked a further departure from the 1916 pattern. The 1928 election showed the sharpest deviation as the crosscurrents of that campaign played havoc with past voting patterns. Yet in 1932, the counties moved back toward their preexisting ranking.

[24] Tests of the index of political predisposition of the Erie County study of 1940 against national samples in the elections of 1944 and 1948 illustrate the problem. (See Lazarsfeld, Berelson, and Gaudet, *op. cit.*, pp. xv–xviii; and Morris Janowitz and W. E. Miller, "The Index of Political Predisposition in the 1948 Election," *Journal of Politics*, vol. 14 (1952), pp. 710–727.) An index descriptive of the association between particular social characteristics and political preference among the electors of a particular locality at a particular election did not fit so well national samples at other elections. To round out the theory of the determinism of social characteristics, it would be necessary to devise a scheme to account for the shifting political significance of these characteristics. If they do change in significance, no index in terms of particular characteristics could be expected to have much predictive value save under conditions of a highly stable politics or over the relatively short run.

[25] For a statement of other directions of development, see B. R. Berelson, "Democratic Theory and Public Opinion," *Public Opinion Quarterly*, vol. 16 (1952), pp. 313–330.

[26] It should be noted for the record that this essay was completed essentially in its present form in June 1953. It therefore does not take into account the theoretical advances by Berelson, Lazarsfeld, and McPhee in their *Voting* (Chicago: University of Chicago Press, 1954). Moreover, since the essay was drafted Mr. Munger has completed an intensive analysis of Indiana politics reported in *Two-Party Politics in the State of Indiana* (MS dissertation, Harvard University, 1955). Full utilization of his detailed findings would permit considerable refinement of the factual data underlying the argument.

Analyzing American Voting, 1830–1860:

Methods*

Ronald P. Formisano

3

Correlation of county-level voting returns, while quite illuminating and useful, is only one step in the task of reconstructing the nature of historical voting behavior. Such measurements do reveal general tendencies but since most American counties are socially heterogeneous and politically divided, further refinement is desirable. In the absence of individual polling data this refinement consists primarily of developing further measurable social and electoral information, particularly encompassing the smaller, more homogeneous units within the counties — i.e., the townships, wards, and precincts. Unfortunately, the quantitative data that have survived into the twentieth century are particularly noted for their incomplete and haphazard quality. Nevertheless, as Ronald P. Formisano notes in the following article, historians can combine the quantitative material available with more traditional evidence, systematic methods, and some imagination, to illuminate past voting habits, despite all the problems and gaps. Formisano's own efforts in this direction are contained in his forthcoming study of Michigan popular voting between the mid-1830s and the Civil War. He is currently assistant professor of history at the University of Rochester.

The methods and concepts to be discussed here are informing and shaping a study entitled "Parties and Voters in Michigan, 1835–1860." I shall not discuss its substantive goals, which at their most ambitious are concerned with the nature of American political culture and with Civil War causation, but shall concentrate on methods. The study was conceived in part deliberately to develop methods and concepts of specific and general relevance for American political history. Hopefully, those who will be or are engaged in similar case studies can save time from advice offered here, use the methods, and improve them.

In *The Concept of Jacksonian Democracy: New York as a Test Case* (1961)

SOURCE: Reprinted with permission from *Historical Methods Newsletter*, vol. 2 (March 1969), pp. 1–12.

*An earlier version of this essay was presented at the conference on "American Political Behavior: New Approaches," State University of New York, College at Cortland, October 18–19, 1968.

Lee Benson offered a research design, concepts, and methods for analyzing party formation and mass voting behavior in an antebellum northern state which I took as models to be emulated and improved upon. The study of Michigan began with one county — Wayne. Although Wayne, which included Detroit, was the most heterogeneous county in Michigan, it was necessary to look beyond it to observe the behavior of more social groups than was possible within its confines. From the start, voting and demographic data at the county level were analyzed and compared with township and ward data for Wayne. The study presently rests primarily on voting data for townships and wards and on demographic data for townships and wards from the 1850 and 1860 federal censuses, published and manuscript. Techniques yielding the most precise and credible findings were worked out initially in studying Wayne County.

Professor Benson offered his methods expecting that similar studies would follow and that working critics would push up to and beyond various aspects of his work. The methods and concepts described here are offered in the same spirit: they need working criticism; they need testing; they need improving. This essay hopes to stimulate that activity.

Moreover, it is a plea for some standardization of methods; for some uniformity in the way, for example, that scholars quantify demographic data from the 1850 and 1860 censuses. The case study assumes an ongoing community of scholars addressing themselves, however separately, to similar problems. If their communications with each other and with others are to be effective, some uniformity of language in data handling would help.

Methods inevitably rest on assumptions, whether implicit or explicit. Communication is enhanced and controversy lessened when they are made explicit. So it is necessary to engage now in what Heinz Eulau has aptly called "theorizing activity."

1. A case study can reach beyond the description and classification of the unique. Properly designed, it can help provide, with similar studies, increasingly solid bases for generalizations, and progressively better understanding of "exceptions."

2. Voting behavior is socially determined. A number of variables in their social development and environment cause men to choose a certain party. This is not a euphemism for denying that class or "how a man gains his livelihood" have anything to do with voting, nor is it an assertion that voting is caused uniformly by ethnic and religious influences. It is rather a recognition of the whole man in his total social environment and of many potentially relevant variables bearing on political behavior whose mix can kaleidoscopically shift over time and place.

These assumptions underlie most modern studies of voting. In implementing them political scientists today observe many variables relating to individual voters. They can know not only how individuals voted but can also ask them questions to get at subjective characteristics. No such luxuries exist for the study of voters before the Civil War. Rather, the mass must be viewed from the outside via a relatively limited number of variables. Generalizations about voting must rest primarily on aggregate data for townships and wards, bringing one *close* to the individual voter but, alas, never within reach. With aggregate data one does not even see the individual through a glass darkly. Rather one assembles profiles of aggregates and then infers beyond them to group patterns and tendencies. This is not an act of faith. Although it is an imperfect procedure, it is the only one available in most cases to get at the masses of voters. Fortunately, mid-nineteenth-century settlement patterns in the Northwest tend to provide many townships of homogeneous populations or homogeneous politics. These units provide the most obvious support for inferences about group voting behavior. These methods provide almost no way, however, for making reasonable inferences about individual members of social groups who are dispersed throughout the population and presumably emotionally apart from the group, lacking the group's reinforcement of perceptions and behavior patterns.

3. Aggregate voting data for minor civil divisions in the nineteenth century can usually provide a basis for making inferences about the party loyalties of social groups. Aside from state and county election returns for major elections 1835–1860, *voting profiles* for townships and wards were constructed. Such a profile shows the number, percent, and total vote for parties in each unit in every election year. The election for the highest office in any year was the representative major election for that year. After searching newspapers in various libraries, the rich but incomplete mine of election returns in the Michigan Historical Commission archives (deposited there by the secretary of state's office), and after letters and visits to county courthouses across lower Michigan, voting profiles of townships of some use for thirty-two counties were assembled. Fairly complete returns existed for Detroit's wards for the entire period, and for several large towns which incorporated as cities in the 1850s election returns by ward were available.

What do the voting profiles show? They provide a reasonable basis for making inferences about party loyalty. Simple observation, for example, readily established that most units showed overall a striking consistency in their party loyalties from the late 1830s to 1852. Any drastic voting shifts could usually be attributed to drastic demographic changes. There are ways of quantifying what one sees by simple observation, and describing it statistically. Through interyear correlations one can inquire statistically how closely the distribution of the vote in any given year resembled that in any other year for the same units. This has been done with counties for the state, by presidential elections, and for three selected counties by township, using Democratic percents, 1837–1860.

The persistence of party loyalty as well as periods of realignment may be inferred from such data. But one might well ask, party loyalty for whom? The answer is party loyalty for *voting units*, not necessarily for voters, not even in the aggregate. There is a saying that a man cannot step into the same river twice. Analogous to this is the historian's usually not being able to look into the same township twice in the nineteenth-century American Midwest. If one is comparing the voting of townships in 1837 and 1850, their populations and electorates may have changed considerably in that time. Historians studying mobility in mid- and late nineteenth-century midwestern communities have warned that while published census data may show stability over time with population levels remaining fairly constant, turnover *within* may be going on at a tremendous rate.[1] Studies of an Iowa county and an Iowa township in 1850 and 1860 show horizontal mobility rates to have been extremely high, especially among nonfarm occupations.[2] Data have not been assembled to test adequately the extent to which this was true of Michigan. However, aggregate data was assembled from the manuscript population schedules for socioeconomic, ethnic, and religious groups in Wayne County's towns for both 1850 and 1860. This data, and my impression from intensive study of many Michigan towns over time, suggest that most towns probably formed at an early stage a social character which usually persisted for at least a decade or two. Thus the turnover among Canton township's native Protestants and Ecorse township's Catholic French may have been high, but between 1850 and 1860 Canton remained predominantly native Protestant and Ecorse remained predominantly Catholic French; both persisted as farming communities. One could extend this example to other social variables and one cannot extend it to others. Evidence from the Iowa studies and from Wayne indicates, for example, that as most towns left the frontier stage the great group of "middling" farmers with which they usually began flattened out, with some increase in the top socioeconomic ranks and larger gains among the lowest. There is clearly a need for more studies of mobility and of persistence of social character. Meanwhile, one must say of interyear correlations for antebellum counties and towns that the farther apart in time are the elections being compared the less the party loyalty of voters is being examined, but rather the loyalty of voting units of somewhat similar social composition.

Concepts

For the crucial period of party formation in the 1830s, systematic demographic data is not available and one must rely heavily on impressionistic evidence, a random gazetteer, city directories, and a variety of sources. However piecemeal the data, one must be clear about the concepts with which it should be approached. In the 1830s one can use available data to reconstruct the community being studied in terms of its politically relevant subcultures, or *political subcultures*.[3]

A political subculture is broader than an interest or pressure group. It might have its bases in a mix of variables — ethnicity, class, religion, occupation, environment, and others. The members share experiences and a social and geographic location which gives them a common view of the world. This common view is rooted in shared value systems which are often articulated and thus observable in religious beliefs, and shaped by ethnoreligious heritage, education, occupation, family, and all the other factors influencing political socialization. A political subculture might be said to share a *belief-system* (a term borrowed from Phillip Converse) which tends to unify and make somewhat predictable its response to an ever shifting political scene, and which affords the researcher a primary means of understanding the subculture's *political character*. It can be argued that the assumption of group political character has played a key role, even if implicit and unspoken, in recent studies of nineteenth-century voting which rely on aggregate data to determine group tendencies.[4]

Finally, a related concept of use especially in analyzing party formation is that of the *broad symbolic group*. This is usually an elite group which is perceived by various groups as threatening or reassuring. It may pursue political goals and may affect party alignments because of the way in which voters perceive party attitudes toward the group.

These concepts, within the framework of reference group behavior, can be helpful in analyzing party formation in situations where quantitative data are lacking. They also aid in the explanation of voting patterns — after, of course, demographic data have been quantified, correlated with voting data, and voting patterns determined.

I gathered demographic data describing potential voters in the townships of six counties and in fourteen selected townships ("banner" units) in three other counties representing a fair cross section of lower Michigan. The number of potential voters counted ran into the thousands, over 4900 for Wayne County alone in 1850 not including Detroit for which no count was made because the population schedules had not been recorded by ward.

Ethnic

The 1850 census manuscript listed the state or country of birth of every individual. The tabulation of this information for all potential voters gave the percent of each category or any combination of groups. Correlations of, say, foreign-born percent with Democratic percent in 1850 could be compared with correlations of particular foreign or native groups and Democratic percent. Impressionistic evidence was necessary to use the data to best advantage. For example, many towns had a majority of New York-born voters, but these people could have been of Yorker, Yankee, or mixed heritage. That could be determined only through using township histories or information about, say, churches in particular towns.

Socioeconomic

The description of the individual's occupation and the cash value of his real property, also provided in the 1850 census manuscript, provided the criteria by which he was ranked in one of seventeen basic occupational groups. I constructed, after investigation of occupations, wages, etc., an *occupational-status* scale designed to reflect relative socioeconomic status within two major groups:

Farm	*Urban*
Workers	
1. Laborers	*Blue Collar*
2. Tenants, renters	1. Unskilled
Owners	2. Semi-skilled
3. Farmers with land $500 or under	3. Skilled
4. Farmers with land $501-1000	4. Service
5. Farmers with land $1001-3000	
6. Farmers with land $3001-5000	*White Collar*
7. Farmers with land $5001-9999	5. Sales
8. Farmers with land $10,000 up	6. Clerical
	7. Managers, officials
	8. Professionals
	9. Proprietors

For 1850 this scale is most useful for measuring the distribution of farm "classes" within rural townships. The urban occupations give a measure of the relative "ruralness" (or "urbanness") of towns. The percent of any one or any combination of groups could be calculated and correlations run with party percents. If the 1850 returns were not available an average percent for elections 1848–1852 was used.

It seemed that the best measure of lower-class concentration in the townships was a combination of Farm Occupations, 1–3, that is, farm laborers, tenants, and farmers owning farms worth up to $500, and Urban Occupations 1 and 2, unskilled and semiskilled. The percent of these five categories of occupations in any township was regarded as the percent of Rural Lower Classes (RLC). For all the townships correlations were calculated for RLC and Democratic strength and compared with the correlates of other variables and Democratic strength.[5]

The occupational-status scale is less imperfect than average values for measuring the distribution of "classes" within townships. This can be seen by rank ordering a county's townships by their percent RLC and then by the average cash value of farms and the average value of farm implements and machinery — ("tools"). These values were found by dividing the number of occupied farms in a town into the aggregate values.[6]

The average value of farms (or tools) can be misleading, primarily by disguising poor towns as rich towns. For example, Wayne County's Monguagon township in 1850 had the highest average cash value of farms in the county, according to the data provided in printed census material. But inspection of the manuscript schedules showed that the average potential voter in Monguagon was not prosperous. In contrast to the published data which gave the number of occupied farms as thirty-six (the number which was divided into the total cash value of farms in the town), the manuscript schedules showed 108 potential voters engaged in farm occupations with almost 60 percent of them farm laborers and tenants. Ninety men actually voted in Monguagon's congressional poll of 1850. Monguagon's average values were high because a general level of prosperity *did not* prevail among its population; rather farm ownership was relatively limited and a few farms had very high values. Thus, average values showing "rich" towns should be checked as far as possible with other kinds of data. A disproportionate gap between the number of "occupied farms" and actual voters is one indicator of unreliability. Average values showing poor towns, according to all the evidence I have seen, can generally be relied on. All of the foregoing applies to predominantly farming towns, excluding, for example, those with large manufacturing villages, for which additional measures of overall wealth would be needed.[7]

Religion

The 1850 and 1860 censuses of "Social Statistics" list each church by denomination in every town and give the number of "accommodations" or "seats" in each building (as well as the value of church buildings, of which some use might be made). The number of seats can be used as a relative measure of denominational strength by computing the percent each denomination had of the total seats These percents became the *religious preferences* of each township. Thus

Redford township had three Methodist churches with 450 seats, one Baptist with 250, and one Dutch Reformed with 150 (total 850); its Methodist preference was 53 percent, its Baptist 29 percent, and Dutch Reformed 18 percent. Ecorse with one Catholic church of 200 seats had a Catholic preference of 100 percent. Considering also the number of seats in relation to population, I divided the total number by the town's population to determine the *religiosity* of each town. Redford's 850 church seats in a population of 1642 gave it a 52 percent religiosity. While Ecorse's 200 seats in a population of 631 gave it a 32 percent religiosity.[8]

Impressionistic evidence suggests that while many towns may have had extensive religious activities in 1850, if they had no church building then no record of that activity appeared in the census. A church building might have been located in a village just across a township line while most of the persons who attended it lived in another town. Only careful study of other sources can partly correct the limitations of this method.[9]

Measures of religious preference and religiosity seem best suited to observe differences between major groups, such as Catholics and Protestants. Study of religious sources for Michigan suggested that the Protestant churches could be divided into two groups of potential political relevance, evangelical and non-evangelical. While there were certainly great variations within denominations and even within congregations, the Presbyterians, Congregationalists, and Baptists seemed to be decidedly more evangelical than the other major Protestant churches (Methodist, Episcopalian, Dutch Reformed, Lutheran), that is, more oriented toward moral reform, benevolence, and pietism. Thus strong evangelical towns — with both *evangelical preference* and *religiosity* over 50 percent — could be grouped and observed as to their party preference and other characteristics. I have not run correlations using religious preferences because the crudity of the data, and the necessity of combining it with impressionistic and other evidence would give such correlations a false aura of certitude and definiteness that the data simply do not merit. This was unfortunate for many reasons, but it was still possible, after observing correlations between Democratic strength and, say, ruralness, foreign-born, Yankees, Germans, rural lower classes, prosperous farmers, and so forth, and after observing the party preferences of evangelical towns and their other characteristics, to come to fairly firm conclusions about some of the hypotheses generated from the study of party formation, platforms, appeals, images, and other kinds of political and social records of political and group conflict.

The 1860 population schedules offer the same data as 1850 adding one item: personal property. The schedules were used as in 1850 to construct an occupational-status scale, but only for Wayne County's eighteen townships and ten Detroit wards. The Wayne tabulations involved over 7160 men in the towns and some 10,960 in Detroit. I kept track of over 400 different urban occupations — although many were slight variations of the same job.

Religious preferences were calculated for townships in all counties in 1860, and for all counties other than Wayne average values (farms and tools) were used as socioeconomic indicators for townships. Some county level data proved to be of use as in 1850, but the most reliable indicators of voting patterns were based on township and ward data, and on data collected for two groups of individual voters which will be described below.

There was a lack of religious data for Detroit's wards in 1860; in fact, the only useful religious data for Detroit appeared in the 1853 city directory and was a remarkable census of the nationality and religious groups present in each ward. Any percents of ethnic and religious groups from this table used in correlations were thus based on the percent of those groups in the total population of each ward, not among the potential voters. Thus, foreign-born voting groups probably were underestimated.[10]

The occupational-status scale data for Detroit were supplemented by aggregate economic data, namely average values of carriages, household furniture, personal estate, and real estate. When the wards were ranked poorest to richest using each of these measures and compared with their percent blue collar rankings, there was no exact fit, but there was a close correspondence in the rankings, especially between percent blue collar and the average values of carriages and household furniture. These two average values seem to be the best indicators of average property distribution *within* wards.

Students of nineteenth-century voting may have the good luck to find, as I did, information about the party preferences of individual voters in particular units. So far, two such treasure caches have turned up for antebellum Michigan. In 1856 some political leader in Detroit took the trouble to write in an account book the names of 895 men, grouped alphabetically, with their street address, followed by a check mark in one of four columns headed: Frémont, Buchanan, Fillmore, and Doubtful. By using several Detroit directories available in the 1850s the occupations of 651 of the men were identified. The tabulation of this data then gave a fair picture of the composition of the Detroit parties by occupation as well as the kind of occupations affected by the turmoil and realignment of the mid-fifties. Though the representativeness of the list is moot, it seems reasonable to suppose that men appearing on the list as Frémonters and "Buchaneers" tended to be known for their party loyalties, and thus the list is probably weighted toward the more intense partisans and voters. A greater proportion of the Republicans could be identified, and this fit with other findings bearing on the class composition and mobility of the two groups.

The Detroit lists lay in a book which had been used in the 1860s and 1870s as a scrapbook for clippings on politics from newspapers. What was underneath had to be first guessed at and then discovered by having an expert in such matters steam off the disguise. However, in the Bagley Papers (Michigan Historical Collections) there lay waiting naked for the eye a record book similar to that found for Detroit. This one, for Lansing, 1858 (the Ingham County capital of Michigan by then), contained the names of 814 men, arranged in rough alphabetical order in five groups: Republicans; Democratics; Doubtful with Republican proclivities; Doubtful with Democratic proclivities; and Doubtful with uncertain proclivities. Mr. David Marion Bagley appears to have been, happily, a most methodical politician.

The local Daughters of the American Revolution, to aid genealogists, had typewritten and indexed the 1860 census population schedules for Lansing, making it possible with relatively little work to find, for 425 of the men: age, occupation, personal property, real property, birthplace, ward, and whether or not they headed a household. Once again, as in Detroit, a greater proportion of the Republicans could be identified, especially among the doubtfuls.

The 425 men were not necessarily a representative sample of the electorate, as the initial 814 may not have been, so one must be careful not to generalize about particular groups in the population, for example, laborers, carpenters, Yankees, foreign-born, and so on, since these groups may not have been adequately represented in this particular collection of names. Yet it seems reasonable to assume that the list is a rough approximation of groups in the parties in Lansing in 1858. The initial list was much more complete than the Detroit list; only 712 men actually voted for governor in November 1858 in Lansing, with the Republicans receiving 56.5 percent of that total. Comparing this simply to the relative number of Republicans (233) and Democrats (179) identified in the census, the Republican proportion of 59.6 percent was not far off the actual November division. (See Appendix for the occupational classification system used for the Lansing voters).

Referenda

Also useful were two referenda, an 1850 vote on suffrage for colored people and an 1853 vote on a law prohibiting intoxicating liquors. Correlations were run using county level and township level (wherever available) data to see if opposition to colored suffrage was related to Liberty-Free Soil voting, and if support for prohibition in 1853 was related to Whig-Free Soil voting in 1852 and also to Republican support in 1854. The most interesting methodological finding in both cases was that the correlations shown by county data were strikingly different from those shown by township data. Where, for example, an expected positive correlation from county data was low or insignificant, the township data for several counties would be impressively high.

Conclusion

Can this patchwork of blunt methods, crude quantitative data, good old impressionistic evidence, and part-time correlating be called multivariate analysis? All that can be claimed is that analysis has proceeded as much as possible, to paraphrase Lee Benson, under the control of the *logic* of multivariate analysis. One cannot pretend to have discovered proof or truth — only probabilities, tendencies, and suggestions of more subtle hypotheses than those with which one began.

The use of correlation coefficients should not impart a false aura of empirical certitude. One set of correlations is useful primarily in comparison with another set to suggest the probable relative significance of variables observed. Correlations, as everyone knows, are not causes and do not show causality. Causal relationships can only be inferred by the historian when he is immersed within all the traditional sources relevant to a particular problem.

It is time, however, to begin to work out the best ways of processing data, not only for northwestern states in the antebellum period, but for other states in that and other periods. An array of researchers is at large in the data mines, presumably at work on many case studies, attempting to rebuild American history from the bottom up. They are often aware of projects similar to their own, but they are usually unaware of the methods and concepts employed in data processing and interpretation by other scholars, even while they are all united by the unspoken, collective assumption that their work will probably converge into new explanations or hypotheses for American political history. That assumption will stand more securely to the extent that there is self-conscious, explicit standardization of methods. However far this suggested uniformity proceeds, there is little danger, historians being what they are, that individual scholars will fail to maintain their own flexibility to do their own thing.

Appendix   Occupational Classification Used for Analysis of Lansing Voters, 1858

Unskilled
  laborer, day laborer, common laborer
  drayman
  teamster, hack driver
  stage driver
Semi-skilled
  furnaceman
  gardener
  journeyman shoemaker
  fireman
Service
  nurseryman
  groceryman
Skilled Artisans
  bookbinder
  brewer
  brick maker
  baker
  butcher
  blacksmith
  carriage maker
  cloth dresser
  cabinet maker, manufacturer
  carpenter and joiner, joiner
  chair manufacturer
  fanning mill maker
  glazier
  hatter
  gunsmith
  machinist
  marble engraver, worker
  miller
  millright
  mason, stone, brick & stone
  plasterer
  printer
  mover of buildings
  painter
  saddle, harness maker
  sash maker
  shoemaker
  silk weaver
  stove moulder
  sawyer
  tanner
  tailer
  tinsmith
  tin, sheet iron, stove manufacturer
  upholsterer
  wagon maker, manufacturer

  well digger
  wood turner
  ambrotype artist
  cooper
Sales
  book seller, peddler
  peddler
Clerical
  clerk
  agent (stage, collecting)
  bookkeeper
  scribe
Managers, Officials
  state official
  local official
  assistant superintendent reform school
Professionals
  attorney and counsel, attorney
  clergy
  dentist
  editor
  physician, surgeon, druggist
  horticulturalist
  school superintendent
  teacher
  surveyor
  artist
Proprietors
  banker
  builder
  clothier
  contractor
  druggist
  dealer real estate
  grocer
  hotel keeper
  hardware merchant
  jeweler, watchmaker
  livery stable keeper
  master carpenter
  master builder
  merchant
  harness manufacturer
  printer and publisher
  saloonkeeper
  book merchant
Other
  gentleman
  farmer
  no occupation

NOTES

1 Peter S. Coleman, "Restless Grant County: Americans on the Move," *Wisconsin Magazine of History* (Autumn 1962), pp. 16–20. See also, Merle Curti et al., *The Making of An American Community: A Case Study of Democracy in a Frontier Community* (Stanford: Stanford University Press, 1959).

2 Mildred Throne, "A Population Study of an Iowa County in 1850," *Iowa Journal of History*, vol. 57 (October 1959), pp. 305–330. William L. Bowers, "Crawford Township, 1850–1870: A Population Study of a Pioneer Community," *Iowa Journal of History*, vol. 58 (January 1960), pp. 1–30. Also see James C. Bonner, "Profile of a Late Antebellum Community," *American Historical Review*, vol. 49 (July 1944), pp. 663–680, a study of Hancock County, Georgia, which used the 1850 and 1860 census schedules and dealt with some of the problems faced later by Throne, Bowers, and others.

3 The term is from Frank J. Sorauf, *Political Parties in the American System* (Boston and Toronto, 1964), by way of V. O. Key; see Frank J. Sorauf, "Political Parties and Political Analysis," in William N. Chambers and Walter Dean Burnham, eds., *The American Party Systems* (New York, 1967), pp. 33–55, for changes in Sorauf's general conceptual approach. My intellectual debts, particularly in this section, overwhelm any attempt to sort and list them here.

4 Some studies using the concept of political character implicitly if not unconsciously: Ronald P. Formisano, "A Case Study of Party Formation: Michigan, 1835," *Mid-America*, vol. 50 (April 1968), pp. 83–107; Lee Benson, *The Concept of Jacksonian Democracy: New York as a Test Case* (Princeton, 1961); Paul Kleppner, *The Cross of Culture: A Social Analysis of Midwestern Politics, 1850–1900* (to be published by the Free Press); Samuel T. McSeveney, "The Politics of Depression: Voting Behavior in Connecticut, New York and New Jersey, 1893–1896" (unpublished Ph.D. dissertation, University of Iowa, 1965; to be published by Oxford University Press); Richard J. Jensen, "The Winning of the Midwest: A Social History of Midwestern Elections, 1888–1896" (unpublished Ph.D. dissertation, Yale University, 1967); Frederick C. Luebke, "German Immigrants and the Churches in Nebraska, 1889–1915," *Mid-America*, vol. 50 (April 1968), pp. 116–130.

5 The tenants require some comment. There has been considerable investigation of the status of men described in population schedules as "farmers" but who owned no land and who did not appear in the manuscript for agriculture. In many Michigan towns in 1850 census takers described some men as "farm laborers" including some who owned small amounts of real estate, while they described others as farmers though they owned no real estate. I have concluded that the latter probably were tenants or renters. Others have made a similar guess: Bonner, p. 668; Throne, pp. 310–312; Curti, pp. 59–60; Bowers, pp. 9–10; Paul W. Gates, "Frontier Estate Builders and Farm Laborers," in Walker D. Wyman and Clifton B. Kroeber, eds. *The Frontier in Perspective* (Madison, 1957), pp. 145–47; for a recent discussion with new data, Allan G. Bogue, *From Prairie to Corn Belt: Farming on the Illinois and Iowa Prairies in the Nineteenth Century* (Chicago, 1963), pp. 22–28, 47–66.

6 The data were published in *The Statistics of Michigan*, 1850 (Lansing, 1851), by the Michigan Department of State.

7 Thomas J. Pressly and William H. Scofield, *Farm Real Estate Values in the United States by Counties, 1850–1959* (Seattle, 1965), p. 10.

8 Philip A. Nordquist, "The Ecology of Organized Religion in the United States: 1850" (unpublished Ph.D. dissertation, University of Washington, 1964), calculated religious preferences for all United States counties. Professor Thomas Pressly suggested the calculus of religiosity.

9 The number of seats is obviously not a measure of formal membership. Church rolls suggest that most communicating members of Protestant churches were women, children, and young adults. I have assumed that seat numbers give a relative measure of religious affiliations of dispositions among men. Whether churches were or were not built in developing, rural towns surely was of significance.

10 George A. Boeck, "A Historical Note on the Uses of Census Returns," *Mid-America*, vol. 44 (January 1962), pp. 46–50. Determining the religious composition of city wards in the absence of census data is not insurmountable. For the methods used to estimate relative percents of Catholic and Protestant voters in Pittsburgh in 1860 see Paul Kleppner, "Lincoln and the Immigrant Vote: A Case of Religious Polarization," *Mid-America*, vol. 48 (July 1966), pp. 183–187.

Defining American Popular Voting Behavior,

1800–1860

Part Two

In the first half-century of the American political system under the Constitution, thousands of election contests defined the enduring characteristics of American popular voting behavior. Popular electoral politics had existed to some degree throughout the colonial period. In the early years of the Republic a number of intense clashes over government policy greatly stimulated the political cleavages within the society. Political parties emerged in the 1790s as the characteristic organizers of these conflicts and the resulting electoral behavior. By 1800 Federalists and Republicans faced each other in the national political arena in constant and bitter conflict with each party enjoying a high degree of popular support.

Unfortunately, there has been little quantitative research as yet into the nature of mass voting behavior during the period of this first party system in large part because of the absence of pertinent electoral and demographic data. We do know from the studies of J. R. Pole and Richard P. McCormick that most white males could vote as bars to their participation largely disappeared before 1815. Furthermore, turnout for the many local and state elections was extraordinarily high in the early nineteenth century. (Although there was significantly less voter participation in national elections until 1840.) McCormick's research also indicates that this was a voting system with an uncertain and transient quality to it. Sustained national patterns of electoral behavior had not yet emerged nor did the first political parties last very long. The Federalists disappeared as a national force by 1815 while the Republicans grew increasingly factionalized and divided.

With the emergence of the second American party system beginning in the 1820s, the patterns of electoral politics become visible to the historian. Many scholars have described the politics of this era as reflecting a basic class confrontation between the conservative forces of an older upper class and the newly rising democratic masses of the cities and rural areas. A number of recent quantitative studies of voting patterns cast considerable doubt on this proposition. On the leadership level of politics the two parties may have grown up because of differences over public economic policies. But the research of Lee Benson on New York State, Ronald P. Formisano on Michigan, and Roger Petersen on Pennsylvania all indicate that social tensions triggered by aggressively defended religious and cultural perspectives, rather than economic or class differences, lay at the heart of political divisions among the mass of the electorate. Even in a new country, groups with different national or religious backgrounds persistently maintained their traditional prejudices and antagonisms toward one another and expressed their attitudes in their voting behavior.

By 1840 two major parties, the Whigs and the Democrats, had become firmly rooted in the political system. The two parties were crucial in structuring the behavior of the electorate. Most partisan voters viewed the parties as representing different social attitudes and as mechanisms through which particular cultural values could be maintained and threats to group well-being countered. The resulting party identification was tenaciously held by the individual voter. Patterns of Whig and Democratic association, first developed in the 1820s and 1830s, continued to affect the way people voted long after the immediate reasons for the particular party association had passed away. Each party also enjoyed a substantial following in the electorate. To be sure, there was occasional third-party activity. The Anti-Masons and American Republicans enjoyed some local successes and the Liberty and Free Soil parties entered national campaigns, but none of these parties shook the loyalty of the mass of voters to one or the other major party. This party system was a highly competitive one, reflecting its great success in organizing a closely divided electorate into two national coalitions. Although the Whigs were able to win only two presidential elections, national electoral contests were usually very close. In 1836, for example, the percentage difference between each party's national vote total was only 1.8 percent. In 1844 it was 1.4 percent.

In addition to the stability of attitudes and closeness of elections, this emerging voting system was a nationwide phenomenon. Whatever the social, economic, and other differences between sections of the United States in this period, the Democrats and Whigs enjoyed a large and loyal following in every area of the country, including the South. Scholars have not clearly identified a significant ethnocultural dimension to southern voting behavior but the research of a number of scholars does show the same lack of class-oriented voting that we find in the North, as well as a similar tenacity of party identification despite the presence and rising salience of unique sectional perspectives in the region.

This definitional period of American voting behavior culminated in the 1850s in a major realignment of electoral forces. The Democrats had enjoyed national voting supremacy for a quarter of a century when, beginning in 1853 and 1854, they permanently lost the support of a small but significant number of their partisans. A massive Irish-Catholic immigration profoundly frightened thousands of normally Democratic Protestants in the North away from their traditional party home. Many Whigs were similarly affected. Finding their parties unable or unwilling to deal with the rising alien-Catholic danger, these unhappy groups sought another means of countering the clear threat posed to their values and culture. At first they worked within a third party: the Know-Nothings. But as the revolt widened to encompass other issues, a much broader coalition, the Republican party, replaced both the Whigs and Know-Nothings and welded the revolters together. By the late 1850s, the first significant electoral realignment in American political history had created a new electoral structure, that of the third American party system characterized by a somewhat different configuration of partisan groups. Significantly, this configuration continued to be rooted, as party divisions had been throughout the previous era, primarily in differences engendered by major cultural tensions between conflicting social groups.

Suffrage and Representation in Maryland

from 1776 to 1810: A Statistical Note

and Some Reflections

J. R. Pole

4

Determining the basic conditions of the political climate in America — who was eligible to vote, when they became eligible, and how many participated in specific elections — is an important preliminary step in defining and understanding the nature of our electoral history. Professor J. R. Pole of Cambridge University, England, has made a number of careful quantitative measurements of the extent of the franchise and the amount of participation in elections in the early years of American politics. As he indicates in the following essay, this was an electoral system in which there was a great deal of popular participation and involvement. The franchise, for example, was fairly widespread in most states from the Revolutionary period onward. Throughout the same period large numbers of those eligible to vote turned out at the polls on election day.

The Maryland constitution of 1776 has been described as the result of conservative victory,[1] and certainly of the early state constitutions it was one of the most carefully calculated to protect conservative interests.[2] Yet as early as 1801, the state adopted universal free white manhood suffrage, subject only to a residence requirement of twelve months in the state and six months in the county;[3] and by a constitutional amendment ratified in 1810, all property qualifications for public office were abolished.[4] The state constitution, once renowned and indeed admired for its conservatism,[5] was thus swiftly transformed into an instrument that was democratic from top to bottom.

The scale and rapidity of this process call for careful examination. Both before and after the Revolution, Maryland was governed by a comparatively small band of powerful families who, though they sometimes found it expedient to enlist popular support, did not relax their control of policy. Even the agitation

SOURCE: Reprinted with permission of the Managing Editor from *The Journal of Southern History*, vol. 24 (May 1958), pp. 218–225. Copyright 1958 by the Southern Historical Association. The table entitled "Maryland Election Statistics, 1790–1814" was originally published by the University of California Press and is reprinted by permission of The Regents of the University of California.

for a paper currency during the postwar economic crisis was led by Samuel Chase, one of the conventional political leaders of the state. The distinguishing feature, indeed, of the leaders of this movement was not social inconspicuousness but the fact that they had purchased confiscated Tory property on a large scale.[6] In the political and constitutional conflicts that arose over this issue, the state Senate, a most conservative body, succeeded both in resisting the paper money movement and in defending its own independence against the claim that voters might exercise a constitutional right to instruct their senators.[7] The fact that the radicals gave way, after a series of bitter disputes between House and Senate, is a remarkable tribute to the power of the upper chamber. It does not seem at all likely that either party at this stage would have anticipated the reforms that were to be provided by constitutional amendment in 1810. Under the constitution of 1776, the property qualification for membership of the House was one year's residence in the county and the possession of property worth £500 current money in real and personal property, in the state; for the Senate, three years' residence and £1,000 such property, again in current money. The Senate was elected by an electoral college that made it more remote than the House from direct responsibility to the voters.[8] Even the members of the House were distinguished in general by the possession of superior means and social position.[9]

That this society, apparently so stable, and secured both by its initial structure and by constitutional safeguards, came to be so rapidly transformed, is obviously not a subject for facile explanations; but the problem will at least be rendered more manageable if we look beyond the constitutional forms and suggest that the transformation may have been less radical, and less of a social upheaval, than it appears. This seems justified when one recalls that Maryland was not the only state in which constitutional reform followed rather than anticipated a good deal of unauthorized local practice.

Under the proprietary government, the qualification for voting in assembly elections was the ownership of a fifty-acre freehold, or of forty pounds worth of personal estate valued in sterling.[10] Nonfreeholders could thus qualify to vote by the ownership of ordinary property; and there is evidence both that the common voters could exert distinct influence over the assembly, and also that these common voters might include a high proportion of the white male population.[11] Catholics, however, had been disfranchised in 1718.[12]

The constitution of 1776 abolished religious discrimination and made one change in the property qualifications of great prospective — perhaps of great immediate — significance. The alternative to a fifty-acre freehold was reduced from personal estate of forty pounds in sterling to thirty pounds in current money. In view of the perpetual shortage of hard currency and the relatively depreciated level of provincial currencies, this change must in itself have brought more people at once within the fold of the voters; but that was not the final nor the most instructive result. Before the end of the war, three new types of money were in fact "current" in Maryland, the "Continental state money" and the "black money," both issued in 1780, and the "red money" of 1781[13] — in addition to Continental dollars and the notes and currencies of other state authorities. There is no need to repeat the history of the wartime depreciation of the currency: its effect on voting qualifications expressed in current money can only have been to give every owner of ordinary personal possessions enough property to enable him to vote. A similar situation developed in New Jersey, where the decisive step taken in 1776 was the removal of the freehold tenure qualification, leaving the franchise open to all owners of fifty pounds worth of estate in proclamation money. The currency depreciated violently, and within a very few years practically no one could be excluded from the polls on grounds of insufficient property. In due course the monetary position returned to stability, and those people who had recently been enfranchised by virtue of currency depreciation rather than constitutional intent ought, in the logic of the case, to have been disfranchised once more. But of such a development there was no sign in either of the two main sources of such information, legislative petitions or evidence produced in election disputes. The property qualification disappeared as an issue of political contention as soon as the freehold tenure clause was dropped in 1776, and disappeared for good.[14]

In New Jersey, the evidence produced in election disputes shows clearly that all serious thought of property qualifications was abandoned long before constitutional reform formally did away with them;[15] in Maryland, the evidence of disputed elections remains indecisive. Want of property was occasionally alleged against voters by a defeated candidate; on one occasion at least, in Calvert County in 1782, a disappointed aspirant to the office of sheriff alleged that "Many persons who were assessed to twenty odd pounds were refused their suffrage altho' they offered to make Oath they were worth 'Thirty.' " The successful candidate was also said to lack sufficient property; but later the objection was withdrawn.[16] It is clear from a case arising in Queen Annes County in 1788 that the suffrage restrictions could still be a live issue. John Ritchie, petitioning against the election of his rival, Peter Mantz, stated that Mantz had influence in the town of Frederick, and had decided that if Ritchie objected to any voter — many in the town not being qualified — then he, Mantz, would declare in public that in his opinion all men were and ought to be privileged to vote; if Ritchie persisted after this it was expected to cause him great unpopularity. Mantz was said to have told the judges that he himself would object to no one because he held that every freeman should have the privilege of voting. But, again, the objections of the plaintiff were withdrawn.[17] In Cecil County in 1785 a disappointed candidate, in a letter to Governor William Paca, alleged that laborers, digging to make the Susquehanna navigable, had been admitted to vote; in his opinion, as tax commissioner for the county, not less than two hundred bad votes were admitted.[18] In Queen Annes County in 1788, two candidates reached an agreement not to challenge voters on grounds of property.[19] If any general inference can be drawn from the records of election disputes under the 1776 constitution, it would seem to be that technically unqualified persons frequently participated in elections, but that the practice was not so universally accepted as to be free from challenge by disappointed candidates — who, however, did not always substantiate their allegations.

As in New Jersey, some of the most striking evidence as to the state of the suffrage is provided by the figures of participation in elections; in New Jersey, without any legal or constitutional amendment to the provisions of 1776, we find 80, 90, even 100 percent of the adult males voting after about 1800;[20] in Maryland, the figures are impressive at an even earlier date;[21] and again, these evidences of high popular participation emerged before the constitution had been amended to broaden the suffrage. As early as 1790, there were seven counties in which 50 or more percent of the free adult white males voted, the figure in Baltimore Town being almost all it could be. Two years later the same was true of nine counties. The elections of 1800 produced percentage figures of more than 60 in six counties, while the records of 1808 show a degree of participation that was seldom surpassed in other states even in the Jacksonian period. All this was achieved, of course, under conditions of transport that at the best were never good and at the worst were primitive. It is generally reasonable to assume, even in good conditions, that considerably more people are entitled to vote than take advantage of the privilege. This, of course, is true today; and it was only in or about 1800 that political excitement began as a rule to stir large numbers of Americans to vote. The suffrage amendment of 1801 did not at once produce spectacular results, but there can be little doubt that it made way for the situation in 1808 when eleven counties showed voting percentages in the seventies, eighties, and nineties. (Prince Georges and Calvert counties distinguished themselves with over 100 percent.) Negro suffrage, of course, was another matter, and the contrast is revealed in the separate columns of percentage figures.

This, however, is only half the picture. The abolition, at one stroke, of the elaborate safeguards of property in the legislative structure seems, on the face of it, more dramatic and unexpected than the sanctioning of voting practices which before the advent of suffrage reform, though probably quite common, had been irregular, unconstitutional, and liable to be overturned in the legislature. In these conditions, the problems of leadership and control assumed new forms and called for new and more professional techniques in the growing science of political management.[22]

Maryland Election Statistics
1790-1814[a]

Year	County	Free Adult White Males	Total Free Adult Male Popn.	Election	Votes	Per- centage F.A.W.M.	Per- centage Total
1790	Allegheny	886	—	Cong.	408	46	—
	Anne Arundel	2,336	—	Cong.	166	7	—
	Baltimore Town	3,072	—	Cong.	3,048	99	—
	Baltimore County	4,214	—	Cong.	2,486	57	—
	Calvert	880	—	Cong.	238	27	—
	Caroline	1,365	—	Cong.	690	50	—
	Cecil	2,236	—	Cong.	901	40	—
	Charles	2,184	—	Cong.	1,018	46	—
	Dorchester	2,087	—	Cong.	549	26	—
	Frederick	5,610	—	Cong.	688	12	—
	Harford	2,352	—	Cong.	1,285	54	—
	Kent	1,428	—	Cong.	635	44	—
	Montgomery	2,592	—	Cong.	1,419	54	—
	Prince George's	2,113	—	Cong.	975	46	—
	Queen Anne's	1,681	—	Cong.	499	29	—
	St. Mary's	1,819	—	Cong.	380	20	—
	Somerset	1,760	—	Cong.	181	10	—
	Talbot	1,512	—	Cong.	297	19	—
	Washington	3,040	—	Cong.	1,152	37	—
	Worcester	1,600	—	Cong.	280	17	—
1792	Allegheny	1,021	—	Cong.	148	14	—
	Anne Arundel	2,350	—	Cong.	1,275	54	—
	Baltimore Town	3,422	—	Cong.	1,209	35	—
	Baltimore County	4,500	—	Cong.	1,433	31	—
	Calvert	858	—	Cong.	493	57	—
	Caroline	1,370	—	Cong.	497	36	—
	Cecil	2,094	—	Cong.	1,204	57	—
	Charles	2,128	—	Cong.	1,166	55	—
	Dorchester	2,041	—	Cong.	582	28	—
	Frederick	5,611	—	Cong.	438	7	—
	Harford	2,390	—	Cong.	1,166	49	—
	Kent	1,388	—	Cong.	765	55	—
	Montgomery	2,432	—	Cong.	1,119	46	—
	Prince George's	2,069	—	Cong.	1,192	57	—
	Queen Anne's	1,655	—	Cong.	1,119	67	—
	St. Mary's	1,739	—	Cong.	514	29	—
	Somerset	1,784	—	Cong.	256	14	—
	Talbot	1,516	—	Cong.	1,066	71	—

[a]The population figures have been taken from the federal census returns. For years falling between census years, the lesser has been subtracted from the greater of the two census reports, and the remainder has been divided by ten; one tenth of this remainder has then been added for each intervening year. In cases where the population has declined, it has been necessary to subtract. To estimate the number of white males over twenty-one, and also the total number of adult males including colored, a similar principle has been applied to the census information. Where, for example, the census breaks the information at age groups sixteen and twenty-six, I have taken the total between these ages, divided it by two, and added one half to give the age group from twenty-one to twenty-six. Where necessary, this method has been varied according to the type of information available. (I am indebted to Mr. N. H. Carrier, Reader in Demography in the London School of Economics, for his guidance in matters of statistical method when dealing with populations. He is not, of course, responsible for my arithmetic or my inferences.)

The voting figures have been taken from the Executive Papers in the Maryland Hall of Records.

Year	County	Free Adult White Males	Total Free Adult Male Popn.	Election	Votes	Percentage F.A.W.M.	Percentage Total
1792	Washington	3,126	—	Cong.	321	10	—
	Worcester	1,756	—	Cong.	778	44	—
1794	Allegheny	978	—	Cong.	679	69	—
	Anne Arundel	2,364	—	Cong.	1,141	48	—
	Baltimore Town	3,772	—	Cong.	160	4	—
	Baltimore County	4,786	—	Cong.	43	1	—
	Calvert	836	—	Cong.	578	69	—
	Caroline	1,377	—	Cong.	530	38	—
	Cecil	1,952	—	Cong.	1,289	66	—
	Charles	2,072	—	Cong.	1,264	61	—
	Dorchester	1,995	—	Cong.	1,176	59	—
	Frederick	5,612	—	Cong.	924	16	—
	Harford	2,428	—	Cong.	1,256	51	—
	Kent	1,348	—	Cong.	695	51	—
	Montgomery	2,272	—	Cong.	1,102	48	—
	Prince George's	2,025	—	Cong.	635	31	—
	Queen Anne's	1,629	—	Cong.	1,004	61	—
	St. Mary's	1,659	—	Cong.	525	31	—
	Somerset	1,808	—	Cong.	468	25	—
	Talbot	1,520	—	Cong.	651	42	—
	Washington	3,212	—	Cong.	1,211	37	—
	Worcester	1,912	—	Cong.	699	36	—
1796	Allegheny	1,024	—	Pres.	649	63	—
	Anne Arundel	2,378	—	Pres.	390	16	—
	Baltimore Town	4,122	—	Pres.	765	18	—
	Baltimore County	5,072	—	Pres.	731	14	—
	Calvert	814	—	Pres.	266	32	—
	Caroline	1,383	—	Pres.	162	11	—
	Cecil	1,810	—	Pres.	392	21	—
	Charles	2,016	—	Pres.	442	21	—
	Dorchester	1,949	—	Pres.	583	29	—
	Frederick	5,613	—	Pres.	1,917	34	—
	Harford	2,460	—	Pres.	618	25	—
	Kent	1,308	—	Pres.	774	59	—
	Montgomery	2,112	—	Pres.	1,310	62	—
	Prince George's	1,981	—	Pres.	1,226	62	—
	Queen Anne's	1,603	—	Pres.	538	33	—
	St. Mary's	1,579	—	Pres.	419	25	—
	Somerset	1,832	—	Pres.	24	1	—
	Talbot	1,524	—	Pres.	581	38	—
	Washington	3,298	—	Pres.	2,035	61	—
	Worcester	2,068	—	Pres.	133	6	—
1800	Allegheny	1,115	1,140	Pres.	571	51	50
	Anne Arundel	2,406	2,796	Pres.	1,218	50	43
	Baltimore Town	4,820	5,512	Pres.	1,935	40	35
	Baltimore County	5,641	6,014	Pres.	1,077	19	17
	Calvert	768	844	Pres.	221	28	26
	Caroline	1,392	1,542	Pres.	560	40	36
	Cecil	1,524	1,617	Pres.	1,015	66	62
	Charles	1,904	2,046	Pres.	621	32	30
	Dorchester	1,858	2,449	Pres.	850	45	30
	Frederick	5,614	5,732	Pres.	3,808	68	66

Year	County	Free Adult White Males	Total Free Adult Male Popn.	Election	Votes	Percentage F.A.W.M.	Percentage Total
1800	Harford	2,539	2,875	Pres.	808	31	28
	Kent	1,230	1,676	Pres.	758	61	45
	Montgomery	1,788	1,853	Pres.	1,267	71	68
	Prince George's	1,893	2,055	Pres.	1,192	63	58
	Queen Anne's	1,555	1,811	Pres.	824	53	45
	Somerset	1,881	2,027	Pres.	302	16	14
	St. Mary's	1,421	1,576	Pres.	340	24	21
	Talbot	1,536	1,933	Pres.	689	44	35
	Washington	3,471	3,556	Pres.	2,122	61	59
	Worcester	2,379	2,491	Pres.	530	22	21
1801	Allegheny	1,130	1,155	Cong.	641	56	55
	Anne Arundel	2,421	2,854	Cong.	1,189	49	41
	Baltimore Town	5,253	6,013	Cong.	1,254	23	20
	Baltimore County	5,538	5,912	Cong.	460	8	7
	Calvert	768	847	Cong.	387	50	45
	Caroline	1,392	1,552	Cong.	261	18	16
	Cecil	1,599	1,706	Cong.	407	25	23
	Charles	1,871	2,009	Cong.	805	43	40
	Dorchester	1,876	2,474	Cong.	343	18	13
	Frederick	5,652	5,777	Cong.	2,561	45	44
	Harford	2,585	2,943	Cong.	909	35	30
	Kent	1,230	1,681	Cong.	286	23	17
	Montgomery	1,819	1,894	Cong.	850	47	45
	Prince George's	1,846	2,115	Cong.	954	51	45
	Queen Anne's	1,567	1,860	Cong.	405	25	21
	St. Mary's	1,407	1,562	Cong.	339	24	21
	Somerset	1,928	2,040	Cong.	285	14	14
	Talbot	1,540	1,948	Cong.	220	14	11
	Washington	3,462	3,551	Cong.	2,052	59	57
	Worcester	2,383	2,510	Cong.	269	11	10
1803	Allegheny	1,160	1,185	Cong.	952	82	80
	Anne Arundel Baltimore Town and County	11,453	11,925	Cong.	8,284	72	69
	Calvert	769	853	Cong.	607	79	71
	Caroline	1,392	1,572	Cong.	653	47	41
	Cecil	1,748	1,884	Cong.	782	44	41
	Charles	1,804	1,935	Cong.	1,063	59	55
	Dorchester	1,912	2,524	Cong.	681	35	27
	Frederick	5,728	5,867	Cong.	4,728	82	80
	Harford	2,676	3,079	Cong.	1,821	68	59
	Kent	1,230	1,691	Cong.	625	50	36
	Montgomery	1,880	1,976	Cong.	1,369	72	69
	Prince George's	1,752	2,235	Cong.	940	53	42
	Queen Anne's	1,592	1,976	Cong.	892	56	45
	St. Mary's	1,379	1,534	Cong.	509	36	33
	Somerset	1,921	2,066	Cong.	580	30	28
	Talbot	1,548	1,978	Cong.	595	38	30
	Washington	3,444	3,541	Cong.	2,505	73	71
	Worcester	2,390	2,548	Cong.	584	24	23
1804	Allegheny	1,175	1,200	Cong.	341	29	28
	Anne Arundel	2,527	3,208	Cong.	900	35	28

Year	County	Free Adult White Males	Total Free Adult Male Popn.	Election	Votes	Percentage F.A.W.M.	Percentage Total
1804	Baltimore Town and County	11,784	13,122	Cong.	2,888	24	22
	Calvert	770	856	Cong.	322	41	37
	Caroline	1,393	1,582	Cong.			
	Cecil	1,823	1,973	Cong.	382	21	19
	Charles	1,770	1,898	Cong.	304	17	16
	Dorchester	1,930	2,549	Cong.	1,002	52	39
	Frederick	5,765	5,912	Cong.			
	Harford	2,721	3,147	Cong.	1,272	46	40
	Kent	1,230	1,696	Cong.	389	31	22
	Montgomery	1,911	2,017	Cong.	918	48	45
	Prince George's	1,705	2,295	Cong.	704	41	30
	Queen Anne's	1,604	2,031	Cong.	341	21	16
	St. Mary's	1,365	1,520	Cong.	631	46	41
	Somerset	1,918	2,079	Cong.	1,217	63	58
	Talbot	1,553	1,993	Cong.	862	55	43
	Washington	3,435	3,536	Cong.	502	14	14
	Worcester	2,394	2,567	Cong.	2,014	84	78
1806	Allegheny	1,206	1,230	Cong.	496	41	40
	Anne Arundel	2,597	3,144	Cong.	1,820	70	57
	Baltimore Town and County	12,446					
	Calvert	771	862	Cong.	368	47	42
	Caroline	1,393	1,602	Cong.	1,014	72	63
	Cecil	1,973	2,151	Cong.	1,155	59	58
	Charles	1,703	1,822	Cong.	818	48	44
	Dorchester	1,966	2,599	Cong.	1,841	94	71
	Frederick	5,839	6,002	Cong.	3,519	60	58
	Harford	2,813	3,281	Cong.	1,868	66	57
	Kent	1,230	1,706	Cong.	729	59	42
	Montgomery	1,972	2,100	Cong.	1,712	86	81
	Prince George's	1,611	2,414	Cong.	1,432	89	59
	Queen Anne's	1,630	2,140	Cong.	1,009	61	46
	St. Mary's	1,337	1,493	Cong.	529	39	35
	Somerset	1,910	2,105	Cong.	1,203	63	57
	Talbot	1,562	2,021	Cong.	1,200	77	59
	Washington	3,417	3,526	Cong.	2,012	59	57
	Worcester	2,401	2,604	Cong.	1,771	73	68
1808	Allegheny	1,235	1,260	Cong.	892	72	70
				Pres.	843	[b]34	33
	Anne Arundel	2,670	3,260	Cong.	1,557	58	47
				Pres.	636	[b]12	10
	Baltimore Town	8,292	9,523	Cong.	3,952	47	41
				Pres.	2,848	[b]17	15
	Baltimore County	4,811	5,195	Cong.	3,706	77	71
				Pres.	1,780	37	34
	Calvert	772	865	Cong.	783	100+	91
				Pres.	728	94	84
	Caroline	1,393	1,622	Cong.	1,099	78	67
				Pres.	898	64	55

[b]See notes to 1812.

Year	County	Free Adult White Males	Total Free Adult Male Popn.	Election	Votes	Percentage F.A.W.M.	Percentage Total
1808	Cecil	2,122	2,330	Cong.	1,919	90	82
				Pres.	881	41	37
	Charles	1,640	1,746	Cong.	1,111	67	63
				Pres.	398	24	22
	Dorchester	2,003	2,655	Cong.	1,047	52	39
				Pres.	1,014	50	38
					(incomplete)		
	Frederick	5,914	6,095	Cong.	4,983	84	81
				Pres.	4,809	[b]41	40
	Harford	2,905	3,419	Cong.	1,919	66	56
				Pres.	1,158	39	33
	Kent	1,229	1,713	Cong.	1,154	93	67
				Pres.	467	37	27
	[c]Montgomery	2,034	2,185	Cong.	1,559	77	71
	Prince George's	1,516	2,534	Cong.	1,396	92	55
				Pres.	1,154	76	45
	Queen Anne's	1,651	2,251	Cong.	1,344	81	59
				Pres.	431	26	19
	St. Mary's	1,308	1,465	Cong.	713	54	48
				Pres.	321	24	21
	Somerset	1,890	2,131	Cong.	1,001	52	46
				Pres.	741	39	34
	Talbot	1,572	2,050	Cong.	1,281	81	62
				Pres.	1,057	67	51
	Washington	3,400	3,516	Cong.	2,568	75	73
				Pres.	2,590	[d]38	37
	Worcester	2,410	2,641	Cong.	1,460	60	55
				Pres.	864	35	32
1810	Allegheny	1,266	1,294	Cong.	317	25	24
	Anne Arundel	2,738	3,376	Cong.	1,669	61	49
	Baltimore Town	9,158	10,525	Cong.	5,075	36	32
	Baltimore County	4,611	4,995	Cong.			
	Calvert	773	870	Cong.	386	50	44
	Caroline	1,394	1,644	Cong.	893	64	54
	Cecil	2,272	2,508	Cong.	1,022	45	40
	Charles	1,569	1,672	Cong.	567	41	39
	Dorchester	2,038	2,704	Cong.	938	46	34
	Harford	2,997	3,552	Cong.	1,401	47	39
	Kent	1,229	1,723	Cong.	511	41	29
	Montgomery	2,096	2,265	Cong.	374	17	16
	Prince George's	1,423	2,654	Cong.	1,369	96	51
	Queen Anne's	1,681	2,365	Cong.	665	39	28
	St. Mary's	1,279	1,438	Cong.	457	35	31
	Somerset	1,894	2,158	Cong.	572	30	26
	Talbot	1,580	2,080	Cong.	781	49	37
	Washington	3,382	3,502	Cong.	757	22	21
	Worcester	2,416	2,679	Cong.	1,890	78	71
1812	Allegheny	1,344	1,372	Cong.	1,085	80	79
				Pres.	950	[d]35	34

[c]See notes to 1812.
[d]Under the election law of 1806, ch. xcvii, these counties were arranged in districts each of which chose two electors, so that each voter was entitled to cast two votes. The percentage figures have accordingly been halved.

Year	County	Free Adult White Males	Total Free Adult Male Popn.	Election	Votes	Percentage F.A.W.M.	Percentage Total
1812	Anne Arundel	2,816	3,474	Cong.	2,127	75	61
				Pres.	1,266	d23	18
	Baltimore Town	9,576	11,105	Pres.	3,467	e18	16
				Cong.	4,273	44	38
	Baltimore County	4,793	5,211	Cong.		g61	
				Pres.	2,394	50	45
	Calvert	780	888	Pres.	599	76	67
				Cong.	367	47	41
	Caroline	1,406	1,664	Pres.	1,111	79	66
				Cong.	1,245	88	75
	Cecil	2,346	2,620	Pres.	1,549	66	59
				Cong.	972	41	37
	Charles	1,596	1,650	Pres.	451	28	27
				Cong.	1,189	74	72
	Dorchester	2,061	2,704	Pres.	1,113	54	41
				Cong.	1,927	93	71
	Frederick	6,242	6,509	Pres.	4,717	e38	36
				Cong.	5,500	88	84
	Harford	2,917	3,424	Pres.	1,410	48	41
				Cong.	1,602	55	46
	Kent	1,219	1,709	Pres.	984	80	57
				Cong.	576	47	33
	fMontgomery	2,010	2,255				
				Cong.	1,564	77	69
	Prince George's	1,512	2,544	Pres.	1,109	73	43
				Cong.	1,539	100+	60
	Queen Anne's	1,719	2,293	Pres.	1,127	65	49
				Cong.	1,182	68	51
	St. Mary's	1,287	1,448	Pres.	311	24	21
				Cong.	517	40	35
	Somerset	1,942	2,252	Pres.	766	39	33
				Cong.	1,545	79	68
	Talbot	1,596	2,076	Pres.	1,392	87	67
				Cong.	1,446	90	69
	Washington	3,554	3,676	Pres.	2,304	h32	31
				Cong.	2,910	81	79
	Worcester	2,396	2,681	Pres.	988	41	35
				Cong.	1,930	80	71

dUnder the election law of 1806, ch. xcvii, these counties were arranged in districts each of which chose two electors, so that each voter was entitled to cast two votes. The percentage figures have accordingly been halved.
eSee notes to 1812.
fUnder the election law of 1806, Montgomery County was divided between a district electing one, and a district electing two electors, making it impossible to infer the number of voters from the number of votes cast.
gSee David Hackett Fischer, *The Revolution of American Conservatism* (New York, 1965), p. 189.
hSee notes to 1812.

NOTES

[1] Allan Nevins, *The American States during and after the Revolution* (New York, 1924), p. 157.

[2] Philip A. Crowl, *Maryland during and after the Revolution* (Baltimore, 1943), pp. 34–37.

[3] *Laws of Maryland, 1811–1812* (with index 1800–1812) (Annapolis, 1812). Sess. 1801, chap. 90.

[4] Francis N. Thorpe, *Federal and State Constitutions, Colonial Charters, and Other Organic Laws* (7 vols, Washington, 1909), vol. 3, p. 1705.

[5] Crowl, *Maryland during and after the Revolution*, pp. 34–37.

[6] *Ibid.*, pp. 96–97.

[7] *Ibid.*, pp. 104–109.

[8] Thorpe, *Federal and State Constitutions*, vol. 3, p. 1693.

[9] Crowl, *Maryland during and after the Revolution*, pp. 33–34.

[10] Charles A. Barker, *The Background of the Revolution in Maryland* (New Haven, 1940), p. 171.

[11] *Ibid.*, 171–77. In 1752 there were 992 votes cast in a Baltimore County election. The number of free white males was reported in the census of 1775 as 2630. If about one half of the population was of age, then this figure would stand for some 75 percent of the free adult white males.

[12] Barker, *Background of the Revolution in Maryland*, p. 172.

[13] Crowl, *Maryland during and after the Revolution*, pp. 86–87.

[14] J. R. Pole, "Suffrage Reform and the American Revolution in New Jersey," in *Proceedings of the New Jersey Historical Society* (Newark, 1847–   ), vol. 74 (July 1956), pp. 173–194.

[15] AM Papers (New Jersey State Library).

[16] Petition of Alexander Somervell, Calvert County, October 13, 1782, in Executive Papers (Maryland Hall of Records).

[17] Petition of John Ritchie, Frederick County, October 18, 1788, *ibid.*

[18] Samuel Veazey to Governor William Paca, October 20, 1785, *ibid.*

[19] Remonstrance of John Price, Queen Annes County, October 1788, *ibid.*

[20] J. R. Pole, "The Suffrage in New Jersey, 1790–1807," in *Proceedings of the New Jersey Historical Society*, vol. 71 (January 1953), pp. 54–61. See, in general, Richard P. McCormick, *The History of Voting in New Jersey* (New Brunswick, 1953).

[21] See appended table.

[22] This problem, with special reference to the Federalist attitude towards it, is discussed with regard to a neighboring state in J. R. Pole, "Jeffersonian Democracy and the Federalist Dilemma, New Jersey, 1800–1812," in *Proceedings of the New Jersey Historical Society*, vol. 74 (October 1956), pp. 260–292.

Suffrage Classes and Party Alignments:

A Study in Voter Behavior

Richard P. McCormick

5

Richard P. McCormick's quantitative examination of the composition and partisan distribution of the American electorate in the 1820s and 1830s has significantly challenged a number of traditional ideas about popular voting in Jacksonian America. In one study of patterns of voter turnout in the nation, he has questioned whether the rise of the Jacksonians to power in the 1820s actually stimulated an upsurge of mass political participation in American society. McCormick has also found little evidence, as he indicates in the following article, for the usual notion that economic class differences were the primary influence on popular voting. Rather, he suggests, regardless of rhetorical flourishes about Democratic identification with the common man, the lower classes did not uniformly support the Democratic party.

The traditional ingredients of American political history have been personalities, classes, sections, parties, and issues. The voter, except in so far as he has been regarded as an element of a class or a section, has received relatively little attention. More recently, because of dwindling confidence in the efficacy of the hypotheses of Beard and Turner, we are less sure of our ability to conceive of the electorate in terms of classes and sections. Consequently, we are impelled to reexamine the entire field of voter behavior in order to obtain new understandings of the role of the electorate in the democratic process. In attacking one aspect of this large problem, this study deals with certain limited but critical questions related to the composition and behavior of the electorate in the early national period. More specifically, it is an analysis of the degree to which certain types of property qualifications restricted the size of the electorate and of the relationship of the economic status of voters to their party affiliation.[1]

It is generally understood that in the decades before the Civil War property qualifications for voting existed in most states.[2] What is not known with any degree of precision is the extent to which these barriers excluded adult males

SOURCE: Reprinted with permission from *The Mississippi Valley Historical Review*, vol. 46 (December 1959), pp. 397–410.

from the polls. Neither is it clear what effect extensions of the franchise to lower economic segments of the population had on the relative strength of competing political parties. Equally clouded is the larger question of whether the electorate tended to divide between the major parties along lines of economic cleavage. It is doubtful whether these questions can be answered with assurance for most states, because the nature of the evidence is often such as to preclude methodical inquiry. There are, however, two states that provide highly favorable conditions for analyses of the type proposed, and for that reason they have been selected as the basis for this study.

These states — North Carolina and New York — have been chosen, then, not because they are necessarily typical, but because they afford more reliable and relevant data than can be secured for other states. Both states were unusual in that they had, for varying periods, dual property qualifications for voting. That is, voters having the minimum qualifications could vote for limited categories of officials, whereas those meeting higher qualifications were eligible to vote for all elective officials. This feature, together with others that will be considered, makes it possible to measure not only the restrictive effect of certain property qualifications but also the party affiliations of the different classes of electors.

It is convenient to examine first the experience of North Carolina. Its constitution of 1776 created a dual suffrage system. Only adult freemen possessed of fifty acres of land within the county in which they voted could vote for a member of the state senate. But all freemen — including the fifty-acre freeholders — who had paid county or state taxes were eligible to vote for members of the house of commons. After 1835, when the office of governor became elective by popular vote, the lesser franchise requirement was extended to apply also in gubernatorial elections. Not until 1856 was this dual arrangement replaced by general taxpayer suffrage.[3] For eighty years, then, the fifty-acre freeholders can be distinguished as a separate electoral class in North Carolina. In any state election within that period it is possible to analyze the ratio of fifty-acre electors to those voters meeting only the taxpayer qualification. The party preferences of the two suffrage groups can also be determined. For the most reliable results, however, it is desirable to select a period when party lines were distinct and strong and when something approaching a maximum vote was registered.[4] These conditions maintained between 1836 and 1856.[5]

During those years the Whig and Democratic parties contested on a nearly even basis in North Carolina, with the Whigs dominant by a slight margin down to 1848. Voter participation was high, averaging 77 percent of the adult white male population. By comparing the size of the vote cast county-by-county for governor with the comparable vote for state senators, it is possible to measure the proportion of the total electorate that could not meet the fifty-acre requirement (see Table 5.1). Then, by examining the distribution of each class of the electorate between the two major parties it can be determined whether economic status influenced party affiliation.

Table 5.1 indicates that approximately one-half of the total electorate lacked the amount of property required to vote for state senators. In 1840, for example, 57,460 votes were cast for governor and 31,241 for senator in the forty-six counties for which returns were available. Thus 45.6 percent of the voters lacked the fifty-acre freehold required of senatorial electors. The fact that a vote equivalent to 83 percent of the total adult white male population of the state was

Table 5.1   Size of Electoral Classes in North Carolina, 1835-1856[*]

Year	Number of Counties in Sample	Vote for Senators	Vote for Governor	Senate Vote as % of Vote for Governor	Governor Vote as % of Adult White Males
1835-1836	26 of 64	18,532	33,066	56.0	67.1
1840	46 of 68	31,241	57,460	54.4	83.0
1844	22 of 73	15,209	31,481	48.3	78.7
1856	46 of 82	30,205	62,915	48.0	79.3

[*]The only available source of returns of elections of members of the state senate are the contemporary newspapers, and their coverage was not complete. The elections that I cite were chosen mainly because returns were found for a fairly large number of counties in various parts of the state. Because the returns for the 1836 senatorial elections were inadequate, I have used the returns for the 1835 election and have compared them with the 1836 gubernatorial returns. For the other three elections, the voting for governor and senators took place at the same time. Voting was by paper ballot and elections were held biennially in August. All returns are from the Raleigh *North Carolina Standard*, and can be found in the several issues following each election.

polled for governor in 1840 would suggest that the requirement that voters must have paid a state or county tax was not a serious limitation on the franchise.[6] Even in states where unrestricted manhood suffrage existed, voter participation did not ordinarily exceed the 80 percent level.[7] The conclusions regarding the proportion of taxpayers excluded from voting for senator is based on a sample ranging from 38.3 percent to 71.7 percent of the total state vote, and some degree of error could result from this lack of a complete enumeration. But the proportions are sufficiently consistent from election to election to indicate that the true figure would not be far from 50 percent. This reasoning is confirmed by the observations of the editor of the Raleigh *Standard* in 1848 that there were "between thirty and forty thousand freehold voters" in the state, and that the total electorate was "about eighty thousand."[8]

The precise relationship of fifty-acre freeholders to taxpayers varied somewhat from county to county, although a one-to-one ratio prevailed in a remarkably high number of instances. Detailed studies could readily be made to determine whether the proportion of freehold voters was greater in some sections than in others, and such an analysis would be relevant to any intensive investigation of the North Carolina political environment. Table 5.2 indicates the pat-

Table 5.2   Size of Electoral Classes in Wake County, North Carolina[*]

Year	Vote for Senator	Vote for Governor	Senate Vote as % of Vote for Governor
1838	946	1857	50.9
1840	1006	2187	46.0
1842	1020	2138	47.7
1844	1083	2344	46.2
1846	992	2161	45.9
1848	1023	2284	44.8

[*]The vote figures are from the Raleigh *North Carolina Standard* in August of each election year.

tern in Wake County, in which Raleigh was situated. The ratio between the two electorates was quite stable, and it was fairly close to the statewide average.

Because of the dual suffrage system, it is an easy matter to compare the party affiliations of the fifty-acre freeholders with those of the lower electoral class. How wide an economic margin separated the two politicoeconomic classes is a matter for conjecture — or further research — but it would seem reasonable to assume that there was an appreciable distinction in status. The question, then, is whether the fifty-acre freeholders, as an upper-level economic group, differed markedly in their party affiliations from the remainder of the electorate.

Table 5.3 presents the results of a study of three state elections. In the first two columns are given the party distribution of votes cast for senator and for governor in the counties that comprised the sample. Column three gives the assumed vote of the nonfreehold electors for governor and has been obtained by subtracting the senatorial vote of each party from the gubernatorial vote.[9] The next three columns show the percentage distribution of the party vote cast by the senatorial electors, by the total electorate, and by the nonfreeholders, respectively.

Table 5.3 Distribution of Party Affiliation by
Electoral Classes in North Carolina*

Year	Party	Vote for Senators	Vote for Governor	Nonfreehold Voters	% by Party Senators Vote	% by Party Governors Vote	% by Party Nonfreehold Vote
1840	Whig	16,760	30,594	13,834	53.7	53.2	52.7
	Dem.	14,481	26,866	12,385	46.3	46.8	47.3
1844	Whig	8,053	16,430	8,377	52.9	52.2	51.4
	Dem.	7,156	15,051	7,895	47.1	47.8	48.6
1856	Whig	13,231	27,035	13,804	43.8	43.0	42.2
	Dem.	16,974	35,880	18,906	56.2	57.0	57.8

*The votes have been compiled from the returns in the Raleigh *North Carolina Standard*.

In each of the three elections the fifty-acre freehold voters were divided between Whigs and Democrats in almost exactly the same proportions as those who met only the taxpaying qualification. In 1840, for example, 53.7 percent of the freehold electors were Whigs, as were 52.7 percent of the less qualified electors. In none of the elections was there as much as a 2 percent difference in the party distribution of the two classes of voters. Indeed, the similarity of the party affiliations of the two groups was so nearly identical as to be astonishing. The fifty-acre freeholder class was from one to two percentage points more strongly Whig than the less privileged voters, a differential so small as to be inconsiderable. Thus, whether or not a man owned fifty acres or more of land seemingly had little or no influence on his party affiliation. Or, to express it differently, the economic distinction implicit in the dual suffrage system had no substantial significance as a factor in determining party alignments in these North Carolina elections.

The similarity of party distribution within the two classes of electors existed in almost every county; it is not the fabrication of an averaging process. In the 1840 election the same party that obtained a majority of votes in the senatorial election also received a majority in the gubernatorial contest in forty-three of the forty-six counties.[10] In each of the three exceptional cases the vote was extremely close, and local circumstances may well have produced a majority for one party in the election of a senator and for the other in the gubernatorial election. What this means, of course, is that if the election of a governor had been determined by the fifty-acre freeholders alone, the same candidate would have been elected with almost precisely the same percentage of the total vote.

The implications of this analysis are both intriguing and suggestive. If it was true that in North Carolina the restriction of the suffrage to fifty-acre freeholders would have produced the same results as extending the franchise to all taxpayers, what happened in other states when the suffrage was broadened? Is there convincing evidence that when lower economic strata of the population were given the vote there resulted some measurable change in party alignments? Did the new voters, presumably homogeneous in their economic status, tend to move as a group into one of the two major parties?

Certain more or less ideal conditions must exist before this question can be answered with assurance for any state. There should be a marked reduction in suffrage qualifications occurring at a time when party lines were distinct and stable and when voter participation was at a sufficiently high level that the effect of the change in suffrage could be measured. The first condition is found in a number of states, but not usually in association with the two others. Most of the lowering of suffrage barriers in the United States took place before 1824 in a period when party alignments were unstable, weak, or nonexistent.[11] After 1824, Rhode Island, Louisiana, Mississippi, and Virginia broadened the franchise, but in the first three states the increase in the proportion of adult white males voting was so small as to be inconsiderable. In Virginia the liberalization was accomplished in two steps, in 1830 and 1850, which rather lessened the impact of the change.[12]

Probably the state which most nearly fulfills the specified conditions is New York. Moreover, because that state also had a dual suffrage system, it lends itself to analyses similar to those made for North Carolina. Under the New York Constitution of 1777, only those men who owned freeholds valued at £100 were eligible to vote for governor, lieutenant-governor, and state senator. Those who had freeholds worth £20, or who rented tenements with a yearly value of forty shillings and paid public taxes, could vote for assemblymen and members of Congress. This dual system ended when a new constitution, effective February 28, 1822, conferred franchise privileges on all adult male citizens who paid county or state taxes, performed (or were exempted from) militia duty, or labored on the public highways. In 1826 all property and taxpaying requirements for voting in New York were eliminated.[13]

There is no difficulty in determining how many electors were in each of the two suffrage classes. New York conducted censuses of electors at least once in every seven years between 1790 and 1821, and from these records the restrictive effect of the various suffrage qualifications can be computed and tabulated.

The data in Table 5.4 indicate that prior to 1822 roughly two-thirds of the adult white male population could vote. The £100 freeholders averaged about 38 percent of the adult white male population. Between one-quarter and one-third of the adult white males possessed only the lower of the two suffrage qualifications and were therefore unable to vote for governor, lieutenant-gover-

Table 5.4   Size of Electoral Classes in New York, 1801-1835 [*]

Year	Adult White Males	Total Electors	Total Electors as % of Adult White Males	£100 Electors	£100 Electors as % of Adult White Males	Other Electors	Other Electors as % of Adult White Males
1801	125,000	85,907	68.7	52,058	41.6	33,849	27.1
1807	170,000	121,289	71.3	71,159	41.8	50,130	29.5
1814	239,000	151,846	63.5	87,491	36.6	64,355	26.9
1821	299,500	202,510	67.6	100,490	33.5	102,020	34.1
1822	312,700	259,387	82.9				
1825	352,300	296,132	84.0				
1835	467,000	422,034	90.3				

[*]New York (State), Secretary of State, *Census of the State of New York for 1855* (Albany, 1857), ix-x, xli-xliii. The 1855 census contains a compendium of all preceding electoral censuses, giving the number of electors in each category by counties. This remarkably detailed information has been surprisingly neglected by students of voter behavior. Several other states, among them Ohio, Louisiana, Kentucky, and Tennessee, also conducted censuses of electors, but none was comparable in excellence to those of New York.

nor, and senator. Approximately one-third of the adult males lacked the qualifications to vote in any elections before 1822. As a result of the constitutional change in the suffrage in 1822, the total electorate rose sharply to include 83 percent of the adult white males. Most important is the fact that the number of those eligible to vote for governor rose from 100,490 to 259,387, an increase of almost 160 percent. The elimination of the taxpaying requirement after 1825 had a relatively slight effect on the size of the electorate. In general terms, the economic-electoral classes within the population of New York in 1821 can be described as follows: the top third enjoyed full franchise privileges; the middle third had limited privileges; and the bottom third was disfranchised.

We can, as in the case of North Carolina, inquire whether the two suffrage classes in New York differed in party alignment. The election held in April 1816, at which time a governor and members of Congress — as well as legislators — were chosen, saw the Federalists making their final full-scale effort against the Republicans.[14] Because complete returns by counties for both the gubernatorial and congressional contests are available, it is possible to use these votes to determine the party alignments within the two suffrage classes (see Table 5.5). The governor was elected by the £100 freeholders alone; the total electorate was eligible to vote for members of Congress.

Table 5.5 would seem to show that the nonfreehold voters were only slightly more biased toward the Republican party than were the elite electors. Two circumstances, however, make interpretations of these data hazardous. If the voting figures are taken at face value, they indicate that 93 percent of those eligible to vote for governor actually went to the polls. This percentage is so suspiciously high as to suggest that many who lacked the £100 freehold may have voted in the gubernatorial election. Again, the figures imply that only 48 percent of the eligible nonfreehold electors cast their ballots. If this was indeed the case, the question arises as to whether such a low turnout constitutes a realistic

Table 5.5 Distribution of Party Affiliation by
Electoral Classes in New York, 1816[*]

Party	Vote for Governor	% by Party	Vote for Congress	% by Party	Nonfreehold Voters Congress	% by Party
Republican	45,412	54.0	67,757	54.9	22,345	57.0
Federalist	38,647	46.0	55,514	45.1	16,867	43.0

[*]The returns for both the gubernatorial and congressional elections, which were held at the same time, are from the Albany *Advertiser*, June 15, 1816. The results of the congressional election were used because those returns were complete and those for the assembly districts were not. The estimates of the numbers of nonfreehold voters participating in the congressional elections has been computed with the same procedure that was used in the North Carolina analysis.

sample.[15] The safest conclusion to be drawn is that the presence at the polls of the nonfreehold electors — as evidenced in the congressional vote — did not significantly alter the party alignments manifested in the gubernatorial election.

The final problem to be examined is the effect of a marked broadening of the electorate on party alignments in New York. The liberalization of the suffrage in 1822 increased the number of those eligible to vote for governor from approximately 33 percent of the adult white males to 84 percent. The two parties in New York at this period were the Republicans and the Clintonians — the candidate of the latter for the governorship in 1820, 1824, and 1826 being De Witt Clinton. In 1820, prior to the expansion of the electorate, Clinton received 50.9 percent of the total gubernatorial vote of 93,437. In 1824, when lowered suffrage requirements resulted in a total vote of 190,545, his percentage was 54.3. In 1826 he polled 50.9 percent of the 195,920 votes cast.[16] There is every reason to assume that the increased vote came from those electoral classes that previously had either lacked the vote entirely or had been ineligible to vote for governor.[17]

According to the most recent authoritative survey of New York history, Clinton was regarded by the conservative forces as their champion; and the "liberal elements, whose strength was augmented by the widened suffrage, followed the leadership of the Albany Regency."[18] Yet the foregoing analysis of the voting in New York demonstrates that the only observable effect of the extension of the suffrage was a very slight increase in Clinton's majority. Certainly the New York experience offers no support for the belief that even a drastic enlargement of the electorate resulted in any measurable change in party alignments.[19] On the contrary, it gives added weight to the view that economic status as defined in suffrage restrictions had little or no influence on the party affiliations of voters. The new voters, drawn from an economic level that had previously been barred from the polls, apparently divided fairly evenly in party preferences between the Republicans and the Clintonians.

Perhaps Erastus Root was right when, speaking in the New York constitutional convention in 1821 in defense of manhood suffrage, he rejected the notion that the propertyless must be held in check because their interests were antagonistic to those of men of substance. "We have," declared Root, "no different estates, having different interests, necessary to be guarded from encroachments by the watchful eye of jealousy. We are all of the same estate — all commoners."[20]

This analysis of suffrage conditions and voter behavior in North Carolina and

New York suggests several conclusions and raises some questions that merit further investigation. It is quite clear that in both of these states property qualifications effectively limited the size of the electorate. In North Carolina nearly one-half of those who went to the polls to vote for governor were unable to vote for state senators because they lacked the requisite fifty-acre freehold. In New York prior to 1821 approximately one-third of the adult white males were totally excluded from voting and another third was not qualified to vote for governor.

In both states the abandonment of property tests led to a sharp and immediate rise in the number of votes cast for those offices that had previously been elective by voters possessed of special qualifications. In New York, however, it seems quite probable that the constitutional restrictions were not rigidly enforced, with the result that a sizable number of inadequately qualified voters participated in gubernatorial elections. Moreover, when the suffrage was liberalized, the newly enfranchised voters manifested considerable apathy toward the exercise of their newly gained privilege.

Studies of other states — most notably New Jersey and Massachusetts — have tended to minimize the importance of property requirements as a factor limiting the size of the electorate.[21] Obviously, for the period studied, this was not the case in New York or North Carolina. The point is that the experience of each state must be carefully investigated before any sweeping generalizations are made. The particular definitions of the suffrage qualifications must be examined, as well as the practical arrangements that existed for enforcement of the legal or constitutional requirements.

Although North Carolina and New York are not cited as "typical," they were two important — and even representative — states. Consequently, the conclusion that the upper economic-electoral class in each state divided between the major parties in almost the same proportions as the lower economic-electoral class raises significant questions about the general validity of economic-class interpretations of political behavior. Of course, the fact that parties did not reflect lines of economic cleavage in the periods under investigation does not necessarily imply that in other periods the same condition maintained. Here, again, is a field for further study.

It does not appear that the liberalization of the franchise had any measurable effect on the relative strength of the contending parties in either of the states investigated. To put it even more bluntly, when the common man was enfranchised in New York after 1821, he did not upset the political balance by throwing his weight heavily on the side of one party. Either he did not vote, or he showed as much preference for one party as for the other. If the broadening of the franchise did result in a major realignment of parties in any other state, that fact, I believe, has yet to be demonstrated.

The behavior of the voters of the lower electoral class in both North Carolina and New York indicates that there was little reason for the more substantial voters to fear the consequences of entrusting the masses with the franchise.[22] How important was this fear factor, actually, in delaying the general movement toward white manhood suffrage in other states? Conversely, how vociferous were those who lacked the franchise in demanding voting privileges? Neither of these questions has been studied sufficiently in individual states to permit any firm general conclusions.

Finally, preoccupation with such matters as franchise restrictions and the influences shaping a voter's party preference should not result in neglect of the equally relevant problem of what stimulated voters to go to the polls. In North Carolina nearly all of the eligibles participated in elections. In New York a considerable fraction — around one-third in 1824 — did not choose to vote. Such large variations in the rate of voter participation from state to state require explanation. It may well be that the factor most responsible for increasing the size of the actual electorate after 1824, for example, was not the elimination of suffrage barriers but rather the surge to the polls of voters who previously had not been sufficiently stimulated to cast their ballots. The voter, then, must be added to the traditional ingredients of American political history. Studies of his behavior hold some promise of adding a new dimension to our perception of the nature of our democracy.

NOTES

[1] Grateful acknowledgment is made to the Social Science Research Council for a grant that made possible an investigation of early American political behavior, of which this study is one product.

[2] Despite its many inaccuracies, the standard work on the subject is Kirk H. Porter, *A History of Suffrage in the United States* (Chicago, 1918). For an adequate brief summary, see Charles O. Paullin, *Atlas of the Historical Geography of the United States* (Washington, 1932), pp. 126–127.

[3] Francis N. Thorpe (comp.), *The Federal and State Constitutions, Colonial Charters, and Other Organic Laws of the States, Territories, and Colonies* (7 vols., Washington, 1909), vol. 5, pp. 2790, 2796–2797, 2799. Neither of the two standard histories of the suffrage in North Carolina makes any attempt to examine the actual restrictive effect of the dual qualifications. John S. Bassett, "Suffrage in the State of North Carolina (1776–1861)," *Annual Report of the American Historical Association, 1895* (Washington, 1896), pp. 271–285; John W. Carr, "The Manhood Suffrage Movement in North Carolina," *Historical Papers of the Trinity College Historical Society* (Durham), vol. 11 (1915), pp. 47–78. See also J. G. de Roulhac Hamilton, *Party Politics in North Carolina, 1835–1860* (Chapel Hill, 1916), pp. 77, 84, 117–121. Bassett, Carr, and Hamilton all agree that prior to 1848, when the Democratic candidate for governor unveiled the suffrage issue in the campaign, there was no indication of a popular demand for the elimination of the freehold requirement.

[4] If there were no discernible party lines, or if such lines were indistinct, it would obviously be impossible to relate parties to definable groups within the electorate. If voter turnout was extremely low, the vote might not represent accurately the dimensions of each class of electors. Connecticut provides an illustration of both points. Almost simultaneously with the liberalization of the suffrage in 1818, the Federalist party collapsed, political activity declined, and the percentage of adult white males participating in elections fell off sharply. Such conditions would not be ideal for analyzing the effects of a liberalized franchise. For an excellent study of early Connecticut politics, see Norman L. Stamps, "Political Parties in Connecticut, 1789–1818" (Ph.D. dissertation, Yale University, 1952).

[5] General guides to the political history of North Carolina in this era are Hamilton, *Party Politics in North Carolina*, and Clarence C. Norton, *The Democratic Party in Ante-Bellum North Carolina, 1835–1861* (Chapel Hill, 1930).

[6] One factor that explains the high proportion of taxpayers to adult white males was the imposition of a poll tax on every free male between the ages of twenty-one and forty-five. Thorpe (comp.), *Federal and State Constitutions*, vol. 5, pp. 2799.

[7] Vermont, Indiana, and Georgia, for example, all had no property or taxpaying qualifications, but they never — prior to 1840 — registered votes in excess of 80 percent of their adult white males. Delaware, on the other hand, had taxpayer suffrage but polled 81.9 percent of its adult white males as early as 1804. These and subsequent references to the percentages of adult white males participating in elections are based on a compilation that I have made of statewide votes for governor, President, and, in some states, congressmen. This collection, which

is being prepared for publication, includes the voting records down to 1860 of those states admitted to the Union by 1836, except South Carolina. I have computed for each election the percentage of adult white males voting.

[8] Raleigh *North Carolina Standard*, July 5, 1848. Similar conclusions are set forth in John C. Vinson, "Electioneering in North Carolina, 1800–1835," *North Carolina Historical Review* (Raleigh), vol. 29 (April 1952), pp. 171–188. Although it might be suggested that the low vote for senators was attributable to voter apathy toward that office, this does not seem to have been the case, for after 1856 the senatorial vote was equal to the vote for governor. See, for example, the returns for the state election of 1860 in the Raleigh *Weekly Standard*, August 15, 22, 1860.

[9] This calculation is necessarily based on the assumption that the freehold voters cast their ballots for the same party candidate for senator and governor. This assumption would seem to be a valid one, for there is little evidence of split-ticket voting. Relying on this assumption, it can be calculated that if in 1840 there were 16,760 freehold votes for the Whig gubernatorial candidate out of the total of 30,594 Whig votes cast, then the remainder — 13,834 — would have come from those who lacked fifty-acre freeholds.

[10] It is pertinent to mention that the parties in North Carolina were not highly sectionalized; both parties had strength in all sections of the state. See William S. Hoffmann, *Andrew Jackson and North Carolina Politics* (Chapel Hill, 1958); Hamilton, *Party Politics in North Carolina*, pp. 40, 66.

[11] I have particular reference to the changes that were made between 1800 and 1824, most notably in Maryland in 1802, in New Jersey in 1807, in Connecticut in 1818, and in Massachusetts in 1821. It would be difficult, I believe, to demonstrate that the reduction of suffrage barriers in the last three states resulted in any marked expansion of the electorate.

[12] Rhode Island altered its suffrage requirements in 1842, and there was a marked temporary rise in the percentage of adult white males voting, but even with the increase there was only one occasion (1843) prior to 1860 when as many as half of the adult white males voted. In Louisiana, similarly, voter participation normally remained below the 50 percent level despite suffrage changes in 1845 and 1852. In 1832, Mississippi, which had previously required militia service or the payment of a state or county tax, conferred the franchise on free white male citizens. Not until 1839, however, was there any significant upward surge in voter participation. With respect to Virginia, there was a considerable jump in voter participation between the presidential elections of 1836 (35.1 percent) and 1840 (54.6 percent), several years after the redefinition of suffrage qualifications in 1830. Voter participation in the 1848 presidential election was 47.9 percent of the adult white males. This figure rose to 61 percent in the 1851 gubernatorial election, which followed the suffrage liberalization of 1850. The Democrats received 50.8 percent of the total vote in 1848 and 52.3 percent in 1851. Many other factors would have to be considered, but on the basis of these figures it is not apparent that the increase in the size of the electorate had much effect on party alignments. Detailed studies of votes by counties in the state elections might produce sounder evidence for evaluating the effect of suffrage changes than do these statewide figures. For a recent analysis of the suffrage in Virginia see J. R. Pole, "Representation and Authority in Virginia from the Revolution to Reform," *Journal of Southern History* (Lexington, Ky.), vol. 24 (February 1958), pp. 16–50. Pole does not attempt to estimate the extent to which the electorate was increased by the suffrage changes of 1830 and 1850.

[13] Thorpe (comp.), *Federal and State Constitutions*, vol. 5, pp. 2630–2633, 2642, 2652. The 1822 constitution made a distinction between white and colored voters. The latter had to be citizens of the state for three years and possess a freehold of $250, upon which taxes were paid, in order to vote. *Ibid.*, pp. 2642–2643.

[14] Dixon Ryan Fox, *The Decline of Aristocracy in the Politics of New York* (New York, 1919), pp. 188–193.

[15] It can be calculated from the electoral census that approximately 172,300 men were eligible to participate in the election of members of Congress and 90,440 in the election of the governor, leaving 81,860 electors who lacked the £100 freehold requirement. It is from these base figures that the proportions of each electoral class participating in the 1816 elections have been computed. The question that should be resolved before the New York returns can be used with confidence is whether the suffrage qualifications were rigorously enforced. It would seem doubtful that they were.

[16] The gubernatorial vote figures are from Edgar A. Werner (comp.), *Civil List and Constitutional History of the Colony and State of New York* (2nd ed., Albany, 1886), p. 164.

[17] It is pertinent to note that the newly enfranchised voters were slow to exercise their privilege. Approximately 84 percent of the adult white males were eligible to vote for governor in 1824, as indicated in Table 5.4. But the actual voter turnout was only 56.1 percent of the adult white males. This was a considerably higher proportion than had ever voted in the state before, but it implies that nearly one-third of the eligibles did not vote. In view of this manifest apathy

on the part of the new voter, it is relevant to raise the question of how eager the disenfranchised class was to obtain the vote.

[18] David M. Ellis, James A. Frost, Harold C. Syrett, and Harry J. Carman, *A Short History of New York State* (Ithaca, 1957), p. 148.

[19] It is recognized that party alignments in this era exhibited the confusion that was typical of New York politics and that voter participation was well below the maximum potential level. Consequently, the conditions stipulated for an ideal situation were not completely fulfilled. However, the general attributes of the New York situation are relatively satisfactory when compared with those of other states.

[20] Quoted in Ellis *et al.*, *Short History of New York*, p. 147.

[21] See Richard P. McCormick, *The History of Voting in New Jersey, 1664–1911* (New Brunswick, 1953); Robert E. Brown, *Middle-Class Democracy and the Revolution in Massachusetts, 1691–1780* (Ithaca, 1955); and J. R. Pole, "Suffrage and Representation in Massachusetts: A Statistical Note," *William and Mary Quarterly* (Williamsburg), 3rd ser., vol. 14 (October 1957), pp. 560–592.

[22] This point is most ably developed in Louis Hartz, *The Liberal Tradition in America* (New York, 1955), pp. 106–110.

Ethnocultural Groups and Political Parties

Lee Benson

6

As class explanations of voting behavior in Jacksonian America have lost their appeal among some political historians, a number of them, led particularly by Professor Lee Benson of the University of Pennsylvania, have stressed the importance of ethnocultural influences on voting patterns instead. In America, Benson argues, political attitudes shaped by different national origins and contrasting religious perspectives have sharply affected group voting behavior on election day whatever have been the great issues discussed during the campaign. In the following selection, reprinted from his pioneering quantitative study, *The Concept of Jacksonian Democracy: New York as a Test Case* (Princeton, 1961), Benson details the impact of this cultural polarization in the presidential election of 1844. Cleavages between people of different national origins, he notes, primarily affected partisan choice in that year. Conversely, religious differences did not have as strong an impact on individual voting. A decade later, as we shall see, religious conflict was to be much more influential in determining electoral behavior.

The present study rejects the economic determinist interpretation that Frederick J. Turner and Charles A. Beard impressed upon American political historiography.[1] It also rejects the proposition that American political differences are random in character, that they reflect not group patterns, but the clashing ideas held by individual voters about the "community interest." And it rejects the proposition that socioeconomic cleavages are the obvious place to begin a study of American voting behavior. A counterproposition is advanced here: that at least since the 1820s, when manhood suffrage became widespread, ethnic and religious differences have tended to be *relatively* the most important sources of political differences. No attempt is made to "prove" that sweeping proposition, but this chapter and the following will try to show that it holds for New York in 1844. (Since the United States is highly heterogeneous, and has

SOURCE: Reprinted by permission of Princeton University Press from *The Concept of Jacksonian Democracy: New York as a Test Case* (copyright © 1961 by Princeton University Press; Princeton Paperback, 1970), pp. 165–185.

high social mobility, I assume that men tend to retain and be more influenced by their ethnic and religious group membership than by their membership in economic classes or groups.)

To anyone familiar with the literature, it will come as no surprise to read that the Democrats were the party of the immigrants and of the Catholics, the Whigs of the native Protestants, particularly those of New England stock. Unfortunately that statement is almost as inaccurate and misleading as it is unoriginal. Collection and analysis of the relevant data reveal that the sharpest political cleavages occurred, not between immigrants and Yankees, *but between different groups of immigrants.*

By 1844, New York's population was remarkably heterogeneous. Thus before the relationships between ethnocultural group and voting behavior could be ascertained, it was necessary to work out a detailed classification system. The term *ethnocultural* is used in preference to *ethnic*, because the latter term lumps together men who came from the same "stock" but who, like the English in New England and New York, had developed considerably divergent cultures in the New World.[2] Classifying men according to their membership in ethnocultural groups, however, enables us to uncover significantly different voting behavior patterns — patterns that are hidden or obscured when men are grouped according to ethnic attributes only.

Brevity was sacrificed to clarity when it came to labeling the two main categories of the classification system: "Groups in United States by 1790" (hereafter called "natives"); "Groups arriving in significant numbers after 1790" (hereafter called "immigrants"). Both the natives and the immigrants are subdivided, but our present concern is with the latter groups. For convenience, they are labeled "New British" and "New non-British." The former consisted of the northern or Protestant "Irish," the Welsh, Scots, and English. Among others, the New non-British included the southern or Catholic Irish, the Germans, French, and French Canadians. (The "Irish" religious divisions actually corresponded closely with ethnic divisions, but the traditional terms of Protestant and Catholic Irish will be used hereafter.)[3]

How Did the Immigrants Vote?

If the Democratic party really had been the party of the immigrants, the ethnocultural groups identified above should have voted more or less alike. But they did not. Except for the Negroes, the New British were by far the strongest Whigs of any group in New York, the New non-British by far the strongest Democrats.

Protestant Irish and Welsh

Numerically the smallest of the New British groups,[4] the Protestant Irish and the Welsh were probably the most homogeneous politically. Because the Protestant Irish failed to constitute a distinct, significant group in rural towns or urban wards, it is necessary to rely primarily upon contemporary observations for estimates of their party affiliation. Although precise estimates obviously cannot be verified, because contemporary observers agreed so unanimously, it seems safe to say that about 90 percent of the Protestant Irish voted Whig. (As is true of all such estimates presented below, that figure is not intended to be taken literally. Assigning groups a specific percentage enables us to indicate their *relative* party support.) The *Tribune* claimed "almost every Protestant Irishman" for the Whigs;[5] the *New York Plebeian* (Democratic), the *Evening Post* (Democratic), and the *Freeman's Journal* (official Catholic organ) emphasized the "nativist," "anti-Catholic" proclivities that led the members of the group to vote against the Democrats.

According to the *Plebeian*, "every Orangeman" in the city voted American Republican in the 1844 mayoralty election, when the Whigs deserted their own nominees and voted for that party.[6] Commenting upon this election and the 1844 anti-Catholic Irish riots in Philadelphia, the *Freeman's Journal* argued that "the most active, although not the most prominent of the Native Americans in New York, and probably in Philadelphia also, have been Irish Orangemen. They alone have been capable of furnishing the antisocial views with which our young *Natives* have been inoculated."[7] The *Post* agreed that the "Orangemen" stood in the forefront of the "nativist" movement and, in effect, it wrote them off for the Democrats.[8] Actually, as early as 1832 a Catholic Irish paper in Albany, which was devoted to the Republican (that is, Jacksonian) cause, claimed that any "Orange Irish" who may once have been attached to that party were now "apostates."[9] There seems to be no reason to doubt that claim or to believe that it was less accurate after 1832, particularly not in 1844 when the Whigs coalesced with the American Republicans in several counties and the Democrats identified themselves more closely than ever with the Catholic Irish.[10]

Although the Welsh had outposts throughout the state, they were most heavily concentrated in Oneida County. The first Welsh families came to the Oneida hills in 1795, and by 1808 they had formed a significant element in the population of the area.[11] The high Whig vote in the predominantly Welsh agricultural town of Remsen bears out the *Tribune*'s claim that "hardly one of them [was] a Loco-Foco." Remsen was the lowest ranking Democratic town in the county, and in 1844, when the median Democratic unit registered 50.8 percent, Remsen gave that party only 32.8 percent; in 1840, 25.6 percent. Since many voters in Remsen belonged to groups that did not strongly support the Whigs (including some Catholic Irish), the *Tribune* apparently was not exaggerating Welsh anti-Democratic sentiment.[12] A reasonable estimate seems to be that about 90 percent of them *usually* cast Whig ballots (that is, unless abolitionist candidates were running).

English and the Scots

It is not possible to estimate precisely the number of voters of English and Scots descent, but they almost certainly constituted a much larger proportion of the electorate than the other two New British groups. The *Tribune* claimed nearly all the Scots and a "large portion" of the English for its party.[13] Significantly, the *Evening Post* conceded the accuracy of that claim in a campaign editorial which argued that nativism would cost the Whigs many votes: "There is a large number of naturalized citizens in the interior counties of the state, and in all the western states, mostly English or Scotch by birth, who have hitherto [1844] voted with the Whigs. Not being gregarious in their manner of settlement, like the Irish and Germans, they do not pass for so large a portion of our population as they are found upon enquiry to make." [14]

The *Post* erred in one respect, for the Scots were markedly "gregarious in their manner of settlement," and formed a respectable proportion of the population in counties as far apart as Washington, Fulton, Delaware, and Livingston. "Scots" towns comprised the lowest Democratic units in three of those counties and the second lowest (33.7 percent) in Fulton; the Scots were also well represented in the lowest (Johnstown, a manufacturing area). Putnam was the lowest ranking Democratic town (18.5 percent) in Washington as well as in the state. In 1844 it was overwhelmingly a community of Scots, as was York in Livingston, where the Democrats received only 23.0 percent of the total vote. Perhaps the clearest indication of the group's voting pattern is this: not a single town in which the Scots were clustered gave the Democrats a majority, *even in the strongest Democratic counties.*[15]

Delaware County, for example, was a longtime Democratic stronghold. Yet the towns in which the Scots formed either a majority or a large minority of the population were the highest-ranking Whig units in the county. Hamden gave the Whigs 68.2 percent of its vote, followed closely by Andes which gave them 67.5 percent. Even Bovina, with 59.1 percent, was a "strong anti-Democratic" town. Such figures in traditionally Democratic Delaware County support the observations of the *Tribune* and *Evening Post* and justify the estimate that, like the Protestant Irish and the Welsh, about 90 percent of the Scots voted Whig.

The *Post* noted that the English were not "gregarious," and it has been possible to locate only two towns in which they formed a significant proportion of the population. Stockport in Columbia County and Stafford in Genesee were both "very strong Whig" communities. But they had voted much the same way before the English came and might well have continued to do so whether or not they contained any sizable number of English "adopted citizens." As noted previously, Stockport was a manufacturing town; and Stafford had been an Anti-masonic stronghold prior to the arrival of immigrants from Devonshire. But it is at least suggestive that both towns were even more strongly Whig after sufficient time had elapsed for the English to make their presence felt. In Stockport, the Whigs received 69.6 percent of the vote in 1834, and 76.8 percent in 1844. In Stafford they received 69.0 percent and 70.1 percent, respectively. Thus there is no reason to doubt the *Post*'s and *Tribune*'s description of the English as Whig sympathizers. Moreover, other contemporary observers agreed that they shared the antipathy to the Catholic Irish that was characteristic of all the New British groups, and that they voted their antipathies.[16] Nevertheless, there are nuances in *Tribune* editorials that suggest the English were *relatively* less homogeneous politically than the Protestant Irish, Welsh, and Scots. Since the *Tribune* editorials indicate that workers of "Radical" (Chartist) background tended to support the Democrats, it seems safer to estimate that only [sic] about 75 percent of the English voted Whig.[17]

very glossy

Catholic Irish

Though precise figures are not available, by 1844 the Catholic Irish undoubtedly formed the single largest immigrant group in New York.[18] Contemporary observations suggest that about 95 percent of the Catholic Irish who participated in the 1844 election cast Democratic ballots.[19] But that group had not always formed so solid a bloc. During the late 1830s, enough Catholic Irish supported the Whigs to raise the expectations of men like Weed, Seward, and Greeley. Their expectations were badly blighted in 1840, however, when even Seward conceded that "the Irishmen . . . voted against us generally, and far more generally than heretofore." [20] Desertions increased after 1840, and by November 1844 the *Albany Evening Journal* was printing letters that claimed, for example, that out of about 100 Catholic Irish voters in the city of Hudson, all were "against us except two or three."[21] (Whether the Catholic Irish voted along ethnocultural or religious lines will be discussed later.)

Affiliation of the *urban* Catholic Irish to the Democratic party has long been noted, although little attention has been given to changes in their voting behavior over time. What has tended to be overlooked is that the Catholic Irish voted Democratic in New York State, whether they lived in urban or rural communities, whether they were day laborers or freehold farmers — in short, their voting pattern represented an ethnocultural or religious group, not a place or class, phenomenon.

Most Catholic Irish lived in cities and large villages, but by 1844 many could be found in rural areas scattered throughout the state. Wherever they constituted a substantial proportion of the population, they voted as a bloc and made their presence felt politically. For example, in Franklin County "Irish [Catholic] settlers began to swarm into Bombay about 1825 . . . Mr. Hogan, the younger [the town's landowner], is said to have received these [settlers] with great kindliness, and to have located them upon what was then regarded as the very best lands in the town, which location came to be known as the 'Irish ridge.' " [22] As the local historian noted, thanks to the solid Irish attachment to the Democrats,[23] Bombay was a "strong Democratic" town in a traditionally Whig county.

Similarly, in 1844 in the Antimasonic and Whig county of Wyoming in western New York, the only town that gave the Democrats enough support to place it in a category above "neutral" was Java (58.6 percent). After the advance guard of Catholic Irish arrived in 1829, its farmlands began to attract many others. By 1844 substantial numbers of Irish Catholics must have lived there, for by 1855 the *Freeman's Journal* was proudly claiming that in Java and the adjoining town of China, "*there are one thousand Catholic families engaged in farming,* most of whom have already paid for their land." [24] Though concentrated in Java, enough of those families lived in China to make it another high-ranking Democratic town.

Few agricultural towns contained as heavy concentrations of Catholic Irish as Bombay and Java. But the *Evening Journal* and the *Tribune* emphasized that the Catholic Irish were sufficiently numerous to aid the Democrats materially in about half the counties of the state.[25] Thus, once it is recognized that the Catholic Irish voted overwhelmingly Democratic wherever they lived and whatever their occupation, it follows that their voting behavior cannot be attributed to conditions peculiar to urban areas or to particular occupations.

Germans

Of the New non-British groups, the second largest, the Germans, were also strongly attached to the Democratic party. Unlike the others, however, they divided into three distinct religious segments, Catholics, Protestants, and "Rationalists," or free thinkers. A credible source estimates that nearly one half the German settlers in New York State before the Civil War were Catholics; the remainder were divided among the Protestants and Rationalists.[26]

Pending an intensive study, firm statements are unwarranted, but the available data suggest that the Protestant Germans, particularly the Prussian Lutherans, voted less strongly Democratic than the other two groups.[27] Yet in the 1840s this difference in German voting behavior was apparently only a matter of degree, and Democratic papers claimed the Germans almost exclusively for their party. In Syracuse, for example, during the 1844 campaign, the *Argus* reported that "no Dutchman [sic] could be found to carry Gen. Granger's Banners, at the recent coon [Whig] celebration." [28] Even before the nativist issue developed intensity, the Whigs conceded that the "great majority" of German voters were arrayed against them. From the *Tribune*'s admission — and it appealed strongly for German support — as well as from other evidence, it seems clear that they voted Democratic irrespective of religious affiliation.[29] Nonetheless, the Catholic Germans probably voted most Democratic, the Protestants probably least Democratic.[30]

A highly "gregarious" group, the Germans are easily detected in the rural areas. In Croghan, Lewis County, they appear to have constituted a larger proportion of the population than in any other New York town.[31] Croghan was the highest ranking Democratic unit in the county (83.2 percent), and the second highest in the state. As part of its campaign to get the vote of "adopted citizens," the *Albany Argus* highlighted the presence of naturalized German citizens from Croghan at the Democrat's main rally in Lewis County. They were assigned a prominent place in the parade and their float's banner emphasized a favorite party theme: "The Naturalized Citizens of Croghan — Have Not We the same rights as Natives?" [32]

Croghan, with its large proportion of Germans, was an extremely "poor" town in a Democratic county; Tonawanda (in Erie) and Irondequoit (in Monroe), each with large numbers of Germans, were "prosperous" agricultural towns in Whig counties. Both were the highest-ranking Democratic units in their counties, giving sizable majorities to the party (65.6 percent and 58.6 percent, respectively), even though Erie and Monroe were longtime Antimasonic and Whig strongholds. With the exception of two towns settled by Prussian Lutherans,[33] all towns in New York containing significant numbers of Germans were found to be high-ranking Democratic units. The estimate that approximately 80 percent of the Germans voted Democratic is based upon my analysis of the statistical data and the impressionistic evidence of contemporary observers, for example, "The victory of the Loco-Focos is not that of *Americans* but a triumph of *Irishmen* and *Germans* over *Americans*." [34]

Catholic French

Though few in number and concentrated largely in New York City,[35] the Catholic French also contributed to the 1844 Democratic victory. Under the headline, "A New Foreign Ally Brought into the Field," the *American Republican* added the French to the Catholic Irish and German "foreign battalions," long mustered under Tammany banners. According to the *Express*, an ardently nativist Whig paper, the French as a group "since time immemorial," had abstained from political participation. But "this year they have wakened," the paper observed; and its tone suggested that the awakening would not bring joy to Whig politicians. Unwilling to concede the French to the Loco-Focos before election, the *Express* included them afterwards in its angry denunciation of "the avalanche of Germans, Irish, Swiss, Prussians, French, Russians, and Poles" that had rolled over the Whigs on election day. The *Herald*, an independent paper, also presented evidence sustaining the view that the French voted *en masse* for the Democrats in 1844.[36]

Perhaps the most significant aspect of the solid French support for the Democrats relates to their socioeconomic status. In his illuminating study of New York immigrant life, Robert Ernst has noted that, unlike the Irish and the Germans, "there were few laborers or shanty dwellers among them [the French]." Also unlike those groups, a relatively sizable percentage of the French were merchants, some of whom "grew rich from the increasing trade between New York, Le Havre and Paris." [37] Since they probably voted as solidly Democratic as the Catholic Irish, and since their socioeconomic status was much higher than the latter's, French voting behavior strengthens the claim that in 1844 the New non-British acted along ethnocultural (and religious) rather than economic group lines.

French Canadians

The smallest of the New non-British groups, and the latest to arrive in the United States (after 1837), the French Canadians were highly concentrated in a few Northern Tier counties.[38] Their small number and late arrival makes it difficult to estimate their 1844 party allegiance from statistical data. But the *Tribune* in effect conceded them to the Democrats.[39] An impressionistic estimate that they voted along the lines of the Catholic Irish (95 percent Democratic) is probably not far off the mark. The 1852 data support that estimate, since by then enough time had elapsed for the voting statistics to reflect their presence. Clinton, where they were more highly concentrated than anywhere else in the state, gave the Democrats 74.1 percent of its vote and thereby became the party's banner unit in the county. (By 1860 the French Canadians comprised an even higher proportion of the electorate in Clinton, and the Democrats received 85 percent of the town vote in that strong Republican county.) Similarly, Chateaugay in Franklin County was another French Canadian center, and its Democratic vote (72.7 percent in 1852) was even higher than Bombay's (60.1 percent), where many Catholic Irish lived.[40]

Summary

As noted above, the purpose of estimating group percentages is to suggest the relative rather than actual support given the major parties by different groups. The group estimates appear to be roughly accurate, at least, and they discredit the claim that the Democratic party was the party of the immigrants. That claim may be literally accurate, but it is thoroughly misleading. The New non-British strongly supported the Democratic party; the New British just as strongly opposed it. Because the former considerably outnumbered the latter in the state, it is undoubtedly true that many more "adopted citizens" voted Democratic than Whig.[41] But that statistic is a demographic accident. Had migration been larger from New British areas than from New non-British, it seems reasonable to assume that the reverse situation would have developed in the state — as, in fact, it did in many localities.

How Did the Natives Vote?

Shifting attention to differences in voting behavior *between immigrant groups and native groups*, we find a significant phenomenon that will be noted here and commented upon in later chapters. Although all immigrant groups voted as solid blocs, the natives divided *relatively* closely between the two major parties (except for two small groups identified below).

Yankees

Contrary to the traditional view that voters of New England descent voted strongly Whig, the estimate here is that for the state as a whole they split about 55 percent Whig, 45 percent Democratic. (This estimate counts Liberty party voters according to their previous affiliations.) That the generic term *Yankee* refers to men who derived from heterogeneous social and cultural backgrounds is suggested by this finding: unlike every immigrant group, and to a greater extent than any other native group, the Yankees varied widely in their voting behavior in different parts of the state and in different towns within the same county.

The small Whig margin among the Yankees actually derived from the original Antimasonic strength in western New York. That extensive region constituted a "colony from New England," [42] and the party that dominated it politically contained necessarily a large proportion of Yankees. But in many New York counties where the Antimasonic movement had failed to penetrate or had produced a counterreaction, the Democrats received strong Yankee support.

Since Yankees constituted about 65 percent of the state's electorate,[43] it follows logically that they must have been closely divided in their party allegiance. Had the Whigs received much more than 55 percent of that group's vote, their opponents would invariably have been beaten badly on the state level, unless all other groups cast solid Democratic ballots. But logical deduction need not be relied on; "New England" counties and towns are easily located.

For example, the county of Suffolk, directly across Long Island Sound from Connecticut, was "completely Yankee in population." [44] Traditionally a Democratic stronghold, in 1844 it ranked as the third-highest Democratic county and gave the party 57.8 percent of its total vote. Within the county, however, the descendants of Connecticut Yankees differed widely in political allegiance. Easthampton, an "unusually prosperous" agricultural town ($883), was the banner Democratic unit with 75.7 percent of the vote; Southhampton, a "very prosperous" agricultural, whaling, and fishing town ($632) was the lowest-ranking Democratic unit with 34.0 percent. (The voting record of the latter nicely illustrates the proposition stated in Chapter VII about the conditions under which economic interests are most likely to influence political behavior. A local Democratic newspaper explained its party's poor showing in Southhampton by citing the specific attractions that Whig policies held for its substantial nonagricultural interests.)[45]

Much the same situation obtained in Delaware County (southeastern New York) as in Suffolk on eastern Long Island. Except for the Scots (and some Dutch in a couple of towns), Delaware was overwhelmingly Yankee. And yet, despite the solid Scots support for the Whigs, Delaware was the sixth-highest Democratic county in the state (57.3 percent). Again, striking variations in Yankee voting patterns appear on the town level. For example, Franklin, unmistakably a transplanted Connecticut community, gave the Democrats 72.9 percent of its total vote. Stamford, just as clearly an outpost of Fairfield County, Connecticut, gave them only 44.9 percent.[46] Contrary to what the economic determinist interpretation of voting behavior would lead one to expect, both Franklin ($441) and Stamford ($473) were "prosperous" agricultural towns.

To an even greater extent than Delaware, Otsego County in central New York was settled by Yankees. The historian of that area noted, as late as the Civil War, that "the vast majority of the inhabitants traced their ancestry to New England."[47] Yet "wool-growing" Otsego was traditionally Democratic and gave that party 54.5 percent of its vote in 1844. Moving up to the North Country, we find that Warren and St. Lawrence were other Yankee counties that traditionally voted Democratic. The former trailed Delaware closely in the party's honor roll with 55.1 percent, the latter ranked just above Otsego with 54.7 percent. And even in western New York many New England towns voted strongly Democratic. Prattsburg in Steuben County serves as a good example, since its settlers "were peculiarly a homogeneous population." Its pioneers were nearly all of Congregational background and "originally from Connecticut, of the best Puritan stock."[48] In this "prosperous" agricultural town, the Democrats received 61.3 percent of the total vote.

Other examples would only belabor the point. The data, I believe, warrant these conclusions: (1) In no county did Yankee voting behavior resemble the bloc pattern characteristic of all immigrant groups; (2) In some counties the Yankees voted strongly Whig; (3) In other counties they divided more or less evenly; (4) In still others they voted strongly Democratic. Contrary to traditional assumptions, the group's voting behavior shows no significant class differences. Put another way, unless one knew *where* well-to-do or poor Yankees lived, or knew certain other information noted below, one would have little basis for predicting party affiliations. Yankee voting in New York during the 1830s and 1840s was heterogeneous, suggesting that so wide a variety of factors over time and space had influenced them that easy generalizations are exceedingly dangerous.[49]

Negroes and Huguenots

Aside from the Yankees, I estimate that only two native groups cast Whig majorities in New York, the Negroes and the Huguenots (Protestant French). Unlike all other natives, members of each of these small groups had experienced or were experiencing "persecution," and each voted as a solid bloc.

Because of the property restrictions upon Negro suffrage which the Van Buren faction had written into the 1821 state constitution, only about one thousand "persons of color" were eligible to vote in 1844.[50] An analysis of the parties' opposing positions during the 1840s on the proposed constitutional amendment removing Negro suffrage restrictions strongly confirms Dixon Ryan Fox's conclusion that Negroes voted solidly Whig.[51] To estimate that they supported the Whigs as solidly as the Catholic Irish supported the Democrats (95 percent) does not appear to be an overstatement.

Like the Negroes, the Huguenots were among the earliest inhabitants of New York province. An estimate based upon the best available study indicates that they comprised about 3 percent of the state's population in 1790. By 1844, however, as a result of the influx of native and foreign migrants to New York, they probably comprised less than 1 percent of the electorate and cast about 4000 votes.[52] Though it seems reasonably certain that they strongly supported the Whigs, the estimated figure of 75 percent is frankly impressionistic. Clusters of Huguenots lived in Ulster, Richmond, Westchester, New York, and Kings counties, but only in the town of New Paltz, Ulster County, did they form a substantial part of the population. Unfortunately for our purposes, that town also contained many Dutch — a group that tended to vote Democratic. It is difficult, therefore, to draw any credible inferences from the 52.3 percent the Whigs received in New Paltz. Contemporary references to enthusiastic Huguenot participation in the 1844 anti-Catholic campaign suggest, however, that the 75 percent Whig figure is not too inaccurate an estimate of their group voting pattern.

The *American Republican* carried frequent and glowing reports concerning "the progress of Americanism" in the "old Huguenot county of Ulster." Both New Paltz and Hurley (another Huguenot center) were "all right" and ready to do their part at the polls. An editorial hailing the group's contribution to the success of an "immense" Fourth of July party rally in Ulster is revealing. "That county may be considered as the Huguenot county of the State. It is filled with a class of people who appreciate all the blessings of liberty, and are sensitively alive to anything that threatens danger to the Protestant faith." Although resolutions passed at the July rally denounced the Whigs as well as the Democrats for "truckling to papal interests," [53] the *Tribune* later revealed that before the campaign was over the Whigs and American Republicans had practically merged in Ulster.[54] Nonetheless, a not insignificant proportion of Huguenots must have voted Democratic or that party's vote would have been lower in New Paltz.

Other "Yorkers"

The Huguenots comprise one of four native groups classified here as "Yorkers," the descendants of men who came directly to the province of New York rather than migrated to it after first settling in New England, New Jersey, or elsewhere. The Dutch, the Palatine Germans, and the "Old British" complete the list. This latter group is really a composite and includes the English, Welsh, Scots, and Scotch-Irish living in New York by 1790. Long residence in the country as well as behavior patterns and traditions associated with Revolutionary and early national struggles differentiated them from the post-1790 "New British."

Like the Huguenots, the other Yorker groups were largely clustered in eastern portions of the state that had been settled before the Revolution, particularly in the Hudson, Mohawk and Schoharie valleys.[55] But, contrary to the Huguenot pattern, I estimate that roughly 60 percent of the Dutch, Palatines, and Old British voted Democratic. (Only a study that examined the evidence microscopically could isolate their separate voting patterns.) The estimate 60 percent is supported by the comfortable Democratic majorities in most Yorker counties and communities. Thus they comprised either a majority or a substantial minority of the population in the *highest-ranking Democratic towns in fourteen counties; they comprised either a majority or a substantial minority of the population in the lowest-ranking Democratic towns in only two counties.*

Dutch, Palatine, and Old British majorities for the Democrats powerfully discredit the traditional assumption that the Whigs represented primarily the prosperous farmers living on better soils or along good transportation routes. Having arrived early, the Yorker families had decades, often centuries, to pick out the best sites, accumulate wealth (and status), and pass it along to descendants. This is not to imply that all Yorkers in 1844 were well-to-do. But as a group, their early arrival had given them relatively high places on the economic scale. For example, as a local historian observed, long devotion to agriculture by the Dutch in Rockland County had paid off handsomely. "Wealth brought with it grand and comfortable homes. Money begat money. 'Money saved is money made' was the Dutchman's motto. It was not an unusual thing for a farmer, a generation ago [that is during the 1850s], to be worth from $50,000 even up to $100,000 in cash, besides a fine farm to leave to his posterity."[56]

As noted previously, the solidly Dutch, "very prosperous" agricultural community of Clarkstown in Rockland County was the state's leading Democratic unit (89.9 percent). In contrast, the "prosperous" agricultural town of Ramapo, settled largely by twice-transplanted Connecticut Yankees from Hempstead, Long Island, was the county's lowest-ranking Democratic unit (56.5 percent). Another "very prosperous" Dutch agricultural community, Coeymans in Albany County, cast 71.4 percent of its vote for the Democrats. The predominantly Yankee "marginal" town of Knox in the same county cast only 34.0 percent for the Democrats. (It is worth noting here that the pattern of high Yorker and low Yankee support for the Democrats was not limited to Rockland and Albany, but tended to persist in almost all counties where "restless" Yankees came to disturb the peace of "conservative" Yorkers.)

Other "Dutch" towns heading their county's Democratic list were Lexington in Greene (79.1 percent), Deerpark in Orange (67.7 percent), Greenbush in Rensselaer (64.7 percent), Newton in Queens (60.3 percent), Shawangunk in Ulster (60.1 percent), and Sullivan in Madison (53.1 percent). In every case, these towns were "prosperous" or "very prosperous" agricultural communities. The two Yorker communities at the tail-end of their county's Democratic list were Catskill in Greene (42.3 percent) and Esopus in Ulster (32.7 percent). Catskill, a "very prosperous" commercial and agricultural town on the Hudson, was settled originally by the Dutch, but the heavy Yankee influx after the Revolution makes it difficult to determine whether the Yorker element actually predominated by 1844. Similarly, Esopus on the Hudson was a "prosperous" old Dutch agricultural town, but it contained many Huguenots who may have been responsible for its low Democratic vote.

Arriving in the lower Hudson Valley early in the eighteenth century, many of the "poor German Protestants" from the Palatine migrated soon afterwards to the "fat lands" along the Mohawk and Schoharie rivers.[57] Although by 1844 the post-Revolutionary Yankee invasion had drastically changed the ethnocultural composition of Herkimer, Schoharie, and Montgomery counties, the Palatines still formed at least a substantial minority element in those reliably Democratic counties. Certainly they formed the numerically dominant element in the highest-ranking Democratic towns in all three counties.

The town of Herkimer in the county of Herkimer, named after the Palatine's revolutionary hero (General Nicholas Herkimer), was "unusually prosperous" and contained the "German Flats," widely renowned for their enduring fertility. It gave the Democrats 70.5 percent of its vote, slightly more than the "prosperous" Palatine agricultural towns of Sharon in Schoharie (66.0 percent) and St. Johnsville in Montgomery (65.6 percent) gave them. Of the highest-ranking Democratic towns dominated by the Palatines (and Dutch), Taghanic in Columbia County (70.1 percent) was the only one of "marginal" status.

As was true in general of the three Yorker groups we are now considering, not all Palatine towns voted heavily Democratic. For example, although the "very prosperous" town of Schoharie in Schoharie County strongly resembled Herkimer in socioeconomic composition and other characteristics, it voted only 52.0 percent Democratic. Schoharie shows that the group's voting pattern varied somewhat in different areas, but does not weaken the finding that Palatine communities characteristically gave the Democrats comfortable majorities.

Yonkers, an Old British (English) town, led the Democratic ranks in Westchester (70.3 percent). Nearness to New York City had long given its farmers an excellent market for produce, and land values soared after 1842 as Yonkers increasingly became a suburban community. The "marginal" town of Putnam Valley in adjoining Putnam County presented an exception to the general rule of Yorker prosperity, but it was another Old British community long devoted to the Democratic cause (83.2 percent). Across the Hudson in Orange County, the flourishing agricultural towns of Crawford (Scotch-Irish), Hamptonburg (English and Scotch-Irish), and New Windsor (English and Scotch-Irish) also registered comfortable Democratic majorities (65.8, 59.3, and 57.5 percent, respectively).

Although I estimate that the three groups voted about 60 percent Democratic, undoubtedly differences existed among the Dutch, Palatine, and Old British patterns. The significant point, however, is that those groups enjoyed relatively high socioeconomic status in their communities and definitely sided with the Democrats in the political wars.

Penn-Jerseyites

Like the Old British, the last ethnocultural group to be considered here is a composite one. Particularly after the Revolution, Scotch-Irish, Germans, and Dutch from Pennsylvania and New Jersey came to take up unoccupied lands in New York. Although they tended to locate in southeastern and Southern Tier counties, many of them pushed father north. Seneca County in western New York, for example, was as much a Penn-Jersey center as Chemung on the Pennsylvania line and Orange on the New Jersey line.[58]

Analysis of county and town statistics leads to the conclusion that the Penn-Jerseyites tended to divide evenly between the parties. Unlike the Yankees, however, this native group leaned to the Democratic side, and I estimate that about 55 percent of them voted "Loco-Foco." Thus the Democrats had a majority in counties such as Chemung (58.1 percent) and Steuben (55.0 percent), and the Whigs had a majority in no Penn-Jersey county. Even in Seneca, where the Antimasonic "blessed spirit" had manifested itself, the Democrats received 51.6 percent of the total vote. Nevertheless, both the highest- and the lowest-ranking Democratic towns in Seneca, Tioga, and Tompkins counties were Penn-Jersey centers that resembled each other in many respects; it seems clear, therefore, that the group was closely divided politically.[59]

Summary

Perhaps the most dramatic way to summarize and delineate the ethnocultural basis of party divisions in New York in 1844 is to bring together the estimated group voting percentages. The table below illustrates the main point: party affiliations were extremely polarized among immigrants, and native voters tended to be relatively evenly divided. It is worth noting that the "deviant" behavior of Negroes and Huguenots strengthens rather than weakens the conclusion that native groups had not yet developed polarized voting patterns. Like the immigrants, members of those two groups were influenced by certain ethnic and religious factors that differentiated them from the great bulk of the native electorate.

Table 6.1   Estimated Party Percentages,
New York Ethnocultural Groups, 1844

	"Natives"			"Immigrants"	
	Whig %	Dem. %		Whig %	Dem. %
Negroes	95.0	5.0	Catholic Irish	5.0	95.0
Huguenots	75.0	25.0	French Canadian	5.0	95.0
Yankees	55.0	45.0	French	10.0	90.0
			New German	20.0	80.0
Penn-Jerseyites	45.0	55.0			
Old British	40.0	60.0	English	75.0	25.0
Dutch	40.0	60.0	Scots	90.0	10.0
Old German	40.0	60.0	Welsh	90.0	10.0
			Protestant Irish	90.0	10.0

NOTES

[1] See Lee Benson, *Turner and Beard* (Glencoe, Ill., 1960), *passim*. The systematic errors that the traditional economic determinist interpretation makes are less harmful than the confusion which results when voters are identified haphazardly according to a variety of attributes, for example, when "workers" are identified as Democrats and then Catholics are identified as Democrats, but little or no attempt is made to identify the voting patterns of different social strata of Catholics. In short, I accept Francis Bacon's observation: "Truth emerges more easily from error than from confusion."

[2] For a brilliant analysis of the cultural differences between people of English stock living in New England and New York, see Dixon Ryan Fox, *Yankees and Yorkers*, *passim*. By the time

Fox came to deliver these lectures, he had sharply revised the views concerning "the economic interpretation" of American history which he had expressed in *Decline of Aristocracy in the Politics of New York*. Unfortunately, that doctoral dissertation has tended to be treated as Fox's last word on the subject of New York history. In my opinion, *Yankees and Yorkers* corrects many of the oversimplifications and errors in his pioneer (and pioneering) study which have seriously misled later historians.

[3] For a succinct, informative discussion of the different ethnic stocks included in the "British" migration to the United States, see Rowland T. Berthoff, *British Immigrants in Industrial America* (Cambridge, Mass., 1953), pp. 1–11.

[4] The New York State *Census for 1845* listed under one heading all inhabitants born in Great Britain or its possessions; the 1855 *Census*, however, had a much more precise breakdown. Impressionistic evidence suggests that the totals for 1855 accurately indicate the rank order of the several groups in 1845; Ireland, 469,753; England, 102,286; Scotland, 27,523; Wales, 8557. According to an analysis made by the Irish Emigrant Society of the immigrants arriving in New York in May and June 1844, the Irish numbered 10,668, the English and Scots combined, 3992. (*Freeman's Journal*, August 24, 1844, p. 60.) The Protestant Irish were not listed separately in the census data. For informed estimates concerning them and other British immigrants, see Berthoff, *British Immigrants*, pp. 1–11.

[5] A sizable group of Protestant Irish had settled in Lisbon, St. Lawrence County. Out of twenty-eight towns in that traditionally Democratic county, Lisbon ranked twenty-sixth on the party's list, with 42.2 percent. Actually, that figure is somewhat misleading, for Silas Wright's popularity in his home county undoubtedly swelled the Democratic vote. Without Wright on the ticket, the Democrats received only 34.0 percent in 1834 and 28.4 percent in 1840. See also *New York Tribune* (w.), March 22, 1845, p. 5.

[6] See Louis D. Scisco, *Political Nativism in New York State*, p. 47.

[7] *Freeman's Journal*, May 11, 1844, p. 364. A week later, the paper printed a letter charging that the "Native American Party" was the "spawn" of the American Protestant Association, an "Orange" organization. Letter signed "A Catholic Native American," *ibid.*, May 18, 1844, p. 373. See also the quotation from a Pittsburgh Democratic newspaper asserting that on July 12, the anniversary of the Battle of Boyne, the Orange amended their traditional slogan and cried out "For King William and [Henry] Clay." *Ibid.*, August 3, 1844, p. 37.

[8] *Evening Post for the Country*, March 29, 1845, p. 3.

[9] Letter to the editor of the *Irish Republican Shield*, quoted in the *Albany Argus* (s.w.), September 21, 1832.

[10] *Albany Argus* (w.), June 15, 1844, p. 205; November 2, 1844, p. 356; November 9, 1844, p. 366; *Brooklyn Eagle* (d.), October 16, 18, 26; November 6, 9, 1844, p. 2.

[11] Millard F. Roberts, *History of Remsen . . . Including Parts of Adjoining Steuben and Trenton* (n.p., 1914), 1–18, 116–117; Pomeroy Jones, *History of Oneida County* (n.p., 1851), pp. 306–307.

To quote Jones: "The reports of these early foreign immigrants to their friends in Wales, of the cheapness and fitness for dairying of the lands in this section has induced these ancient Britons to emigrate in such numbers that competent residents of the town [Remsen] believe that at least three-fourths of its population are Welsh. It is said that Remsen, Steuben, Trenton, and portions of Deerfield, Marcy, and Boonville, are almost as well known in Wales as in Oneida County." Jones's estimate is probably essentially correct, but somewhat exaggerated; Roberts estimated that in 1857 "they comprised nearly, if not quite, two-thirds of the community," *Remsen*, pp. 116–117.

[12] *New York Tribune* (w.), March 22, 1845, p. 5. The Welsh probably comprised about 65 percent to 75 percent of Remsen's electorate in the mid-1840s. (See n. 11). Since political abolitionism attracted some of them (Roberts, *Remsen*, p. 128), the town's devotion to the Whig party is best seen by presenting the percentages for 1834 (69.4 percent) and 1840 (69.5 percent), as well as 1844 (57.0 percent). Moreover, as will be shown below, Irish Catholics throughout the state voted overwhelmingly Democratic and the New Englanders tended to be closely divided; the Whig vote among the Welsh in Remsen must therefore have been extremely high. Fortunately, it is not necessary to rely solely on logical deduction. Long agitation by the Welsh finally paid off in 1869 when the northern half of Remsen was set off as the town of Forestport; it contained most of the Irish Catholics. The party percentages before and after the division tell their own story: In 1868 Remsen voted Republican 62.5 percent, Democratic 37.5 percent. Four years later, Remsen voted Republican 85.4 percent, Democratic 14.6 percent; Forestport voted Republican 48.2 percent, Democratic 52.8 percent. See Roberts, *Remsen*, pp. 37–38, 108, for the division of the town in 1869. As a Democratic newspaper noted during the 1844 campaign, the Whigs published a Welsh paper in Utica and "wooed" the Welsh with pamphlets in New York City. *Morning News*, October 29, 1844, p. 2.

[13] *New York Tribune* (w.), March 22, 1845, p. 5.

[14] *Evening Post for the Country*, October 12, 1844, p. 2.

[15] Together with the leads provided by the 1845 and 1855 Census data, the detailed description of settlement patterns and churches in the appropriate regional, county and town histories and gazetteers made it possible to estimate the ethnocultural composition of the towns identified in this section. The New York Public Library and the New York Historical Society have excellent collections of these histories and gazetteers. They vary greatly in quality, but at least one useful history has been published for every county in the state.

[16] See, in particular, the calculated attacks upon the English and the defense of the Irish in a leading Democratic newspaper, the *Brooklyn Eagle* (d.), August 9; September 16, 19, 28; October 26, 1844, p. 2. The paper noted that "no exception" was taken to the English or Scotch by nativist Whigs; the Irish in particular, not British immigrants in general, were the targets of Whig fury. *Ibid.*, November 9, 1844, p. 2. See also the praise for the "intelligent English naturalized citizens" in the *American Republican*, November 4, 1844, p. 2; the attacks upon the Protestant Irish, English, and Scotch merchants of New York in the Irish Catholic organ, the *Freeman's Journal*, October 15, 1844, p. 108, and the answer to this in the *American Republican*, December 12, 1844, p. 2, letter signed "Junius."

[17] For example, the *Tribune* (w.) claimed that some workers were Democrats because "a good many of our workmen in factories, forges, etc., are English Radicals, who have been led to attribute the depression of the Laboring Classes in Europe to Protection, and who never ask nor think whether the circumstances and the essence of the thing are the same here as there, but cry out for this 'Free Trade' here which would inevitably reduce their own wages to the European standard." August 3, 1844, p. 4. See also *ibid.*, September 12, 1846, p. 3. Moreover, as noted below, free thinkers strongly tended to vote Democratic, and in the 1830s English immigrants were stigmatized as the "worst atheists in the country." Albert Post, *Popular Freethought in America, 1825–1850* (New York, 1943), pp. 86, 32–33.

[18] See n. 4 above.

[19] *New York Herald* (d.), November 9, 1844, p. 4; *Evening Post for the Country*, November 23, 1844, p. 1; *New York Express*, November 6, 1844, p. 1; *New York Tribune* (w.), November 16, 1844, p. 5; *New York Courier and Enquirer*, November 18, 1844, p. 2.

[20] William Seward to B. S. [Benjamin Squire?], November 12, 1840, in George E. Baker, ed., *The Works of William H. Seward*, vol. 3, pp. 386–387.

[21] *Albany Evening Journal* (d.), November 15, 1844, p. 2. See also *ibid.*, November 8, 1844, p. 2.

[22] Frederick J. Seaver, *Historical Sketches of Franklin County* (Albany, 1918), pp. 186–187.

[23] *Ibid.*, pp. 104–106.

[24] F. W. Beers and Co., *History of Wyoming County, N.Y.* (New York, 1880), pp. 204–211; *Freeman's Journal*, October 27, 1855, p. 4.

[25] *Albany Evening Journal* (d.), November 11, 1844, p. 2; *New York Tribune* (w.), November 16, 1844, p. 5.

[26] Alexander Flick, *History of The State of New York* (New York, 1933), vol. 7, pp. 43–44; Carl Wittke, *We Who Built America* (New York, 1940), pp. 222–229; Post, *Popular Freethought in America*, pp. 197–198.

[27] Both Clarence in Erie County and Wheatfield in Niagara County contained large settlements of Prussian Lutherans. Unlike other towns in which Germans made up a large or significant proportion of the population, they cast very low Democratic votes: 22.9 percent and 36.3 percent, respectively. See Truman White, *Erie County* (Boston History Company, n. p., 1898), vol. 1, pp. 516–519; William Pool, ed., *Landmarks of Niagara County, New York* (D. Mason Company, n. p., 1897), pp. 338–359. For an interesting discussion of the conflicts between German and Irish Catholics, and between Protestant and Catholic Germans, see John T. Horton, et al., *History of Northwestern New York*, vol. 1, pp. 143–148.

[28] *Albany Argus* (w.), August 3, 1844, p. 261; July 27, 1844, p. 253; October 5, 1844, p. 327; October 26, 1844, p. 348; November 16, 1844, pp. 369, 370, 372.

[29] *New York Tribune* (w.), April 6, 1844, p. 6; *New York Herald* (d.), November 9, 1844, p. 4.

[30] Immediately after the election, Millard Fillmore wrote that the "foreign vote" went against the Whigs in Erie County; several days later he was more precise and twice referred to the "foreign Catholics" as the cause of the Whig defeat in New York. Fillmore to Weed, November 6, 1844, Fillmore to Clay, November 11, 1844, in Frank H. Severance, ed., "Millard Fillmore Papers," vol. 11, pp. 267–268.

[31] "In 1849, this town had a population of 1168 of whom 646 were Americans and Irish, and 522 French, Germans, and Swiss." These designations refer to country of origin. Actually, the immigrants were from German areas then under French domination, and from the German cantons of Switzerland. A large majority were Catholics. Franklin Hough, *History of Lewis County* (New York, 1860), pp. 74–79.

[32] *Albany Argus* (w.), October 19, 1844, p. 340.

[33] See n. 27 above.

[34] *New York Express*, November 9, 1844, p. 2.

[35] In 1855, of the state's 18,366 residents born in France (including the Germanic provinces),

more than one third lived in New York City. New York State, *Census for 1855*, pp. 175–176.

[36] *American Republican*, November 1, 1844, p. 2; *New York Express*, October 29; November 11, 1844, p. 2; *New York Herald* (w.), November 2, 1844, p. 346.

[37] Ernst, *New York Immigrant Life*, pp. 44–45, 94–95.

[38] Marcus L. Hansen, *The Mingling of the Canadian and American Peoples* (New Haven, Conn., 1940), pp. 115–126. Using the data for 1855 as a guide, the three counties with the highest proportion of French Canadians were Clinton, Franklin, and Essex.

[39] *New York Tribune* (w.), August 3, 1844, p. 6; September 13, 1845, p. 3.

[40] See D. H. Hurd, compiler, *History of Clinton and Franklin Counties* (Philadelphia, 1880), pp. 300–302; Seaver, *Franklin County*, pp. 238–249. According to the *Freeman's Journal*, October 19, 1844, pp. 124–125, the Catholics in Chauteaugay were principally French-Canadian.

[41] My estimate is that the Democrats outnumbered the Whigs among the immigrants by about two to one.

[42] David M. Ellis, "The Yankee Invasion of New York, 1783–1850," *New York History*, vol. 32, p. 3 (January 1951).

[43] The basis for that estimate is given in Appendix III.

[44] Ellis, in *New York History*, vol. 31, p. 4.

[45] See the *Greenport Watchman's* analysis reprinted in *Brooklyn Eagle*, December 3, 1844, p. 2.

[46] David Murray, ed., *Delaware County, New York* (Delhi, N.Y., 1898), pp. 48–49, 120; Jay Gould, *History of Delaware County* (Roxbury, N.Y., 1856), pp. 199.

[47] James P. Frost, *Life on the Upper Susquehanna: 1783–1860* (New York, 1951), pp. 99–100 and 7–16.

[48] W. W. Clayton, *History of Steuben County* (Philadelphia, 1879), pp. 355–363; James H. Hotchkin, *A History of the Purchase and Settlement of Western New York* (New York, 1848), pp. 463–467.

[49] Even a cursory study of the county statistics in New England indicates the scant basis which exists for the notion of a solid "Yankee" vote. See, for example, the 1844 returns in *The Whig Almanac . . . for 1845* (New York, 1845), p. 42.

[50] See n. 33 in Chapter VII.

[51] Fox, in *Political Science Quarterly*, vol. 32, pp. 263–275. Compare *New York Tribune* (w.), January 4, 1845, p. 5; June 14, 1845, p. 3, March 25, 1846, p. 5; April 4, 1846, p. 3; November 28, 1846, p. 5; *New York Morning News*, June 2, 7, 11, 1845, p. 2; *Evening Post for the Country*, September 23, 1845, p. 3; *Albany Atlas* (s.w.), October 27, 1846, p. 2.

[52] These estimates are discussed in Appendix III.

[53] *American Republican*, July 9; September 2, 5; October 30, 1844, p. 2.

[54] *New York Tribune* (w.), November 16, 1844, p. 5.

[55] David Ellis, et al., *A Short History of New York State* (Ithaca, N.Y., 1957), pp. 60–67.

[56] David Cole, *History of Rockland County* (New York, 1884), p. 99.

[57] Walter A. Knittle, *The Early Eighteenth-Century Palatine Migration* (Philadelphia, 1936), pp. 144–210.

[58] Whitney R. Cross, *The Burned-over District*, pp. 67–68; McNall, *Agricultural History of Western New York*, pp. 68–69. New York State *Census for 1845* provided an excellent clue to the location of the Penn-Jerseyites by dividing native migrants in New York according to their birth in "New England" and "Other States." Research in county and town histories revealed that the latter category consisted overwhelmingly of Penn-Jerseyites.

[59] The highest- and lowest-ranking Democratic towns in the three counties were: Lodi 67.7 percent, Ovid 36.9 percent (Seneca); Barton 74.1 percent, Nichols 39.0 percent (Tioga); Lansing 68.8 percent, Ulysses 37.4 percent (Tompkins).

The Basis of Alabama's

Antebellum Two-Party System*

Thomas B. Alexander
Peggy Duckworth Elmore
Frank M. Lowrey
Mary Jane Pickens Skinner

7

Despite often aggressively articulated sectional rhetoric, the general similarity of antebellum southern popular voting behavior to that of the rest of the country is striking. Although hampered by the absence of much electoral and demographic data, Professor Thomas B. Alexander of the University of Missouri and his students have made a number of rather sophisticated quantitative assessments of pre–Civil War voting in the state of Alabama. As the following summary of their work makes clear, the same basic two-party system as in the North structured voting patterns between 1840 and 1860. In addition there was the same decided absence of economic class voting and the same marked stability of voting behavior over time. Even amid the intense sectional pressures of 1860, previous party identification significantly shaped the vote on the secession question.

In the 1836 presidential election a new political party made its debut into the United States political scene.[1] The Jacksonian Democratic party, which for almost a decade had dominated American political life, had begun to splinter into factions, even in the South. Anti-Jackson elements of the South joined with surviving Federalists and with National Republicans to form the Whig party as an effective nationwide opposition to the Democrats. From 1836 until 1860 this organization, long known in the South as Whig but in 1856 as American and in 1860 as Constitutional Union, held a place of significance as the opponent of Jacksonian Democracy. Until after the presidential election of 1852 this opposition retained its national unity, but before 1856 the bulk of the northern Whigs assumed the name Republican and departed from organized cooperation with their southern brethren.

Alabama became a two-party state with the first election in which the na-

SOURCE: Reprinted with permission from *The Alabama Review*, vol. 19, no. 4 (October, 1966), pp. 243–276. Copyright © 1969 by the University of Alabama Press.

* "The Basis of Alabama's Two-Party System," A Case Study In Party Alignment And Voter Response In The Traditional Two-Party System Of The United States By Quantitative Analysis Methods.

tional Whig organization appeared, that of 1836. The Alabama Whigs never won the presidential vote of their state, but they came within 1 percent of victory in 1848 and 5 percent in 1840. Despite the troubles which beset Alabama Whigs as the sectional controversy worsened, they managed to retain well above one-third of the popular vote in the presidential elections of 1852 and 1856, and almost one-third in 1860.[2]

For a generation prior to 1824 individual political decisions had been closely tied to family tradition and regional heritage. But between 1824 and 1836 political alignment of the individual voter was a far more personal decision. No longer could he rely on family or neighborhood attitudes as a guide; he had to turn to the appeals of the new parties and decide which group offered the most satisfactory answers to the problems he viewed as important — or, perhaps, simply react favorably toward those national or local leaders who more effectively aroused his enthusiasm. It is important to discover what factors were influential in the political decisions of this period, for it is one of the rare instances in United States political history in which the momentum of habit and the weight of tradition could not dominate voter preference.

Discovery of influential factors in choice of party alignment for a period when individuals were remarkably free to follow personal inclinations should be valuable in assessing the significance of the two-party system as a United States political institution. This system has been widely extolled and credited with being an indispensible part of our democratic political process. Americans have, indeed, so completely identified two-party politics with democracy that we often grow impatient with emerging political systems in Africa and Asia unless they incorporate a reasonable facsimile of our party structure, sometimes even denouncing as nondemocratic a new nation-state without our arrangement. Perhaps such criticism is well founded; perhaps our party arrangements and traditions are truly necessary components of stable democratic government. It behooves us to be very sure about the nature of our political institutions, however, to discern as well as we can which elements are vital and whether any are transitory or unique to our particular culture and tradition, before we measure and judge other political patterns by the yardstick of our own. And despite the decades of interest and investigation, disturbingly little is yet known about why, without family political tradition, a voter aligns himself with one party or another, or what circumstances can wrench him out of his party commitment. Hence, there is no adequate measure of the extent to which decision-making political leaders are constrained by voter response or expectation of voter reaction, and we are far from knowing what real difference it makes in the development and implementation of our governmental policies that we have a two-party system instead of some other form of election structuring. Placing Alabama Whigs and their partisan opponents under intensive scrutiny is offered, then, as a modest step in pursuit of significant new knowledge.[3]

The prevailing interpretations of party alignment in the United States have emphasized economic consideration. One of the pithiest statements of this view may be found in the 1956 edition of a distinguished college textbook of United States history: " . . . the Democrats became the party of poverty and numbers, and the Whigs the party of property and talents."[4] It is commonly assumed among students of the antebellum South that the Whig party of the region was dominated primarily by wealthy, aristocratic planters and merchants and con-trasted significantly with a Democratic party supposed to have been composed of small farmers and artisans — "strong in the pine barrens and areas of high illiteracy of the white population, of low land values, and of small proportion of slaves." [5] This economic interpretation, applied directly to the individual voter, has been accepted by students of antebellum Alabama party division. The Whigs of Alabama have been designated a "broadcloth party" which "drew its strength from the men of slaves and means who lived in the Black Belt and in the western counties of the Tennessee Valley and the business interests affili-ated with them." [6] There has been, however, some evidence presented in recent years which casts doubt on the validity of the economic basis of antebellum party division in the South.[7]

In comparing Alabama Whigs with Democrats, evidence has been sought to sustain, modify, or discredit economic interpretations in several ways and from several types of sources. The first of the approaches used is simple but tedious and time consuming. Individual Whigs and Democrats have been identified by searching newspaper accounts of local or state political meetings, political peti-tions, or other political activity. Each individual has then been searched out in the original returns for the United States census so as to locate such informa-tion as was recorded by the census-taker who called at his residence. The 1840 census contained too little information to justify the labor of more than limited search, but both the 1850 and the 1860 censuses yielded valuable information about the economic status, age, and birthplace of each individual.[8]

Tables 7.1 through 7.5 present the analysis of characteristics of identified Whigs and Democrats in Alabama based on information located in the original census returns. The men used in the comparison were from Autauga, Greene, Jefferson, Lowndes, Montgomery, and Tuscaloosa counties. Almost one thou-sand men whose party identification could be established were included in the analysis by occupation, age, and place of birth, and approximately seven hun-dred in the real estate and slaveholding comparisons. This number is large enough to go beyond what twentieth-century political scientists define as a po-litical elite and which they have found to be drawn from the same socioeco-nomic levels for both major parties. Whether or not such similarity was the case a century ago is not the problem here confronted, but rather whether distinc-tions existed between Democrats and Whigs of rank and file levels. And, al-though party identification could be discovered only for those whose names appeared in print, chiefly in newspapers, it was still possible to reach far below leadership levels. This is true because newspapers of the antebellum period were party organs and made a practice of printing long lists of names from local party mass gatherings or from petitions or endorsements. The number of men employed in this study from Autauga and Montgomery counties is a substantial portion of the total number of voters there.[9]

Table 7.1 presents a comparison of Whigs with Democrats based on value of real estate owned.[10] The outstanding fact is the overall similarity of the two groups. In the highest category employed, $20,000 and above, 21 percent of the Whigs and 27 percent of the Democrats were found.[11] In each of the other cate-gories the percentages for Whigs and Democrats are very close. Such slight differences as appear suggest, if anything, that those in both the highest and the lowest wealth classifications had the same slight tendency to prefer the Demo-cratic side.

Table 7.1 Percentage of Identified Whigs and of Identified Democrats in Each
Economic Level as Determined by the Dollar Value of Real Estate Owned
*Politically Active Men of Autauga, Greene, Jefferson, Lowndes, Montgomery,
and Tuscaloosa Counties*

almost agricultural only

Dollar Value of Real Estate Owned	Percentage of Party Group	
	Whigs (291 men)	Democrats (436 men)
$20,000 and over	21	27
$10,000 and under $20,000	20	16
$5000 and under $10,000	21	20
$1000 and under $5000	29	25
Under $1000	7 20 *people*	12 52

The customary interpretation that slaveholding and Whig alignment went together has been tested in the analysis summarized in Table 7.2. At the level of
ownership of one hundred or more slaves were found 7 percent of the identified
Democrats as contrasted with only 3 percent of the identified Whigs, the reverse of expectations engendered by the "broadcloth party" view. The small
and middle-sized planters, with slaves numbering from twenty to ninety-nine,
comprised a very slightly higher proportion of the Whig group than of the Democratic; and the same was true of the larger farmer with one to four slave families (or owning less than twenty slaves).

neither able considered time change

Table 7.2 Percentage of Identified Whigs and of Identified Democrats in Each
Slaveholding Level
*Politically Active Men of Autauga, Greene, Jefferson, Lowndes, Montgomery,
and Tuscaloosa Counties*

Number of Slaves Owned	Percentage of Party Group	
	Whigs (268 men)	Democrats (407 men)
100 and over	3	7
50-99	12 } 42	11 } 40
20-49	27	22
10-19	→ 21 } 49	16 } 39
1-9	28	23
None	9	21

None of these distinctions is significantly large, however, and in total impact
their slightness raises further doubt that economic characteristics distinguished
Whigs from Democrats. The nonslaveholding group among the identified voters,
on the other hand, requires further comment. On the last line of Table 7.2 is
recorded a large differential: nonslaveholders comprised only 9 percent of the
identified Whig group but 21 percent of the Democratic. One should here take
into account the age differential between party groups. As shown in Table 7.3,
decidedly a larger proportion of the Democrats than of the Whigs were very
young voters. Acquisition of slaves, whether by inheritance or by purchase,

generally occurred after a man was established and probably older than thirty. The large difference between Whigs and Democrats among the nonslaveholders may, therefore, be attributed chiefly to the age differential. In general, slave-holding information fails to confirm an economic basis of party alignment.

Table 7.3 Percentage of Identified Whigs and of Identified Democrats
in Each Age Bracket
Politically Active Men of Autauga, Greene, Jefferson, Lowndes, Montgomery, and
Tuscaloosa Counties

Age	Percentage of Party Group	
	Whigs (350 men)	Democrats (609 men)
61 and over	9	9
51 to 60	17	14
41 to 50	30	25
31 to 40	33	30
21 to 30	12	22

	Percentage of Party Group			
	1840 or 1850		1860	
Age	Whigs (250 men)	Democrats (332 men)	Whigs (100 men)	Democrats (277 men)
61 and over	7	9	15	9
51 to 60	15	11	21	17
41 to 50	26	22	40	30
31 to 40	39	33	18	27
21 to 30	14	26	6	17

Age distinctions are offered in Table 7.3. In the top section of the table, in which are lumped together all data from the censuses of 1840, 1850, and 1860, the similarity between Whigs and Democrats is striking for all but the youngest group. There is strong evidence that men in their twenties were more drawn to the Democratic ranks. In each age category from thirty-one to sixty, in turn, a very slightly larger percentage of Whig supporters was found. The lower section of Table 7.3 distinguishes between age information taken from the censuses of 1840 and 1850 and that from 1860. The comparison based on 1860 figures alone reveals a significantly greater contrast in the lowest age bracket. Whereas less than twice as large a percentage of Democrats as Whigs in the total tabulation and in that for 1840 and 1850 were thirty or less, almost three times as large a percentage of Democrats as of Whigs were in the youngest category among the men located in the 1860 census (17 percent to 6 percent). Furthermore, men from thirty-one to forty comprised a substantially larger portion of the Democratic group in this latter comparison (27 percent to 18 percent). Not only did the Democrats appeal more effectively to the young voter from the beginning of party division in Alabama, but in addition that appeal grew greater as the years passed, so that age emerges as a meaningful basis of party distinction.

As another index to possible economic or other distinctions, a voter's occupation should be revealing. As shown in Table 7.4, precisely the same percentage

T. B. Alexander / P. Elmore / F. Lowrey / M. Skinner   103

of the identified Whigs and Democrats were farmers or planters (shown as 48 percent on the first line of information in Table 7.4). The merchants of the counties studied, however, presented a slightly different picture, in which it appears that the Whig party was more attractive than the Democratic — but the difference even here may be less significant than the similarity (19 percent for the Whigs to 13 percent for the Democrats). No other occupational category shows enough variation between Whigs and Democrats to suggest that this factor led men to different political parties. Occupation emerges as little if any explanation of party alignment.

Table 7.4   Percentage of Identified Whigs and of Identified Democrats
in Each Occupation
Politically Active Men of Autauga, Greene, Jefferson, Lowndes, Montgomery, and Tuscaloosa Counties

	Percentage of Party Group	
Occupation	*Whigs (338 men)*	*Democrats (542 men)*
Farmers and planters	48	48
Merchants	19	13
Lawyers	11	11
Artisans	6	6
Doctors and druggists	6	7
Clerks, bookkeepers, and managers	4	4
Editors, printers, and publishers	2	3
Public officials	2	3
Ministers	1	1
Overseers	1	1
Teachers	1	1
Bankers	0	0
Other professions and occupations	0	1
Tailors	0	0
Collectors	0	0

The original census returns provide information on the place of birth for each individual, which for the counties under consideration shows several differences between Whigs and Democrats (Table 7.5). A larger segment of the Democrats was from the group born in Alabama, a fact compatible with the discovery that younger men were disproportionately Democrats. Alabama was so new as an area of settlement in 1840 that few voters were natives of the state. Even by 1850 not a great proportion were Alabama-born; and the voters who were born in the state were necessarily the younger voters. Although the Georgians comprised a slightly higher percentage of the Whigs than of the Democrats, the dominant image projected from Table 7.5 is that political choice was very little related to the southern state a voter claimed as his birthplace. The northern-born voter was decidedly inclined to be Whig, and the foreign-born Democratic.

The most serious deficiency of the group of individuals here analyzed is that it includes too few very small farmers or others with little wealth. Whereas it was typical for half or more of the family heads of an Alabama county in 1860 to report wealth of less than $1000, only a small percentage of the Whigs and

Table 7.5 Percentage of Identified Whigs and of Identified Democrats
Born in Each State or Area
*Politically Active Men of Autauga, Greene, Jefferson, Lowndes, Montgomery, and
Tuscaloosa Counties*

| | Percentage of Party Group | |
State or Area	Whigs (347 men)	Democrats (544 men)
Alabama	8	15
Georgia	23	17
Kentucky	2	1
Maryland	1	1
North Carolina	12	14
South Carolina	21	21
Tennessee	3	3
Virginia	15	13
Northern U.S.	13	6
Foreign	3	9

Democrats in the present comparison reported as little wealth as this. There is not much probability that further search would turn up any substantial number of names from among the lowest wealth category. Another approach, also employing the original census returns, has, therefore, been made to estimate the political alignment of the less wealthy half of the potential voters. For nine Alabama counties a tabulation has been made of the wealth reported for the 1860 census by every family head or individual living apart from a family. These nine counties include two from the Tennessee Valley, two from the Hill Country, two from the Black Belt, and three from the Pine Barren or Coastal Plain portion of Alabama. Table 7.6 makes available a comparison of the percentage of those reporting less than $1000 in wealth with the percentage of the Democratic vote for each of these nine counties. If a substantially larger portion of the men lowest in wealth voted Democratic rather than Whig, there ought to be considerable correlation between the two sets of percentages in Table 7.6. There is not, however, any such correlation. Although Greene County turns out to be lowest in both percentage of low-wealth families and in percentage of Democratic voters, in general there is little relationship — as the two right-hand columns of the table illustrate. The coefficient of correlation between these two sets of percentages is an insignificant +.276 and can offer no basis for assuming that any large majority of those reporting wealth of less than $1000 favored the Democratic party.

The original census returns, together with a generous listing of Whigs and Democrats in the contemporary newspapers, have made possible scrutiny of some economic and other characteristics of individual Alabama voters. The same data have made possible very close reckoning of party tendencies for the less wealthy voters who were not adequately represented among the individuals identified and studied. Similarity rather than difference has been discovered, particularly with regard to economic considerations. Youthfulness or foreign birth inclined one toward the Democratic party; birth in a northern state had the opposite effect; but personal economic status was not a significant basis of

Table 7.6 Party Preference Tendencies of Low-Wealth
Alabama Voters, 1844-1860
*Percentages of Family Heads or Individuals without Family Reporting Wealth of
Less than $1000 for the Census of 1860 Compared with Average Democratic Party
Percentage of the Total Vote, 1844-1860
For Autauga, Baldwin, Barbour, Bibb, Coffee, Coosa, Greene, Lawrence,
and Morgan Counties*

Counties Arranged in Descending Order by Percentage of Family Heads or Individuals Reporting Wealth of Less than $1000 for the Census of 1860	Per- centage Less than $1000	Average Percentage Democratic Vote† Presidential Elections 1844-1860	County Rank by Per- centage Less than $1000	County Rank by Per- centage Democratic Vote
Barbour	68	53	1	6 tie
Baldwin	65	48	2	8
Lawrence	59	55	3	4 tie
Coffee	57	64	4	2
Bibb	52	55	5	4 tie
Morgan	52	67	6	1
Coosa	44	63	7	3
Autauga	39	53	8	6 tie
Greene	20	44	9	9

*The tabulations upon which this table is based were made for a seminar paper by Lewis D. Tyler and are in the possession of Professor Thomas B. Alexander, Department of History, University of Alabama.

†The average percentage Democratic party vote was calculated on the basis of five presidential elections (1844 through 1860), except that third-party vote distorted the proportions too far to permit meaningful use in two counties for the 1852 election (State Rights party vote) and in five counties for the 1860 election (large vote for Stephen A. Douglas, the northern Democratic party candidate, who attracted considerable numbers of Whigs as well as Unionist Democrats to his ranks in the 1860 election).

party alignment in Alabama.

It will never be possible to determine the vote of every individual voter in a county for the antebellum period. The total vote of a county, on the other hand, is rarely very useful for simple observation of economic factors in relation to voter preferences because the parties were often fairly closely balanced in a county, and the various neighborhoods may have differed greatly in soil characteristics and other aspects of economic significance. The smallest unit of election returns to be found for the period under study is the voting district, or beat, or box, which often involved less than one hundred voters, usually was far more decidedly aligned with one party than was a whole county, and sometimes comprised a very homogeneous neighborhood in terms of economic development. Unfortunately, beat election returns are scarce and can be located in official returns or newspapers for only scattered beats and few elections. It is, furthermore, very difficult to identify the location of beats of a century and more ago, many of which were called by names no longer used or even associated with a particular locality, and some of which were merely assigned numbers. Despite these handicaps, a significant number of beat returns have been ferreted out and employed in seeking to discover whether the

Whig-dominated neighborhoods were noticeably wealthier than the Democratic ones.

The results of studies of beat election returns for Lowndes and Tuscaloosa counties appeared in *The Alabama Review* for January, 1963; consequently, only brief reference will be made to these counties.[12] Lowndes County beat election returns for the presidential elections of 1836 and 1860 and for the state and congressional elections of 1851 and 1855 revealed that the only consistent Whig beats were in the southern portion of the county, an area characterized by steep hills and deep ravines, and not suitable for large-scale cotton production. Democratic strength displayed itself more strongly in the black prairie portions of the county. This is, of course, the reverse of expectations suggested by the prevailing interpretations of party alignment. It should be noted, furthermore, that a large minority vote appeared in almost every beat and that often the division between parties was very close.

From the available beat returns of Tuscaloosa County, it would appear that during the 1840s this county conformed fairly well to the prevailing interpretation in so far as rank and file of voters were concerned. During the 1850s, however, the county was tending to divide along the Black Warrior River into a Democratic southeastern portion and a Whig northwestern segment, with some unstable beats in the middle and eastern portion. Beat returns for the 1857 congressional election and the 1860 presidential election, therefore, reveal a party division which in some measure cut across soil considerations in such a way as to weaken association of Whiggery with plantation economy.

Montgomery County has served as an excellent case study in beat analysis.[13] About two-thirds of this county lies in the Alabama Black Belt. Bordering on the north of the Black Belt section of the county and extending along the Alabama and Tallapoosa rivers are the river bottom lands. These river bottom lands, along with the black prairie, contain the greater part of the better cotton-producing lands of the county. The southern quarter of Montgomery County is in a range of hills and not suitable for cotton plantations. Another highland area was in the extreme northeast corner of the county north of the Tallapoosa River, an area which in 1866 became part of Elmore County.

Ten of the fourteen beats of Montgomery County in 1848 were identified. The beat returns for these do not reveal any particular voting patterns. The strongest Whig beat was in the hill section of the southern part of the county, and the northern hill section furnished the strongest Democratic beat. In the total vote of the located beats, 84 percent of the Whig votes came from the Black Belt section of the county, and 87 percent of the Democratic votes came from this same section.

Fourteen of the sixteen 1852 beats have been located, although in four of these beats no election was held. The strongest Whig beat, Jackson's (87 percent Whig), was located in the southern hill section of the county. The strongest Democratic beat (60 percent Democratic), was Butler's Mills, lying in the Black Belt section of the county. A scrutiny of the beat returns as a whole, however, does not reveal any significant voting patterns in 1852. Although, among the located beats holding an election, five of the six Whig beats were in the Black Belt and only one of the three Democratic beats was in this section, in the aggregate vote of these beats 89 percent of the Whig votes and 83 percent of the Democratic votes came from the Black Belt section of the county.

It has been possible to locate ten voting beats in Montgomery County for the presidential election of 1856. Six of the ten gave a majority of votes to the American candidate, former Whig President Millard Fillmore. Two of the American beats were in the hill country of the south, and the remainder were in the Black Belt and river bottom lands. Three of the Democratic beats were in the Black Belt, and one was in the northern hill section. Again, no significant voting pattern based on geographic location may be observed in the county.

Eleven 1860 beats have been located. Ten of the eleven were in favor of John C. Breckinridge, the nominee of the Southern Democratic party. The chief opponent of Breckinridge in Montgomery County was John Bell, nominee of the Constitutional Union party, the continuation of the Whig organization in the South. In the located beats in 1860, the Black Belt section of the county gave slightly more support to Breckinridge than to Bell — 78 percent for Breckinridge and 72 percent for Bell. These percentages are much too close, however, to justify generalization.

In the composite of all the located beats holding elections in the presidential contests considered in this study of Montgomery County, 82 percent of the Whig votes and 82 percent of the Democratic votes came from the Black Belt section of the county. Thus, it can be concluded that in all probability geographic location was an unimportant factor in choice of party for most voters of Montgomery County.

A study has been made of beat election returns of Pickens County for the presidential election of 1860.[14] About one-third of Pickens County — the southern and southwest portion — lies in the Black Belt, whereas the northern portion of the county is hill country. For the presidential election of 1860, seventeen beats with returns have been located, all but two of which returned majorities for Breckinridge. The two Bell beats were located in the hill country just to the north of the Black Belt area. Two Black Belt beats showed about 40 percent Bell strength, but most of the beats with large minorities for Bell were in the hill section. Most of the beats with the lowest percentage of Bell votes were also in the hill section. The strongest Breckinridge beat was in the Black Belt. It would not appear, then, that the division between Bell and Breckinridge was particularly associated with the division of the county into the Black Belt and hill sections.

Between 1836 and 1860 no significant voting patterns based on geographic location may be observed in the counties considered in this study. In all probability, geographic location was not a major consideration in party choice by most voters in these four counties.

Correlation studies, carried out with information at the county total level, have been made in an attempt to discover what relationship prevailed between Whig voting strength and economic characteristics of the counties as shown in the published abstracts of the United States censuses. The informative censuses of 1850 and 1860 and sensitive correlation procedures, which are based on precise percentage calculations for each county, have been employed. If Whigs were the economic upper half, there ought to be a significantly high positive relationship between percentages of Whig vote and prevalence of economic prosperity as shown by land values, production levels, slaveowning or any of the clues to advanced economic development and affluence. In oversimplified statement, a primitive county ought to have been predominantly Democratic and a prosperous one largely Whig. Correlation analysis can make possible management of quantities of information entirely beyond the capacity of informal analysis, as well as more perceptive study of relationships, and can, furthermore, reduce the sets of relationships to terms simple enough to grasp and discuss.

Most of the correlation analysis employed for study of associations between politics and economic or other measurable factors for geographic districts, such as counties, has been of a rudimentary nature and has compared only two variables at a time. Even this type of correlation (bivariate) can be oppressively laborious if many counties or other units are to be compared. This level of analysis, laborious and useful as it is, is dotted with pitfalls. It may appear from bivariate analysis alone, for example, that members of a certain religious denomination overwhelmingly vote Republican in the mid-twentieth century, when, in fact, it is the ruralism of the Middle West, where these voters are concentrated, that is strongly and positively correlated with Republicanism. By studying relationships between this religious group and Republican voting apart from the distinction between urbanism and ruralism, it may be discovered that their religious connection gives them no special tendency to vote Republican or even may impel them more often to vote Democratic. It is exceptional to be able to locate counties, or other voting districts, in useful numbers in which all factors other than the one to be studied are identical. When such a fortunate set of observations can be located, the uncontaminated relationship between two variables may be determined with considerable confidence by two-variable correlation analysis.

In almost all real situations, how two things are related to each other, if all other factors were equal, can only be discovered by statistical procedures which simultaneously take into account many different variables and attempt to calculate the effect of all of the independent variables lumped together on a single dependent variable and then to calculate the relation of each separate variable to the changes in that dependent variable. This is termed multiple correlation and partial correlation. The mathematical formula for entertaining the enormously complicated sets of relationships involved in multiple and partial correlation can only be used with crushing expenditures of effort and time, and only on very limited numbers of observations, without electronic computer assistance. Computer programs which can manage these intricate and extensive calculations have, themselves, been so difficult to design that only very recently has computer assistance become available. Multiple and partial correlation procedure will yield more precise information if all data are in strictly comparable form. No attempt was made to correlate bales of cotton with numbers of swine, nor total value of all farms in each county with the number of slaves in each county. It was decided, instead, to reduce to percentage form the election and census information employed.

Tables 7.7 through 7.9 contain the results of these multiple and partial correlation analyses.[15] Tables 7.7 and 7.8 show the coefficient of correlation existing between each possible pair of the economic factors included from the 1850 and the 1860 census, respectively. This figure is customarily shown as a positive or negative fraction, in decimal form, ranging from a maximum positive relationship approaching a full $+1$ in instances of perfect positive correlation to a -1 for the maximum negative relationship. As a simple example, assuming

Table 7.7 Coefficients of Correlation Between Each Pair of Economic
Characteristics Among Ten Selected from the 1850 Census
for All of the Counties of Alabama

	Cotton Production	Corn Production	Number of Swine	Number of Cattle	Value of Livestock	Value of Farms	Value of Farms per Acre	Value of Farm Implements	Total Population	Percent Slaves of Total Population
Cotton production	1.00									
Corn production	.89	1.00								
Number of Swine	.82	.92	1.00							
Number of cattle	.47	.30	.39	1.00						
Value of livestock	.95	.94	.89	.50	1.00					
Value of farms	.94	.95	.85	.33	.94	1.00				
Value of farms per acre	.47	.55	.39	−.14	.45	.63	1.00			
Value of farm implements	.92	.90	.84	.40	.94	.93	.45	1.00		
Total population	.85	.85	.77	.40	.91	.89	.67	.85	1.00	
Percent slaves of total population	.80	.66	.54	.51	.74	.73	.33	.69	.65	1.00

adequate rainfall and soil fertility, cotton production would correlate positively and very highly with length of growing season and very negatively with annual snowfall.[16]

The immediately notable and very significant element in these matrices of correlation coefficients is that all but one single coefficient are positive and that the great majority are significantly high, many approaching nearly perfect positive correlation (in the high 80s or 90s). The evident conclusion from this pattern is that total population increase in a county generally brought more corn production, more cattle and swine, more slaves, and roughly a higher percentage standing for the county in every one of the elements here studied.

Table 7.9 shows the multiple and partial correlation coefficients expressing the relationship between the economic factors and political party alignment. In the first place, almost all of the coefficients of multiple correlation, relating the collective economic elements to politics, are significantly high. The coefficient of determination, also shown for each correlation, statistically purports to estimate what part or portion of the political behavior is actually explained by the collective impact of the entire group of economic factors used in the

Table 7.8 Coefficients of Correlation Between Each Pair of Economic
Characteristics Among Ten Selected From the 1860
Census for All of the Counties of Alabama

	Cotton Pro- duction	Corn Pro- duction	Num ber of Swine	Num- ber of Cattle	Value of Live- stock	Value of Farms	Value of Farms per Acre	Total Popu- lation	Percent Slaves of Total Popu- lation	Percent Slave- holders of Male Adult Free Popu- lation
Cotton production	1.00									
Corn production	.90	1.00								
Number of swine	.85	.87	1.00							
Number of cattle	.71	.61	.64	1.00						
Value of livestock	.90	.89	.81	.62	1.00					
Value of farms	.95	.94	.82	.67	.91	1.00				
Value of farms per acre	.86	.86	.69	.56	.79	.93	1.00			
Total population	.77	.76	.74	.63	.74	.78	.75	1.00		
Percent slaves of total population	.84	.70	.64	.69	.70	.80	.81	.61	1.00	
Percent slaveholders of male adult free popu- lation	.86	.71	.67	.69	.72	.81	.81	.65	.96	1.00

multiple correlation analysis. It will be noted that these coefficients of determination shown as the bottom line of Table 7.9 (ranging about .50, or 50 percent, for most of the correlations), suggest that perhaps half of the political behavior can be attributed to these economic considerations. But the other half goes unexplained and cannot properly be attributed to the influence of factors here used. The conclusion is indicated that these economic considerations played a critically important general role in determining party alignment, but that other factors, economic or otherwise, played an equally important role.

The coefficients of partial correlation for each of the factors separately, on the other hand, show that not one of the factors alone is highly related to political alignment. Individually, most of these economic elements show so close to a zero correlation as to be meaningless as explanations. The percentage of slaves in the population, a good index to general economic development, correlated significantly positively with Whig strength, and corn production significantly negatively. The general point is, however, that none of these is county level too aggregate

Table 7.9 Coefficients of Multiple and Partial Correlation Between Each of
Ten Economic Characteristics Selected From the Census of 1850 or 1860
and Political Party Division of the Popular Vote in Presidential Elections
From 1840 through 1860 for All of the Counties of Alabama

Economic Characteristics	Economic Characteristics from the Census of 1850 — Partial Correlation with:				Economic Characteristics from the Census of 1860 — Partial Correlation with:				
	Whig % 1840	Whig % 1844	Whig % 1848	Whig % 1852	American Party % 1856	Douglas Faction % 1860	Breckinridge % 1860	Bell Whig % 1860	Douglas and Bell % 1860
Cotton production	.09	.11	.05	.17	−.12	−.06	.15	−.11	−.15
Corn production	−.35*	−.30	−.34*	−.33*	−.37*	.05	.25	−.33*	−.25
Number of swine	.00	−.11	.09	.14	.12	−.21	.04	.20	−.04
Number of cattle	.00	.06	.13	−.05	.14	−.45*	.26	.28	−.26
Value of livestock	.21	.30	.27	.27	.12	.02	−.20	.19	.20
Value of farms	−.02	−.07	.04	−.26	.18	−.03	.06	−.01	−.06
Value of farms per acre	−.10	−.03	.13	.08	−.25	.12	−.18	.02	.19
Value of farm implements	−.04	−.11	−.08	.03					
Total population	.09	.04	−.14	.02	.32*	.19	−.21	.05	.21
Percent slaves of total population	.38*	.37*	.11	.51*	.45*	.16	−.43*	.30*	.43*
Percent slaveholders of male adult free population					−.16	−.10	.20	−.06	−.20
Multiple Correlation with:									
Multiple correlation coefficient†	.78	.81	.66	.83	.78	.67	.67	.72	.67
Multiple coefficient of determination	.59	.65	.43	.68	.61	.44	.45	.52	.45

*For any of these partial correlation coefficients which are high enough to indicate significant relationship, it is important to know what level of confidence exists that the relationship is not an accidental one. Computed t values are provided by the computer program employed, and these values can be converted to a level of confidence. Only five of the above partial correlation coefficients have t values indicating better than an .01 level of confidence, or only 1 percent probability that the relationship is a chance one. Another nine coefficients are at the .05 level, or only 5 percent probability of chance relationship. These fourteen coefficients are marked with an *. Six additional coefficients are at the .10 level, but almost half have t values indicating less than .50 level, or more than a one-half probability that the relationship discovered is accidental.

†The level of confidence for the multiple correlation coefficients, as shown by the F values provided by the computer program employed, is in every case above the .01 level, with the probability of chance relationship less than 1 percent.

economic elements alone can be said to be consistently controlling determinants. The very nearly zero correlation coefficients relating the proportion of slaveowners among the free male adults with political alignment is an excellent case in point, powerfully suggesting that slaveowners as such were no more inclined to be Whigs than to be Democrats.

Combining the insights acquired through these research procedures, a general conclusion about political alignment and economic development is suggested. In the counties with the more advanced stages of general economic development, with the greater cash cropping and the greater commercial contacts with the outside world, in short, in the counties more nearly in the mainstream of the national and world economy, Whig party appeals were more effective. And these appeals were more effective to all types of voters regardless of individual economic status. It is not that a planter with many slaves or an affluent merchant was more likely to be a Whig than was a carpenter or small farmer or blacksmith; it is simply that all of these men were more likely to be Whigs if they lived in well developed economic communities rather than in frontier, or isolated, or more nearly self-sufficient communities.

As a warning against oversimplified conclusion, it should not be forgotten that wide latitude remains for unmeasured influences on voter preferences. Effectiveness of local political leadership, decisions by that leadership for very personal, or family, or temperamental reasons, and individual voter response for equally personal reasons remain in the background, probably as very significant determinants of political choice.

In a further effort to discover whether significant differences existed between Whigs and Democrats in Alabama, a statistical estimate was made of voting consistency between the presidential election of November 1860 and the December 1860 election of delegates to the Alabama secession convention. It was not possible to estimate voter performance in the secession convention election from county-total election information. The following estimates, therefore, are based on analysis of returns from 199 beats from fifteen counties. The statistical method used is the least squares estimate of voting behavior. In plain English, this means that the two-variable correlation analysis mentioned above was applied to the electoral units (beats or counties) to study the relationship between party strength and secessionist strength.

In the presidential election of 1860 in Alabama approximately half of the voters supported the southern Democratic candidate, Vice-President John C. Breckinridge of Kentucky. A third of the voters were for John Bell, the Whig candidate running under the southern Whig party label of 1860, the Constitutional Union party. The other sixth voted for the northern Democrat, Stephen A. Douglas. The great bulk of the Breckinridge men were Democrats, although a few in his camp were States Rights Whigs of South Alabama. Undoubtedly, those who supported Bell were Whigs. The support for Douglas was difficult to identify with precision because some prominent Whigs decided to support him as the best candidate to avoid a sectional rift or worse after the election. Some well-known Alabama Whigs even accepted places on the Douglas electoral ticket, and they surely influenced considerable numbers of Whigs. The remainder of the Douglas men were strongly Anti-Secessionist Democrats, chiefly in North Alabama.

In the election of a state convention to consider secession, held in the month following the presidential election, voters had essentially three possible courses of action. They could vote for candidates running as Cooperationists (the Alabama catchall label for every group opposed to immediate secession), if such a candidate for the convention entered the race. They could support an Immediate Secessionist, and such candidates were running in every county. Or they could refrain from voting. The Secessionists made such a strenuous effort to arrange a solid front in the state that they convinced or discouraged Anti-Secessionist leadership to the extent that no opposition officially announced for convention seats in several South Alabama counties. It was in these counties that the decline in voter turnout was greatest; but varying degrees of abstention from voting occurred in other counties.

Under these circumstances the problem of determining how Breckinridge, Bell, and Douglas voters behaved in the secession convention election proved to be a difficult one. In most counties the balance between the parties was close enough that almost any degree of intermingling of parties in support of immediate secession could have existed as far as inspection of county-total returns could reveal. In Black Belt counties such as Montgomery, for instance, in which only about half the voters participated in the convention election and in which Whigs and Democrats were fairly evenly balanced, theoretically it might have been men from either party or some from both parties actually voting for the Immediate Secessionist candidates. With beat election returns, however, least squares estimates have been made of the action taken by each party group in the secession convention election throughout the state.

Beat returns had to be located for the same beats for both the presidential election of November 1860 and the convention election of December 1860 before statistical calculations could be applied to making the estimates. An exhaustive search of the official returns in the Alabama State Department of Archives and History and of the contemporary newspapers provided such sets of returns for 199 beats from fifteen counties, fortunately well scattered over the state: Madison and Marshall in the Tennessee Valley; Pickens, Tuscaloosa, Chambers, and Tallapoosa principally in the Hill Country; Autauga, Greene, Lowndes, Montgomery, and Sumter of the Black Belt; and Butler, Clarke, and Mobile in the southernmost portion. The Mobile beat returns were from the city only.[17]

Estimates from these sets of beat returns have been based on numerous combinations for correlation. The pattern employed for correlation calculations consisted of four percentages from the presidential election returns (Bell percent, Breckinridge percent, Douglas percent, and the combined Bell and Douglas percent) and five percentages from the secession convention election (Cooperationist percent, Secessionist percent, abstention percent, Cooperationist and abstention percents combined, and Secessionist and abstention percents combined). Each of the four presidential election figures was correlated with each one of the five figures drawn from the secession convention election. This was done for each of the following: all 199 beats, 96 North Alabama beats, 103 South Alabama beats, 141 beats in which there were opposing convention candidates, 58 beats in which only a Secessionist candidate ran, and finally all the beats except the 16 in principal towns.

As an additional safeguard, all correlations were calculated not only on the beat data alone but also on the same information weighted to account for the

abstention in now considered ?

fact that some beats had less than twenty-five voters while others had several hundred. The total number of sets of percentages correlated in this weighted analysis was 1156 for all beats, 494 for North Alabama beats, 662 for South Alabama beats, 829 for beats with opponents for the convention seats, and 327 for beats with only Secessionist candidates. Correlation studies were also made for each county separately, employing the weighted-beat sets of percentages.

These correlation analyses were used to make least squares estimates of the

Table 7.10   Voter Consistency in Alabama Presidential and Secession
Convention Elections of 1860
*An Estimate by Least Squares Method**

Of Those Voting for	Percentage Voting for Secession	Percentage Voting for Cooperation	Percentage Not Voting	Percentage Voting for Cooperation or Not Voting
Alabama: 199 Selected Beats Comprising Fifteen Counties				
Breckinridge	73	0	31	27
Bell or Douglas	15	62	23	86
Bell	28	33	40	73
Douglas	12	76	11	88
North Alabama: 96 Selected Beats Comprising Seven Counties				
Breckinridge	76	1	23	26
Bell or Douglas	0	90	12	100
Bell	29	60	12	72
Douglas	1	84	16	99
South Alabama: 103 Selected Beats Comprising Eight Counties				
Breckinridge	70	0	35	30
Bell or Douglas	30	37	33	70
Bell	21	13	67	79
Douglas	30	69	2	72
Elections with Opposing Candidates: 141 Selected Beats				
Breckinridge	70	11	18	30
Bell or Douglas	15	67	18	85
Bell	26	62	13	74
Douglas	17	64	22	85
Elections with Only a Secessionist Candidate: 58 Selected Beats				
Breckinridge	75		26	
Bell or Douglas	20		77	
Bell	17		79	
Douglas	4		97	

*The estimates provided in this set of tables are based on weighting the observations to compensate for the wide variation of numbers of voters among the beats. The numbers of observations, therefore, are much greater than the numbers of beats given (1156 instead of 199 for all the beats employed, for example). No substantial differences were found between weighted and nonweighted calculations, however.

behavior of Whigs, Douglas Democrats, and Breckinridge Democrats in the convention election. Table 7.10 represents a selection from the findings which illustrate the conclusions as well as some of the problems encountered. One problem which emerged in almost every set of correlations was the fact that erratic and impossible-to-determine proportions of Whigs voted for Douglas in many of the heats, particularly in North Alabama. This distorted the pattern of Whig strength, apparently even inverting it in some groups of beats, so that strong Whig beats appeared to be weak ones because the Whigs there voted for Douglas instead of for Bell, while less strong Whig beats in which no swing to Douglas developed, appeared as relatively strong Whig ones. Scattergrams such as the one used to illustrate the least squares method of estimating voter behavior, and similar to the one shown in Figure 7.1, made it clear what distortions of the Bell vote estimates were involved. The most nearly valid least squares estimates were found to be those made from dividing the electorate into two parts only (Breckinridge voters and a combination of Bell and Douglas voters). These two-fold divisions appear as the top two lines of each of the sections of Table 7.10. In addition, Table 7.10 includes the faulty estimates of the Bell group for contrast and the somewhat more trustworthy estimates of the Douglas group.

The Table of Least Squares Estimates indicates that for all Alabama the Breckinridge supporters tended to divide about 73 percent for Secession and 31 percent abstaining from voting, with no tendency to vote for Cooperation. It should be noted here that these are estimates of central tendencies. It is perfectly evident from the original beat election returns that some Breckinridge men did vote for Cooperationist candidates. What this estimate of zero support for Cooperationists means is simply that, while in some beats a few Breckinridge men were Cooperationists, in other beats the Breckinridge contingent brought some of their opponents in the presidential election over to their side and produced a Secessionist proportion greater than their own numbers. These two tendencies cancelled each other to yield the least squares estimate of central tendency for Breckinridge men not to furnish any support for Cooperation.

By following the Breckinridge voters through the subsequent sections of Table 7.10, one can note that in North Alabama, where contests occurred in every county, the Breckinridge tendency to vote Secessionist was a bit higher (76 percent) than for the state as a whole, and conversely in South Alabama, where several counties had no real contest to create a turnout, it was slightly lower (70 percent). In neither area, however, does any significant support for Cooperation emerge from the estimates, only the non-voting percentages vary to compensate for Secessionist vote differences. If the table is examined for the beats with opposing candidates, Breckinridge men still show 70 percent Secessionist vote, but here an 11 percent Cooperationist vote is estimated. Freed from the effects of the fifty-eight beats with no real contests, the statistical estimate here evidently differs enough from the previous ones to warn against drawing very precise conclusions from the least squares estimate. It is nonetheless true that no combination of the data yielded any significantly high estimate of the number of Breckinridge men supporting Cooperationist candidates. Examining the last section of the table, for the fifty-eight beats with no real contest, it is evident that the Breckinridge pattern estimates are consistent, still in the range of 70 to 75 percent Secessionist, with the remainder abstention.

By returning to the first section of Table 7.10 to examine the combined Bell and Douglas vote, it may be noted that for the entire state the estimate is 15 percent for Secession and 86 percent either for Cooperation or not voting. The next two sections of the table, on North and South Alabama respectively, make it evident that the abstention from voting (23 percent for the whole state) was smaller in North Alabama than in South (12 percent as contrasted with 33 percent). The reason for this is made manifest in the next two sections which con-

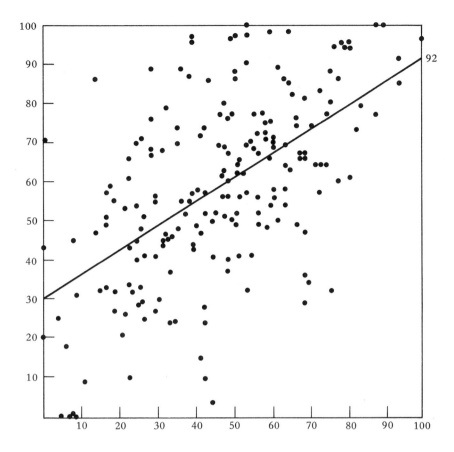

Figure 7.1 *Relation Between Party Preference and Unionism in Alabama in 1860.**

*Scattergram of comparison of combined Bell and Douglas vote with combined vote for the Co-operationist candidates for seats in the Alabama secession convention and abstention from voting in the convention election (decline from presidential election totals): 199 selected beats comprising fifteen counties — unweighted.

Numerals indicate percent of vote within each beat, and each beat is indicated by a dot.

For each beat, the combined percent vote for Cooperation and abstention from voting is the number at the left margin opposite the dot. The combined percent vote for Bell and Douglas is the number at the base line directly below the dot.

Dots close to an imaginary line running from the lower left corner to the upper right corner represent beats in which these two percentage figures are almost identical, suggesting that almost all Bell and Douglas voters either voted for Cooperation or did not vote. Dots above and to the left of such a line represent beats in which more voters supported Cooperation or refrained from voting than had voted for Bell or Douglas; dots below and to the right represent opposite instances.

The line appearing on the scatterplot is the line of best fit (least squares line) for the pattern of the dots. Any point along the line offers the least squares estimate of what percentage Cooperation or decline would be anticipated for the indicated percentage of Bell and Douglas voters. For example, in beats with 50 percent combined Bell and Douglas voters, the estimate of percentage for Cooperation combined with decline would be approximately 60 percent. At the right margin of the plot, where Bell and Douglas voters are indicated at 100 percent, the least squares line intercepts at 92 percent on the Cooperation and decline scale. This provides the least squares estimate that the central tendency of Bell and Douglas supporters was for 92 percent to vote for Cooperation candidates for the convention or not to vote at all.

trast the beats with opposing candidates and those with no real contest. In the former abstention was estimated at 18 percent, in the latter at 77 percent.

In tracing the Bell or Douglas support of Secessionist candidates, it is evident that the 15 percent estimate for the whole state is the result of virtually no such support in North Alabama blended with 30 percent support in South Alabama. It is significant that the Bell or Douglas voters in the 141 beats with real contests showed a tendency to give only 15 percent of their votes for Secession. It was only in the Black Belt and other South Alabama beats with no contests that Whigs even to the extent of an estimated 20 percent actually voted for Secessionists.

From the point of view of summarizing the opposition to Secession among Bell and Douglas supporters, the right-hand column of the Table 7.10, showing the combined percentage voting for Cooperation or not voting, is the most useful. From this column can be read the estimates that, in the state as a whole, 86 percent of Bell and Douglas men were anti-Secession, that the tendency was for all of them in North Alabama and 70 percent of them in South Alabama to be so, and that wherever a real contest existed anywhere in the state 85 percent of the Bell or Douglas supporters could be counted on not to support Secession.

The 199 beats which could be employed represented only about one-third of the state. It was possible that the one-third used was far from typical of the state as a whole, although such a large sample selected as randomly as the counties for which election returns just happen to have survived is reasonably trustworthy. Nonetheless, a test of acceptability is possible by applying the percentage performance estimates to the known total number of Bell, Breckinridge, and Douglas voters in the state to discover whether this will produce a total vote for Secession, vote for Cooperation, and abstention number corresponding to the actual state vote in the convention election. This test has been applied, using the information and estimates for the entire state and for North Alabama and South Alabama separately, and it appears that the least squares estimates calculated from the 199 beats will apply very closely to the entire state or to its northern or southern half. For the whole state the estimate is slightly larger in the Secession column, meaning that the 199 beats had a slightly stronger Secessionist tendency than did the other beats of the state. This modest deviation from a pattern that might have resulted from having every beat in the correlation analysis appears confined to the North Alabama area. In South Alabama the beats employed were the source of more than average Cooperationist votes. This probably means that this set of beats had more actual election contests than was typical of South Alabama. It does not imply an underestimate of the Secessionist tendency of the Bell or Douglas men but only slight underestimate of their abstention tendency. The combined estimated Cooperation vote and abstention percentages work out almost precisely for South Alabama actual election results.

The conclusion is offered with considerable confidence that approximately 75 percent of the 49,019 Breckinridge voters in Alabama voted for Secessionist candidates for the convention, and that almost all of the remainder did not vote. On the other hand, in North Alabama 90 percent of the Bell and Douglas voters voted for Cooperation and the remainder did not vote, while in South Alabama more than one-third of these men voted for Cooperation, somewhat less voted for Secession, and the remaining third did not vote (chiefly in those counties where no Cooperationist candidate announced). Previous party alignment was the overwhelming factor in determining the votes of Alabamians in the convention election, and not even the defection to Immediate Secession of some of the most prominent Whigs of South Alabama could swing very many of the voters from their traditional party attitudes.

The admittedly incomplete image of political-economic relationships emerging from this entire set of investigations is compatible with the image of the Whig party projected by Henry Clay and by most of the leading national Whig figures — that of a party aware of broad national interests, of change and the need to promote and direct that change, of the need for cooperation even to the extent of Federal legislation overriding localism, and, above all, of the necessity for Union and broad functions for the United States government to advance the general welfare of all of the people. The voting behavior of Alabama Whigs and Democrats in the secession crisis buttresses the image of Whigs as more aware of outside considerations, national interests and needs, and the value of preserving the Union intact.

At the risk of falling back into a pit as deep as the one in which it was said that the "Democrats became the party of poverty and numbers, and the Whigs the party of property and talents," as sharp but a different distinction is offered for further study: perhaps Democratic votes were more likely to come from those preoccupied with the way of life of their immediate place and time, while Whig support came predominantly from those whom environment, access to information, and temperament inclined toward an awareness of a way of life beyond their horizons of space and time.

NOTES

[1] This study was presented in the form of four papers at the annual meeting of the Alabama Historical Association, Anniston, April 22, 1966. Professor Alexander wishes to acknowledge support from the University of Alabama Research Committee for assistance to a broader project of which this study is a part.

[2] State- and county-total election returns are from W. Dean Burnham, *Presidential Ballots, 1836–1892* (Baltimore, 1955).

[3] Very stimulating findings of survey research on the subject of voter preference and related problems may be found in Angus Campbell et al., *The American Voter* (New York, 1960).

[4] Samuel E. Morison and Henry S. Commager, *The Growth of the American Republic* (New York, 1956), vol. 1, pp. 554–555.

[5] Clement Eaton, *A History of the Old South* (New York, 1949), p. 304. See also Charles G. Sellers, Jr., "Who Were the Southern Whigs?" *American Historical Review*, vol. 59, p. 346 (January 1954).

[6] Albert B. Moore, *History of Alabama and Her People* (Chicago, 1927), vol. 1, pp. 216–217.

[7] Paul Murray, *The Whig Party in Georgia, 1825–1853* (Chapel Hill, 1948), p. 2; Grady McWhiney, "Were the Whigs a Class Party in Alabama?" *Journal of Southern History*, vol. 23, pp. 510–522 (November, 1957); Thomas B. Alexander, et al., "Who were the Alabama Whigs?" *Alabama Review*, vol. 16, pp. 5–19 (January, 1963); Richard P. McCormick, "Suffrage Classes and Party Alignments: A Study in Voter Behavior," *Mississippi Valley Historical Review*, vol. 46, pp. 398–403 (December, 1959). Many detailed investigations into state or local political situations have exposed the weakness of economic interpretations of party alignment, but these have little affected general accounts.

[8] Identification of individual Whigs and Democrats and location of information on these men in the original manuscript United States census returns has been reported in the following unpublished M.A. theses at the University of Alabama: Kit C. Carter, "A Critical Analysis of the Basis of Party Alignment in Lowndes County, Alabama, 1836–1860," 1961; Frank M. Lowery, "A Critical Analysis of the Relation Between Selected Factors and Party Affiliation in Montgomery County, Alabama, 1840–1860," 1964; Jerry C. Oldshue, "The Secession Movement in Tuscaloosa County, Alabama," 1961; Mary Jane Pickens, "A Critical Analysis of the Basis of Party Alignment in Autauga County, Alabama, 1836–1860," 1963; Winfred G. Sandlin, "A Critical Analysis of the Traditional View of Whiggery in Alabama," 1960. Additional

data of this nature for Tuscaloosa County was compiled by Jack R. Lister for a project available from the files of Professor Thomas B. Alexander, Department of History, University of Alabama.

[9] Furthermore, a comparable study for Mississippi, involving more than one-third of the voters in several counties, has yielded results strictly comparable to those here offered for Alabama. See David N. Young, "The Whig Party in Mississippi" (forthcoming Ph.D. dissertation, University of Alabama, 1967).

[10] It is elementary that percentages should be based on what is offered as the independent variable, assuming that the research design and the data available can be ideal. It would, therefore, be proper to show in these tables what percentage of wealthy, or of large slave-holders, or of men sixty-one and over were Whigs and what percentage were Democrats, if the available data had made possible a research design in which wealthy men or old men were identified and then their party affiliation determined. In point of fact, however, this design was not feasible because no sources for party affiliation exist which could be consulted for men selected to comprise all of those sixty-one or older, or men selected to comprise all or a suitable sample of the men of a county falling into any of the economic or other categories employed. It was necessary to obtain names of Democrats and of Whigs, never in the same numbers nor even in numbers proportional to party voting divisions within the counties studied. It was, therefore, decided to present the tables in the form shown as the most meaningful structure under the less-than-ideal circumstances. An alternate possibility was to weight the figures for the party group which was smaller than its total proportion of the vote justified and then run the percentages according to the independent-variable categories such as wealth. When several such weighted comparisons showed approximately the same pattern as the one herein used, it was decided to offer the unweighted data, and in the form shown, as the most nearly valid analysis of the thrust of this material.

[11] Real estate values employed for this tabulation came from both the 1850 and the 1860 censuses. Although census takers of 1860 were instructed to use strikingly different bases of estimating value from those employed for the 1850 census, it was found that the patterns were so nearly identical in tabulations for the two census years separately that the total image could be offered in one table.

[12] Alexander, et al., "Who Were the Alabama Whigs?"

[13] Lowrey, "A Critical Analysis of the Relation between Selected Factors and Party Affiliation in Montgomery County, Alabama, 1840–1860."

[14] Peggy J. Duckworth, "The Role of Alabama Black Belt Whigs in the Election of Delegates to the Secession Convention" (unpublished M.A. thesis, University of Alabama, 1961), pp. 115–118.

[15] Information for each Alabama county was taken from *Seventh Census of the United States: 1850* (Washington, 1853), and *Eighth Census of the United States: 1860* (Washington, 1864–1865). Election returns are from Burnham, *Presidential Ballots*. Multiple and partial correlation calculations were performed by electronic computer using a program from W. J. Dixon, ed., *Biomedical Computer Programs* (Health Science Computing Facility, Department of Preventive Medicine and Public Health, School of Medicine, University of California, Los Angeles, 1965), Program BMDO3R, pp. 258–275. The University of Alabama Computer Center staff provided perceptive, encouraging, and indispensable assistance for several phases of this study. Appreciation is especially due Mrs. Betty J. Whitten, who adapted the data herein employed to the computer programs used for correlation work and for least squares estimate procedure.

[16] The procedure used to reduce the information from the censuses to ratio data (percentage form for this study) was to identify the county with the maximum production or value and consider it as 100 percent, expressing the information for each of the other counties as a percentage of the maximum figure. Percentage of slaveholders in the male adult free population was estimated by dividing the total free white population by four to obtain an estimate of the number of such men, and then calculating the percentage of this number represented by the number of slaveholders as recorded in the census. Since some women and some minors were slaveowners, this procedure is not precise; but precise data was not available and this method should not vary enough from the actual situations to affect the correlation results.

[17] All beat returns employed are tabulated by actual vote in Duckworth, "The Role of Alabama Black Belt Whigs in the Election of Delegates to the Secession Convention." Correlation calculations and regression line identifications were accomplished by computer, employing a program originally designed by David McGonagle and Don Siegal, Linear Correlation, Stepwise Multiple Regression Program, for the University of Pennsylvania (available through the I.B.M. Share Program Library as CRRG, SDA 3205). Modifications and adaptations have been provided by the staff of the University of Alabama Computer Center, including identification of intercept and slope of the regression line, which is the line used for least squares estimates.

The Power of Political Frenzy

Michael F. Holt

8

The political realignment that shook the United States in the mid-1850s began in the off-year elections of 1853 and 1854 in a number of northern states. In his analysis of that period in Pittsburgh, Pennsylvania, Michael F. Holt argues that neither slavery nor sectional economic differences were primarily responsible for the new political alignments. Rather, traumatic cultural tensions continued to determine much popular voting behavior. Confronted with extraordinary social changes prompted by the great wave of Catholic immigration, a significant number of Democrats forsook their traditional loyalties to join with the bulk of the Whigs in a new party directed against both "the hated Catholics and [the] impudent South." In the following selection abstracted from his book, *Forging a Majority: The Formation of the Republican Party in Pittsburgh, 1848–1860* (New Haven, 1969), Holt describes the early stages of this dramatic process of political change.

The standard interpretations of the rise of the Republican party do not suffice for Pittsburgh. . . .

Most people disliked slavery and the South, and the anti-southern free-soil appeal of the Whigs and Republicans undoubtedly won them votes. But politics did not revolve exclusively around those issues just as politics today does not revolve around communism, although most people dislike it. Instead, social, ethnic, and religious considerations often determined who voted for whom between 1848 and 1861. Divisions between native-born Americans and immigrants and between Protestants and Catholics, rather than differences of opinion about the tariff or the morality of slavery, distinguished Whigs and Republicans from Democrats. Until 1853 the Whig party ordinarily triumphed in local, state, and national elections. The city's business and social elite who shared many economic and private interests also shared the leadership of its majority party. The bulk of Whig voting strength, however, came from middle- and working-class

SOURCE: Reprinted with permission of Yale University Press from *Forging A Majority: The Formation of the Republican Party in Pittsburgh, 1848–1860*, pp. 5, 7–8, 135–136, 138–142, 144–154, 167–174, 312–313, 339–343. Copyright © 1969 by Yale University.

native-born Americans. The minority Democratic party, hampered by the unpopular platforms of the national party, drew its support primarily from poorer Catholic and immigrant groups. A combination of hostility to the slave power and antagonism toward immigrants apparently accounted for the Whig success, but after the passage of the Kansas-Nebraska Act in 1854 these sentiments divided the components of the coalition into competing groups. Debates about the violation of the Sabbath by Catholics, temperance laws, the allocation of public school taxes to support parochial schools, and the role of Catholics in politics sharply rent the community and even cut across ethnic lines so that Protestant Irishmen and Germans repudiated their Catholic countrymen and voted differently from them. Anti-Catholic sentiment fostered the nativist Know-Nothing party which initially overshadowed the fledgling antislavery Republican party as the opponent of the Democracy. Only in 1856 when the Republican party wooed Know-Nothing support did it combine the foes of the Democrats into a winning alliance. By carefully maintaining that partnership in 1860 the Republicans continued the Whig hegemony in the city. Apparently most Republicans in Pittsburgh voted not for Negro equality but against the hated Catholics and the impudent South, both of which the Democracy represented.

Interpreting the rise of the Republican party in the North solely in terms of hostility to slavery or economic issues is, therefore, too simplified. While Republicans inherited the free-soil position of the Whigs, they also inherited the ethnic antagonisms from which Whigs had benefited. Moreover, the smoldering anti-Catholic bias, which was fanned by events in the 1850s, brought additional voters into the Republican ranks and became a vital element of the party. Because national and state platforms focused on national events does not mean that these issues attracted the support the parties won. In Pittsburgh and probably in many other areas, local conditions and the mutual dislike by the members of one party for those of the other fixed traditional voting patterns that contributed as much to Republican strength as did national questions.

In the first few months of 1854 the Whigs expressed as much anti-Catholic sentiment as they did antislavery feeling. The resolutions of the Whig county convention in early February which only included a line against the Nebraska Bill also declared:

> That we are in favor of a *liberal system of education,* and to effect the promotion of civil and religious liberty, we pledge ourselves to support, with unfeigned effort, the *Common School System,* as the great bulwark of our Institutions.

In other words, they would brook no division of the public school fund. The Whig state platform declared that universal education and religious liberty should be goals of all state legislation, and the address of the Whig state central committee charged that Governor Bigler favored a division of the school fund.[1]

In the first part of 1854, the Whig press also blatantly identified the Whig party with Protestantism and the Democrats with Catholicism. White boasted, "The Whig party always was and is, the standard bearer of Protestantism and Free Soilism, whilst the Democratic party represents the opposite principles." Later he insisted "that the great mass of Catholic voters in this county are members of the Democratic party" and "that the papers and leaders of that party have always been ready to yield to the wishes and demands of Popery as far as they could venture without driving away their Protestant supporters." Earlier White had denounced Franklin Pierce's appointment of James Campbell as Postmaster General as a blatant appeal to Catholic support and warned that he would live to regret the favoritism of that denomination. During the campaign he commented that major reasons for opposition to Bigler were his connection with Campbell, whom he had appointed State Attorney General, and the widespread disgust with the political power of Catholics. Combining the issues, White insisted that the gubernatorial canvass would turn on the Nebraska Bill and opposition to popery.[2]

After the passage of the Nebraska Act in May, however, the Whigs ceased to agitate the anti-Catholic issue and concentrated solely on slavery expansion in order to form an anti-Nebraska coalition. As early as March the *Gazette* called for a fusion of all northern opponents of slavery extension into a sectional party. . . .

But when the Whigs dropped their anti-Catholic appeal, another movement emerged which stressed it. It is not exactly certain when the Know-Nothing order, a secret organization dedicated to the proscription of foreigners and Catholics from public office, was first formed in Pittsburgh, but newspapers first referred to its existence around the beginning of July. Although the order had political goals, it was organized initially in fraternal lodges whose membership was drawn from all the old political parties. Gradually, however, the order evolved into a political organization as its members were sworn by oath to support the candidates selected by the lodges. It must be emphasized at this point that the new Know-Nothing order was a separate and distinct entity from the Native American party which had existed since the late 1840s, had far fewer supporters than the Know-Nothings, and was open in its organization.[3] Throughout the 1850s this Native American party maintained its open existence and held open conventions, while the larger Know-Nothing order chose its candidates secretly. For a variety of reasons this new political order rivaled the Whig party for the anti-Democratic vote.

For one thing, many native-born citizens who had voted Whig were genuinely outraged at Catholics and immigrants. Not only Catholic aggressions but certain evils attributed to immigrants aroused native-born Protestants in these years. Immigrants filled the poorhouse, huckstered illegally in the city's marketplace, drank on Sundays, and increased the crime rate, cried editors in Pittsburgh.[4] To escape the seemingly pernicious impact of aliens, the wealthy native-born citizens who could afford to moved away from their old strongholds, the first, second, and fourth wards, and were replaced by Germans. Newspapers commented that because of the much improved means of transportation offered by the plank roads and passenger railroads the men of means moved to country homes to escape the crowded city.[5]

Because the actual increase in the numbers of immigrants in Pittsburgh between 1850 and 1860 was so small, the virulent nativism which appeared in 1853 and 1854 probably resulted from anger at the increasing political participation by the foreign-born and Catholics. Forbidden to vote until the five-year naturalization period expired, many Germans and Irishmen who had come over in the late 1840s were beginning to vote in the early and mid-1850s. J. Heron Foster, an admitted Know-Nothing, later declared that resentment of the political power of foreigners and Catholics, and especially of the courting of the foreign-born vote by both old parties, had been a primary motive for starting the movement. Because the Know-Nothings were dedicated to the proscription of Catholics and immigrants from political office and demanded a total repeal of naturalization laws or the extension of the period to twenty-one years, they seemed a more likely vehicle than the Whigs to redress the grievances of native-born Americans.[6]

Another reason why men joined the Know-Nothings was to clean up politics. Not only bloc voting by immigrants but the corruption of the ward primary meetings and of the county nominating conventions by party bosses angered many citizens. Foster wrote in 1855:

> One great reason the American orders swelled so rapidly in numbers was the profound disgust every right-thinking man entertained for the corrupt manner in which the machinery of the party had been perverted to suit the base purpose of party wireworkers — an evil they honestly believed the orders would remedy.

A correspondent wrote Simon Cameron that the Democrat J. K. Moorhead defected to the Know-Nothings because of disgust "with the trickery and rascality of the old parties." In brief, many complained that ward primary meetings were infiltrated by outsiders and that county conventions were dominated by professional politicians who often chose candidates distasteful to the party's voters.[7]

Through secrecy and a direct primary system the Know-Nothings hoped to correct these faults. They kept a tight discipline on party membership through oaths and then had direct primaries in the wards in which every member of the order handed in a ballot with his choices for all the nominations on the county ticket. An executive committee then named as the ticket the men who had received the most votes for the respective offices.[8]

In 1854 the movement was new, and it secretly selected its slate of candidates from the tickets of the three existing parties — Whig, Democratic, and Native American. Secrecy was so tight that the *Gazette*, which knew of the arrangement, was far wide of the mark in its predictions of the number of Democrats and Native Americans the Know-Nothings would support. In 1855 the party held secret primaries before the mayoral and county elections, but announced the tickets publicly before the elections.[9]

The very newness of the Know-Nothings combined with their expression of nativist hostilities and desire for political reform to make the party an attractive alternative for Whigs and Democrats. Many Whigs who opposed slavery may have preferred the American party to their altered organization because the Whigs were clearly dead as a national party while the Know-Nothings appeared on the rise. This growing strength became especially apparent after the Know-Nothing victories in 1854 in Massachusetts, Pennsylvania, and New York. Moreover, to many Whigs, Know-Nothingism probably seemed a better way to rally antislavery sentiment against the Democrats than the Whig anti-Nebraska coalition. By joining the Know-Nothings, native-born citizens could express simultaneously their nativist antipathies, their desire for political reform, and their free-soil hostility to the South. The new Whig party was less attractive because it campaigned after June on the slavery issue alone. To Democrats who wanted to leave their party for any reason, the Know-Nothings as a new and amorphous party were more appealing than an anti-Nebraska coalition controlled by their old foes — the Whigs. . . .[10]

By the time of the election, then, several issues, not just the Nebraska Act, commanded attention. White appealed to the opponents of slavery to vote solidly for the coalition of Whigs and Free-Soilers, and proclaimed, "The great conflict *is hastening to its final and desperate issue*. Freedom and Slavery cannot exist much longer together. These differences are irreconcilable and vital." On the day of the election, however, he angrily complained that the Know-Nothings had prevented a clear-cut vote on the Nebraska Act.[11] Trying to avoid the slavery-expansion issue, the Democrats posed as the defenders of Catholics, foreigners, and open political action. Finally, the murky Know-Nothing organization ignored the slavery issue and recommended political action and proscription to stem the tide of immigration and remedy evils attributed to the immigrant and Catholic populations.

Nor did the results of the election in October reveal an overwhelming anti-Nebraska outrage which swept the Democrats out of office. True, both James Pollock and David Ritchie, the Whig gubernatorial and congressional candidates, won crushing victories, but the Know-Nothings backed both men. On the other hand, of the ten remaining men on the Whig state and county tickets, only two assemblymen won office, and these, as the *Gazette* later admitted, also were supported by Know-Nothings. The election for members of the state assembly should particularly have revealed the impact of anti-Nebraska sentiment, for the legislature was to choose a new United States Senator, who could presumably take a strong stand for the repeal of the Nebraska Act. For the five openings in the assembly from Allegheny County, each of the three parties had nominated five men. Two Native Americans, one Democrat, and only two Whigs were elected, and all five had Know-Nothing support. William E. Stevenson, the Free-Soiler placed on the Whig ticket explicitly to fuse and rally anti-slavery sentiment, had the smallest vote of all five Whig assembly candidates. Thus of a total of twelve men elected in 1854, four were Whigs, three were Democrats, and five were Native Americans. Since all had Know-Nothing backing, the election was hardly a triumph for the anti-Nebraska party.[12]

Because Stevenson lost so decisively and because the Democrats won almost as many offices as the Whigs, the *Post* asserted that the Kansas-Nebraska Act had nothing to do with the result. It was clearly a Know-Nothing victory. A lieutenant of Bigler's blamed his chief's defeat on "excited religious prejudice." "It is idle to talk of *causes* for the result," he wrote. "There was but one, and that was the momentary supremacy of bigotry and prejudice. It was the power of political frenzy."[13] These assertions, however, are exaggerated. At least one editor argued that the Know-Nothings received votes from many unsuspecting Whigs and Democrats who had been handed ballots at the polls by their old party friends, secret members of the order, and who had voted for what they thought it was the regular party ticket.[14] Moreover, although the Know-Nothings backed two Democrats who had supported the Nebraska Bill, many Whigs in the order probably did so only because they were under oath. More than likely many of these Whigs opposed the Nebraska Act as well as the political power of Catholics.

In the vote for governor, the Whigs and Know-Nothings almost reestablished the coalition which carried Pittsburgh for William F. Johnston in 1851.[15] Native Americans, both rich and poor, employer and employee, tended to vote for Pollock. Pollock's support from the wealthy business leaders and shopkeepers, however, was somewhat less solid than that given Whigs in previous elections, and perhaps the desertion of old Whig principles and the adoption of the free-soil platform frightened away some of the conservative businessmen who once voted Whig. Indeed these men may have voted for the Democrats, who had wooed their votes.

Pollock's vote as a whole did not tend to come from the poor Irish and German workers, but the Democrats for once failed to win any united support from those groups.[16] What probably happened was that the immigrant vote divided along religious lines as Protestants voted against the Catholic countrymen they hated. Pollock had Know-Nothing support, and almost every newspaper analyst both before and after the election agreed that the Protestant immigrants, organized in the secret Protestant Association or another group known as the Muscovies, voted with the Know-Nothings against the Democrats. Members of these groups had taken oaths to oppose any political party which gave Catholics nominations. These organizations of foreign Protestants cooperated with the Know-Nothings only so long as there was hope they would drop their nativism and convert the order solely into an anti-Catholic body. When it became evident that they opposed foreigners too, the Irish and German Protestants swung back to the Democratic, or anti-Know-Nothing, party in the mayoral election of 1855.[17]

While the Whigs benefited from anti-Catholic animosities and American support in the gubernatorial election of 1854, the Know-Nothing movement, not free-soil sentiment, actually destroyed the Whig majority coalition. In the election for state supreme court judge in which the Whigs, Democrats, and Know-Nothings all ran a separate candidate, the parties split and the traditional alignment of votes disappeared. None of the three parties won the bloc support of any ethnic, economic, or occupational group. One may reasonably assume that the vote split along religious lines with native-born citizens and Protestants tending to divide between the Whigs and the Know-Nothings. Indeed, the combined vote of the Whig and Know-Nothing candidates almost duplicated that of Pollock. Most newspapers pointed to the election for judge as a model to show the respective strength of the three parties, and one can estimate roughly how many voters the old parties contributed to the Know-Nothings if he compares these returns with those for state supreme court judge in 1852. Between the two elections, the Democrats lost about 350 votes while the Whigs lost around 800. If one assumes these voters joined the secret order and then adds the 200 votes which the Native American party normally drew, he has a total of 1350 which closely approximates the Know-Nothing vote in 1854. In short, of the original Know-Nothing vote, about 25 percent came from the Democrats and about 60 percent came from the Whigs. Unfortunately this estimate is very crude because one cannot tell how many Whigs abstained and how many new voters from the working classes the Know-Nothings drew out. Nor can one tell how many of the Democratic converts were foreign-born Protestants who voted with but did not belong to the order.[18]

Examination of the election for clerk of courts, another three-way race, reveals equally significant voting trends. In this election, the native-born Americans again split their vote between the Know-Nothings and the Whigs. The wealthy among them and the professional groups, however, supported the Whigs. The Whigs did not tend to draw votes from the poor, and the Democrats apparently won the support of the Germans, the propertyless, and the unskilled laborers. It is evident, however, that since most of the poor were German and Irish, the Native American workers probably voted Know-Nothing; many native-born citizens, except the wealthy, tended to vote that way. Moreover, many skilled artisans who resented economic competition from immigrants also seem to have voted for the Know-Nothings, although that group did not tend to vote as a bloc for them.[19]

Various factors contributed to the decision of old Whig voters to support the new party or remain loyal to the transformed Whig organization. Allan Nevins has suggested that many of the conservative Whigs went into the American party because it was the only alternative to the more radical anti-Nebraska coalitions which became the Republican party, and because they were disgusted with the apparent results of immigration. In Pittsburgh, however, what distinguished those Whigs who refused to join the Know-Nothings from those who did join was that, as most newspapers pointed out, many of the former were old Antimasons, while the latter were not. Until 1853 the Whig county convention always assembled under the name "Antimasonic and Whig," and Antimasons were a powerful element in the party. Traditionally antislavery men, they voted for the stiff free-soil, anti-southern platform of the Whigs in 1854. They could not join the Know-Nothings because they "abhor[red] secret, oath-bound political societies."[20]

On the other hand, there was also some economic basis to the split between the Whigs and Know-Nothings. Some of the wealthy native-born citizens, who could afford to, moved out of the city in the face of the immigrant invasion. Those who did not, but whose wealth protected them from direct social and job competition with Catholic foreigners, voted for their old party, the Whigs. In contrast, the poorer and middle-class native-born citizens, more exposed to competition from newcomers and possibly more susceptible to the sensational anti-Catholic propaganda which had pervaded the country for years, went into the Know-Nothing movement immediately. Alexander K. McClure, a Whig, asserted that the Baptists and Methodists, many of whom were poor, joined the Know-Nothings more readily than other Protestant sects because they were more aggressively anti-Catholic. Too poor to move away from the immigrants, these native-born Protestants found a political channel for their hostility to foreigners. Along with them voted the Protestant Irish and Germans. In this first appearance then, the Know-Nothing vote seems essentially to have been an anti-Catholic rather than a nativist one.[21]

Desire to stamp out the Know-Nothing flare-up caused both Whigs and Democrats to abandon their separate organizations in the mayoral election of 1855. Warning that the Whigs should hold no more formal conventions because the Know-Nothings controlled their primaries, White urged them to fuse with all the other opponents of the secret order to rid the party and the city of the menace. The Democratic city executive committee announced that the Democrats would not nominate a separate candidate and told the Democrats to support an independent. Both Democrats and Whigs signed a long petition and persuaded incumbent Whig Mayor Volz to run as an Independent Fusion candidate against B. T. C. Morgan, who all knew was the Know-Nothing candidate. White emphasized that there was only one issue in the municipal election — whether the secret society would gain control of the city government.[22]

Both parties waged a bitter campaign. White warned that the Know-Nothings would try to stir up the anti-Catholic prejudices of the German and Irish Protestants, but he confidently predicted that "the foreign Protestants of this city know that Mr. Morgan has sworn to proscribe *all* foreigners whether Protestant or Catholic, and simply *because* they are foreigners." He cautioned that Know-Nothings intended to vote early and then challenge all voters, particularly foreigners. Also they would try to insult immigrants and provoke fights to keep them from the polls. The other Whig paper, the *Daily Commercial Journal*, whose editor had joined the Know-Nothings, came out for Morgan. Foster campaigned openly for him and appealed to the temperance sentiments of native Protestants by criticizing Volz for his lack of vigor in enforcing liquor laws and preventing huckstering. He complained that the Fusion tickets were "selected by a few wireworking politicians" while the ostensibly secret Know-Nothing tickets were nominated by the mass of American Protestants in the respective wards.[23]

Though the Fusion party elected the mayor and the bulk of the city councilmen, the Know-Nothing vote showed an increase of almost 55 percent since the previous October as more native-born Whigs joined the party. Dedicated free-soil men, these new converts could not stomach an alliance with pro-Nebraska Democrats. Other Whigs, many of whom were former Antimasons, joined the fifteen hundred Democrats in supporting the Fusion ticket. Foster moaned that the Democrats, Roman Catholics, foreign Protestants who had once supported Pollock in order to proscribe Catholics, and former Antimasons who wanted "to oppose the secresy [sic] of Know Nothingism" backed Volz.[24] Most native-born Americans tended to move into the Know-Nothing camp while most immigrants — Protestants and Catholics — combined to oppose the order.[25]

Estimating the makeup of the parties is difficult. It would seem that about nine hundred of the Whig and Antimasonic remnant joined the Fusion coalition while five hundred now went into the Know-Nothing party. But foreign Protestants who had backed Know-Nothing, not Whig, candidates in October 1854 also switched, so that it is probably more correct to estimate that about six hundred Antimasonic Whigs and three hundred foreign Protestants went into the Fusion party while about eight hundred more Whigs joined the Know-Nothings. Although the *Post* later asserted that the Democrats lost many more voters to the Know-Nothings than they gained from the Whigs, the vast bulk of Know-Nothing voters by 1855 were probably former Whigs, since most native-born Protestants had voted for that party. A former Democrat in the order complained to Simon Cameron, who joined the Know-Nothings in 1854,

> It requires the most indomitable energy to overcome the deeprooted Whig *prejudices* that still exist in this county *notwithstanding* the change which has occurred through the influence of the new organization. There are nearly 8000 order men in this *county*, but the bloated visage of Whiggery still peers from under the cloak of Americanism. . . .[26]

The Democrats tried desperately to hold together the anti-Know-Nothing coalition of January, [1855] and, as they had done in 1854, they concentrated on winning the votes of those groups most alienated by the order. After the formal attempt to prolong the Fusion party failed, the Democratic county executive committee adopted a resolution pledging that its members were not and never had been members of secret political societies, although some on that committee complained that it would proscribe foreigners who had been Muscovies or had belonged to the Protestant Association. The Democratic state platform denounced the Know-Nothing party by name and insisted that citizens should not be discriminated against because of place of birth or religion. Obviously these planks were aimed at immigrants and Catholics. Less clearly, but equally important, by establishing their anti-Know-Nothing pedigree, the Democrats, like the Republicans, courted the Antimasonic Whigs. Because of the secrecy and ineffectiveness of the Know-Nothings in the legislature, boasted the *Post*, staunch old-line Whigs as well as Democrats, old and young, were out campaigning to rid the city of the Know-Nothing plague.[27]

The election results bore out the editor's confidence. The Democrats carried their entire ticket over the Know-Nothings, and the hapless Republicans, despite White's calls to Armageddon to do battle against the advance of slavery in Kansas, received only a small fraction of the vote. If one assumes that the separate Native American vote came from men who voted Know-Nothing in January, then about 330 Know-Nothings joined the Republicans, and about 330 antislavery Whigs left the Fusion ranks for the new party.[28] Many who voted Republican were evidently Antimasonic Whigs who could not accept coalition with either Democrats or Know-Nothings. In any case, the failure of the Republicans to draw enough votes away from the Know-Nothings brought their defeat.

Explanations for the Know-Nothing loss varied, but all agreed that the result revealed a disgust with the Americans rather than any particular preference for Democratic principles. Both the *Gazette* and the *Post* maintained that many Whigs joined the Democrats to overthrow the Know-Nothings.[29] If one assumes that three hundred former Whigs left the Fusion party between January and October, about six hundred former Whigs and foreign-born Protestants remained with the Democrats. An anti-Know-Nothing coalition had been continued in fact, if not in name. Contrary to predictions, the antislavery sentiment could not keep Whigs and Democrats from acting together when a local issue, the presence of the Know-Nothings, seemed more vital and relevant to them than the crisis in Kansas.

Indeed, the voting followed the same patterns as in January when there had been an open effort to demolish the order.[30] Native-born Protestants again tended to vote for the Know-Nothings while Germans and Irishmen, indeed, most immigrants, apparently voted against them.[31] Even though the Know-Nothings adopted Whig economic positions, they failed to win the unified support of the wealthy businessmen who formerly voted for the Whigs.[32] On the other hand, the other native Americans in the community who lacked the wealth to give them social status superior to the immigrant Catholics continued to vote Know-Nothing.[33] The *Post* pointed out that while many Know-Nothings were more antislavery than nativist, many others, while opposing slavery extension, had "joined the new party for other purposes" and would not join an "abolitionist Republican party" which did not aim at those purposes — i.e., proscription of Catholics and immigrants.[34] In short, the Americans continued to win a nativist, anti-Catholic vote which the single-purpose Republican party could not capture.

Thus the voting in 1855 turned on one's opinion of the Know-Nothings. Commenting on the election a year later, a Democrat testified that German and Irish

Protestants voted with their Catholic countrymen against the nativist order. Right after the election, another Democrat wrote Bigler that "the result here is mainly owing to the strong foreign vote, to the Catholic vote, to the liquor movement, and to the fact that a Republican ticket was in the field. It needed all these elements to break down the power of the opposition in this country."[35] Devoted to opposing slavery alone and hostile to the secrecy of the Know-Nothings, the Republican party was swamped in an election for canal commissioner and local offices where slavery was an irrelevant issue. To note this fact is not to say that many in the ranks of all parties were not opposed to the extension of slavery, but to argue that because other issues were important to people at this time in this election, a party based on that issue alone could not succeed. Once again, local issues and differences prevented the reestablishment of the old nativist and anti-southern Whig majority of 1848 and 1852.

The Americans, however, were not destroyed, and they captured the mayor's office in the election of 1856. The anti-Know-Nothing coalition split when many Democrats refused to support Volz again and supported a separate Democrat. The anti-Know-Nothings, though, had majorities in both councils.[36] Significantly, the Republican party, aborted after the defeat of 1855, did not even enter a candidate. Russell Errett, the other editor of the *Gazette*, dismally reported to Salmon P. Chase after that defeat about Republican chances: "The short and long of the matter is that, as things are now, I have no hope of Pennsylvania. I cannot see how all parties can cooperate here without a sacrifice of principle or loss of votes sufficient to insure defeat."[37] At the beginning of 1856 the Pennsylvania Republicans had not found a formula for successful organization. The Know-Nothings had undermined the initial attempts to form an anti-Nebraska Republican party just as they had ruined the last efforts to rally the Whig party on that issue in 1854.

Before 1853 the Whigs in Pittsburgh had flourished on a combination of nativism and an antislavery, anti-southern sentiment which was strengthened by the Antimasonic tradition. When the local Whig party began to collapse at the time of the passage of the Kansas-Nebraska Act, new parties appeared which drove apart the elements that had joined in the Whig party. At first it appeared that the Whigs would be rejuvenated as an anti-Nebraska party. Then the secret Know-Nothing order arose in response to a very real hostility to Catholics and immigrants. To many Whigs who were convinced their old party was dead, this nativist order seemed the best way to oppose the Democracy and to achieve political reform. It also attracted those native-born and, at first, foreign-born Protestants whose hatred of Catholics determined how they voted. For many former Antimasons among the Whigs, however, the methods of the Know-Nothings were obnoxious. At first, they remained in the transformed Whig party; then they joined a Fusion party with the Democrats solely in order to defeat the Americans. In the fall of 1855 they followed divided counsels. Many sincere antislavery men joined the new Republican party which tried to preserve Antimasonic principles by condemning secret political action. Others, however, remained with the Democrats in an anti-Know-Nothing coalition, for to them the menace of secret proscriptive orders seemed more real than the threat of slavery expansion in Kansas. If any one factor destroyed the Whig party in Pittsburgh, it was not the Kansas-Nebraska Act, which actually strengthened Whigs there. It was the strength and form of organized anti-Catholic sentiment.

While the Whig party was shattering, a combination of grievances coincided with the Kansas-Nebraska Act to destroy party loyalty among Democrats. Party regulars disliked Bigler's patronage policies or the influence of Catholics within the party. Moreover, out politicians had reached the limit of their patience with the control of the in Buchanan-Bigler faction. Just at the moment when public wrath boiled over at the Nebraska Act, these disgruntled elements bolted from the party. Particularly important in their decision to switch allegiance was the availability of the American party, into which most of them went. It provided a much greater opportunity for advancement than did the anti-Nebraska coalition, led by old Whig chiefs.

By the beginning of 1856 political alignments remained confused. The Democrats had gained strength from Whigs and foreign Protestants who detested Know-Nothings. The Know-Nothings had won a large part of the Whig coalition, but their methods alienated a vital portion of it, and they could not muster a majority. The incipient Republican party had failed to rally all the anti-Nebraska voters, for it defied rather than wooed Know-Nothings and did not attract the poorer and middle-class Protestant native-born Americans who wanted to express their hostility to immigrant Catholics emphatically when they voted. As a Pittsburgh Know-Nothing wrote to Simon Cameron, the way to succeed in Pennsylvania was to drop secrecy and "step on two planks of a new platform and carry the state with a rush — viz. Americanism and antislavery."[38] In January 1856 no party had yet followed this advice. . . .

The appeals and voting behavior in Pittsburgh create doubts about how much the moral issue of slavery shaped political patterns in the North in the 1850s. First, it is unclear that sectional and partisan differences grew out of a fundamental cleavage over the morality of slavery. Not the oppression of the slave, but slavery extension which threatened to bring the hated Negro into the territories and which apparently involved southern aggression on northern rights seems to have been the major popular grievance against the South in the North. Second, it is not certain that even sectional issues, let alone moral indignation, motivated northern voters. Some local factors in Pittsburgh like the railroad tax crisis may have been unique, but in almost every city of the North local conditions may also have importantly shaped the nature of the Republican and Democratic parties. Anti-Catholic and nativist elements were probably fundamental blocs of Republican coalitions in other areas where the Know-Nothings had flourished.[39] One can accept Richard P. McCormick's conclusion that the second American party system "could survive only by avoiding regionally divisive issues"[40] and agree that sectional animosity intensified by the issue of slavery extension destroyed the old national party system and brought about the replacement of the Whig party in the North by the Republican party without agreeing that sectional antagonism alone explains either the defection of northern Whigs from their party or the voting support of the new party. Why the Republican party emerged and why people voted for it are two different questions which do not necessarily have the same answer. Southerners were correct to interpret the vote for Lincoln as an assault on their section, but it represented as well the continuation of voting patterns which had formed in the 1850s because of traditional party loyalties and bitter religious hatreds.

Table 8.1 Party Vote and Party Percentage of Vote in Pittsburgh, 1854-1856*

Election	Whig	Democratic	Know-Nothing	Republican	Others
1854 (Mayor)	2166	1132			465
	(57.5%)	(30%)			(12.5%)
1854 (Governor)	2786	1505			155
	(62.6%)	(33.6%)			(3.8%)
1854 (Congress)	2795	1529			
	(64.6%)	(35.4%)			
1854 (Supreme Court Judge)	1457	1583	1281		
	(33.7%)	(36.6%)	(29.7%)†		
1854 (Clerk of Courts)	1412	1241	1392		
	(34.9%)	(30.7%)	(34.4%)†		
1854(County Register)‡	1787	1668			403
	(46.3%)	(43.2%)			(10.5%)
	Fusion				
1855 (Mayor)	2406		1944		
	(55.3%)		(44.7%)		
1855 (Canal Commissioner)		2111	1503	653	108
		(48.2%)	(34.3%)	(14.9%)	(2.6%)
	Volz	*Irwin*			
1856 (Mayor)	1030	1115	1499		234
	(26.5%)	(28.7%)	(38.6%)		(6.2%)

*These election returns may be found in the *Gazette*, Oct. 16, 1854, Jan. 13, Oct. 17, 1855; and Jan. 9, 1856; the *Post*, Jan. 11, 1854.

†In these elections the Native American candidates received the Know-Nothing vote.

‡In this election the Democratic candidate who had the Know-Nothing vote won a majority in the county as a whole although he failed to carry Pittsburgh.

Table 8.2 Product-Moment Coefficients of Correlation Between the Whig Votes and Variables, 1854*

Variable	Mayor 1854	Governor 1854	Supreme Court Judge 1854	Clerk of Courts 1854
Ethnic				
Native American	+.23	+.71	−.07	+.45
Irish	.00	−.32	+.13	+.16
German	−.54	−.74	−.21	−.71
Property Holdings				
$10,000 plus	+.20	+.50	+.13	+.52
$5000-9999	+.43	+.48	−.10	+.42
None	−.31	−.45	−.10	−.83
Occupation				
Manufacturers, merchants, & bankers	+.13	+.50	+.03	+.40
Clerks and shopkeepers	+.25	+.52	−.18	+.33
Professional	+.36	+.54	.00	+.54
Skilled artisans	−.50	−.51	−.54	−.62
Unskilled laborers	−.12	−.48	+.30	−.27

*The socioeconomic indices used in this table were the same as those used in Chapter 2.

Table 8.3 Product-Moment Coefficients of Correlation Between the Democratic Votes and Variables, 1854-1855*

Variables	Mayor 1854	Governor 1854	Supreme Court Judge 1854	Clerk of Courts 1854	Fusion† Mayor 1854	Canal Commissioner 1855
Ethnic						
Total immigrant‡	+.26	+.57	+.34	+.67	+.67	+.49
Irish	+.41	+.42	+.34	+.13	+.65	+.43
German	+.04	+.41	+.15	+.61	+.22	+.22
Property Holdings						
$10,000 plus	−.08	−.32	−.16	−.36	−.40	−.31
None	−.12	+.29	.00	+.54	+.26	+.31
Occupation						
Skilled artisans	+.09	+.37	+.11	+.08	+.10	+.23
Unskilled laborers	+.11	+.29	+.10	+.54	+.52	+.27

*These figures are calculated from the socioeconomic indices based on the manuscript census of 1850.
†This column of figures represents the correlations between the variables and the Fusion vote for mayor in 1855.
‡These figures are exactly opposite what the correlation between the Democratic votes and the percentage of Native Americans would be since the group "Total immigrants" includes all white males over twenty-one who were not natives. Hence, the correlation between the Democratic vote for governor in 1854 and the Native Americans was −.57.

Table 8.4 Product-Moment Coefficients of Correlation Between the
Know-Nothing Votes and Variables, 1854-1855*

Variables	Supreme Court Judge 1854	Clerk of Courts 1854	Mayor 1855	Canal Commissioner 1855
Ethnic				
Native American	+.37	+.45	+.67	+.64
Irish	−.41	−.30	−.65	−.52
German	+.05	−.16	−.22	−.42
Property Holdings				
$10,000 plus	.00	−.02	+.40	+.37
$5000-9999	+.10	+.19	+.36	+.41
None	+.04	+.05	−.26	−.47
Occupation				
Manufacturers, merchants, & bankers	+.07	−.04	+.40	+.34
Professional	−.10	.00	+.21	+.26
Clerks and shopkeepers	+.18	+.30	+.43	+.38
Skilled artisans	+.37	+.45	−.10	−.45
Unskilled laborers	−.32	−.45	−.52	−.38

*These figures are calculated with the same tables and in the same way as those in Tables 8.2 and 8.3. For the mayoral election of 1855, they are exactly opposite in sign but equal in number to the correlations between these variables and the Fusion vote for mayor. Hence, the correlation between the professional groups and the Fusion vote was −.21.

Table 8.5 Changes in the Absolute Numbers and Proportions of Various
Ethnic Groups in Pittsburgh's Wards Between 1850 and 1860*

Ward	Natives	Germans	Irish	British
First	− 89 (−7.7%)	+31 (+2.3%)	+40 (+3.1%)	+3 (−1.3%)
Second	−152 (−1.6%)	−18 (+1.2%)	−24 (−2.9%)	−28 (−.4%)
Third	+39 (+1.8%)	+119 (+5.1%)	−22 (−1.6%)	−66 (−3%)
Fourth	−80 (−6.2%)	+43 (+3.7%)	−52 (−11.3%)	−37 (−3.1%)
Fifth	−29 (−.8%)	+314 (+15.5%)	−261 (−11.3%)	−90 (−3.7%)
Sixth	+108 (+6.1%)	+101 (+6.5%)	−150 (−10.7%)	−18 (−1.4%)
Seventh	+110 (+9.3%)	+85 (+8.6%)	−6 (−11.8%)	−23 (−6.6%)
Eighth	+66 (+8.4%)	+7 (+3.4%)	−126 (−7.8%)	−67 (−4%)
Ninth	+437 (+23.2%)	+43 (−12.1%)	+122 (+1%)	+30 (−1.9%)
Totals				
1850	4137 (35.8%)†	2229 (19.3%)	4089 (35.4%)	1102 (9.5%)
1860	4547 (38.1%)	2954 (24.8%)	3610 (30.3%)	805 (6.8%)

*This table is based on counts of the white males over twenty-one in the manuscript censuses of 1850 and 1860. The percentage difference listed for each group in each ward represents the change in the portion each group constituted of the total adult male population of each ward between 1850 and 1860 rather than the percentage change in each group represented by the increase or decrease in absolute numbers in that group. For example, in the first ward, the native Americans formed 53.2 percent of the population in 1850 and only 45.5 percent of the population in 1860. Hence, the decrease was −7.7 percent.

†The percentages listed in the total sections are not changes, but are the proportions which the ethnic groups constituted of the total adult white male populations of the city in 1850 and 1860.

[1] *Gazette*, Feb. 2, Mar. 20, 1854; *Post*, July 21, 1854.

[2] *Gazette*, Mar. 3, 1853, Mar. 20, Ap. 1, 10, Sept. 4, 1854.

[3] *Post*, July 3, 12, 1854. See reports of the American county conventions in the *Gazette*, May 3, July 19, 1855. See also the *Dispatch*, May 3, Sept. 18, 1855.

[4] *Dispatch*, Sept. 11, 1854; *Gazette*, June 3, 1853, Mar. 15, 1855; *Journal*, Jan. 5, 1855. For a summary of the resentment of the immigrants, see Billington, pp. 322–344.

[5] See Table 8.5 and note that the numbers of native-born men and Germans over twenty-one increased between 1850 and 1860 while the numbers of Irishmen and Englishmen dropped. Still, the increase in the percentage and numbers of Germans in each ward was small. Note also the decline in the numbers of native Americans in the four old wards and their replacement by Germans. For other evidence that wealthy native-born citizens moved out of the city into the country, see the *Dispatch*, Aug. 14, Sept. 16, 1856, Nov. 9, 1858; the *Post*, June 8, 1860; Edward McPherson to J. B. McPherson, Pittsburgh, Apr. 28, 1856, Edward McPherson MSS (LC); and Charles C. Arensberg,"Evergreen Hamlet," *Western Pennsylvania Historical Magazine*; vol. 38 (1955), pp. 117–133. Other reasons than the influx of immigrants also prompted men to move out of the city. Two of the main ones were probably high taxes and smoke.

[6] *Dispatch*, Sept. 5, 1855. For the Know-Nothing program, see the national American platform framed in 1855 and Foster's editorial comments in the *Gazette*, June 18, 1855; *Dispatch*, Jan. 4, 9, 1855.

[7] *Dispatch*, Sept. 15, 1855; see also the *Dispatch*, Sept. 5, 1855, and the *Gazette*, July 25, Sept. 26, 1855. John B. Guthrie to Simon Cameron, Pittsburgh, Dec. 10, 1854, Cameron MSS.

[8] *Gazette*, Aug. 5, 1854, Sept. 19, 26, 1855; *Dispatch*, Sept. 18, 20, 24, Oct. 17, 1855.

[9] *Gazette*, Oct. 2, 1854; *Dispatch*, Jan. 4, May 3, Sept. 18, 1855.

[10] In his reminiscences, Alexander K. McClure, an old Pennsylvania Whig and Republican leader, says that when the Kansas-Nebraska Act aroused antislavery sentiment among the Democrats, the Know-Nothings found a wide field for recruitment among them. McClure, *Old Time Notes of Pennsylvania* (2 vols. Philadelphia, 1905), vol. 1, p. 196.

[11] *Gazette*, Sept. 8, Oct. 10, 1854.

[12] *Post*, Oct. 4, 9, 12, 26, 1854; *Gazette*, Oct. 16, 1854, July 25, Sept. 26, 1855. See Table 8.1. It should be noted that in certain instances, for example the campaigns for the clerk of courts and county register, the Whig candidate had a plurality in the city of Pittsburgh but lost in the county as a whole, in the first case to a separate Know-Nothing candidate (i.e., Native American) and in the second case to a Democrat with Know-Nothing support. In general, the Know-Nothings were much stronger in the small boroughs and rural townships than they were in Pittsburgh and Allegheny City, probably because there were more Catholics in the cities and because the ties to the Whig party were stronger there. The Know-Nothings boasted that their main strength was in the rural areas of the county. See the *Gazette*, July 19, Sept. 26, 1855.

[13] *Post*, Oct. 16, 1854; Alfred B. McCalmont to William Bigler, Pittsburgh, Oct. 16, 1854, Bigler MSS.

[14] See the discussion of the 1854 Know-Nothing vote in the *Gazette*, July 25, Sept. 26, 1855.

[15] The correlation between the vote for Pollock in 1854 and the vote for Johnston in 1851 was $+ .82$.

[16] See Tables 8.2 and 8.3. See Appendix B for a discussion of possible difficulties in correlating 1854 and 1855 voting returns with socioeconomic indices based on the 1850 census.

[17] *Gazette*, Sept. 12, 1854, July 25, Sept. 26, 1855; *Post*, Sept. 21, Oct. 4, 1854; *Dispatch*, Jan. 4, 9, 1855.

[18] There were no significant correlations between the vote for any of the three candidates and any ethnic or economic group. See Tables 8.2, 8.3, and 8.4. Again, the possible unreliability of correlations with the indices based on the 1850 census must be noted.... Compare Tables 8.1 and 8.2 to see the 1852 and 1854 returns. See also John B. Guthrie to James Buchanan, Pittsburgh, Sept. 8, 1856, Buchanan MSS (HSP).

[19] See Tables 8.2, 8.3, and 8.4. Note the fairly high correlation between the Know-Nothing vote and the skilled artisans. It is possible that since the Germans seem to have voted as a bloc for the Democrat, some only deserted that party in the vote for governor because Bigler was specifically associated with favoritism of Catholics and held responsible for the dismissal of Ryser from the Western Penitentiary. On the other hand, the correlation figures may be suspect.

[20] Nevins, *Ordeal of the Union*, vol. 2, p. 330; *Gazette*, July 25, 1855. See especially the *Post*, Oct. 5, 1854. Lee Benson correctly emphasizes the lingering influence of Antimasonry in shaping voting in New York state in the 1840s in *The Concept of Jacksonian Democracy*, pp. 155–156, 312–313. Moreover, one should recall Butter's letter to Cameron in which he emphasized that opposition to abolitionism and Antimasonry were both political suicide in

Pittsburgh. The standard work on the Antimasonry party stresses its continuing influence in Pittsburgh, but the author's assertion that because Antimasons hated Catholics they became a primary source for Know-Nothings seems incorrect. McCarthy, *The Antimasonic Party*, pp. 470, 482, 502. McCarthy does point out, however, that United Presbyterians, who were a major part of the Antimasonic strength, were forbidden by their church to belong to secret organizations. These men, who hated Catholics, may have constituted the bulk of those Whigs who adamantly refused to join the Know-Nothings and later started the Republican party.

[21] McClure, *Old Time Notes*, vol. 1, p. 240; *Dispatch*, Jan. 4, 1855.

[22] *Gazette*, Dec. 12, 18, 22, 25, 28, 1854; *Post*, Dec. 21, 1854.

[23] *Dispatch*, Jan. 4, 6, 9, 1855; *Gazette*, Jan. 9, 1855; *Journal*, Jan. 5, 1855.

[24] *Post*, Aug. 4, 1855; *Gazette*, Sept. 26, 1855; *Dispatch*, Jan. 9, 1855.

[25] See Tables 8.1, 8.3 and 8.4. The apparent insignificant correlation between the Germans and the Fusion vote may have resulted from the fact that many Germans could not or did not vote, rather than the fact that they split their vote between the two parties. In other words, most of the Germans who voted supported the Fusion ticket, but not enough voted for the Germans to appear as a bloc vote. Contrary to Foster's commentary, the Catholic vote may not have been solidly Democratic, for the correlation between the percentage of Catholics in 1860 and the Fusion vote was only +.36. Since this index of Catholics was based on the 1860 census and other calculations, it may not have accurately described the proportional strength of Catholics in 1855 and therefore may not be valid for correlation with the 1855 vote. It is also possible that many of the Catholics listed in 1860 were unnaturalized immigrants in 1855. For the proportions of Protestants and Catholics in Pittsburgh's wards, I relied on Table 3 in Paul J. Kleppner, "Lincoln and the Immigrant Vote: A Case of Religious Polarization," *Mid-America*, vol. 48 (1966), pp. 176–195. Kleppner explains in detail how he ingeniously constructed this index reproduced in my Table 35.

[26] *Post*, Jan. 30, 1860; James A. Dean to Simon Cameron, Allegheny City, June 1, 1855, Cameron MSS; Erwin Stanley Bradley, *Simon Cameron*, p. 93.

[27] *Gazette*, July 9, Aug. 16, 1855; *Post*, Oct. 6, 1855.

[28] See Table 8.1 and the *Gazette*, Oct. 11, 1855. White, however, asserted that none of the Republican votes came from Know-Nothings. If so, the 330 votes probably came from Antimasonic Whigs who abstained in January.

[29] See *Post*, Oct. 10, 1855; *Gazette*, Oct. 11, 1855; Edward McPherson to J. B. McPherson, Pittsburgh, Oct. 12, 1855, McPherson MSS; John M. Kirkpatrick to Simon Cameron, Pittsburgh, Oct. 31, 1855, Cameron MSS; *Dispatch*, Oct. 17, 1855.

[30] The correlation between the Know-Nothing vote for canal commissioner in October and the Know-Nothing vote for mayor in January was +.87. The correlation between the Democratic vote for canal commissioner in October and the Fusion vote for mayor in January was +.92.

[31] See Tables 8.3 and 8.4. Because of the year 1855, I also correlated the election results with socioeconomic indices based on the manuscript census of 1860. See Appendix B for the method of constructing these indices. The correlation between the Know-Nothing vote for canal commissioner and the percentage of Native Americans in 1860 was +.82; between that vote and the percentage of Irish in 1860, it was −.40; and between that vote and the percentage of Germans in 1860, it was −.71. The correlation between that Know-Nothing vote and the percentage of Protestants in 1860, according to Kleppner's scale, was +.66. Conversely, the correlation between that vote and the Catholics was −.66. The Know-Nothings obviously drove immigrants into the Democratic ranks, and the correlations with the 1860 indices are probably more accurate than those in Table 8.3. The correlations between the Democratic vote for canal commissioner in 1855 and the proportions of total immigrants, Irish, and Germans in 1860 were +.84, +.44, and +.50 respectively.

[32] See Tables 8.3 and 8.4. The correlations of the Know-Nothing vote with the indices based on the 1860 census are: with those owning $10,000 or more worth of property, +.14; with those owning property valued between $5000 and $10,000, +.11; with merchants, manufacturers, and bankers, +.49; with professional men, +.09; with clerks and shopkeepers, +.30.

[33] See Tables 8.3 and 8.4. The vote of the poor probably split on an ethnic basis. The indices of property holdings from the 1860 census produced two groups of poorer men — those who owned property valued between $100 and $999 and those who owned property worth less than $100. The correlations with these two groups of poorer voters contrasted sharply. For example, the correlation between the Know-Nothing vote and the group owning less than $100 was +.70, indicating that the poorest people voted Know-Nothing, but the correlation between that vote and the group owning $100–$999 was −.66. Moreover, the latter group seems to have voted Democratic, for the correlation between it and the Democratic vote was +.51. These figures are of course imprecise, particularly when one remembers that the composition of the population may have been different in 1855 than in 1860, but it seems reasonable to conclude that the poorer a native American was, the more likely he was to vote Know-Nothing to express his resentment against the economic and social competition of

Catholic immigrants. On the other hand, it is difficult to believe that Irish and German Catholics among the poorest group voted for the Know-Nothings. This paradox is explained in part by the fact that the group owning $100–$999 tended to be immigrant while the poorest group tended to be native American. See Appendix B for a further discussion of the construction of these indices and of the ethnic makeup of the two poor groups.

[34] *Post*, Aug. 4, 1855.

[35] A. B. McCalmont to William Bigler, Pittsburgh, Oct. 10, 1855, Bigler MSS. See Tables 8.3 and 8.4. The correlations between the Democratic vote and the percentages of immigrants, Irish, Germans, and Catholics in 1860 were +.84, +.44, +.50, and +.46, respectively.

[36] *Gazette*, Dec. 27, 1855, Jan. 9, 1856; *Post*, Jan. 4, 5, 15, 1856.

[37] Russell Errett to Salmon P. Chase, Pittsburgh, Nov. 16, 1855, Chase MSS.

[38] James A. Dean to Simon Cameron, Allegheny City, June 22, 1855. Cameron MSS. I disagree with Ray Billington's contention (*The Protestant Crusade*, p. 262) that Americans sublimated their hatred of Catholics and foreigners in the latter part of 1854 to sectional stands on the slavery issue. Not only did the Know-Nothing party continue through 1855 and into 1856 in Pittsburgh, but the religious and ethnic tensions reflected in its rise continued to influence voting behavior long after the party merged with the Republicans. The Republican party in 1856 was just as much a vehicle for anti-Catholic sentiment as it was for antislavery

[39] This view finds support in an excellent essay in Joel H. Silbey, *The Transformation of American Politics, 1840–1860* (Englewood Cliffs, N.J., 1967), pp. 1–34.

[40] Richard P. McCormick, *The Second American Party System: Party Formation in the Jacksonian Era* (Chapel Hill, N.C., 1966), p. 15.

Stability and Realignment:

Cultural and Depression Politics,

1860–1896

Part Three

For more than three decades, from 1860 through 1892, the nation's political order owed its basic shape to the political realignment of the 1850s. Intense two-party competition characterized this third party system as it had the second, the Republicans narrowly holding the upper hand before 1874, the Democrats even more narrowly doing the same thereafter. Rival political organizations were active on the local level in both urban and rural areas; competing partisan newspapers flourished even in small cities. Significantly, the political system continued to involve the mass of eligible voters as well as the political elites. Year in and year out, impressive numbers of rank-and-file voters demonstrated their loyalty to one or the other political party by voting straight party tickets. Even the frequency of political campaigns and elections, which were annual affairs in many states, served to keep partisan feelings running high. As Walter Dean Burnham has put it (in an article reprinted in Part Four): "The late-nineteenth-century voting universe was marked by a more complete and intensely party-oriented voting participation among the American electorate than ever before or since."

Cultural differences continued to divide the popular coalitions that supported the rival parties. Since 1854, as noted in the previous section, the Republican party had derived its strongest support from old-stock and immigrant pietistic Protestants, for example, Methodists, Congregationalists, many Presbyterians, and some Lutherans. On the other hand, the Democratic party depended most heavily on Catholics (regardless of nationality) and Protestants, both native and foreign-born, who were not pietists, for example, Episcopalians, most Lutherans, and some Presbyterians. Within the South, on the other hand, whites, including the pietists among them, generally voted Democratic; they did not give the Republicans support comparable to that they had given the Whigs during the second party system. Blacks, where free to vote, usually supported the Republicans. Northern pietists sought to protect the moral order against alien threats (for example, Irish Catholic and beer-drinking German immigrants) and to purify it by uprooting evils such as slavery. They worked within the Republican party, which espoused active government, to abolish slavery, win civil rights for blacks, achieve prohibition, force observance of the Sabbath, and maintain the public schools as instruments of Americanization. Those threatened by pietistic crusades turned to the Democratic party to protect their institutions and practices by restricting the authority of government. One must bear in mind that this cultural conflict involved a whole range of issues. Even in the election of 1860, in which the slavery extension question was allegedly crucial, the analysis by George H. Daniels included in this part reveals that issues such as nativism and temperance continued to have an important influence on popular voting behavior.

Changing circumstances and conflicts within the rival coalitions sometimes led specific groups to increase or decrease their commitment to the party with which they identified. Pietistic southern whites who moved to the Midwest no longer lived in an area where the racial issue was paramount. Most of them continued to vote Democratic, but a sizable minority came to vote Prohibitionist or Republican when they perceived the Democracy as the party of rum and Romanism, rather than as the white man's party. German Lutherans shared the fears of other Protestants regarding Roman Catholicism. They increased their support of the Republican party when Protestant-Catholic conflict was politically salient. But they shifted toward the Democracy as the party of "personal liberty" when their German language schools and "continental Sundays" were attacked by pietists. Under these circumstances, the German Lutherans became an important political swing group.

The period witnessed the emergence of numerous protest parties, which expressed the position of groups that felt they could not realize their objectives through the major parties. Pietists who were particularly angered by the equivocation of Republican politicians over the liquor question founded the Prohibition party. Marxists formed the Socialist Labor party. Economically discontented laborers and farmers established a number of parties, the most important of which was the People's or Populist party, whose strength lay in the agrarian West and South and the silver-producing Rocky Mountains.

The second electoral realignment in the nation's history occurred during the 1890s. An economic depression that began in 1893, affecting urban as well as rural areas, generated sufficient unrest to weaken decisively the Democratic coalition that had battled the Republicans on relatively even terms for over thirty years. Essays by Paul Kleppner on the Midwest and Samuel T. McSeveney on the Northeast included in this part indicate, however, that there were important sectional differences in voting during this period. As a result of the voter realignment of the 1890s the Republican party established its political hegemony in the nation. But unlike the 1850s a major party did not disappear from the scene. Rather the Democratic party survived as the minority opposition.

Immigrant Vote in the 1860 Election:

The Case of Iowa

George H. Daniels

9

In focusing on the political behavior of one ethnic group in one state in one election, Professor George H. Daniels of Northwestern University sheds light on the persistent importance of cultural conflict in American politics. The presidential election of 1860 marked the end of a period of voting realignment and the beginning of a period of political stability in the United States. The election has long been interpreted in terms of the slavery expansion issue. But in his analysis of German voting in Iowa in 1860, Daniels demonstrates that voting patterns in that election cannot be understood without reference to other issues, specifically temperance and nativism. His essay makes particularly clear the danger of interpreting mass political behavior solely on the basis of research in sources generated by articulate members of the community and the necessity for basing such interpretations on the quantitative analysis of election data.

The influence of the immigrant vote in the presidential election of 1860 has been a subject of continuing controversy since the date of the election. The disagreement, though, is not usually in terms of how a given immigrant group voted; it is in terms of how much influence its vote exerted on the outcome of the election. There is a consensus of opinion among historians about the partisan leanings of every major immigrant group. The starting point of this paper was the recognition that there is still some question on the more fundamental level; before it is reasonable to dispute about the influence of a group's vote, the most elementary considerations require that one first determine how the group voted. No adequate evidence has yet been offered on this basic question. This paper is an effort to determine as exactly as possible, on the basis of a study of township voting returns, how the major immigrant groups in Iowa voted in the election of 1860.

When historians try to analyze political trends, there are a number of courses open to them; they may reach a judgment on the basis of an impressionistic

SOURCE: Reprinted with permission from *Mid-America*, vol. 44 (July 1963), pp. 142–162.

survey of the data; they may — in the manner of the modern pollster — accept the judgment of contemporary opinion; or they may use statistical analysis of the votes on the question at issue. Although the third of these alternatives seems to have much to commend it, statistical analysis has not, until recently, been widely used.

Lee Benson has suggested that a closer analysis of voting on the precinct level might reveal the unsoundness of many of our commonly accepted impressionistic judgments about past political behavior. By simply using state voting statistics, he was able, for instance, to disprove the generalizations of Allan Nevins about the Cleveland victory of 1884 and that of Arthur M. Schlesinger, Jr., concerning the Jackson victory of 1824. But he was not able, using the figures available to him, to do more than show that the generalizations of German influence in the election of 1860 were not proved.[1]

The German vote is usually credited with being a major factor in Lincoln's victory in 1860, and on the surface at least, there is a great deal of evidence for this viewpoint. The seven states then known as the Northwest are generally regarded as a crucial area in that election. The area was just emerging from the frontier stage, its population was rapidly increasing, and it represented more than enough electoral votes to determine the outcome of the election. The total vote in Illinois, Indiana, Iowa, Michigan, Minnesota, Ohio, and Wisconsin increased by 440,223 in the quadrennium 1856–1860. In the same period, 976,678 immigrants arrived, many of whom went to the Northwest and most of whom were Germans.[2] Since Lincoln captured the sixty-six electoral votes in these states, winning them all by narrow margins over Douglas, a large bloc of united voters in this area could very easily have carried the election to Douglas. Lincoln's plurality in the Northwest was only 149,807 — far less than the most conservative estimate of the number of German voters in the area.

Addressing the Chicago Republican Convention in 1860, the German-American politician Carl Schurz promised the party 300,000 German votes in the Northwest.[3] Since that time, it has been traditional to assert that the immigrants in general, and in particular the Germans, were largely responsible for Republican success in 1860. Both panegyrists who wished to laud the immigrants for their peculiar humanitarian concern for liberty, and apologists who wished to blame "foreigners" for Democratic losses in the Midwest and for the purely American chaos which followed the election of Lincoln in 1860, have advanced the claim continuously. The Des Moines Valley Whig of Lee County remarked in October, 1859: "Verily, Germany is a power in Lee County."[4] The editorial observed that there were no Germans campaigning for the Democrats and estimated that over three-fourths of Lee County Germans had gone over to the Republican party. On the unfriendly side, the Sioux City Register predicted that if the Republicans "refuse to accede to the demands of their German allies they will be defeated in every state west and north of the Ohio."[5]

Historians have generally fallen in line with the thinking of contemporary observers. When they have not maintained that the Germans were responsible for the victory in 1860, they have, at least, listed them as an important factor. The most extreme claim was that of Schrader, who, basing his estimate on German immigration into the Northwest between 1856 and 1860, estimated the German Republican vote in those states in 1860 to be nearly 450,000.[6] Faust, in his two-volume study of German immigrants, maintained that a large majority of

German immigrants joined the Republican party in an "unselfish effort to advance the interests of humanity, i.e., to banish slavery from the country."[7] Faust based his conclusion on a study of the spokesmen of the German community, who undoubtedly did, both in Iowa and the Midwest generally, campaign vigorously for the Republican party. The same type of evidence led Herriot to conclude that the Germans voted heavily Republican in the Iowa gubernatorial election of 1854,[8] and, more recently, two historians to conclude that midwestern Germans poured into the Republican party en masse during the decade in a "spontaneous overflow of powerful emotions."[9]

Among all of these studies, only Herriot actually made an effort to determine how the German masses voted, but since his analysis was on the county level, he had to confess that the returns were "somewhat perplexing."[10] Dissent from the majority opinion first came in 1942 when Dorpalen tentatively concluded that the Germans were generally conformists, tending to vote as their neighbors did.[11]

Following the suggestion in Benson's essay, this study was specifically designed as a test of the thesis that Germans were overwhelmingly Republican in 1860. For reasons that will appear later in the essay, this could not effectively be done without at the same time considering the other population groups. I selected Iowa purely as a matter of convenience on the grounds that it would serve quite as well as any of the others. The situation in Iowa at that time was similar to that in the other midwestern states. It had been solidly Democratic in 1850 and subsequent elections began showing a marked Democratic decline. Whig strength increased, the Free Soil party registered small percentages in 1852 in several counties, and the first opposition success came in 1854 with the election of James W. Grimes as governor on a combined Whig and Free Soil platform. The Grimes supporters were later active in forming the Republican party, which carried every election in Iowa from 1856 until long after the Civil War. The period of Republican rise coincided with the period of greatest increase in Iowa's population, and also with a definite shift in the focus of immigration from the southern states and the southern part of the Ohio Valley, to the Northern Ohio Valley, the Middle Atlantic states, and Europe. In 1850, the population stood at 192,214, and by 1856 had reached 517,875. Thereafter, immigration from all quarters greatly decreased, and by 1860 only another 150,000 was added to the population. Native Germans in 1860 formed 5.79 percent of the entire state population of 674,913.[12]

In order to apply systematic data in the analysis of a political problem, it is first necessary to translate the question of what happened into a question of who (what voting groups) caused it to happen. In this case, we have a state which over a period of ten years changed its political allegiance from one party to a rival party. The German-Americans allegedly were a causal factor in the change. If this be the case, one would hypothesize that in a national election at the end of the transition period, a relationship would be found between the Republican vote and the presence of large numbers of German-Americans in a given area. The hypothesis can be tested by listing the various nativity groups, or at least the larger ones, found in Iowa at the time and comparing the vote in areas of their dominance. If place of origin does, indeed, play a determining role in the way one votes, a clear pattern should emerge when a large number of areas are compared.

Still, there is one other difficulty which could interfere with the validity of the results. If a historian selects a group and then studies only those areas where it is numerically strong, he will be in danger of neglecting other groups in other areas, equally or more important as causal agents for the trend. For this reason, the author has not considered population as a factor in selecting the areas of study. The only criterion was intensity of partisanship. In making this kind of selection, the only necessary assumption is that if a group be notably partisan, it will be almost certain to emerge in a tabulation of extremes.

Two methodological conclusions emerged quite early in this study: first, that the township was the largest political unit that could yield the desired answers, and second, that total population figures were untrustworthy as guides to political strength. On the county level, population groups are so evenly divided and so many changes are occurring at once that no pattern can readily emerge. If, for example, the vote is fairly well split on the county level, as it was in Lee County in the presidential election of 1860 when 51.5 percent of the vote went to the combined Democratic parties; and if no one group of voters is clearly dominant, as was also the case in Lee County, there is little that the historian can properly deduce about the election. But the Democratic vote in the townships of Lee County ranged from 14 percent to 74 percent, and since groups originating from the same locality did tend to settle close together, a clearly dominant group can be distinguished in most of the townships.

The only disadvantages in this approach are in the labor involved and in the difficulty of locating returns by townships. In most cases, the counties themselves did not retain the returns for any great length of time, and one must resort to newspapers for their report. Where no newspaper existed, or where the newspaper did not choose to print such returns, the historian must usually admit failure and try another county. Although this lack of complete evidence does make it impossible to utilize any normal scientific sampling methods, it does not make it necessary to leave the existing material unstudied. The historian must, rather, make the best use he can of the materials he can find. This has been the procedure followed in this study. Township returns for twenty-six counties were located for the presidential election of 1860, and eleven more for the gubernatorial election of 1859. In addition to these, there were twenty-two counties so sparsely populated that for election purposes they were regarded as comprising one township each, and they can be so regarded by the investigator. The fifty-nine counties (from a total of ninety-nine) are distributed throughout the state, and they contained in 1860 over 70 percent of the total population of Iowa. Considering the present state of scientific sampling techniques, it can be seriously argued that covering this large a percentage of the total population is at least as conducive to accuracy as any sample could be.

While the desirability of pursuing one's study in terms of townships is hardly a controversial issue, there is a deficiency of the census that has not been so often remarked. A look below the surface of the county returns drives one to the conclusion that census figures showing the total population do not necessarily reflect the distribution of voting power. In studies of group voting behavior, historians have characteristically assumed that there is a real relationship between total and voting population, but the results of this study show not only that it is not necessarily so, but also that in a frontier community, it is highly unlikely to be so.[13]

A comparison of the two kinds of population statistics for any of Iowa's counties will demonstrate that the formal ethnic divisions of the census do not reflect voting power. Comparative figures for Clay County, a particularly revealing example, are shown below [Table 9.1]:

Table 9.1   Voting Strength in Clay County

	Percent of Total Population	Percent of Potential Voters
Middle Atlantic	28.0	20.0
Ohio Valley	20.0	13.3
Germany	22.0	46.7

In other words, the census showed that the Middle Atlantic natives were the largest group and the Ohio Valley group followed closely behind the Germans, while in terms of the voting population, the Germans greatly outnumbered the two combined. In all of the other cases, the greatest discrepancies occurred along the normal migration lines of the most numerous group outside the Ohio Valley, and discrepancies increased in direct relation to proximity to Iowa. Missouri and Illinois were consistently overrated by the census and the immigrant groups consistently underrated in terms of their actual voting power. In cases where, for example, New England was listed as the birthplace of a large percentage of adult males, the Middle Atlantic states without exception received disproportionate representation in the census.[14]

The meaning of all this, so far as this particular study is concerned, is clear. Although we have no way of determining who actually did vote, it is apparent that in order to determine the relative strength of those who could possibly have voted, it will be necessary to count only adult males. This has been done in all the townships used.

The analysis in the remainder of this paper is largely based upon the group of counties for which township returns are available for the election of 1860. The other categories are used as a check upon the conclusions and will only be mentioned when necessary for clarification. While the desirability of including materials for an earlier period is unquestionable, returns before 1859 are so extremely fragmentary that they could add very little to the study.

In order to have a large number of townships for comparison, all those voting over 65 percent Democratic and all those voting less than 25 percent Democratic were tabulated along with the most Democratic and the most Republican townships in each county. The only significance which is attached to these percentages is that they undoubtedly deviate a great deal from the state averages and that they yield an equal number of Democratic and of Republican townships (forty each). These, then, are the extremes and their populations are compared in Table 9.2. According to the table, the Middle Atlantic states of New York, Pennsylvania, and New Jersey supplied the most consistent Republicans.[15] The Ohio Valley states were split, while Germans, Irish, and southerners were clearly Democratic. There are no other groups which appear often enough in a dominant position for one to judge.

These results were taken a step further on Table 9.4 which shows that in every case, an increase in the dominance of a nativity group increased the trend

Table 9.2 Largest Nativity Groups in Most Democratic and Most Republican Townships
Presidential Election of 1860

Nativities	Most Democratic Townships	Most Republican Townships
New England	0	1
Middle Atlantic	3	21
Upper Ohio Valley	21	16
South	4	0
Germany	7	0
Great Britain	1	0
Ireland	4	0
Scandinavia	0	1
Holland	0	1

Table 9.3 Largest Nativity Groups in Most Democratic and Most Republican Townships
Gubernatorial Election of 1859

Nativities	Most Democratic Townships	Most Republican Townships
New England	0	1
Middle Atlantic	2	4
South	0	0
Upper Ohio Valley	7	5
Germany	1	1
Ireland	2	0

of the township vote. The first entry on the table shows the median Democratic vote of all the townships studied which contain more than 20 percent of a given nativity group; the second entry shows the median vote of townships containing more than 40 percent of the group. In townships where the Germans, for example, supplied over 20 percent of the voting population, the median Democratic vote was 70 percent. But if one considers only those townships where Germans numbered more than 40 percent of the population, the median Demo-

Table 9.4 Median Democratic Vote of Townships According to the
Percentage Distribution of Selected Nativity Groups
Presidential Election of 1860

Nativity	+20% of Voting Population Median Vote		+40% of Voting Population Median Vote	
Ireland	86.7	83.0	89.2	86.7
Germany	70.0		81.1	
South	67.1	66.3	75.1	
Upper Ohio Valley	56.4	56.0	68.4	67.7
Middle Atlantic	22.2		22.2	17.8

cratic vote rose to 81.1 percent. This is a clear indication that Germans in these townships did contribute to the Democratic vote.

Every item on the chart, except that pertaining to the Germans, is in accord with the standard interpretation and will require little further comment. It does seem worthwhile to remark that if the known Republicanism of immigrants from the Middle Atlantic states and their known influx into the midwest during the decade 1850–1860 be considered in connection with the migration pattern alluded to in this study, historians will in all probability find that their migration into the midwest was the sole cause for the political shift. Although the percentage of population from the Ohio Valley was also increasing phenomenally at the same time, these immigrants were, as it seems, mostly women and children who could have had no immediate political influence. The fact that townships dominated by Ohio Valley immigrants were evenly divided reflects the divided sympathies of their background. There only remains the problem of reconciling the conflict between the statistics on German voting and other types of evidence.

Even though all of the German townships located in this study were Democratic in 1860, the theory of Dorpalen, which was endorsed by Benson is suggestive when it is applied to the Germans in Iowa's large cities. In all of the German townships studied, there was really no chance for the Germans to conform to anything; conformity requires frequent contact in order for the political attitude to be transferred. The situation in all seven of the townships precluded such contact and transfer, for the Germans all lived and worked in purely German communities. Iowa's two largest cities, Davenport and Dubuque, were also the cities which contained the largest number of Germans in an urban environment, where contact, and presumably outside political influence would be almost a daily occurrence. And, the Germans in both cities seemed to adopt the prevailing political attitudes. Dubuque voted Republican only once in the thirteen statewide elections between 1850 and 1860, and Davenport voted Democratic only twice during the same period. The Germans entering between 1852–1854 seemed to do no more than increase the already prevailing trend in each case. According to a census taken in 1858, there were approximately 496 Germans who could have voted in Davenport in that year, and the Republican majority of that year was 438 out of the total 1864 votes cast for Representative in Congress.[16] While similar population figures for Dubuque (Julian Township, Dubuque County) do not exist, contemporary reports indicate that the German population must have been about the same as in Davenport. Here the Democratic majority in 1858 was 503 out of 2339. It would require a great stretch of the imagination to believe that either city would have voted differently had there been no Germans in them.

Although the situation in Dubuque and Davenport may be explained in terms of conformity, as Dorpalen and Benson would have it, outside of these two areas, the great majority of Germans in Iowa were not diffused throughout the population. Instead, they normally formed communities of their own and enjoyed relative political isolation. In these cases, they did not conform to the political attitudes of the counties in which they lived; in every instance this study shows that they were a great deal more Democratic than their neighbors in 1860. The seven Democratic townships in which Germans formed the largest group were in six different counties, four of which were Republican in 1860, and one of which was only slightly Democratic. In this connection it is significant to note that while 21 percent of Scott County's population in 1860 was German, Germans did not appear as a large group in any of the highly Republican townships in that county. On the other hand, in Dubuque County, which contained only 15.6 percent Germans, they were the largest group in two townships which voted more than 80 percent Democratic. The one German township voting Republican in the election of 1859 (Amana, Iowa County) is easily explained on the grounds that being a pietistic religious colony, it would have little ideological affiliation with other German groups in the state.

Any way the problem is approached, except by taking the word of interested politicians, German intellectuals and newspapers, it seems that Iowa Germans were definitely inimical to Republican aspirations in the election of 1860, and the indications are that a study would show that the same was true in 1856.[17]

Actually there were two very potent reasons why German-Americans should have been attracted to the Democratic party during that particular decade. Republicanism was linked, at least in the popular mind, with Know-Nothingism, and in Iowa it was also linked to prohibition. Democrats, on the other hand, tended to favor free liquor, and in their convention of 1856, had roundly denounced native Americanism and read the Know-Nothing element out of the party. Events outside the Midwest also reflected a basic difference between the two parties in their treatment of immigrants, and the Iowa Democratic press seized every opportunity to play up Know-Nothingism in the Republican ranks. When the "two year" amendment was passed by the heavily Republican Massachusetts legislature in March 1859, every Democratic paper in Iowa featured it in their editorials. Obviously aimed at eliminating immigrant influence at the polls, the Massachusetts amendment provided that naturalized citizens must have resided in the state for two years before being eligible to vote. Iowa papers claimed that the Massachusetts action demonstrated that Republican love for humanity extended only so far as the African, while the Democratic party, "places the adopted citizen . . . on a basis of perfect and entire equality with the native."[18] The *Weekly Independence Civilian* prophesied that if the Republicans of Iowa "were strong enough to do without foreign votes, they would soon be walking in the steps of Massachusetts."[19]

In answer to the Republican defense that the nativist attitude was purely local, not reflecting any national Republican attitudes, the Democrats pointed out that the New York and the Connecticut Republican party were sponsoring a similar proscriptive amendment.[20] Democrats also claimed that the union of the American and the Republican parties in Hamilton, Ohio, proved that Know-Nothingism was not a local element in the Republican party.[21]

There is abundant evidence that German-Americans in Iowa were aroused by the nativist tendencies in the Republican party. One German immigrant, a resident of Burlington, Iowa, wrote a lengthy public letter to the press, urging Germans not to vote for the party of nativism and prohibition.[22] Denunciatory resolutions were drawn up by an association of Germans in Scott County,[23] and a group of German political leaders submitted a questionnaire to the congressional delegation from Iowa asking them, in effect, if they condemned the Massachusetts legislation.[24]

All historians who considered the subject have noted these less attractive — at least from the German viewpoint — features of the Republican party, but have insisted that because of their love of liberty, the Germans overlooked these minor points. Speaking of the German intellectuals, this seems to be perfectly true; and the masses were also lovers of liberty. But like masses everywhere, the rank and file Germans who did the bulk of the voting considered their own liberty to be of paramount importance. Apparently ignoring the advice of their leaders, they cast their ballots for the party which consistently promised them liberty from prohibition and native-American legislation.

At least one German-American businessman expressed the same opinion just before the election of 1860. Samuel Stern of Boston, in an open letter to Carl Schurz, claimed that he had been in the Revolution of 1848, and had learned enough of "radicalism and idealism to learn to be conservative and look after my own interests." Although he offered no statistics to prove his contention, Mr. Stern's experience had convinced him that the bulk of the Germans who had become adopted citizens and could vote were largely Democratic. Only the newly arrived masses, he said, were fooled by Schurz and the other politicians who were really thinking of their own advancement.[25] Although Mr. Stern could hardly be called a disinterested observer, his analysis is suggestive, and would seem to be largely borne out by the results of this study. An editorial in the *New York Demokrat* which was widely reprinted in midwestern newspapers, although it did not speak so frankly of conservatism and self-interest, came to roughly the same conclusions. The editor described German-Americans who were still voting Republican after all the kicks they had received as "stupid."[26] Whatever the merits of the arguments of Stern and the *New York Demokrat*, it is evident that large numbers of German voters, at least in Iowa, must have taken them seriously.

Although the prohibition issue was undoubtedly a factor, it was probably not as important as Republican native-Americanism. Had a split occurred over prohibition, one would expect a religious pattern to emerge. But an inspection of the *Census of 1860, Social Statistics* and the appropriate county histories indicates that the German Democrats ranged from Roman Catholic in Dubuque and Johnson Counties to Methodist-Episcopal and Mennonite in Lee, and Baptist in Des Moines. Any religious issues were apparently subordinated to the general German hatred of native-Americanism.

Even though it be granted that Iowa Germans were largely Democratic in 1860, it does not automatically follow that Germans throughout the Midwest were Democratic. Conclusions drawn from a study of one state cannot be automatically applied elsewhere, for it is possible that there were conditions peculiar to Iowa which caused the split between the German spokesmen and the German masses, but this conclusion is important for another reason. In a sense, this paper has been a case study in the relationship between the pronouncements of group spokesmen and the actions of group members. And, since no significant relationship existed in this case, it does call into question all generalizations about group voting based upon the opinions of leaders. Historians, accepting the statements of contemporary observers as true, had found reasonable grounds for assigning a large majority of the German vote to Frémont and to Lincoln. That they were wrong in at least one case has been demonstrated in this study; for well over half the Germans in Iowa lived in the six counties where the most Democratic townships were dominated by Germans. It is important to recognize that in every case conclusions of German Republicanism have been made on the same ground — acceptance of contemporary opinion. The broadest generalizations that can be made from this study are that the masses do not necessarily vote the way their spokesmen are campaigning, and that contemporary opinion, including that of newspapers, is a poor guide. If the historian would discover how any group actually voted, he must turn to an analysis of voting returns in terms of the smallest possible units. Only in a unit the size of a township can groups be isolated with enough precision for the historian to be sure that his conclusion is correct. If this study has any applicability outside of the immediate area considered, it is only in adding evidence to Benson's claim that historians must utilize systematic data in political studies if their statements are to bear scrutiny.

Appendix A   The Democratic Vote by Townships According to Nativity Groups
Presidential Election of 1860

MIDDLE ATLANTIC TOWNSHIPS

Township	County	Democratic Vote (%)
Putnam	Fayette	9.4
Fremont	Buchanan	13.6
Jefferson	Butler	17.3
Boardman	Clayton	18.6
Scott	Johnson	16.4
Wayne	Jones	17.8
Cue	Benton	20.0
St. Claire	Benton	21.2
Taylor	Dubuque	35.4
Liberty	Scott	25.7
Union	Boone	31.4
Amity	Page	2.2
Douglas	Page	22.2
Fulton	Muscatine	22.7
Mitchell	Mitchell	9.9
Albion	Butler	17.5
Fremont	Butler	25.0
Sumer	Buchanan	18.8
Ohio	Webster	24.1
Washington	Webster	22.0
Harlan	Fayette	25.0
Clear Creek	Johnson	66.3
Auburn	Fayette	56.4
Rockingham	Scott	57.9

UPPER OHIO VALLEY TOWNSHIPS

Township	County	Democratic Vote (%)
Wayne	Henry	0.8
Gower	Cedar	11.3
Yellow Springs	Des Moines	16.9
Brown	Linn	20.7
Bruce	Benton	7.3
Harrison	Benton	23.6
Cedar	Lee	24.8
Valley	Page	11.4
Indiana	Marion	32.5
Milford	Story	30.0
Center	Pottawattamie	20.8
Crawford	Washington	15.2
Clay	Washington	14.7
Richmond	Wayne	27.6
Drakeville	Davis	43.5
Springdale	Cedar	17.2
Jefferson	Lee	73.9
Roscoe	Davis	71.6
Dodge	Boone	67.1
March	Boone	78.7
Buffalo	Linn	63.3
Jackson	Jones	60.0
Augusta	Des Moines	73.1

UPPER OHIO VALLEY TOWNSHIPS (Cont.)		
Township	*County*	*Democratic Vote (%)*
Massilon	Cedar	57.2
Jackson	Butler	71.4
Baltimore	Henry	70.9
Buchanan	Page	70.8
Pierce	Page	68.4
Polk	Marion	79.2
Jefferson	Mahaska	70.7
Collins	Story	56.0
Rocky Ford	Pottawattamie	67.3
Pleasant Grove	Des Moines	67.7
Salt Creek	Davis	81.9
Lick Creek	Davis	73.0
Marion	Davis	74.5
SOUTHERN TOWNSHIPS		
Fabius	Davis	88.7
Clay	Wayne	66.1
Fox River	Davis	75.1
Yell	Webster	63.2
NEW ENGLAND TOWNSHIPS		
Denmark	Lee	13.7
GERMAN TOWNSHIPS		
West Point	Lee	70.0
Liberty	Dubuque	86.6
Mossalem	Dubuque	81.1
Liberty	Johnson	83.2
Clayton	Clayton	56.6
Benton	Des Moines	66.7
Moscow	Muscatine	55.8
IRISH TOWNSHIPS		
Prairie Creek	Dubuque	83.0
Iowa	Dubuque	89.2
Union	Benton	86.7
Washington	Jones	93.4
SCANDINAVIAN TOWNSHIPS		
Cedar	Mitchell	1.4
DUTCH TOWNSHIPS		
Black Oak	Mahaska	31.7

Appendix B   The Democratic Vote and Dominant Nativity Groups by Townships
Gubernatorial Election of 1859

Township	County	Democratic Vote (%)	Dominant Nativity Group
Butler	Jackson	100.0	Irish
Washington	Clinton	88.9	Irish
Warren	Keokuk	84.6	Ohio Valley
Sioux City	Woodbury	69.5	Middle Atlantic
Clear Creek	Jasper	69.4	Ohio Valley
Walnut	Jefferson	63.7	German
Iowa	Iowa	60.2	Ohio Valley
Columbia	Tama	59.0	Ohio Valley
Sugar Creek	Poweshiek	57.4	Ohio Valley
Green	Wapello	77.8	Ohio Valley
Union	Black Hawk	70.0	Ohio Valley
Amana	Iowa	3.2	German
Buckingham	Tama	8.1	Middle Atlantic
Richland	Jasper	8.6	Ohio Valley
Grinnell	Poweshiek	13.9	New England
Berlin	Clinton	19.9	Ohio Valley
Prairie	Keokuk	21.9	Ohio Valley
Richland	Wapello	23.4	Ohio Valley
Correctionville	Woodbury	25.0	Middle Atlantic
Monmouth	Jackson	25.7	Middle Atlantic
Liberty	Jefferson	33.5	Ohio Valley
Black Hawk	Black Hawk	15.4	Middle Atlantic

Appendix C   Democratic Vote and Dominant Nativity Groups of Counties Not
Organized into Townships
Presidential Election of 1860

County	Democratic Vote (%)	Dominant Nativity Group
Audubon	55.1	Upper Ohio
Sac	72.7	Upper Ohio
Clay	61.9	German
Ida	60.0	Middle Atlantic
Palo Alto	87.9	Irish
Kossuth	23.8	Middle Atlantic
Grundy	11.9	Middle Atlantic
Hancock	12.1	Middle Atlantic
Dickinson	13.2	Middle Atlantic
Humbolt	24.7	Middle Atlantic
Emmet	0.0	Middle Atlantic
Crawford	39.7	Middle Atlantic
Cherokee	23.1	New England
Shelby	39.0	Upper Ohio
Plymouth	15.8	Upper Ohio
Pocahontas	32.3	Irish

NOTES

1 Lee Benson, "Research Problems in American Political Historiography," in Mirra Komarov-sky, *Common Frontiers in the Social Sciences*, Glencoe, Illinois, 1957, pp. 113–183.

2 Frederick F. Schrader, *The Germans in the Making of America*, Boston: 1924, p. 195.

3 Charles W. Emery, "Iowa Germans in the Election of 1860," unpublished M.A. Thesis, State University of Iowa, 1940, p. 28.

4 *Des Moines Valley Whig*, October 17, 1859, p. 1.

5 *Sioux City Register*, vol. 1, no. 47, June 16, 1859.

6 Schrader, *The Germans in the Making of America*, p. 195.

7 Albert B. Faust, *The German Element in the United States*, Boston, 1909, pp. 130–131.

8 Frank I. Herriot, "A Neglected Factor in the Anti-Slavery Triumph in Iowa in 1854," *Deutsch-Americanische Geschictsblatter; Jahrbuch der Deutsch-Amerikanischen Historischen Gesell-schaft von Illinois*, vol. 18–19, 1918, 1919, pp. 174–335.

9 Lawrence S. Thompson and Frank X. Braun, "The Forty-Eighters in Politics," in Adolf E. Zucker, *The Forty-Eighters*, New York, 1950, p. 120.

10 Herriot, "A Neglected Factor," p. 342.

11 Andreas Dorpalen, "The German Element and the Issues of the Civil War," *Mississippi Valley Historical Review*, vol. 29, no. 55, June 1942.

12 *Population of the United States in 1860; Compiled from the Original Returns of the Eighth Census*, Washington, 1864.

13 After submission of this manuscript, George A. Boeck's "A Historical Note on the Uses of Census Returns" appeared in the January [1963] edition of this journal [*Mid-America*], in which he made the same observations that occur in the above and the following three paragraphs. Doctor Boeck's work and my own were done independently and in total ignorance of each other. Had I known of Doctor Boeck's work earlier, it would have saved me a great deal of labor; but at this point I can only say that I agree completely with all that Doctor Boeck observed about the dangers inherent in working with the census returns. Since my examples were all newly settled frontier areas, and Doctor Boeck's a relatively stable urban area in the same frontier state, the two, taken together, provide a base for a rather broad generalization.

14 The three frontier counties of Boone, Decatur, and Marshall, which in 1850 had 2051 residents were used to determine whether this kind of distribution was peculiar to the later period in Iowa, or whether it could be applied more generally to frontier communities. Four hundred seventeen, or about one-fifth of the total residents were adult males and could possibly have voted in the gubernatorial election of that year. The same pattern is found as in 1860. At one extreme is the foreign group, which had 33 potential voters from a total foreign population of 55, and at the other extreme are the neighboring states of Missouri, Indiana, and Illinois which together furnished only 42 voters out of a total of 802 immigrants from those states.

15 Although New Jersey is included as a Middle Atlantic state, only an insignificant number from this state ever came to Iowa. New Yorkers and Pennsylvanians are about equally repre-sented. No differences were noted when the Ohio Valley states were considered separately.

16 The census returns can be found in Franc B. Wilkie, *Davenport Past and Present*, Davenport, 1858, p. 325.

17 At least five of the seven German townships found in the election of 1860 were also highly Democratic in 1856. Records do not exist for the other two.

18 *Iowa Weekly Democrat*, Sigourney, Iowa, vol. 1, no. 10, March 25, 1859.

19 *Weekly Independence* (Iowa) *Civilian*, vol. 4, no. 40, May 12, 1859.

20 *Sioux City* (Iowa) *Register*, vol. 1, no. 49, June 30, 1859.

21 *Page County Herald*, Clarinda, Iowa, vol. 1, no. 10, July 29, 1859.

22 *Weekly Independence* (Iowa) *Civilian*, vol. 4, no. 45, June 16, 1859.

23 *Iowa Weekly Democrat*, Sigourney, Iowa, vol. 1, no. 17, May 13, 1859.

24 *Weekly Maquoketa* (Iowa) *Excelsior*, vol. 4, no. 10, May 17, 1859.

25 *Mississippi Valley Register*, Guttenberg, Iowa, November 1, 1860, p. 4.

26 *Ibid.* (reprint) October 6, 1859, p. 2.

Northern Voters and Negro Suffrage:

The Case of Iowa, 1868

Robert R. Dykstra / Harlan Hahn

10

Referenda on proposals extending the suffrage to blacks in the mid-nineteenth century, like similar votes on open housing proposals and the civilian review of police activities in our own period, provide scholars with one useful measure of public attitudes toward race. Among post–Civil War referenda on black suffrage, only the one in Iowa in 1868 has been quantitatively analyzed. The struggle in Iowa reveals much about the political standing and consequent strategy of the two rival national parties in the post–Civil War period and the relative importance of various determinants of voting behavior. The Democrats attempted not only to block black suffrage, but also to undermine the Republicans' majority coalition in that state by playing on the racism of many Republicans. The Republicans sought to maintain their dominance and achieve black suffrage by appealing to the party loyalty and conscience of their adherents, not by arguing for social equality for blacks per se. In Iowa the Republicans held enough of their normal partisan support to win despite some significant defections over the race issue. In several closely contested states, on the other hand, their stand sometimes cost them dearly. Professor Dykstra teaches history at the University of Iowa, Professor Hahn, political science at the University of California.

Although American race prejudice is usually viewed as a southern-born phenomenon that came north only with urbanization, northern prejudice itself has a long history. Formal discrimination against the Negro in the North was probably most severe in the decades before the Civil War.[1] But the wartime triumph over slavery did not automatically bring an end to northern discrimination. The result in many ways was a widespread crisis of conscience: having fought a war to preserve the Union that had developed into a crusade against slavery, would northerners yield to the moral implications of their victory and grant full civil rights — everywhere — to the Negro?

Between Appomattox and the promulgation of the Fifteenth Amendment in 1870, proposals that would allow Negroes to vote became burning political issues

SOURCE: Reprinted with permission from *The Public Opinion Quarterly*, vol. 32 (Summer 1968), pp. 202-215.

in several northern states. The confrontation of views on the suffrage question during this period has been too long neglected by scholars interested in the relationship of race prejudice to the history of Negro civil rights.[2] While attitudes on Negro suffrage may not have been *precisely* related to race prejudice, it seems a proper if unverifiable assumption that those opposed to suffrage extension were opponents of racial equality. An examination of the Negro suffrage question of the 1860s, therefore, should lend insights into an important area of social relations in a historical era as well as perhaps help clarify more recent social and political behavior.

On the eve of the Civil War, only five New England states permitted Negroes to vote. New York had a limited provision for Negro suffrage. Four other states had altered their constitutions to exclude Negroes from the franchise, and in eight northern states Negroes had always been legally deprived of the right to vote.[3] Opposition proved so strong prior to the Civil War that, in the estimation of one student, "the problem of Negro suffrage eclipsed the problem of the foreigner."[4] The question, however, was not resolved by the war. Between 1865 and 1870 proposals for Negro suffrage were defeated in at least fourteen northern states.[5] In addition, Colorado Territory jeopardized its admission to the Union in 1865 by a favorable referendum vote on a constitution restricting the franchise to "every white male citizen of the age of twenty-one and upward."[6] In New Jersey the question of Negro suffrage was never submitted to a referendum, although the state's legislators rejected it decisively by a vote in 1867[7] and by a subsequent resolution denouncing Negro enfranchisement.[8]

Rejection of Negro suffrage by northern states in the Reconstruction era placed the Republican "radicals" in Congress in a serious dilemma. At the same time that most of them demanded the right to vote for southern Negroes, some on the grounds of principle, others to establish a Republican foothold in the South, their constituents blocked similar plans in the North.[9] The political advantages of the situation were not lost on President Andrew Johnson, who taunted northern congressmen for the inconsistencies in their position.[10] One of the relatively few prominent radicals who urged that Negroes universally be permitted to vote was Senator Charles Sumner of Massachusetts. Many other Congressmen, however, championed Negro suffrage in the South without risking the political consequences of advocating a similar program for the North. In these circumstances the Fifteenth Amendment, by prohibiting racial qualifications for voting in any state, provided a means to resolve the embarrassing issue without the need for various state constitutional referenda, although the battle still had to be waged in the state legislatures.[11]

Meanwhile, expressions of public opinion on Negro suffrage gave the radicals little encouragement. Since politicians generally were reluctant to decide the issue themselves, franchise extension became a frequent subject of referendum voting in the late 1860s. The percent of the vote in opposition to Negro suffrage in nine northern state referenda is contained in Table 10.1. There was no decided trend in favor of extending the franchise to Negroes. Although border states evidenced somewhat more resistance to Negro suffrage than states farther north, the years in which the referenda were held seemed to have little effect on the outcome. In general, there were few differences in the outcome of referenda held in 1868 and those held earlier.

While most northern states confronted the issue directly, proponents of

Table 10.1   Percent of the Vote in Opposition to Negro Suffrage in Nine
State Referenda, 1865-1868

State	Percent Against Negro Suffrage
District of Columbia (1865)	99.5
Connecticut (1865)	55.2
Wisconsin (1865)	54.4
Kansas (1867)	65.1
Ohio (1867)	55.2
Minnesota (1867)	51.2
Michigan (1868)	53.1
Missouri (1868)	57.3
Iowa (1868)	33.5

Source: *Annual Cyclopaedia*, 1865-1870.

Negro suffrage in a few states attempted relatively circuitous methods of gaining approval for the measure. In Michigan, for example, voters were presented with a totally new constitution that quietly omitted the word "white" from the qualifications for voting.[12] In Illinois, a Negro suffrage amendment had been overwhelmingly defeated in 1862. Six years later, Illinois voters endorsed a plan for a constitutional convention by a scant majority of 704 out of 444,860 ballots cast.[13] The convention delegates struck the word "white" from the suffrage requirements of the new constitution but refused to refer the issue to the voters as a separate amendment, thus forestalling its rejection.[14]

The presidential election of 1868 represented a peak time for voting on Negro suffrage. In that year voters approved franchise extension in Iowa and Minnesota, but rejected it in Michigan and Missouri.[15] In Minnesota, Negro enfranchisement was adopted, after two previous defeats in referenda, only when the question was submitted to voters as "an amendment of section 1, article 7, of the Constitution" — without any direct reference to impartial suffrage.[16] Negro suffrage also won in Wisconsin that year, but through a decision of the state supreme court rather than a popular vote.[17] Thus the only straightforward victory for Negro suffrage in 1868 occurred in Iowa; and as the only state that adopted franchise extension by means of a single, uncomplicated referendum, Iowa appears to offer productive opportunities for investigating postwar popular attitudes toward Negro rights in the North.

The analysis of voting returns is a particularly appropriate method of studying historical public opinion.[18] Even though previous research suggests that aggregate election data may not correlate precisely with individual opinions,[19] voting statistics remain the only quantitative measure of "grass roots" attitudes before the twentieth century. Clearly the alternative to using election statistics is to ignore them entirely and continue to place exclusive emphasis on random estimates of public opinion — usually highly subjective — hazarded by contemporary politicians and journalists. While one may, of course, lament the nonexistence of such ideal aids as opinion surveys, much more historical election data can be recovered than is sometimes imagined, and much can be accomplished with it through the use of modern analytical techniques.

The principal sources of data for this study were the election returns from 97 counties and 437 townships for Iowa's 1868 referendum on the Negro suffrage question. Surprisingly, the location of voting statistics proved a much less severe problem than anticipated. County election returns were recovered from the state archives and the township reports were obtained from an exhaustive review of extant local newspapers. The statistics were then internally verified to ensure their accuracy.

Census material comprised a second important source of data for this study, especially the published state censuses of 1867 and 1869 and the federal manuscript census of 1870. Unfortunately, the unusual mobility of the Iowa population in the late 1860s required the exercise of considerable caution at some points, especially in positing relationships between the 1868 voting and 1870 demographic characteristics. Yet, the overall richness of the census data greatly facilitated the research. When the analysis of voting and demographic patterns was supplemented by information from newspapers and other historical records, a relatively comprehensive picture emerged.

The issue of Negro suffrage was first presented to Iowans in 1857. After the 1854 election of a Whig as governor had dislodged Democrats from control of public offices in the state, considerable agitation developed for a new constitution that would remove the prohibition on banks and effect other changes. An ensuing constitutional convention produced a number of important alterations in the basic framework of Iowa government, but disagreement over a Negro suffrage proposal proved sufficiently intense to inspire the delegates to refer it to the voters as the only separate amendment to the new constitution.[20] Although Iowans approved the new constitution by a slight majority, they turned down the proposal to strike the word "white" from its suffrage provisions by an overwhelming margin of 85.4 percent. But at the same time, more than one-fourth of the people who cast ballots on the new constitution failed to vote on the suffrage amendment.

An examination of the 1857 voting returns by area permits some interesting insights. Only two counties in the state recorded a majority for the amendment. . . . By arbitrarily dividing the state along geographic lines, the location of centers of support and opposition becomes apparent. Counties in the northern half of the state, for example, provided nearly 10 percent fewer votes in opposition to franchise extension than southern counties, in which settlers from below the Mason-Dixon Line predominated. The largest vote against Negro suffrage was recorded in southeastern Iowa, which contained the state's earliest and most southern settlements.[21]

Resistance to Negro rights was manifested in several areas of Iowa during the Civil War, although the attitudes of many residents undoubtedly underwent profound changes during the war years. Iowa, for example, contributed more men per capita to the Union army than any other state. As an area subjected to the agitations and dislocations of the war during a formative period of its history, perhaps Iowa was particularly affected by doctrines and arguments promulgated in support of the Union position.

The results of the second referendum in 1868 suggested that a major shift in opinion had occurred. The vote for Negro enfranchisement increased from 14.6 percent in 1857 to 66.5 percent in 1868. Furthermore, the total vote cast on

Negro suffrage was within 5 percent of the total vote in the 1868 presidential contest, which was on the ballot at the same time.

The 1868 referendum presented voters with five different amendments to strike the word "white" from the Iowa constitution. The first amendment removed the qualification of race from voting requirements; the second, third, and fourth amendments eliminated similar restrictions from census and apportionment regulations; and the fifth amendment voided racial limitations on the composition of the state militia. A sixth discriminatory clause in the state constitution, confining membership in the legislature to free whites, was overlooked in the haste to prepare amendments, but voters repealed this provision in 1880 by a margin of 63.4 percent.[22] The 1868 vote on the five amendments varied by only 202 out of more than 186,000 cast. Consequently, the vote on the first amendment has been employed as the principal measure of attitudes in this analysis.

Since the vote for Negro suffrage varied by 5 percent or less between different sections of the state in 1868, more precise statistics were examined. The associations between the vote for franchise extension and several major political, social, and economic variables by county have been recorded in Table 10.2. Perhaps the most striking feature of the table is the high association between party preferences and voting on Negro enfranchisement. The township voting statistics also revealed the strength of this association. In 367 out of the 437 townships, there was a difference of only 10 percent or less between the vote on suffrage and the presidential returns. At the township level, the coefficient of correlation between the percentage of the vote for U. S. Grant, the Republican candidate for President, and the percentage of the vote in favor of Negro suffrage was +.91. This correlation probably reflects the success of Republican leaders who sought to identify their party with the cause of extending additional liberties to Negroes in the postwar era.

Table 10.2   Correlation Between Vote for Negro Suffrage in 1868 and Political, Social, and Economic Characteristics, by County

Political, Social, and Economic Characteristics	Correlation with Vote for Negro Suffrage	p
Percent of vote for Republican candidate for Secretary of State (1867)	+.92	.001
Percent of vote for Republican candidate for Governor (1867)	+.84	.001
Percent of vote for Republican candidate for President (1868)	+.86	.001
Percent of eligible voters in incorporated towns (1867)	−.32	.01
Percent of population Negro (1867)	−.23	.05
Per capita value of manufactures (1868)	−.26	.05
Value of farm produce sold per unit of production (1868)	+.31	.01
Average value of land per acre (1868)	−.30	.01

As early as 1866, Iowa was the only state in which the Republican party had strongly endorsed Negro suffrage.[23] The particular zealousness of Iowa Republicans on the suffrage question also probably reflected the bitter factional dispute between James Harlan, Secretary of the Interior in Lincoln's Cabinet, and war-time Governor Samuel J. Kirkwood, who, along with General Grenville M. Dodge, led the radical reconstructionists of Iowa. Agitation for the radical cause in the party became so intense that Congressman John A. Kasson, Lincoln's First Assistant Postmaster General, was purged by Dodge at least in part for his failure to espouse Negro suffrage.[24] The power of the radical faction in the Iowa Republican party of 1868 was implicitly echoed by one Republican editor, who proclaimed, "A vote for Grant and Colfax in Iowa, is *not a true, honest, Republican, vote,* unless it contain[s] the clause striking the word 'White' from the Constitution." [25] The high association between the vote for Republican candidates and for suffrage extension indicates that a large number of Iowa Republicans heeded such exhortations.

Party regularity, however, does not provide the only explanation for the remarkable discipline the parties apparently exerted on the referendum vote. The balloting on Negro suffrage also was somewhat related to settlement patterns. Several measures of population characteristics suggest that the greatest support for Negro enfranchisement was concentrated in rural or farming regions and that its principal opponents were located in the relatively urbanized or densely settled areas of the state. Both the proportion of eligible voters living in incorporated towns and the per capita value of manufacturing were negatively related to the vote for Negro suffrage. On the other hand, a positive association was found between support for franchise extension and such rural indices as the percentage of enclosed areas devoted to the cultivation of wheat (+.41) and the proportion of rural voters in the county population (+.34).

A somewhat clearer picture of the differences between urban communities and farming areas emerged from an examination of the vote in the 437 townships by type of population unit. Small towns (2500 population or less) gave slightly more support to the Republican party and to Negro suffrage, and they had higher levels of voter participation in both the election and the referendum, than either farm areas or large towns (more than 2500 population).[26] Although the amazingly large percentages of eligible voters who everywhere cast ballots on both questions are consistent with the findings of prior research on voter turnout in the late nineteenth century, the data did not support the conclusion that rural or farm settlers voted in greater proportions than the residents of urban communities generally.[27]

The tendency of small towns to support both the Republican candidate for President and Negro suffrage in 1868 is consistent with previous research indicating that the residents of small towns are less likely to depart from traditional party orthodoxy than other segments of the voting population.[28] A number of special factors probably influenced the vote in both rural townships and relatively large communities, where the pro-suffrage total was 10 percent below the state plurality for Negro suffrage. Large towns normally contained large concentrations of Democratic voters, who, as Democrats, had little sympathy for Republican-sponsored proposals to secure Negro rights. On the other hand, the relative lack of enthusiasm for Negro suffrage displayed in farm townships perhaps was affected by the special status of the Negro in a rural environment. By the end of the Civil War, the few Negroes in Iowa, who constituted only one-half of 1 percent of the population of the state, had begun to filter thinly into the Iowa countryside. Many of them, perhaps lacking the skills and training qualifying them for work in populous areas, were probably compelled to perform marginal work without steady employment. There did not seem to be a role for the Negro in a rural economy. In these circumstances, the farmer whose status was subject to the fluctuations of an unpredictable market perhaps had little difficulty in conjuring a vision of colored immigrants flooding the rural landscape from outside the state, attracted by guarantees of equal rights.

Support for the idea that rural areas facing the specter of economic insecurity were the most susceptible to fears of displacement through Negro immigration was discovered in documents from that era. The 1868 campaign rhetoric reflected both intense partisan disagreements and a possible explanation for the strong correlation between party preferences and positions on the suffrage question. While Republicans enlisted the "bloody shirt" and appeals to conscience in their efforts to enfranchise the Negro, Democrats often sought to arouse fears concerning economic status as a means of stimulating opposition to the measure. Some Democratic spokesmen attempted to expose Negro suffrage as a device for attracting cheap labor with which white voters would be forced to compete. For example, a stumpspeaking innkeeper from Clayton County, the seat of a large concentration of foreign-born voters with Republican proclivities, admonished his fellow citizens to vote for "a free white Democratic ticket." His argument was a cunning amalgamation of "populist" economic rhetoric and appeals to race prejudice:

> You voted for "Abraham Lincoln;" this made you "loyal;" you freed the negro; you put down that awful curse *"negro* slavery" and fastened eternal white slavery upon yourselves and children by lowering and knuckling to the most absolute, despotic and exacting, intruding slave driver, that ever marked the poor man's path — the Giant God of Moloch — the monied mon[o]polies of the country. Good bye laboring man! The bondocracy of New England have fixed your status.[29]

This was a somewhat circumlocutory appeal to white status panic with respect to the Negro; and, in fact, few such Democratic exhortations were issued straightforwardly and openly. But Republican spokesmen acknowledged them to be a potent factor affecting the decisions of white voters. *"That man is a Coward who fears Negro suffrage,"* argued the Republican editor quoted previously. ". . . It is not the color of the skin you fear, it is the fear you have, that the negro will outstrip you in the race of life."[30] Another Republican editor addressed the question at some length. "A Democratic friend in Edenville," he wrote,

> . . . contends that he wants laws passed which shall give him a better chance in life than is given the colored man. He thinks it should be made by law easier for him to get his living — that in the race and struggle of life he should have advantages, while the black, already borne down by the prejudice of color, should be made to labor under positive disabilities. . . . Either our Edenville friend is very uncharitable at heart, or he is afraid that "the nigger" will get the start on him in the race of life and in the struggle for preferment. . . . How narrow, contemptible, illiberal, unjust and mean, is the prejudice, which would hamper the colored man in the pursuit of an industrious livelihood. . . .[31]

Since the economic consequences of extending Negro rights were debated primarily by party spokesmen, the effectiveness of appeals to white anxieties over the threat of economic displacement is difficult to assess. By removing the influence of partisan considerations, however, some indications can be gained about the independent impact of the argument. Table 10.3 contains the partial correlations between the vote for Negro suffrage and several social and economic variables by county, controlling on the percentage of the vote for the Republican candidate for secretary of state in 1867. Table 10.3 reveals that, with the effect of the Republican vote eliminated, the associations between variables measuring agricultural prosperity and positions on Negro suffrage are altered considerably. The correlations with the indicators of urbanization and the percentage of Negroes are substantially reduced. But the relation between farm prosperity as measured by the relative value of farm produce and the suffrage vote is strengthened. Perhaps even more striking is the coefficient of correlation between the average value of land per acre and the vote in favor of Negro enfranchisement, which changes from a negative to a positive direction when the Republican vote is introduced as a control. Apparently, support for Negro suffrage was related to economic success in rural areas, independent of the effects of partisan allegiances. Since rural workers in relatively prosperous areas had less to fear from economic displacement than those in poor farming areas, they seemed to be more resistant to the imagined threat of Negro immigration.

Table 10.3 Partial Correlations Between Vote for Negro Suffrage in 1868 and Social and Economic Characteristics, by County

Social and Economic Characteristics	Partial Correlation with Vote for Negro Suffrage*	p
Percent of eligible voters in incorporated towns (1867)	+.15	n.s.
Percent of population Negro (1867)	−.01	n.s.
Per capita value of manufacturers (1868)	−.16	n.s.
Value of farm produce sold per unit of production (1868)	+.49	.001
Average value of land per acre (1868)	+.23	.05

*Controlling on the percent of the vote for the Republican candidate for Secretary of State in 1867.

In addition, the township data were used to measure the association between the difference in the vote on Negro suffrage and the Republican presidential vote, and the percentage of the population that was Negro. In farm townships, but in neither small nor large towns, the Negro proportion of the population correlates positively and significantly with the size of this difference. Only in rural areas was it found that the greater the relative number of Negroes, the greater was the difference between the percentage of the vote for Grant and the percentage for Negro suffrage. Although the relation between the fear of economic competition and race prejudice among the residents of large towns and cities has been popularly accepted, patterns in the 1868 Iowa vote indicate that similar conclusions may be equally and perhaps particularly applicable to rural areas.

The results of the 1868 referendum and the partisan elections of the 1860s also indicate that immigrant townships, which were perhaps most vulnerable to anxieties about Negro economic competition, were more consistently opposed to both Republican candidates and Negro suffrage than native American areas.

The mean percentage of the vote in selected townships of Iowa for three elections is contained in Table 10.4. Fortunately, information on the predominant ethnic composition of Iowa townships is contained in a prior study, which discovered that townships dominated by Irish and German voters provided overwhelming support for Democratic candidates before the Civil War.[32] By comparing the vote in various townships, it is possible to determine areas of support and opposition to Negro suffrage and changes in voting patterns that may have occurred over time.

Table 10.4 Vote in Townships, by Native Origins of Voters, in Three Elections in Iowa, 1860-1868

Townships*	Number of Townships	Percent for Grant (1868)	Percent for Negro Suffrage (1868)	Percent for Lincoln (1860)
Upper Ohio Valley (voted Republican by 75 percent or more in 1860)	8	81	77	82
Upper Ohio Valley (voted Democratic by 60 percent or more in 1860)	7	42	37	31
German (voted Democratic by 60 percent or more in 1860)	5	22	18	23
Irish (voted Democratic by 60 percent or more in 1860)	4	16	12	12

*As identified by George H. Daniels, "Immigrant Vote in the 1860 Elections: The Case of Iowa," *Mid-America*, vol. 44 (July 1962), pp. 159-162.

German and Irish townships not only expressed the greatest opposition to Negro suffrage, but they also were least inclined to depart from Democratic allegiances. Townships dominated by natives of the Upper Ohio Valley that had voted overwhelmingly for Lincoln in 1860 gave the most support to Grant and Negro suffrage in 1868. But while the Republican vote in *Democratic* townships dominated by voters from the Upper Ohio Valley increased markedly between 1860 and 1868, the presidential vote and the vote on Negro suffrage in Irish and German townships remained relatively stable. Thus townships with a high proportion of foreign-born voters yielded more opposition both to Republican candidates and to Negro suffrage than even traditionally Democratic townships settled by native Americans from the Upper Ohio Valley.

Another measure of the opposition of immigrant groups to Negro enfranchisement was provided by isolating the several townships casting the heaviest vote against the referendum proposal. So far as is known, all of the townships that voted less than 10 percent for Negro suffrage also were among the most Democratic townships in the state in both the 1860 and the 1868 elections. Even more striking, however, the electorates of all were over 48 percent foreign-born in 1870. Voters of Irish birth dominated five, Germans one, and Irish and Norwegians shared dominance in another.[33]

Although partisan loyalties and ethnic group identifications overlapped to a great extent in Iowa during this period, it was possible to identify three traditionally Republican townships in which foreign-born voters predominated over residents of native birth. Two of the townships were dominated by Germans, and the other by Norwegians. In all three, the discrepancy between the Republican vote in 1868 and the vote in support of Negro suffrage exceeded, though slightly, the state average.[34] Despite the limited amount of evidence, therefore, the data did suggest a cautious finding that even Republican immigrant voters gave somewhat less support to franchise extension than native Americans.

The explanation of these phenomena is not difficult to discern. A ranking of ethnic backgrounds reveals that the three largest foreign-born groups in Iowa in 1870 were the Germans, the Irish, and the Scandinavians. They constituted 9 percent, 6 percent, and 3 percent, respectively, of the total labor force in the state. In many of the jobs requiring few skills, however, they congregated in larger numbers than their relative proportions of the working population. More than 37 percent of the common laborers in Iowa at this time were German, Irish, and Scandinavian. Nearly 25 percent of all railroad employees were Irish, and 13 percent were Scandinavian.[35] Consequently, immigrants were less immune to fears of economic displacement should Negroes be attracted to Iowa by the extension of suffrage than were native Americans who held occupations providing greater security and status.

Referenda on Negro rights in the years after the Civil War created major problems and conflicts for many groups of voters. Perhaps the group that experienced the greatest difficulty with the Negro suffrage question in that period was the Republican party. While congressmen who endorsed radical Reconstruction programs demanded Negro suffrage in the South, they experienced serious resistance to the imposition of Negro suffrage on their own northern constituencies. In Iowa the suffrage vote was closely related to partisan loyalties. Republican discipline may have been less effective in some other northern states. Yet, significantly, opinions on Negro suffrage everywhere were clearly divided along party lines during this period. Republicans generally endorsed the extension of Negro rights, and Democrats frequently were obliged to defend themselves against charges of anti-Negro prejudice.[36] The Democratic strategy of opposing Negro suffrage as a potential invitation to the influx of cheap labor was directed particularly at immigrant groups, which most feared economic competition.[37] Probably appeals contrived to portray Negro rights as a social and economic threat contributed to Democratic strength in the predominantly Republican era of the 1860s.

The results of Iowa's referendum voting indicate that Democrats generally were successful in arousing antipathy to Negro suffrage among immigrants. The vote on Negro suffrage also was closely related to social and economic characteristics. Although small towns cast somewhat larger majorities in favor of Negro suffrage than rural townships or urban areas, the only positive association between the presence of Negroes in the population and the Republican presidential vote minus the vote for Negro suffrage was found in farming areas. The white farmer in Iowa apparently experienced a reaction to potential Negro competition similar to the response of other groups enjoying few economic privileges.

Whether the case of Iowa in 1868 was or was not typical for the North in the 1860s is a question that can be answered only by similar research for other states. The historical bases of race prejudice, despite the complexities involved in attempting to assess them, are certainly worthy of continued investigation. The analysis of popular referenda on Negro suffrage held prior to the Fifteenth Amendment would appear to be one fruitful approach.

No attempt to find a pattern in Repub. opposition to Black suffrage - no concern for religious identification.

NOTES

[1] See Leon F. Litwack, *North of Slavery: The Negro in the Free States, 1790–1860*, Chicago, University of Chicago Press, 1961. For the intellectual bases of race prejudice in the United States in the nineteenth century, see especially William Stanton, *The Leopard's Spots: Scientific Attitudes Toward Race in America, 1815–1859*, Chicago, University of Chicago Press, 1960; Thomas F. Gossett, *Race: The History of an Idea in America*, Dallas, Southern Methodist University Press, 1963, chaps. 4–13.

[2] For a brief overview, see Leslie H. Fishel, Jr., "Northern Prejudice and Negro Suffrage, 1865–1870," *The Journal of Negro History*, vol. 39, 1954, pp. 8–26. See also James M. McPherson, *The Struggle for Equality: Abolitionists and the Negro in the Civil War and Reconstruction*, Princeton, Princeton University Press, 1964, pp. 236–237, 333–334, 377, 382–383, 419ff.

[3] Litwack, *op. cit.*, pp. 74–93; Kirk H. Porter, *A History of Suffrage in the United States*, Chicago, University of Chicago Press, 1918, pp. 89–92; Stephen B. Weeks, "The History of Negro Suffrage in the South," *Political Science Quarterly*, vol. 9, 1894, p. 677.

[4] Porter, *op. cit.*, p. 62.

[5] James Albert Hamilton, *Negro Suffrage and Congressional Representation*, New York, Winthrop Press, 1910, pp. 21–23.

[6] *The American Annual Cyclopaedia and Register of Important Events of the Year 1865*, New York, D. Appleton and Co., 1866, p. 178.

[7] *Annual Cyclopaedia* (1867), p. 539.

[8] *Annual Cyclopaedia* (1868), pp. 541–542.

[9] Eric L. McKitrick, *Andrew Johnson and Reconstruction*, Chicago, University of Chicago Press, 1960, pp. 55–58.

[10] Charles H. Coleman, *The Election of 1868: The Democratic Effort to Regain Control*, New York, Columbia University Press, 1933, p. 19. For the most important recent scholarship on the party conflict over a Reconstruction policy for the defeated South, see LaWanda Cox and John H. Cox, *Politics, Principle, and Prejudice, 1865–1866: Dilemma of Reconstruction America*, New York, Free Press, 1963; W. R. Brock, *An American Crisis: Congress and Reconstruction, 1865–1867*, New York, St. Martin's, 1963; Kenneth M. Stampp, *The Era of Reconstruction, 1865–1877*, New York, Knopf, 1965; David Donald, *The Politics of Reconstruction, 1863–1867*, Baton Rouge, Louisiana State University Press, 1965.

[11] For the most recent book-length study of the Fifteenth Amendment issue, see William Gillette, *The Right to Vote: Politics and the Passage of the Fifteenth Amendment*, Baltimore, Johns Hopkins University Press, 1965. For a recent article taking issue with the prevailing view that most national Republican figures were cynically political in their approach to the Negro suffrage question see LaWanda and John H. Cox, "Negro Suffrage and Republican Politics: The Problem of Motivation in Reconstruction Historiography," *Journal of Southern History*, vol. 33, 1967, pp. 303–330.

[12] Fishel, *op. cit.*, pp. 20–21.

[13] *Annual Cyclopaedia* (1868), p. 351.

[14] *Annual Cyclopaedia* (1870), p. 392.

[15] Coleman, *op. cit.*, p. 18.

[16] *Annual Cyclopaedia* (1868), p. 505.

[17] *Annual Cyclopaedia* (1865), p. 823.

[18] For a comprehensive discussion of the application of such methods to historical problems, see Samuel P. Hays, "New Possibilities for American Political History: The Social Analysis of Political Life," unpublished paper presented at the meeting of the American Historical Association, Washington, D. C., December 29, 1964; see also William O. Aydelotte, "Quantification in History," *American Historical Review*, vol. 71, 1966, pp. 803–825.

[19] W. S. Robinson, "Ecological Correlations and the Behavior of Individuals," *American Sociological Review*, vol. 15, 1950, pp. 351–357; Herbert Menzel, "Comment on Robinson's 'Ecological Correlations and the Behavior of Individuals,' " *ibid.*, p. 674.

[20] Carl H. Erbe, "Constitutional Provisions for the Suffrage in Iowa," *The Iowa Journal of History and Politics*, vol. 22, 1924, pp. 185–207.

[21] Alice Lucile Hahn, "Exercise of the Electoral Franchise in Iowa in Constitutional Referenda,

1836–1933," Des Moines, Drake University, unpublished master's thesis, 1933, pp. 63–66.

[22] *Ibid.*, pp. 74–76.

[23] Fishel, *op. cit.*, p. 17.

[24] Edward Younger, *John A. Kasson*, Iowa City, State Historical Society of Iowa, 1955, pp. 182–206.

[25] Davenport *Western Soldier's Friend*, Oct. 24, 1868.

[26] In small towns, 98 percent of the population voted in the 1868 presidential election and 95 percent on the Negro suffrage question; 65 percent of the vote went to Grant and 61 percent for Negro suffrage. In rural townships, 89 percent voted in the presidential election and 87 percent in the suffrage referendum; 62 percent voted for Grant and 56 percent for Negro suffrage. In large towns, 84 percent voted in the presidential election and 80 percent in the suffrage referendum; the vote for Grant and for Negro suffrage was, respectively, 61 and 56 percent.

[27] Walter Dean Burnham, "The Changing Shape of the American Political Universe," *American Political Science Review*, vol. 59, 1965, pp. 16–17.

[28] Harlan Hahn, "One-partyism and State Politics: The Structure of Political Power in Iowa," unpublished doctoral dissertation, Cambridge, Harvard University, 1964.

[29] McGregor *North Iowa Times*, Sept. 30, 1868. For the speaker's personal characteristics, see *History of Clayton County, Iowa*, Chicago, Inter-State Publishing Co., 1882, pp. 819–820. A summary of the economic issues in the 1868 campaign is given by Coleman, *op. cit.*, pp. 24–44.

[30] Davenport *Western Soldier's Friend*, Oct. 24, 1868.

[31] Marshalltown *Times*, Sept. 26, 1868.

[32] George H. Daniels, "Immigrant Vote in the 1860 Election: The case of Iowa," *Mid-America*, vol. 44, 1962, pp. 159–162.

[33] The townships were: Washington Twp., Clinton County; Iowa Twp., Liberty Twp., Prairie Creek Twp., Washington Twp., all in Dubuque County; Butler Twp., Jackson County; and Washington Twp., Jones County. The mean percentage of the vote for Negro suffrage in the seven townships was 5.0, the mean percentage of the vote for Grant was 7.1, and the mean percentage of foreign-born voters in 1870 was 71.9.

[34] These townships were: Garnavillo Twp., Volga Twp., and Marion Twp., all in Clayton County.

[35] Calculated from *United States Census* (1870), vol. 1, p. 733.

[36] Horace Samuel Merrill, *Bourbon Democracy of the Middle West, 1865–1896*, Baton Rouge, Louisiana State University Press, 1953, pp. 13–17.

[37] Frank L. Klement, *The Copperheads in the Middle West*, Chicago, University of Chicago Press, 1960, pp. 13–14, 105.

The Religious and Occupational

Roots of Party Identification:

Illinois and Indiana in the 1870s

Richard Jensen

11

Richard Jensen's study of selected midwestern voters during the 1870s is unusual in that it rests on data relating to the ethnocultural and economic background of individuals rather than of large groups. Political scientists base much of their research into contemporary politics on such data but historians are generally unable to do so. Only occasionally has political information about individuals in eras before the advent of polls and surveys survived into our own time. Historians, therefore, usually have had to rely on aggregate data revealing group, but not individual, characteristics in their analyses. Jensen's article thus provides a unique opportunity for students to compare the findings of research into individual historical behavior with those of scholars who have had to rely solely on aggregate data. Professor Jensen teaches at the University of Illinois (Chicago Circle). His book, *Winning of the Midwest: Social and Political Conflict, 1885–1896*, was published in August 1971.

"Religion comes very little into the American party," declared James Bryce. "Roman Catholics are usually Democrats. . . . Congregationalists and Unitarians . . . are apt to be Republicans. Presbyterians, Methodists, Baptists, Episcopalians . . . have no special party affinities. They are mostly Republicans in the North, Democrats in the South."[1] With these brief, tidy generalizations the foremost commentator on late-nineteenth-century American politics dismissed the relationship between religion and partisanship, and steered generations of scholars away from the topic.[2]

Bryce was wrong. One of the most accurate ways to determine a voter's choices in the late nineteenth century was to ascertain his religious preferences (except in the South, where one ascertained his race). Table 11.1, showing the partisanship of the inhabitants of the small northern Illinois town of Geneseo, indicates that over 90 percent of the Congregationalists, Unitarians, Methodists, Baptists, Swedish Lutherans and Swedish Methodists were Republican, and

SOURCE: Reprinted with permission from *Civil War History*, vol. 16 (December 1970), pp. 325–343.

over 90 percent of the Catholics were Democrats.[3] Table 11.2, which cross-classifies the old-stock voters in Geneseo (i.e., those not identifiable as immigrants or sons of immigrants) according to church membership and occupation, indicates that quite apart from his religion, a man's occupation also was related to his party preference. These patterns, which held for a sample of other towns and rural areas in Illinois and Indiana in the 1870s, and probably for the Midwest as a whole, are too strong to be dismissed with Bryce's vague assertions. Religion, and to a lesser extent occupation, constituted the basic roots of party identification for the average citizen.

Table 11.1 Party, by Ethnic-Religious Groups, Geneseo City and Township, 1877

Ethnic	Denomination	% Republican (of Two-Party Total)	N
Old Stock	Congregationalist	96.5	74
	Unitarian	96.0	25
	Methodist	91.4	70
	Baptist	90.9	22
	Presbyterian	72.5	29
	Other	80.0	20
	No denomination given	69.0	400
German	Lutheran	66.7	60
	Other Protestant	52.2	67
	Roman Catholic	25.0	16
Irish	Roman Catholic	0.0	52
Other	Roman Catholic	7.7	13
Swedish	Lutheran, Methodist, and other	96.3	72
Total		70.1	920
Actual Vote	(Governor, 1876)	68.1	827

Table 11.2 Party, by Occupational and Religious Status, Geneseo Old Stock, 1877
(Percent Republican of Two-Party Total)

	Church Affiliated		Not Church Affiliated		All	
	% Rep.	N	% Rep.	N	% Rep.	N
Business & professional	95.4	151	75.4	221	86.4	372
Urban labor	72.7	11	55.3	74	57.6	85
Farmer	84.6	78	67.6	105	74.9	183
All	90.8	240	69.0	400	77.2	640

The data for Geneseo, and all the other places tabulated, comes from recently discovered county directories published in the mid-1870s. The compilers attempted to ascertain the name, address, occupation, nationality, religious affiliation and party identification of every voter and taxpayer. The value of any farm holdings in Illinois, and in Indiana information on age, birthplace and year of arrival, were also included. Each of the directories seems to have canvassed the population quite thoroughly. Probably unskilled workers and farm laborers were frequently overlooked, but the possible bias in this deficiency can be largely overcome by grouping the men into occupational categories.[4]

The overwhelming Republicanism of the old-stock denominations in Geneseo is striking, especially the 95 percent level for the business and professional men. Equally impressive is the homogeneity of the Republican Swedes and the Democratic Catholics (occupation made little difference here!). Nor was this pattern confined to Geneseo; all the Swedish communities in the Midwest were heavily Republican, and all the Catholic settlements heavily Democratic. The Protestant Germans (mostly Lutherans) were the only religious group that was politically divided. Indeed, the German voting patterns across the Midwest were constantly in flux, except for the small number of German Methodists and Baptists, who were consistently Republican. Analysis of aggregate election returns suggests that whenever prohibition was the salient issue, the Germans voted heavily Democratic; whenever the money question was uppermost (as in 1896) they swung toward the GOP.

Church affiliation, as Table 11.2 shows, added 20 points to the Republicanism of old-stock professionals and businessmen, and 17 points to the Republicanism of old-stock urban laborers and farmers. The partisan spread between high and low occupational status groups in each religious category was about 20 points, with farmers midway between the high and low groups. Thus church affiliation was as important a factor as occupational status among the old stock in this city.

The Geneseo patterns are quite similar to those in the nearby city of Princeton, Illinois, as displayed in Table 11.3. For Princeton the coding scheme was slightly different, with skilled workers (like carpenters and bakers) and clerks grouped with the laborers instead of with the businessmen as in Geneseo. (The problem was the difficulty in deciding whether skilled artisans owned their own shops.) Church affiliation added 15 points to the Republicanism of high status old-stock Princeton voters, and 19 points to the low status men, while high status itself added only 2 to 5 points to the Republicanism of each religious group. Church affiliation, therefore, was just as influential in Princeton as in Geneseo, but occupational status was less important. (The difference was not caused by the coding change, however.) The various denominations divided in Princeton much the same as they did in Geneseo, except that the Protestant Germans in each occupational category were 2:1 Democratic, in contrast to Geneseo where they were 3:2 Republican.

Table 11.3 Party, by Occupational and Religious Status, Princeton City Old Stock, 1876 (Percent Republican of Two-Party Total)

	Church Affiliated		Not Church Affiliated		All	
	% Rep.	N	% Rep.	N	% Rep.	N
Business & prof.	83.0	88	67.5	200	72.3	288
Blue collar	80.8	47	62.1	208	65.6	255
All	82.2	135	64.7	408	69.1	543

Partisanship in Illinois and Indiana will be analyzed further with fresh data (excluding Geneseo and Princeton), but first a theoretical explanation of the results so far obtained is necessary so that a hypothesis will be available for testing.

Religion was relevant to social and political behavior in three ways. First, different theological positions produced different interpretations of morality and of the behavior most appropriate for the Christian citizen. Second, organized religious bodies formed fundamental social groups of the highest importance to their adherents. The members of a particular congregation or denomination knew other members intimately — they worshiped together, intermarried, and probably discussed political issues with each other over long periods of time. Thus a strain toward political uniformity within a particular religious group would not be unexpected. If like the German Lutherans a particular religious group was sufficiently inwardly directed, they might be said to constitute a distinct subculture. This usually happened in the case of immigrant groups sharing a common religion.[5] Thirdly, the denominations as formal groups sometimes took active parts in political controversies. Thus the Methodists before the Civil War came to adopt a semiofficial antislavery stance through the actions of respected elders, ministers, bishops, educators, and editors. These positions were transmitted to the general membership through voluntary association, special meetings, regular sermons, and an influential network of church periodicals.[6] By working with denominations rather than specific congregations, the three modes of religious influence can all be incorporated into an interpretation of how religious differences generated political differences.

The importance of religion in nineteenth-century America cannot be overestimated. In 1789 the United States was a largely de-Christianized nation. Wave after wave of revivals, from the 1790s to World War I, converted the major part of the population to Protestantism. The depth and breadth of the revivals forced a revamping of the fundamentals of Protestant theology. The revivalists, led by a few powerful intellectuals at Yale and Oberlin and hundreds of preachers in the field, rejected the orthodox Calvinist theory of predestination, and the Catholic-Anglican-Lutheran established church styles of theology which emphasized patience, gradualism and incrementalism and which made no allowance for massive and sudden revivals. The antirevivalists fought back bitterly and often brilliantly, producing major theological and liturgical renaissances in the Episcopalian, Presbyterian, Reformed, Lutheran and Catholic denominations. The result was a century-long conflict between the revivalist or "pietistic" outlook, and the antirevivalist or "liturgical" outlook.

While this conflict was not the only divisive force in American religion,[7] it was the most intense and long-standing. By the end of the century, when the revivalist circuit riders had dismounted and ministers searched for new methods to tend their flock, the pietistic-liturgican conflict rapidly faded in the major denominations. This in turn set off another wave of formation of new sects and denominations by men who felt the dimension was all-important.

The liturgical (or "ritualistic" or "high church") outlook stressed the institutionalized formalities and historic doctrines of the established churches of Europe — Calvinist, Catholic, Lutheran and Anglican. Salvation required faithful adherence to the creed, liturgy, sacraments, and hierarchy of the church. The quintessence of liturgical style could be found in Catholicism's lavish use of ornamentation, vestments, esoteric languages, ritualized sacraments, devotion to the saints, and vigorous pursuit of heretics, all directed by an authoritarian (and after 1870 infallible) hierarchy. Comparable ritualism became firmly established among Episcopalians and Orthodox Jews. German Lutherans (of the Missouri Synod, especially) and orthodox Calvinists (the "Old School" Presbyterians and many Baptists) similarly fixed ritualistic practices, clung to old theologies, and rejected both revivals and the manifestations of pietism.

One key element in the liturgical outlook was particularism, the conviction that their denomination was the one true Church of God, and most outsiders were probably damned. This attitude was strong not only among Catholics, but also among orthodox Calvinists, who clung to predestination, high church Episcopalians, Missouri Synod Lutherans and Landmarkean Baptists. For the liturgicals, moralistic social action groups that were not an integral part of the church structure were illegal, unscriptural, and unnecessary; the church could attend to all matters of morality without outside help. Thus the orthodox Calvinists ejected half the Presbyterian membership in 1837; the Baptists split over missionary societies in the 1830s; the Catholics underwent a great crisis in the 1890s regarding missions to Protestants; and the Episcopalians ordered their Church Temperance Society to disband in the 1920s.

Heresy, pride, and innovation, rather than impure behavior, were the cardinal sins for the liturgicals. Consequently they responded to pietism by stressing orthodox theology and developing seminaries and parochial schools to preserve their faith unchanged. Catholics and German Lutherans relied on their parochial schools to the exclusion of public schools, thus opening a line of political battle that climaxed in 1890 in intensely bitter elections in Wisconsin and Illinois. The courageous pursuit of duty was the highest virtue for liturgicals, and the most outstanding exemplar of this trait was the son of a Calvinistic Presbyterian minister, Grover Cleveland.[8]

The pietistic outlook rejected liturgicalism. It had little respect for elaborate ceremonies, vestments, saints, devotions, and frequently opposed organ music in church. Theologically the key to pietism was the conviction (called Arminianism) that all men can be saved by a direct confrontation with Christ (not with the Church) through the conversion experience. The revival was the basis of their strength — the preaching of hellfire, damnation, and Christ's redeeming love, the anxious bench for despondent sinners, the moment of inner light wherein a man gained faith and was saved. While the liturgicals routinely baptized all the children in their community, and then went out to baptize heathens, the pietists insisted on the conversion experience before membership could be granted, and demanded continuous proof in the form of pure behavior. The Methodists, for example, did not hesitate to expel a member whose conduct was unbecoming to a true believer. Creeds and formal theology were of little importance, and heresy was not a major concern. Denominational lines were not vital either, and pietists frequently switched churches. The pietists fostered interdenominational voluntary societies to distribute Bibles, conduct missionary work, abolish slavery and promote total abstinence.

Every major denomination was torn by conflicts between liturgical and pietistic members in the nineteenth century. In most cases one group or the other gained the upper hand, often after heresy trials, thus driving the minority to silence, schism, or transfer to another denomination. By the 1860s, the midwestern Congregationalists, Disciples of Christ, Methodists, and Quakers were over-whelmingly pietistic. The Episcopalians and Catholics were predominantly liturgical, although a sort of pietism had considerable support among Catholic bishops and intellectuals. The Presbyterians were fragmented, with liturgicals concentrated in the "Old School" assemblies, and pietists in control of the "New School" and Cumberland groups. (The Old and New Schools merged in 1869, and Cumberland joined in later.) The Baptists were fragmented, too. The Free Will Baptists were pietistic, the Primitive Baptists liturgical. However, the largest group of Regular Baptists contained both elements, since there was no central authority to insure theological uniformity. Lutherans divided into three camps: liturgicals (led by the Missouri Synod Germans), pietists (Scandinavians and old stock), and a middle-of-the-road group of diverse membership. Likewise, the Jews divided into Orthodox, Reform, and Conservative camps. Round after round of schisms, mostly based on the pietistic-liturgical dimension, produced a proliferation of smaller denominations.[9]

The bridge linking theology and politics was the demand by pietists that the government actively support the cause of Christianity by abolishing the sinful institutions that stood in the way of revivals. Specifically, midwestern pietists demanded that the government halt the spread of slavery (or even abolish it), overthrow the saloon and the sale of liquor, and (among many pietists) restrict the "pernicious" and "corrupting" flood of Catholic immigration. (Nearly all the abolitionists were prohibitionists, and most were anti-Catholic.) Antiliquor, antislavery and nativism were the immediate causes of the realignment of parties in the mid-1850s that produced the third party system, pitting Republicans against Democrats.[10]

Liturgicals, as a rule, opposed prohibition, denounced abolitionists (even if they disliked slavery), and avoided the nativist agitation. The intrusion of government into affairs of morality was, in their eyes, a threat to the primacy of the Church in the spiritual realm, and an unconstitutional abridgment of individual liberties. Although the liturgicals did not favor the pernicious evils of the saloon any more than did pietists, they did not demand total abstinence of their members, nor did they discipline their slaveholding adherents. While the major pietistic denominations each suffered a North-South rupture *before* the Civil War, none of the liturgical churches was divided. The liturgicals feared that "fanatical" (their favorite epithet) pietists would use the government to further their moralistic crusades.

The liturgical fears were well grounded. Beginning with the Maine Law of 1851, a wave of prohibition legislation swept the country, instigated by the pietists, first through the Whig party, and then through the Know-Nothings and Republicans. After 1854 the slavery issue became paramount, and the pietists of the North mobilized into the moralistic, crusading Republican party. The Democrats, who had always claimed the support of most liturgical voters, sought to blunt the Republican attack by vigorously defending a wet, antinativist, anti-abolitionist position. During the Civil War itself, the pietists were the mainstay of the Union war effort, while the liturgicals held back. Catholics, both Irish and German, rioted against the draft and emancipation; Old School Presbyterians refused to fly the American flag at their 1863 convention; and not a few Episcopalians were denounced as Copperheads. The Episcopalian church in Indianapolis was even ridiculed as the "Church of the Holy Rebellion." The only appeal that finally gained liturgical support for the war was Lincoln's emphasis on loyalty, patriotism, and nationalism.

It seems reasonable to hypothesize that when party lines reformed in the 1850s, the great majority of pietists in the Midwest became Republicans, and liturgicals Democrats, and that the phenomenon of political inheritance through families and long-term stability of individual partisan identification maintained this basic division for the remainder of the century. This hypothesis has to be modified slightly in view of the fact that after 1869 and the victory of Radical Reconstruction, the temperance issue reemerged as the most salient political issue on the state and local level throughout the Midwest. In the mid-1870s, with the formation of the Woman's Christian Temperance Union, the prohibition movement again attained the status of a continuous crusade. Thus the religious-political correlation established before the Civil War was reinforced afterwards. (The Republicans, furthermore, used the "bloody shirt" issue, and the anger of Methodists about southern religious developments, to maintain the Civil War cleavages.)

The postwar temperance movement brought religious tensions sharply to the fore. Denouncing the wicked saloon as the father of drunkenness, the cause of disease, crime, poverty, and urban decay — and the base of power of Catholic politicians — the pietists opened a crusade that finally triumphed in 1919. As one Democratic leader complained:

> The preachers of Iowa with the exception of those in the ritual churches and a few [Old School?] Presbyterians . . . have been on the stump for legal prohibition, declaring that the use of alcoholic drinks is the source of all sin.[11]

The liturgicals bitterly opposed the prohibitionists. The Episcopalian bishop of Iowa sneered at "the disappointments and disasters, the illiberal fanaticism and unwarranted license, of the so-called temperance reform."[12] A leading German Catholic priest in Cincinnati sounded the liturgicals' favorite charges of fanaticism and hypocrisy:

> The American nationality . . . is often the hotbed of fanaticism, intolerance, and radical, ultra views on matters of politics and religion. All the vagaries of spiritualism, Mormonism, freeloveism, prohibition, infidelity, and materialism, generally breed in the American nationality. While the Irishman will get drunk and engage in an open street fight, and the German drink his beer in a public beergarden, the American, pretending to be a total abstainer, takes his strong drink secretly and sleeps it off on a sofa or in a club room.[13]

More loftily, the Missouri Synod found "the real principle involved in prohibition is directly adverse to the spirit, the method and the aim of Christian morals."[14]

The Republican party, responding to the demands of its rank and file, supported efforts to control the saloon. In 1886 and 1888, for example, Republican platforms endorsed temperance positions in twenty-seven states, and opposed them only in California. The Democratic party, nationally and in each midwestern state, repeatedly endorsed wet positions.[15] As one party leader explained, "The Democratic party has never posed as the great and only party of morality and temperance. The Republican party has."[16]

One by one the pietistic denominations moved from endorsements of total abstinence to demands for temperance legislation, soon including total prohibition of the manufacture and sale of all alcoholic beverages. The Methodists were the most vigorous, as their official declaration in 1888 suggests:

> The liquor traffic is so pernicious in all its bearings, so inimical to the interests of honest trade, so repugnant to the moral sense, so injurious to the peace and order of society, so hurtful to the homes, to the church and to the body politic, and so utterly antagonistic to all that is precious in life, that the only proper attitude toward it for Christians is that of relentless hostility. It can never be legalized without sin. No temporary device for regulating it can become a substitute for prohibition.[17]

In 1883 the Presbyterians officially denounced the liquor traffic as "the principle cause of . . . drunkenness and its consequent pauperism, crime, taxation, lamentations, war, and ruin to the bodies and souls of men," and advised its members to "persevere in vigorous efforts" for total prohibition.[18] The Scandinavian Lutherans insisted it was the "duty" of the Christian voter to abolish intoxicating drinks by law.[19] In some smaller denominations, and even among Methodists, many ministers switched out of the Republican party to support the Prohibition party candidates. In 1888 the annual conference of the small Free Methodist denomination went so far as to assert "that it is the solemn duty of the ministers and laymen . . . to give to the National Prohibition party our hearty support in every proper way, and especially to vote its ticket."[20]

The effect of the prohibition issue in differentiating liturgical and pietistic voters of similar background can be traced in aggregate election returns. Most Norwegians in Iowa were pietistic Lutherans and voted 90 percent Republican year in and year out. In Winneshiek County, however, liturgical Norwegian Lutherans predominated. The three towns of Pleasant, Glenwood, and Madison voted 93 percent Republican in 1881, before the temperance issue became salient. In 1882, the same towns voted 55 percent against a prohibition amendment to the state constitution and, as the temperance crusade continued, the Republican share of the vote slipped 33 points to 60 percent in 1891. In 1893, after the prohibition issue had been temporarily resolved to the satisfaction of the liturgicals, the vote in the towns shot up to 76 percent. In heavily liturgical-German Dubuque, where the Republicans had taken 50 percent of the vote in 1881, the prohibition amendment received only 15 percent of the vote, and the Republican vote plunged at the next election to 28 percent. (Dubuque's ward five, a German center, which had been 63 percent Republican, voted 94 percent wet, and the Republican vote then plunged to 22 percent.)[21] The professionals in the Republican party finally learned that support for prohibition meant defeat at the polls and after 1891 generally refused to permit the pietists to dictate dry platforms.[22]

Religious outlook seems also to have affected occupational status. The pietistic faith, by placing heavy emphasis upon individual initiative and responsibility for salvation, attracted entrepreneurs, while the passive liturgical faith was more amenable to less adventuresome men. One study of the split between Old School and New School Presbyterians in Philadelphia shows that from 60 to 80 percent of the merchants, manufacturers, professional men and retailers chose New School (pietistic) congregations, while 75 percent of the artisans and laborers moved into Old School congregations. Furthermore, the New School artisans were significantly more economically secure than the Old School artisans.[23] As Seymour M. Lipset has observed, "The Arminian [pietistic] emphasis on the personal attainment of grace, perhaps even more than the Calvinist stress on the existence of an 'elect,' served as a religious parallel to the secular emphasis on equality of opportunity and achievement."[24]

Occupational status had a more direct connection with politics; the Republican party always offered a comfortable home to the businessman, while the Democrats throughout the century consistently attacked the wealthy and the privileged. For example, in 1876, the leading Democratic newspaper in Illinois, noting that the Republican candidate for governor "speaks of Mr. Seward, the democratic candidate, as the 'barnyard' candidate," retorted:

> The men of the shops and of the farms, the laborers of the cities and towns, in short, the workingmen, are the real owners of the country. They fight its battles in war and support its revenues in peace; the man who works in his barn-yard has a better claim upon the suffrages of his fellow citizens than has the banker who clips off coupons and shaves notes.[25]

A few years later, a Republican newspaper in Indianapolis proclaimed, "In this community the majority of people who occupy the foremost walks of life, as preachers, lawyers, doctors, merchants . . . are republicans." The leading Democratic organ immediately denounced this "snobbery" as "insults to every honest wage-worker," and as "un-American, undemocratic and monstrous" to boot.[26]

So far, men without religious affiliations have not been accounted for. The very fact that they did not belong to a church in an age of revivals suggests that most of these men would either be young voters who had not yet been converted, or else were reluctant to join in voluntary organizations. It can therefore be expected that their partisanship would be weak. And since they lacked religious affinities toward either party, they should be located midway between pietistic Republicans and liturgical Democrats. Furthermore, the two parties were very closely matched before 1894 and election campaigns very intensely fought. As every extra vote counted, both parties probably endeavored to enlist these men, thus dividing them 50–50. If they were in business or professional occupations, however, they might be drawn to the Republicanism of their colleagues and repelled by the antibusiness animus of the Democracy. If they were factory workers, the Republican high-tariff position would be especially appealing. If they were laborers or farmers, they might have been drawn to the Democracy as the party of the common man. All of these possibilities can be explored with interview data.

The detailed analysis of one urban and seven rural townships in northern and central Illinois, and six rural townships in central Indiana[27] reaffirm the patterns displayed in Geneseo and Princeton and support the hypotheses drawn from that data. Table 11.4 shows the partisan distributions by denomination for the Indiana townships, where the coverage was unusually good (in part because the editors lived in one of the townships); all names were included except for twenty-four (1.5 percent) who failed to return any information on party or religion, and who usually had no age data listed. Less than 25 percent of the eligible men were missed by the canvassers here and, according to aggregate election returns, they voted the same way as the men who were included. Table 11.5 shows the party breakdown by denomination for the Illinois data. In this case, only Republicans and Democrats listed in the directories were included; otherwise coverage was comparable to that in Indiana.

The four most Republican denominations, Quakers, Congregationalists, Disciples, and Methodists, were strongly pietistic in the Midwest. The Presbyterians

Table 11.4 Party, by Denomination, Hendricks County, 1874

Denomination	% Rep.	% Dem.	% None or Other	N
Friends (Quaker)	96.4	1.2	2.4	83
Christian (Disciples)	73.6	23.7	2.7	291
Methodist*	72.8	21.9	5.2	232
Presbyterian	64.3	31.4	4.3	70
Missionary Baptist	57.4	38.6	4.0	101
Misc. Prot. denoms.	52.1	39.1	8.7	23
No denomination given	47.0	48.3	4.6	699
Regular Baptist	17.0	78.7	4.3	94
Roman Catholic	4.2	83.3	12.5	24

*Methodist Episcopal plus African Methodist.

Table 11.5 Party, for Pietistic Denominations, Eight Illinois Townships, 1877-1878
(Percent Republican of Two-Party Total)

Denomination	% Rep.	N
Congregationalist	82.0	39
Methodist	75.2	289
Disciples, Christians & Cumberland Presbyterian	71.8	220
Lutheran (pietistic synods only)	60.5	38
Presbyterian	57.7	108
Baptist	55.7	61

were predominantly pietistic, but the traces of Old School liturgical Democracy were evident.[28] The Baptists present an interesting special case. The Missionary Baptists were pietists, while most of the "Regular" Baptists in Hendricks County clung to orthodox Calvinist views and were especially hostile to missionary and temperance societies.[29] Only 4.2 percent of the Hendricks County men were independent — including several "Greeley Republicans," two Grangers, three Prohibitionists, and one "Old Whig." Occupationally, only half the independents were farmers, in contrast to over three-fourths of the partisans; the independents were also a bit younger, but the small N's prevent more exact conclusions. The "Civil War" generation (born 1832 to 1845) in Hendricks County was only slightly more Republican than other age cohorts, controlling for religion and occupation, although 189 of the 236 Union veterans in the county (80 percent) in 1880 were reportedly Republicans, with Democrats outnumbering Greenbackers two to one among the remainder.[30] Sectional origins were not significant in Hendricks — the great majority of all the voters had been born in the South or had fathers born in the South. Southern origins, less than a decade after the Civil War, did not affect the partisanship of these Hoosiers; the effect in Illinois was very small.

The interview records do not, of course, specify whether a man was pietistic or liturgical in orientation. Some oversimplification is necessary: all members of predominantly liturgical denominations must be classified as liturgicals, and all members of pietistic denominations as pietists. Obviously some men will be misclassified, but the effect of this error will be to weaken the true patterns. That is, if the hypothesis is true, most of the true liturgicals misclassified as pietists would be Democrats, and the misclassification therefore lowers the observed proportion of pietists who were Republicans. If the errors of misclassification could somehow be rectified, the estimated proportion of Republicans among pietists (already high) would be further increased and the estimated proportion of Republicans among liturgicals (already low) would be further lowered.[31]

All members of Protestant denominations were classified as pietistic with the exception of Episcopalians, German Lutherans, Old School Presbyterians, Primitive Baptists, and Anti-Missionary Baptists. Everyone else, including the handful of Jews, was classified as liturgical. Table 11.6 shows the aggregate totals by religious and party groups for the eight Illinois townships. The small number (73) of liturgical Republicans were mostly (56 percent) German Lutherans; possibly some may have actually belonged to one of the pietistic Lutheran groups. Of the 262 pietistic Democrats, a disproportionate number were farmers (56 percent versus 43 percent of other Democrats), or were born in eastern states (26 percent versus 10 percent of other Democrats). This suggests that pietistic Democrats were older men who had first been socialized into politics during the second party system and had never abandoned the Jacksonian Democracy. This hunch is partially confirmed by the age data in Hendricks County. Half the pietistic Democrats (50.6 percent) were born before 1833 and thus came of voting age before the Republican party was formed; however, almost as many pietistic Republicans (44.5 percent) had also been born before 1833.

Table 11.6 Party and Religion, Eight Illinois Townships, 1877-1878

| | Religious Grouping | | | |
	Pietistic	Not Affiliated	Liturgical	All
Republican	515	549	73	1137
Democrat	262	504	333	1099
No party, other	45	510	56	611
All	822	1563	462	2847

The Illinois returns for each religious and political group are shown by their occupational distributions in Tables 11.7 and 11.8. Bear in mind that low-status occupations probably were under-represented in the directories. Several striking patterns appear. An urban-rural split occurs on party identifications. The great majority (83 percent) of independents were nonfarmers, while Democrats were somewhat more likely to be farmers than Republicans (51 percent versus 41 percent). There was, however, no urban-rural difference between liturgicals and pietists, while nonmembers were slightly more likely to be nonfarmers. Age probably accounted for this — young men, who had not yet been converted, were leaving the farms for the nearby towns.

Among the nonfarmers (not all of whom lived in towns or cities), the Republicans were especially strong and liturgicals weak. This was the age of the Yankee mechanic, and the Republican protective tariff. To scotch one old myth,

Table 11.7 Nonfarm Occupation, by Party and Religion, Eight Illinois Townships, 1877-1878 (Read Down)

	% All	Party			Religion		
		% Rep.	% Neither	% Dem.	% Piet.	% None	% Lit.
Professional	8.5	9.6	8.9	6.8	13.4	7.3	4.6
Business	21.1	24.0	25.5	13.3	23.3	21.6	15.3
White collar	6.8	6.9	7.3	6.3	5.8	7.6	5.3
Skilled blue collar	32.7	36.0	30.4	30.9	33.8	35.2	21.4
Unskilled blue collar	8.2	5.8	7.1	12.0	3.1	8.2	16.5
Unskilled common labor	15.2	10.2	13.6	22.9	11.0	13.2	30.4
Unknown	7.5	7.5	13.2	7.8	9.6	6.9	6.5
Total	100.0	100.0	100.0	100.0	100.0	100.0	100.0
N	1717	669	506	542	447	1009	261

Table 11.8 Farm Occupation, by Party and Religion, Eight Illinois Townships, 1877-1878 (Read Down)

	% All	Party			Religion		
		% Rep.	% Neither	% Dem.	% Piet.	% None	% Lit.
Farm owners	75.2	76.0	73.3	74.9	78.9	70.5	81.5
Sons of owners	9.7	10.5	8.6	9.3	9.6	12.3	3.0
Renters & laborers	15.1	13.5	18.1	15.8	11.5	17.2	15.5
Total	100.0	100.0	100.0	100.0	100.0	100.0	100.0
N	1129	467	105	557	374	553	201
Farmers as % of all voters	39.7	41.1	17.2	50.6	44.5	35.5	43.5

blacksmiths (in Indiana) were just as religious and partisan as anyone else, though it is true that the only "naturalist" and the "free and easy" independent in Hendricks County were both blacksmiths. The pietists were especially strong among professionals and weak among unskilled labor, with just the reverse for liturgicals. The religious literature of late-nineteenth century is full of warnings that the Protestant churches had abandoned the lower classes to the "Romanists."

By removing the political independents (and nonresponders) the relative party strength among occupational groups, controlling for religion, can be discriminated. Table 11.9 shows the Republican share of the two-party vote for each occupational group by religious subgroups.

The basic pietistic-liturgical correlation with party holds true for every occupational group, with two exceptions. Among high-status businessmen, Republican liturgicals barely outnumbered Democrats. Among low-status farm renters and laborers pietistic Democrats outnumbered Republicans. The unchurched groups hovered around the 50–50 mark, except among businessmen, white col-

Table 11.9 Party Strength by Occupation and Religion, Eight Illinois Townships,
1877-1878
(Percent Republican of Two-Party Total)
(N in parentheses)

Occupation	% Pietists	% Not Affiliated	% Liturgicals	% All
Professional	75.9 (N = 58)	50.0 (34)	33.3 (9)	63.4 (101)
Business	81.4 (97)	62.8 (105)	51.5 (31)	69.1 (233)
White collar	60.0 (25)	61.9 (42)	38.4 (13)	57.5 (80)
Skilled blue collar	73.1 (145)	55.6 (218)	30.4 (46)	58.9 (409)
Unskilled	65.0 (60)	48.0 (123)	8.0 (113)	36.1 (296)
Unknown	65.9 (38)	52.6 (38)	31.2 (16)	54.4 (92)
All nonfarm	72.9 (423)	55.1 (560)	22.8 (228)	55.3 (1211)
Farm owner	59.1 (279)	49.1 (348)	13.1 (145)	46.1 (772)
Sons of owner	70.6 (34)	41.0 (61)	0.0 (6)	48.5 (101)
Renters & laborers	42.5 (40)	52.4 (84)	7.4 (27)	41.7 (151)
All farm	58.4 (353)	48.7 (493)	11.8 (178)	45.6 (1024)
All	66.2 (776)	52.2 (1053)	18.0 (406)	50.9 (2236)

lar workers and, inexplicably, among adult sons living on their fathers' farms.
The unchurched fell midway politically between the pietists and liturgicals in
every occupation except white collar workers (but the N is small), and among
those farmer renters and laborers. (The reason here is that only 3 of 35 Republican farm laborers were pietists, in contrast to 14 of 28 renters.) Note also that
farmers were 10 points less Republican than nonfarmers (14.5 points for pietists, 6.4 points for nonmembers, 11.0 points for liturgicals). As far as age is
concerned, a random sample ($N = 314$) from Indiana gives a median age of 36 or
37 for the Republican farmers and nonfarmers, and for the Democratic nonfarmers, but a median age of 44 for Democratic farmers — indicating again the
special affinity for Jacksonian Democracy among older farmers.

The four rows in Table 11.9 representing the largest nonfarm occupational
groups, businessmen, professionals, skilled blue-collar workers, and unskilled
laborers, illustrate the complex relationship among party, religion, and occupation. (White-collar clerks, for whom the numbers are small, are somewhat exceptional.) The Republican strength in the four groups ranged from 65 to 81
percent among pietists, from 48 to 63 percent among unaffiliated, and from 8
percent to 52 percent among liturgicals. Three factors account for these patterns, and for the similar patterns in Tables 11.2 and 11.3: religion itself, occupation itself, and the joint effect (interaction) between religion and occupation.

For each occupational group taken separately, the Republican strength depended greatly on religious grouping. Pietists were 30 points more Republican
than liturgicals among businessmen, and a remarkable 57 points more Republican among the unskilled. Secondly, among men in the same religious group,
there was a wide range between the most and least Republican occupation, with
businessmen highest and unskilled lowest for each group. Among pietists, businessmen were 16 points more Republican than laborers, while among liturgicals

the businessmen were 43 points more Republican. Occupation was thus more influential among liturgicals than among pietists or the unaffiliated. Clearly religion and occupation were both "real" factors that cannot be explained away by statistical controls. The independent effects of religion and occupation added together so that pietistic businessmen had the extra Republicanism of pietists added to the extra Republicanism of businessmen, and were amazing 73 points more Republican than unskilled liturgicals. This immense range between two polar groups living in the same community was far greater than the average differences in voting patterns between different communities. Considering the farmers too, the 2236 voters in the eight townships who expressed a political preference were almost exactly divided between the parties (50.9 percent Republican versus 49.1 percent Democratic). In aggregate terms, therefore, the townships hovered around 50–50, yet the constituent groups typically hovered around the 75–25 level (except for the nonaffiliated group which was 50–50). Any analysis of the social correlates of partisanship that depends upon aggregate election returns will miss the most important dimension of midwestern voting patterns, the deep internal conflicts, because the votes of the various religions and occupational groups were usually mixed together in aggregate data.

The factors of religion and occupation interacted so that the liturgical concentrated in the heavily Democratic low-status occupations (see Table 11.7). Thus the nonfarmer pietists, taken all together, were 50 points more Republican than the liturgicals (72.9 versus 22.8), which is larger than the spread in any occupation group except unskilled. It is impossible to explain the reasons for this interaction, but the theological and social group functions of religion were factors, along with positive antiliturgical job discrimination. If the interaction had not existed and the pietists, liturgicals, and unaffiliated had been proportionately represented in each occupation, then the pietists would have been 71.5 percent Republican instead of 72.9 percent, the unaffiliated would have been 54.8 percent instead of 55.3 percent, and the liturgicals would have been 29.8 percent instead of 22.8 percent for a range of 71.5–29.8 = 42 points instead of 72.9–22.8 = 50 points.[32] Thus, different occupational profiles increased the political difference between pietists and liturgicals from 42 to 50 points, an increase of 20 percent. *Playing wt numbers; no significance*

Conversely, if the religious profile of each occupational group had been identical, the businessmen would have been 67.1 percent Republican instead of 69.1 percent, and the unskilled would have been 46.4 percent Republican instead of 36.1 percent. Thus the different religious profiles of the occupations stretched the difference between businessmen and unskilled from 67.1–46.4 = 21 points to 69.1–36.1 = 33 points, an increase of over 50 percent. Hence, the religious distribution produced relatively greater effects than the occupational distribution did or, in other words, religion exacerbated the political tension between high and low status occupations.

The 21 point spread between the Republicanism of businessmen and unskilled laborers which remains after correction for the lopsided religious distribution has been made stands in need of further explanation. Unfortunately, no profound insights can be squeezed out of the tables. A variety of hypotheses could explain the result. Perhaps the Republicans were simply the party of the classes and the Democrats the party of the masses. This may be true, but it merely restates the results and does not explain when, how, and why such a difference emerged. If the pattern first emerged after the Civil War, it could be best explained in terms of Reconstruction race and economic policies and, perhaps, the effects of the depression of 1873–1877. If the pattern first emerged during the war, emancipation policies, conscription, economic conditions and Republican appeals to patriotism would seem to offer the best leads. If the patterns first emerged before the war, a different set of explanations is required. Until the dating problem is solved, the occupational differences cannot be explained.

New data is also needed to settle conclusively whether the relationships among religion, occupation and party can be generalized for the entire country. Clearly a different framework of analysis is necessary to explain the racially-oriented patterns of partisanship in the postwar South. The political history of the northern states was relatively uniform in the 1850s, 1860s, and early 1870s, but the East differed sharply from the Midwest by its more industrialized occupational profile and the tendency in some denominations (Congregationalists, Quaker, Presbyterian) for liturgical elements to be stronger than they were in the Midwest. Congregationalists in New England in the 1850s, for example, were less committed to temperance and antislavery than their counterparts in the Midwest.[33] The tentative conclusion is that the strong links among religion, occupation and politics that existed in Illinois and Indiana were typical of the Midwest, and perhaps the Northeast too, but not the South.

NOTES

[1] James Bryce, *The American Commonwealth* (New York, 1894), vol. 2, pp. 37; cf. Seymour M. Lipset, "Religion and Politics in American History," in Earl Raab (ed.), *Religious Conflict in America* (Garden City, 1964), p. 72. The author is indebted to George Shockey for coding the Illinois data analyzed in Tables 11.5–11.9.

[2] Although Frederick Jackson Turner and several of his students were aware of the ethnic basis of partisanship, recent interest dates from Samuel Lubell, *The Future of American Politics* (New York, 1952), and Samuel P. Hays, "History as Human Behavior," *Iowa Journal of History*, vol. 58 (1960) pp. 193–206. See Richard Jensen, "American Election Analysis: A Case History of Methodological Innovation and Diffusion," in Seymour Martin Lipset (ed.), *Politics and the Social Sciences* (New York, 1969), pp. 226–243.

[3] Only men listed as Republicans or Democrats were tabulated in Tables 11.1, 11.2, 11.3, and 11.5, because the Illinois directories sometimes neglected to ask party identification. The nonpartisans are examined in detail later. Although Geneseo had a population of just 3000, only one-sixth of the inhabitants of Illinois and Indiana lived in larger cities.

[4] The directories, not to be confused with "mugbooks" that charged for inserting laudatory biographies, were: *The People's Guide: A Business, Political and Religious Directory of Hendricks Co., Indiana* (Indianapolis, 1874); *The History of Henry County, Illinois, Its Taxpayers and Voters* (Chicago, 1877); *The History of Logan County, Illinois* (Chicago, 1878); *The Past and Present of Rock Island County, Illinois* (Chicago, 1877); and *The Voters and Taxpayers of Bureau County, Illinois* (Chicago, 1876). At least a dozen more of these directories exist for Illinois and Indiana. Cf. Ronald P. Formisano, "Analyzing American Voting, 1830–1860: Methods," *Historical Methods Newsletter*, vol. 2 (March 1969), pp. 1–12.

[5] See Frederick Luebke, *Immigrants and Politics: The Germans of Nebraska, 1880–1900* (Lincoln, 1969) for an excellent discussion.

[6] Donald G. Mathews, "The Methodist Schism of 1844 and the Polarization of Antislavery Sentiment," *Mid-America* vol. 51 (1968), pp. 3–23.

[7] Anti-Catholicism was widespread among Protestants. Most Catholics were Democrats, but so too were most anti-Catholic German Lutherans and Southern Baptists. Thus the political overtones of anti-Catholicism were muted; see Clifton J. Phillips, *Indiana in Transition: 1880–1920* (Indianapolis, 1968), p. 463; Paul Kleppner, *The Cross of Culture: A Social Analysis of Midwestern Politics, 1850–1900* (New York, 1970), pp. 103–129, analyzes the importance of anti-Catholicism in Ohio and Wisconsin.

8 Robert Kelley, *The Transatlantic Persuasion* (New York, 1969), is especially interesting on Cleveland. Woodrow Wilson was another good example.

9 The few studies of nineteenth-century pietistic-liturgical conflicts are Winthrop Hudson, *Religion in America* (New York, 1965); Timothy Smith, *Revivalism and Social Reform* (New York, 1957); H. Shelton Smith, Robert T. Handy, and Lefferts A. Loetscher (eds.), *American Christianity* (New York, 1963), especially vol. 2, chs. 12, 13, 15, 18; and Frank S. Mead, *Handbook of Denominations* (New York, 1965); statistical returns appear in H. K. Carroll, *The Religious Forces of the United States* (New York, 1896).

10 See Joel Silbey, *The Transformation of American Politics, 1840–1860* (Englewood Cliffs, N.J., 1967). On the state level, see Floyd Streeter, *Political Parties in Michigan: 1837–1860* (Lansing, 1918); Arthur C. Cole, *The Civil War Era, 1850–1873* (Springfield, Ill., 1919); and Emma Lou Thornbrough, *Indiana in the Civil War Era* (Indianapolis, 1965).

11 John P. Irish, former Democratic state chairman, quoted in Des Moines *Iowa State Register*, July 12, 1882.

12 *Twenty-Ninth Annual Convention, Diocese of Iowa* (Davenport, 1882), pp. 56–57.

13 Anton Walburg, *The Question of Nationality* (Cincinnati, 1889), quoted in Robert Cross (ed.), *The Church and the City* (Indianapolis, 1967), p. 118.

14 *Lutheran Witness*, vol. 7 (Feb. 7, 1889), p. 131.

15 For details of the temperance crusades, see Charles E. Canup, "The Temperance Movement in Indiana," *Indiana Magazine of History*, vol. 16 (1920), pp. 112–151; Ernest Bogart and Charles Thompson, *The Industrial State: 1870–1893* (Springfield, Ill., 1920), pp. 42–50, 139–147; and for dry detail, *The Standard Encyclopedia of the Alcohol Problem* (Westerville, Ohio, 1924–1930); for party platforms, see *Cyclopedia of Temperance and Prohibition* (New York, 1891), pp. 152–153, 592–593.

16 From 1895 speech in Indiana Senate by John Kern (Bryan's running mate in 1908, and later majority leader in the United States Senate), in Claude Bowers, *The Life of John Worth Kern* (Indianapolis, 1918), p. 104.

17 *Cyclopedia of Temperance*, p. 426.

18 *Ibid.*, p. 494.

19 See Henry E. Jacobs and John Haas, *The Lutheran Encyclopedia* (New York, 1899), p. 395.

20 *Voice*, Sept. 27, 1888 (this was the Prohibition party newspaper); see issues of Sept. 6, 27, Oct. 4, 25, 1888; *Cyclopedia of Temperance*, p. 186; and *One Hundred Years of Temperance* (New York, 1886), pp. 96, 98, 344, 351, 414, 423, for details of third-party activity among Methodist, United Presbyterian, United Bretheran, Church of God, Quaker, Swedish Baptist, Free Will Baptist, and Free Methodist clergy. In 1889 one pietistic Ohio Lutheran synod endorsed the Prohibitionist nominee for governor. *Lutheran Witness*, vol. 8 (Nov. 21, 1889), p. 93.

21 Election returns and ethnic details based on the *Iowa Census of 1885* (Des Moines, 1885) and the Dubuque *Herald*.

22 See Richard Jensen, *The Winning of the Midwest: Social and Political Conflict, 1888–1896* (Chicago, 1971) for details.

23 Robert Doherty, "Social Bases for the Presbyterian Schism of 1837–1838," *Journal of Social History*, vol. 2 (1968), pp. 69–79.

24 Seymour Martin Lipset, *The First New Nation* (New York, 1963), p. 185; Lipset has a valuable chapter on the importance of religion in the nineteenth century.

25 Springfield *Illinois State Register*, Oct. 25, 1876, quoted in Bogart and Thompson, *Industrial State*, pp. 118–119.

26 Indianapolis *Sentinel*, Oct. 18, 1888.

27 Lincoln city, Elkhart, Sheridan, and Chester townships, Logan County, Illinois; Black Hawk, Buffalo, Prairie, Port Byron and Rural townships, Rock Island County, Illinois; Liberty, Lincoln, Marion, Middle, Union and Washington townships, Hendricks County, Indiana. See note 4 for list of sources.

28 Suppose half the Presbyterians had been pietistic New School members and had voted 90 percent Republican, while the other half had been liturgical Old School members and had voted only 40 percent Republican. Then about 65 percent of all the Presbyterians would be Republican, or about the same as the actual results in Tables 11.1 and 11.4.

29 See John F. Cady, *The Origin and Development of the Missionary Baptist Church in Indiana* (Berne, Ind., 1942).

30 "The number of Ex-Union Soldiers in Indiana and their Politics in 1880," manuscript poll in Benjamin Harrison Papers, Library of Congress (series 14, reel 143 of the microfilm edition).

31 The proportion of Republicans among pietists would be mistakenly exaggerated only if the true liturgicals misclassified as pietists were more than 80 or 90 percent Republican, an extremely unlikely situation. Conversely the proportion of Democrats among liturgicals would be mistakenly high only if the true pietists misclassified as liturgicals were nearly

100 percent Democrats, an equally implausible situation.

[32] The first column of Table 11.7 shows the occupational profile of all 1717 nonfarmers; the last three columns show the profile for each religious group. If the occupational profile for each religious group had been identical, 8.5 percent of the pietists, nonmembers, and liturgicals would be professionals, of whom 75.9 percent, 50.0 percent and 33.3 percent, respectively, would be Republicans (according to the first row of Table 11.9). Arithmetically, the proportion of pietists who would then be Republicans is: $8.5\% \times 75.9\% + 21.1\% \times 81.4\% + \ldots + 7.5\% \times 65.9\% = 71.5\%$. This procedure, called "standardization," was repeated for each religious group, and a similar standardization by religion was computed for each occupational group.

[33] Charles C. Cole, *The Social Ideas of the Northern Evangelists: 1826–1860* (New York, 1954), pp. 196–197; Richard R. Wescott, "A History of Maine Politics 1840–1856: The Formation of the Republican Party" (Ph.D. dissertation, Univ. of Maine, 1966), pp. 13–14; Whitney R. Cross, *The Burned-Over District* (Ithaca, 1950), pp. 222–223; John Niven, *Connecticut for the Union* (New Haven, 1965), p. 7; Lewis Vander Velde, *The Presbyterian Churches and the Federal Union 1861–1869* (Cambridge, 1932) pp. 62–63; Gilbert H. Barnes, *The Antislavery Impulse, 1830–1844* (New York, 1933), pp. 91, 242 n.10.

The Political Revolution of the 1890s:

A Behavioral Interpretation

Paul Kleppner

12

The voting realignment of 1893–1896 ended some thirty years of political stalemate. In this essay, originally presented before the convention of the Midwest Political Science Association in 1968, Paul Kleppner analyzes "the social bases of midwestern politics," 1860–1892, as well as "the political revolution of the 1890s." He delineates differences between: (1) the religious perspectives of groups committed to one or the other major party through 1892; and (2) voter shifts in the midterm elections of 1894 and the presidential election of 1896. Particularly noteworthy are his discussions of the continued importance of cultural issues during the political realignment of the 1890s and the remarkable partisan shifts of mutually hostile cultural groups in 1896. Professor Kleppner's book, *The Cross of Culture: A Social Analysis of Midwestern Politics, 1850–1900* (New York, 1970), elaborates on the points made in this paper. Professor Kleppner teaches at Northern Illinois University.

Political historians have consistently displayed a unique fascination with the quadrennial contests for the American presidency. In monographs, articles, and survey texts, they devote their energies to an explanation of the results of these elections. These explanations, unfortunately, suffer from three major types of inadequacies.

First, historians have rarely attempted to assess the relationship between a particular election and those which preceded and followed it. They have focused on the episodic, the dramatic, but they have failed to locate a particular set of election results in a broader time series of data. From this shortcoming have come some ingenious explanations. For example, political historians have attempted to explain the adverse impact of the 1884 Blaine candidacy, when, in fact, Blaine ran a stronger race than the Republican presidential candidates who preceded or followed him. By using that dimension of analysis which is

SOURCE: Reprinted with permission of the author. The table is reprinted with permission of The Macmillan Company from *The Cross of Culture* by Paul Kleppner. Copyright © 1970 by The Free Press, a Division of The Macmillan Company.

uniquely the historian's, analysis over time, political history can obviate this shortcoming and can discern those elections in which major changes in the balance of political forces have occurred.

Second, political historians have displayed little interest in systematically determining the social bases of support of the contesting parties. All too frequently, they have accepted as factual, descriptions of social support emanating from partisan contemporaries. Thus, since Carl Schurz insisted that German voters were opposed to slavery, political historians have described the shift of the German vote to the Republicans in 1860. Or, since farmers somehow appeared to have been "conservative," it has been assumed that they provided a solid phalanx of support for the "conservative" Republican party in the 1870s and 1880s. No basis in fact exists for either of these claims. A systematic comparison of election and demographic data can provide historians with solid answers to factual questions concerning the social bases of political support. Only when these low-level types of questions have been answered is it possible to generate the more useful analytical questions.

Third, political historians have used inadequate models of explanation. Indeed rarely have they made their design of proof explicit. But there is a common pattern of implicit assumptions which permeates most historical explanations. Underlying these explanations is the notion that the stands taken by parties on public issues somehow or another serve as determinants of popular voting behavior. Thus, when the party of "tariff reform" wins over that of "tariff protection," historians explain the result in terms of public receptivity to one of these divergent tariff positions. The explanation assumes that the voter perceives the relationship between his own economic position and the tariff; that the voter further perceives the relationship between his tariff attitude and party positions on that question; and that the voter minimizes all other factors and makes his decision on the basis of these perceived relationships. In short the explanation assumes that the voter translates a policy belief into a partisan selection. This is an adequate explanation of the behavior of the highly issue-oriented voter. When a voter is aware of an issue or has an opinion about it, when that issue arouses at least a minimal intensity of feeling, and when he perceives that one party represents his position better than others, he is likely to react in this way. But these are highly specific conditions which must be present in order to elicit an issue-oriented response. There is no reason to assume, as historians generally have, that such conditions are always and everywhere satisfied.

The combined impact of these shortcomings has been to produce a grossly inadequate view of the politics of the 1890s. Accepting the notion that a "dramatic" election must somehow be a "significant" one, historians have seen the 1896 contest as a political turning point. Its nomination of William Jennings Bryan, the admixture of Jacksonian Democrat and Populist yeoman, and its espousal of free silver placed the Democratic party squarely on the side of "the people" in a battle against the very personification of the business interests, the political puppet of Mark Hanna, William McKinley. But as a result of a combination of manipulation, corruption, and coercion, "the people" lost and McKinley was elected to the Presidency.

Imbedded in this view of the 1890s are all of the shortcomings which characterize historical political analysis generally. Failure to view the 1896 results in the context of a longer time series of data obscures the changes in voting behavior which had taken place prior to that election. The failure to systematically describe the social bases of support prior to and after the 1890s makes it impossible to determine *who*, i.e., what social groups, were responsible for the political change. Focusing on free silver as a substantive economic issue overlooks the broader, noneconomic implications of the ideology.

Rather than concentrating further on the negative aspects of past analyses, I want to suggest here an alternative hypothesis. This hypothesis derives from a research design which explicitly attempted to overcome the weaknesses of the traditional approach. The design borrows heavily from work in political science, political sociology, and social psychology. It attempts to combine a quantitative analysis of election and demographic data, in time series, with the use of standard historical sources. Specifically, I have analyzed county-level voting and demographic data for five states, Illinois, Indiana, Michigan, Ohio, and Wisconsin, from 1848 through 1936, and minor civil division data for three states, Michigan, Ohio, and Wisconsin, for over 4000 voting units from 1870 to 1900. Through a systematic, multivariate analysis of these data, it is possible to describe the social bases of party support in terms of class, ethnic, and religious factors. It is possible, too, to determine *when* political realignment began and which groups were responsible for it.

Between 1860 and 1892 there were no persisting changes in the social bases of midwestern politics. During the three decades, the gap between Republican and Democratic party percentages narrowed considerably. This was not the product of a voter group realignment, secular or otherwise, but resulted from changes in the composition of the electorate and the impact of minor parties. By 1892 those groups which were very strongly Democratic constituted a much larger proportion of the midwestern electorate than they had in 1860. Simultaneously the Republican party had lost voters to the persevering Prohibitionist party. The combined impact of these two trends was to produce a situation in which election results were much closer than they had been three decades earlier, and in which *neither* major party commanded the loyalty of a majority of the region's voters.

Even more important, the analysis of minor civil division voting and demographic data affirms that there had been no realignment of social groups over the three decades. In general, those groups which had been "very strongly" Republican in 1860 remained so in 1892, and to about the same degree. The same was true of those social groups which offered disproportionate support to the Democracy.

The distribution of political support across social groups was not a random one. The social bases of politics in this period of equilibrium has a very clear and discernible central tendency. Regardless of degree of economic prosperity, regardless of occupational category, irrespective of rural or urban place of residence, those religious groups interested in a moral reconstruction of society offered very strong support to the Republican party. These pietistic religious groups, who aimed at extending their own canons of social behavior to the broader society through prohibitory legislation and laws keeping holy the Sabbath, included native-born Methodists, Congregationalists, and Presbyterians, acting in unison with Norwegian and Swedish Lutherans, Dutch Reformed voters, and Germans who were Methodists, United Brethren, or members of the

Evangelical Association. The Democracy was a social coalition of Catholic voters, of all types of ethnicity, a small majority of German Lutherans, and voters with southern kin-group connections. For estimates of the relative degree of support given to each party see Table 12.1.

Table 12.1   Estimated Party Percentages, 1870-1892, by Ethnocultural Groups*

	Immigrants			Natives	
	Dem. %	*Rep. %*		*Dem. %*	*Rep. %*
Catholic Irish	95.0	5.0	Free Will		
Catholic Polish	95.0	5.0	Baptists	5.0	95.0
Catholic Germans	85.0	15.0	N.Y. Methodists	10.0	90.0
Catholic Dutch	85.0	15.0	Congregationalists	10.0	90.0
Catholic Bohemians	80.0	20.0	Quakers	15.0	85.0
French Canadians	75.0	25.0	Presbyterians	30.0	70.0
Old French	70.0	30.0	N.Y. Baptists	45.0	55.0
Lutheran Germans	55.0	45.0			
Reformed Germans	55.0	45.0			
Lutheran Danes	45.0	55.0	Presbyterians, southern	55.0	45.0
True Reformed Dutch	45.0	55.0	Baptists, southern	60.0	40.0
Sectarian Germans	35.0	65.0	Disciples	60.0	40.0
Reformed Dutch	30.0	70.0			
Lutheran Norwegians	30.0	70.0			
Methodist Cornish	25.0	75.0			
English Canadians	15.0	85.0			
Lutheran Swedes	10.0	90.0			
Protestant Irish	5.0	95.0			
Methodist Welsh	5.0	95.0			
Haugean Norwegians	5.0	95.0			

*Such figures should not be construed literally. An estimate, for example, of 90.0 percent Democratic does not mean that nine out of ten members of the group invariably voted Democratic; but it does mean that the group was more Democratic than one to which an estimate of 70.0 percent is assigned. For a discussion of this point and the utility of making such estimates, see Lee Benson, *The Concept of Jacksonian Democracy: New York as a Test Case* (New York: Atheneum Publishers, 1964), pp. 167, 184-185.

What cohesive force enabled a variety of disparate groups to cooperate politically within each of the major parties? More than any other, that force was a general attitude toward social control; and that attitude, in turn, derived from religious perspectives. The Republican groups shared in common the desire to re-form society, to purge it of godlessness. These were groups whose religious perspective inclined them to activism, predisposed them to reach out and try to change the world, to bring it into conformity with their conception of the good and moral society. Collectively, they could support the Republican party as the "party of great moral ideas." The groups supporting the Democracy shared in common the status of "reformee." It was their social customs and habits which the pietists sought to change. To conserve their value systems, these groups turned to the Democracy as the "party of personal liberty."

It was not the events of the 1870s or 1880s which produced these political coalitions of social groups. The functional realignment of social groups in the

1850s had been responsible for that. The political contests of the three subsequent decades served to reactivate latent party loyalties and to reinforce these partisan commitments. Whether the battle was over a Sunday-closing law, a local option measure, laws aimed at closing the parochial schools, Bible reading in the public schools, or the election of Catholics to local school boards, the effect was to perpetuate a partisan division of social groups which accorded, not with class differences or differences in ethnicity, but with differing religious perspectives.

This was the political division of social groups which marked the beginning of the 1890s. By 1900 the social bases of politics differed markedly from that which had persisted for nearly half a century. The voting shifts of the 1890s altered the political juxtaposition of social groups. Those which had been strongly Democratic prior to 1892 were less strongly so, or even mildly anti-Democratic, eight years later. Conversely, groups which had been steadfastly anti-Democratic showed a greater propensity to move in the direction of the Democracy than the party's usual supporters.

The political realignment of social groups which occurred during the 1890s was not solely the product of the Bryan-McKinley confrontation. It was produced by two clearly different types of political shift.

The first of these began under the impact of an urban-industrial depression. What began as a financial panic on Wall Street in the late spring of 1893 broadened, by the early summer, into a major depression. Indices of factory employment began to drop in June, and the rate of decline increased in July and August. During the winter of 1893–1894, unemployment hovered around three million, and was sustained at that level throughout most of the following year.

The economic downturn depressed the political fortunes of the Democracy. In the 53rd Congress, elected in 1892, 61.2 percent of the members of the House of Representatives were Democrats. In the 1894 congressional elections the Democrats lost 113 seats in the House, and were reduced to only 29.4 percent of the membership in the 54th Congress. Democratic losses in the Midwest were diffused evenly throughout the region. The 1894 Democratic regional mean vote was 9.9 percentage points below its 1892 level, and 6.1 percentage points lower than the previous nadir in 1872.

As the spatial distribution of the Democratic losses implies, the party suffered declines among all types of social groups. Regardless of ethnic group membership or religious orientation, irrespective of place of residence, type of occupation, or degree of economic prosperity, voters reacted negatively to the "party of hard times."

This was the political context in which Bryan and McKinley contested for the Presidency in 1896. Bryan was the standard-bearer of a party which had already been reduced to a minority position, and McKinley was the nominee of the party which had benefited from the negative reactions of voters to the "party of depression." But the 1896 voter movement was not a continuation of that which characterized the 1894 elections. The relevant first difference correlations show a strong negative relationship.

Midwestern Democratic percentage strength in 1896 increased over the disastrously low levels of 1894. The party's regional mean rose from 37.0 percent to 43.6 percent. But the spatial distribution of the Democratic gains displays a totally unexpected pattern. The gains came in areas which had been traditionally anti-Democratic. In Michigan, for example, the most pronounced Democratic gains, 21.6 and 15.5 percentage points, came in the Republican strongholds in the Old Stock and Dutch counties. In Ohio the Democracy registered its best gains in the counties which constituted bastions of Republicanism; they gained 15.7 percentage points on the Western Reserve, and 14.4 percentage points in the counties of the Ohio Land Company Purchase. At the same time Bryan's Democracy continued to lose support in areas populated by normally strong Democratic voter groups. Even the steadfast who had resisted the 1893–1894 movement shifted away from the "new Democracy."

The 1896 voter movement was a bipolar one. One set of social groups moved towards Bryan's Democracy; and another moved away from the Democracy. That observation is not very arresting in itself, but it becomes so when one realizes that the movement was precisely what would not have been expected on the basis of a knowledge of partisan identifications. The groups reacting most negatively to Bryan were precisely the ones which had been consistently loyal to the Democracy, the party of "personal liberty," for half a century; and the groups offering new support to Bryan were the ones which had been most strongly anti-Democratic. Expressed in specific terms, those groups which offered lower levels of support to the Democrats in 1896 than they had in either 1892 or 1894 included German Lutherans and Catholics of all ethnic varieties, except the Irish. Bryan drew greater support than any nineteenth-century Democratic candidate had among native Methodists, Norwegian and Swedish Lutherans, Dutch Reformed voters, and German Evangelicals. This pattern of voter movement persists even when place of residence, size of urban place, type of occupation, degree of economic prosperity, and region of state are held constant.

Contrary to the usual "explanations," the outcome of the 1896 election cannot be understood in terms of conflicting class, or economic, identifications among voter groups. Bryan's campaign strategy and rhetoric were designed to unite the "toiling masses," farmers and urban workers, in a political coalition against the Republicans. However well conceived, this attempt to attract workers and farmers as economic groups, to produce a class polarization in politics, failed.

The political configuration which Bryan envisaged did not involve an extension of the old social bases of political action, but the creation of an entirely new one. Late nineteenth-century midwestern partisan identifications were not rooted in economic class identifications. Voting behavior was not significantly determined by differences in relative degrees of economic prosperity. To polarize voting behavior along economic lines required that large numbers of voters not only accept a new set of priorities, one which placed economic considerations above ethnic and religious ones, but that they structure entirely new political perspectives. Essentially Bryan was asking Democrats to view their party not as a preserver of their religious value system, not in the way in which they had seen it since the 1850s, but as a vehicle through which they could implement class objectives. His aim was to orient traditional Democrats to a pattern of values and a basis of party identifications which was specifically in conflict with their time-honored political perspective and its attendant values and definitions. In formal terms such rhetoric was disruptive rather than reactivating.

Instead of polarizing politics along class lines, the Bryan-McKinley confrontation elicited a voter response along cultural lines, a response which cut across long-standing partisan identifications. While depression and unemployment had shaken the loyalty of large numbers of Democratic voters in 1893 and 1894, it had least affected the partisanship and resolve of German Lutheran and Catholic voters. As long as the Democracy remained a political vehicle through which to defend their religious values, these groups remained committed. It was only when they perceived that the Democracy had ceased to fulfill that function, when they perceived that it was no longer the defender of "personal liberty" against the encroachments of imperialistic pietism, that they broke away from their political allegiance, rejected the "Democracy of Bryan," and turned to the Republicanism of McKinley.

Any realistic model designed to explain the results of the 1896 election must take into account three significant findings. First, voter groups which had been anti-Democratic over fifty years offered greater than usual support to Bryan. Second, usually strong Democratic voter groups gave lower levels of support to Bryan than they had to earlier Democratic candidates. Third, these usually Democratic voter groups opted, not for a third party or nonvoting, but for the Republicanism of William McKinley.

Partially these findings can be explained by the fact that in 1896 the two major parties each projected an image which was at variance with its historical role. In the hands of William Jennings Bryan the Democracy was not the "traditional Democracy," not the party of the "saloon interests," and the Catholics, but a vehicle through which those groups interested in a moral reconstitution of society could pursue their goals. The Republican party of McKinley was not the agency of rabid evangelical Protestantism that it had been for the temperance, sabbatarian, and abolitionist crusaders of the 1850s; instead, it was an integrative mechanism whose leaders overtly and primarily sought to minimize latent cultural animosities among its subcoalitional elements in order to broaden its social base of support. To a major extent these "new departures" mirrored the political and social backgrounds and commitments of each party's standard bearer.

Bryan had been born and raised in Salem, in Marion County, Illinois. His perspectives, especially his religious outlook, were rooted in this small-town evangelical Protestant background. That religious perspective was one which focused on the integral connection between *right belief* and *right behavior*. The Christian did not compartmentalize his behavior, he did not demarcate between the secular and the spiritual; rather he evaluated all activities in terms of their consonance with God's maxims.

From the blending of the ultraenthusiastic emotionalism of the Methodist with the Calvinistic doctrine of the natural depravity of man, Bryan's religious perspective attained social relevance. He viewed "progress" as the establishment of a truly religious relationship between God and man. Society would steadily march toward "progress" were it not for man's depravity and the plethora of the devil's temptations in the world about him. The Christian's duty was to abolish these temptations, to create a "safe" atmosphere for the religious and the potentially religious. This was not a passive orientation which accepted the world as it was, but an imperialistic one which sought to change man's behavior, to bring it into conformity with religiously sanctioned norms. It was not that those whose behavior was to be circumscribed would in this way be "saved" but that a pure and moralistic social atmosphere would be created in which the righteous would not be lead astray from the path of "progress." Bryan's religious zeal did not concern itself with uplifting the downtrodden but with safeguarding and exacting the righteous.

This type of perspective, with its emphasis of the "oneness" of all human activity, did not make it possible for Bryan to distinguish readily between "political" and "religious" activities. To him these were not two unrelated spheres of endeavor, but two aspects of the same battle, the battle between good and evil, between the Christian and the sources of temptation which abounded in his social environment. Thus because he did not compartmentalize his behavior, because his religious perspective led him to see the connection between the power of government and the purification of society, Bryan could enter a political battle with the same righteous self-assurance, the same rhetoric, and the same goals, as when he did battle for the literal integrity of Holy Writ against the assaults of the evolutionists. "From the fight against gold to the fight against the ape," there had been no change in Bryan's religious perspective.

Bryan's commitment to the pietistic canons of right behavior, his perception of evil in all that did not contribute to their implementation, and his view of the essential "oneness" between his religious values and his political goals, stood in sharp contrast to the political attitudes of William McKinley. While of Scotch-Irish ancestry and a communicant in the Methodist Episcopal Church, McKinley did not perceive the same type of inexorable relationship between religious attitudes and secular activity that characterized Bryan's perspective. Bryan's experience had reinforced his religious values; McKinley's exerted a cross-pressuring influence.

In Salem, Illinois, a community whose population was a mixture of Baptists, Methodists, and Cumberland Presbyterians who shared a common commitment to evangelical Protestantism and its canons of behavior, Bryan's personal religious values had found social reinforcement. McKinley spent his early years in Niles, in Trumbull county, and in Poland Village, in Mahoning County. Both of these communities were socially heterogeneous, communities in which there was no commonly shared religious outlook.

Nor did McKinley's involvement in Stark County politics reinforce his religious commitment. The county's voting population included a relatively large proportion of German Lutheran, and German and Irish Catholic voters. As McKinley learned from his successful race for the office of prosecuting attorney in 1869, and his unsuccessful reelection bid in 1871, political success for a Republican in the county depended upon preventing the coalescence of Catholic and German Lutheran voters into a solid voting bloc. This in turn meant that Republican politicians had to minimize the pietistic goals with which the party was publicly identified. The party had to be used not as an ideologically instrumental mechanism through which pietistic groups could seek the implementation of their norms of right behavior, but as an integrative one enlisting the support of a broad range of social groups.

That pietistic voters frequently perceived themselves to be Bryan's "kind of people," while religious traditionalists rejected him for McKinley's Republicanism, can only be partially explained by the social and political backgrounds of the candidates, the perspectives to which these gave rise, and the personal elements, but they were relatively less important in evoking a voter response than other types of considerations.

That Bryan could draw new support from normally anti-Democratic voter groups was due not merely to his personal image but to the functional affinity and organizational relationships which existed between the Bryan movement and older norm-oriented movements. That movement of former Prohibition party voters and the "1892 Populists" into the Democratic ranks accounted for the major portion of the new strength which Bryan brought to the Democracy. These were voters who shared a common pietistic religious perspective, and who sought to implement their religious values through political action. Precisely because they had perceived relatively little hope of realizing their goals through the major political parties, they had earlier rejected them and turned instead to minor party organization. In 1896 the Bryan candidacy gave them new hope. They turned to Bryan because they saw in his evangelism their best hope for reconstituting the social order to conform to the norms which their religious commitments sanctified. They were responsive to Bryan because he, as they, did not seek to structure a *new* set of social values, but to restore an older one. He, as they, sought the restoration of the moral society.

In 1896 there was more than inchoate affinity among "reform" groups. Organizations and leaders who had endorsed the "cold water" cause and had long been identified with it came to the support of Bryan's Democracy. Of greater consequence in the actual mobilization of voters was the fusion not only between the Democrats and Populists, but at the county level between Democrats and Prohibitionists. This enabled Prohibition party voters who were attracted to Bryan to cast a straight ticket for him and at the same time to give support to their own local leaders. It also meant that the local Prohibitionists could cooperate with the Democrats in enlisting support for Bryan without weakening their own local party structure.

While later historians have concentrated on the economic nature of the Bryan crusade, his contemporary supporters showed a greater interest in its moral aspects. Populist and Prohibition papers in the Midwest, which supported Bryan, devoted more of their symbolism to the crusade for moral reform than they did to a discussion of economics. In depicting Bryan's crusade, they identified him with pietistic virtues; they denounced the "saloon power," with which they claimed McKinley was identified; and they argued that Bryan's election would guarantee the advent of "a grander civilization," of the "moral society." The party which they had characterized in 1894 as the "party of corruption," and the "Catholic party," in 1896 they hailed as the "party of piety."

While enlisting new supporters from the ranks of the pietists, Bryan was uniquely unsuccessful in reactivating the latent partisan loyalties of normally Democratic voter groups. For over fifty years, Catholic and German Lutheran voters, religious traditionalists, had been steadfastly Democratic. This commitment was the political expression of their religious perspective. From that perspective, one which concentrated on *right belief* as opposed to *right behavior*, they did not regard as sinful those social customs which pietists, in the name of morality, sought to eradicate. The repeated conflicts between the two types of religious groups, although occurring over a variety of substantive issues, were ones between two divergent sets of religious values. Each group had to resort to the political structure of society to resolve the conflict in its favor. As the pietists sought government *action* to create the moral society, the anti-Pietists espoused government *inaction* as a means of resisting such encroachments. The personal liberty theme of the Democracy was at once an apt political expression of the religious perspective of the traditionalists and an ideology through which that perspective could be translated into a partisan commitment. In 1896 it was precisely because traditionalists perceived that the Democracy had ceased to be the "old Democracy," had ceased to be the defender of "personal liberty" and negative government, that they rejected it.

Because they were relatively more concerned with conversion than with reactivation or reinforcement of old commitments, both Bryan and his midwestern supporters deemphasized their Democratic lineage and their connections with the old Democratic ideology. The image they projected of themselves was not that of "negative government," but of a government dedicated to the use of positive action to remedy social inequalities. This was not the Democracy whose usual program was a litany of "thou shalt nots," but a Democracy espousing that very type of government which for over half a century had repelled religious traditionalists.

Democratic voters were not very likely to expose themselves to campaign propaganda emanating from Prohibition and Populist sources. It is reasonable to assume that their exposure was to partisan Democratic sources. Most of the regularly Democratic papers in the Midwest opposed Bryan in 1896. The fact that they devoted a significant proportion of their symbolism to projecting basically the same *kind* of image of Bryan as did those organs which supported him is highly important. It suggests that the old-line Democratic strategists, aware of the underlying reasons for the commitment of voter groups to their party, saw in the pro-Bryan themes much that would repel normally Democratic voters. It suggests that the very causes which led pietistic voters to respond favorably were the ones which induced religious traditionalists to reject Bryan.

When anti-Bryan Democratic papers set out to attack the candidate's free silver program, they did not concentrate on economic arguments. Instead, they simply argued that Bryan was not a "real" Democrat, and that free silver was not a Democratic doctrine. This line of attack suggests that these strategists were relatively less concerned with the appeal of free silver as an economic ideology to normally Democratic voters than they were with that of party identification. Since they aimed at defeating Bryan, they concentrated on undermining his identification *as a Democrat*. The specific line of argument which they used for that purpose is revealing. Stripped of its hyperbolic allusions, these anti-Bryan Democratic papers presented an argument with whose essence the Bryanites could have agreed. Bryan was not a Democrat, and his Democracy was not the "old Democracy," they argued, because his program would magnify the regulatory power of government. This was a violation of the "personal liberty" for which the Democratic party had always stood, it was another attempt "to regulate things . . . and to propose laws governing the habits, pursuits and beliefs of men."

The third important finding is that these normally Democratic voter groups not only rejected Bryan, but voted for McKinley. The anti-Bryan Democratic leaders, or "gold bugs" as they were normatively labeled by Bryanites, organized a separate party as a haven for "real" Democratic voters. But despite being provided with this "safe" third party haven, most of the Catholic and Lutheran German voters who abandoned Bryan's Democracy chose to cast a ballot for the Republican party. Whatever Bryan and his supporters and opponents proposed or did could not have accounted for the decision to support the Republicans. This decision was ultimately contingent upon the voter's perception of that party and its aura. In 1894 Democratic Catholic and German Lutheran voters had been the groups least likely to shift to the Republicans. When they defected in 1894 they more often than not sought a third party as a means through which to express their dissatisfaction with the Democracy while not giving a stamp of approval to the Republicans. That they did not react in the same way in 1896 suggests that their perception of the Republican party then was different than it had been in 1894.

Republican party strategists recognized the discontent of these voter groups with Bryan's candidacy and sought to recruit them to the support of McKinley. Since the 1850s the Republicans had had the support of a strong majority of pietistic voters. The strength of party identification, despite the appeals of the Bryanites, could be counted on to assure that a significant proportion of these would remain loyal. In addition, Republicans attempted to attract Catholic and German Lutheran voters. This type of coalition was possible only if the party's strategists were willing to tolerate a high degree of ideological noncongruence among its subcoalitional elements. This "price" McKinley Republicans were certainly willing to pay.

Throughout the Midwest, and probably elsewhere as well, Republican leaders employed precisely the strategy which McKinley had used successfully in earlier elections in Ohio. They avoided identification with those cultural symbols with which the party had usually identified itself. They presented to defecting Democrats an image of the party as a culturally safe vehicle through which they could express their dissatisfaction with Bryan. Democrats need not reject the Republican party as the "party of pietism." If they could not vote for it as the "party of personal liberty," they could support it as the "party of prosperity." In the hands of McKinley, the Republican party was a much different social organism than it had been in 1892. It was no longer the vehicle of pietism; but an intergrative mechanism which sought to avoid subcoalitional conflicts by minimizing cultural questions and addressing itself to a commonly shared concern with "prosperity."

Thus by examining the 1896 election in the context of a broader time series of data, by systematically determining which social groups were responsible for the political realignment, and by adopting a more realistic explanatory model, we can gain an insight into the political revolution of the 1890s that would be impossible through the traditional approach. If political history is ever to rise from the mire of subjective relativism, these are the methods and approaches which must be adopted. To produce meaningful history the practitioners of the art must abandon their time-honored tradition of "splendid isolation" from developments in other disciplines, and must frankly and overtly borrow concepts and models from political science, sociology, and social psychology. But the relationship should not be thought of as one-sided; for historians, atuned to seeing events and developments in a broad time perspective, are thereby equipped to make a meaningful contribution to the other social sciences. Indeed, whether historian, political scientist, sociologist, or psychologist, we should all see the wisdom in the maxim that to be credible any explanation of human behavior must be a *historical* explanation.

Voting in the Northeastern States

During the Late Nineteenth Century

Samuel T. McSeveney

13

Cultural and economic issues have influenced mass political behavior throughout the United States, but regional variations in the religious, ethnic, racial, and socioeconomic characteristics of the population have often created regional differences in popular voting behavior. Such was the case during the political realignment of the 1890s. Samuel T. McSeveney of Brooklyn College here examines various aspects of political behavior during that critical decade. He deals with differences between Republican gains in the midterm elections of 1894 and the presidential election of 1896 in Connecticut; the persistence and significance for voting patterns of Democratic factionalism in New York (a phenomenon without parallel in other states); and the nature and electoral consequences of cultural conflicts in these states and New Jersey. A slightly different version of this paper was read before the University of Wisconsin Political and Social History Conference in 1968. Professor McSeveney's book on the 1890s, *The Politics of Depression*, is forthcoming.

The dramatic Bryan-McKinley campaign has long dominated historical thinking regarding the 1890s. Some years ago, V. O. Key termed the election of 1896 "critical," but evidence points to a politically "critical period" rather than a single "critical election." The importance of this "critical period" of realignment cannot be overestimated: it ended decades of stalemate and ushered in an era of Republican dominance. Accordingly, I studied intensively the period between the onset of economic depression in 1893 and the presidential election of 1896. Concerned with the responses of voters as well as public figures to developments during this period, I worked sources of local election data (official and unofficial) and information (hard and soft) relating to the composition of the electorate in these political units, in addition to the traditional sources mined by political historians.[1]

I do not propose to summarize my research in this paper. Rather, after sketching the pre-1893 political scene, I shall deal with a number of themes

---

(specifically the successive stages in the popular shift toward the Republican party and the political roles played by factional and cultural conflict) and one sharp economic conflict that are important to my analysis of the period. In developing these themes I shall emphasize the contribution the study of local election data made to my understanding of politics during the 1890s and suggest possibilities for further exploration along these lines. My study focuses on Connecticut, New York, and New Jersey. We frequently think of the late-nineteenth-century Democracy in terms of the rural-agricultural South and Border, but these three states gave the party a base in the urban-industrial Northeast. Each of the closely contested states usually voted Democratic. No voting realignment took place in this area from 1860 through 1892. Rather the Democrats benefited from the relative growth of population groups that normally voted Democratic while the GOP suffered from the emergence of the Prohibition party, which recruited among pietistic Protestants who normally voted Republican. Embarrassed by such defections, the Republican party sometimes sought safety by moving to drier ground. This shift involved risks, for it alienated German Lutherans, many of whom voted Republican, and German Catholics, some of whom did likewise. As these remarks suggest, the basic differences between the rival parties' supporters were cultural, not economic. Though cultural conflicts in the Northeast were not as intense as those in the Midwest over the schools, foreign languages, and prohibition, they did contribute to a Democratic upswing at the end of the 1880s that seemed on the way to dissolving the long political stalemate.

This picture began to change in 1893. For the purposes of analyzing the two-step shift toward the Republicans, which involved GOP victories over first the Cleveland Democrats and then the Bryan Democrats, I shall focus on Connecticut, which held its first depression elections in 1894. As elsewhere the important midterm campaign resolved itself into a struggle between the new politics of depression and the old cultural politics. Both parties were "sound" on the money question in the Northeast: the Republicans hammered at Democratic tariff policy in assigning blame for hard times. Cleveland Democrats sought to meet these charges, but on the state and local levels hard-pressed Democratic politicians played up the cultural issues that had defined politics for decades, identifying the Republicans with anti-Catholicism (the American Protective Association in particular), prohibition, and rural dominance.

The Connecticut GOP swept to its greatest victory since 1865; Democratic percentage strength fell in towns of all sizes and characteristics. If a few Irish-Catholic towns ran counter to this trend, so did a few old-stock ones. In the towns containing the state's eleven largest cities, which had accounted for nearly one-half of the vote and 127 percent of the Democrats' plurality in 1892, the party's decline was only fractionally greater than elsewhere.[2] The Democrats fared worst in urban wards where economic and cultural issues worked against them, but even loyal Irish Catholic wards broke under the impact of the depression. A campaign that reinforced traditional identifications may have helped in the Irish wards, but it did not save the day — and it probably hurt elsewhere. The Democrats' best showing in a non-Irish ward in New Haven came in the old-stock upper income First, where neither depression nor religious strife was as important as elsewhere.

Analysis of local election data enables us to locate focal points of cultural conflict in at least two Connecticut cities: New Haven where the American Protective Association ran a slate in school board elections; and New Britain, where a series of liquor license, local, and state elections involved shifting religious and ethnic coalitions. In both cities anti-Catholic groups were stronger among some immigrants (e.g., Swedes, Britons, British-Canadians, Germans) than among old-stock Americans. Data on similar local elections in other areas undoubtedly exist, particularly in contemporary newspapers. This data should be studied. I do not contend that we can grasp the full significance of anti-Catholicism in this way, but we can broaden our understanding of its political dimensions through such analyses.

The elections of 1894 reduced the Connecticut (indeed the northeastern) Democracy to a minority party. The presidential election of 1896 submerged it under a tide of Republican votes. (Bryan's reference to "the enemy's country" was accurate enough.) Percentage shifts exceeded those of 1894 in Connecticut; they also fell into a different pattern. The Republicans gained most in rural towns, villages, and lesser cities. The National or Gold Democrats also flourished in the smaller towns.[3] The Gold Democrats are frequently referred to as urbanites, but whatever the origin of the leaders, the Connecticut rank-and-file was not. Frankly, one cannot distinguish culturally or economically between strong and weak Gold Democratic towns. Differences in local political leadership accounted for different voting patterns among otherwise similar towns.

Connecticut's major cities neither shifted as violently toward the Republicans nor supported the Gold Democrats as strongly as the rest of the state. As in 1894, Irish Catholic districts were the most loyally Democratic; unlike 1894, the Republicans (and Gold Democrats, too) fared best in upper class, old-stock wards such as New Haven's First, which housed the Yale and financial-business communities. Bryan certainly failed to win over eastern laborers, but neither did he alienate them to the degree he did "the better element," for whom the depression alone had not been reason to abandon the Democracy.

A comparison of registration and voting data reveals that the rate of participation fell somewhat from earlier elections, particularly in smaller towns. Abstaining or voting Gold Democratic can best be understood as options open to Democrats who disapproved of Bryan but could not bring themselves to vote Republican. Such halfway measures were easiest to take in noncritical areas. Thus, Gold Democratic strength was greatest in the South and Northeast. Even then, fear of Bryan prompted some to vote for McKinley, then for Gold Democratic state tickets — which generally ran ahead of the national ticket. Similarly the rate of participation declined slightly in northeastern states for which we have data, but not in the bitterly contested Middle West. I do not wish to mislead: turnout was high in the Northeast throughout this period; there was no large pool of nonparticipants waiting to be tapped. Thus, as V. O. Key pointed out, the realignment of the 1890s, unlike that of 1928, depended almost exclusively on voter shifts from one party to the other.

One final observation regarding Connecticut: in 1894, the Democrats lost popular support, but their organization remained intact; in 1896, many old-line leaders, financial contributors, and newspapers deserted Bryan. Defections hurt, particularly in smaller, old-stock towns, where the Democracy depended for leadership upon the bolting social elements. In cities, however, Irish politicians helped fill the void. They and not the veterans of assorted reform causes who flocked to Bryan were the ultimate beneficiaries of the Nebraskan's candidacy — as regulars strengthened their party position at the expense of defecting "respectables." In this connection, the comparative analysis of the composition of state and local party committees of the pre-1896 Democrats, the 1896 regular and Gold Democrats, and the post-1896 Democrats sheds light on the changing leadership of a party in flux. A few such quantitative analyses have been made; more are needed.

Insofar as basic economic and cultural issues of 1893–1896 were concerned, New York and New Jersey resembled Connecticut. At the same time, analysis of local election data revealed other factors worthy of attention. In New York, for example, Democratic factionalism (which I sorely underestimated early in my research) was politically important before the divisive Bryan campaign. With their hero safely in the White House, Cleveland Democrats renewed the factional warfare that had racked the state party before the harmony compaign of 1892. They supported the Republican candidate for the State Court of Appeals in 1893, ran an Independent Democratic gubernatorial candidate in 1894, and backed Gold Democratic national and state tickets in 1896. They also opposed party regulars in municipal elections in Brooklyn (1893, 1895) and New York City (1894). The voting base of the Cleveland Democrats in statewide contests lay in the seven counties of the metropolitan New York City area: these ranked highest in percentage strength in 1893, 1894, and 1896. Within New York City, votes of 1893 and 1894 were positively and strongly correlated: their assembly district rank-order correlation was +.734; the latter vote correlated at +.667 with the Fusion (anti-Tammany) vote for mayor the same year.[4] Though assembly district boundary shifts bar direct comparisons with 1896, analysis of maps and returns reveals that the same areas supported the Gold Democrats. Clearly, any account of New York's Gold Democrats that treats them exclusively in terms of party developments during 1896 disregards the existence of an identifiable Cleveland Democratic faction before that year.

The factional split had considerable impact in 1893: Isaac Maynard, the judicial candidate under Clevelandite attack, actually ran farther behind his running mates than they fell behind the 1892 ticket. Though the Democrats lost some ground in most rural counties, they suffered their major setbacks in Buffalo and Brooklyn, where anti-machine campaigns were waged.[5] (In cities free of such fights — Syracuse, Albany, Troy, and most importantly, New York City — the Democrats declined slightly or gained percentage strength.) In Brooklyn, other Republican candidates for state office gained most in wards where defections to Maynard's opponent ran high and the vote against the city machine even higher. In New York City, the assembly district rank-order correlation between across-the-board GOP shifts and the anti-Maynard vote was +.762. Voting data shed light on the bases of support of the Cleveland Democrats: the districts most heavily involved in the 1893 shifts were silk-stocking or middle-class, rather than working class; old-stock and/or German, rather than Irish or East European Jewish. Statewide Democrats other than Maynard had been defeated, not routed; in New York City, they remained dominant.

The following year — 1894 — the Republicans won a decisive statewide victory, almost capturing New York City, while a Fusion municipal ticket wrested the city from Tammany Hall. The Republicans' showing in New York City was impressive: unlike 1893, they gained in every district, scoring most heavily in one Tammany stronghold (the East European Jewish and German Lower East Side) and advancing even in Tammany's Irish bailiwicks. As elsewhere the politics of depression paid off in 1894; these gains were negatively correlated with those of the previous year's anti-Maynard race (—.762) and with the Independent Democratic gubernatorial vote (—.199, Kendall's tau), which was greatest in old-stock middle- and upper-class assembly districts.

The Democrats declined sharply in other cities that had been untouched by anti-machine revolts the previous year, while in Brooklyn they lost further ground. In Buffalo the election was a standoff. In Brooklyn and Buffalo the Republicans gained, if slightly, in Democratic strongholds (which had contributed least to the reform campaigns of 1893) and declined, if slightly, in the "better" neighborhoods (where the reform campaigns had had their greatest success). Thus the New York Democratic urban decline of 1893–1894 can be related to factors arising out of the depression (as elsewhere in the Northeast) and to tensions within the state party. Each deserves attention. The aforementioned urban shifts underlay the Republican upsurge in New York State. Percentage shifts in rural counties fell within a much narrower range: most or all towns in such counties moved in the same direction at about the same rate, the Republicans gaining at the expense of the Democrats and minor parties.

The Republican tide reached a temporary high-water mark in the Northeast in 1894, receding slightly in off-year elections the following year. New Jersey illustrated a common pattern in 1895: the Democrats gained slightly in districts of all descriptions as some voters who had shifted during 1893–1894 returned to traditional voting habits. New York did not fit this pattern: there the Democrats regained lost ground in the future Greater New York City, failed to improve their position in other cities, and suffered additional losses to the Republicans and Prohibitionists in most rural counties. This two-way shift differed from that in New Jersey; and for the only time during this period, metropolitan New York moved in one direction while all upstate regions moved the opposite way.

Divisive cultural conflicts, which Republican leaders had sought to avoid, contributed to this development. The New York City and Brooklyn reform coalitions had been united by their opposition to Democratic machines; they did not agree on the shape "reform" was to take. Time prevents me from discussing all their disagreements here, but I will note the central one: to pietistic Protestants "reform" meant the Sunday closing of taverns; to Germans "reform" meant freeing the Sunday flow of beer from both corrupt and "puritanical" influences. The urban reform administrations were divided on the issue; rural drys stampeded the GOP state convention into declaring for vigorous enforcement of Sunday laws. Evidence from New York City and Brooklyn points to this renewal of an old conflict as working to the local advantage of the Democrats, who, less disunited than in 1894, campaigned in behalf of "personal liberty."

I hasten to add that another pietistic crusade — which involved no conflict with the German community — worked to the net advantage of the Republicans. Methodist ministers led a protest against racetrack legislation in New Jersey during 1893. Voting shifts against racetrack legislators were marked in rural assembly districts, particularly where old-stock Methodists predominated, and were even greater in culturally homogeneous Methodist towns. This uprising was no indirect expression of depression discontent: the sole Republican pro-racetrack assemblyman (he represented Atlantic County) from the inflamed area was roundly defeated in the face of the GOP trend. Sharp shifts in rural assembly districts inflated the statewide GOP gain in 1893; one year later as broader issues came to the fore and the racetrack issue faded, the Republicans lost some ground in counties (for example, Cape May) where they had gained the previous year and the Democrats lost disastrously in Atlantic as that county moved into line with shifts in the rest of the state.[6] (Analysis of assembly district returns was essential in studying the racetrack issue: shifts occurred within assembly districts; conflicting trends within multi-district counties rendered data from such counties meaningless.)

In 1896 the Republicans more than wiped out the Democrats' modest recovery of 1895. In New York State, as two years earlier, the GOP gained most in the metropolitan area: in Queens, Richmond, Rockland, Suffolk, and Westchester counties, these percentage shifts exceeded the earlier ones; in Kings and New York counties, they did not quite match those of 1893 and 1894, respectively. Silk-stocking and middle-class assembly districts responded sharply to Bryan's candidacy, both the Republicans and Gold Democrats scoring best in such assembly districts; elsewhere in the city the shift toward the GOP was more broadly based than that toward the Gold Democrats. Still there was a positive, if weak, correlation (+.355, Kendall's tau) between Republican gains and defections to the Gold Democrats; in 1894, the correlation between Republican gains and defections to the Independent Democrats had been negative (−.199, Kendall's tau). Upstate cities did not respond as intensely to the Bryan–McKinley campaign. For the first time during the period of realignment rural areas of the state pulled apart in their voting. Eastern New York counties and towns generally moved toward the Republicans. In western New York Bryan gained percentage strength — more at the expense of the Prohibition and Populist parties than of the Republicans. Bryan's gains within the Burned-Over District, the New England settlers of which had given themselves to many earlier "reform" causes, did not sweep the region into Democratic hands — for it had long been the stronghold of New York Republicanism. Thus the final act in the Democratic decline involved further losses in the populous one-time strongholds of the party and a reversal of fortunes in the heart of Republican country. No such development occurred in New Jersey: there, only a traditionally Democratic rural area withstood the Republican storm.

In one respect my research into state politics during the depression drew a blank: I found no partisan debate regarding state economic policies during the depression on which to base an analysis; it was as if politicians regarded depression and recovery exclusively as functions of federal tariff and financial policies. Still, in New York at least, politicians dealt with one long-standing economic issue, the state canals, study of which demonstrates the potency under certain circumstances of such issues. Thwarted in the legislature, New York City mercantile interests and a variety of allies along the canals sought from the New York State Constitutional Convention of 1894 an amendment authorizing improvement of the canals. Groups from the interior of the state opposed the canals, which basically carried eastward the products of out-of-state competitors along routes supported by taxes levied on the property of New Yorkers. Republican leaders drafted a compromise amendment: viewing the constitution as an instrument to assure GOP control of the state through legislative reapportionment and other amendments, they feared that a strong canals amendment would alienate the rural hinterland on which party strength rested. (Even the People's party divided on the issue. Populists from the interior of the state disagreed with the New York City Populists, who shared with merchants the view that the canals checked the monopolistic railroads. Obviously, they also disagreed with western Populists regarding interregional transportation rates. So much for the harmony of interests among the toiling masses.)

In November 1894 Empire State voters ratified the compromise canals amendment, the legislative apportionment proposal, and the body of the revised constitution. The canals amendment fared best in mercantile and rural counties that depended on the canals, lagging elsewhere. The dispersion of county-level voting support for the canals was greater than for apportionment and the main section of the constitution.[7] Still, the compromise amendment dampened the ardor of friends and foes of the canals alike; the thrust of the apportionment article may have softened opposition to the canals amendment in the interior, and conversely, increased it in commercial counties. (The correlation between the vote on the two proposals was +.702, remarkably strong when one considers that urban and rural spokesmen had taken opposing stands on both reapportionment and the canals.)

The following year, the legislature — dividing along lines similar to those in the constitutional convention — approved a canals improvement bill, subject under the new constitution to approval by the electorate. This time the issues were clear: supporters knew the improvements involved, opponents the costs; no other questions complicated matters. Though turnout in statewide elections declined by 8.2 percent, the vote on the canals increased by 19.7 percent — and markedly polarized.[8] Support for the canals rose from 57.5 percent to 65.0 percent, but a heavy favorable shift in major cities accounted for this: pro-canals strength actually ebbed in thirty-seven of fifty-nine counties. (The correlation between the successive votes on the canals was +.646, between the Republican statewide and pro-canals vote +.179 in 1894 and −.424 in 1895.) The polarity of the second canals vote suggests that large numbers of voters believed that they recognized their interests in the canals issue as defined in 1895 and voted accordingly. Such polarity was not characteristic of partisan contests, in which policy differences were often blurred and the strong party identification of voters generally militated against sweeping shifts in party preference. (I would suggest that we pay increased attention to constitutional votes and referenda. Studies of votes on black suffrage have already appeared. Other possibilities — prohibition, woman suffrage, open housing — come to mind.)

In this talk I have sought to develop a number of themes which ran through the period of realignment in the Northeast. Obviously the deep, widespread, and (for many) enduring voting shift toward the Republicans was the central development of the 1890s. But close analysis of local election data enables us to appreciate underlying realities of the period. First, the Republicans exploited economic issues throughout the depression, but some districts shifted sharply toward the GOP in 1894, others not until 1896, and still others shifted slowly in a series of elections. Different groups perceived the issues of 1894 and 1896 in different ways. Second, Republican politicians in general (and William McKinley — the advance agent of prosperity, the candidate of the full dinner pail — in particular) sought to assure their party's success on economic issues by playing down cultural issues that had plagued it for years. They could (and did) reduce these tensions; they could not eliminate them, for the very basis of differences between the parties was cultural: each party contained cultural groups that sought to attain their goals through politics. Therefore in the final analysis the political analyst must seek to understand the cultural factors and persistent party identifications that make for continuity in political behavior as well as the factors (of whatever nature) that make for change during periods such as 1893–1896.

NOTES

[1] I am grateful to the Social Science Research Council, whose fellowships made possible the research on which this paper is based.

[2] The 1892–1894 Democratic percentage loss in towns containing the state's eleven most populous cities was 8.1 points, the Republicans' gain 7.5 points. In other towns, the respective percentage point shifts were −7.1 and +7.6. The Democratic defection ratio (i.e., percentage point loss as a percentage of percentage strength in the previous election) was 15.1 percent in the eleven major towns and 15.0 percent elsewhere.

[3] The 1894–1896 percentage point shifts in the eleven major towns were: Democratic −6.1; Republican +6.0. In other towns, the shifts were −15.0 and +12.7 points, respectively. The respective Democratic defection ratios were 13.4 percent and 37.3 percent. The National Democrats received 1.6 percent of the total vote in the eleven major towns and 3.5 percent elsewhere.

[4] The measure of rank-order correlation employed here was Kendall's tau. Unless indicated, Spearman's measure was used.

[5] Democratic percentage point losses were greater and the off-year election decline in voter turnout was smaller in Buffalo and Brooklyn than elsewhere in New York State:

Unit	Democratic Point Loss (1892–1893)	Decline in Turnout
Brooklyn	−11.1	−0.2%
Buffalo	− 8.5	−4.6%
Rest of state	− 1.8	−17.6%
New York State	− 3.2	−14.9%

[6] Analysis of a time series of election data from New Jersey makes clear that the anti-racetrack crusade produced voting patterns in 1893 unlike those in other elections during the period. Correlations among the elections of 1892, 1893, 1894, 1895, 1896, and 1900 indicate the election of 1893 to have been more weakly correlated with each of the others than any other election. Indeed the strongest correlation between the election of 1893 and another election was weaker than the weakest correlation between any other pair of elections. This held true for both the Republican and Democratic parties.

[7] The respective coefficients of variability were: .148, .105, and .111.

[8] The coefficients of variability increased from .148 in the 1894 vote to .428 in the 1895 vote.

The Republican Era,

1896–1928

Part Four

The political realignment of the 1890s was followed by an era of Republican dominance that lasted with but brief interruption until the Great Depression and New Deal. During much of this period two-party competition was virtually nonexistent in most states, the Republicans smothering their opposition in all areas but the South, where the Democrats held a monopoly of political power. (Republican strength in the South ebbed badly from the 1880s onward; the serious challenge of the Populists was turned back by the Democrats during the 1890s.) This fourth party system differed from the second and third systems in that a high level of voter turnout, characteristic of elections since the 1840s, now gave way to a lower level of popular participation. In the main, the falling off in voter turnout seems to have been a consequence of the collapse of political competition across the nation. Institutional developments may have contributed to the nationwide decline as well. The replacement of party ballots (distributed by the rival parties and listing only the slate of the distributing party), for example, by official ballots (distributed by the government and listing the candidates of all parties) deprived the political parties of a device by which their workers had regularly gotten out the vote and placed responsibility for turning out on election day upon the citizenry itself. The systematic disfranchisement of blacks in the South between 1890 and World War I further contributed to the decline in voting in that region. Significantly, not even the political realignment of the 1930s could fully restore popular participation in American elections to its 1840–1896 level.

Insofar as the fortunes of the political parties themselves during the early twentieth century are concerned, our present understanding is partial. Cultural politics, reflecting differences among ethnic, racial, and religious groups continued to be significant from the 1890s through the 1920s, but we do not know as much about some aspects of this subject as we should. The electoral behavior of the various "new" immigrant groups (i.e., those from eastern and southern

Europe) during the years before America's entry into World War I is a relatively unknown quantity. Similarly, the political behavior of women in the states that granted them the suffrage before 1920 is only partly understood.

A Democratic revival, reflected in congressional strength, began in 1906 but its grass roots origins are hazy. The Republican party was plagued by factionalism during the presidency of William Howard Taft (1909–1913), but the Democrats had begun to gain ground in the House of Representatives before 1909 and continued to do so afterward even in areas where Republican internal strife was not significant. Woodrow Wilson won the presidency in 1912 not because his Democratic party had become the nation's majority party but because Theodore Roosevelt, who ran as the candidate of the Progressive party, and Taft split the normal Republican vote. In a two-party race four years later, Wilson pieced together a coalition that narrowly won him a second term in the White House. John Shover (whose article is included here) and Michael Rogin have illuminated important aspects of Democratic strength in the 1916 presidential election in California, but much remains to be discovered regarding Wilson's popular base in other states.

The successful Democratic coalition of 1916 disintegrated during the immediate postwar years. The Republicans registered a landslide victory in the presidential election of 1920. Central to this GOP restoration — as indicated by the research of John M. Allswang on Chicago, J. Joseph Huthmacher on Massachusetts, and David Burner on the Democratic party — was the disaffection of several ethnic groups with the Wilson administration as a result of wartime government policies. The Democratic downswing persisted through the presidential election of 1924 as the party continued to be plagued by internal ethnocultural difficulties and an inability to take advantage of the factionalism besetting the Republicans.

Third parties were quite active during the Republican era. The Socialists received nearly one million votes in 1912 and again in 1920. Theodore Roosevelt polled over four million votes for the Progressive party of 1912 and Robert La Follette did likewise as the candidate of a second Progressive party twelve years later. Each of these third parties differed from the others in regard to its sources of popular support. Ethnocultural factors clearly affected third party, as well as major party, voting patterns. The Socialist party, for example, derived greater support from East European Jews and Germans than from other groups in urban, working-class districts. Though we do not yet possess analyses of the Socialist and two Progressive parties in all sections of the country, the essays included here suggest fruitful channels of inquiry into the electoral base of "reform" parties during the first quarter of the twentieth century.

The presidential election of 1928 marked the final success of the Republican party during its period of dominance. Early quantitative studies of the election suggested that even in defeat, Al Smith, the Democratic candidate, an Irish Catholic with deep roots in New York City, laid the groundwork for the subsequent success of his party by putting together a powerful ethnic coalition in urban centers of "new" immigrant population. But in the final article of this part, Jerome M. Clubb and Howard W. Allen suggest the limitations of this interpretation and place the presidential election of 1928 in a somewhat different historical perspective. Their essay underscores the significance of the Great Depression and the New Deal in the voting realignment that restored the Democracy as the nation's majority party during the 1930s.

The Changing Shape of the American Political Universe

Walter Dean Burnham

14

Most quantitative studies of popular voting behavior emphasize the partisan distribution of the vote. Walter Dean Burnham's article, however, reveals the contributions that analysis of other aspects of that behavior — voter turnout, vote drop-off and roll-off, split-ticket voting, and mean partisan swing — can make to our understanding of the operation of the American political system over time. Burnham argues convincingly that the collapse of the third-party system during the 1890s was followed by a decline in the proportion of the electorate regularly involving itself in politics and in the influence of the political parties on the voting decisions of the electorate. (No such developments had followed the breakup of the second-party system during the 1850s.) Burnham also suggests that so fundamental have been changes in American political behavior during the twentieth century that some of the findings of survey research into contemporary voting behavior may be irrelevant to the study of earlier eras. Walter Dean Burnham teaches political science at the Massachusetts Institute of Technology. He is the author of *Critical Elections and the Mainsprings of American Politics* (New York, 1970).

In the infancy of a science the use even of fairly crude methods of analysis and description can produce surprisingly large increments of knowledge if new perspectives are brought to bear upon available data. Such perspectives not infrequently require both a combination of methodologies and a critical appraisal of the limitations of each. The emergence of American voting-behavior studies over the last two decades constitutes a good case in point. Studies based on aggregate election statistics have given us invaluable insights into the nature of secular trends in the distribution of the party vote, and have also provided us with useful theory concerning such major phenomena as critical elections.[1] Survey research has made significant contributions to the understanding of motivational forces at work upon the individual voter. As it matures, it is now reaching out to grapple with problems which involve the political system as a whole.[2]

SOURCE: Reprinted with permission from *The American Political Science Review*, vol. 59 (March 1965), pp. 7–28.

Not at all surprisingly, a good deal of well-publicized conflict has arisen between aggregationists and survey researchers. The former attack the latter for their failure to recognize the limitations of an ahistorical and episodic method, and for their failure to focus their attention upon matters of genuine concern to students of politics.[3] The latter insist, on the other hand, that survey research alone can study the primary psychological and motivational building blocks out of which the political system itself is ultimately constructed. Not only are both parties to the controversy partly right, but each now seems to be becoming quite sensitive to the contributions which the other can make. As survey scholars increasingly discover that even such supposedly well-established characteristics of the American voter as his notoriously low awareness of issues can be replaced almost instantaneously under the right circumstances by an extremely pronounced sensitivity to an issue, the importance of the time dimension and factors of social context so viewed become manifest.[4] Students of aggregate voting behavior, on the other hand, are turning to the data and methods of survey research to explore the structure and characteristics of contemporary public opinion.[5] A convergence is clearly underway. One further sign of it is the construction of the first national election-data archive, now underway at the Survey Research Center of the University of Michigan.[6] The completion of this archive and the conversion of its basic data into a form suitable for machine processing should provide the material basis for a massive breakthrough in the behavioral analysis of American political history over the last century and a half.

If controversies over method accompany the development of disciplines, so too does the strong tendency of the research mainstream to bypass significant areas of potential inquiry, thus leaving many "lost worlds" in its wake. One such realm so far left very largely unexplored in the literature of American politics centers around changes and continuities in the gross size and shape of this country's active voting universe over the past century. Key, to be sure, made contributions of the greatest significance to our understanding of the changing patterns of party linkage between voters and government. Moreover, he called attention to the need for quantitative analysis of political data other than the partisan division of the vote for leading offices.[7] E. E. Schattschneider's discussion of the struggle over the scope of political conflict and his functional analysis of the American party system remain a stimulus to further research — not least in the direction of examining the aggregate characteristics of the American electorate over time.[8] Other recent studies, for example of the turnout of voters in Canada and Indiana, have added to our knowledge of contemporary patterns of mass political involvement.[9] The fact remains, however, that no systematic analysis over lengthy time periods has yet been made of the massive changes of relative size and characteristics in the American voting universe, despite their obvious relevance to an understanding of the evolving political system as a whole.

This article does not purport to be that systematic study. It is, rather, a tentative reconnaissance into the untapped wealth of a whole range of political data, undertaken in the hope of showing concretely some of the potentialities of their study. The primary objective here is the preliminary exploration of the scope of changes since the mid-nineteenth century in turnout and other criteria of voting participation, and the possible substantive implications of such changes.

There is also a second objective. The day is not far distant when a major effort will be undertaken to relate the findings of survey research to contemporary aggregate data and then to examine the aggregate data of past generations in the light of these derived relationships. Before such inquiry is undertaken, it will be a matter of some importance to ascertain whether and to what extent the basic findings of survey research about the present American electorate are actually relevant to earlier periods of our political history. Firm conclusions here as elsewhere must await much more comprehensive and detailed study. Even so, enough can be learned from the contours of the grosser data to warrant posting a few warning signs.

I

Several criteria of voting participation have been employed in this analysis: (1) estimated turnout; (2) drop-off; (3) roll-off; (4) split-ticket voting; (5) mean partisan swing. Turnout, the most indispensable of these criteria, is also unfortunately the "softest." A number of errors of estimate can arise from the necessary use of census data. For example, interpolations of estimates for intercensal years can produce significant error when abnormally large increases or decreases in population are bunched together within a few years. Estimates of the alien component in the total adult male population must also necessarily remain quite speculative for the censuses from 1880 through 1900, and are impossible to secure from published census data prior to 1870. No doubt this helps explain why students of voting-behavior research have avoided this area. But we need not reject these admittedly imprecise data altogether, because of their imperfections, when secular changes in turnout levels and variabilities from election to election are of far too great a magnitude to be reasonably discounted on the basis of estimate error.[10]

Moreover, the other criteria employed in this study not only share a very similar directional flow over time, but are directly derived from the voting statistics themselves. Free from the estimate-error problem, they are ordinarily quite consistent with the turnout data.[11] What is called "drop-off" here is the familiar pattern of decline in the total vote between presidential and succeeding off-year elections. The drop-off figures usually presented below are reciprocals of the percentage of the presidential-year total vote which is cast in the immediately following off-year election. If the total vote for the two successive elections is the same, drop-off is zero; if the total vote in the off-year election exceeds that cast in the immediately preceding presidential election, drop-off is negative. Secular increases in the amplitude of drop-off could be associated with such factors as a declining relative visibility or salience of off-year elections, or with an increasing component of active voters who are only marginally involved with the voting process as such.

"Roll-off" measures the tendency of the electorate to vote for "prestige" offices but not for lower offices on the same ballot and at the same election. If only 90 percent of those voting for the top office on the ticket also vote for the lesser statewide office receiving fewest votes at the same election, for example, the roll-off figure stands at 10 percent. Secular increases in this criterion of voting participation could be associated with such variables as a growing public indifference to elections for administrative offices which might well be made appointive, or with a growing proportion of peripheral voters in the active elec-torate; or with changes in the form of ballots. Split-ticket voting has been mea-sured rather crudely here as the difference between the highest and lowest per-centages of the two-party vote cast for either party among the array of statewide offices in any given election. Zero on this scale would correspond to abso-lute uniformity in the partisan division of the vote for all offices at the same election. The amplitude of partisan swing is computed in this study without reference to the specific partisan direction of the swing, and is derived from the mean percentage of the two-party vote cast for either party among all statewide races in the same election. Both of these latter criteria are more directly related to changes in the strength of partisan linkage between voters and government than are the others employed in this study.

Two major assumptions underlie the use of these criteria. (1) If a secular de-cline in turnout occurs, and especially if it is associated with increases in drop-off and roll-off, we may infer that the active voting universe: (a) is shrinking in size relative to the potential voting universe; and (b) is also decomposing as a relative increase in its component of peripherally involved voters occurs. Op-posite implications, of course, would be drawn from increases in turnout ac-companied by decreases in these rough indices of voter peripherality. (2) If split-ticket voting and the amplitude of partisan swings are also increasing over time, we may infer that a decline in party-oriented voting is taking place among a growing minority of voters. Reductions in these criteria would suggest a resur-gence of party-oriented voting.

A recent study by Angus Campbell tends to support the view that the above criteria are actually related to the component of marginal voters and voters with relatively weak partisan attachments in today's active electorate.[12] Campbell argues that surge and decline in voting participation and in partisan distribution of the vote result from two major factors: the entrance into the active electorate of peripherally involved voters who tend to vote disproportionately for such beneficiaries of partisan surges as President Eisenhower, and then abstain from the polls in subsequent low-stimulus elections; and the temporary movement of core voters with relatively low levels of party identification away from their nominal party allegiance, followed by their return to that allegiance in subse-quent low-stimulus elections. Campbell's study reveals that split-ticket voting in the 1956 election tended to be heavily concentrated among two groups of voters: those who voted Republican for President in 1956 and did not vote in 1958, and those who voted Republican in 1956 but Democratic in 1958 — in other words, among those with peripheral involvement in the political process itself and those with borderline partisan commitments. Moreover, roll-off — the fail-ure to vote a complete ticket in 1956 — was heavily concentrated among the nonvoters of 1958. It is also suggestive that the level of drop-off in Campbell's panel from 1956 to 1958, 23 percent, very closely approximates the level of drop-off as measured by the aggregate voting data.[13]

II

Even the crudest form of statistical analysis makes it abundantly clear that the changes which have occurred in the relative size and shape of the active electorate in this country have not only been quantitatively enormous but have followed a directional course which seems to be unique in the contemporary universe of democratic polities. In the United States these transformations over the past century have involved devolution, a dissociation from politics as such among a growing segment of the eligible electorate and an apparent deterioration of the bonds of party linkage between electorate and government. More precisely, these trends were overwhelmingly prominent between about 1900 and 1930, were only very moderately reversed following the political realignment of 1928–1936, and now seem to be increasing once again along several dimensions of analysis. Such a pattern of development is pronouncedly retrograde compared with those which have obtained almost everywhere else in the Western world during the past century.

Table 14.1   Decline and Partial Resurgence: Mean Levels of National Turnout and Drop-Off by Periods, 1848-1962*

Period (Presidential Years)	Mean Estimated Turnout	Period (Off Years)	Mean Estimated Turnout	Mean Drop-Off
	(%)		(%)	(%)
1848-1872	75.1	1850-1874	65.2	7.0
1876-1896	78.5	1878-1898	62.8	15.2
1900-1916	64.8	1902-1918	47.9	22.4
1920-1928	51.7	1922-1930	35.2	28.7
1932-1944	59.1	1934-1946	41.0	27.8
1948-1960	60.3	1950-1962	44.1	24.9

*Off-year turnout data based on total vote for congressional candidates in off years.

Probably the best-known aspect of the changing American political universe has been the long-term trend in national voter turnout: a steep decline from 1900 to about 1930, followed by a moderate resurgence since that time.[14] As the figures in Table 14.1 indicate, nationwide turnout down through 1900 was quite high by contemporary standards — comparing favorably in presidential years with recent levels of participation in Western Europe — and was also marked by very low levels of drop-off. A good deal of the precipitate decline in turnout after 1896 can, of course, be attributed to the disfranchisement of Negroes in the South and the consolidation of its one-party regime. But as Table 14.2 and Figure 14.1 both reveal, non-southern states not only shared this decline but also have current turnout rates which remain substantially below nineteenth-century levels.[15]

The persistence of mediocre rates of American voting turnout into the present political era is scarcely news. It forms so obvious and continuing a problem of our democracy that a special presidential commission has recently given it intensive study.[16] Two additional aspects of the problem, however, emerge from a perusal of the foregoing data. In the first place, it is quite apparent that the political realignment of the 1930s, while it restored two-party competition to many states outside the South, did not stimulate turnout to return in most areas to nineteenth-century levels. Even if the mere existence of competitiveness precludes such low levels of turnout as are found in the South today, or as once prevailed in the northern industrial states, it falls far short of compelling a substantially full turnout under present-day conditions. Second, drop-off on the na-

Table 14.2 Sectionalism and Participation: Mean Turnout in Southern and
Non-Southern States in Presidential Elections, 1868-1960

Period	Mean Turnout: Eleven Southern States	Period	Mean Turnout: Non-Southern States
	(%)		(%)
1868-1880	69.4	1868-1880	82.6
1884-1896	61.1	1884-1896	85.4
1900 (transition)	43.4	1900	84.1
1904-1916	29.8	1904-1916	73.6
1920-1948	24.7	1920-1932	60.6
1952-1960	38.8	1936-1960	68.0

Figure 14.1 *Patterns of Turnout: United States, 1860–1964, by Region, and
Selected Western European Nations, 1948–1961.*

tional level has shown markedly little tendency to recede in the face of increases in presidential-year turnout over the last thirty years. The component of
peripheral voters in the active electorate has apparently undergone a permanent

expansion from about one-sixth in the late nineteenth century to more than one-quarter in recent decades. If, as seems more than likely, the political regime established after 1896 was largely responsible for the marked relative decline in the active voting universe and the marked increase in peripherality among those who still occasionally voted, it is all the more remarkable that the dramatic political realignment of the 1930s has had such little effect in reversing these trends.

At least two major features of our contemporary polity, to be sure, are obviously related to the presently apparent ceiling on turnout. First, the American electoral system creates a major "double hurdle" for prospective voters which does not exist in Western Europe: the requirements associated with residence and registration, usually entailing periodic re-registration at frequent intervals, and the fact that elections are held on a normal working day in this employee society rather than on Sundays or holidays.[17] Second, it is very probably true that nineteenth-century elections were major sources of entertainment in an age unblessed by modern mass communications, so that it is more difficult for politicians to gain and keep public attention today than it was then.[18] Yet if American voters labor under the most cumbersome sets of procedural requirements in the Western world, this in itself is a datum which tends to support Schattschneider's thesis that the struggle for democracy is still being waged in the United States and that there are profound resistances within the political system itself to the adoption of needed procedural reforms.[19] Moreover, there are certain areas — such as all of Ohio outside the metropolitan countries and cities of at least 15,000 population — where no registration procedures have ever been established, but where no significant deviation from the patterns outlined here appears to exist. Finally, while it may well be true that the partial displacement by TV and other means of entertainment has inhibited expansion of the active voting universe during the past generation, it is equally true that the structure of the American voting universe — i.e., the adult population — as it exists today, was substantially formed in the period 1900–1920, *prior* to the development of such major media as the movies, radio and television.

III

As we move below the gross national level, the voting patterns discussed above stand out with far greater clarity and detail. Their divergences suggest something of the individual differences which distinguish each state subsystem from its fellows, as their uniformities indicate the universality of the broader secular trends. Five states have been selected for analysis here. During the latter part of the nineteenth century two of these, Michigan and Pennsylvania, were originally competitive states which tended to favor the Republican party. They developed solidly one-party regimes after the realignment of 1896. These regimes were overthrown in their turn and vigorous party competition was restored in the wake of the New Deal realignment. In two other states, Ohio and New York, the 1896 alignment had no such dire consequences for two-party competition on the state level. These states have also shown a somewhat different pattern of development since the 1930s than Michigan and Pennsylvania. Our fifth state is Oklahoma, where a modified one-party system is structured heavily along sectional lines and operates in a socioeconomic context unfavorable to the classic New Deal articulation of politics along ethnic-class lines of cleavage.

Michigan politics was marked from 1894 through 1930 by the virtual eclipse of a state Democratic party which had formerly contested elections on nearly equal terms with the Republicans. The inverse relationships developing between this emergent one-partyism on the one hand, and both the relative size of the active voting universe and the strength of party linkage on the other, stand out in especially bold relief.

Table 14.3 Michigan, 1854-1962: Decay and Resurgence?

Period	Mean Turnout		Mean Drop-Off	Mean Roll-Off	Mean Split Ticket Voting	Mean Partisan Swing	Mean % D of Two-Party Vote
	Pres, Years	Off Years					
	(%)	(%)	(%)	(%)	(%)	(%)	
1854-1872	84.8	78.1	7.8	0.9	0.8	3.2	43.9
1878-1892	84.9	74.9	10.7	0.8	1.6	2.2	48.0
1894-1908	84.8	68.2	22.3	1.5	5.9	4.7	39.6
1910-1918	71.4	53.0	27.2	3.0	9.8	4.1	40.4*
1920-1930	55.0	31.5	42.9	6.0	10.0	7.3	29.8
1932-1946	63.6	47.3	25.9	6.7	6.0	7.4	47.9
1948-1962	66.9	53.6	19.1	4.1	5.8	4.9	51.0

*Democratic percentage of three-party vote in 1912 and 1914.

A decisive shift away from the stable and substantially fully mobilized voting patterns of the nineteenth century occurred in Michigan after the realignment of 1896, with a lag of about a decade between that election and the onset of disruption in those patterns. The first major breakthrough of characteristics associated with twentieth-century American electorates occurred in the presidential year 1904, when the mean percentage Democratic for all statewide offices reached an unprecedented low of 35.6 and the rate of split-ticket voting jumped from almost zero to 17.1 percent. A steady progression of decline in turnout and party competition, accompanied by heavy increases in the other criteria of peripherality, continued down through 1930.

The scope of this transformation was virtually revolutionary. During the Civil War era scarcely 15 percent of Michigan's potential electorate appears to have been altogether outside the voting universe. About 7 percent could be classified as peripheral voters by Campbell's definition, and the remainder — more than three-quarters of the total — were core voters. Moreover, as the extremely low nineteenth-century level of split-ticket voting indicates, these active voters overwhelmingly cast party-line ballots. By the 1920s, less than one-third of the potential electorate were still core voters, while nearly one-quarter were peripheral and nearly one-half remained outside the political system altogether. Drop-off and roll-off increased sixfold during this period, while the amplitude of partisan swing approximately doubled and the split-ticket-voting rate increased by a factor of approximately eight to twelve.

For the most part these trends underwent a sharp reversal as party competition in Michigan was abruptly restored during the 1930s and organized in its contemporary mode in 1948. As the mean Democratic percentage of the two-party vote increased and turnout — especially in off-year elections — showed a marked relative upswing, such characteristics of marginality as drop-off, roll-off, split-ticket voting and partisan swing declined in magnitude. Yet, as the means for the 1948–1962 period demonstrate, a large gap remains to be closed before anything like the *status quo ante* can be restored. Our criteria — except, of course, for the mean percentage Democratic of the two-party vote — have returned only to the levels of the transitional period 1900–1918. As is well known, exceptionally disciplined and issue-oriented party organizations have emerged in Michigan since 1948, and elections have been intensely competitive throughout this period.[20] In view of this, the failure of turnout in recent years to return to something approaching nineteenth-century levels is all the more impressive, as is the continuing persistence of fairly high levels of drop-off, roll-off and split-ticket voting.[21]

The Michigan data have still more suggestive implications. Campbell's discussion of surge and decline in the modern context points to a cyclical process in which peripheral voters, drawn into the active voting universe only under unusual short-term stimuli, withdraw from it again when the stimuli are removed. It follows that declines in turnout are accompanied by a marked relative increase in the component of core voters in the electorate and by a closer approximation in off years to a "normal" partisan division of the vote.[22] This presumably includes a reduction in the level of split-ticket voting as well. But the precise opposite occurred as a secular process — not only in Michigan but, it would seem, universally — during the 1900–1930 era. Declines in turnout were accompanied by substantial, continuous increases in the indices of party and voter peripherality among those elements of the adult population which remained in the political universe at all. The lower the turnout during this period, the fewer of the voters still remaining who bothered to vote for the entire slate of officers in any given election. The lower the turnout in presidential years, the greater was the drop-off gap between the total vote cast in presidential and succeeding off-year elections. The lower the turnout, the greater were the incidence of split-ticket voting and the amplitude of partisan swing. Under the enormous impact of the forces which produced these declines in turnout and party competitiveness after 1896, the component of highly involved and party-oriented core voters in the active electorate fell off at a rate which more than kept pace with the progressive shrinking of that electorate's relative size. These developments necessarily imply a limitation upon the usefulness of the surge-decline model as it relates to secular movements prior to about 1934. They suggest, moreover, that the effects of the forces at work after 1896 to depress voter participation and to dislocate party linkage between voters and government were even more crushingly severe than a superficial perusal of the data would indicate.

Pennsylvania provides us with variations on the same theme. As in Michigan, the political realignment centering on 1896 eventually converted an industrializing state with a relatively slight but usually decisive Republican bias into a solidly one-party GOP bastion. To a much greater extent than in Michigan, this disintegration of the state Democratic party was accompanied by periodic outbursts of third-party ventures and plural party nominations of major candidates, down to the First World War. Thereafter, as in Michigan, the real contest between competing candidates and political tendencies passed into the Republican primary, where it usually remained until the advent of the New Deal. In both states relatively extreme declines in the rate of turnout were associated with the disappearance of effective two-party competition, and in both states these declines were closely paralleled by sharp increases in the indices of peripherality.

Table 14.4   Voting Patterns in Pennsylvania, 1876-1962: Decline and Resurgence?

Period	Mean Turnout		Mean Drop-Off	Mean Roll-Off	Mean Split Ticket Voting	Mean Partisan Swing	Mean D of Two-Party Vote
	Pres. Years	Off Years					
	(%)	(%)	(%)	(%)	(%)	(%)	
1876-1892	78.5	69.3	9.4	0.6	0.6	1.4	47.7
1894-1908	75.7	64.7	12.2	5.2	1.3	6.3	38.5
1910-1918	64.0	51.4	20.0	4.3	4.7	5.8	43.6*
1920-1930	50.4	39.5	28.0	5.2	8.9	7.1	32.8
1932-1948	61.5	51.9	14.9	2.2	1.4	6.1	49.0
1950-1962	67.5	56.3	12.2	1.8	3.1	3.3	49.3

*Combined major anti-Republican vote (Democrat, Keystone, Lincoln, Washington).

As Table 14.4 demonstrates, the parallel behavior of the Michigan and Pennsylvania electorates has also extended into the present; the now-familiar pattern of increasing turnout and party competition accompanied by marked declines in our other indices has been quite visible in the Keystone State since the advent of the New Deal. On the whole, indeed, a better approximation to the *status quo ante* has been reached in Pennsylvania than in Michigan or perhaps in most other states. But despite the intense competitiveness of its present party system, this restoration remains far from complete.

A more detailed examination of turnout and variability in turnout below the statewide level raises some questions about the direct role of immigration and

Table 14.5   Differentials in Aggregate Turnout and Variations of Turnout in Selected Pennsylvania Counties: Presidential Elections, 1876-1960*

County and Type	N	% Foreign Stock, 1920	1876-1896		1900-1916		1920-1932		1936-1960	
			Mean Turn-out	Coef. Var.	Mean Turn-out	Coef. Var.	Mean Turn-out	Coef. Var.	Mean Turn-out	Coef. Var.
		(%)	(%)	(%)	(%)	(%)	(%)		(%)	
Urban:										
Allegheny	1	56.6	71.8	6.75	56.7	2.45	43.8	10.11	68.9	5.82
Philadelphia	1	54.3	85.2	4.61	72.9	6.42	50.5	12.57	68.8	4.40
Industrial-										
Mining:	4	49.0	88.1	4.48	72.8	4.41	54.2	11.63	64.7	10.88
Rural:	8	13.5	88.5	3.12	76.4	3.63	56.0	8.09	65.2	13.20

*The coefficient of variability is a standard statistical measure; see V. O. Key, Jr., *A Primer of Statistics for Political Scientists* (New York, 1954), pp. 44-52. Since secular trends, where present, had to be taken into account, this coefficient appears abnormally low in the period 1900-1916. During this period many counties registered a straight-line decline in turnout from one election to the next.

woman suffrage in depressing voter participation. It also uncovers a significant transposition of relative voter involvement in rural areas and urban centers since about 1930.

It is frequently argued that declines in participation after the turn of the century were largely the product of massive immigration from Europe and of the advent of woman suffrage, both of which added very large and initially poorly socialized elements to the potential electorate.[23] There is no question that these were influential factors. The data in Table 14.5 indicate, for example, that down until the Great Depression turnout was consistently higher and much less subject to variation in rural counties with relatively insignificant foreign-stock populations than in either the industrial-mining or metropolitan counties.

Yet two other aspects of these data should also be noted. First, the pattern of turnout decline from the 1876–1896 period to the 1900–1916 period was quite uniform among all categories of counties, though the rank order of their turnouts remained largely unchanged. It can be inferred from this that, while immigration probably played a major role in the evolution of Pennsylvania's political system as a whole, it had no visible direct effect upon the secular decline in rural voting participation. Broader systemic factors, including but transcending the factor of immigration, seem clearly to have been at work. Second, a very substantial fraction of the total decline in turnout from the 1870s to the 1920s — in some rural native-stock counties more than half — occurred *before* women were given the vote. Moreover, post-1950 turnout levels in Pennsylvania, and apparently in most other non-southern states, have been at least as high as in the decade immediately preceding the general enfranchisement of women. If even today a higher percentage of American than European women fail to come to the polls, the same can also be said of such population groups as the poorly educated, farmers, the lower-income classes, Negroes and other deprived elements in the potential electorate.[24] In such a context woman suffrage, as important a variable as it certainly has been in our recent political history, seems to raise more analytical problems than it solves.

Table 14.6 Urban-Rural Differences in Stability of Political Involvement: 1936-1960 Mean Turnout and Variability of Turnout as Percentages of 1876-1896 Mean Turnout and Variability of Turnout, Pennsylvania

County and Type	N	1936-1960 Turnout / 1876-1896 Turnout	1936-1960 Variability / 1876-1896 Variability
Urban:		(%)	(%)
Allegheny	1	95.9	86.2
Philadelphia	1	80.8	95.4
Industrial-Mining:	4	73.4	249.6
Rural:	8	73.7	447.4

Particularly suggestive for our hypothesis of basic changes in the nature of American voting behavior over time is the quite recent transposition of aggregate turnout and variations in turnout as between our rural sample and the two metropolitan centers. In sharp contrast to the situation prevailing before 1900, turnout in these rural counties has tended during the past generation not only to

immigration & women suffrage not the causes

be slightly lower than in the large cities but also subject to far wider oscillations from election to election. In Bedford County, for example, turnout stood at 82.5 percent in 1936, but sagged to an all-time low of 41.2 percent in 1948. The comparable figures in Philadelphia were 74.3 and 64.8 percent, and in Allegheny County 72.5 percent (in 1940) and 60.6 percent.

A major finding revealed by survey research is that the "farm vote" is currently one of the most unstable and poorly articulated elements in the American electorate.[25] It is said that since rural voters lack the solid network of group identifications and easy access to mass-communication media enjoyed by their city cousins, they tend to be both unusually apathetic and exceptionally volatile in their partisan commitments. As rural voting turnout was abnormally low in 1948, its rate of increase from 1948 to 1952 was exceptionally large and — fully consistent with Campbell's surge–decline model — was associated with a one-sided surge toward Eisenhower. A restatement of the data in Table 14.5 lends strong support to this evaluation of the relative position of the rural vote as a description of the *current* American voting universe.

But the data strongly imply that virtually the opposite of present conditions prevailed during the nineteenth century. Such variables as education level, communications and non-family-group interaction were probably much more poorly developed in rural areas before 1900 than they are today. Not only did this leave no visible mark on agrarian turnout; it seems extremely likely that the nineteenth-century farmer was at least as well integrated into the political system of that day as any other element in the American electorate. The awesome rates of turnout which can be found in states such as Indiana, Iowa, and Kentucky prior to 1900 indicate that this extremely high level of rural political involvement was not limited to Pennsylvania.[26] As a recent study of Indiana politics demonstrates, the primarily rural "traditional vote" in that state was marked prior to 1900 by an overwhelming partisan stability as well.[27]

Perhaps, following the arguments of C. Wright Mills and others, we can regard this extraordinary change in rural voting behavior as a function of the conversion of a cracker-barrel society into a subordinate element in a larger mass society.[28] In any event, this rural movement toward relatively low and widely fluctuating levels of turnout may well be indicative of an emergent political alienation in such areas. It is suggestive that these movements have been accompanied generally in Pennsylvania as in states like West Virginia by a strongly positive Republican trend in these agrarian bailiwicks during the last thirty years.[29] The impression arises that the political realignment of the 1930s, which only imperfectly mobilized and integrated urban populations into the political system, had not even these limited positive effects in more isolated communities.

The behavior of the Ohio electorate down to about 1930 closely paralleled the patterns displayed in its neighbor states, Michigan and Pennsylvania. Since then a marked divergence has been manifest.

Two-party competition here was far less seriously affected by the sectional political alignment of 1896–1932 than in most other northern industrial states. Of the eighteen gubernatorial elections held in Ohio from 1895 to 1930, for example, Democrats won ten. But here as elsewhere are to be found the same patterns of decline in turnout and sharp increases in indices of voter peripherality after 1900. Indeed, while turnout bottomed out during the 1920s at a point considerably higher than in Michigan or Pennsylvania, it had also been consid-

Table 14.7 Patterns of Voter Participation in Ohio, 1857-1962:
Decline Without Resurgence?

| Period | Mean Turnout | | Mean Drop-Off | Mean Roll-Off | Mean Split-Ticket Voting |
	Pres. Years	Off Years			
	(%)	(%)			
1857-1879	89.0	78.4	9.7	0.6	0.5
1880-1903	92.2	80.5	11.2	0.8	0.6
1904-1918	80.4	71.2	9.2	2.5	3.3
1920-1930	62.4	45.8	24.1	7.9	9.9
1932-1946	69.9	49.1	27.2	7.6	6.5
1948-1962	66.5	53.3	19.0	8.2	11.1

erably higher than in either of them during the nineteenth century. Here too such variables as woman suffrage seem to have played a smaller role as causal agents — at least so far as they affected the growing tendencies toward peripherality among active voters — than is commonly supposed. Drop-off from presidential to off-year elections began to assume its modern shape in Ohio between 1898 and 1910. As Figure 14.2 shows, roll-off — an especially prominent feature in contemporary Ohio voting behavior — emerged in modern form in the election of 1914.

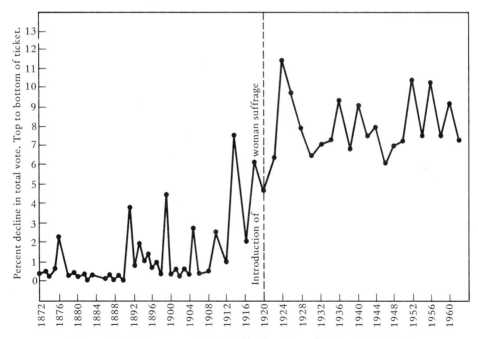

Figure 14.2 *Increases in Roll-Off: The Case of Ohio, 1872-1962.*

Ohio, unlike either Michigan or Pennsylvania, has demonstrated only an extremely limited resurgence since the realignment of the 1930s. Presidential-year voting turnout in the period 1948–1960 actually declined from the mean level of 1932–1944, and was not appreciably higher than it had been in the trough of the 1920s. If mean drop-off has declined somewhat in recent years, it still stands at a level twice as high as in any period before 1920. Moreover, roll-off and the

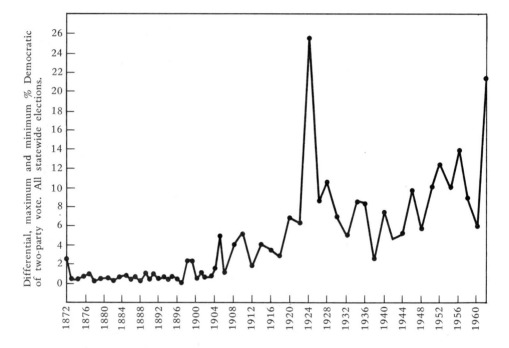

Figure 14.3 *Increases in Split-Ticket Voting: The Case of Ohio, 1872-1962.*

rate of split-ticket voting have actually increased to unprecedented highs since 1948. By 1962 the latter ratio touched an all-time high of 21.3 percent (except for the three-party election of 1924), suggesting that Ohio politics may be becoming an "every-man-for-himself" affair. This pattern of behavior stands in the sharpest possible contrast to nineteenth-century norms. In that period turnout had reached substantially full proportions, drop-off was minimal and well over 99 percent of the voters cast both complete ballots and straight party tickets — an achievement that may have been partly an artifact of the party ballots then in use.[30] The political reintegration which the New Deal realignment brought in its wake elsewhere has scarcely become visible in Ohio.

Two recent discussions of Ohio politics may shed some light upon these characteristics. Thomas A. Flinn, examining changes over the past century in the partisan alignments of Ohio counties, concludes that until the first decade of the twentieth century the state had a set of political alignments based largely on sectionalism within Ohio — a product of the diverse regional backgrounds of its settlers and their descendants. This older political system broke down under the impact of industrialization and a national class-ethnic partisan realignment, but no new political order of similar coherence or partisan stability has yet emerged to take its place.[31] Flinn's findings and the conclusions which Lee Benson has drawn from his study of New York voting behavior in the 1840s are remarkably similar.[32] In this earlier voting universe the durability of partisan commitment and the extremely high levels of turnout appear to have had their roots in a cohesive and persistent set of positive and negative group referents. These, as Flinn notes, provided "no clear-cut class basis for statewide party following from the time of Jackson to that of Wilson."[33]

John H. Fenton, discussing the 1962 gubernatorial campaign, carries the argument one step further.[34] Basic to Ohio's social structure, he argues, is an unusually wide diffusion of its working-class population among a large number of middle-sized cities and even smaller towns. The weakness of the labor unions and the chaotic disorganization of the state Democratic party seem to rest upon this diffusion. Ohio also lacks agencies which report on the activities of politicians from a working-class point of view, such as have been set up by the United Automobile Workers in Detroit or the United Mine Workers in Pennsylvania or West Virginia. The result of this is that to a much greater extent than in other industrial states, potential recruits for a cohesive and reasonably well-organized Democratic party in Ohio live in an isolated, atomized social milieu. Consequently they tend to vote in a heavily personalist, issueless way, as the middle and upper classes do not. Such a state of affairs may provide clues not only for the relative failure of voter turnout to increase during the past generation but for the persistent and growing indications of voter peripherality in Ohio's active electorate as well.

The development of the voting universe in New York is more analogous to the situation in Ohio than in either Michigan or Pennsylvania. In New York, as in Ohio, two-party competition was not as dislocated by the 1896–1930 alignment as a hasty survey of the presidential-election percentages during that period might suggest. Democrats remained firmly in control of New York City, and this control helped them to capture the governorship eight out of eighteen times from 1896 through 1930. There were other parallels with Ohio as well, for here too this persistence of party competition did not prevent the normal post-1896

Table 14.8   New York Voting Patterns, 1834-1962: Decline Without Resurgence?

Period	Mean Turnout (Pres. Years)	Mean Drop-Off	Mean Roll-Off	Mean Split-Ticket Voting	Mean Partisan Swing	Mean % D of Two-Party Vote
	(%)	(%)	(%)	(%)	(%)	
1834-1858	84.8	3.3	1.6	1.2	1.7	50.9*
1860-1879	89.3	7.9	0.4	0.6	2.6	50.1
1880-1898	87.9	10.4	1.2	1.6	5.0	50.5
1900-1908	82.5	8.3	1.1	2.2	3.7	47.2
1910-1918	71.9	10.9	5.1	3.3	3.8	46.2
1920-1930	60.4	17.3	5.5	9.5	8.3	49.6
1932-194.-	71.3	22.5	4.9	3.4	3.2	53.2†
1948-1962	67.8	20.6	3.6	6.5	5.8	47.3†

*Elections from 1854 to 1858 excluded because of major third-party vote.
†The American Labor party, 1936-1946, and the Liberal party, 1944-1962, are included in Democratic vote when their candidates and Democratic candidates were the same.

voting syndrome from appearing in New York. Nor has there been any pro-nounced resurgence in turnout levels or convincing declines in the other vari-ables since the 1930s. Drop-off, roll-off, split-ticket voting and partisan swing are not only quite high in New York by nineteenth-century standards, but have been twice as great as in neighboring Pennsylvania during the past decade. This relative failure of political reintegration is revealed not only by the data pre-sented in Table 14.8 but — in much more dramatic fashion — by the rise and persistence of labor-oriented third parties which are centered in New York City and have enjoyed a balance-of-power position between the two major party es-tablishments. The existence of the American Labor and Liberal parties, as well as the continuing vitality of anti-Tammany "reform" factions, are vocal testi-mony to the failure of the old-line New York Democratic party to adapt itself successfully to the political style and goals of a substantial portion of the urban electorate.

Curiously enough, examination of the data thus far presented raises some doubt that the direct primary has contributed quite as much to the erosion of party linkages as has been often supposed.[35] There seems to be little doubt that it has indeed been a major eroding element in some of the states where it has taken root — especially in states with partially or fully one-party systems where the primary has sapped the minority party's monopoly of opposition. But com-parison of New York with our other states suggests the need of further concen-trated work on this problem. After a brief flirtation with the direct primary be-tween 1912 and 1921, New York resumed its place as one of the very few states relying on party conventions to select nominees for statewide offices, as it does to this day. Despite this fact, the post-1896 pattern of shrinkage in turnout and increases in our other indices of political dissociation was virtually the same in New York as elsewhere. To take a more recent example, New York's split-ticket voting ratio was 16.1 percent in 1962, compared with 21.3 in Ohio, 7.1 in Michigan and 6.8 percent in Pennsylvania. The overall pattern of the data sug-gests that since 1932 the latter two states may have developed a more cohesive party politics and a more integrated voting universe with the direct primary than New York has without it.

If the data thus far indicate some link between the relative magnitude of voter nonparticipation and marginality with the cohesiveness of the local party system, even greater secular trends of the same sort should occur where one of the parties has continued to enjoy a perennially dominant position in state poli-tics. Oklahoma, a border state with a modified one-party regime, tends to sup-port such an assumption.[36] The relatively recent admission of this state to the union naturally precludes analysis of its pre-1896 voting behavior. Even so, it is quite clear that the further back one goes toward the date of admission, the closer one comes to an approximation to a 19th-century voting universe. In Oklahoma, curiously enough, the secular decline in turnout and increases in the other indices continued into the New Deal era itself, measured by the off-year elections when — as in a growing number of states[37] — a full slate of statewide officers is elected. Since 1946 very little solid evidence of a substantial resur-gence in turnout or of major declines in drop-off, roll-off or split-ticket voting has appeared, but there is some evidence that the minority Republican party is atrophying.

The magnitude of drop-off and roll-off has become relatively enormous in

Table 14.9 Voter Peripherality and Party Decay? Oklahoma, 1907-1962

Period	Mean Turnout (Off Years)	Mean Drop-Off	Mean Roll-Off*	Mean Split-Ticket Voting*	% of State and Congressional Elections Uncontested by Republicans	
					Percent	Mean N†
	(%)	(%)	(%)	(%)		
1907-1918	52.9	12.1	6.1	3.6	2.1	32
1922-1930	40.1	13.0	13.9	9.7	2.1	31
1934-1946	37.1	32.2	16.4	8.1	14.8	32
1950-1962	44.5	26.3	14.0	10.5	41.3	29

*Roll-off and split-ticket voting are computed for contested elections only.
†Mean number of state and congressional races in each off-year election.

Oklahoma since the 1920s, with a very slight reduction in both during the 1950–1962 period. While turnout has correspondingly increased somewhat since its trough in the 1934–1946 period, at no time since 1914 have as many as one-half of the state's potential voters come to the polls in these locally decisive off-year elections. Still more impressive is the almost vertical increase in the proportion of uncontested elections since the end of World War II. The 1958 and 1962 elections, moreover, indicate that the trend toward decomposition in the Republican party organization and its linkage with its mass base is continuing. In 1958 the party virtually collapsed, its gubernatorial candidate winning only 21.3 percent of the two-party vote. Four years later the Republican candidate won 55.5 percent of the two-party vote. The resultant partisan swings of 34.2 percent for this office and 22.0 for all contested statewide offices was the largest in the state's history and one of the largest on record anywhere. But while 1962 marked the first Republican gubernatorial victory in the state's history, it was also the first election in which the Republican party yielded more than half of the statewide and congressional offices to its opposition without any contest at all. Even among contested offices, the Oklahoma electorate followed a national trend in 1962 by splitting its tickets at the unprecedented rate of 17.3 percent.

As Key has suggested, the direct primary has almost certainly had cumulatively destructive effects on the cohesion of both parties in such modified one-party states as Oklahoma.[38] The rapidly spreading device of "insulating" state politics from national trends by holding the major state elections in off years has also probably played a significant role. Yet it seems more than likely that these are variables which ultimately depend for their effectiveness upon the nature of the local political culture and the socioeconomic forces which underlie it. Pennsylvania, for example, also has a direct primary. Since 1875, it has also insulated state from national politics by holding its major state elections in off years. Yet since the realignment of the 1930s, both parties have contested every statewide office in Pennsylvania as a matter of course. Indeed, only very infrequently have elections for seats in the state legislature gone by default to one of the parties, even in bailiwicks which it utterly dominates.[39]

These five statewide variations on our general theme suggest, as do the tentative explorations below the statewide level in Pennsylvania, that an extremely

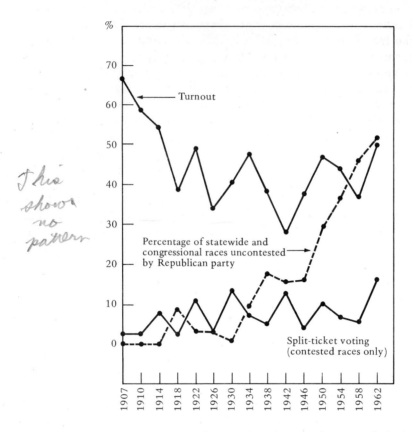

This shows no pattern

Figure 14.4 *Patterns of Political Evolution: The Case of Oklahoma, 1907–1962.*

important factor in the recent evolution of the voting universe has been the extent to which the imperatives of the class-ethnic New Deal realignment have been relevant to the local social structure and political culture. In the absence of an effectively integrating set of state political organizations, issues and candidates around which a relatively intense polarization of voters can develop, politics is likely to have so little salience that very substantial portions of the potential electorate either exclude themselves altogether from the political system or enter it in an erratic and occasional way. As organized and articulated in political terms, the contest between "business" and "government" which has tended to be the linchpin of our national politics since the 1930s has obviously made no impression upon many in the lowest income strata of the urban population. It has also failed to demonstrate sustained organizing power in areas of rural poverty or among local political cultures which remain largely pre-industrial in outlook and social structure.

IV

The conclusions which arise directly out of this survey of aggregate data and indices of participation seem clear enough. On both the national and state levels they point to the existence and eventual collapse of an earlier political universe in the United States — a universe in many ways so sharply different from the one we all take for granted today that many of our contemporary frames of analytical reference seem irrelevant or misleading in studying it. The late nineteenth-century voting universe was marked by a more complete and intensely party-oriented voting participation among the American electorate than ever before or since. Approximately two-thirds of the potential national electorate were then "core" voters, one-tenth fell into the peripheral category, and about one-quarter remained outside. In the four northern states examined in this survey the component of core elements in the potential electorate was even larger: about three-quarters core voters, one-tenth peripherals and about 15 percent nonvoters.

In other ways too this nineteenth-century system differed markedly from its successors. Class antagonisms as such appear to have had extremely low salience by comparison with today's voting behavior. Perhaps differentials in the level of formal education among various groups in the population contributed to differentials in nineteenth-century turnout as they clearly do now. But the unquestionably far lower *general* level of formal education in America during the last century did not preclude a much more intense and uniform mass political participation than any which has prevailed in recent decades. Though the evidence is still scanty, it strongly implies that the influence of rurality upon the intensity and uniformity of voting participation appears to have been precisely the opposite of what survey-research findings hold it to be today. This was essentially a preindustrial democratic system, resting heavily upon a rural and small-town base. Apparently, it was quite adequate, both in partisan organization and dissemination of political information, to the task of mobilizing voters on a scale which compares favorably with recent European levels of participation.

There is little doubt that the model of surge and decline discussed above casts significant light upon the behavior of today's American electorate as it responds to the stimuli of successive elections. But the model depends for its validity upon the demonstrated existence of very large numbers both of peripheral voters and of core voters whose attachment to party is relatively feeble. Since these were not pronounced characteristics of the nineteenth-century voting universe, it might be expected that abnormal increases in the percentage of the vote won by either party would be associated with very different kinds of movements in the electorate, and that such increases would be relatively unusual by present-day standards.

Even a cursory inspection of the partisan dimensions of voting behavior in the nineteenth century tends to confirm this expectation. Not only did the amplitude of partisan swing generally tend to be much smaller then than now,[40] but nationwide landslides of the twentieth-century type were almost nonexistent.[41] Moreover, when one party did win an unusually heavy majority, this increase was usually associated with a pronounced and one-sided *decline* in turnout. Comparison of the 1848 and 1852 elections in Georgia and of the October gubernatorial and November presidential elections of 1872 in Pennsylvania, for example, makes it clear that the "landslides" won by one of the presidential contenders in 1852 and 1872 were the direct consequence of mass abstentions by voters who normally supported the other party.[42] Under nineteenth-century conditions, marked as they were by substantially full mobilization of the eligible electorate, the only play in the system which could provide extraordinary majorities had to come from a reversal of the modern pattern of surge and decline — a depression in turnout which was overwhelmingly confined to adherents of one of the parties.[43]

This earlier political order, as we have seen, was eroded away very rapidly after 1900. Turnout fell precipitately from nineteenth-century levels even before the advent of woman suffrage, and even in areas where immigrant elements in the electorates were almost nonexistent. As turnout declined, a larger and larger component of the still-active electorate moved from a core to a peripheral position, and the hold of the parties over their mass base appreciably deteriorated. This revolutionary contraction in the size and diffusion in the shape of the voting universe was almost certainly the fruit of the heavily sectional party realignment which was inaugurated in 1896. This "system of 1896," as Schattschneider calls it,[44] led to the destruction of party competition throughout much of the United States, and thus paved the way for the rise of the direct primary. It also gave immense impetus to the strains of antipartisan and antimajoritarian theory and practice which have always been significant elements in the American political tradition. By the decade of the 1920s this new regime and business control over public policy in this country were consolidated. During that decade hardly more than one-third of the eligible adults were still core voters. Another one-sixth were peripheral voters and fully one-half remained outside the active voting universe altogether. It is difficult to avoid the impression that while all the forms of political democracy were more or less scrupulously preserved, the functional result of the "system of 1896" was the conversion of a fairly democratic regime into a rather broadly based oligarchy.

The present shape and size of the American voting universe are, of course, largely the product of the 1928–1936 political realignment. Survey-research findings most closely approximate political reality as they relate to this next broad phase of American political evolution. But the characteristics of the present voting universe suggest rather forcefully that the New Deal realignment has been both incomplete and transitional. At present, about 44 percent of the national electorate are core voters, another 16 [percent] or so are peripheral, and about 40 percent are still outside the political system altogether. By nineteenth-century standards, indices of voter peripherality stand at very high levels. Party organizations remain at best only indifferently successful at mobilizing a stable, predictable mass base of support.

The data which have been presented here, though they constitute only a small fraction of the materials which must eventually be examined, tend by and large to support Schattschneider's functional thesis of American party politics.[45] We still need to know a great deal more than we do about the specific linkages between party and voter in the nineteenth century. Systematic research remains to be done on the causes and effects of the great post-1896 transition in American political behavior. Even so, it seems useful to propose an hypothesis of transition in extension of Schattschneider's argument.

The nineteenth-century American political system, for its day, was incomparably the most thoroughly democratized of any in the world. The development of vigorous party competition extended from individual localities to the nation itself. It involved the invention of the first organizational machinery — the caucus, the convention, and the widely disseminated party press — which was designed to deal with large numbers of citizens rather than with semiaristocratic parliamentary cliques. Sooner than the British, and at a time when Prussia protected its elites through its three-class electoral system, when each new change of regime in France brought with it a change in the size of the electorate and the nature of *le pays légal*, and when the basis of representation in Sweden was still the estate, Americans had elaborated not only the machinery and media of mass politics but a franchise which remarkably closely approached universal suffrage. Like the larger political culture of which it was an integral part, this system rested upon both broad consensual acceptance of middle-class social norms as ground rules and majoritarian settlement (in "critical" elections from time to time), once and for all, of deeply divisive substantive issues on which neither consensus nor further postponement of a showdown was possible. Within the limits so imposed it was apparently capable of coherent and decisive action. It especially permitted the explicit formulation of sectional issues and — though admittedly at the price of civil war — arrived at a clear-cut decision as to which of two incompatible sectional modes of social and economic organization was henceforth to prevail.

But after several decades of intensive industrialization a new dilemma of power, in many respects as grave as that which had eventuated in civil war, moved toward the stage of overt crisis. Prior to the closing years of the century the middle-class character of the political culture and the party system, coupled with the afterglow of the civil-war trauma, had permitted the penetration and control of the cadres of both major parties by the heavily concentrated power of our industrializing elites. But this control was inherently unstable, for if and when the social dislocations produced by the industrial revolution should in turn produce a grassroots counterrevolution, the party whose clienteles were more vulnerable to the appeals of the counterrevolutionaries might be captured by them.

The take-off phase of industrialization has been a brutal and exploitative process everywhere, whether managed by capitalists or commissars.[46] A vital functional political need during this phase is to provide adequate insulation of the industrializing elites from mass pressures, and to prevent their displacement by a coalition of those who are damaged by the processes of capital accumulation. This problem was effectively resolved in the Soviet Union under Lenin and Stalin by vesting a totalitarian monopoly of political power in the hands of Communist industrializing elites. In recent years developing nations have tended to rely upon less coercive devices such as nontotalitarian single-party systems or personalist dictatorship to meet that need, among others. The nineteenth-century European elites were provided a good deal of insulation by the persistence of feudal patterns of social deference and especially by the restriction of the right to vote to the middle and upper classes.

But in the United States the institutions of mass democratic politics and universal suffrage uniquely came into being *before* the onset of full-scale industrialization. The struggle for democracy in Europe was explicitly linked from the outset with the struggle for universal suffrage. The eventual success of this movement permitted the development in relatively sequential fashion of the forms of party organization which Duverger has described in detail.[47] In the United States — ostensibly at least — the struggle for democracy had already been won, and remarkably painlessly, by the mid-nineteenth century. In consequence, the American industrializing elites were, and felt themselves to be, uniquely vulnerable to an anti-industrialist assault which could be carried out peacefully and in the absence of effective legal or customary sanctions by a citizenry possessing at least two generations' experience with political democracy.

This crisis of vulnerability reached its peak in the 1890s. Two major elements in the population bore the brunt of the exceptionally severe deprivations felt during this depression decade: the smaller cash-crop farmers of the southern and western "colonial" regions and the ethnically fragmented urban working class. The cash-crop farmers, typically overextended and undercapitalized, had undergone a thirty-years' decline in the prices for their commodities in the face of intense international competition. With the onset of depression in 1893, what had been acute discomfort for them became disaster. The workers, already cruelly exploited in many instances during this "take-off" phase of large-scale industrialization, were also devastated by the worst depression the country had thus far known. Characteristically, the farmers resorted to political organization while the workers sporadically resorted to often bloody strikes. The industrializers and their intellectual and legal spokesmen were acutely conscious that these two profoundly alienated groups might coalesce. Their alarm was apparently given quite tangible form when the agrarian insurgents captured control of the Democratic party in 1896.

But the results of that great referendum revealed that the conservatives' fears and the anti-industrialists' hopes of putting together a winning coalition on a Jacksonian base were alike groundless. Not only did urban labor *not* flock to William Jennings Bryan, it repudiated the Democratic party on an unprecedented scale throughout the industrialized Northeast. The intensity and permanence of this urban realignment was paralleled by the Democrats' failure to make significant inroads into Republican strength in the more diversified and depression-resistant farm areas east of the Missouri River, and by their nearly total collapse in rural New England. The Democratic-Populist effort to create a coalition of the dispossessed created instead the most enduringly sectional political alignment in American history — an alignment which eventually separated the southern and western agrarians and transformed the most industrially advanced region of the country into a bulwark of industrialist Republicanism.

This realignment brought victory beyond expectation to those who had sought to find some way of insulating American elites from mass pressures without formally disrupting the preexisting democratic-pluralist political structure, without violence and without conspiracy. Of the factors involved in this victory three stand out as of particular importance:

1. The depression of 1893 began and deepened during a Democratic administration. Of course there is no way of ascertaining directly what part of the decisive minority which shifted its allegiance to the Republican party reacted viscerally to the then incumbent party and failed to perceive that Cleveland and Bryan were diametrically opposed on the central policy issues of the day. But contemporary survey findings would tend to suggest that such a component in a realigning electorate might not be small. In this context it is especially worth noting that the process of profound break with traditional voting patterns began in the fall of 1893, not in 1896. In a number of major

states like Ohio and Pennsylvania the voting pattern of 1896 bears far more resemblance to those of 1893–1895 than the latter did to pre-1893 voting patterns. Assuming that such visceral responses to the Democrats as the "party of depression" did play a major role in the realignment, it would follow that the strong economic upswing after 1897 would tend to strengthen this identification and its cognate, the identification of the Republicans as the "party of prosperity."

2. The Democratic platform and campaign were heavily weighted toward the interests and needs of an essentially rural and semicolonial clientele. Considerably narrowed in its programmatic base from the farmer–labor Populist platform of 1892, the Democratic party focused most of its campaign upon monetary inflation as a means of redressing the economic balance. Bryan's viewpoint was essentially that of the smallholder who wished to give the term "businessman" a broader definition than the easterners meant by it, and of an agrarian whose remarks about the relative importance of farms and cities bespoke his profound misunderstanding of the revolution of his time. Silver mine owners and depressed cash-crop farmers could greet the prospect of inflation with enthusiasm, but it meant much less to adequately capitalized and diversfied farmers in the Northeast, and less than nothing to the depression-ridden wage earners in that region's shops, mines and factories. Bryan's appeal at base was essentially Jacksonian — a call for a return to the simpler and more virtuous economic and political arrangements which he identified with that bygone era. Such nostalgia could evoke a positive response among the native-stock rural elements whose political style and economic expectations had been shaped in the faraway past. But it could hardly seem a realistic political choice for the ethnically pluralist urban populations, large numbers of whom found such nostalgia meaningless since it related to nothing in their past or current experience. Programmatically, at least, these urbanites were presented with a two-way choice, only one part of which seemed at all functionally related to the realities of an emergent industrial society. With the Democrats actually cast in the role of reactionaries despite the apparent radicalism of their platform and leader, and with no socialist alternative even thinkable in the context of the American political culture of the 1890s, the Republican party alone retained some relevance to the urban setting. In this context, its massive triumph there was a foregone conclusion.

3. An extremely important aspect of any political realignment is the unusually intense mobilization of negative-reference-group sentiments during the course of the campaign. 1896 was typical in this respect. Profound antagonisms in cultural and political style between the cosmopolitan, immigrant, wet, largely non-Protestant components of American urban populations and the parochial, dry, Anglo-Saxon Protestant inhabitants of rural areas can be traced back at least to the 1840s. Bryan was virtually the archetype of the latter culture, and it would have been surprising had he not been the target of intense ethnocultural hostility from those who identified with the former. He could hardly appeared as other than an alien to those who heard him in New York in 1896, or to those who booed him off the stage at the Democratic convention — also in New York — in 1924. Moreover, his remarks about the Northeast as "the enemy's country" — anticipating Senator Goldwater's views about that region in 1964 — could only intensify a broadly sectional hostility

to his candidacy and deepen the impression that he was attacking not only the Northeast's industrializing elites but the Northeast itself. Both in 1896 and 1964 this region gave every visible evidence of replying in kind.

As Schattschneider has perceptively observed, the "system of 1896" was admirably suited to its primary function. One of its major working parts was a judiciary which proceeded first to manufacture the needed constitutional restraints on democratic political action — a development presaged by such decisions as the Minnesota railroad rate case of 1890[48] and the income tax cases of 1894–1895[49] — and then to apply these restraints against certain sensitive categories of national and state economic legislation.[50] Another of the new system's basic components was the control which the sectional alignment itself gave to the Republican party, and through it the corporate business community, over the scope and direction of national public policy. Democracy was not only placed in judicial leading-strings, it was effectively placed out of commission — at least so far as two-party competition was concerned — in more than half of the states. Yet it was one of the greatest, if unacknowledged, contributions of the "system of 1896" that democratic forms, procedures and traditions continued to survive.[51] Confronted with a narrowed scope of effective democratic options, an increasingly large proportion of the eligible adult population either left, failed to enter or — as was the case with southern Negroes after the completion of the 1890–1904 disfranchisement movement in the Old Confederacy — was systematically excluded from the American voting universe. The results of this on the exercise of the franchise have already been examined here in some detail. It was during this 1896–1932 era that the basic characteristics associated with today's mass electorate were formed.

These characteristics, as we have seen, have already far outlived the 1896 alignment itself. There seems to be no convincing evidence that they are being progressively liquidated at the present time. If the reemergence of a competitive party politics and its at least partial orientation toward the broader needs of an urban, industrialized society were welcome fruits of the New Deal revolution, that revolution has apparently exhausted most of its potential for stimulating turnout or party-oriented voting in America. The present state of affairs, to be sure, is not without its defenders. The civics-minded have tended to argue that the visible drift away from party-oriented voting among a growing minority of voters is a sign of increasing maturity in the electorate.[52] Others have argued that mediocre rates of turnout in the United States, paralleled by the normally low salience of issues in our political campaigns, are indicative of a "politics of happiness."[53] It is further contended that any sudden injection of large numbers of poorly socialized adults into the active voting universe could constitute a danger to the Republic.[54]

But there is another side to this coin. The ultimate democratic purpose of issue-formulation in a campaign is to give the people at large the power to choose their and their agents' options. Moreover, so far as is known, the blunt alternative to party government is the concentration of political power, locally or nationally, in the hands of those who already possess concentrated economic power.[55] If no adequate substitute for party as a means for mobilizing nonelite influence on the governing process has yet been discovered, the obvious growth of "image" and "personality" voting in recent decades should be a matter of some concern to those who would like to see a more complete restoration of the democratic process in the United States.

Moreover, recent studies — such as Murray Levin's examinations of the attitudes of the Boston and Massachusetts electorate — reveal that such phenomena as widespread ticket-splitting may be associated quite readily with pervasive and remarkably intense feelings of political alienation.[56] Convinced that both party organizations are hopelessly corrupt and out of reach of popular control, a minority which is large enough to hold the balance of power between Republicans and Democrats tends rather consistently to vote for the lesser, or lesser-known, of two evils. It takes a mordant variety of humor to find a kind of emergent voter maturity in this alienation. For Levin's data are difficult to square with the facile optimism underlying the civics approach to independent voting. So, for that matter, are the conclusions of survey research about the behavior of many so-called "independent" voters.[57]

Findings such as these seem little more comforting to the proponents of the "politics of happiness" thesis. Granted the proposition that most people who have been immersed from birth in a given political system are apt to be unaware of alternatives whose explicit formulation that system inhibits, it is of course difficult to ascertain whether their issueless and apathetic political style is an outward sign of "real" happiness. We can surmise, however, that the kind of political alienation which Levin describes is incompatible with political happiness, whether real or fancied. A great many American voters, it would seem, are quite intelligent enough to perceive the deep contradiction which exists between the ideals of rhetorical democracy as preached in school and on the stump, and the actual day-to-day reality as that reality intrudes on his own milieu. Alienation arises from perception of that contradiction, and from the consequent feelings of individual political futility arising when the voter confronts an organization of politics which seems unable to produce minimally gratifying results. The concentration of socially deprived characteristics among the more than forty million adult Americans who today are altogether outside the voting universe suggests active alienation — or its passive equivalent, political apathy — on a scale quite unknown anywhere else in the Western world. Unless it is assumed as a kind of universal law that problems of existence which can be organized in political terms must fade out below a certain socioeconomic level, this state of affairs is not inevitable. And if it is not inevitable, one may infer that the political system itself is responsible for its continued existence.

Yet such an assumption of fade-out is clearly untenable in view of what is known about patterns of voting participation in other democratic systems. Nor need it be assumed that substantial and rapid increases in American voting participation would necessarily, or even probably, involve the emergence of totalitarian mass movements. The possibility of such movements is a constant danger, to be sure, in any polity containing so high a proportion of apolitical elements in its potential electorate. But it would be unwise to respond to this possibility by merely expressing the comfortable hope that the apoliticals will remain apolitical, and by doing nothing to engage them in the system in a timely and orderly way. It is much more to the point to seek a way, if one can be found, to integrate the apolitical half of the American electorate into the political system before crisis arises.[58] Such integration need not be out of the question. The United States, after all, enjoyed intense mass political involvement without totalitarian movements during the last part of the nine-teenth century, as do other Western democracies today.

No integration of the apoliticals can be carried out without a price to be paid. Underlying the failure of political organizations more advanced than the nineteenth-century middle-class cadre party to develop in this country has been the deeper failure of any except middle-class social and political values to achieve full legitimacy in the American political culture. It may not now be possible for our polity to make so great a leap as to admit non-middle-class values to political legitimacy and thus provide the preconditions for a more coherent and responsible mode of party organization. But such a leap may have to be made if full mobilization of the apolitical elements is to be achieved without the simultaneous emergence of manipulative radicalism of the left or the right. The heart of our contemporary political dilemma appears to lie in the conflict between this emergent need and the ideological individualism which continues so deeply to pervade our political culture. Yet the present situation perpetuates a standing danger that the half of the American electorate which is now more or less entirely outside the universe of active politics may someday be mobilized in substantial degree by totalitarian or quasi-totalitarian appeals. As the late President Kennedy seemed to intimate in his executive order establishing the Commission on Registration and Voting Participation, it also raises some questions about the legitimacy of the regime itself.[59]

NOTES

[1] The leading work of this sort thus far has been done by the late V. O. Key, Jr. See, e.g., his "A Theory of Critical Elections," *Journal of Politics*, vol. 17 (1955), pp. 3–18, and his *American State Politics* (New York, 1956). See also such quantitatively oriented monographs as Perry Howard, *Political Tendencies in Louisiana, 1812–1952* (Baton Rouge: Louisiana State University Press, 1957).

[2] The most notable survey-research effort to date to develop politically relevant theory regarding American voting behavior is Angus Campbell, Philip E. Converse, Warren E. Miller and Donald E. Stokes, *The American Voter* (New York, 1960), especially chap. 20.

[3] V. O. Key, Jr., "The Politically Relevant in Surveys," *Public Opinion Quarterly*, vol. 24 (1960), pp. 54–61; V. O. Key, Jr., and Frank Munger, "Social Determinism and Electoral Decision: The Case of Indiana," in Eugene Burdick and Arthur J. Brodbeck, eds., *American Voting Behavior* (Glencoe, Ill., 1959), pp. 281–299.

[4] Warren E. Miller and Donald E. Stokes, "Constituency Influence in Congress," [*American Political Science Review*], vol. 57 (1963), pp. 45–56. The authors observe that in the 1958 Hays-Alford congressional race in Arkansas, the normally potential nature of constituency sanctions against representatives was transferred under the overriding pressure of the race issue into an actuality which resulted in Hays's defeat by a write-in vote for his opponent. The normally low issue- and candidate-consciousness among the electorate was abruptly replaced by a most untypically intense awareness of the candidates and their relative positions on this issue.

For an excellent cross-polity study of voting behavior based on comparative survey analysis, see Robert R. Alford, *Party and Society* (Chicago: Rand McNally, 1963).

[5] V. O. Key, Jr., *Public Opinion and American Democracy* (New York, 1961) based largely on survey-research data at the University of Michigan.

[6] This effort, to which the author was enabled to contribute, thanks to a Social Science Research Council grant for 1963–1964, has been supported by the Council and by the National Science Foundation. This article is in no sense an integral part of that larger project. But it is proper to acknowledge gratefully here that the S.S.R.C., by making it possible for me to spend a year at the Survey Research Center, has helped to provide conditions favorable to writing it. Thanks are also due to Angus Campbell, Philip E. Converse, Donald E. Stokes and Warren E. Miller for their comments and criticisms. They bear no responsibility for the defects of the final product.

[7] V. O. Key, Jr., *American State Politics, op. cit.*, pp. 71–73, 197–216.

[8] E. E. Schattschneider, *Party Government* (New York, 1942) and *The Semi-Sovereign People* (New York, 1960), pp. 78–96.

[9] Howard A. Scarrow, "Patterns of Voter Turnout in Canada," *Midwest Journal of Political Science*, vol. 5 (1961), pp. 351–364; James A. Robinson and William Standing, "Some Correlates of Voter Participation: The Case of Indiana," *Journal of Politics*, vol. 22 (1960), pp. 96–111. Both articles — one involving a political system outside of but adjacent to the United States — indicate patterns of contemporary participation which seem at variance with the conclusions of survey studies regarding the behavior of the American electorate. In Canada rural turnout is higher than urban, and no clear-cut pattern of drop-off between federal and provincial elections exists. Voter participation in Indiana apparently does not increase with the competitiveness of the electoral situation, and does increase with the rurality of the election jurisdiction. With the possible exception of the relationship between competitiveness and turnout, all of these are characteristics associated with nineteenth-century voting behavior in the United States; see below.

[10] In computing turnout data, note that until approximately 1920 the criteria for eligibility to vote differed far more widely from state to state than they do now. In a number of states west of the original thirteen — for example in Michigan until 1894 and in Wisconsin until 1908 — aliens who had merely declared their intention to become citizens were permitted to vote. Woman suffrage was also extended piecemeal for several decades prior to the general enfranchisement of 1920. The turnout estimates derived here have been adjusted, so far as the census data permit, to take account of such variations.

[11] If one computes the off-year total vote of the years 1950–1962 as a percentage of the total vote cast in the preceding presidential election, ʌ virtually identical correspondence is reached with estimated off-year turnout as a percentʌɡ ɔf turnout in the immediately preceding presidential year:

Year	Total Off-Year Vote as Percent of Vote in Last Presidential Year	Estimated Off-Year Turnout as Percent of Turnout in Last Presidential Year
1950	82.9	80.4
1954	69.2	67.5
1958	73.9	72.1
1962	74.4	73.6

[12] Angus Campbell, "Surge and Decline: A Study of Electoral Change," *Public Opinion Quarterly*, vol. 24 (1960), pp. 397–418.

[13] *Ibid.*, p. 413. The percentage of drop-off from 1956 to 1958, as computed from aggregate voting data, was 25.6 percent.

[14] See, e.g., Robert E. Lane, *Political Life* (Glencoe, Ill., 1959), pp. 18–26.

[15] There are, of course, very wide divergences in turnout rates even among non-southern states. Some of them, such as Idaho, New Hampshire and Utah, have presidential-year turnouts which compare very favorably with European levels of participation. A detailed analysis of these differences remains to be made. It should prove of the utmost importance in casting light upon the relevance of current forms of political organization and partisan alignments to differing kinds of electorates and political subsystems in the United States.

[16] *Report of the President's Commission on Registration and Voting Participation* (Washington, 1963), especially pp. 5–9. Hereafter cited as *Report*.

[17] *Ibid.*, pp. 11–14, 31–42.

[18] See, e.g., Stanley Kelley, "Elections and the Mass Media," *Law and Contemporary Problems*, vol. 27 (1962), pp. 307–326.

[19] E. E. Schattschneider, *The Semi-Sovereign People, op. cit.*, pp. 102–103.

[20] Joseph La Palombara, *Guide to Michigan Politics* (East Lansing, Mich.: Michigan State University Press, 1960), pp. 22–35.

[21] This recalls Robinson and Standing's conclusion that voter participation in Indiana does not necessarily increase with increasing party competition. Of the eight Michigan gubernatorial elections from 1948 to 1962 only one was decided by a margin of 55 percent or more, while three were decided by margins of less than 51.5 percent of the two-party vote. Despite this intensely competitive situation, turnout — while of course much higher than in the 1920s — remains significantly below normal pre-1920 levels.

[22] Angus Campbell, "Surge and Decline," *op. cit.*, pp. 401–404.

[23] Herbert Tingsten, *Political Behavior* (Stockholm, Stockholm Economic Studies, no. 7, 1937), pp. 10–36. See also Charles E. Merriam and Harold F. Gosnell, *Non-Voting* (Chicago, University of Chicago Press, 1924), pp. 26, 109–122, for a useful discussion of the effect of woman suffrage on turnout in a metropolitan area immediately following the general enfranchisement of 1920.

[24] Survey-research estimates place current turnout among American women at 10 percent below male turnout. Angus Campbell et al., *The American Voter, op. cit.*, pp. 484–485. The sex-related difference in participation is apparently universal, but is significantly smaller in European countries which provide election data by sex, despite the far higher European level of participation by both sexes. The postwar differential has been 5.8 percent in Norway (1945–1957 mean), 3.3 percent in Sweden (1948–1960 mean), and 1.9 percent in Finland (1962 general election). While in 1956 only about 55 percent of American women went to the polls, the mean turnout among women in postwar elections was 76.1 percent in Norway and 79.4 percent in Sweden.

[25] *Ibid.*, pp. 402–440.

[26] The estimated rates of turnout in presidential elections from 1876 through 1896, mean turnout in the period 1936–1960 and estimated turnout in 1964 were as follows in these states:

State	1876	1880	1884	1888	1892	1896	1936–60 (Mean)	1964 (Prelim.)
Indiana	94.6	94.4	92.2	93.3	89.0	95.1	75.0	73.3
Iowa	89.6	91.5	90.0	87.9	88.5	96.2	71.7	72.0
Kentucky	76.1	71.0	68.0	79.1	72.6	88.0	57.6	52.6

[27] V. O. Key, Jr., and Frank Munger, "Social Determinism and Electoral Decision," *op. cit.*, pp. 282–288.

[28] C. Wright Mills, *The Power Elite* (New York: Oxford University Press, 1956), pp. 298–324. See also Arthur J. Vidich and Joseph Bensman, *Small Town in Mass Society* (New York, 1960), pp. 5–15, 202–227, 297–320.

[29] John H. Fenton, *Politics in the Border States* (New Orleans: Hauser Press, 1957), pp. 117–120.

[30] However, Ohio's modern pattern of split-ticket voting, formed several decades ago, seems to have been little (if at all) affected by the 1950 change from party-column to office-block ballot forms. See Figure 14.3.

[31] Thomas A. Flinn, "Continuity and Change in Ohio Politics," *Journal of Politics*, vol. 24, (1962), pp. 521–544.

[32] Lee Benson, *The Concept of Jacksonian Democracy* (Princeton: Princeton University Press, 1961), pp. 123–207, 288–328.

[33] Flinn, *op. cit.*, p. 542.

[34] John H. Fenton, "Ohio's Unpredictable Voters," *Harper's Magazine*, vol. 225, (1962), pp. 61–65.

[35] This would seem to suggest a limitation on Key's findings, *American State Politics, op. cit.*, pp. 169–196.

[36] This designation is given the state's political system in Oliver Benson, Harry Holloway, George Mauer, Joseph Pray and Wayne Young, *Oklahoma Votes: 1907–1962* (Norman, Okla.: Bureau of Government Research, University of Oklahoma, 1964), pp. 44–52. For an extensive discussion of the sectional basis of Oklahoma politics, see *ibid.*, pp. 32–43, and V. O. Key, Jr., *American State Politics, op. cit.*, pp. 220–222.

[37] In 1936, 34 states (71 percent) elected governors for either two- or four-year terms in presidential years, and the three-year term in New Jersey caused major state elections to coincide with every fourth presidential election. By 1964, only 25 of 50 states (50 percent) still held some of their gubernatorial elections in presidential years. Two of these, Florida and Michigan, are scheduled to begin off-year gubernatorial elections for four-year terms in 1966.

[38] *American State Politics, op. cit.*, pp. 169–196.

[39] In the period 1956–1962 there have been 840 general-election contests for the Pennsylvania House of Representatives. Of these all but six, or 0.7 percent have been contested by both major political parties. No Pennsylvania state Senate seat has been uncontested during this period. Despite the 1962 Republican upsurge in Oklahoma, however, there were no contests between the parties in 11 of 22 Senate seats (50.0 percent) and in 73 of 120 House seats (60.9 percent). All the uncontested Senate seats and all but two of the uncontested House seats were won by Democrats.

[40] Mean national partisan swings in presidential elections since 1872 have been as follows: 1872–1892, 2.3 percent; 1896–1916, 5.0 percent; 1920–1932, 10.3 percent; 1936–1964, 5.4 percent.

[41] If a presidential landslide is arbitrarily defined as a contest in which the winning candidate received 55 percent or more of the two-party vote, only the election of 1872 would qualify among the 16 presidential elections held from 1836 to 1896. Of 17 presidential elections held from 1900 through 1963, at least eight were landslide elections by this definition, and a ninth — the 1924 election, in which the Republican candidate received 54.3 percent and the Democratic candidate 29.0 percent of a three-party total — could plausibly be included.

[42] The total vote in Georgia declined from 92,203 in 1848 to 62,333 in 1852. Estimated turnout declined from about 88 percent to about 55 percent of the eligible electorate, while the Democratic share of the two-party vote increased from 48.5 percent in 1848 to 64.8 percent in 1852. The pattern of participation in the Pennsylvania gubernatorial and presidential elections of 1872 is also revealing:

Raw Vote	Governor, Oct. 1872	President, Nov. 1872	Absolute Decline
Total	671,147	562,276	−108,871
Democratic	317,760	213,027	−104,733
Republican	353,387	349,249	−4,138

Estimated turnout in October was 82.0 percent, in November 68.6 percent. The Democratic percentage of the two-party vote was 47.3 percent in October and 37.9 percent in November.

[43] The only apparent exception to this generalization in the nineteenth century was the election of 1840. But this was the first election in which substantially full mobilization of the eligible electorate occurred. The rate of increase in the total vote from 1836 to 1860 was 60.0 percent, the largest in American history. Estimated turnout increased from about 58 percent in 1836 to about 80 percent in 1840. This election, with its relatively one-sided mobilization of hitherto apolitical elements in the potential electorate, not unnaturally bears some resemblance to the elections of the 1950s. But the increase in the Whig share of the two-party vote from 49.2 percent in 1836 to only 53.0 percent in 1840 suggests that that surge was considerably smaller than those of the 1950s.

[44] The Semi-Sovereign People, op. cit., p. 81.

[45] Ibid., especially pp. 78–113. See also his "United States: The Functional Approach to Party Government," in Sigmund Neumann, ed., Modern Political Parties (Chicago: University of Chicago Press, 1956), pp. 194–215.

[46] Clark Kerr, John T. Dunlop, Frederick S. Harbison, and Charles A. Myers, Industrialism and Industrial Man (Cambridge, Mass.: Harvard University Press, 1960), pp. 47–76, 98–126, 193, 233. Walt W. Rostow, The Stages of Economic Growth (Cambridge: Cambridge University Press, 1960), pp. 17–58.

[47] Maurice Duverger, Political Parties (New York, 2d. ed., 1959), pp. 1–60.

[48] Chicago, Milwaukee & St. Paul Railway Co. v. Minnesota, 134 U. S. 418 (1890).

[49] Pollock v. Farmers' Loan & Trust Co., 157 U. S. 429 (1895); (rehearing) 158 U. S. 601 (1895).

[50] The literature on this process of judicial concept-formulation from its roots in the 1870s through its formal penetration into the structure of constitutional law in the 1890s is extremely voluminous. Two especially enlightening accounts are: Benjamin Twiss, Lawyers and the Constitution (Princeton: Princeton University Press, 1942), and Arnold M. Paul, Conservative Crisis and the Rule of Law (Ithaca: Cornell University Press, 1960).

[51] Paul, ibid., pp. 131–158.

[52] See, among many other examples, Congressional Quarterly Weekly Report, vol. 22 (May 1, 1964), p. 801.

[53] Heinz Eulau, "The Politics of Happiness," Antioch Review, vol. 16 (1956), pp. 259–264; Seymour M. Lipset, Political Man (New York, 1960), pp. 179–219.

[54] Ibid., pp. 216–219; Herbert Tingsten, Political Behavior, op. cit., pp. 225–226.

[55] V. O. Key, Jr., Southern Politics (New York, 1949), pp. 526–528; E. E. Schattschneider, The Semi-Sovereign People, op. cit., pp. 114–128.

[56] Murray B. Levin, The Alienated Voter (New York, 1960), pp. 58–75, and his The Compleat Politician (Indianapolis, 1962), especially pp. 133–178. While one may hope that Boston and Massachusetts are extreme case studies in the pathology of democratic politics in the United States, it appears improbable that the pattern of conflict between the individual's expectations and reality is entirely unique to the Bay State.

[57] Angus Campbell et al., *The American Voter, op. cit.*, pp. 143–145.

[58] The line of reasoning developed in this article — especially that part of it which deals with the possible development of political alienation in the United States — seems not entirely consistent with the findings of Gabriel A. Almond and Sidney Verba, *The Civic Culture* (Princeton: Princeton University Press, 1963), pp. 402–469, 472–505. Of course there is no question that relatively high levels of individual satisfaction with political institutions and acceptance of democratic norms may exist in a political system with abnormally low rates of actual voting participation, just as extremely high turnout may — as in Italy — be associated with intense and activist modes of political alienation. At the same time, the gap between American norms and the actual political activity of American individuals does exist, as Almond and Verba point out on pp. 479–487. This may represent the afterglow of a Lockean value consensus in an inappropriate socioeconomic setting, but in a policy quite lacking in the disruptive discontinuities of historical development which have occurred during this century in Germany, Italy and Mexico. Or it may represent something much more positive.

[59] Whereas less than 65 percent of the United States population of voting age cast ballots for Presidential electors in 1960; and

"Whereas popular participation in Government through elections is essential to a democratic form of Government; and

"Whereas the causes of nonvoting are not fully understood and more effective corrective action will be possible on the basis of a better understanding of the causes of the failure of many citizens to register and vote..." [emphasis supplied]. The full text of the executive order is in *Report*, pp. 63–64. Compare with Schattschneider's comment in *The Semi-Sovereign People, op. cit.*, p. 112: "A greatly expanded popular base of political participation is the essential condition for public support of the government. This is the modern problem of democratic government. The price of support is participation. The choice is betwee.. participation and propaganda, between democratic and dictatorial ways of *changing consent into support, because consent is no longer enough*" [author's emphasis].

A Portrait of Ethnic Politics:

The Socialists and the 1908 and 1910 Congressional

Elections on the East Side[1]

Arthur Goren

15

During the early twentieth century, the Socialist party easily outpolled its older rival, the Socialist Labor party. No other Socialist or Communist party has since matched its showing. Ironically, as Arthur Goren points out, the Socialist party captured a congressional seat in the Lower East Side of New York City only when its leaders recognized the marked sensitivity of the district's Russian Jews to issues relating to their shared experiences in Russia and the United States. Socialist politicians, like politicians of the major parties long before them, had to learn to appreciate the importance of religious and ethnic factors in electoral politics. On the other hand, the Socialist party also gained considerable support in the Southwest and West, areas where East European Jews and Germans were few in number. Unfortunately, we lack quantitative analyses of this vote comparable to Goren's study. Professor Goren teaches American Studies at the Hebrew University in Israel.

Introduction

In the course of the first two decades of the twentieth century the Socialist party gained relatively important footholds in two metropolitan areas, German-populated Milwaukee and the Jewish Lower East Side of New York. Both districts sent Socialists to Congress in the latter half of this period and in Milwaukee notable victories were registered in municipal elections.

By 1900, the Ninth Congressional District of New York, carved out of the heart of the Lower East Side, had become the most densely populated area of Russian-Jewish immigration.[2] It had also acquired its reputation as the habitat of a vigorous, young radical movement. The year 1904 saw the District's Socialist candidate poll 21 percent of the vote.[3] Two years later Morris Hillquit raised the Socialist share of the vote to 26 percent.[4] Eventually, Hillquit's successor as candidate, Meyer London, was elected to Congress from the East Side.[5]

SOURCE: Reprinted with permission from *Publication of the American Jewish Historical Society*, vol. 50 (March 1961), pp. 202–238.

The political campaigns in the Lower East Side attracted considerable attention. Progressives saw the Socialist "David" pitted against the Tammany "Goliath." Others, disquieted by the frenzied agitation of the East European radicals, found support for their immigrant restriction stand. Americanized coreligionists of the Jewish immigrant populace feared anti-Semitic repercussions that would ultimately endanger their hard won position.

Of all the parties in the ghetto, the Socialist party was least responsive to the ethnic interests of the residents of the ghetto. Cosmopolitan in outlook and faithful to its class allegiance, the party was hostile to what it considered to be the conflicting loyalties invoked by "nationality." Furthermore, despite the ethnic locale, in its political ambition to embrace the American working-class it sought to avoid the suspicion of domination by "foreign groups."

The central theme of this investigation of the 1908 and 1910 political campaigns on the Jewish East Side is the impact of an ethnic-centered, new immigrant community of a political ideology posing imperatives transcending the ghetto parochialism. The unexpected dimensions of Morris Hillquit's defeat in 1908 and his replacement in 1910 by Meyer London indicate the conflict and the compromise the Socialist politician was compelled to make in his encounter with the immigrant community. The two campaigns also form part of a transition period in the history of the Socialist party. By 1910, the East Side radicals were elevated to the status of a "serious threat." As this study will indicate the new show of strength was possible only when due recognition was given to the local interests of the ghetto.

The 1908 Campaign: Profile of Victory

On October 31, 1908, the Socialist *New York Evening Call* carried on its front page in large type and framed in a black border Eugene Debs's "A final word to you on the eve of battle."[6] Debs did not address his order of the day to all the socialist forces. He singled out the voters of the Ninth Congressional District of New York for these special words of encouragement.

> The East Side is destined to be a historic battleground. It is here that capitalism has wrought its desolation, here that it has spread its blighting curse, like a pestilence, to destroy manhood, debauch womanhood and grind the blood and flesh and bones of children into food for Mammon.
>
> It is here on the East Side where the victims of capitalism struggle and suffer, that the hosts of freedom must spring from the soil, fertilized by the misery of their class.
>
> Hillquit, the working class candidate for Congressman can and should be elected so that the working class may have its first representative in the national Congress.[7]

There were other indications besides Debs's unparalleled appeal to the voters of a particular district that the Socialist party had mounted a major offensive on the East Side. In the two Assembly Districts, the Sixth and Eighth, which made up much of the Lower East Side, Hillquit's running mates were Robert Hunter and James Graham Phelps Stokes. The three were drawn from the first echelon of the national leadership.

"The Ninth" offered the best chances for a breakthrough. In the logic of the Socialist analysis it possessed the basic elements needed for victory: the "desolation capitalism has wrought" was nowhere more evident; its Socialists were alert, militant and numerically significant; and they were appealing to a public consisting by and large of impoverished wage earners.

To this Socialist dialectic, Hillquit, in an interview granted to a *New York Times* reporter, appended an analysis of the political balance of power in the district which he predicted would spell out his election.[8] The Democratic vote for Congressman would be reduced by these factors: the stringent new election law decreasing the number of enrolled voters in the District would eliminate Tammany floaters and repeaters;[9] the Presidential campaign would preclude the Republican machine "voting openly" for the Democratic candidate for Congress as in 1906; and finally, the Hearst candidate would remain in the field at Tammany's expense.[10] Thus, four candidates were vying for 11,000 votes. The one receiving 4000 votes, Hillquit reasoned, was assured of election. In the light of this campaign arithmetic, Hillquit needed to improve his 1906 showing by 300 votes to win. The reporter compared the "lukewarmness" of the other campaigns to the "enthusiasm, buoyant and bubbling over, among the Socialists of the lower East Side." . . . "Republican and Democratic leaders," he concluded, "see much truth in Morris Hillquit's prediction."

The stir created by the Debs campaign and the support of a stronger local ticket were additional sources of Hillquit's optimism. However, aside from such political variables he undoubtedly postulated the uncompromising support of the growing Socialist movement in the Jewish quarter. The Jewish trade union movement provided functionaries and rank-and-filers who were gaining political experience in each succeeding campaign.[11] The Socialist *Forward*, surmounting earlier vicissitudes to become a leading Yiddish daily by 1908, possessed organizational resources of consequence,[12] and particularly striking was the growth of the *Arbeiter Ring*, a fraternal order of Jewish workingmen sympathetic to the Socialist party. Its New York City membership increased from 5103 in 1906 to 10,233 in 1908.[13] Meanwhile, the booming Russian immigration brought reinforcements of highly literate, "ready-made" Socialists.[14]

The Socialists conducted their most vocal and best organized campaign to date.[15] Outside help augmented the party's district organization. Hillquit, in his autobiography, tells of the "hordes of young intellectuals" who "came down daily to speak at street corners."[16] William Dean Howells endorsed the Socialist ticket.[17] Lincoln Steffens remembered his days on the East Side as a police reporter and backed Hillquit and his comrades as the only way of breaking the evil machine.[18] Charles Edward Russell chose the week before election to join publicly the Socialist party and endorse Hillquit.[19] In the final weeks of the campaign the Socialist party was averaging twenty-five meetings a night with audiences aggregating 25,000, the *New York Times* estimated.[20] The *New York Evening Call* found confirmation of the effectiveness of the East Side campaign in the dissension and panic reportedly rampant in Timothy ("Big Tim") Sullivan's downtown Tammany domain.[21] "Tammany Hall on East Side Panicky," one story ran ten days before election.[22] A week later a page one headline read, "Tammany Heelers are Desperate."[23] A sense of confidence unusual for Socialist leaders led them to expect the votes of sympathizers reluctant in the past to waste their ballots on a Socialist candidate with no chance of winning.[24] Impressed by their own showing in 1906, convinced they were cheated out of victory then by an eleventh-hour deal, the East Side Socialists anticipated sending the first Socialist congressman to Washington.[25] A week before election Hillquit felt certain enough of victory to declare that were the opposition to combine behind a single candidate he would still be able to win.[26] The *New York Times* in a survey of the congressional election campaign saw no likelihood of change in New York with the exception of the "Ninth."[27]

Yet, when the returns were counted, Hillquit ran a distant second behind Tammany's Henry Mayer Goldfogle. His total vote was nearly a third less than his 1906 showing and one had to look back to the lean election years of the first part of the decade to find a comparably bad showing.[28] The post-mortems offered by the Socialist commentators were quick to explain the defeat: a deal between the Democrats and the Republicans to defeat the Socialist at all costs.[29] Tammany terror;[30] the continual movement of Socialists out of the East Side to Brownsville and the Bronx leaving a mounting residue of Tammany-dependent shopkeepers and peddlers.[31] One *Forward* commentator appended a psychological explanation: The Old World antipathy of the Russian Jew for all bureaucratic activity explained his indifference to becoming naturalized, registering and finally voting.[32] However, in their analysis of the defeat, the Socialist commentators chose to ignore those issues which revolved around the ethnic interests of the population of "the Ninth."[33]

The Alleged Special Interests

"The Ninth" was not merely the district of tenement houses, sweatshops and immigrant radicals. The heart of the Jewish ghetto and the point of concentration of Yiddish-speaking Russian Jews served as the unofficial reception center of the newly arrived immigrants during the decade of their highest influx into this country.[34] An uninhibited, self-contained social and, in certain respects, economic life, eased the ordeals of its inhabitants. Four Yiddish daily newspapers and a score of periodicals published on the East Side, offered the comfort of the familiar word and the full range of political and literary tastes.[35] "Here a man was ... safe among his own kind."[36] This sentiment found expression in the preeminence of the *Landsmannschaft* in the ferment of East Side institutional life.[37] However, the ascendancy of the *Landsmannschaft* in Jewish life represented not merely nostalgia for the warmth of the "old home." It also indicated an overwhelming concern for the kinsmen left behind in the *shtetl* [small East European town]. Consequently, not only the synagogue and the mutual aid society were established on the *Landsmannschaft* principle but the great majority of the socialist-oriented *Arbeiter-Ring* branches, as well, despite the Socialist injunction calling for the unity of the working class.[38] Just as the Yiddish press coverage revealed the apprehension of the newly-arrived immigrant for the well-being of his family and townsmen on the "other side," so the functions of the *Landsmannschaft* were attuned to their transportation, reception and initial settlement.[39] We must bear in mind that the four years prior to the 1908 campaign witnessed a new wave of pogroms in Russia and the extinction of all radical and progressive hopes for a more liberal Russian policy. The tempo of relief work rose sharply.[40] Prominent individuals, including radical intellectuals heretofore passive in Jewish communal life, now accepted a more active role.[41] Immigration figures continued to climb. The prevalent feeling was stronger than ever that the Jews of Russia had no alternative but emigration.

This atmosphere of crisis coincided with the public discussion on immigration: the renewed attempt to enact a literacy test, the establishment of the Dillingham Commission, the negotiations on Japanese immigration, Russia and the American passport debate.[42] Jewish organizations, ambitious to play a role in Jewish communal life, joined in the fight against the "restrictionists."[43] Thus, on the individual and institutional plane the note of anxiety and fear lest the doors of asylum close dominated the new immigrant ghetto. This anxiety expressed itself in a high-pitched sensitivity to the immigration restriction issue. One can appreciate, then, the shrillness of the debate when this very issue was injected into the campaign in the Ninth Congressional District and the accusation of supporting the restrictionist stand was hurled at the downtown Socialists.

Not unrelated to the immigration issue was a second theme which ruffled the pride of the Jewish quarter. For the social reformer, immigration restrictionist, socialist and uptown coreligionist, the ghetto of the Lower East Side epitomized a host of evils — crime, prostitution, disease, machine politics at its worst, and cultural backwardness. Though much of this picture of the degrading conditions of the ghetto was drawn by those wishing its inhabitants well, the Jewish quarter rebelled against this image. Characteristic of this sensitivity was the reaction on the East Side to an article by the Commissioner of Police, General Theodore Bingham which appeared in the September, 1908 issue of the *North American Review*. By implication the Commissioner attributed 50 percent of all crimes committed in New York City to Jews.[44] While Louis Marshall and other respected Jewish citizens from "uptown" cautioned restraint and sought to deal with the incident away from the public's eye, protest meetings were held on the East Side.[45] The *Tageblatt* called for mass demonstrations demanding Bingham's resignation for besmirching the name of the Jews of the East Side.[46] The good intentions of Lincoln Steffens' muckraking letter or Debs's rhetoric on behalf of Hillquit emphasizing the need to "clean up" the abominations of the East Side were equated by many with Bingham's accusation.[47]

At the first Hillquit rally in the 1908 campaign, which Abraham Cahan, editor of the *Forward*, chaired, the candidate for Congress said:

> The issues thus defined by the Socialist party in its National platform are also the issues in the Congressional District of New York. . . .
>
> It is true that our district is inhabited largely by a foreign-born population. . . . [That] the naturalized citizen of Russian-Jewish origin is as much a citizen as the native American of Dutch or Puritan origin is fact as well as theory.
>
> The interests of the workingmen of the Ninth Congressional District are therefore entirely identical with those of the workingmen of the rest of the country, and if elected to Congress, I will not consider myself the special representative of the alleged special interests of this district, but the representative of the Socialist party and the interests of the working class of the country so understood and interpreted by my party. . . ."[48]

The irony of two Russian Jews, Morris Hillquit and Abe Cahan, solemnly declaring they recognized "no special interests" in the Lower East Side may have been lost to the socialist audience of Russian Jews. The rhetoric delivered by known citizens of the ghetto in the language of the ghetto obscured the anomaly. Nevertheless, in the maze of ghetto organizations dedicated in one fashion or another to ethnic continuity, socialism was unique in preaching an involvement in American life and concern for issues transcending the ethnic group.

The Arraignment

On the day before election, Louis Miller, Abe Cahan's old comrade and now archtraitor of the downtown Socialists, wrote in his *Warheit*:

> The American people has one position of high honor, the office of the President. For this highest office it seeks out its finest, most famous, most devoted and loyal son. We Jews in the quarter possess only the office of Congressman. It is not much, perhaps, but it is all we have. To whom shall we give this office, to a person who has always been with us, or to a person who never cared to know us and has no desire to know us now, who when he comes among strangers denies that he is a Jew, who was, is and will always remain a renegade. Morris Hillquit's coming to us Jews when he wants our vote should by itself be sufficient reason for not voting for him.[49]

With the refrain, Where was Morris Hillquit when . . ." the *Warheit* itemized its charges of indifference to the interests of the Jewish quarter: the strike of tenants over the raising of rents in January, 1908;[50] the organized boycott of the kosher meat wholesalers who raised prices in 1907;[51] Julia Richman's campaign urging deportation of immigrants guilty of violating the pushcart ordinance;[52] the bankrupcy of fraternal and benevolent funds during the 1907–1908 crisis;[53] Commissioner of Police Bingham's accusation of criminality among the Jews.[54]

The catalogue of indifference concluded with this accusation:

> Where was Morris Hillquit in the days of the pogroms when old, infirm people marched and women threw their jewels into the collection plates to help? When the entire Jewish people, radicals and conservatives, young and old, united in brotherhood in the great day of tragedy.[55]

The reference was to the burst of mass meetings and appeals for funds triggered by the Kishineff pogrom in 1903. Months of agitated activity had reached a climax on December 4, 1905, when 125,000 Jews dressed in mourning garb marched to Union Square from the Lower East Side.[56] A young, American-born Reform rabbi, Judah L. Magnes, headed the sponsoring organization, "The Jewish Defense Assocation." Serving on the Executive Committee was the Reverend Zevi Hirsch Masliansky, renowned Orthodox Jewish preacher. A Jewish labor leader and former Socialist candidate for Congress from the Ninth Congressional District, Joseph Barondess, acted as Grand Marshal of the procession.[57] Jacob H. Schiff, philanthropist banker, personification of propriety and Americanism, made his contribution to a fund avowedly buying arms for clandestine Jewish defense units in Russian towns.[58] For the moment it appeared that fraternal factionalism and strife had been forgotten in the name of "brotherhood in the great day of tragedy." Three years later the *Warheit* reminded the voters of Morris Hillquit's abstention.[59]

The crime of indifference became one of outright treason in the conservative *Tageblatt*'s arraignment.

> Morris Hillquit belongs to those who hide their Jewish nationality . . . who crawl after the Gentiles on all four. It was not enough for him to change his name . . . not only did he run away from his people, he . . . backed closing the door of the land of freedom to those who like himself wished to find a home in America.[60]

"The assimilationist, alienated from his people, ashamed of his nationality" Morris Hillquit could not represent the million Jews of New York!

Every right-thinking Jew will recognize that the Jews of New York should have as their representative in Congress a Jew who bears in mind Jewish interest. If Morris Hillquit were to be elected it would mean that New York Jewry would have no representative in the Congress of the United States.[61]

In the broader campaign the Jew had the same interest as any other citizen.[62] The campaign within "the Ninth," however, was unabashedly a Jewish campaign.[63] It became so the moment Morris Hillquit declared it was not.

With muckraking zeal, Hillquit and his supporters exposed the ignorance, crime, and moral depravity of the East Side, depicting it as the ultimate proof of decadent capitalism.[64] The picture of the ghetto the Socialist campaign presented to the American public appeared so slanderous in the eyes of the *Tageblatt* that it rose to defend not only the good name of the East Side's Jewish quarter but of American Jewry at large. From this ethnocentered outlook, alone, the paper criticized the campaign tactics of the Socialists. "We are greenhorns. We must guard our honor and the fate of those who must yet come."[65] Such propaganda, the *Tageblatt* declared, was ammunition in the hands of the enemies of the Jews:

> They [the Socialists] must show how low society has fallen under the present system. They tell the whole world that they come to rehabilitate the filthy, backward Jews. . . . No wonder the anti-Semite hurls his lies at the East Side. No wonder the public considers the East Side a center of crime. It is enough for a Gentile to hear Morris Hillquit's speech to label the East Side the hell of America and the Jews who live there the worst of all nationalities in America.[66]

In this manner, "the Socialist Bingham," as the *Tageblatt* dubbed Hillquit, would speak to Congress endangering the Jews of America.[67]

> We are as well off as others. . . . It is the lowest lie that the East Side is immoral or is as poor as the "comrades" say. . . . We must not allow the East Side to be so portrayed. . . . We are citizens, as upright and as honest as others. . . .[68] He who says the East Side is filled with corruption, neglect and filth must not represent the East Side.[69]

Morris Hillquit was certainly the commanding figure of the Socialist party in the East. A person of consequence at party conventions, delegate to International Congresses, leading theorist, his interests and ambitions lay on a national plane. As Debs himself had put it, his election would give Congress a representative of the working class.[70] He had long outgrown the confining parochialism of local politics. The opposition, however, campaigned on no other level.

Sensational appeals to ethnic sentiments could in part be met by Morris Hillquit's national reputation and his fame as a lawyer, a socialist version of the American success story: Russian immigrant, formative years amidst the poverty of the East Side, early struggles to improve conditions there, on to law school to become a fighter for the oppressed of the world. Running mates Max Pine, in the Fourth Assembly District, veteran organizer of the United Hebrew Trades, and Jacob Panken, popular orator in the Eleventh Senatorial District, together with Abe Cahan and his *Forward*, spoke the language of the ghetto.[71] The Socialists did take up the cudgel of race pride sufficiently to be rebuked by the *Tageblatt* for their brazenness in appealing for Morris Hillquit as a Russian Jew.[72]

But interlaced through the diatribes appeared the dominant strand of the immigration issue. A leader of American socialism, he was now held accountable for all actions of his party. An exponent of a moderate position in the party, he was now roundly rebuked for his own ambivalence on immigration and tagged a restrictionist and enemy of the immigrant workingman.

Rebuff and Post Mortem

David Shannon has aptly summarized the Socialist party's official policy on immigration as a straddling of two opposing principles.[73] On the one hand, the socialist scripture called for the international solidarity of the working class. On the other hand, cooperating with the trade unions and wooing the American laborer required a stand favoring immigration restriction.

In 1904, Morris Hillquit, representing the American Socialists at the International Socialist Congress in Amsterdam, supported the minority resolution of restriction of immigration from "backward races." Hillquit went to the 1907 Socialist Congress in Stuttgart, instructed by the national executive of the American party to "combat importation of cheap labor calculated to destroy labor organization, lower the standard of living of the working class and retard ultimate realization of socialism."[74] When Hillquit wrote that he opposed the immigration of workers from industrially backward countries "who are incapable of assimilation with the workingmen of the country of their adoption," he was referring to Asiatic immigration.[75] Its applicability to Russian immigration was not overlooked on the East Side. Just five months before the 1908 campaign, the Chicago Socialist Convention had avoided acting on a Resolutions Committee draft of an anti-immigration plank by voting to appoint an investigating committee to report to the next convention. The delaying action did not conceal the vigorous restrictionist sentiment at the convention.[76]

At the opening rally of the campaign, Hillquit deftly sought to identify the socialist restrictionist sentiment with the problem of Asiatic immigration.

> As for the question of Asiatic exclusion, it may be an issue for the workingmen of the Pacific slope . . . but the workingmen of this congressional district have but a remote abstract interest.

By referring to a basic tenet of international socialism, the demand "that the doors of all civilized countries be left open to the unfortunate workingmen . . . especially the victims of political oppression," he sought to deflect the attack.[77]

In Daniel De Leon, the Socialist Labor party's candidate, Hillquit had a shrewd and knowledgeable opponent who waged his campaign with single-minded purpose: to embarrass and abuse his old adversary, Morris Hillquit. Fully aware of Hillquit's vulnerability on the question of the Socialist party's position on immigration, De Leon adopted a double line of attack. The Socialist party had violated socialist canon and Hillquit had inspired that policy.[78] Louis Miller's widely-read *Warheit* trumpeted the De Leon exposés throughout the ghetto. Hillquitian proposals made to convention committees were exhumed from protocols. *Bund* [Jewish Social Democratic party in Russia] representatives were quoted as saying that Hillquit's resolution at Stuttgart "was like a knife plunged into live flesh."[79]

In the closing weeks of the campaign immigration had become the pivotal issue. The rebuttal Hillquit delivered on October 23 revealed a master debater arguing the more difficult side of the proposition.[80] Referring to the 1907–1908 depression with the resulting decrease in immigration and sharp increase in departing immigrants Hillquit declared:

> Immigration is not an issue in this campaign.... The problem ... is how to stop emigration.[81]

He offered the following syllogism: "The capitalist system forces the worker to emigrate from land to land in search of bread; this cannot be stopped as long as capitalism exists"; hence the Socialists by destroying capitalism will solve the immigration issue. As in his earlier speech, he invoked socialist human- itarianism as assurance that the party stood for an open door "especially for the sufferers of economic exploitation, race and political attacks, refugees like the Russian Jews."[82] The Socialist party, however, was against "the abuse of immigration." Capitalist shipping companies artificially stimulated emigration of European workers. Socialists and union men had been called upon at Stuttgart to prevent the importation of strike-breakers and contract labor, thus recognizing that immigration was not always desirable.[83]

Establishment of a category of "undesirable immigration," however, was not likely to allay the fears of the Jewish quarter. A single desperate logic ruled the immigrant community: an open door for immigration; restriction in any form would eventually affect Russian immigration.[84] In such a situation, however brilliantly Hillquit couched his reservations, the Jewish quarter insisted on an unqualified stand for unrestricted immigration. As a spokesman of American socialism, Hillquit could not meet this sectional demand. He spoke with the circumspection of a presidential nominee and not with the regional partiality expected of a congressional candidate.

In the course of the acrimonious campaign, the incumbent, Congressman Henry M. Goldfogle, received slight attention in the pages of the Republican- inclined *Tageblatt*, the Hillquit-flaying *Warheit*, and the Socialist *Forward*. The radical, Hillel Rogoff, a keen observer of the East Side, has provided us with a partial explanation:

> Campaigning was done almost exclusively by the Socialists, Tammany relying upon the effective work of their henchmen on Election Day.[85]

Goldfogle may not have found it necessary to conduct an active campaign and hence the opposition's denunciation of Tammany as the villain and Goldfogle as a mere tool. The disregard for the latter, however, may have reflected other considerations than disdain or lack of newsworthiness. Goldfogle, as repre- sentative of the East Side, was not particularly vulnerable. In the tradition of American political life, the Congressman championed the special interests of his District. As a freshman in Congress, he introduced the "Goldfogle Resolution" which called on the President to use his good offices for equal treatment of all American passport holders.[86] The representative of the Lower East Side in Congress thereafter became the advocate of naturalized Jewish citizens of Russian birth discriminated against while traveling in Russia. He thus became chief protagonist of the honor of the American passport, placing principle above material gain, America's egalitarianism above Czarist prejudice. Vicariously he struck a blow for the downtrodden.[87] On the other hand, socialist ire was not likely to be aroused by a fight to abrogate an 1832 Treaty of Commerce and Navigation with Russia. The issue, nevertheless, touched the sense of dignity and belonging of the new American of the East Side. Similarly, the day in December 1905 when the Jews mourned the victims of Russian pogroms, Goldfogle offered a resolution to the effect that the House of Representatives express its profound sorrow and horror at the massacres and that the President use his good offices to prevent such outrages.[88] When Police Commissioner Bingham's article incensed New York Jewry in September 1908, Congressman Goldfogle addressed an emergency conference of communal leaders.[89] Goldfogle's vulnerability to attack lay not in his record but in his connection with the machine. Tammany, therefore, became the more likely villain.[90]

Observers miscalculated the Socialist strength by employing the faulty index of campaign ardor. "Whenever we had a Socialist procession march through the streets the enthusiasm was tremendous and spontaneous," Charles Edward Russell wrote in retrospect. "When election day came around . . . we had the cheering and the old parties had the votes."[91] In the aftermath of the 1908 election when the campaign processions no longer marched, M. Baranof, a Socialist journalist of the East Side, explained the phenomenon of loud cheers and few votes. He wrote:

> It would be a good thing if the comrades of down-town would establish a committee whose task would be helping Jewish workers become citizens. It now seems that we Jews make the most noise before the elections and make fools of ourselves when we can't vote on election day.[92]

The Census of 1910 bore out what East Siders knew so well. Only 18.6 percent of the foreign-born males of voting age in the Second, Fourth, and Eighth Assembly Districts were naturalized.[93] The new wave of Russian Jewish immigrants, containing many influenced by the Jewish Socialist movement in Russia and seared by the Russian Revolution of 1905, was bringing ready-made Socialists to America.[94] These Socialists were in all likelihood attending the campaign meetings but they would not be going to the polls in significant numbers until after 1910.

Yet despite the debacle, Hillquit nevertheless ran well ahead of his party's standard bearer, Eugene Debs. The East Side voter was splitting his ballot. Hillquit claimed that the Republican machine, seeing no hope for its candidate and fearing a Socialist upset, connived with Tammany, instructing its followers to "split for Goldfogle."[95] An examination of the election returns for offices in the Ninth Congressional District other than that of Congressman discloses an amazing pattern of party irregularity. The Republican presidential nominee, William Howard Taft, ran 5 percent ahead of his running mate for governor, Charles Evans Hughes. Undoubtedly, Taft's favorable statement on the passport issue, made from an East Side platform late in the campaign, together with the goodwill harbored for Theodore Roosevelt, contributed to Taft's stronger showing in the Jewish quarter.[96] More difficult to explain was the 7 percent difference in the Socialist vote and the 11.5 percent difference in the Republican vote for assemblymen in neighboring districts.[97] Obviously, personalities weighed heavily with the East Side voter. As the Jewish immigrant boy who made good and as the advocate of the laboring man, Morris Hillquit carried an appeal beyond the Socialist ranks. Thus, we can understand his 21.23 percent of the vote compared to Debs's 13.56 percent in the Ninth Congressional District.[98] On the other hand, Morris Hillquit appeared in too controversial and equivocal a light to command the broad support of the population of the Jewish quarter. The hard political facts pointed to his 1133 loss in votes compared with his 1906 total rather than to his 897 lead over running mate Debs.[99]

That the Socialist party was in the process of learning the lessons of the campaign was borne out by the new candidate it offered to the electorate of the Jewish quarter in 1910. With Meyer London, the Socialists strove to avoid a conflict of interest. The party began to recognize grudgingly what an increasing number of Jewish Socialists were agitating for: that socialism operating in the ghetto must acknowledge the legitimacy of the ethnic loyalties of its inhabitants. The Jewish Socialists coming in the new wave of immigration were making their presence felt within the Jewish labor movement and in the periodical press. The lines of ideological conflict were evident. Newer immigrants, radical but committed to the Jewish group, opposed the older, cosmopolitan leadership anxious to merge with their American radical comrades.

The 1910 Campaign: New Tactics

At the Socialist Congress held in May, 1910, Meyer London was one of two delegates representing the Jewish Agitation Bureau which was organized in 1907 for the purpose of recruiting Jewish workers for the Socialist party and trade unions. It was suspected of Jewish "nationalistic" tendencies by the "old guard."[100] When London raised the question at the Congress of the voting rights of the Bureau's delegates, Morris Hillquit, the chairman, ruled that representatives of foreign language organizations were not delegates. They had only advisory status, and were unable to vote or serve on committees.[101] Weeks later, Meyer London received the Socialist nomination in the Ninth Congressional District. Hillquit, high in the inner councils of the party, was replaced by London who never rose above leader of the East Side. Hillquit was enmeshed in the compromises of national politics while London, single-mindedly, served the interests of his constituency. His biographer, possibly with Hillquit in mind, said this of London.

> The older labor and socialist leaders on the East Side considered his presence among them as temporary. It was expected that he would gradually attach himself to the general American movement and go into the non-Jewish sections to live. But he did not. London was drawn more and more into the East Side Socialist and trade union activities. He remained on the East Side because his services were needed there, because his heart was there.[102]

It was London who served as legal counsel of the *Arbeiter-Ring*, the radical fraternal order, thereby earning its undeviating loyalty.[103] And it was London who was invited to attend the conference of the Joint Board of Cloakmakers Unions in August 1908, to consider the calling of a general strike. In the throes of union disorganization and financial distress, the union leaders convened in an air of utter despondency. London's role in encouraging them became legendary.[104] In the summer of 1910, as counsel for the cloakmakers he stood at the helm of the "revolt of the 70,000."[105] London emerged in the fall of 1910 as a popular hero of the Jewish labor movement and his party's leading candidate for public office. The *Forward* boasted that the Socialist party

has proven it is a "workers' party" . . . with brilliant possibilities of winning the campaign . . . because this year [the party] established close ties of cooperation with the broad laboring masses. . . .[106]

At the Socialist convention in Chicago, the immigration issue, sent to committee two years before for further study, was again discussed. The majority report submitted called for "unconditional exclusion" of all Mongolian races. Refusal to exclude certain races and nationalities

would place the Socialist party in opposition to the most militant and intelligent portion of the organized workers of the United States, whose assistance is indispensable to the purpose of elevating the Socialist party to political power.[107]

From the floor of the convention, Hillquit offered a substitute resolution which placed the party on record favoring legislative measures to "prevent the immigration of strikebreakers . . . and the mass importation of workers . . . for the purpose of weakening the organization of American labor. . . ." The resolution, at the same time, opposed the "exclusion of any immigrants on account of their race or nationality" and demanded that the United States be "maintained as a free asylum" for the persecuted.[108] The resolution was accepted 55 to 50. David Shannon in his history of the Socialist party wrote pointedly that

the first paragraph . . . was one that might have been written by an American Federation of Labor convention; the second paragraph might have been written by an International Congress of Marxists.[109]

Meyer London opposed any form of immigration restriction. He supported the Hillquit compromise because it rejected race as a basis for exclusion.[110] The Socialist-Zionists who opposed Hillquit in 1908 in protest of the Socialist party's position on immigration still found the convention's immigration resolution unsatisfactory. It would, however, campaign for London who openly favored free immigration.[111] No longer was the local candidate being identified with the entire party.

A colleague of Cahan and Hillquit in the early days of Socialist activity, the pragmatic, undogmatic London had allied himself with the vital movements on the East Side. He could make his bid for the support of the undoctrinated, the downtrodden as well as the liberate Socialists. During the campaign, the *Forward* carried the following interview of a storekeeper:

As a businessman I will work and vote for Meyer London. Our interests demand this. . . . The politicians sap the blood of us businessmen. . . . The honest businessman must have someone who will take his part, [someone] the politicians will fear. . . . When Meyer London will be elected he will be under no obligation to anyone. As a citizen of the East Side he will be in a position to accomplish a great deal. He will liberate us from graft. . . .

The East Side has no father or mother, no spokesman. . . . When Meyer London is elected to Congress he will be the spokesman of the Jewish Quarter both in Washington and in New York.[112]

We have no way of verifying that such an interview did take place. This would not alter the fact that in 1908 the *Forward* had not appealed to "storekeepers and businessmen." It had conceived of Hillquit as representing the "working class" in Congress and not the Jewish quarter. The *Forward*'s interview was indicative of a change in campaign tactics as different from 1908 as the candidates were different.

Following the 1910 election, a series of letters to the editor of the *New York Evening Call* in response to Louis Boudin's article, "Milwaukee and New York" corroborated the change in tactics. In Milwaukee, there had been less than a 10 percent difference between the highest and lowest vote polled on the Socialist ticket. In the Ninth Congressional District, London had run more than two to one ahead of the party's candidate for governor. According to Boudin,

> In the London campaign, racial and subracial prejudices of voters were appealed to. The Russian Jews were appealed to because Comrade London was also a Russian Jew.[113]

A member of London's campaign committee replied that London had been selected to run because of his "tremendous popularity with the workers of the East Side." As for the accusation of appealing to "racial prejudices," the campaign worker wrote,

> We have not made any stronger use of it notwithstanding the temptations which came from the enemy.[114]

Other letters indicated that an effort had been made to appeal to nonsocialists. A Professional League had been organized. The *Arbeiter-Ring* and the Cloakmakers Union established campaign committees. The propaganda published by these committees, one letter explained, did not present socialism as the issue. The campaign highlighted Meyer London's character, and Gold-fogle's infamy. As one writer put it,

> The keynote of the campaign was "split for London" and with this race prejudice was appealed to, nationality was appealed to, and, in fact, everything except the class consciousness of these workers.[115]

It was freely admitted that the vote of the small businessman and professional had been energetically pursued.[116]

London's 33.09 percent of the vote was 11.86 percent better than Hillquit's 1908 showing.[117] In 1908, except for Congressman, the Socialist vote in the Ninth Congressional District for other city and state offices ranged from a high of 17.87 percent to a low of 12.88 percent. In 1910, again excluding the vote for Congressman, the Socialist vote carried from 15.78 percent to 15.12 percent.[118] A consolidation and a moderate gain in the straight-ticket party vote had taken place. The growth in Socialist strength did not preclude London receiving two votes for every one the remainder of his ticket received. The London campaign and London's appeal had reached well beyond the regular Socialist following.

What the Boudins and Hillquits regarded as a "pestilential atmosphere generated by the appeal to national or race feelings ... [and] unsocialistic practice ..." denoted, rather, recognition by the local party that "special interests" indeed existed.[119] The impassioned debate two years before had revealed the depths of these "national and race feelings." Anguish for the fate of brethren left behind and dedication to the task of their removal to America transcended other loyalties. These emotions together with the continued efforts at restricting immigration heightened group allegiances. Rather than expose conditions on the East Side, the representative of the Ninth Congressional District was expected to defend the good name of his District and its citizens. The Socialist, London, rooted in the East Side, responded to these demands. Finally elected to Congress in 1914, Meyer London told his victory rally:

> When I take my seat in Congress I do not expect to accomplish wonders. What I expect to do is take to Washington the message of the people. . . . I want to show them what the East Side of New York is and what the East Side Jew is.[120]

Reelected in 1916 and elected for a third term in 1920, Meyer London dominated the political scene on the Jewish East Side for most of the decade. This period witnessed the crystallization of the "Jewish Socialist Federation," the last of the Socialist language federations to be organized. The Federation's organization, so long prevented by the "old guard," indicated the ascendancy of the newer immigrants committed to ethnic continuity. Beginning with 1910, the energetic Jewish labor movement entered its period of gigantic growth. London had been associated with both. The "old guard" Socialists became inactive in the Jewish quarter or underwent a change of heart and accepted the ethnic factor as a legitimate one. The 1908 and 1910 campaigns on the Lower East Side illustrate the most striking development in this process.

Appendix: Statistical Data

Table 15.1   Percentage of Total Population According to Ethnic Groups

A. Second, Fourth, and Eighth Assembly District of the Borough of Manhattan, New York City, 1910;

B. Sixth Assembly District of the Borough of Manhattan, New York City, 1910*

Ethnic Group	A	B
Born in Russia	41.69	26.52
Natives, parents born in Russia	15.12	7.96
Born in Roumania	.78	1.69
Born in Austria	12.85	26.80
Natives, parents born in Austria	5.82	12.36
Born in Italy	6.89	.68
Natives, parents born in Italy	1.50	.34
Born in Ireland	1.03	.19
Natives, parents born in Ireland	1.50	.23
Natives, both parents native	2.02	1.07
Others: (Negro, Indian, Cuba, Canada, France, Germany, Norway, Turkey, etc.)	10.80	22.22
Total	100 percent	100 percent

*Based on the United States Bureau of the Census, *Thirteenth Census of the United States: 1910. Abstract with Supplement for New York*, pp. 635-636. The Ninth Congressional District of New York consisted of the 12th, 13th, 14th, 15th, 16th, 17th, 19th, and 20th Election Districts of the Second Assembly District; the 5th, 6th, 7th, 8th, 9th, 10th Election Districts of the Fourth Assembly District; and the entire Eighth Assembly District. The smallest division for which the 1910 United States Census provides statistics for "Composition and Characteristics of the Population" is the Assembly District. By considering the 2nd, 4th and 8th Assembly Districts as a unit, one arrives at a fairly accurate ethnic portrait of the Jewish Lower East Side and of the Ninth Congressional District which lay within these Assembly Districts. Though the Sixth Assembly District was outside of the "Ninth" it was treated by the population, press and political parties as part of the campaign in the "Ninth." The ethnic composition as well as election results of the Sixth Assembly District are therefore included in the tables. For boundaries of the Assembly Districts and the Ninth Congressional District see the Election Notices of the *New York Times*, October 27, 1908, p. 13.

It should be noted that the majority of those listed as of Austrian birth were most likely Yiddish-speaking Jews from Galicia and should be considered East European Jews.

Table 15.2 Composition and Characteristics of the Population

A. Composite of the Second, Fourth and Eighth Assembly Districts of the Borough of Manhattan, New York City, 1910;

B. Sixth Assembly District of the Borough of Manhattan, New York City, 1910*

	A		B	
Total Population		300,337		99,228
Native white — native parentage		6,059		1,067
Native white — foreign or mixed parentage		90,187		30,803
Foreign-born white		203,825		67,322
Others: Negro, Indian, Chinese		266		46
Foreign-born white: born in				
Ireland	3,079		192	
Italy	20,677		678	
Russia	125,220		26,317	
Austria	38,586		26,593	
Roumania	2,352		1,913	
Others: Canada, Cuba, Norway, Sweden, France, England, Germany, Turkey, etc.	13,911		11,629	
Native white: both parents born in				
Ireland	4,505		230	
Italy	10,004		338	
Russia	45,422		7,901	
Austria	17,491		12,267	
Others: Canada, Cuba, Norway, Sweden, France, England, Germany, Turkey, etc.	23,012		10,067	
Males of voting age				
Total number		85,803		27,398
Native white — native parentage	1,784		173	
Native white — foreign or mixed parentage	4,901		1,346	
Others: Negro, Chinese, Indian	174		25	
Foreign-born — white	78,944		25,844	
Naturalized	14,672		5,445	

*United States Bureau of the Census, *Thirteenth Census of the United States: 1910. Abstract with Supplement for New York,* pp. 635-636.

Table 15.3 Selected Election Results in the Ninth Congressional District of New York, 1908*

	Republican	No. of Votes	Percent of Whole Vote	Democrat	No. of Votes	Percent of Whole Vote	Socialist	No. of Votes	Percent of Whole Vote	Ind. League	No. of Votes	Percent of Whole Vote	Soc. Labor	No. of Votes	Percent of Whole Vote	Whole Vote	Percent of Whole Vote
President	William H. Taft	3,821	32.66	William J. Bryan	5,789	49.49	Eugene V. Debs	1,586	13.56	Thomas L. Hisgen	646	5.52	August Gillhaus	94	0.80	11,698	100
Governor	Charles E. Hughes	3,247	27.76	Lewis Stuyvesant Chandler	6,133	52.43	Joshua Wanhope	1,507	12.88	Clarence J. Shearn	505	4.32	Leander A. Armstrong	91	0.91	11,698	100
Congressman	Louis I. Cherry	2,312	19.18	Henry M. Goldfogle	6,194	52.95	Morris Hillquit	2,483	21.23	Morris Salem	329	2.81	Daniel De Leon	151	1.29	11,698	100
State Engineer and Surveyor	Frank M. Williams	3,602	30.80	Phillip P. Farley	5,927	50.67	F. Wilton James	1,604	13.71	Mario J. Cafiero	246	2.15	George Luck	92	0.79	11,698	100
Total Assembly Vote in Ninth Cong. District		3,233	27.65		5,804	49.62		2,091	17.87		243	2.08		75	0.64	11,698	100

*Official Canvas of the Vote Cast in the County of New York, The City Record, Board of the City Record, City of New York, December 31, 1908, pp. 1-4, 18-20, 34-36, 50-52, 82-84, 98, 122, 146, 158.

Table 15.4 Election Results of the Second, Fourth, Sixth and Eighth Assembly Districts of New York County, 1908*

	Republican	No. of Votes	Percent of Whole Vote	Democrat	No. of Votes	Percent of Whole Vote	Socialist	No. of Votes	Percent of Whole Vote	Ind. League	No. of Votes	Percent of Whole Vote	Soc. Labor	No. of Votes	Percent of Whole Vote	Whole Vote	Percent of Whole Vote
Second Assembly District	Bernard Robinson	1,572	21.75	Alfred E. Smith	4,703	65.06	William Mailey	657	9.09	Jere F. Butler	171	2.37	Abraham Levine	19	0.26	7,229	100
Fourth Assembly District	Louis Rosenzweig	1,239	21.06	Aaron J. Levy	3,688	62.86	Max Pine	680	11.56	Bernard Fliasmick	131	2.23	Joseph Schlossberg	43	0.73	5,883	100
Sixth Assembly District	David Robsen	2,396	38.34	Adolph Stern	2,714	43.42	Robert Hunter	806	12.93	Charles Schifter	155	2.48	Sigmond Moskowitz	65	1.04	6,250	100
Eighth Assembly District	Joseph Segal	1,699	26.84	Moritz Graubard	3,073	48.55	J. G. Phelps Stokes	1,252	19.78	Max Perlman	144	2.27	James T. Hunter	45	0.71	6,330	100

*Ibid., p. 158.

Table 15.5 Selected Election Results in the Ninth Congressional District of New York, 1910*

	Socialist	Number of Voters	Percent of Whole Vote	Democrat	Number of Voters	Percent of Whole Vote	Republican	Number of Voters	Percent of Whole Vote	Whole Votes	Percent of Whole Vote
Governor	Charles Edward Russell	1,518	15.12	John A. Dix	5,254	52.34	Henry L. Stimson	2,702	26.92	10,038	100
Congressman	Meyer London	3,322	33.09	Henry M. Goldfogle	4,606	45.89	Jacob W. Block	1,850	18.43	10,038	100
State Engineer and Surveyor	William Lipellt	1,556	15.50	John A. Bensel	5,156	51.36	Frank M. Williams	2,612	26.02	10,038	100
Total Assembly Vote		1,581	15.75		5,228	52.08		2,782	27.71	10,038	100

*Official Canvass of the Vote Cast in the County of New York, The City Record, Board of the City Record, City of New York, December 31, 1910, pp. 1, 39, 57, 70-71. Socialist Labor party and Independent League did not run full tickets and are not herein tabulated.

Table 15.6 Election Results of the Second, Fourth, Sixth and Eighth Assembly Districts of New York County, 1910*

	Socialist	Number of Voters	Percent of Whole Vote	Democrat	Number of Voters	Percent of Whole Vote	Republican	Number of Voters	Percent of Whole Vote	Whole Vote	Percent of Whole Vote
Second Assembly District	Max Mysell	551	8.94	Alfred E. Smith	4,180	67.86	Henry H. Silver	1,807	39.33	6,160	100
Fourth Assembly District	Abram Caspe	646	12.85	Aaron J. Levy	3,165	62.95	Max Bernfeld	940	18.69	5,028	100
Sixth Assembly District	Algernon Lee	537	9.64	Harry Kopp	2,631	47.21	Sol. H. Eisler	2,302	41.31	5,573	100
Eighth Assembly District	William Karlin	812	15.23	Moritz Graubard	2,758	51.74	Louis Jacobson	1,636	30.69	5,330	100

*Ibid., pp. 70–71.

NOTES

[1] The author is greatly indebted to Professor William E. Leuchtenburg of Columbia University for his thorough reading of this paper and the resulting criticism and suggestions. He also benefited from a number of discussions with Dr. Lloyd P. Gartner of the American Jewish History Center.

[2] The smallest geographic division for which the United States Census of 1900 has published statistics on country of birth of foreign-born population, and foreign-born parents of native population, is the city, hence the difficulty in arriving at an accurate picture of the population composition of the East Side for 1900. The United States Census for 1910 supplies these statistics for Assembly Districts in New York allowing a fairly precise view of the East Side's population makeup. See Appendix, Tables 15.1 and 15.2. *The Jewish Encyclopedia* (New York: Funk and Wagnalls Co., 1905), vol. 9, p. 284, mentions a census taken in May 1904 by David Blaustein who arrived at a figure of 320,000 Jewish inhabitants of the East Side. In *University Settlement Studies*, October 1905–June 1906, p. 106, the figure of 450,000 Jews living on the East Side is suggested.

[3] *The Worker* (New York), Nov. 10, 1906, p. 1: *Zukunft*, vol. 13 (December 1908), p. 768.

[4] See note 25.

[5] Lawrence H. Fuchs's study, *The Political Behavior of American Jews* (Glencoe, Ill.: The Free Press, 1956), is a helpful survey of the subject. On pp. 47–55 and 121–129, Fuchs covers in more general terms aspects of the subject of this study. Several inaccuracies deserve to be corrected. Henry Mayer Goldfogle served in Congress sixteen years, but not beginning in 1910. He was elected for the first time to the 57th Congress in 1900, served continually through the 63rd and again in the 66th Congress (March 4, 1919 to March 3, 1921) [page 48]. In 1910, Meyer London and not Morris Hillquit ran for Congress from the Ninth Congressional District [page 127]. Hillquit could not always count on "about 40 percent of the total vote in Jewish congressional districts," [page 127]. In his first two campaigns running from the Ninth Congressional District, he received 26 percent in 1906 and 21 percent in 1908. For his three later campaigns running from the 20th Congressional District in 1916, 1918 and 1920 Fuchs is correct. Goldfogle, not London, was elected from the Ninth, and not the Twelfth Congressional District in 1910 [page 128]. London was not defeated by Goldfogle in 1914 but was elected to Congress for his first term [page 128].

[6] Reported also in *New York Times*, Nov. 1, 1908, p. 5.

[7] This was the only direct appeal made by Debs to a particular district that appeared in the *New York Evening Call* during the entire 1908 campaign.

[8] *New York Times*, Oct. 19, 1908, p. 2.

[9] The new law required the signature of the voter on registration and election days. If the voter claimed he could not write he was required to answer identifying questions. *New York Times*, Oct. 4, 1908, p. 5; Oct. 13, 1908, pp. 1–2.

[10] *New York Times*, Oct. 19, 1908, p. 2; *New York Evening Call*, Oct. 13, 1908, p. 6; also see note 25 below.

[11] Morris Hillquit, Meyer London, Max Pine, Jacob Panken were some of the more prominent Socialist candidates for office with trade union experience; also see note 12 below; Melech Epstein, *Jewish Labor in U. S. A.* (New York, 1950) vol. 1, p. 344, suggested that the depression of 1907–1908 weakened labor union activity and stimulated efforts on the political front.

[12] N. W. Ayer and Sons' *American Newspaper Annual* (Philadelphia: N. W. Ayer and Sons, 1907), p. 1129 estimates the *Forward's* circulation for 1906 at 52,190. Ayer's *Annual*, 1909 edition, p. 1143, gives the *Forward's* circulation for 1908 as 53,539. The *Forward* which had begun stating its circulation daily over the masthead gave its circulation on September 1, 1908 as 72,353. Abraham Cahan discusses the progress of the *Forward* in *Bleter fun Mein Leben*, vol. 4 (New York: *Forward*, 1908), pp. 536–538. From 1907 on, its financial situation improved and its circulation rose. On the role of the *Forward* in the trade union and Socialist movement on the East Side during the period, see, Cahan, *op. cit.*, pp. 542–543, 547 and 549; M. Osherowitch, "Di Geschichte fun Forverts: 1897–1947" [typescript, New York Public Library], pp. 136–140.

[13] The figures were computed from the branch membership totals in the *Sixth Annual Report for the Year 1906 and Proceedings of the Seventh Annual Convention of the Workmen's Circle*, General Executive Committee (New York: Workmen's Circle, 1907), pp. 43–44, and *Eighth Annual Report of the Workmen's Circle* for the year 1908, General Executive Committee (New York: Workmen's Circle, 1909), pp. 77–81.

[14] Hillquit explained the growth of Socialism on the East Side and the large number of first-time voters who registered as Socialists as resulting from "ready made Socialists who came from Russia." *New York Times*, Oct. 19, 1906, p. 2; see also A. Cahan, vol. 4, p. 547; see also A. Menes, *The Jewish People: Past and Present*, vol. 4 (New York): *Jewish Encyclopedic*

Handbooks, 1955), pp. 360–363.

15 *New York Times*, Oct. 19, 1908, p. 2; *Zukunft* [Yiddish], Nov. 1908, p. 714. A. Cahan, vol. 4, p. 548; On the organization of the campaign see *New York Evening Call*, Sept. 18, 1908, p. 1; Oct. 17, p. 1; Oct. 24, p. 1.

16 Morris Hillquit, *Loose Leaves from a Busy Life*, (New York: Macmillan, 1934), p. 115; Harry Rogoff, *An East Side Epic* (New York: Vanguard, 1930), p. 57.

17 Hillquit, *op. cit.*, p. 115.

18 *New York Evening Call*, Oct. 28, 1908, p. 1.

19 *Ibid.*, Oct. 28, 1908.

20 *New York Times*, Oct. 26, 1908, p. 3.

21 *New York Evening Call* (1908), Oct. 8, p. 1; Oct. 13, p. 1; Oct. 17, p. 1; Oct. 21, p. 1; Oct. 22, p. 2; Oct. 23, p. 1; Oct. 26, p. 1; Oct. 30, p. 1. Sullivan was described as losing his grip on the party machine for the following reasons: the loss in Democratic registration; his candidate was defeated for a Tammany nomination; inability to protect his alleged gambling and narcotics activities from police action. See also *New York Times*, Oct. 27, 1908, p. 4, for further indication of dissension within the Democratic Party and the demands of insurgent leaders for new tactics in party campaigning on the Lower East Side.

22 *New York Evening Call*, Oct. 23, 1908, p. 6.

23 *Ibid.*, Oct. 30. p. 1.

24 *New York Times*, Oct. 19, 1908, p. 2; *New York Evening Call*, Oct. 13, 1908, p. 6.

25 The results of the 1906 election for Congressman of the Ninth Congressional District of New York were:

Henry M. Goldfogle [Democrat and Independence League]	7265
Charles Adler [Republican]	2733
Morris Hillquit [Socialist]	3616

New York Times, Nov. 8, 1906, p. 3; *The Worker*, Nov. 10, 1906, p. 1. The campaign attracted wide attention, see *New York Times*, Nov. 7, 1906, p. 6. Goldfogle succeeded in running on Hearst's Independence League ticket despite court action by the Socialists to remove his name. *New York Times*, Oct. 21, 1906, p. 2. Hillquit claimed that in a four-cornered race the Hearst candidate would have pulled enough votes from the Democrats' Goldfogle to give the Socialists the victory. Hillquit, *op. cit.*, pp. 109–115. See also Charles Edward Russell, *Bare Hands and Stone Walls* (New York: Scribner's, 1933), p. 200; A. Cahan, *op. cit.*, vol. 4, p. 548; *Forward*, Oct. 29, 1908, p. 4.

26 *New York Times*, Oct. 26, 1908, p. 3.

27 *Ibid.*, Nov. 1, 1908, p. 3.

28 *Zukunft*, Dec. 1908, p. 768.

29 The *Forward's* headline, Nov. 4, 1908, was, "Tammany Does Business with Republicans and Wins over Hillquit." This was based on a *New York Times* report, Nov. 3, 1908, p. 1, of a deal between the Democrats and Republicans whereby Republican regulars would vote for Goldfogle to insure Hillquit's defeat. See also *Forward*, Nov. 4, 1908, p. 8; *New York Evening Call*, Nov. 4, 1908, p. 1; *Zukunft*, Dec. 1908, p. 768.

30 *New York Evening Call*, Nov. 5, 1908, p. 5.

31 *Forward*, Nov. 5, 1908, p. 1; The *Zukunft*, Dec. 1908, p. 768, remarked that "as the ships bring the greenhorns the moving vans move out the radicals."

32 *Forward*, Nov. 9, 1908, p. 4.

33 Nachman Syrkin's analysis of the election in the Ninth Congressional District emphasized the immigration issue as the cause of Hillquit's defeat. *Zukunft*, Dec. 1908, p. 748. Syrkin, ideological mentor of the Socialist-Zionists, was not fully accepted in Socialist circles. The closest a Socialist came to admitting publicly the primacy of the immigration issue in the defeat of Hillquit was when M. Baranof wrote:

> Such questions should not be raised at a time when the proletariat must unite to fight the always united enemy. The immigration question must be discussed in quieter times. Let the comrades . . . have an effective answer ready for the time when they will again appeal to the members [of the Socialist Party] in a referendum . . . The Socialist Party, if it erred, will not be afraid to admit it [*Forward*, November 12, 1908, p. 4].

34 See Appendix, Tables 15.1 and 15.2.

35 N. W. Ayer and Sons' *Annual*, 1909 edition, p. 1143 lists the following Yiddish dailies with their circulations: *Tageblatt* (68,442), *Jewish Morning Journal* (67,664), *Forward* (53,539), and *Warheit* (59,522). The *American Jewish Year Book, 1909–1910* (Philadelphia: Jewish Publications Society, 1909, p. 219, lists the following weeklies or monthlies which were published in New York in December 1908: *Arbeiter, Freie Arbeiter Stimme, Der Kibetzer, Dos Naye Leben, Der Yiddisher Kempfer, Die Zukunft*. I have not included the weekly editions of the daily newspapers which appeared under separate titles.

[36] Oscar Handlin, *Adventure in Freedom* (New York: McGraw-Hill, 1954), p. 103.

[37] Lamed Shapiro, "Immigration and the Landsmannschaft," *The Jewish Landsmannschaften in New York* [Yiddish] (prepared by the Yiddish Writers Group of the Federal Writers Project, Works Progress Administration) (New York: I. L. Peretz Yiddish Writers Union, 1938), pp. 27–30. According to Shapiro's statistics 255 societies were established in New York City on the *Landsmannschaft* principle between 1906 and 1910. For the organization of federations of *Landsmannschaften* at this time, see Samuel Margoshes, "The *Verband* Movement in New York City," *Jewish Communal Register* (New York: The Jewish Community of New York, 1917/1918), p. 1286, also Samuel Schwartz, "Landsmannschaft Federations," *Jewish Landsmannschaften in New York*, pp. 52 ff.

[38] Between 1906 and 1910, eighty-five *Landsmannschaft* branches of the *Arbeiter-Ring* were founded according to Lamed Shapiro, *Jewish Landsmannschaften*, p. 32; see also Melech Epstein, *op. cit.*, p. 307.

[39] Samuel Schwartz, in *Jewish Landsmannschaften*, pp. 52, 53; Lamed Shapiro, in *Jewish Landsmannschaften*, p. 27.

[40] During this period the "National Committee for the Relief of Sufferers of Russian Massacres," the "American Jewish Relief Committee," "The Jewish Self Defense Fund," were organized, not to mention collection of funds through the fraternal orders and *Landsmannschaft* groups.

[41] On the effect of the Kishineff pogrom in 1903 and the Russian Revolution and pogroms in 1905 on Jewish radical intellectuals, see Samuel Niger's succinct summary, "Yiddish Culture," *The Jewish People*, vol. 4, pp. 362–363. The organization of the American Jewish Committee in 1906 should be seen as part of a heightened sense of responsibility on the part of the leaders of the settled Jewish community. Nathan Schachner, *The Price of Liberty: A History of the American Jewish Committee* (New York, 1948), p. 7 f.

[42] John Higham, *Strangers in the Land* (New Brunswick: Rutgers University Press, 1955), pp. 128–129, 162–163; *American Jewish Year Book*, *1909–1910*, pp. 29–41. Twenty-five bills to restrict immigration were introduced into the House of Representatives alone from July 1907 to August 1908. *American Jewish Year Book*, 1908–1909, pp. 74–76.

[43] Among the organizations dealing with the question were: Jewish Immigration Committee of New York, American Jewish Committee, Board of Delegates of the Union of American Hebrew Congregations, Union of Jewish Orthodox Congregations, National Council of Jewish Women, the Independent Order Brith Abraham, the *Arbeiter-Ring*, the Federation of Galician and Bucovinian Jews, Federation of Roumanian Jews, Federation of Russian-Polish Hebrews of America, Federation of Jewish Organizations, Hebrew Sheltering and Immigrant Aid Society.

[44] In part, Bingham wrote:

> ... It is not astonishing that with a million Hebrews, mostly Russian, in the city (one quarter of the population), perhaps half of the criminals should be of that race, when we consider that ignorance of the language, more particularly among men not physically fit for hard labor, is conducive to crime.... The crimes committed by the Russian Hebrews [are those of] ... burglars, firebugs, pickpockets, and highway robbers — when they have the courage.... The juvenile Hebrew emulates the adult in the matter of crime percentage [*North American Review*, vol. 188, Sept. 1908, pp. 383–384].

[45] On the series of meetings on the East Side which culminated in the "Clinton Hall Conference for the Organization of the Jewish Community of New York," Oct. 11 and 12, 1908 (*American Hebrew*, vol. 83, Oct. 16, 1908, p. 583), see *American Hebrew*, Sept. 11, 1908, p. 449; *Warheit*, Sept. 14, 1908, p. 1; *Tageblatt*, Sept. 14, 1908, p. 1. On the position of the "Uptown Jews" see the editorial "Jewish Sensitiveness" in the *American Hebrew*, Sept. 11, 1908, p. 444, and the rejoinder in the *Tageblatt*, Sept. 14, 1908, p. 4. For Marshall's reply see *American Hebrew*, Sept. 25, 1908, p. 502.

[46] *Tageblatt*, Sept. 16, 1908, p. 4.

[47] A *Tageblatt* editorial entitled "The Socialist Bingham's Calumnies against the East Side" saw Lincoln Steffens', Robert Hunter's and Morris Hillquit's "preachings on the immorality of the East Side" as giving credence to Bingham's accusations [Oct. 30, 1908, p. 4].

[48] *New York Evening Call*, Sept. 12, 1908, p. 3.

[49] *Warheit*, Nov. 3, 1908, p. 4. Mordecai Soltes, *The Yiddish Press: An Americanizing Agency* (New York, 1925) pp. 22–23, gives the political complexion of the *Warheit* as Democratic. A. Cahan, vol. 4, p. 502, records that Louis Miller, editor of the *Warheit*, began to fight the Socialist Party and her candidate and then went on to become "Tammany's energetic defender ... among the Yiddish-speaking public." Founded in 1905 in opposition to the *Forward* by Louis Miller, the *Warheit* tried to capture part of the Socialist following of the *Forward*. In its opposition to the *Forward*, it developed Jewish nationalist sympathies. Ber Borochov, Chaim Zhitlowsky, Nachman Syrkin contributed to its columns. See D. Kaplan's

article, "The Warheit" in *75 Years Yiddish Press in the United States of America, 1870–1945* [Yiddish], ed. Jacob Gladstone, Samuel Niger, Hillel Rogoff, pp. 62–83. In the 1908 campaign, the *Warheit* fought the *Forward* accusations of having been bought by the Democratic Party [*Warheit*, Sept. 10, 1908, p. 1, Sept. 13, 1908, p. 4, Sept. 18, 1908, p. 4, Nov. 1, 1908, p. 4, Oct. 25, 1908, p. 4]. Whatever the truth there is in the *Forward's* claim that Miller's support of the Socialist Labor party candidate was a maneuver to confuse and split the socialist vote in Tammany's interests, the *Warheit's* editorials attacked Hillquit as a betrayer of Socialism and the "Jewish people," appealing to the public as a Socialist newspaper in 1908. See *Forward*, Oct. 28, 1908, p. 4 and *Warheit*, Nov. 2, 1908, p. 4.

50 *Ibid.*, p. 4. On the rent strike see *New York Times* (1908), Jan. 1, p. 3; 2, p. 8; 3, p. 2; 5, p. 9; 6, p. 7; 8, p. 16; 9, p. 16; 11, p. 8. A Socialist "Committee of Ten" attempted to direct the strike to reduce rents in the tenement houses. Jacob Panken, Mr. and Mrs. J. G. Phelps Stokes are the prominent Socialists mentioned in connection with the Committee.

51 *American Hebrew*, Sept. 25, 1908, p. 493.

52 *Ibid.*, April 3, 1908, p. 552. A District School Superintendent on the East Side, her appeal to Police Commissioner Bingham evoked a furor in the Yiddish press and a petition was circulated for her removal. *Louis Marshall, Champion of Liberty*, 2 vols., ed. Charles Reznikoff (Philadelphia: Jewish Publication Society, 1957), pp. 1125–1126; *Warheit*, Sept. 12, 1908, p. 4.

53 *The Hebrew Standard*, vol. 52, April 3, 1908, p. 6. *American Hebrew*, Aug. 28, 1908, p. 395; Sept. 25, 1908, p. 493; *Fifty Years of Social Service: The History of the United Hebrew Charities of New York City* (New York, 1926), pp. 70–72.

54 See note 47 above.

55 *Warheit*, Nov. 3, 1908, p. 4.

56 *New York Times*, Dec. 5, 1905, p. 6; *American Hebrew*, vol. 78, Dec. 8, 1905, p. 73.

57 On Magnes, see Norman Bentwich, *For Zion's Sake: A Biography of Judah L. Magnes* (Philadelphia: Jewish Publication Society, 1954), p. 38. On Barondess and Masliansky see L. Shpizman (ed.), *History of the Labor Zionist Movement of North America* [Yiddish] (New York: Yiddisher Kempfer, 1954), p. 103.

58 Bernard G. Richards, "Amul iz Geven a Kehillah," *Zukunft*, vol. 50, Feb. 1945, p. 83.

59 See note 50 above. In 1903, following the Kishineff and other pograms, the executive committee of the Socialist party of New York warned Jewish Socialists not to desert Socialism and be swept along by the stream of Jewish nationalism (*The Worker*, July 12, 1903, p. 1).

60 *Tageblatt*, Oct. 26, 1908, p. 4. Hillquit had changed his name from Hilkowitz. The *Tageblatt* as a rule supported the Republican party and its candidates. Soltes, *op. cit.*, pp. 22–23. In the 1908 campaign, while overtly for the national and state Republican ticket, the paper passed silently over the party's candidate for Congressman from the Ninth Congressional District and concentrated its entire attack on Hillquit.

61 *Ibid.*, Nov. 2, 1908, p. 4.

62 *Ibid.*, p. 4.

63 *Ibid.*, p. 4. See also editorial, "The Jewish Vote," *ibid.*, Oct. 23, 1908, p. 4.

64 *New York Evening Call*, Oct. 28, 1908, p. 1; *Tageblatt*, Oct. 30, 1908, p. 4.

65 *Tageblatt*, Oct. 30, 1908, p. 4.

66 *Ibid.*, Nov. 1, 1908, p. 4; see also Oct. 30, 1908, p. 4.

67 *Ibid.*, Nov. 1, 1908, p. 4.

68 *Ibid.*, Oct. 30, 1908, p. 4.

69 *Ibid.*, Nov. 1, 1908, p. 4.

70 *New York Evening Call*, Oct. 31, 1908, p. 1. At his ratification rally, Hillquit said: "If elected [I will consider myself] . . . the representative of the Socialist party and the interests of the working class of the country . . ." *New York Evening Call*, Sept. 12, 1908, p. 2.

71 Hillquit's native tongues were Russian and German. He learned to write Yiddish on the East Side but did not use it on the speaker's platform. *Loose Leaves from a Busy Life* (New York, 1934), pp. 32–34; A. Cahan, vol. 4, p. 549.

72 *Tageblatt*, Oct. 26, 1908, p. 4. Several years later Louis Boudin criticized Socialist tactics in the East Side campaign denouncing "the pestilential atmosphere generated by the appeal to national and race feelings." *New York Evening Call*, Dec. 15, 1910, p. 6.

73 David Shannon, *The Socialist Party in America* (New York: Macmillan, 1955), pp. 47–48; see also Ira Kipnis, *The American Socialist Movement 1897–1912* (New York: Columbus Press, 1952), pp. 276–288.

74 *Ibid.*, pp. 277–278; L. Shpizman, *op. cit.*, pp. 206–207. In *The Worker*, Nov. 9, 1907, p. 3, Hillquit in an article, "The Stuttgart Resolution on Labor Immigration," wrote that the resolution of the national executive of the American Socialist party was a compromise.

75 Kipnis, *op. cit.*, p. 277.

76 *Ibid.*, pp. 206 and 279; Shannon, *op. cit.*, p. 49.

77 *New York Evening Call*, Sept. 12, 1908, p. 3.

[78] *Warheit*, Sept. 10, 1908, p. 1: "The 'agitation' against immigration is directed mainly against the Jews and this is a crime. It is also a crime against Socialism. There are no 'progressive' races and 'backward' races. There is only a capitalist class and a workers' class. To divide the workers into races is the doing of capitalists. . . . " From DeLeon's speech, *Warheit*, Oct. 22, 1908, p. 1.

[79] *Ibid.*, Oct. 29, 1908, p. 4. See also, *ibid.*, Sept. 13, 1908, p. 4.

[80] Indication of the importance of the speech may be found in the *New York Evening Call* announcing that a Yiddish translation would be distributed to all the voters of the District (Oct. 24, 1908, p. 1). The *Warheit's* longest and most vitriolic attack against Hillquit appeared in answer to this speech. Oct. 24, 1908, p. 4.

[81] *Forward*, Oct. 23, 1908, p. 4. See also *New York Evening Call*, same date.

[82] *Forward*, Oct. 23, 1908, p. 4.

[83] *New York Evening Call*, Oct. 22, 1908, p. 2.

[84] See John Higham, *op. cit.*, pp. 128–129, 160–165, C. Reznikoff, *Louis Marshall*, pp. 109–115.

[85] Hillel Rogoff, *op. cit.*, p. 57.

[86] *Journal of the House of Representatives*, First Session of the Fifty-Seventh Congress, p. 541. A pamphlet entitled, "Russian Persecution and American Jews," a translation of Goldfogle's speech into Yiddish was distributed throughout the East Side.

[87] *The American Jewish Year Book, 1909–1910*, summarizes the Congressional activity on the passport issue in which Goldfogle's legislative work is particularly clear (pp. 29–64). See also C. Reznikoff, *Louis Marshall*, pp. 49–108. On Goldfogle's role in Congress as spokesman of the "Jewish interests," see Jacob Magidoff, *The Mirrors of the East Side* [Yiddish] (New York: published by the author, 1923), pp. 117–131.

[88] *New York Times*, Dec. 6, 1905, p. 6.

[89] *American Hebrew*, Sept. 11, 1908, p. 449; *Warheit*, Sept. 14, 1908, p. 1.

[90] J. Magidoff, *op. cit.*, pp. 122–125.

[91] Charles Edward Russell, *op. cit.*, p. 206.

[92] M. Baranof, *Forward*, Nov. 12, 1908, p. 4. Rogoff in his biography of London writes:

> During the campaign weeks the East Side districts rocked with socialistic agitation. The Socialist candidates were hailed as Messiahs. The open air meetings were monster demonstrations of public confidence and affection. The whole city knew it. . . . The marvels of the Socialist strength would grow until the day of election. Then during the twelve hours between the opening of the polls and their closing the strength would melt away [Rogoff, *op. cit.*, p. 16].

[93] See Appendix, Table 15.2. Percentages have been computed on the basis of the U. S. Bureau of the Census, *Thirteenth Census of the United States: 1910 Abstract with Supplement for New York*, pp. 635–636.

[94] See note 14 above. See also Jacob S. Hertz, *The Jewish Socialist Movement in the United States of America* [Yiddish] (New York: *Der Wecker*, 1954), pp. 123–128.

[95] M. Hillquit, *op. cit.*, p. 116; also see note 29 above.

[96] See Appendix, Table 15.3. For Taft's speech at the Thalia Theater, Oct. 28, 1908, see *New York Times*, Oct. 29, 1908, p. 1.

[97] Robert Hunter and J. G. Phelps Stokes were the Socialists running for Assembly in neighboring districts while David Robsen and Joseph Segal were the Republicans. Socialist Robert Hunter despite charges of allegedly harboring anti-Semitic sentiments, *Warheit*, Oct. 30, 1908, pp. 1 and 4; Nov. 3, 1908, p. 4, ran slightly ahead of Max Pine, veteran organizer for the United Hebrew Trades and a fellow Socialist candidate for Assembly in an East Side district.

[98] Louis Boudin in his criticism of the local Socialist campaign strategy mentioned that during the Hillquit campaign circulars were distributed with instructions of how to vote Democrat, Independent and Republican and "split for Hillquit" [*New York Evening Call*, Dec. 15, 1910, p. 6]. Boudin implied that this tactic emanated from Hillquit's campaign headquarters. If it did, it ran counter to the type of campaign Hillquit waged. See also Appendix, Table 15.3.

[99] See Appendix, Table 15.3; also see notes 25 and 29 above.

[100] From the Bureau's inception, the leadership of the Socialist party organization in New York City was antagonistic to it. Hertz, *op. cit.*, pp. 91–107. In December 1908, the National Executive hired an organizer for Yiddish-speaking elements. In January 1909, Hillquit moved to have the organizer recalled. Hertz, *op. cit.*, p. 112. At the 1910 convention, when concessions were made to foreign language groups, the Jewish Agitation Bureau, influenced by the cosmopolitan outlook of the older Jewish Socialists, was the only foreign language body which did not take advantage of the resolution. Hertz, *op. cit.*, p. 118. For a contemporary view of the conflct between "nationalists" and "cosmopolitans" and the Jewish Agitation Bureau, see *Zukunft*, vol. 14, March 1909, p. 187, and Zivyon (Ben Zion Hofman), "The Jewish Agitation Bureau," *Zukunft*, May 1909, pp. 274 ff.

[101] Hertz, *op. cit.*, p. 117.

[102] Rogoff, *op. cit.*, p. 18.

[103] *Ibid.*, p. 52.

[104] *Ibid.*, p. 19; Melech Epstein, *op. cit.*, p. 398.

[105] Rogoff, *op. cit.*, p. 29; Cahan, *op. cit.*, vol. 4, p. 544.

[106] *Forward*, Oct. 3, 1910, p. 1.

[107] Kipnis, *op. cit.*, pp. 282–288.

[108] Shannon, *op. cit.*, pp. 49–50.

[109] *Ibid.*

[110] Kipnis, *op. cit.*, p. 285. For London's report of the Convention, see *Zukunft*, vol. 15, July 1910, p. 401 ff.

[111] Shpizman, *op. cit.*, p. 208. For the position of the Socialist-Zionists in the 1908 campaign see *Warheit*, Sept. 2, 1908, p. 2.

[112] *Forward*, Oct. 20, 1910, p. 1.

[113] *New York Evening Call*, Nov. 25, 1910, p. 6.

[114] *Ibid.*, Nov. 29, 1910, p. 6.

[115] *Ibid.*, Dec. 3, 1910, p. 6; Dec. 6, 1910, p. 6; Dec. 7, 1910, p. 6.

[116] *Ibid.*, Dec. 6, 1910, p. 6.

[117] In 1910, Hillquit was the Socialist candidate for Associate Justice of the Court of Appeals and received 1,581 votes in the Ninth Congressional District, 15.78 percent of the votes cast for that office. *Official Canvass of the Vote Cast, The City Record, City of New York*, Dec. 31, 1910, p. 41. See Appendix, Table 15.5.

[118] See Appendix, Tables 15.3, 15.4, 15.5, 15.6.

[119] *New York Evening Call*, Dec. 15, 1910, p. 6.

[120] *New York Times*, Nov. 9, 1914, p. 14. The boundaries of the Ninth Congressional District were slightly redrawn prior to the 1912 elections to include parts of the 2nd, 4th, 6th, and 8th Assembly Districts and renumbered the Twelfth Congressional District. The results of the 1912 election for Congressman of the Twelfth Congressional District were:

Henry Goldfogle [Democrat]	4,592	[39.42% of the whole vote]
Alex Wolf [Republican]	839	[7.18% of the whole vote]
Meyer London [Socialist]	3,646	[31.22% of the whole vote]
Henry Moskowitz [Progressive]	2,602	[22.18% of the whole vote].

See *Official Canvas of the Vote Cast in the County of New York, The City Record*, Board of the City Record, City of New York, Dec. 31, 1912, p. 177.

The results of the 1914 election for Congressman of the Twelfth Congressional District were:

Benjamin Borowsky [Republican]	1,133	[8.67% of the whole vote]
Meyer London [Socialist]	5,969	[47.98% of the whole vote].
Henry Goldfogle [Democrat]	4,947	[37.98% of the whole vote]

See *ibid.*, Dec. 31, 1914, p. 59.

The Progressives and the Working Class

Vote in California

John L. Shover

16

Quantitative research into popular voting behavior during the Progressive era has modified our earlier belief that the basic source of Progressive strength lay in the middle class. As John L. Shover shows in the following article, Hiram Johnson, California's most important Progressive, received his strongest support in working-class, not middle-class, districts. Shover's conclusions strongly suggest the necessity for further studies of elections involving other California Progressives and Progressives in other states. Professor Shover teaches history at the University of Pennsylvania. With Michael Rogin, who teaches political science at the University of California, Professor Shover is co-author of *Political Change in California, Critical Elections and Social Movements, 1890–1966* (New York, 1970).

Wageworkers were the forgotten men of the Progressive years, if current historical interpretations are to be accepted. Progressivism was a middle-class movement, and while its leaders might strive to remedy the crassest abuses of industrial society, they were as fearful of concentrated labor power as of unregulated monopoly capitalism. In their zeal for moral reform and efficiency, they were often thrown into conflict with labor and immigrant-dominated political machines in cities. Consequently, we should expect few labor leaders to declare their sympathy for the reformers' cause; we should anticipate far less voting strength for Progressive candidates in working-class districts than in middle-class or exclusive residential neighborhoods.[1]

The case is made even stronger for California. The leading authority on the California reformers writes: "Admitting in theory that the union was a necessary organization in the industrial world, the Progressives' bias against labor was always greater than against the large corporation." One of the most influential interpreters of the Progressive movement asserts: "And wherever labor was genuinely powerful in politics — as it was, for instance, in San

---

SOURCE: Reprinted with permission from *Labor History*, vol. 10 (Fall 1969), pp. 584–601.

Francisco, a closed-shop town where labor for a time dominated the local government — progressivism took on a somewhat anti-labor tinge."[2] The Progressive leaders of Southern California were affected by the open-shop militancy of the *Los Angeles Times*; and when they faced political crises in 1911 and 1913, they joined forces with reactionaries to defeat the mayoralty candidacy of a labor-backed Socialist candidate.[3]

The legislatures of 1911 and 1913, guided by Progressive Governor Hiram Johnson, passed significant legislation for the benefit of California working people. Yet Professor Mowry stresses that any concessions to labor were always ringed with compromises. In the 1911 session legislation was approved limiting the working day for women to eight hours, but only after the bill had been amended to exclude farm labor, canning, and packing-house workers. A labor-endorsed anti-injunction bill passed the Senate but died in the Assembly.[4] The 1913 legislature made workman's compensation compulsory; it established an Industrial Welfare Commission empowered to regulate maximum hours, minimum wages, and standard working conditions for women and children; and it set a minimum wage for contract work of the state. However, legislation legalizing peaceful picketing, a bill to provide jury trials in contempt cases arising from labor disputes, and a second anti-injunction measure were defeated.[5] Even this moderate labor legislation distressed Progressive leaders from the conservative Southland; some of the early and prominent supporters of reform attempted to foil the tempered eight-hour day measure and they vigorously resisted the anti-injunction bills.[6] Governor Johnson dispatched four companies of the National Guard to Wheatland, north of Sacramento, after migratory farm workers organized by the IWW had clashed with a sheriff's posse. When Kelley's army of unemployed was disbursed and driven from the capital city by volunteer deputies, the Governor remained silent but, Professor Mowry adds, "there is no question that his sympathies were with the city officials."[7]

The interpretation that represents progressivism as a political move by a disaffected middle class, as reformers frightened by the power of monopolistic corporations and fearful of organized labor, rests upon inferences drawn from public statements and, in a few instances, private thoughts of a leadership elite. Few attempts have been made to examine the other side of the coin and determine the response of labor leaders and the labor press. The conclusion that progressivism was a middle-class movement has not been adequately tested against the voting records of metropolitan areas. It is the hypothesis of this paper that leaders of organized labor in California strongly endorsed progressivism and that, though progressivism was originally sustained by middle- and upper-class voters, after 1914 the major political support for Progressives came from the working-class districts of the state's two principal cities.

Progressive insurgency and the factionalism it wrought in the dominant Republican party were the central issues in California politics from 1910 until 1930. California progressivism was more than Hiram Johnson, but there can be little doubt that the forceful Governor (and later Senator) was the prime representative of the movement in the state. Although Progressive leadership was fractured after 1920, Johnson still laid claim to the mantle to reform leadership and neither his supporters nor his enemies were inclined to deny him the title. To focus principally upon the political support for Johnson therefore provides a good index of the nature of the Progressive voting constituency. During the period considered here, 1910 to 1924, Johnson appeared as a candidate on the California ballot ten times: in the Republican primary for governor and as Republican candidate for governor in 1910; Progressive vice-presidential nominee in 1912; Progressive candidate for governor in 1914; candidate in two senatorial primaries and Republican nominee in two general elections, 1916 and 1922; delegations pledged to him were entered in the presidential primaries of 1920 and 1924. Johnson lost the state in only one election, the presidential primary of 1924.[8]

If California Progressives harbored a bias against labor it was obvious neither to contemporary labor nor to political leaders. True, no labor leaders were among Hiram Johnson's top advisors, but this apparently had little effect upon their support for the Governor. Paul Scharrenberg, long-time executive secretary of the California State Federation of Labor and a central figure in the San Francisco labor movement, was asked in 1954: "Do you think Johnson was pro-labor generally?" He replied:

> Oh, there was no question about it. Some of Mowry's statements in here are perfectly ridiculous. Hiram Johnson was started on his career by the teamsters' union of San Francisco. He'd been their attorney for some time, And John P. McLaughlin, who was secretary of the Teamsters' Union and was later appointed Labor Commissioner by him, he was the boy that rounded them up. And I was one of the first converts. (I was inclined to be for Bell, you know.[9] I was a Democrat then.) I swung in line and so did all the other leaders, but the rank and file in the labor districts of San Francisco, they were Democrats. And they couldn't just switch over because some new guy appeared on the horizon and said, "Here, vote for me." So when someone told Mowry that the leaders of labor were not for Johnson, he's got the thing upside down. The leaders of labor were for Johnson, they dragged the rank and file along. After the election and one or two sessions of the legislature, then the rank and file didn't have to be persuaded any more. They came along all right — on state issues. On national issues, that's something else again.[10]

Scharrenberg also recalled that the labor movement in San Francisco had backed the Progressive initiative and referendum measures.[11]

Frank Havenner, who served as Hiram Johnson's private secretary, managed his California campaign in the presidential primary of 1924 and later served as Congressman from a San Francisco district, commented:

> Johnson through his policies as governor won strong support from organized labor and I think that after that the organized labor forces of San Francisco supported Johnson.... As Hiram Johnson gradually acquired the support of organized labor in Northern California ... he began to lose some of his old anti-labor so-called Progressive support in Southern California.[12]

Chester Rowell, once designated by Johnson as his heir-apparent[13] but by 1920 at bitter odds with the Senator over the League of Nations, appraised the political situation in California before the Hoover-Johnson presidential primary of 1920. He noted that Johnson had the labor vote and that of the political Irish and Catholics. He had the support of all important labor leaders and of both the Old Guard and Progressive machines in San Francisco,[14] while Hoover was endorsed by housewives, the Protestant church, anti-Irish and anti-Catholics voters, and both the old Guard and Progressive machines in Southern California.[15]

Organized labor, particularly in San Francisco, generally refrained from partisan political endorsements. Nevertheless, the sympathies of the labor press for Hiram Johnson were scarcely veiled. *The Labor Clarion*, organ of the San Francisco Central Labor Council, quoted Scharrenberg that Johnson's "uncompromising attitude for an effective Workman's Compensation Act ... should ever endear him to the men and women of labor."[16] *The Clarion* refrained from comment during the campaign of 1914, though after the balloting "rejoiced" in the reelection of Governor Johnson.[17] The paper also offered discreet blessings for Johnson during his first senatorial campaign in 1916.[18]

When the California State Federation of Labor took a political stance in the 1920s, its support for Senator Johnson was unequivocal. During the 1924 presidential primary, a flyer signed by the President and Secretary of the State Federation urged all members who registered Republican to cast their ballot for Johnson.[19] *The Southern California Labor Press* (Los Angeles) editorialized on March 21: "The labor movement of California always has supported Mr. Johnson, on account of his record as governor." The four labor councils of Los Angeles — central labor, building trades, metal trades and allied printing trades — unanimously endorsed Johnson's presidential candidacy. The *Sacramento Bee* remarked that the labor councils had taken this stand "in every campaign in which Senator Johnson has figured."[20]

Did the workers of California, organized and unorganized, follow the lead of union leaders and the labor press? The extent of working class support for Johnson and progressivism can best be determined by examining voting statistics from California's two major metropolitan centers, San Francisco and Los Angeles.

The two counties[21] provided upwards of 40 percent of the total vote cast in any California election.[22] Both cities contained a large working-class population, but here the similarity ended. San Francisco, though predominantly Catholic, was ethnically diverse; in 1920, 28 percent of its population was foreign-born, with Irish and Italians forming the largest groups. Los Angeles was peopled by immigrants, but they were mostly Protestant Anglo-Saxons from the small towns and farms of the South and Midwest. Only 18 percent of the country's population was foreign-born, and a quarter of these were from England and Canada.[23] San Francisco was a closed-shop town; union membership at its peak in 1918 totaled approximately 100,000.[24] In contrast, Los Angeles was virtually an open-shop city; 40,000 belonged to unions in 1919.[25] Labor influence loomed large in San Francisco city politics. Abe Reuf's Union Labor party, built independently of formal union support, was broken by the graft prosecutions of 1906, but P. H. McCarthy, head of the powerful Building Trades Council, managed to pick up the pieces and win election as mayor in 1909. By 1911, however, the San Francisco Labor Council, a rival organization that had supported the graft prosecutions and opposed McCarthy, emerged as the dominant power group in San Francisco labor. More cosmopolitan than the locally-centered Building Trades, the Labor Council lobbied in Sacramento and its leaders, Paul Scharrenberg among them, identified with the Progressive administration of Johnson.[26] On the other hand, Los Angeles labor, locked in a futile battle with powerful anti-labor interests, took up a more radical posture. Job Harriman, a Socialist supported by labor, barely lost the race for mayor in 1911, and several Socialist assemblymen won seats in Sacramento. Although weak, Los Angeles labor was far from politically impotent. Labor-endorsed candidates usually held several posts on the city council and, in May 1925, eight of eleven labor-approved candidates were elected.[27]

In the reapportionment of 1911, San Francisco was allotted thirteen assembly districts. Voting returns were tabulated by assembly district and, since there was no further reapportionment until 1929, political boundaries remained fixed through the Progressive period. To characterize the political constituency of the various San Francisco assembly districts is relatively easy. Tradition has it that the working class lived south of Market Street along the bayshore and in the Mission District, while the nabobs peered down upon them from Nob Hill, Russian Hill, and Pacific Heights in the north, and an upwardly mobile middle class resided in the trim row houses of Sunset and Richmond on the ocean side of the city. The accuracy of these impressions can be confirmed by such indices as the vote on an anti-picketing referendum in 1916 (an indication of where labor sentiment was strongest), the vote for Socialist candidates, and ethnic data from the 1920 census (also tabulated by assembly district).[28]

When Hiram Johnson, prosecutor of the Reuf machine and opponent of the Southern Pacific Railroad, first sought the governorship in 1910, he was not popular in his home town. Contesting with five other candidates in the Republican primary, he ran second with 36 percent of the vote while carrying Los Angeles County by a clear majority of 52 percent.[29] Johnson carried, all by plurality, only three of San Francisco's eighteen assembly districts;[30] these three encompassed the Sunset and Richmond areas, Pacific Heights, and an apartment-house district stretching north from the present Civic Center toward Nob Hill. He ran weakest in the working-class areas south of Market and in the Mission District. His 43 percent of the vote won him San Francisco County in a three-way race in November, but at the same time garnered him 46 percent in Los Angeles. Johnson carried ten assembly districts but won a majority only in A.D. 41 and 42, the silk-stocking Pacific Heights and midtown apartment house areas. The election was complicated by the presence on the ballot of a Socialist,[31] who received 8 percent of the city's vote but won more than 20 percent in five of the "south of the slot" working-class districts.[32] Although Johnson carried five of the districts south of Market, the votes that won for him ranged from a low of 38 percent to a high of 44 percent. Johnson's victories in 1910 owed little to San Francisco; he had won the "better" neighborhoods, but the vast majority of the working-class population had voted their preference for Democratic or Socialist candidates.[33]

An abrupt change in the Progressive voting constituency took place in 1914. Campaigning as a Progressive party candidate in his bid for reelection and opposed by both major parties, Johnson polled 55 percent of the vote in San Francisco and 53.5 percent in Los Angeles. More important was the vote distribution.[34] Johnson secured a majority in nine of the thirteen assembly districts, including all those south of Market and in the Mission. For example, in 1910 Johnson polled 38 percent of the vote in the assemnly district situated in the Potrero Hill area; in 1914 in the new A.D. 22, which circumscribed much the same area, he received 67 percent of the vote. The Socialist vote there in 1910 had been 24 percent; in 1914 it was down to 7 percent. Johnson's poorest showing in the entire city (39.5 percent) was in A.D. 31 located in the Pacific Heights area, its boundaries only slightly modified from the district that had given him 52 percent of its vote in 1910. In addition he ran below his city average in A.D. 27 (Sunset), 28 (Richmond), 32 (Russian Hill, downtown apartment house area), 30 (Western Addition) and 33 (Italian, North Beach). Thus Johnson won San Francisco with a base of support quite different from that which placed him in the State House four years earlier. His success resulted from strong new support in working-class districts, which more than compensated serious losses in the more exclusive residential areas.

The voting patterns of 1914 became a permanent part of the San Francisco political landscape. As Table 16.1 indicates, in seven contests between 1914 and 1924, Johnson's landslide victories derived most from the vote in A.D. 21 through 26 and 29 — all but two of them south of Market or in the Mission.[35] With minor exceptions, Johnson's vote was always below the mean of his San Francisco vote in A.D. 27, 28, 31, 32, and 33; the Sunset, Richmond, Pacific Heights, Nob Hill, Russian Hill, and North Beach areas.[36] The differential was most obvious in primaries, less so in general elections because of traditional

Table 16.1   Johnson's Percentage Vote in San Francisco

	Governor 1914	Senator Primary 1916	Senator 1916	Presidential Primary 1920	Senator Primary 1922	Senator 1922	Presidential Primary 1924
City	54.6	59.2	71.9	73.4	60.7	67.9	59.7
Working Class Assembly Districts							
21	60.0	70.1	68.2	80.5	70.8	64.5	67.5
22	67.7	77.3	77.5	84.2	75.6	70.2	78.8
23	66.3	75.2	72.7	87.5	78.7	70.4	79.9
24	66.5	72.9	74.3	84.1	73.5	71.8	70.6
25	62.6	64.2	74.9	84.9	73.6	75.6	75.2
26	56.2	60.0	73.8	79.7	67.0	69.0	64.3
29	59.4	63.3	70.7	80.3	71.6	71.4	70.4
Middle and Upper Class							
27	53.7	55.9	71.1	71.8	58.7	67.6	50.7
28	51.1	53.6	70.8	68.8	50.7	68.0	43.5
30	46.5	57.5	67.7	74.8	61.7	65.7	57.4
31	39.5	42.2	71.3	52.7	38.7	60.7	31.5
32	45.4	49.1	70.0	62.0	48.0	62.6	38.6
Italian Working Class							
33	47.4	57.0	74.3	63.7	52.3	67.1	48.0

party loyalty. Even so, working-class districts were casting a more preponderant vote for Hiram Johnson by 1922, when he was a Republican party candidate, than were the residents of Pacific Heights.[37]

The Johnson voting constituency in San Francisco can be defined more precisely by correlating the percentage votes in the thirteen assembly districts over a series of elections.[38] Correlations with votes before 1911 are impossible because of the reapportionment that took place in that year. However, comparison of the votes for Theodore Roosevelt, first in the presidential primary and then in the general election of 1912, with the vote for Hiram Johnson in 1914 strongly suggests that a major realignment took place between these two elections. The vote for Roosevelt in the Republican presidential primary of 1912 correlated a low .484 with the vote for Johnson in the general election of 1914; and the vote for Roosevelt, the Republican presidential candidate in California in 1912, correlated negatively (−.48) with the Johnson vote in the general election of 1914.[39] The alignment first evident in 1914 was amazingly stable. As Table 16.2 indicates, it persisted regardless of embroilments and defections within the Progressive leadership. Johnson's vote for governor in 1914, for example, correlated a high .93 with his vote in the presidential primary of 1924.

Table 16.2   Correlation Matrix, Johnson's San Francisco Vote

	(1) Governor 1914	(2) Primary 1916	(3) Senator 1916	(4) Primary 1920	(5) Primary 1922	(6) Senator 1922	(7) Primary 1924
(1)							
(2)	.944						
(3)	.514	.683					
(4)	.939	.909	.330				
(5)	.938	.936	.351	.994			
(6)	.818	.649	.583	.801	.764		
(7)	.936	.939	.427	.983	.996	.782	

Most important, the correlation figures underscore the close relationship of the vote for Hiram Johnson with pro-labor sentiment in San Francisco. In the election of 1916 the city's voters passed by a narrow margin Charter Amendment #8, an anti-picketing ordinance modeled on that of Los Angeles and supported by business interests determined to limit union power.[40] The vote for Johnson in the primary correlated .949 with the votes "no" on this crucial index of labor sentiment. In the general election of 1914 and in each primary in which Hiram Johnson was a candidate, the correlation of his vote with the vote "no" on the anti-picketing ordinance was above .90.

Table 16.3   Johnson Vote and Pro-Labor Sentiment in San Francisco

	Governor 1914	Primary 1916	Senator 1916	Presidential Primary 1920	Senator Primary 1922	Presidential Primary 1924
Charter Amendment #8	.921	.949	.358*	.914	.947	.959

*This correlation is low since votes in the general election might include loyal Republicans unsympathetic to labor.

The fact that Johnson absorbed the Socialist vote in San Francisco indicates further the political inclination of areas where he gathered his most loyal supporters. His percentage in 1914 correlated .67 with the percentage for Eugene V. Debs in the 1912 election; in 1920, when Johnson was a candidate in the May presidential primary and Debs was in the November election, the correlation was .88.

Johnson's working-class backers in San Francisco recognized Progressives regardless of the party label they wore. Woodrow Wilson carried the city in 1916 with 52 percent of the vote; Robert LaFollette, listed on the California ballot in 1924 as a Socialist, won 46 percent of the San Francisco vote. The distribution of Wilson's 1916 vote by assembly district correlated .905 with that of Johnson in the Republican primary and .245 with his Republican senatorial vote in November (Table 16.4). The latter figure is especially significant. As against the normal expectation of a close identity between a party's presidential and senatorial candidate, Johnson's vote correlated positively with that of Wilson and negatively (−.245) with that of Hughes.[41] Given the decisive importance of the close California vote in 1916, if Charles Evans Hughes had ridden Johnson's coattails in San Francisco he would have become President of the United States.

Table 16.4   Correlation: Johnson, Wilson, LaFollette

	Governor 1914	Primary 1916	Wilson 1916	Charter Amendment #8	Primary 1920	Primary 1922	Primary 1924
LaFollette 1924	.888	.935	.922	.971	.926	.967	.986
Wilson, 1916	.911	.905		.912	.943	.953	.931

The high correlation of .986 between the backing given Johnson in the 1924 presidential primary and the vote for LaFollette in the general election demonstrates an almost complete identity of support. Examined in time series (Table 16.4), LaFollette's strength in San Francisco was in the same districts that had overwhelmingly endorsed Johnson, opposed the anti-picketing ordinance, and voted most heavily for Wilson in 1916.[42]

There was an important ethnic element in Hiram Johnson's vote. In general, the greater the number of foreign-born and first generation immigrants in an assembly district, the higher the vote for Johnson. (See Table 16.5.) Most striking was the high relationship between the number of foreign-born Irish[43] and the Johnson vote. The Irish population was diffused throughout San Francisco with slightly higher concentrations in A.D. 21, 24, and 25, the former south of Market on the bayshore and the latter two in the Mission. All three were Johnson political strongholds.[44] One ethnic group, representing the largest foreign-born component in the city, however, was little attracted to Progressivism. A.D. 33, where 19 percent of the population were native Italians, ran consistently below the city average for Johnson and voted 60.2 percent "Yes" on the 1916 anti-picketing ordinance.[45] The Irish, foreign-born and first generation were concentrated in working-class districts; whether they voted as they did because they were members of a nationality group or because they were part of the laboring class cannot be accurately determined. But the higher correlation figures indicate that the vote against the 1916 anti-picketing ordinance would have been a better gauge of the future political behavior of a district than the percentage of Irish or non-native white population.

Table 16.5   Correlation: Nativity, Foreign Born, and the Progressive Vote

	Nativity* 1920	Foreign-Born Irish	Foreign-Born German
Johnson, Governor, 1914	.545	.796	.545
Johnson, Primary, 1916	.756	.692	.455
Johnson, Senator, 1916	.432	.469	.07
Wilson, 1916	.522	.751	.630
Charter Amendment #8	.703	.733	.530
Johnson, Primary, 1920	.524	.780	.686
Johnson, Primary, 1922	.687	.747	.613
Johnson, Senator, 1922	.305	.604	.414
Johnson, Primary, 1924	.644	.735	.578

*"Nativity" refers to the percent of the total population of the city or an A.D. who were *not* native whites of native white parentage.

San Francisco voting returns lend scant support to any hypothesis that progressivism in California was sustained by middle-class votes. Alleged bias against unions did not deter the great majority of San Franciscans who voted "no" on the anti-picketing ordinance from also marking their ballot for Hiram Johnson. As governor and senator, Johnson had amazing drawing power in San Francisco and the ability to win middle-class votes, particularly in general elections. Yet, as 1910 demonstrated, his base was weak when these constituted his principal support. A new Progressive constituency centered in working-class assembly districts emerged in 1914; it carried the city for Johnson every time he was a candidate; it won the city — and the presidency — for Woodrow Wilson in 1916; it provided the core of LaFollette's support in 1924. As the Progressives gained strong labor support, they were deserted by voters in "better" neighborhoods. Had Johnson lacked the urban lower-class support that allowed him to garner huge majorities in San Francisco to offset losses in Southern California, his political career would have been terminated at an early date.

Analysis of the support for Hiram Johnson in Los Angeles County must first take into account the fact that the original enthusiasm Southern California voters demonstrated for progressivism waned rapidly after 1914.[46] In the 1910 primary, Johnson ran 20 percentage points ahead of the strongest of his four opponents and carried Los Angeles County with a 52 percent majority. In the general election, his 46 percent was ten percentage points above that of the Democratic candidate.[47] The governor far outdistanced the field in 1914, winning 53.5 percent of the county's vote against Republican, Democratic, Prohibition and Socialist opponents. In the four ensuing primaries, two senatorial and two presidential, while Johnson was winning more than 60 percent of the San Francisco Republican vote in each, he failed to carry Los Angeles County once.[48]

The study of Los Angeles County voting returns is complicated by methodological problems.[49] Any conclusion drawn from the returns must be more generalized and less precise than those from San Francisco data. A few comparisons, however, are possible. Votes within the City of Los Angles, the urban heart of the county, can be distinguished from the combined vote of the suburbs. It is also possible to extract from the voting ledgers the approximate vote of Long Beach and Pasadena, the two largest suburban communities.

The impressive majority that Hiram Johnson compiled in Los Angeles County in the 1910 primary owed more to votes cast in the suburban communities than in the urban central city. In Pasadena, a wealthy garden city, he amassed 58 percent of the vote; in Long Beach, largest of the suburbs and haven for midwestern émigrés, he won 61.4 percent. The voting pattern was comparable to that of San Francisco in 1910: Johnson ran proportionately better in middle- and upper-class districts.

Changes in the distribution of votes in Los Angeles are less dramatic than those in San Francisco, but a similar trend appears. Between 1910 and 1914, support for Johnson increased sharply in the City. As Table 16.6 shows, while his voting percentage dwindled throughout the county after 1916, the greatest losses were in the suburbs and were most severe in Pasadena and Long Beach. By 1920 Johnson was distinctly a more popular candidate among the residents of the older, less exclusive homes and apartments in the heart of the city than with the more affluent in Pasadena or Long Beach.

Table 16.6   Percentage Vote for Johnson in Los Angeles County

	Primary 1910	Governor 1910	Governor 1914	Primary 1916	Primary 1920	Primary 1922	Primary 1924
Los Angeles County	51.9	45.7	53.5	41.8	49.7	44.1	34.5
City	49.7	41.5	54.9	41.0	53.7	47.0	37.6
Suburbs	55.7	52.1	51.5	43.2	44.5	40.0	30.8
Long Beach	61.4	54.1	52.9	46.7	46.4	34.2	25.7
Pasadena	58.0	55.9	52.8	49.7	33.0	30.2	19.8

Other variations in voting behavior suggest differences between the City of Los Angeles and the suburbs. The City tended to be more favorable to Socialist candidates: J. Stitt Wilson tallied 20 percent of the City vote in 1910 and only 12 percent in the suburbs. Los Angeles County was a Republican stronghold, but the City was less so than the suburbs. In 1916 Woodrow Wilson won 47.4 percent in the City and 42.6 percent in the suburbs.[50] The most distinct difference was the vote on a 1916 state prohibition initiative: the City voted 46 percent in favor: the suburbs, 64 percent. Johnson received his best support in Los Angeles County after 1916 from areas that tended to be against prohibition, slightly more Democratic, and more inclined to vote for an attractive Socialist candidate.[51]

Ethnically, Los Angeles County was more homogenous than San Francisco, and population distinctions between City and suburbs represent shadings rather than clear differences. Fifty-five percent of the county's residents in 1920 were native whites born of native parents, compared to 33 percent in San Francisco. Nonetheless, a few variations appear in this predominately white, Anglo-Saxon mosaic. Table 16.7 shows that Los Angeles City was slightly more diverse than the suburbs, and particularly more so than Long Beach and Pasadena. Even the figures of 15 percent and 12 percent foreign-born in the latter two cities are deceiving, for in Pasadena, 39 percent and Long Beach 47.5 percent of the foreign born were natives of England or Canada.[52] Nativity statistics from Los Angeles County, though indecisive, support the conclusion that Hiram Johnson ran proportionately stronger after 1916 in more ethnically diverse areas — that is, urban Los Angeles — and, in general, the greater the percentage of native whites of Anglo-Saxon background, the weaker the support for Johnson.

Table 16.7   Ethnic Background, Los Angeles County (in Percentages)

	Native White	Native White of Native Parentage	Foreign Born
San Francisco County	69.0	33.0	27.7*
Los Angeles County	77.4	55.1	17.8
City	75.4	51.1	19.4
Suburbs	79.7	60.0	14.8
Long Beach	86.8	68.2	12.1
Pasadena	81.5	61.7	15.0

*California Compendium, 1920, pp. 34-35, 39-43.

To determine if there were differences in the extent of support for Johnson within the boundaries of the City an attempt was made in one election, the primary of 1922, to equate the official vote tabulations by precinct with the seven assembly districts in the City.[53] By this estimate, the percentage vote for Johnson was greatest in A.D. 71 (61 percent compared to 47 percent in the City as a whole), located to the south of the City's center adjacent to Long Beach, incorporating the harbor area at San Pedro and stretching north in a narrow corridor along Main and Central Avenue.[54] Johnson ran above his city average by more than 10 percentage points in two assembly districts just south of the present Civic Center. His weakest showing in the City was in the two districts located west of Figueroa Street, a traditional boundary line that separates "better" residential areas to the west from downtown. In general, Johnson's vote in the City was greatest in the most distinctly working-class areas to the south and near the city center, and diminished as one moved westward across the City.

Los Angeles voting returns reveal a pattern similar to, though less distinctive than, San Francisco's. Whether this less distinctive pattern is the result of actual voting returns, or of the more generalized data from Los Angeles County employed here, cannot be determined. Suburban voters, particularly in Pasadena and Long Beach, like those in San Francisco's Richmond District and Pacific Heights, abandoned Hiram Johnson in increasing numbers on election day. As his popularity in the state's largest county declined, those who remained his most steadfast supporters were residents of urban neighborhoods which not vague impressions but such concrete data as skepticism toward prohibition, occasional support for Socialists, and diverse ethnic composition would identify as working class.

To accept the conclusion of this paper, coupled with those of two recent and complementary studies by Michael P. Rogin and Alexander Saxton,[55] would require a recasting of widely accepted interpretations of the Progressive movement. Neither the statements of politicians and labor leaders, nor the voting records from California's two major metropolitan centers, sustain the thesis that progressivism was primarily a middle-class movement. The rank-and-file urban voters who consistently backed Progressive candidates lived in working-class areas. In consequence, the hypothesis that the California Progressive represented a particular strain of middle-class individualist who became militant when he felt himself hemmed in between the battening corporation and the rising labor union seems scarcely tenable. Any anti-labor tinge in the thought of leaders of California progressivism appears to have had little political significance.

A reevaluation of progressivism taking into account its urban lower-class support would necessitate a new focus upon the social reform programs of Progressive governors and legislators — certainly in California, and perhaps elsewhere.[56] Between the years 1911 and 1915, *some* factor transformed working-class voters from apathy to vigorous support of progressivism and, by the same token, *some* factor incited the suspicions of middle- and upper-class electors, causing them to drift away.

If the testimony of labor leaders and the evidence from the labor vote is to be accepted, the working class and its leaders considered the social legislation of the Progressives important positive achievements. While this legislation was often qualified and tempered, the labor constituency was obviously more impressed by the gains they had made, rather than by the demands, such as an anti-injunction bill, they had lost.

In like fashion, it would appear that in 1910, when the Progressive program was largely a negative one aimed at destroying the power of the Southern Pacific machine, there were among its leaders — and perhaps voting supporters — individuals, particularly from Southern California, who had little sympathy with the demands of labor. As the Johnson legislative program unfolded, these anti-labor elements fell by the wayside, and by 1916 the main line of California progressivism was firmly tied to a working-class base. In this perspective, the humanitarian and labor legislation of the first Johnson administration assume major political significance.

A reinterpretation that credits the urban-laboring population with a central political role in the Progressive movement will restore a sense of continuity to the study of American reform. Hence, the upsurge of working-class and immigrant power that dominated American politics during the depressions and at least a decade thereafter would no longer appear as a sudden phenomenon that burst forth in an Al Smith revolution in 1928.[57] In California, the political upheaval of the thirties marked the augmenting and coming to power of the same groups that had sustained Johnson, Wilson, and LaFollette, buttressed the Progressive reforms of two decades earlier, and kept what remained of reform politics alive through the 1920s.

NOTES

[1] George E. Mowry, "The California Progressive and His Rationale: A study in Middle Class Politics," *Mississippi Valley Historical Review*, vol. 36 (September 1949), pp. 239–250; Richard Hofstadter, *The Age of Reform* (New York, 1955), pp. 131–270.

[2] George E. Mowry, *The California Progressives* (Encounter paperback ed., Chicago, 1963), p. 92. Hofstadter, *op. cit.*, p. 239.

[3] Mowry, *California Progressives*, pp. 51, 143, 201.

[4] *Ibid.*, pp. 144–147.

[5] *Ibid.*, p. 155.

[6] *Ibid.*, pp. 144, 146–147.

[7] *Ibid.*, pp. 195, 198.

[8] Johnson won reelection by landslide in 1928; in 1932 and 1940 he crossfiled, and won both Republican and Democratic nominations. Eugene C. Lee, *California Votes, 1928–1960* (Berkeley, 1963), pp. A-50, A-55, A-60.

[9] Theodore Bell, Democratic candidate for governor, 1910.

[10] Paul Scharrenberg, "Paul Scharrenberg Reminiscences" (Transcript of tape recorded interviews, Bancroft Library, Berkeley, 1954), pp. 54–55.

[11] *Ibid.*, pp. 56–61.

[12] Franck R. Havenner, "Franck Roberts Havenner Reminiscences" (Transcript of tape recorded interviews, Bancroft Library, 1953), pp. 61.

[13] Hiram Johnson to Chester Rowell, March 19, 1916. Johnson papers. Bancroft Library.

[14] 1920 was the only election in which the San Francisco "Old Guard" endorsed Johnson. See *San Francisco Chronicle*, May 1, 2, 1920.

[15] Rowell to Mark Sullivan, April 29, 1920. Rowell papers, Bancroft Library.

[16] May 16, 1913.

[17] November 6, 1914.

[18] September 1, October 27, 1916.

[19] Copy in Johnson papers, Part III, Carton 10, Bancroft Library.

[20] April 12, 1924.

[21] Boundaries of the city and county of San Francisco are contiguous.

[22] For example, in the 1918 gubernatorial election, 38.7 percent; 1920 presidential, 42.8 percent; 1922 gubernatorial, 40.2 percent, 1924 presidential, 47.6 percent.

[23] U. S. Department of Commerce, Bureau of the Census, *Fourteenth Census of the United States, State Compendium: California* (Washington), 1932, pp. 39–40, 41, 43. (Hereinafter cited, *California Compendium*, 1920.)

[24] Robert Edward Lee Knight, *Industrial Relations in the San Francisco Bay Area, 1900–1918* (Berkeley, 1960), p. 369.

[25] Louis B. Perry and Richard S. Perry, *A History of the Los Angeles Labor Movement, 1911–1941* (Berkeley, 1963), pp. 107–108.

[26] Alexander Saxton, "San Francisco Labor and the Populist and Progressive Insurgencies," *Pacific Historical Review*, vol. 34 (November 1965), pp. 427–430.

[27] Perry and Perry, *op. cit.*, p. 215.

[28] See Table 16.3. Saxton, *loc cit.*, pp. 423–424 uses different indices and arrives at almost the same characterization.

[29] All San Francisco voting statistics are from Official Statement of Vote, City and County of San Francisco (in the files of Registrar of Voters, City Hall). Maps of assembly districts are in the same office. Percentages have been calculated by the author; all figures in the text except those ending .5 have been rounded to nearest whole number.

[30] The 1910 election preceded reapportionment; San Francisco had eighteeen assembly districts.

[31] J. Stitt Wilson, elected mayor of Berkeley in 1911.

[32] Refers to the cable car "slot" that ran down Market Street.

[33] A vote for the Democrat, Bell, was not a vote against reform. His platform denounced the Southern Pacific. Mowry, *California Progressives*, p. 130.

[34] The primaries of 1914 are ignored; Johnson was unopposed for the Progressive party nomination.

[35] A.D. 29 was intersected by Market Street west of City Hall; the bulk of the district lay south in the upper Mission. A.D. 26 was immediately west and extended north from Market to Fulton Street.

[36] On A.D. 33, see *infra*.

[37] The "better" residential areas had not lost their Republican loyalty. Harding polled more than 70 percent in A.D. 27, 28, 31, 32 and 33; his city mean was 65 percent. The victorious Republican gubernatorial candidate in 1922, conservative Friend W. Richardson, lost the city but carried AD. 28, 31, and 32.

[38] A correlation coefficient measures the relationship between two variables. The higher the number, the closer the relationship. A high coefficient would indicate that where one variable was high, the second would be high; and where the first was low, the second would also be low. Coefficients for San Francisco election returns are very high. As a rule of thumb, a coefficient of .90 would explain 81 percent of the variance. All computations are by the author.

[39] Woodrow Wilson carried every San Francisco A.D. in 1912; his largest margins were in nonworking class 30, 31 and 32. Like Johnson's, his support diverged; the vote that won Wilson the city in 1916 correlated —.88 with his vote in 1912.

40 An adjunct of this same campaign was the Preparedness Day parade in July 1916 where the bomb exploded that led to the Mooney-Billings case. Knight, *op. cit.*, pp. 304–318.

41 Where there are two candidates only, a + correlation with the vote of the Democrat would mean the inverse, a — correlation with the vote of the Republican.

42 The same constituency also supported Progressive initiative and referendum measures. One of the most important of these, the Water and Power Act of 1922, was designed to put state credit behind public ownership of water and hydroelectric facilities. It was defeated, but in San Francisco the vote "Yes" correlated .94 with the "No" vote on anti-picketing and .97 with Johnson's vote in the 1922 primary. On the Act itself see Franklin H. Hichborn, "California Politics, 1891–1939" (unpublished manuscript, Haynes Foundation, Los Angeles), pp. 1958–2013.

43 An inference is made that the larger the number of foreign-born Irish, the more Irish a district. *California Compendium*, 1920, p. 43.

44 See Table 16.1.

45 Any explanation of the deviation in the Italian community is beyond the scope of this paper. A.D. 33 voted nearly as strongly for Old Guard Republicans as Pacific Heights, but the district shifted in 1928.

46 Michael P. Rogin, "Progressivism and the California Electorate," *Journal of American History*, vol. 55 (September 1968), pp. 297–314.

47 There were three candidates in the 1910 general election.

48 All Los Angeles County returns are from, Minutes of the Board of Supervisors, County of Los Angeles, Record of Elections (in Files Section, Board of Supervisors, County Administration Building).

49 Election results are not totaled for Assembly Districts but are tallied in units of 60 precincts, the number recorded on a single page of the voting ledger. Precincts are arranged in numerical order for the City of Los Angeles; for outlying areas of the county, all cities with the return from each of their precincts are listed alphabetically. Since precinct boundaries were often modified and new precincts added, correlations are possible only in the rare cases when no changes were made between a primary and general election in the same year. This study made use of the recapitulation of the vote in the ledgers only.

50 Johnson's November vote in 1916 correlated .509 with Wilson's November vote, a coefficient higher than in San Francisco.

51 Differences still exist. In 1966, Governor Brown in losing the county won 53 percent of the vote in the City but only 36 percent in the suburbs. Frank M. Jordan, compiler, *California Statement of Vote and Supplement: November 8, 1966 General Election*, pp. 86–87.

52 Cf. 22 percent of the foreign-born in the city native to England or Canada.

53 No attempt was made to recompute the 600 odd precincts into A.D. totals. Totals used were from the ledger pages and are proximations. E.G., A.D. 74 consisted of precincts 65–104, 275–282. The totals used here to proximate A.D. 74 are 61–120, therefore including twenty precincts contiguous to but not a part of A.D. 74 and eliminating eight precincts. Precinct maps are not available. For A.D. boundaries in Los Angeles, 1911–1929 see Don A. Allen, Sr., *Legislative Sourcebook: The California Legislature and Reapportionment, 1849–1965* (Sacramento, 1966), p. 140.

54 This area is now largely inhabited by Negroes.

55 Rogin, *loc. cit.*, Saxton, *loc. cit.*, pp. 421–438.

56 Such a reevaluation is underway. Several recent studies question the "elitist" interpretation of progressivism by suggesting that many Progressive leaders were motivated by the genuine needs of the urban working class and that workers and union organizations in California and elsewhere reciprocated by providing Progressives with electoral support. See J. Joseph Huthmacher, "Urban Liberalism and the Age of Reform," *Mississippi Valley Historical Review*, vol. 49 (September 1962), pp. 231–241 and by the same author, *Senator Robert F. Wagner and the Rise of Urban Liberalism* (New York, 1968); Spencer C. Olin, Jr., "The Social Conscience of the Hiram Johnson Administration," paper delivered at the annual meeting. Organization of American Historians, Chicago, 1967 and Olin's later book, *California's Prodigal Sons: Hiram Johnson and the Progressives, 1911–1917* (Berkeley, 1968); Gerald D. Nash, "The Influence of Labor on State Policy, 1860–1920: The Experience of California." *California Historical Society Quarterly*, vol. 47 (September 1965), pp. 241–257; Saxton, *loc. cit.*, pp. 430–435.

57 John L. Shover, "Was 1928 a Critical Election in California?" *Pacific Northwest Quarterly*, vol. 58 (October 1967), pp. 196–204.

Immigrant Ethnicity in a Changing Politics:

Chicago from Progressivism to FDR

John M. Allswang

17

Between the 1890s and 1920s, large numbers of immigrants from eastern and southern Europe settled in several major northern cities. By the 1920s, members of the immigrant communities were voting in large enough numbers to transform the electorate and political scene in many cities. John M. Allswang analyzes this trans-formation in one such city, Chicago, focusing in particular on the interaction between the established political parties and the new immigrant groups. He argues that in Chicago at least, a dominant "ethnic Democratic coalition" came into existence before the Great Depression. Professor Allswang teaches at California State College, Los Angeles. His book, *A House for All Peoples: Ethnic Politics in Chicago, 1890–1936* (Lexington, Ky., 1971) has just appeared.

Chicago is an excellent microcosm for ethnic studies: it had a good variety of immigrant groups in considerable numbers, and at least after World War I most of their members were able to vote. The ethnic balance was constantly chang-ing, via in-migrations, thus it was not static, and interchange and conflict were always present. Seventy-two percent of Chicago's people were foreign stock in 1920; 64 percent in 1930; add to the latter figure 7 percent Negroes, and it is obvious that the old stock was a distinct minority.

Total adult population and voting population are not the same, and for this reason one must be careful in generalizing about newer immigrant voting behav-ior before the war. For example, of numbers present in 1930, over half the Rus-sians, Czechs, Poles, Lithuanians, Italians, and Yugoslavs arrived after 1900.[1] And if we add to this a mean-time-to-naturalization of ten years,[2] it is obvious that many of the newer immigrants were naturalized and voting only during and after the war. In 1920, for example, only 35 percent of Chicago's Italians and 34 percent of its Poles were naturalized.[3] Thus we can only note the voting of the

SOURCE: Reprinted with permission of the author. Presented before the Eighty-Fifth Annual Meeting of the American Historical Association, Boston, Massachusetts, December 1970. All figures and tables reprinted with permission of the publisher from *A House for All Peoples: Ethnic Politics in Chicago, 1890–1936* (Lexington, Ky.: The University Press of Kentucky, 1971).

areas in which newer immigrants lived before the war. And for this and other data-related reasons, I have used different methodologies for my pre- and post-war analyses.[4]

An inquiry into immigrant ethnicity in politics logically breaks down into two foci. First, I want to describe immigrant political behavior, especially voting; this will necessarily be cursory since most viable measures of political behavior are quantitative and one cannot all be covered in a paper of this nature. Second, I shall try to point out some of the causes of this behavior — specifically those forces which resulted in strong ethnic Democratic voting by the end of the 1920s, voting that became a tradition, the so-called Roosevelt or New Deal coalition.[5]

Between 1890 and 1916 the two major parties shared Chicago's vote pretty evenly, although at the presidential level the Republicans beat the Democrats five to one; and Theodore Roosevelt received a plurality in 1912. National and state voting were quite close, but local voting was separate, and dominated by the Democratic Carter H. Harrisons, father and son, each of whom was elected mayor five times.

The mean vote of the seven ethnic groups studied to 1916 followed the Chicago vote, although consistently somewhat more Democratic; for example, the ethnic mean vote was Democratic for president in 1900 and 1916, while the city mean was not. As the newer immigrants poured into Chicago, they were entering a city with a mixed political tradition, two strong parties and conflicting pulls.

The Progressive-involved campaigns of 1912–1916 were not without effect in Chicago. In 1912 Roosevelt received a plurality with 38 percent to 31 percent for Wilson, 18 percent for Taft and 13 percent for Debs. In state-level races of that year the Democrats won by pluralities. Again in 1914 the Progressive vote permitted a Democrat to win with a plurality for the Senate. But by 1916 this was over and the Republicans won again, except for one state office where another strong Socialist vote resulted in another Democratic plurality. Apart from a strong response to Roosevelt, immigrant voters remained constant relative to the city's vote; they were not really affected by progressivism. And it appears that Progressive votes, and even most Socialist votes, came from Republican voters who returned to their traditional party in 1916 and after. Progressivism was a phenomenon within the Republican party — a temporary indisposition — and of no real moment to ethnics voting at the time.

The voting of individual groups reinforces these conclusions. Outside of 1912 the progressive era elections saw no change at all in the voting of newer immigrant areas, and only slight change for the Germans and Swedes. As the war descended on the United States, most of Chicago's ethnics lacked a clear political tradition. Germans and Scandinavians, as well as Negroes, were pretty firmly Republican, and the Czechs, Poles and Italians were settling into areas which tended to be Democratic; the Jewish ghetto's political tradition was very mixed. For the newer immigrants the postwar decade would witness their first real partisan loyalties, not a testing of previous ones.

Between 1918 and 1932 voting patterns become clearer. There are fewer methodological problems, and increasingly larger proportions of the newer immigrants naturalized and voting. For this period I have been able to study the political behavior of Germans, Swedes, Czechoslovakians, Poles, Italians, Lith-

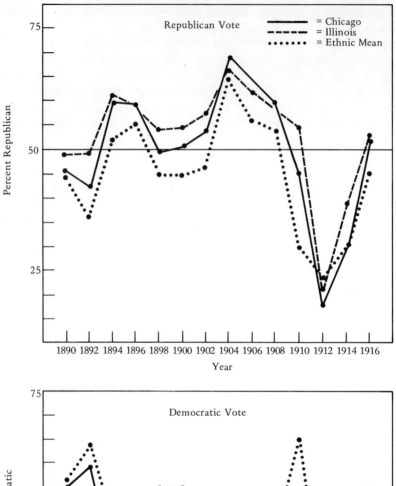

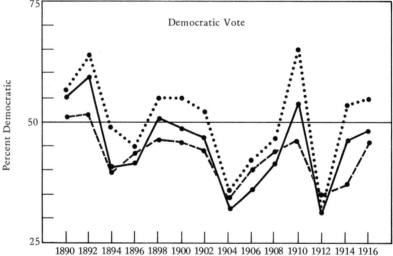

Figure 17.1   *Chicago, Illinois and Ethnic Mean National and State Voting, 1890-1916.* *

*Calculated on basis of Democratic and Republican percentage of two-party vote, except for 1912 (four-party) and 1914 (three-party).

uanians, Yugoslavs and Jews, and for comparison, of Negroes and old-stock whites.

The period saw considerable voting change, primarily from strong Republicanism for most groups at its start to even stronger Democratic loyalty at its conclusion. For example, in 1920 and again in 1932, the races for president, senator and governor for the eight immigrant groups comprise twenty-four con-

Table 17.1 Democratic Vote of Nine Ethnic Groups and Native-Americans in Chicago Elections, 1918-1932 (Percentage Democratic)*

Year and Office	Czecho-slovaks	Poles	Lithu-anians	Yugo-slavs	Ital-ians	Ger-mans	Swedes	Jews	Negroes	Native-Amer-icans
1918:										
Senator	84	71	77	61	71	54	44	60	35	46
Congressman	79	64	76	51	65	46	32	45	28	—
Sheriff	86	66	75	57	65	47	36	54	30	—
1919:										
Mayor	73	55	76	52	61	51	35	40	22	42
1920:										
President	43	39	53	22	31	18	17	15	11	20
Senator	44	41	54	23	28	23	22	20	12	23
Governor	49	46	57	25	36	31	34	31	19	45
1923:										
Mayor	76	76	82	52	80	45	42	57	53	43
1924:										
President	40	35	48	20	31	14	15	19	10	16
Senator	59	49	58	36	39	37	33	39	20	35
Governor	51	42	54	28	35	30	37	41	19	50
1927:										
Mayor	59	54	57	36	42	37	38	39	7	55
1928:										
President	73	71	77	54	63	58	34	60	23	40
Senator	82	75	77	58	62	64	41	64	21	43
Governor	70	66	71	49	52	52	34	53	19	40
1930:										
Senator	89	85	85	74	68	85	73	83	24	68
Congressman	82	78	61	70	59	72	52	70	19	—
Pres.-Cnty. Bd.	85	81	67	73	63	75	54	77	20	56
1931:										
Mayor	84	70	62	64	47	58	53	61	16	61
1932:										
President	83	80	84	67	64	69	51	77	21	43
Senator	81	76	80	62	59	65	42	73	19	39
Governor	81	75	78	59	57	67	53	83	20	63

*Percentage Democratic of the two-party vote except for 1924 — of the three-party vote.

tests. In 1920 only three of the twenty-four went Democratic; in 1932, twenty-three of the twenty-four did so. Since the 1920 and 1932 results are both common to their eras, and the latter would prevail for a generation, it is obvious that changes had taken place between them. State-level voting corresponded to national, but local voting was quite separate and less consistent.

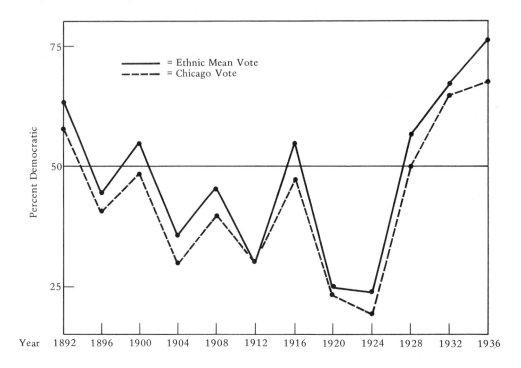

Figure 17.2   *Chicago and Ethnic Mean Democratic Presidential Vote, 1892-1936.**

*Ethnic mean vote = mean of the means of each of the groups involved (seven, 1892-1916; nine, 1920-1936), see Appendix. Calculated on basis of Democratic percentage of two-party (1924: three-party) vote.

The newer immigrant groups — Czechs, Poles, Italians, Lithuanians, and Yugoslavs — voted quite similarly: strongly pro-administration in 1918, but strongly Republican in 1920. Their low Democratic voting continued into succeeding national/state elections, but they remained Democratic in local voting in 1919 and 1923. Republican and Democratic percentages both fell in 1924, due to La Follette's mean of 18 percent among them. And in 1927 their mayoral voting also fell to the Republican side of the balance, leaving them Republican at all levels. The 1928 presidential vote, however, saw a mean Democratic increase over 1924 of 33 percentage points, and over 1920 of 30 points. This Dem-

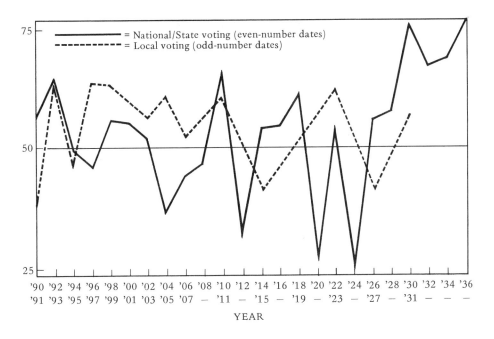

Figure 17.3 *Ethnic Mean Democratic Vote for National/State and Local Elections, 1890-1936.**

*Calculated on basis of Democratic percentage of two-party vote, except for 1891, 1897, 1912, and 1924 — Democratic percentage of total vote.

ocratic switch persisted and increased in the 1930 and 1932 elections, and in the 1931 mayoralty, yielding a new and firm coalition behind the Democrats.

Germans and Swedes tended to vote similarly, although the Swedes were generally more Republican. For example, in 1918 the Germans were 54 percent Democratic for senator and the Swedes only 44 percent. In other contests of that year both groups were, as usual, Republican. Both groups voted over two-thirds Republican in all major 1920 contests, and over 80 percent Republican for president. This Democratic ebb fell even further in 1924, but so did the Republican percentage, as La Follette received 33 percent from the Germans and 19 percent from the Swedes. Both groups were firmly Republican for mayor in 1923, and even more so in 1927. But in 1928 the two groups were further apart in their voting than at any other time, the Germans giving Smith 58 percent (an increase over 1920 of 40 points) and the Swedes giving him only 34 percent. German Democratic voting, like that of the newer immigrants, grew greater over succeeding elections, and even the Swedes were Democratic in most contests in 1930 and 1932. And both went Democratic in the 1931 mayoralty. Thus by 1932 it appeared that the Germans had firmly coalesced in Democratic voting with the newer immigrants, and that the future loyalties of the traditionally more Republican Swedes were unclear.

The Jewish vote was very like the German, but even more dramatic in the extent of its shift. In 1920 the Jews were the most Republican group in the city, voting 85 percent for Harding. Democratic voting increased very slightly in 1924, and the Jews gave La Follette 27 percent, but this still left a Republican majority. This selectivity was reflected locally as well, where the Jews were Republican in 1919, Democratic in 1923 and Republican in 1927 — in each case with strong majorities.

In 1928 the Jews voted 60 percent for Smith, a 41-point increase over 1924, and 45 points over 1920. With the Germans they showed the greatest such increase; and thus the two highest La Follette voters were the two greatest pro-Democratic shifters in 1928. As with other groups, the Jews increased their Democratic percentages in 1930 and 1932, and voted Democratic for mayor in 1931.

Thus there was overall agreement in immigrant voting during the period, pointing to 1928 as, in V. O. Key's model, a "critical election."[6] We might note in passing that Negro and old stock white voting were quite distinct; the former went Democratic only once and was generally Republican on the order of 80 percent or more; and in 1932 Negroes as well as old-stock whites remained outside this new coalition.

Another kind of "voting" that can be considered is that of the ethnic press, a not unimportant indicator of ethnic political behavior.[7] While I must avoid detail on this measure here, my own extensive study of the foreign language press indicates that overall their loyalties reflected those of their readers. (Table 17.2.)

Table 17.2   Election Recommendations of Chicago Ethnic Newspapers for Leading Contests, 1918-1932 (Party of Leading Candidate)*

Election	Dziennik Chicagoski	Dziennik Zwiaz-kowy	L'Italia	La Trib. Ital. Trans-Atlan-tica	Abend-post	Svenska-Trib.-Nyheter	Jew-ish Cour-ier	Jew-ish For-ward	De-fender
1918: Senator	D	—	N	R	D	—	D	S	R
1919: Mayor	D	—	R	—	(R)	—	D	S	R
1920: President	D	(R)	R	R	R	R	D	S	R
1923: Mayor	D	—	—	D	R	—	D	S	N
1924: President	D	N	R	R	(P)	R	D	P	R
1927: Mayor	D	N	R	D	N	—	D	S	R
1928: President	D	N	N	D	D	R	D	S	D
1930: Senator	D	N	—	R	D	—	D	S	N
1931: Mayor	D	D	R	R	D	—	D	S	N
1932: President	D	(D)	R	—	D	—	D	S	(R)

*D = Democratic
R = Republican
P = Progressive
S = Socialist
N = Neutral
— = no interest or missing
() = leaned but did not specifically endorse

I have tried to systematize and render clearer a great deal of quantitative data through the use of several statistical measures of central tendency, relationship, and dispersion. I want to offer only a few highlights here, to avoid tedium. In part I am hoping to develop an ethnic variant of the Key model of criticality, and the first step therein is the employment of correlation coefficients for a systematic picture of the relationship of ethnic voting from one election to another. A correlation table for Democratic presidential voting among Chicago's ethnic groups 1920–1936 does supply an ethnic model of a major part of Key's definition of criticality; for 1928 it produces a change in pattern and correlates at a higher order with succeeding elections than with preceding ones. (Table 17.3.) And when we expand the measure to cover presidential elections from

Table 17.3 Coefficients of Correlation of Presidential Elections, 1920-1936, for Nine Ethnic Groups*

	1920	1924	1928	1932	1936
1920	—	.99	.82	.69	.65
1924		—	.84	.72	.71
1928			—	.95	.95
1932				—	.96
1936					—

*Calculations of Pearson's r for percentage Democratic of vote of each of nine ethnic groups for each election with each other election. For clarity only one side of table is given, since the two sides are identical.

1892 to 1936, the model holds — not until we get as far back as 1900 is there a relationship with 1928 as high as 1928–1932 or 1928–1936. (Table 17.4.) It is

Table 17.4 Coefficients of Correlation of Presidential Elections, 1892-1936, for Seven Ethnic Groups*

	1892	1896	1900	1904	1908	1912	1916	1920	1924	1928	1932	1936
1892	—	.96	.98	.79	.87	.74	.93	.90	.94	.94	.87	.88
1896		—	.95	.85	.85	.75	.83	.92	.94	.83	.73	.73
1900			—	.73	.82	.76	.93	.90	.94	.95	.83	.87
1904				—	.94	.82	.72	.60	.67	.61	.61	.61
1908					—	.90	.88	.64	.73	.75	.76	.80
1912						—	.83	.52	.67	.62	.53	.66
1916							—	.73	.84	.92	.86	.95
1920								—	.99	.82	.69	.65
1924									—	.84	.72	.71
1928										—	.95	.95
1932											—	.96
1936												—

*Calculations of Pearson's r for percentage Democratic vote of each of seven ethnic groups for each election with each other election. For clarity only one side of table is given, since the two sides are identical.

interesting to note the overall high level of correlation for the 44-year period, suggesting the consistency of party as a force of political decision making. This is broken somewhat by the progressive era elections; but these variations are only a ripple in overall consistent pattern, suggesting again that the political upheavals of that period had no long-term effects on ethnic voters, and thus were not critical.

When one adds off-year elections to the correlation tables the picture becomes less clear. I think this reflects the inadvisability of comparing different types of election to one another — their constituencies are not the same.[8] (Table 17.5.)

Table 17.5   Coefficients of Correlation of National/State Elections, 1918-1936, for Nine Ethnic Groups*

	1918	1920	1922	1924	1926	1928	1930	1932	1934	1936
1918	—	.87	.94	.90	.93	.95	.71	.87	.93	.88
1920		—	.94	.99	.80	.82	.53	.69	.81	.65
1922			—	.95	.91	.94	.71	.86	.93	.83
1924				—	.84	.84	.54	.72	.85	.71
1926					—	.93	.84	.91	.94	.88
1928						—	.81	.95	.99	.95
1930							—	.94	.77	.84
1932								—	.92	.95
1934									—	.94
1936										—

*Calculations of Pearson's r for percentage Democratic of vote of each of nine ethnic groups for each election with each other election. For clarity only one side of table is given, since the two sides are identical.

Correlation coefficients also minimize conclusions about the effect of the La Follette candidacy as a way-station between Republican and Democratic voting. And they suggest the absence of any relationship between the progressivisms of 1912 and 1924.

The reverse of central tendency is dispersion — the dispersion of the vote between ethnic groups, or between the various areas comprising the sample for any individual ethnic group. Dispersion can be very illuminating, and to measure it I rely primarily on the standard deviation: the lower the standard deviation, the less the dispersion, or greater the agreement.

For all the immigrant groups together, the standard deviation is higher for 1918–1932 than before; and within this period it is highest 1928–1932. This points to a period of voting change and polarization. On the other hand, this pattern reverses when we look only at the five newer immigrant groups — their voting was becoming more and more similar, and was most in agreement in 1928. Thus the Smith campaign did serve to pull these groups together. This is true also of the 1931 mayoralty — pulling this coalition down to the local level. (Table 17.6.)

Within each group the same forces prevail. For newer immigrants standard deviation decreases in 1928, but for earlier immigrants it does not; these latter, then, were less united in their political behavior in the transitional period.

I will now leave the description of political behavior, the dependent variable, and move on to the independent ones — the causes of that behavior.

A variety of typologies have been created for categorizing issues, and for our purposes we can speak of two kinds: *issues of ethnic interest* and *ethnic issues*.[9] The former are matters of substantive concern to the ethnics; the latter are matters of group definition, acculturation, and survival, and provide the strongest motivation.

A good example of an issue of ethnic interest exists in the variety of forces

Table 17.6 Standard Deviation for Ethnic Group Democratic Voting, 1890-1936

Election	s for all groups*	s for Five Recent Immigrant Groups
1890: State treasurer	10.0	
1892: President	9.7	
1894: State treasurer	7.2	
1896: President	8.7	
1898: State treasurer	8.2	
1900: President	10.0	
1902: State treasurer	9.7	
1904: President	6.8	
1906: State treasurer	11.4	
1908: President	8.9	
1910: State treasurer	14.3	
1912: President	5.0	
1914: Senator	15.4	
1916: President	17.7	
1918: Senator	15.8	8.5
1920: President	14.6	11.8
1922: State treasurer	18.0	14.5
1924: President	12.4	10.6
1926: Senator	15.2	11.8
1928: President	18.0	9.2
1930: Senator	20.0	8.8
1932: President	20.0	9.4
1934: State treasurer	17.6	11.4
1936: President	14.8	4.9
Mayoralties		
1891	8.7	
1893	9.6	
1895	7.6	
1897	9.4	
1899	7.2	
1901	9.1	
1903	7.9	
1905	10.6	
1907	11.2	
1911	8.4	
1915	11.7	
1919	17.5	8.5
1923	15.8	12.1
1927	15.6	10.1
1931	18.6	13.4

*Computed for seven ethnic groups, 1890-1916, and for nine ethnic groups, 1918-1936; s computed for the Democratic vote percentage of each of the groups per election.

involved in World War I and the peace which followed. German–Americans were the most concerned of Chicago's ethnic groups, and their reaction can suggest the role of such an issue. From 1914 to 1917 Chicago's Germans were increasingly united in support of their homeland, and voted for Hughes to show their displeasure with Wilson's neutrality policies.[10] American entry into the war, and then the issuance of the Fourteen Points and the "Peace without Victory" business changed this. As the Chicago *Abendpost*, which had been very critical of Wilson before 1917, put it in 1918: Wilson was a "man of peace" who had gone to war "only against the German government, not the German people."[11] And the German voters agreed, at least to the point of giving Democratic senatorial candidate James Hamilton Lewis a majority of their 1918 vote. But the failure of Versaillles — and the removal of wartime restraints — saw a different situation in 1920. Gone was the Democratic fervor, "Wilson" was a dirty word, and the German press and German voters went strongly Republican.[12]

The dynamism here was similar for other groups; indeed so many were alienated by Wilson's diplomacy that supporters of both sides in the recent war ended up opposing the Democrats. Scandinavians, Italians, and others all felt cheated or otherwise alienated. Even groups with some sympathy for Wilson's efforts, like the Poles and the Jews, had doubts about the Democrats on this issue.[13] The separation of the Negroes, on the other hand, could be seen in a 1920 Chicago *Defender* cartoon, showing Harding and Cox arguing about the League of Nations while a lynched Negro hung from a nearby telephone pole.[14] Overall, the issues of Wilson, the war, and Versailles hurt the Democrats with Chicago's immigrants, and were not rapidly overcome.

The leading example of an ethnic issue — one which involved a group's culture and its very relationship to the dominant society — is Prohibition. It was an old conflict in Chicago, and one which had long divided the immigrant from the old-stock American. In the 1920s it was the most controversial of issues, even, after 1929, pushing the Depression into the background. And, in the long run, it served the Democrats, overcoming the pro-Republican influence of the war and other issues.

It was an issue promoting interethnic cooperation, as in the United Societies for Local Self-Government, founded in 1906 by the editors of several foreign language newspapers, and very active in the 1920s, with the membership of over 1000 ethnic organizations.[15] The secretary of the United Societies from its inception was Anton Cermak, who would come to head the Democratic party in the 1920s, and to defeat William Hale Thompson in the 1931 mayoralty.

Opposition to Prohibition was very strong among Chicago's immigrants. In four opinion elections held between 1918 and 1932, the city voted between 72 percent and 83 percent anti-Prohibition, with some immigrant groups often voting over 90 percent against. The foreign language press was constantly harping on Prohibition and relating it to political choices. A study of the 1919 vote shows unusually high agreement between and within groups on this issue. The standard deviation for nine ethnic groups was lowest here of all elections 1914–1932; and for the five recent immigrant groups, lowest of all elections 1890–1934. Within groups also, dispersion was very slight. Thus the party that came to be identified with leadership in the battle against Prohibition would be in a powerful position with Chicago's ethnics. (Table 17.7.)

The early 1920s offered no clarity on this crucial question. Both parties were

Table 17.7 Percentages and Standard Deviations of Ethnic Group Vote Against Prohibition, 1919*

Group (s)	Percentage Anti-Prohibition	Standard Deviation
Nine ethnic groups	83	10.1
Five recent immigrant groups	88	5.5
Czechoslovaks	95	2.3
Italians	90	4.0
Poles	83	13.2
Lithuanians	91	4.5
Yugoslavs	82	10.7
Germans	93	3.8
Swedes	64	8.7
Jews	77	5.8
Negroes	75	8.6

*Based on percentage voting "No" on proposition, "Shall This City Become Anti-Saloon Territory?" in 1919. Standard deviation computed between ethnic groups and between areas comprising sample of each ethnic group, as indicated.

nationally weak on the issue; and while both expressed formal opposition to it on the local level, neither Thompson nor his opponents emerged as local leaders of anti-Prohibition. 1928, however, saw the issue joined more vigorously, and the ethnic response to Al Smith's anti-Prohibition campaign was simply tremendous. The ethnic press, group leaders, and others responded forcefully and specifically to Smith as a Wet, often breaking strong traditional Republicanism to do so.[16] And this enthusiasm carried over to the voters: a study of correlation coefficients for voting anti-Prohibition in 1919 and voting for leading candidates 1919–1932, finds by far the strongest single relationship was with Smith voting in 1928 (a correlation of .75; second highest was with voting for FDR in 1932: .58). (Table 17.8.)

Table 17.8 Correlations Between Voting Against Prohibition, 1919, and Voting for Leading Candidates, 1919-1932*

Candidate, Office, Year	r with Voting Against Prohibition, 1919
Cox, President, 1920	.62
Davis, President, 1924	.20
La Follette, President, 1924	.25
Smith, President, 1928	.75
Roosevelt, President, 1932	.58
Thompson, Mayor, 1919	−.80
Dever, Mayor, 1923	.60
Thompson, Mayor, 1927	−.52
Cermak, Mayor, 1931	.45
Thompson, Mayor, 1931	−.45

*Calculation of Pearson's r between percentage voting "No" on proposition, "Shall This City Become Anti-Saloon Territory?" in 1919, and percentage voting for named candidate, for nine ethnic groups.

This was not lost on national party leadership, and 1930 and 1932 saw Democratic candidates and party platforms take stronger anti-Prohibition stands. The increasing ethnic Democratic voting of those years showed the wisdom of this position.

Prohibition also eventually served the Democrats locally, when Cermak — the city's leading Wet — took over the party in the late 1920s and then did battle with Thompson in the 1931 mayoralty. Thompson had won reelection to a third term in 1927 in a campaign stressing his opposition to Prohibition, whereas his opponent, the incumbent Democrat, had enforced the law. But he could not maintain the same image against Cermak (one of the reasons his campaign became nativistic): the correlation coefficients for voting anti-Prohibition in 1919 and for the two candidates in 1931, Cermak .45, Thompson —.45, make this clear.

This very brief overview of a complex and most important issue hopefully suggests the way in which an ethnic issue operates. There were one or two others in the decade, especially immigration restriction and other questions of formal or informal nativism. Overall these, too, served the Democrats, since, for example, immigration restriction was passed by Republican congresses and presidents. And one important additional issue of ethnic interest should be mentioned — the depression, which also reinforced Democratic voting. It is indicative of the greater force of ethnic issues that the 1930, 1931, and 1932 campaigns saw far more discussion among immigrants of Prohibition than of depression, although the latter certainly affected these people. My own study persuades me that the political changes outlined above would have come, albeit more slowly, without the depression — by 1930 the forces of coalition were already determined.[17] And issues were central to this determination.

Another important causative force in ethnic politics consists of what we may call political organization — the variety of activities by partisan groups geared to attracting the voter. A number of aspects are involved here, and the most important ones appear at the local level — where politics are most directly related to the immigrant.

One aspect of organizational activity consists of the recognition of ethnic groups through nominations of their members to public office. This was a matter of grave concern to group leaders and spokesmen, who constantly harped on the idea of voting for members of the group (regardless of party), and supporting the party which nominated the greatest number of members of the group.[18]

Consequently I endeavored to tag the names of candidates in Chicago elections, 1918–1932, with any of five ethnicities (German, Scandinavian, Italian, Slavic, Jewish) and look at the patterns in each party. While this measure did not produce an unequivocal pattern, it did show the Democrats better responding to the demands of immigrant groups. Thus in 1918–1922 both parties nominated about the same number of Slavs, but later in the decade the Democratic numbers increased and the Republican ones did not. Between 1918 and 1932 the Democrats nominated forty-one Slavs to the Republicans' twenty. Likewise the Democrats nominated more Jews; the parties were equal on the Italians, the Republicans slightly higher on the Germans (although both parties nominated these in large numbers), and almost all Scandinavians were Republican. (Table 17.9.) A similar measure using ward committeemen — elected party leaders at the ward level — resulted in the same conclusions. And, finally, when I did the same for ward committeemen in ethnic wards (for example, did the parties support Italians for wards with Italian populations?, and so forth) the Democrats were again more responsive, especially after Cermak came into control.

Table 17.9 Ethnic Composition of Party Slates, 1918-1932 (Number of Candidates; D = Democratic; R = Republican)

Election Year and No. of Contests	German		Scandinavian		Italian		Jewish		Slavic		Total	
	D	R	D	R	D	R	D	R	D	R	D	R
1918: 58	5	4	0	3	1	1	2	1	6	5	14	14
1919: 41	7	5	1	1	1	0	1	2	5	7	15	15
1920: 50	6	10	0	5	1	1	4	3	2	1	13	20
1923: 3	0	1	0	0	0	0	0	0	1	0	1	1
1924: 46	6	8	2	4	0	1	2	0	4	1	14	14
1927: 3	0	0	0	1	0	0	0	0	1	0	1	1
1928: 33	3	7	0	8	2	0	1	1	4	1	10	17
1930: 57	9	13	0	3	2	2	3	1	6	2	20	21
1931: 4	1	0	0	0	0	0	0	0	2	0	3	0
1932: 61	5	5	0	2	2	4	4	4	10	3	21	18
Total	42	53	3	27	9	9	17	12	41	20	112	121

Thus on this very important measure — which could be construed as an issue, and an ethnic issue at that — we see another powerful independent variable promoting increased ethnic Democratic allegiance by the late 1920s.[19]

Equally significant aspects of political organization in any urban milieu are the group-oriented activities of the leading parties or factions — in this case the Republican organization of "Big Bill" Thompson and the Democratic one of Anton Cermak. Differences between these two men, their ideas about ethnic politics, and their modes of operation, were of material importance in determining the outcome of ethnic political loyalties.

Thompson had garnered an international reputation for apparent ethnic sensitivity in his first term, when he refused to invite the visiting Joffre mission to Chicago, arguing that some of its citizens would be offended. But Thompson was not as shrewd as many gave him credit for; some group leaders were offended by his apparent pro-Germanism. And his support of Sunday closing in 1915 was a greater blunder. His seeming "ethnic sensitivity" was geared toward those groups which were most traditionally Republican anyway (the Germans, Scandinavians, and Negroes), and thus he was really engaged in a holding action; and his strong alliances with the Negro community, which were central to his power, tended to alienate other groups from him. Equally important in the long run were the nonethnic forces in his organization that served to fragment and divide the local Republican party, and his increasing reputation for malfeasance and corruption which alienated the same middle-class ethnic groups he was trying to hold on to.

Thompson was elected twice (1915, 1919), retired for four years, and in 1927 won again, in another garish and superficially ethnic campaign (this time, "Kick King George in the Snoot")! In fact he did quite well on the whole among the immigrants, but had the barest of majorities among the newer immigrants (50.4 percent). His "wide-open town" pronouncements were probably more important than the threats to King George.

And Thompson ran into increasing trouble in his third term, with the public, the courts, and his own party. Only one year after his reelection his organization was overwhelmingly beaten in the Republican primary, with such stalwart Republican and previously pro-Thompson groups as the Germans, Swedes, and Jews voting heavily against his candidates.

Anton Cermak's career was basically different — much less colorful, more committed to party unity, and from the start predicated on interethnic cooperation. The Irish leadership that preceded him was not ethnically insensitive, but was conditioned by an earlier era, as seen, for example, in its racism. But Cermak just bided his time, serving the party and always supporting harmony. From his first campaign for public office in 1912, through his rule as president of the County Board ("Mayor of Cook County"), Cermak was careful to alienate no ethnic group, but to seek unity, behind himself, of them all. Starting with his own Czechs, then the Jews, then others, he built a personal ethnic organization within the party. His role in the United Societies, and Wet leadership generally, was typical of this. It is not surprising that he ran ahead of Al Smith among seven of eight immigrant groups in 1928, nor that he succeeded to the party's leadership shortly thereafter.

The 1931 campaign between Cermak and Thompson was thus one of political and what one might call "coalitional" belief as well as personality. The marginal nature of Thompson's sense of ethnic complexity became apparent: as his campaign appeared progressively less likely to succeed, it became more nativistic. Almost all his bases of support withered, while Cermak's patient cultivation paid off. As a Polish paper put it, "This campaign is not only against Anton Cermak, but also all of those who are not North Americans."[20] Or, as Cermak himself put it, "It's true I didn't come over on the Mayflower, but I came as soon as I could."

Cermak carried every ethnic group except the Italians and the Negroes (he began to work on these two immediately), and five of the eight immigrant groups voted more heavily Democratic than in any mayoralty of the period, four of these being groups that had gone for Thompson in 1927. And the election had the effect of bringing the changes of 1928–1930 down to the local level, to make the new Democratic coalition vertically complete.

There are other important forces of interethnic coalition which I must gloss over here. Questions of criminal influence in politics, and the reform thereof, for example, were influential in Chicago at this time. Their influence was quite selective, involving primarily the middle and upper classes, and thus only a limited number of immigrants. These questions served the Democrats because of the aura of corruption and malfeasance surrounding the Thompson organization in the city and its state allies, especially Governor Len Small. Thus their main effect was in promoting Democratic voting among the old stock and immigrant middle class — groups that were otherwise most likely to vote Republican. This expanded the size of the new coalition considerably.

Socioeconomic class is itself a significant force, best seen as an intervening causative variable in political behavior. My own conclusions about this variable reflect those of some other historians of American voting, in that socioeconomic position emerges as a far less deterministic force than ethnicity.[21] Its effects were selective and occasional, and at best sometimes conditioned the role of the ethnic variable, but never replaced it.

This paper has tried to extract from a much larger study some of the more important forces in ethnic political behavior in a time of change, seeking to describe the growth of the ethnic Democratic coalition and the forces behind it. Hopefully such a case-study approach — and we need more of them — clarifies some of the major developments of twentieth-century American politics, and the role of ethnic pluralism therein.

NOTES

[1] F. J. Brown, "Meaning and Status of Minorities," in *One America*, eds. F. J. Brown and J. S. Roucek (New York, 1946), pp. 9, 636. See also, John M. Allswang, *A House for All Peoples: Ethnic Politics in Chicago, 1890–1936* (Lexington, Ky.: The University Press of Kentucky, 1971), chap. 2 and Table 2.1.

[2] H. F. Gosnell, "The Chicago Black Belt as a Political Battleground," *American Journal of Sociology*, vol. 39 (November 1933), p. 331; J. P. Gavit, *Americans by Choice* (New York, 1922), pp. 241, 245.

[3] H. F. Gosnell materials (unclassified), Charles E. Merriam papers, University of Chicago.

[4] It is impossible to briefly recapitulate my methodology beyond the cursory description given in the body of this paper. For a complete statement, see Allswang, *A House for All Peoples*, Appendix.

[5] Literature on this phenomenon is steadily increasing. Among more important studies are: S. Lubell, *The Future of American Politics* (Garden City, N. Y., 1952); V. O. Key, Jr., "A Theory of Critical Elections," *Journal of Politics*, vol. 17, no. 1 (February 1955); John L. Shover, "Was 1928 a Critical Election in California," *Pacific Northwest Quarterly*, vol. 58 (October 1967); Duncan MacRae, Jr., and J. A. Meldrum, "Critical Elections in Illinois, 1888–1958," *American Political Science Review*, vol. 54, no. 3 (September 1960); J. J. Huthmacher, *Massachusetts People and Politics* (Cambridge, Mass., 1959); J. M. Clubb and H. W. Allen, "The Cities and the Election of 1928: Partisan Realignment?" *American Historical Review*, vol. 74, no. 4 (April 1969).

[6] Key, "Theory of Critical Elections." The question of criticality is related to that of deviance. Some recent studies of 1928 qualify or dismiss its role as a turning point because of its "deviant" nature (for example, Clubb and Allen, "The Cities and the Election of 1928," especially pp. 1207–1209; Shover, "Was 1928 a Critical Election in California?" especially p. 198). I would suggest that, at least for the period from World War I to the depression, no election is truly ordinary, and all have some measure of deviance. The presidential election of 1916 took place in a fervor of war fears; the 1918 election came on the heels of a successful war effort; the anti-administration ethnic position of 1920 was very similar to the pro-administration one of 1918; 1924 was marked by an unusually strong third-party effort; and so on. Thus we have to take elections as they come; few presidential contests are without some sort of "deviance," and 1928 was no more marked here than many others.

[7] The role of the ethnic press in intragroup communications, and its positions, are discussed in Allswang, *A House for All Peoples*, chaps. 1 and 3.

[8] Some scholars argue that presidential elections should be compared to off-year ones for a truer picture of voting behavior (for example, Clubb and Allen, "The Cities and the Election of 1928," pp. 1209–1212). While I have done it both ways, I am convinced that only in comparing like kinds of elections — in this case presidential ones — do we deal with the same constituencies and thus have a real basis for inference.

[9] For a more extended discussion of typologies of issues, and of issue-effectiveness: Allswang, *A House for All Peoples*, chaps. 7 and 9.

[10] Carl Wittke, *The German Language Press in America* (Lexington, Ky., 1957), pp. 238–243, 255–256, 259–261; A. J. Townsend, *The Germans of Chicago* (Chicago, 1927), pp. 144–148; H. L. Ickes, *The Autobiography of a Curmudgeon* (New York, 1943), p. 186.

[11] Chicago *Abendpost*, November 4, 1918, p. 4.

[12] Townsend, *The Germans of Chicago*, p. 180; Chicago *Tribune*, September 7, 1920, p. 9; Chicago *Abendpost*, November 1, 1920, p. 4.

[13] *Skandinaven*, October 29, 1920, and *Svenska-Tribunen-Nyheter*, October 13 and 17, 1920,

quoted in Works Projects Administration, *Chicago Foreign Language Press Survey* (Chicago, 1942); *L'Italia,* October 10, 1920, p. 1, October 24, 1920, p. 1, October 31, 1920, p. 1; *La Tribuna Italiana Trans-Atlantica,* October 9, 1920, p. 7, October 30, 1920, p. 2; *Dziennik Zwiazkowy,* October 28, 1920, p. 1, October 30, 1920, pp. 5, 6, October 31, 1920, pp. 1, 4, November 2, 1920, p. 4.

[14] Chicago *Defender,* October 23, 1920, p. 12.

[15] Chicago *Abendpost,* June 9, 1919, quoted in W.P.A., *Chicago Foreign Language Press Survey.*

[16] *La Tribuna Italiana Trans-Atlantica,* September 22, 1928, p. 1, October 6, 1928, p. 1, October 20, 1928, pp. 1, 3; *L'Italia,* July 15, 1928, p. 2, October 14, 1928, p. 1, October 21, 1928, p. 1; *Dziennik Chicagoski,* November 2, 1928, p. 7, November 4, 1928, p. 24, November 5, 1928, p. 1ff; Abendpost/Sonntagpost, November 4, 1928, p. 1ff, November 5, 1928, p. 1ff, November 3, 1928, p. 3; *Yiddisher Kuryer,* October 17, 1928, p. 8, November 4, 1928, p. 8. This quite overwhelming quantitative and qualitative evidence for the role of the Prohibition issue in 1928 questions the suggestion that it was not a significant correlate of Smith voting (R. C. Silva, *Rum, Religion and Votes: 1928 Re-Examined* (University Park, Pa., 1962, p. 43).

[17] A different conclusion can be found in Clubb and Allen, "The Cities and the Election of 1928," pp. 1207–1208; I think they are wrong.

[18] On the ubiquitous presence of this phenomenon, see, for example, Chicago *Broad-Ax,* October 23, 1920, p. 3; Chicago *Defender,* September 17, 1932, Part II, p. 2; *L'Italia,* March 30, 1919, p. 1, October 26, 1930, p. 11; *Abendpost,* April 3, 1923, p. 1; *Dziennik Chicagoski,* November 3, 1930, pp. 6–7; *Yiddisher Kuryer,* October 28, 1932, p. 1; A. Gottfried, *Boss Cermak of Chicago: A Study of Political Leadership* (Seattle, 1962), p. 42.

[19] The data on this can be found in tables in Allswang, *A House for All Peoples,* chap. 5.

[20] *Dziennik Zwiaskowy,* April 4, 1931, p. 4.

[21] For example, Lee Benson, *The Concept of Jacksonian Democracy: New York as a Test Case* (Princeton, N.J., 1961) and Paul Kleppner, *The Cross of Culture: A Social Analysis of Midwestern Politics, 1850–1900* (New York, 1970).

The Cities and the Election of 1928:

Partisan Realignment?

Jerome M. Clubb / Howard W. Allen

18

The dramatic contest between Herbert Hoover and Al Smith for the presidency of the United States in 1928 seemed to personify the clash of two political cultures in the United States, one rural–small town, old stock, Protestant, and dry; the other, urban, immigrant, Catholic, and wet. Some quantitative analysts, comparing the Democratic presidential vote of 1928 with that received in 1920 (a Republican landslide), have credited Smith with successfully mobilizing a new Democratic coalition, one destined to become nationally dominant during the 1930s. In their commentary on this literature, Jerome M. Clubb and Howard W. Allen point to the need for examining time series of voting data from lesser as well as presidential elections before characterizing a particular election as "realigning." Their own study of voting data from major cities from 1920 through 1936 suggests that we may have confused the support given Al Smith in many of the cities in 1928 with a major shift in party identification among urban voters. Dr. Clubb is a member of the staff of the Inter-University Consortium for Political Research at the University of Michigan. Howard Allen teaches history at Southern Illinois University.

In recent years students of American political life have assigned particular significance to the presidential election of 1928. Various scholars have examined the voting patterns of the 1920s and have observed that major changes in these patterns occurred in that year. These changes have been interpreted as evidence that the election of 1928 was one of the rare "realigning" or "critical" elections in American political history that marked a lasting reorientation of the political behavior and partisan loyalties of major segments of the electorate. The voting shifts of 1928 have been interpreted, more specifically, as marking the beginning and in some ways providing the basis for the Democratic electoral majority that emerged in the 1930s and that apparently still remains substantially intact.

SOURCE: Reprinted with permission from *The American Historical Review*, vol. 74 (April 1969), pp. 1205–1220.

Samuel Lubell was probably the first to call attention to an "Al Smith Revolution" which antedated the "Roosevelt Revolution" of the 1930s.[1] Lubell noted a sharp increase both in the Democratic presidential vote and in the total vote in 1928 particularly in urban areas characterized by populations with a large immigrant stock. According to Lubell, this change was primarily attributable to the personal characteristics of the Democratic candidates and to peculiarities of the American social scene. As an urban Catholic of immigrant background, Alfred E. Smith was particularly appealing to the resentful and largely disaffected "new" immigrant population of urban America. Prior to 1928 many of these Americans had voted Republican, and more had refrained from participating in the electoral process. But in that year, primarily because of Smith, they went to the polls in unprecedented numbers, voted heavily Democratic, and continued to do so thereafter. Thus one of the crucial elements of the "New Deal Coalition" actually moved into the Democratic camp in 1928.

More recently, various other scholars have submitted evidence that tends to confirm Lubell's findings. Irving Bernstein and Carl Degler have systematically compared the presidential vote in the major cities during the 1920s and have drawn conclusions essentially similar to those of Lubell.[2] Other investigators have also identified the election of 1928 as a "critical election" but with some reservations. On the basis of investigation of the presidential vote in New England, V. O. Key identified the election of 1928 as a "critical election" and concluded that in New England "the Roosevelt revolution of 1932 was in large measure an Al Smith revolution of 1928." Key added, however, that this characterization was "less applicable to the remainder of the country" and suggested that "the great reshuffling of voters that occurred in 1928 was perhaps the final and decisive stage in a process that had been underway for some time."[3] In their study of Illinois voting patterns Duncan MacRae, Jr., and James A. Meldrum also observed significant shifts in 1928, but they demonstrated that for Illinois at least it is more appropriate to speak of a "critical period" rather than a single "critical" or "realigning" election.[4] Although David Burner accepted the view that the election of 1928 had a significant and lasting impact upon the electoral behavior of some groups of immigrant stock, he pointed to the "deviant" nature of that election, as well as the elections of 1920 and 1924, and he raised the possibility that groups of immigrant stock had been deflected from their "normal course" in the presidential voting of the 1920s.[5] And even stronger reservations have been expressed. John L. Shover questioned this interpretation on several general grounds and on the basis of a detailed analysis of voting patterns in California has concluded that no major partisan realignment took place there in 1928.[6] But these reservations aside, the view that major and lasting political realignment occurred in 1928 in large measure because of the peculiar attributes of the Democratic presidential candidate has apparently been widely accepted.

The significance of this interpretation of the political history of the late 1920s and the 1930s is obvious. If it can be demonstrated that major and lasting partisan realignment occurred in 1928 then it may be necessary to modify assessments of the political impact of the Great Depression and the policies of Franklin Roosevelt and the New Deal. This interpretation similarly lends weight to the view that ethnic, religious, and other essentially social factors have constituted major determinants of American political behavior and have perhaps been more important than factors of a more purely economic nature. Studies of contemporary political behavior and of historical voting patterns have suggested, moreover, that for much of the electorate partisan loyalties are deeply seated, intensely held, and remarkably stable over long periods of time.[7] Large-scale changes in party affiliation and habits of electoral participation have been rare and have been identified with times of major national crisis. If realignment came in 1928 as a result of developments less dramatic than national crisis, it may be necessary to modify views of the stability and intensity with which partisan loyalties have been held.

It is possible, however, to entertain doubts as to the adequacy of this general interpretation of the political events of the late 1920s and the 1930s. In the first place, the fact that Democratic successes in certain areas in the presidential election of 1932 were preceded by shifts toward the Democratic party in 1928 in those same areas does not demonstrate that these developments were related. It is possible that Smith's personal appeal brought about an upsurge in the Democratic vote in some areas without changing underlying partisan loyalties or patterns of voting behavior on the part of the groups involved. From this point of view, had it not been for the introduction of a new range of political stimuli by economic depression, the presidential vote would have returned in 1932 to the patterns of the years prior to 1928. Smith's successes may have been no more than a short-term fluctuation in the presidential vote without lasting importance in terms of underlying partisan divisions, and the election of 1928 could be more appropriately described as a "deviating" election rather than a "critical" or "realigning" election.[8]

Various considerations make this alternate interpretation of the election of 1928 at least logically plausible. The immigrant stock groups, which apparently provided the basis for Smith's gains in northern cities, were presumably among the lower income groups hit hardest by the Great Depression. Thus the fact that the Democratic candidate in 1932 was successful in some of the same areas that shifted toward the Democrats in 1928 is compatible with the view that these developments were the result of different and unrelated factors. Large but temporary shifts in voting patterns have occurred, moreover, in American political history. Indeed, as has often been observed, in 1928 Smith split the Solid South. The Democratic vote in that region fell sharply, and large numbers of Democratic voters moved into the Republican column. Few have concluded, however, that the election of 1928 marked a lasting conversion of any significant number of southerners from Democratic to Republican affiliation. Better-known examples of "deviating" elections, perhaps, are those of the 1950s. The overwhelming victories of Dwight D. Eisenhower in 1952 and 1956 were hailed by some as an indication that a new Republican electoral majority had appeared. The events of the 1960s and the continued success of Democrats in their efforts to win election to lesser offices during the 1950s demonstrated that the Eisenhower victories were a tribute to personal popularity unaccompanied by fundamental realignment.

The electoral history of the Eisenhower years suggests a related limitation of the interpretation of the election of 1928 as a "critical" or "realigning" election. With the noteworthy exception of the work of MacRae and Meldrum, assessments of the voting patterns of the 1920s and 1930s, which provide the basis for this general interpretation, have considered only the presidential vote. The vote in 1928 has been compared with the vote in preceding and subsequent presidential elections, and in this way the electoral shifts and changes in voting patterns of 1928 have been identified. Consideration of the nature of the preceding and subsequent elections suggests that this approach may well have its shortcomings. The presidential election of 1924 was marked by the presence of a strong third-party candidate who certainly attracted many normally Democratic voters and who probably cut into Republican strength as well. Most investigators have found it necessary, therefore, to compare the election of 1928 with the election of 1920. It might be argued, however, that the presidential election of 1920 was unusual in character, for that election was a Republican landslide, and the Republican candidate received a larger percentage of the popular vote than any candidate prior to the election of 1936. In this respect the election of 1920 was outside the more normal pattern of American electoral politics. Comparisons with subsequent elections also present difficulties. Both the elections of 1932 and 1936 were conducted under conditions of severe economic stress and might also be considered outside the normal pattern of American elections. In short, the identification of electoral shifts peculiar to the election of 1928 has been based in some measure upon comparisons with elections that were unusual and marked, perhaps, by large but temporary shifts in voting patterns.[9]

The adequacy of the presidential vote as an indication of underlying political attitudes and deep-seated partisan divisions within the electorate can also be questioned on more general grounds. Presidential elections are often "high stimulus" elections that are accompanied by great political sound and fury. The issues of the day and the characteristics of the candidates are brought sharply to the attention of the electorate, and, in the twentieth century at least, voter turnout has usually been higher in presidential elections than in off-year elections. It appears that presidential elections are particularly susceptible to the influence of short-term political forces that may shift the vote toward one or the other of the parties or toward particular candidates without bringing about a lasting change in basic electoral alignments. The circumstances of these elections often prompt some voters to abandon temporarily long-standing partisan loyalties and cross party lines. Conditions of high political stimulation usually bring large numbers of voters to the polls who normally do not vote in other elections, whose level of political interest is low, and whose political preferences are relatively unstable. These considerations work to complicate the voting patterns of presidential elections and lessen their utility as indications of fundamental and lasting divisions and alignments within the electorate.[10]

The voting patterns of subsequent years, therefore, appear to constitute a crucial test of whether major partisan realignment occurred in a particular election. In the case of the election of 1928 this test is, of course, complicated by the presence of a new range of political stimuli presented by the economic adversity of the early 1930s. It also seems, moreover, that the voting patterns of elections to lesser offices, particularly during nonpresidential years, provide a better indication of basic patterns of electoral behavior than do presidential elections. These elections are apparently less subject to short-term and essentially evanescent forces and more clearly reflect underlying partisan divisions and patterns of political participation within the electorate. In both respects, the elections of 1930 should provide a particularly critical indication of whether lasting realignment occurred in 1928.

Studies of the presidential vote during the 1920s and 1930s have shown that the Democratic vote and the total vote increased sharply in particular areas between 1920 and 1928. These increases have been interpreted as indicating that in these areas large numbers of voters came to the polls for the first time and voted disproportionately for the Democratic candidate. That these shifts were particularly noteworthy in urban areas with large immigrant stock populations makes it plausible to conclude that they were due to the peculiar appeal of Smith for dissatisfied Americans of immigrant stock. Even if this interpretation of the presidential returns is accepted, however, it does not follow that lasting changes in partisan affiliation and habits of political participation occurred in 1928. As has been seen, a sharp change in voting patterns associated with a single election does not in itself demonstrate that a permanent realignment has taken place.

These difficulties can be illustrated by examination of the vote in a limited number of areas during the 1920s and the earlier 1930s. Table 18.1 presents the Democratic percentage of the total vote for President in elections from 1920 through 1936 in major metropolitan areas that were characterized by many individuals of immigrant stock and that have been identified as marked by lasting shifts toward the Democratic party in 1928.[11] Inspection of the table clearly suggests that in these areas major shifts toward the Democratic party did take

Table 18.1   Democratic Percentage of the Total Vote for President in Selected Metropolitan Areas, 1920-1936

	1920	1924	1928	1932	1936
Boston	36.3	35.5	66.8	67.1	63.9
Providence	35.3	38.6	52.9	57.4	55.1
New York					
Bronx	24.4	33.6	67.7	70.4	67.2
Kings	25.9	31.9	59.5	66.9	63.6
New York	29.1	39.6	60.8	66.9	67.5
Queens	25.7	31.0	53.4	61.5	61.6
Richmond	33.2	42.0	53.4	61.1	62.6
Buffalo	25.6	21.3	44.9	46.3	52.0
Rochester	24.7	20.5	41.2	44.8	48.2
Newark	25.0	22.3	41.0	45.6	54.7
Jersey City	36.7	47.0	60.2	71.9	77.7
Philadelphia	21.5	12.1	39.5	42.9	60.5
Pittsburgh	20.1	8.7	42.4	52.9	65.2
Cleveland	30.5	9.1	45.6	50.1	65.4
Detroit	17.6	7.1	36.8	57.2	64.5
Chicago	22.1	20.3	46.5	55.2	62.4
Milwaukee	17.8	9.7	53.7	65.6	74.6
Minneapolis	20.6	6.3	38.8	54.8	58.8
St. Paul	30.8	10.1	51.2	61.2	66.0
Seattle	16.2	6.6	31.9	59.1	66.0
San Francisco	22.1	6.4	49.4	64.8	74.1
Oakland	20.3	6.1	33.6	52.1	63.6
Los Angeles	21.6	7.3	28.7	57.3	67.0

place in that year. In all of the areas considered, Smith received a larger proportion of the total vote than did the Democratic candidates in 1920 and 1924. Although in most cases the Democratic vote rose to higher levels in 1932 and 1936, these gains were preceded by shifts toward the Democrats in 1928. In terms of the presidential vote alone in these areas, then, it is plausible to speak of an "Al Smith Revolution" preceding the "Roosevelt Revolution" of the 1930s.

When one examines the Democratic vote for candidates for lesser offices, however, he sees the shifts of 1928 in a different light. As Table 18.2 shows, shifts in the vote for Democratic candidates for lesser offices in the same areas during the same years followed a somewhat different pattern than did shifts in the presidential vote. In most of these areas, the vote for Democratic candidates for the lesser offices was higher in 1928 than in 1920 or 1924.[12] In Rochester, Jersey City, St. Paul, and three of the counties of New York City, on the other hand, the Democratic vote in 1928 was either lower or not significantly greater than in 1924, and in many of the other areas Democratic increases in 1928 were

Table 18.2 Democratic Percentage of the Total Vote for Candidates for Congress in Selected Major Metropolitan Areas, 1920-1936*

	Presidential Year Elections					Off-Year Elections			
	1920	1924	1928	1932	1936	1922	1926	1930	1934
Boston[a]	39.7	57.2	65.4	68.7	62.1	62.9	54.8	66.1	65.4
Providence	36.8	43.6	51.6	58.0	50.7	55.1	44.7	50.9	59.4
New York City									
Bronx	37.0	56.6	67.1	63.6[b]	75.4	57.9	65.1	68.0	68.6[b]
Kings	36.8	53.7	59.4	64.9	71.4	56.2	61.7	59.5	65.8[b]
New York[a]	58.2	70.1	61.0	70.9	61.3	69.6	69.5	67.6	69.1
Queens	45.1	56.9	57.2	63.4	65.0	70.0[a]	63.4	62.8	66.0
Richmond	44.5	63.1	62.0	66.0	65.5	67.7	67.8	67.2	56.4
Buffalo	35.7	32.8	42.6	48.7	46.8	50.3[a]	38.9	45.7	53.5
Rochester	24.1	41.7[a]	34.1	41.7	50.7	46.1[a]	44.5	42.2	53.5
Newark	32.5	30.2	40.3	44.8	50.6	50.8[c]	37.8	36.5	46.2
Jersey City	48.6	59.3	61.0	70.3	75.1	74.5[c]	76.8	70.5	73.2
Philadelphia	21.4	12.8	38.2	40.2	58.1	18.5	11.5	20.9	48.3
Pittsburgh	19.0	12.2	38.1	44.3	61.6	25.8	11.9	15.1	53.2
Cleveland[a]	49.7	41.9	47.9	50.2	48.1	48.8	48.0	55.3	55.8
Detroit	22.1	18.9	34.7	51.7	59.6	40.8	30.6	20.0	54.6
Chicago	27.9	29.5	47.5	54.9	59.7	46.3	43.4	54.7	61.9
Milwaukee	29.6[a]	17.9	27.7	47.2	44.3	d	10.9	16.2	36.5
Minneapolis	9.5	8.4	23.8	23.2[b]	11.6	39.8	8.3	2.6[a]	22.5
St. Paul	34.2	36.9	28.6	24.9[b]	22.9	35.6	3.2	9.0	23.4
Seattle[e]	12.8	20.4	32.2	54.5	62.4	26.3	49.0	40.4	55.9
San Francisco[f]	50.1	d	17.9	32.4	d	53.3	38.1	10.0	38.9
Oakland[f]	41.0	d	17.5	41.0	d	33.9	26.5	14.1	37.7
Los Angeles[f]	36.4	d	18.3	44.1	d	29.2	17.2	34.0	42.0

*In this table the letter designations have the following meanings: [a], vote for governor substituted; [b], at large; [c], vote for senator substituted; [d], no meaningful returns available; [e], vote for first congressional district substituted, 1920-1930; [f], vote for senator, 1920, 1928, and 1932, and for governor, 1922, 1926, 1930, and 1934 substituted.

preceded by gains earlier in the decade and followed by further gains in the 1930s. The data also suggest that in the majority of these urban areas Democratic strength in the 1920s was significantly greater than was indicated by the presidential vote in 1920 and 1924. Several of the areas tended to be predominantly Democratic during much of the 1920s, at least in so far as the vote in elections to lesser offices was concerned. In Boston and Jersey City and in the counties of New York City the Democratic party was apparently the majority party in elections after 1920, and in most areas Democratic candidates for these lesser offices ran well ahead of the Democratic contenders for the presidency in both 1920 and 1924. (See Tables 18.1 and 18.2.) Thus shifts toward the Democratic party in 1928 appear much more moderate when the vote in elections to lesser offices is considered.

In still other respects the data displayed in Table 18.2 do not provide consistent support for the view that major realignment took place in 1928. If political realignment occurred in 1928 in these areas the vote for lesser offices should show two characteristics: the vote for Democratic candidates should have been significantly higher in 1928 than in 1920 and 1924, and, more importantly, the Democratic vote in 1930 should have remained at higher levels than in 1926. If 1928 marked a lasting partisan realignment rather than a temporary fluctuation in the Democratic vote resulting from short-term factors, then the vote in 1930 should reflect the persistence of this realignment when factors idiosyncratic to 1928 were no longer present. Even this test is, of course, clouded by economic depression. It is possible that increases in the Democratic vote in 1930 as compared with 1926 reflected the impact of the depression that began in 1929 rather than the lasting effects of Smith's candidacy.

In these terms, Table 18.2 suggests that lasting partisan realignment may have taken place in some of the metropolitan areas considered. The Democratic vote in Boston, Philadelphia, and Chicago increased by approximately 10 percent between 1926 and 1930, and more moderate shifts toward the Democratic party apparently occurred in Providence, the Bronx, Buffalo, Pittsburgh, Cleveland, Milwaukee, and St. Paul. But despite these gains, the 1930 Democratic vote in four of these cities (Providence, Buffalo, Pittsburgh, and St. Paul) remained at approximately the same level or below that of 1922, and in St. Paul the Democratic vote in 1928 did not increase, but fell below the levels of 1920 and 1924. Shifts in the Democratic vote in the remaining areas provide even less evidence of major partisan realignment in 1928. In several of these areas the Democratic vote in 1930 was lower than in 1926 or 1922, while in others the vote in 1930 was approximately the same as in the earlier mid-term elections. Because of cross-filing and uncontested elections the returns for the far western metropolitan areas of Seattle, San Francisco, Oakland, and Los Angeles are quite inadequate, but such returns as are available suggest that in the California areas the Democratic vote declined in 1928. Only in the case of Los Angeles was the vote higher in 1930 than earlier in the decade. As in the case of St. Paul, it is difficult to associate this 1930 increase with Smith's candidacy in view of the apparent decline in the Los Angeles Democratic vote in 1928. The very low Democratic vote in 1930 in many of these urban areas, including St. Paul, Minneapolis, Milwaukee, and Pittsburgh, suggests, moreover, that whatever happened in 1928 was not significant enough to make the Democratic party a powerful political force. In some of the metropolitan areas considered, then, the Democratic party was apparently stronger in 1930 than it had been during the earlier years of the 1920s. Whether even these gains can be attributed solely to Smith's candidacy is, of course, debatable for it is possible that gains registered by the Democrats in 1930 came in part as a response to economic collapse and had little to do with the presidential election of 1928.

The vote for lesser offices also provides a means to assess the view that in 1928 lasting political realignment came about in part as a result of the movement into the Democratic camp of large numbers of voters who had failed to participate in earlier elections. Examination of the total vote for candidates for lesser offices in these years suggests that in the metropolitan areas considered more voters participated in the election of 1928 than in any election earlier in the decade. Indeed, in several areas the total vote was higher in 1928 than in any election prior to 1936. Many of these urban areas were characterized, however, by rapid population growth in the 1920s, and it is obvious that increases in the total vote were in some measure a reflection of population expansion as well as an indication of changes in patterns of political participation. It is by no means certain, furthermore, that increases in voter participation associated with the 1928 election were solely beneficial to the Democrats; nor is it clear that heavier voter turnout in 1928 marked a lasting increase in voter participation or in either Democratic or Republican strength.

Comparison of the percentage of estimated eligible voters who cast their votes in the mid-term elections of the period provides a basis for at least a suggestive assessment of the impact of the election of 1928 upon patterns of political participation. Again, if the election of 1928 brought about a lasting change in the habits of political participation of significant numbers of former nonvoters, then it could be expected that the rate of voter participation in 1930 would have been higher than in 1926. Table 18.3 suggests that in half of the areas voter turnout was at least moderately higher in 1930 than in 1926.[13] In Providence and Cleveland increases in voter turnout were particularly sharp, while in several of the other cities the vote in 1930, although higher than in 1926, was at approximately the same level as in 1922. In the remaining half of the areas, the level of participation in 1930 was approximately the same or lower than in the mid-term elections of the 1920s. The estimates upon which Table 18.3 is based are by no means precise enough to lend confidence to conclusions based upon small differences, but it appears that on the whole increases in voter participation in mid-term elections were relatively slight prior to 1934 and that participation increased more consistently and more pronouncedly in the earlier 1930s than between 1926 and 1930. In Providence and Cleveland, however, participation increased more sharply between 1926 and 1930 than between 1930 and 1934. In the other metropolitan areas considered, increases in turnout reflected in the elections of the earlier 1930s were of the same magnitude and in many cases were greater than were those that could be associated with the election of 1928.

Although comparison of the vote in 1928 with elections earlier in the decade reveals a substantial increase in Democratic turnout in 1928, it is not certain that this increase was lasting. It is possible that these gains were primarily a response to Smith's personal appeal without permanent significance in terms of the partisan identification or habits of political participation of the voters in-

Table 18.3 Percentage of Estimated Eligible Voters Who Voted for Candidates for Congress in Selected Major Metropolitan Areas, 1922-1934*

	1922	1926	1930	1934
Boston[a]	35	36	41	51
Providence	40	40	51	54
New York City				
Bronx	31	31	30	35[b]
Kings	30	30	31	35[b]
New York[a]	27	27	28	33
Queens	33[a]	36	34	37
Richmond	37	41	42	48
Buffalo	35[a]	37	36	49
Rochester	43[a]	45	44	54
Newark	29[c]	21	28	36
Jersey City	46[c]	42	44	54
Philadelphia	27	31	36	52
Pittsburgh	18	21	25	44
Cleveland[b]	25	21	36	43
Detroit	13	12	18	29
Chicago	36	33	37	49
Milwaukee	d	23	27	38
Minneapolis	42	33	42[a]	55
St. Paul	35	36	40	53
San Francisco[a]	34	29	32	47
Oakland[a]	39	43	41	56
Los Angeles[a]	31	32	32	56
Seattle[d]				

*In this table the letter designations have the following meanings: [a], vote for governor substituted; [b], at large; [c], vote for senator substituted; [d], meaningful returns not available.

volved. It may be that many individuals who shifted into the Democratic column in 1928 returned to the Republican fold or to their former nonvoting habits in later elections when Smith and other factors peculiar to the election of 1928 were no longer present. By comparing Democratic and Republican turnout in 1930 with 1922 and 1926 some indication can be gained of the impact of increases in voter participation in 1928 upon the relative strength of the two parties. Comparison of these elections (Table 18.4) suggests that in only five of the metropolitan areas, Boston, Providence, Philadelphia, Cleveland, and Chicago, can increases in voter turnout in these years be construed as working disproportionately to the advantage of the Democrats. In the remaining areas, despite changes in turnout in the 1928 election, the relative balance of Democratic and Republican voters in 1930 was approximately the same as in 1922 and 1926 or had shifted to the advantage of the Republicans. These comparisons, then, provide little support for the view that lasting political realignment occurred in 1928 because of the movement of large numbers of former nonvoters into the Democratic camp.[14] Indeed, the data presented in Table 18.4 are at least equally compatible with the view that shifts in Democratic turnout and in the Democratic share of the total vote in 1928 were of an essentially short-term nature

Table 18.4 Percentage of Estimated Eligible Voters Who Voted for Democratic and Republican Candidates for Congress in Selected Major Metropolitan Areas, 1922-1934*

		1922	1926	1930	1934
Boston[a]	D	22	20	27	33
	R	12	16	13	15
Providence	D	22	18	26	32
	R	18	22	25	22
New York City					
Bronx	D	18	20	20	24[b]
	R	9	8	6	6
Kings	D	17	18	18	23[b]
	R	11	10	8	8
New York[a]	D	19	19	19	23
	R	7	7	7	8
Queens	D	23[a]	23	22	25
	R	9	13	11	11
Richmond	D	25	28	28	27
	R	11	13	12	13
Buffalo	D	18[a]	15	16	26
	R	14	22	18	21
Rochester	D	20[a]	20	18	29
	R	20	23	24	23
Newark	D	15[c]	8	10	17
	R	14	13	17	19
Jersey City	D	34[c]	32	31	40
	R	11	10	13	14
Philadelphia	D	5	4	8	25
	R	21	27	28	26
Pittsburgh	D	5	2	4	23
	R	11	17	21	17
Cleveland[a]	D	12	10	20	24
	R	13	11	16	18
Detroit	D	5	4	4	16
	R	8	8	14	12
Chicago	D	17	14	20	30
	R	18	19	17	19
Milwaukee	D	d	3	4	14
	R	d	11	12	9
Minneapolis	D	17	3	1[a]	12
	R	25	21	17	18
St. Paul	D	12	1	4	12
	R	21	13	26	19
San Francisco[a]	D	18	11	3	18
	R	15	17	28	24
Oakland[a]	D	13	11	6	21
	R	24	30	33	30
Los Angeles[a]	D	9	5	11	23
	R	20	25	20	26
Seattle[d]					

*In this table the letter designations have the following meanings: [a], vote for governor substituted; [b], at large; [c], vote for senator substituted; [d], no meaningful returns available.

and did not mark a lasting change in the habits of political participation or partisan loyalties of any significant segment of the electorate.

In many of these areas shifts toward the Democratic party were greater in the earlier 1930s than were those associated with the election of 1928 and that might be attributed to the influence of the Democratic candidate in that year. (See Table 18.4.) In the metropolitan areas of Boston, Providence, Cleveland, and Chicago increases in Democratic strength between 1926 and 1930 were of approximately the same magnitude or were greater than the shifts toward the Democrats in the 1930s. In the other areas, however, the increases in Democratic strength between the elections of 1930 and 1934 were greater than were those that could be attributed to changes in patterns of political behavior resulting from the election of 1928.

In short, examination of the vote in elections to lesser offices in metropolitan counties characterized by a population composed of large immigrant stock does not provide consistent support for the view that significant and lasting changes in partisan loyalties and habits of political participation occurred in 1928. The pattern of the vote in several areas, including Boston, Providence, Chicago, Cleveland, and Philadelphia, is at least compatible with that view, although in the last city the Democratic party remained in 1930 a relatively insignificant political alternative. In several other areas the Democratic party enjoyed very small increases perhaps as a result of the Smith candidacy. Whether these gains were of sufficient magnitude to merit characterization as revolution is another matter, and in these as in most of the areas considered the gains of 1928 were followed by more pronounced increases in the elections of the earlier 1930s. Thus, the pattern of the vote in the majority of these metropolitan areas either provides no support for the view that an "Al Smith Revolution" preceded the "Roosevelt Revolution" of the 1930s or is at most inconclusive.

On the basis of the presidential vote alone it could be concluded that in these areas major and lasting partisan realignment occurred in 1928, and it is also possible to conclude that these changes came about in large measure because of the characteristics of Alfred E. Smith and the existing social order. But when the vote in elections to lesser offices is considered, this general interpretation of the electoral history of the 1920s and 1930s appears much less tenable. Indeed, shifts in this vote seem equally consistent with the view that realignment came primarily in the 1930s or with the suggestion that realignment came about in the course of a "critical period" rather than as a result of a single "critical election."

The present examination does not, of course, prove that partisan realignment did not occur in 1928 in these or other areas. Detailed investigation of a larger number of areas employing powerful methods of analysis and taking into consideration, perhaps, the vote for additional offices might provide evidence of major realignment in that year. The areas considered are, moreover, of large size, and it is possible that voting patterns at the county level conceal rather than reveal significant trends and changes. Indeed, examination of the vote in individual congressional districts suggests that changes in the vote in several areas were not evenly distributed, but instead tended to be concentrated in particular districts. Thus it is quite conceivable that investigation of voting patterns at the level of wards and precincts would reveal evidence of lasting partisan change in 1928. Such an analysis might indicate that some immigrant groups defined by religious, economic, and more specific ethnic characteristics did change meaningfully in political behavior while others did not. It may be significant, however, that these shifts, if they occurred, were apparently not of a magnitude sufficient to alter greatly the balance of party strength within most of the metropolitan areas considered here. From a somewhat different point of view, changes in political behavior in 1928 even though not lasting in terms of the election of 1930 may have been a significant or even necessary step in the process of partisan realignment. Deviations in 1928 on the part of some groups from established patterns of partisan identification and political behavior may have increased the likelihood that a more lasting change in the political behavior of these same groups would occur at a latter time.[15]

It is clear, however, that the question of whether major partisan realignment occurred in 1928 can be answered, if it can be answered at all, only through detailed investigation of the voting patterns of 1928 and of earlier and subsequent elections, including the vote for lesser offices as well as the presidential vote.[16] It may be tempting to believe that the impact of Alfred E. Smith upon the electoral patterns of the nation can be established on the basis of other forms of evidence. The thought that Al Smith, the rags-to-riches scion of the Fulton Fishmarket, was responsible for bringing the children of the "new immigration" into an increasingly welfare-oriented Democratic party is in many respects an appealing one. Perhaps in some sense that is what should have happened. That it did happen can be established only through detailed analysis of the actual voting record.

NOTES

[1] Samuel Lubell, *The Future of American Politics* (2d rev. ed., New York, 1956), pp. 35–43. Lubell's findings were anticipated in some respects by Samuel J. Eldersveld in "The Influence of Metropolitan Party Pluralities in Presidential Elections since 1920: A Study of Twelve Key Cities," *American Political Science Review*, vol. 53 (December 1949), pp. 1189–1206.

[2] Irving Bernstein, *The Lean Years: A History of the American Worker, 1920–1933* (Boston, 1960), pp. 75–82; and Carl N. Degler, "American Political Parties and the Rise of the City: An Interpretation," *Journal of American History*, vol. 51 (June 1964), pp. 41–59.

[3] V. O. Key, Jr., "A Theory of Critical Elections," *Journal of Politics*, vol. 17 (February 1955), pp. 3–18.

[4] Duncan MacRae, Jr., and James A. Meldrum, "Critical Elections in Illinois: 1888–1958," *American Political Science Review*, vol. 54 (September 1960), pp. 669–683.

[5] David Burner, *The Politics of Provincialism: The Democratic Party in Transition, 1918–1932* (New York, 1968), pp. 217–243.

[6] John L. Shover, "Was 1928 a Critical Election in California?" *Pacific Northwest Quarterly*, vol. 58 (October 1967), pp. 196–204.

[7] See, *e.g.*, Angus Campbell, Philip E. Converse, Warren E. Miller, and Donald E. Stokes, *Elections and the Political Order* (New York, 1966), especially chaps. II–IV; and Charles Sellers, "The Equilibrium Cycle in Two-Party Politics," *Public Opinion Quarterly*, vol. 29 (Spring 1965), pp. 16–38.

[8] These possibilities are also suggested in Campbell, Converse, Miller, and Stokes, *Elections and the Political Order*, p. 75.

[9] This point is also made by Shover in "Was 1928 a Critical Election in California?" pp. 196–204.

[10] The discussion in this and preceding paragraphs draws heavily upon Angus Campbell, Philip E. Converse, Warren E. Miller, and Donald E. Stokes, *The American Voter* (New York, 1960), *passim*; and *id.*, *Elections and the Political Order*, especially chapters II–IV. These authors, of course, bear no responsibility for our interpretation and use of their findings.

[11] The cities listed in Table 18.1 and the following tables are identified by Degler as marked by major shifts toward the Democratic party in 1928. The cities are those of over 250,000 popu-

lation in 1930 in which, with the exception of Los Angeles, Oakland, and Seattle, immigrant stock population (defined as foreign-born white and native white of foreign or mixed parentage) represented over 50 percent of the total population. Although these groups accounted for less than 50 percent of the population of Los Angeles, Oakland, and Seattle, these cities are included because the population of native stock (defined as native-born white of native parentage) also amounted to less than 50 percent of the total population of each. The balance was made up by colored population. (See Degler, "American Political Parties," pp. 53–56; and Bureau of Commerce, *Statistical Abstract of the United States, 1931* [Washington, D.C., 1931], pp. 22–27.) As in the case of Degler's article, because election returns for the cities themselves are unavailable, the votes given are for the counties in which the cities were located. For purposes of clarity the city rather than the county names are used. The election returns used in this and the following tables were provided by the Inter-University Consortium for Political Research, which bears no responsibility for the analyses and interpretations presented here.

[12] When possible the vote in congressional elections has been displayed in Table 18.2 and subsequent tables. Since these metropolitan areas included more than a single congressional district, the congressional vote given is the Democratic percentage of the total vote for candidates for Congress. Thus the influence of the popularity of an individual candidate is somewhat lessened, and the vote presented in this fashion may more nearly reflect underlying partisan divisions. Because of cross-filing and uncontested elections a comprehensive and valid series of congressional returns is, unfortunately, not available for some of these counties. In these cases, the vote for other offices has been substituted.

[13] For Tables 18.3 and 18.4 the estimates of eligible voters, defined as adults of twenty-one and over, are based upon the assumption that the rate of change in the number of persons in this age category was even across the decades of the 1920s and 1930s. Thus the net change in population in this category between the censuses of 1920 and 1930 and 1930 and 1940 has simply been parceled out evenly across the respective decades.

[14] Observations as to the impact of new voters upon the relative strength of the two parties are subject to a possible fallacy. Increases in the party vote in particular years as reflected in Table 18.4 are, obviously, composed of two elements: voters who had voted in earlier elections and who switched to the opposite party, and voters who had not voted in earlier elections. The relative importance of these two components in the shifts in electoral strength cannot, of course, be determined. Thus it is possible to assume, for example, that the total Republican increase in all areas or in any individual area was disproportionately composed of old voters who switched to the Republicans in 1928 while the Democrats received a heavily disproportionate share of the new voters.

[15] This possibility is raised in Campbell, Converse, Miller, and Stokes, *Elections and the Political Order*, p. 75.

[16] This and related imperatives for the study of political history are discussed in detail in Lee Benson, "Research Problems in American Political Historiography," in *Common Frontiers of the Social Sciences*, ed. Mirra Komarovsky (Glencoe, Ill., 1957), pp. 113–181. It is probable that students of American electoral patterns have based their investigations almost exclusively upon the presidential vote primarily because returns for elections to other offices were not available. County-level returns for elections to the offices of governor, senator, and representative in Congress, as well as presidential returns, for the years from 1824 to the present can now, however, be supplied on a limited basis by the Inter-University Consortium for Political Research, Box 1248, Ann Arbor, Michigan, 48106.

Recent American Voting Behavior:

The New Deal and Beyond, 1932–1970

Part Five

The third and most recent shift in the voting behavior and partisan identification of the American electorate occurred during the 1930s. Out of this political realignment emerged the fifth party system, characterized to the present day by: (1) the first normal Democratic popular majority since the realignment of the 1850s; and (2) a partial reactivation of the electorate, so that voter turnout generally has run higher than at any time since the 1890s. In winning in 1932, Franklin Delano Roosevelt became the first Democratic presidential candidate to receive a majority of the popular vote since Samuel Tilden in 1876. Four years later, Roosevelt won a landslide victory, carrying all but two states. (FDR's second victory led to the modification of a political adage that dated from 1840: "As Maine goes, so goes Vermont.") Democratic congressional strength had begun to increase as early as the first depression elections in 1930; it continued to rise in 1932 and 1934 and reached its peak in 1936. The presidential vote of 1932, cast during the depths of the Great Depression, involved shifts of varying magnitude toward the Democrats among all types of voting groups. In 1936 many rural counties returned to the Republican column but the growing support for the Democrats in urban areas increased their nationwide percentage. The Democratic tide ebbed following 1936. Still Roosevelt was reelected by comfortable, if diminished, margins in 1940 and 1944 and his party retained control of Congress until 1946.

The outlines of mass politics during the New Deal epoch seem clear enough. All the same, we need detailed historical studies of voting behavior in a wide range of settings in order to comprehend the changing socioeconomic and ethnocultural composition of the opposing coalitions. In this connection, analysis of the 1932–1936 period alone will not suffice. To begin with, the Democratic vote during those years was temporarily swollen by Republicans whose protest against hard times did not lead to any lasting shift in party identification. Further, many farmers and prosperous urbanites who voted Democratic during the first years of Roosevelt's New Deal resumed their support of the Republican party when they came to oppose New Deal policies, particularly after 1936. On the other hand, blacks, who were to contribute much to the northern urban Democratic coalition, did not break decisively with the Republican party until 1936 and later. Taken together, voter shifts between 1932 and 1940 produced Democratic and Republican coalitions that differed from each other socioeconomically as well as ethnoculturally. Neither the realignment of the 1850s nor that of the 1890s had had a similar result.

Over the past three decades, the Democratic coalition that was forged during the depression of the 1930s has demonstrated its staying power by surviving profound social and economic changes at home and World War II, the Cold War, and two limited wars abroad. To be sure, the Republicans captured Congress in the postwar midterm elections of 1946, but they scored no victory comparable to those that had destroyed the Wilsonian coalition after World War I. Two years later the Democrats won their fifth consecutive presidential election and recaptured Congress despite Democratic defections to Henry Wallace on the left and J. Strom Thurmond on the right. The vote for Wallace, concentrated in the urban North, was disappointing to him but still the largest received by any candidate to the left of the major parties during the recent period. (Indeed, Socialist, Communist, and other parties of the Left have had negligible support over the past five decades, even during the depression-racked 1930s.) The vote for Thurmond, largely in the rural South, was an early expression of the discontent of southern whites with the national Democratic party that has cost the Democrats southern states in every presidential election from 1948 through 1968.

Democratic grass-roots strength remained impressive during the 1950s, for though Dwight Eisenhower twice decisively defeated Adlai Stevenson for the presidency, he was unable to transfer his own popularity to lesser Republicans even in presidential election years. His party also suffered setbacks in the midterm elections of 1954 and 1958 so that the Democrats commanded majorities in three of four Congresses during Eisenhower's presidency. Finally, polls indicated that among eligible voters, Democratic identifiers continued to outnumber Republican identifiers. Had the partisan preference of most voters not remained Democratic during the 1950s, John Kennedy probably would have lost the presidential election of 1960. The religious issue cost Kennedy many votes, but the Democratic coalition proved strong enough to carry him through to narrow victory.

Democratic strength reached post-1936 heights in the elections of 1964, but Republicans who voted for Lyndon Johnson were rejecting Barry Goldwater, not transferring partisan allegiance. Democratic strength ebbed two years later in the midterm elections and declined sharply in the three-way presidential election of 1968, which is treated by Philip Converse, Warren E. Miller, Jerrold G. Rusk, and Arthur C. Wolfe in the final essay in this section. Observers have particularly noted the unusual instability of popular voting behavior during the 1960s, W. Dean Burnham going so far as to refer to "the end of American party politics." More sanguine students acknowledge the decline in party loyalty during the decade, but contend that partisan identification remains a powerful political influence, particularly in elections other than those for the presidency. Certainly the success of the Democrats in the congressional elections of 1968 and the midterm elections of 1970 suggests that neither party identification as a determinant of popular voting behavior nor the continued strength of the Democratic coalition should be discounted as the nation moves into the 1970s.

The "La Follette Revolution" and

the Pittsburgh Vote, 1932

Bruce Stave

19

Bruce Stave's examination of the antecedents of Franklin Roosevelt's 1932 popular coalition in Pittsburgh raises questions about a number of traditional interpretations of the relationships among various voting coalitions during the first third of the twentieth century. For one, Stave notes a strong positive association between the Al Smith vote of 1928 and the Roosevelt vote. But the correlation between the 1924 vote for Robert La Follette, who ran as a Progressive, and the vote for Roosevelt was even stronger. Thus in Pittsburgh, at least, La Follette had greater success than Smith in mobilizing support among groups that were later to form the New Deal coalition. Professor Stave, who teaches at the University of Connecticut, is the author of *The New Deal and the Last Hurrah, Pittsburgh Machine Politics* (Pittsburgh, 1970).

In the 1932 election the city of Pittsburgh, for the first time since 1856, voted for a Democratic President despite Franklin D. Roosevelt's defeat in the state of Pennsylvania, and the attempt of the local Republican machine to tamper with the ballots.[1] Shocked Republicans and delighted Democrats considered the election results to represent a massive political upheaval in the city's voting behavior. However, analysis of the returns for the Steel City's two previous presidential elections indicates that the Roosevelt New Deal voting coalition had its roots in the support won by Robert M. La Follette during his Progressive campaign of 1924.

The years were lean for the Democratic party prior to 1932. The dearth of party stalwarts in Pittsburgh, where only 5200 out of the city's 175,000 registered voters were listed as Democrats in 1929, played havoc with any formal party organization. From the time in 1912 when the then future Democratic Senator, Joseph F. Guffey, gave an assistant $2500 to pay watchers at the polls and the assistant returned with $1500, unable to find enough people to hire with the money, to the coming of the New Deal, little had changed. As Pittsburgh party boss, David L. Lawrence, noted, "Prior to 1932, just a few old faithfuls

SOURCE: Reprinted with permission from *Mid-America*, vol. 49 (October 1967), pp. 244–251.

stuck by the party. It was a long gap between Wilson and FDR. Before 1932, Democrats always played for the minority places."[2]

Many committeemen, who served during the depression decade, have reminisced that when they first began in politics perhaps only five or six Democrats were registered in their districts; that they had to get Republicans to sit as Democratic election judges; that a mere dozen of the two dozen plus ward chairmen would show up for meetings with Lawrence at Democratic headquarters; and that the party "existed on crumbs from the Republicans." For one Democratic committeeman, the change in party structure, once his candidates began winning, was so great that he left politics. Born a Democrat, and in politics since 1909, he served as 16th ward chairman from 1926 to 1934. "I left in 1934 because after FDR got in, the party became too big. By 1934, everyone was running after me for a job, so I just left," remarked a party worker for whom winning brought too many problems.[3]

Economic conditions stand as the prime cause for the political turnabout. The highly industrialized city felt the brunt of the depression, and as a result, Roosevelt and the local Democrats benefited. The financial strain took its toll on many Pittsburghers. In December 1930, welfare agencies arranged for the unemployed to sell apples without the formality of obtaining a city license. Purchased by the unemployed for $2.00 a box of 88 to 100, they sold on street corners for five cents apiece, grossing $4.40 to $5.00. Men lived in squalid packing boxes on the outskirts of the city, and when police burned them out, a "Shantytown" sprung up in the city's strip district. Named as its honorary mayor, a Catholic priest, Father James R. Cox, presided over his impoverished flock, and ultimately led a "March of the Jobless" on Washington in January, 1932. When the fifteenth census was taken in April of 1930, over 20,000 Pittsburghers were reported out of work and 5000 laid off; nine months later, the special unemployment census of January 1931 found almost 60,000 unemployed and over 19,000 laid off. By 1933, 15.7 percent of all Pittsburgh whites and 43.4 percent of its Negroes could be found on the relief rolls. These percentages topped fourteen other northern and southern cities, all having 50,000 or more Negroes in 1930.[4]

As a result of the economic disaster, the shift from Republican to Democratic allegiance quickly began to snowball. It involved activist party workers as well as the average voter. One precinct committeeman spoke for thousands of Pittsburghers as he remembered: "In 1930, I changed from the Republicans to the Democrats. I guess I was like a cat. I had my eyes open. You had to be hardy and grab a straw. I was a depositor in four banks and all went under. I was in bad shape. I felt we couldn't let the Republicans get away with it." A World War I veteran, active as a precinct official in the city's 20th ward, mirrored the dislikes of other survivors of the American Expeditionary Force. Referring to the rout of the "Bonus Army," he complained, "I disliked Hoover and Mac-Arthur for Anacostia Flats." The Democratic organization picked up new rank and filers, and Roosevelt garnered his vote from an amalgam of dissidents.[5]

Pittsburgh's break from its Republican presidential voting tradition, however, had been building slowly throughout the 1920s, and the election of 1932 cannot be looked upon as merely episodic. The depression quickened a trend that had already begun. In accord with the thesis that "the Republican hold on the cities was broken not by Roosevelt but by Alfred E. Smith," that "before the Roosevelt Revolution there was an Al Smith Revolution," Pittsburgh gave the Pride of New York's Lower East Side 48 percent of its vote. Its foreign born and their children of voting age turned out to cast their ballots for the first Catholic candidate for President. However, an analysis of the voting returns indicates that before the "Smith Revolution" there was a "La Follette Revolution" in Pittsburgh.[6]

After Theodore Roosevelt, running on three tickets, beat the Republican organization in 1912, political normalcy, and then normalcy personified, returned when Hughes won 57 percent of the total Pittsburgh vote in 1916, and Harding captured a phenomenal 71.4 percent in 1920. The landslide of Calvin Coolidge, however, received a jolt in the Steel City when John W. Davis, the Democratic candidate, obtained only 8 percent of the vote, but Progressive Robert M. La Follette, running on a local Socialist-Labor ticket, reaped 36 percent of the vote — 20 percent more than his national average. La Follette's supporters, attacked during the campaign by the Republican county chairman as a "bunch of Reds," brightened when the Wisconsin politician told a local gathering on the Halloween before election day, "It is unnecessary to demonstrate to a Pittsburgh audience that private monopoly does in fact control government and industry. You live here in the shadow of one of the greatest, if not the very greatest, monopoly in the world — the U.S. Steel Corporation." For good measure, he attacked Secretary of the Treasury Andrew Mellon as being "the real President of the United States." "Calvin Coolidge is merely the man who occupies the White House," he declared.[7]

Compared to prior presidential elections dating back to 1912, the La Follette vote bears closest significant relationship to the Debs vote of that year, indicating a firm connection between the support for the Progressive candidate in 1924, and the Socialist standard bearer of a dozen years earlier. (See Table 19.1.) Ironically, however, the 1912 support for Theodore Roosevelt, also run-

Table 19.1   Coefficients of Correlation Between 1912, 1924, 1928 and 1932 Presidential Votes for Pittsburgh Wards

	Debs '12	*TR '12*	*Smith '28*	*FDR '32*
La Follette '24	.75	−.34	.64	.84
Davis '24	—	—	−.40	−.37
La Follette-Davis '24	—	—	.69	.90
Smith '28	—	—	—	.72

*The Correlations for the 1924, 1928 and 1932 votes are based on 28 wards; the correlation for the 1924 and 1912 votes are based on wards 1-27. In 1932 there were thirty-two wards in the city. The formula used for the correlations throughout this article is the Spearman Rank Order Formula, $R = 1 - 6 \, (S \, d^2)/N^3 - N$ where R is the coefficient of correlation, S is the sum of, d is the difference between the rankings of a given ward for the variables being measured and N is the total number of wards. Coefficients of correlation from .5 to 1 and from −.5 to −1 are considered significant.

ning under the Progressive banner, appears much different from La Follette's. In fact, as seen in Tables 19.3 and 19.4, the Bull Moose Progressives in 1912 in Pittsburgh were based in the native white, upper economic elements of the community, while the 1924 Progressives found support among the foreign, lower economic classes of the city.

Compared to the presidential elections of 1928 and 1932, La Follette's impact on Pittsburgh, as evidenced by the 1924 voting returns, must have been greater than described by the Republican oriented newspapers. His vote takes on special significance in the light of the complete Roosevelt breakthrough eight years later. If La Follette's vote is compared with Smith's by ranking their vote by ward, a significant correlation is found. However, the correlation of the 1924 Progressive vote with the 1932 Democratic vote shows an even greater similarity and indicates that both La Follette and Roosevelt drew their support from much the same wards. On the other hand, a comparison of the 1928 Smith vote and the 1932 Roosevelt vote shows a less significant likeness, indicating somewhat different support. Davis's 1924 Democratic backing was poles apart from both Smith's and Roosevelt's. Yet, if Davis's vote is added to La Follette's on the premise that it, too, was a vote against the Republican organization, there is an increase in the positive correlation of the 1924 Democratic–third-party vote combination with both Smith's and Roosevelt's support.

Where the Smith and Roosevelt strength differed most, and the FDR and La Follette support had the most similarity, can be best seen by isolating each candidate's wards of greatest strength. While La Follette's and Roosevelt's heaviest support came from the same wards, although in reversed order, Smith drew best

Table 19.2 Wards Showing Most Support

La Follette '24	Smith '28	Roosevelt '32
16	1	17
24	2	24
17	16	16

in two entirely different wards. One of these, the tightly controlled Republican second ward, gave FDR his least support. The first and second wards, which supplied Smith with his highest ward votes, 77 percent and 75 percent respectively, also housed the highest proportion of foreign-born population of any wards in the city in 1930. One quarter of the population of each ward was foreign born, and of these two thirds were eligible to vote in the first ward and about 60 percent in the second. Italians constituted the largest ethnic group in both districts.[8]

However, if the foreign stock, i.e., foreign born and first generation, is considered, La Follette by polling well in the 16th and 17th wards drew his support from two of the three highest "foreign-stock" wards; his victory in the 24th may reflect that German-American ward's approval of his opposition to the United States' entrance into World War I. La Follette reached the immigrants and their children before Smith, although to a lesser extent. Correlating each candidate's vote by ward with a ranking of the ward's standing with regard to foreign stock, one finds the affinity of the Roosevelt vote and the foreign community to stand between that of La Follette and that of Smith as seen in Table 19.3. La Follette captured the foreign vote and the Democratic hold on that vote reached its zenith with Smith. Roosevelt's foreign support was weaker than the 1928 candidate's, but showed a gain over La Follette's 1924 backing. Concomitantly, all three candidates had a negative relationship with the native white of at least second generation, with Smith doing significantly worse.[9]

Table 19.3 Coefficients of Correlation* Between 1912, 1924, 1928, and 1932
Presidential Votes and Ethnic Variables for Pittsburgh Wards

	TR '12	Debs '12	LaF. '24	Smith '28	FDR '32
Foreign stock	−.62	.31	.55	.87	.67
Native stock (Native white of native parentage)	.58	−.23	−.27	−.70	−.40

*The correlations for the 1924, 1928, and 1932 votes are based on wards 1-28; the correlations for the 1912 votes are based on wards 1-27. In 1932 there were thirty-two wards in the city. For 1912, foreign and native stock is computed from U.S. Census for 1910; for 1924, 1928, and 1932 foreign and native stock is computed from U.S. Census, 1930.

In lower economic working class wards, La Follette set the tone for Smith and Roosevelt as well. When one correlates each candidate's vote in all twenty-eight wards, ranked from highest to lowest by their 1930 median rental, one not only finds no significant difference, but, in fact, a close relationship between the candidates. Each did badly in the high rental, upper economic class districts. Although not realized at the time, the "La Follette Revolution" signaled a sorry turn of the tide for Pittsburgh's Republican machine.

Table 19.4 Coefficients of Correlation* Between 1912, 1924, 1928, and 1932
Presidential Votes and Economic Variables for Pittsburgh Wards

	Most Tenements Actually Occupied, 1912	Median Rental 1930
Debs '12	.01	—
TR '12	−.30	—
La Follette '24	—	−.60
Smith '28	—	−.64
FDR '32	—	−.57

*The 1912 correlations are based on twenty-seven wards; others based on wards 1-28. In 1932 there were thirty-two wards in the city. Comparable informatoin for 1912 and 1930 unavailable. "Most tenements" from City of Pittsburgh, *Annual Report of the Mayor, 1912*. Median Rental from *Social Facts About Pittsburgh and Allegheny County*, vol. 1, *Pittsburgh Wards* (Pittsburgh, 1945).

Viewed over an eight-year period, which witnessed three presidential elections, the Roosevelt victory does not appear as sharp a break from past Pittsburgh voting tradition as it may have to the average Pittsburgher of 1932. The election of 1924 unsettled the laboring city's Republican voting habits. It drew into politics individuals like Thomas J. Gallagher, an Irish-Catholic labor leader, who began his political career as chairman of the working-class 16th and 17th Ward La Follette Campaign Committee. Gallagher, who started work at age 12, claimed firsthand knowledge of "what it meant to be exploited." As a state legislator, he subsequently supported a wide variety of labor and social legislation; in 1933, riding the crest of the Democratic wave, he won election, as a New Deal advocate, to Pittsburgh's City Council. His service as a member of that body would span four decades — the period of Democratic hegemony in the Steel

City. As the foundation for Gallagher's political career was laid in 1924, so, too, did that year's La Follette campaign lay the foundation for the making of the Roosevelt Democratic coalition in Pittsburgh.[10]

NOTES

[1] Joseph F. Guffey, *Seventy Years on the Red Fire Wagon*, privately published, 1952, p. 75.

[2] *Pittsburgh Press*, September 18, 1933; Guffey, *Seventy Years*, pp. 36–37; Interview, David L. Lawrence, April 14, 1964.

[3] Over 100 committeemen, who served the Pittsburgh Democratic party during the depression decade, were interviewed. For reasons of anonymity they are cited by ward and district. Those who made the above or similar remarks are: 6W4, 6W6, 8W8, 11W6, 11W14, 13W3, 14W18, 15W8, 20W15, 21W15, 21W7, 27W2, 29W6; quote is from 16W12.

[4] *Pittsburgh Sun-Telegraph*, December 1, 1930; *Pittsburgh Press*, May 10, 1931, September 27, 1931; *Pittsburgh Post-Gazette*, January 6, 1932; U.S. Bureau of the Census, *Special Census, Unemployment, General Report*, 1931; *Pittsburgh Press*, March 21, 1931; *Negro Year Book*, 1937–1938, p. 21. These cities were: New York, Chicago, Philadelphia, Baltimore, Washington, New Orleans, Detroit, Birmingham, Memphis, St. Louis, Atlanta, Cleveland, Houston, and Richmond.

[5] Interviews, 15W8, 20W15.

[6] The nation's twelve largest cities, of which Pittsburgh was one, gave the Republicans a net party plurality of 1,308,000 in 1924. With the Smith candidacy, this shifted to a Democratic plurality of 210,000. To this day the Democrats have not relinquished their big city plurality. The "Smith Revolution" thesis was popularized by Samuel Lubell, *The Future of American Politics*, 3rd rev. ed., New York, 1965, pp. 148–155, in which figures cited are published. The thesis was perhaps given seminal thought in Samuel J. Eldersveld, "Influence of Metropolitan Party Pluralities on Presidential Elections," *American Political Science Review*, vol. 43 (December 1949), pp. 1189–1206. For a discussion of the 1924 La Follette vote see Richard Hofstadter, *The Age Of Reform*, New York, 1960, p. 284. Ruth C. Silva in *Rum, Religion, And Votes: 1928 Re-Examined*, University Park, Pa., 1962, pp. 9–12, examines the relationship between the La Follette and the Smith vote. Although at one point she notes, "Therefore, it appears that voting for La Follette was a transition from the Republican to the Democratic party for a significant number of voters," Silva qualifies by continuing "Smith's apparently greater (than Hoover's) success in attracting La Follette voters should not be magnified." Admitting that "there was a tendency for Smith to make his gains in states where La Follette had been relatively strong," Silva points to the probability "that Smith's gains resulted largely from the attraction of new voters to the electorate and not merely from winning the support of La Follette voters."

[7] Election returns from *Pennsylvania Manuals* of 1913, 1917, 1921, and 1925 percentaged by the author; *Pittsburgh Post-Gazette*, November 1, 1924; Belle Case and Fola La Follette, *Robert M. La Follette*, vol. 2, New York, 1953, pp. 11–14.

[8] Population statistics based on 1930 from Bureau of Social Research, Federation of Social Agencies of Pittsburgh and Allegheny County, *Social Facts About Pittsburgh and Allegheny County*, vol. 1, *Pittsburgh Wards*, Pittsburgh, 1945. Voting statistics percentaged from returns in *Pennsylvania Manuals* of 1925, 1929, and 1933.

[9] For figures on foreign stock, the number of native white of foreign or mixed parents in each ward was added to the number of foreign born and subtracted from the native white total in each ward. This process provided figures for the population of native parentage only, as well as for foreign stock, that is, foreign born plus first generation. U.S. Bureau of the Census, *15th Census, Pennsylvania, Composition and Characteristics*, Table 23, "Population by Sex, Color, Age, etc., for Cities Over 50,000 or More by Ward, 1930," p. 751; Lubell, *Future of American Politics*, pp. 140–141, notes the link of the 1924 La Follette vote and his opposition to United States' entrance into World War I. This view has not gone unchallenged. For a discussion of the isolationist thesis and further references see R. M. Abrams and L. W. Levine, *The Shaping of Twentieth-Century America*, Boston, 1965, p. 502; Harold F. Alderfer and Robert M. Sigmond, "Presidential Elections by Pennsylvania Counties, 1920–1940," *Pennsylvania State College Studies*, number 10, *College Bulletin*, vol. 35 (June 9, 1941), p. 30, shows that there was a very high correlation between La Follette's vote and the foreign-born white population for all of Pennsylvania's counties in 1924. On the county level for foreign-born whites, the La Follette coefficient was higher than Smith's in 1928.

[10] Interview, Thomas Gallagher, July 27, 1965; clippings, Gallagher file, Pennsylvania Division, Carnegie Library, Pittsburgh, Pa.; obituary, *New York Times*, March 16, 1967.

The Development and Persistence of Ethnic Voting[1]

Raymond E. Wolfinger

20

Since the early 1930s, socioeconomic as well as ethnocultural factors have significantly influenced popular voting behavior in the United States. Italian-Americans, like other Roman Catholic, working-class groups in the Northeast, have usually voted Democratic during this period. Nevertheless, as Professor Raymond E. Wolfinger of Stanford University points out in the following article, Italian-Americans in New Haven, Connecticut, have supported the Republican party to an unusual degree over the past three decades. This has not been because of any change in their socioeconomic position or lessening of their ethnic concerns. Rather it has stemmed from direct Republican appeals to Italian-American ethnic identification and the latter group's positive response thereto.

Mass immigration ended fifty years ago, but national origins continue to be a salient dimension in many people's perceptions of themselves and of others.[2] Where this salience is widespread, ethnicity plays a major role in politics.[3] Ethnicity is often an important independent variable in voting behavior. "Ethnic voting," as I shall call it, has two manifestations.

1. Members of an ethnic group show an affinity for one party or the other which cannot be explained solely as a result of other demographic characteristics. Voters of Irish descent, to take a familiar example, are more likely than other voters of similar economic status to be Democrats.
2. Members of an ethnic group will cross party lines to vote for — or against — a candidate belonging to a particular ethnic group.[4]

This article deals with the development and persistence of ethnic voting. The customary theory holds that ethnic voting is strongest during an ethnic group's earliest residence in this country and subsequently declines from this peak as the group's members make their way out of the working class.[5] This might be

SOURCE: Reprinted with permission from *The American Political Science Review*, vol. 59 (December 1965), pp. 896–908.

called an "assimilation theory." It sees a direct relationship between the proportion of a nationality group in the working class and that group's political homogeneity. As more and more of the group join the middle class, its political unity is progressively eroded. Along with middle-class status, these group members are said to acquire different political interests and to identify more with the majority society and less with their nationality group: in short, they become assimilated. Presumably the end of the process is reached when group members are as occupationally differentiated as the whole population. At this point they are politically indistinguishable from the general population, or from a control group with similar nonethnic characteristics, and ethnicity is no longer a factor in their voting behavior.[6]

This is a plausible argument, but it is not consistent with voting patterns in New Haven, Connecticut.[7] People of Italian descent there comprise about one-third of the city's population. Although the Italians are the poorest segment of the white population, they are also one of the strongest Republican voting blocs. If the assimilation theory held in New Haven, this Italian Republicanism would have been strongest some generations ago when Italians first settled there in numbers, and would have declined with the passage of time. But the overwhelming support that New Haven Italians give to the Republican party is a development of the past twenty-five years. It began when the first New Haven Italian candidate for a major city office won the Republican mayoralty nomination. Since then Italians have been the mainstay of Republican voting strength in New Haven, even in elections with no Italian candidates.

These events may not be as anomalous as they seem. They can be explained by a theory that may also be pertinent to many other places. I will discuss this alternate theory after a detailed description of the development of ethnic voting in New Haven. Finally, I will consider available evidence on the persistence of ethnic voting.

The Conditions of Ethnic Politics

The history of nationality group relations in New Haven is from all accounts typical of many industrial cities in the northeastern states. In the course of the nineteenth and early twentieth centuries the descendants of New Haven's original Anglo-Saxon Protestant settlers were outnumbered by waves of immigrants from Ireland and later from southern and eastern Europe. By 1910, according to the census data, two thirds of the population were first- or second-generation Americans; in 1960 some 42 percent of the population were in these categories. More detailed information on the ethnic composition of the population comes from a sample survey of 525 registered voters conducted in the summer of 1959.[8] White Protestants comprised less than 20 percent of this sample; 31 percent of the respondents were born in Italy or were in the second or third generation of Italian immigrants. Eleven percent were of similarly recent Irish origin,[9] 9 percent were Negroes; and 15 percent were Jews.

Beginning with the first mass Irish immigration the old settlers met the non-Protestant newcomers with hostility, economic exploitation, and religious discrimination. The immigrants were usually penniless and could get only the least desirable jobs. The affronts of everyday life enhanced their ethnic consciousness; so did the obvious gap in wellbeing between them and the old settlers.

In addition to Yankee hostility, other forces tended to maintain ethnic solidarity. For European peasants trying to live in an American city, a familiar language, religion and culture were comforting when so much else was different. Members of any given nationality group usually settled in the same neighborhoods, lived together and married among their kind and not with Yankees or other immigrants, formed nationality associations, and worshiped in national churches.

Needless to say, the ethnics often responded to the Yankees with a hatred that has not yet vanished, while many Yankees continue to look down on the ethnics. Members of each of the major ethnic groups still regard the others with varying amounts of good will, of jealousy and suspicion. As the years have passed, the immigrants and their descendants have moved, in varying numbers, into the middle class. This economic mobility did not result in equivalent geographical dispersion, in part because some of the new prosperity came from neighborhood enterprises such as groceries and mortuaries, in part because of the continuing comforts of ethnic proximity.

One consequence of this history is a persistent emphasis on ethnic differences, which continue to be a major organizing principle in the city's social structure. There are, for example, no less than six Junior Leagues in New Haven, including one each for the not very numerous local young ladies of Swedish and Danish extraction. There are also Jewish organizations with similar functions but different names.[10] The major Catholic ethnic groups have their own national churches.

Ethnic consciousness is an important and pronounced regional characteristic. It is difficult to suggest an objective measure for comparing ethnic salience, much less to find data on this subject, but on the basis of impressionistic evidence it appears that concern with national origins is much greater in the Northeast than in some other parts of the country. The reasons for this regional difference are not immediately apparent. The numerical prevalence of ethnics does not account for it, for the major cities of the West Coast have sizable ethnic populations.[11] San Francisco has about the same proportion of first- and second-generation Americans as New Haven (43 as against 42 percent) but there is no comparison between the two cities with respect to ethnic salience.[12]

This regional difference may be due to the fact that in the Northeast the non-British immigrants came to settled communities with relatively stable class structures and systems of status ascription. Only menial jobs were open to them. The distribution of economic rewards and opportunities reinforced the unambiguous class system. On the other hand, immigrants came to the West at the same time as the Yankees, or on their heels. "The Forty-Niners came from all parts of the world, and foreign accents were as common in the mining camps as American ones."[13] The two groups shared the same pioneering experiences[14] and lived in communities with wildly fluctuating economies and unsettled social systems. Economic advantage was not so closely associated with ethnicity, and class distinctions were not so rigid.

The immigrants in New England were equal to the older settlers in only one relevant respect: they could vote. Little in their previous experience suggested that their opinions had much to do with government, and so their votes had no abstract value to them. But these votes mattered to American politicians, who solicited them with advice, favors, petty gifts, and jobs.

Two typical loci of immigrant politicization were the bosses of casual labor gangs on public works, who owed their positions to their ability to deliver their gangs' votes and their vote-delivering ability to their command of jobs; and the leaders of nationality associations, usually men who were the first to achieve some economic success.[15] Such relationships set the pattern for ethnic politics. Each nationality group in a city had leaders who bargained with politicians, trading their followers' votes for money, favors, and jobs.[16] For their part the politicians found it convenient and efficient to classify the electorate by ethnicity and to dispense rewards on this basis.

The tangible political rewards were limited. Not everyone could be given a job or a Christmas basket. Nor did everyone want such things; or need to get a son out of jail, or a relative into the United States, or a pushcart license from City Hall. But when one Italian was appointed to a public position his success was enjoyed vicariously by other Italians; it was "recognition" of the worth of the Italians. Ethnic solidarity let politicians economize on the indulgences they bestowed. It was unnecessary to do a favor for every individual to win his vote. Rewards given to the few were appreciated by the many. Money or jobs given to a few leaders earned political returns in two ways: (1) through the votes that the recipient could deliver directly; and (2) through appreciation of the "recognition" he had earned. Public office was much the most effective such reward, for it was most visible and hence conveyed most glory.[17]

Certain of New Haven's other political characteristics were (and are) conducive to ethnic politics. In particular, the city's wards were small enough to be ethnically homogeneous. Politicians need schemes for classifying voters and they tend to look for such taxonomies in election returns. In New Haven the ward is the politicians' unit of electoral analysis, which facilitates explaining the outcome of elections on the basis of ethnic preferences.[18] Since results were understood in ethnic terms, strategies were developed in the same terms. Politicians appealed to the electorate on the basis of ethnic rather than class differences. Moreover, many local political issues concerned the allocation of governmental services and facilities among different neighborhoods, and so contests for these rewards could also be interpreted as competition among ethnic groups.

For many years the urban immigrants were mostly Irish and the "outside" politicians were Yankees. In addition to minor rewards for many people, politics offered a few immigrants a path to real wealth and power, a path that was all the more important because prejudice and lack of education drastically narrowed the chances of a lucrative career in legitimate business or the professions. By the time later waves of immigrants arrived, the Irish had attained considerable political influence, largely in the Democratic party. Where this happened they replaced or joined the "outside" politicians with whom the leaders of newer ethnic groups bargained.

Ethnic Politics in New Haven

The first Irishman was elected to the New Haven Board of Aldermen in 1857. Henceforth Irishmen and other ethnics held municipal office in increasing numbers. Democratic mayoralty candidates continued for a while to be Yankee businessmen, demographically indistinguishable from their Republican opponents. The election of 1899 marked the end of Yankee dominance in local politics.

Cornelius Driscoll, born in County Cork, was elected mayor on the Democratic ticket. As the Irish subsequently strengthened their hold on the party, some Yankee Democrats defected to the Republicans.

The Irish were not reluctant to take the spoils of victory. In the early 1930s first- and second-generation Irishmen comprised 13 percent of a sample of 1600 family heads in New Haven, but they accounted for 49 percent of all governmental jobs. The Italians suffered most of all from Irish chauvinism: there were *no* government employees among the 27 percent of the sample who were Italian.[19] These survey data exaggerate the Italians' exclusion from political rewards, but not by very much. In 1930 the proportion of Italians in low-paying municipal jobs was only a quarter of the proportion of Italians in the total population, and the ratio for better city jobs was much lower. By 1940 the Italians had attained half their "quota" of the poorer positions, and only about a fifth in white collar posts.[20] Subsequently their representation in both appointive and elective positions has increased enormously.[21]

The explanation of the New Haven Italians' Republicanism may then be thought to lie here: shut out of the Democratic party, they had no place to go but to the Republicans. This argument has two crippling limitations. (1) The Italians became more Republican during the period when they finally came closer to getting their "fair share" of municipal jobs. (2) Irish control of the local Democratic party is common in Northeastern industrial cities, but the level of Italian Republicanism found in New Haven is not. Allegations about the Republican inclinations of Italians abound in scholarly and journalistic literature, but concrete and systematic evidence for this general proposition is hard to find. Some Italians will split their ballots to vote for an Italian Republican, but the same is true for an Italian Democratic candidate. The best present source of data on this subject is the series of national election studies conducted over the past dozen years by the Survey Research Center of the University of Michigan. I have compared the party identification of the Italian and Irish respondents in the 1952, 1956, and 1958 studies who lived in the New England and Middle Atlantic states. As Table 20.1 shows, the Italians are a little more inclined than the Irish to consider themselves Democrats.[22]

Table 20.1 Party Identification of Italians and Irish in the Northeast, 1952, 1956, and 1958

Party Identification	Irish	Italian
	(%)	(%)
Democratic	51	57
Independent	18	13
Republican	32	30
	—	—
	101*	100
N	152	143

*Does not sum to 100 because of rounding.
Source: Inter-University Consortium for Political Research. I am indebted to Ralph Bisco and Richard T. Lane of the Consortium staff for their assistance.

Since the level of Italian Republicanism found in New Haven is not common in the Northeast, local history is more likely to provide an explanation than are more widespread political events. Two such local causes can be identified. The first was the determined courting of the Italian vote by Louis and Isaac Ullman, the leaders of the New Haven Republican party in the first part of the twentieth century. The Ullman brothers realized that the large and hitherto passive Italian population was an untapped source of potential Republicans. They set out to capture the Italians, using the familiar techniques of ethnic politics. They helped them take out citizenship papers, registered them as voters, found them jobs, used their considerable political influence to smooth over administrative and legal difficulties, subsidized Italian-American fraternal and political clubs, and so on.

It is not too much to say that the Ullman brothers' foresight and political skill kept the Republican party competitive in New Haven. Although the Italians were the poorest part of the population, they were, in the thirty years after 1910, less favorable to Democratic candidates than any other immigrant group, except perhaps the Jews.[23] In the 10th Ward, with the city's heaviest concentration of Italians, the Democratic share of the presidential and mayoralty vote fluctuated around 50 percent. In fact, the 10th voted much like the city as a whole, a remarkable similarity in view of its residents' modest economic position.[24] The other wards in which Italians predominated were also less wholeheartedly Democratic than one would expect from their low income levels. It seems likely that this situation was due largely to the extent and intensity of the Ullmans' proselytizing.

Critical Elections

The Ullman brothers' efforts gave the Republicans a certain advantage with Italian voters. Yet for some thirty years the result was no more than a stand-off; the Italians split their votes more or less evenly between the two parties until the end of the 1930s. Since then they have been very strongly Republican. The big shift in Italian voting habits came when William C. Celentano, a self-made mortician and son of a fruit peddler, won the Republican nomination for mayor in 1939. Celentano was the first New Haven Italian to win either party's nomination for a major city office. He cut 10,000 votes from the enormous majority that the incumbent Democrat, John W. Murphy, had won two years earlier, and came close to winning the election. The Second World War kept Celentano from getting the nomination again until 1945, for the city's Republican leaders did not think it prudent to nominate an Italian while Italy was fighting against the United States. But in that year he defeated Murphy by 6000 votes.

Celentano's candidacy brought thousands of Italians into the Republican party, as the voting history of the heavily Italian 10th Ward illustrates. In 1937 Murphy received 52 percent of the Tenth's vote. Two years later, running against Celentano for the first time, he got 22 percent and fared almost as badly in other Italian neighborhoods.[25] Matters improved somewhat for the Democrats during the war, but Celentano's second candidacy produced an even greater Republican swing; in 1945 Murphy won only 17 percent of the 10th Ward's vote.

In 1947 the Democrats tried to match Celentano's appeal by giving the mayoralty nomination to an obscure Italian dentist. Thereby they recouped most of their losses in Italian neighborhoods — their share of the 10th Ward vote rose from 17 to 42 percent and was about this high in the other Italian wards — but lost heavily elsewhere in the city. Furthermore, a Socialist candidate won a sixth of the total vote and made his best showing in middle-class neighborhoods. Since this was several times greater than any third-party vote in a generation, anti-Italian sentiment may have motivated many of these Socialist votes.[26] The 1947 election was the only one in the city's history in which both major party candidates were Italians.

In every mayoralty election since 1947 the Democratic candidate has been Richard C. Lee, a Catholic of mixed English, Scottish, and Irish descent who, for obvious reasons, emphasizes his Irish side. Lee unseated Celentano in 1953 after two unsuccessful attempts. Celentano did not run for mayor again, preferring to bide his time until Lee left the scene. Since then Lee has defeated a series of Republican candidates, usually by sizable margins.

Although Celentano has not run for office for more than ten years, his impact on the political allegiance of New Haven's Italians appears to have been enduring. In a well-known article some years ago the late V. O. Key suggested "the

Table 20.2 Deviations from New Haven Citywide Democratic Vote by Selected Wards with Concentrations of Various Ethnic Groups — Mayoralty Elections, 1949-1961

Year and Ethnicity of Republican Mayoralty Candidate[a]	Citywide Democratic Vote[b]	10th & 11th Wards (Italian)[c]	16th & 17th Wards (Irish)[d]	19th Ward (Negro)[e]
	(%)	(%)	(%)	(%)
1949 — Italian	46.6	−21.9	8.5	7.9
1951 — Italian	49.9	−24.3	8.0	4.3
1953 — Italian	51.9	−27.3	9.0	8.3
1955 — Italian	65.3	−21.3	8.1	13.4
1957 — Yankee	64.8	−14.4	11.5	14.2
1959 — Italian	61.8	−20.2	11.0	16.3
1961 — Yankee	53.5	−10.7	15.9	24.3
1950 median family income	$3301	$2660 $2318	$3174 $3280	$2117

[a] In all these elections the Democratic candidate was Richard C. Lee.

[b] Percentages are of the total vote cast for mayor.

[c] In 1960 population shifts caused by an urban renewal project began to change the composition of the 10th and 11th wards. By 1963 a substantial fraction of the old residents had been replaced by newcomers, most of whom were neither Italians nor Republicans.

[d] Since about 1958 these wards have had an influx of Negroes.

[e] Negroes comprised 72 percent of the 19th Ward in 1950. Increasing Democratic majorities there may be due *in part* to continued growth of the ward's Negro population.

Sources: Voting returns for 1949-1957 are from official sources; for 1959-1961, from newspapers. Choice of wards was based on a combination of census data and political lore. (Census tracts do not coincide with wards. The 1950 census data were matched with wards, but this was an expensive process and was not repeated for the 1960 census.) One of the three wards with the highest proportion of Italian-born residents, the 12th, has a dissident Democratic organization and was excluded for this reason. Since the first sizable numbers of Irish came to New Haven 120 years ago, census data on the birthplace of present ward residents are an unreliable index of Irish predominance. I have followed the advice of New Haven politicians in choosing the 16th and 17th as the most Irish wards.

existence of a category of elections . . . in which the decisive results of the voting reveal a sharp alteration of the preexisting cleavage within the electorate.
Moreover, . . . the realignment made manifest in the voting in such elections
seems to persist for several succeeding elections."[27] Key called such contests
"critical elections." As the following data show, Celentano's several mayoralty
campaigns were critical elections with respect to the voting behavior of at least
the Italians in New Haven.

Since 1947 the Italian wards have been the most Republican ones in the city.
Table 20.2 shows the citywide Democratic percentage of the vote in mayoralty
elections from 1949 through 1961 and the deviations from this percentage of
wards with the heaviest concentrations of Italians, Irish, and Negroes, respectively. As the table indicates, even a Yankee Republican will make his best
showing in the Italian wards. In fact, the Tenth is the only ward that Lee has
never carried. Since the Italian wards are among the poorest in town, their
marked Republican inclinations can be attributed to ethnic voting.

Italian support for Republican candidates has been so lopsided that the customary relationship between Democratic voting and foreign birth is reversed in
New Haven. The ward-by-ward correlation coefficient (Pearson's r) between

Table 20.3 Democratic Vote for State and National Candidates in New Haven
and in Selected Wards

Year and Election	Citywide Vote	10th Ward (Italian)	17th Ward (Irish)
1956 Presidential	45%	34%	51%
1958 Gubernatorial[a]	69	52	75
1962 Senatorial[b]	65	52	75

[a] The candidates were the incumbent Democrat, Abraham A. Ribicoff, and Fred Zeller.
[b] The candidates were Ribicoff and Horace Seely-Brown.
Source: Official voting returns.

Table 20.4 Percentage in Working Class Occupations and Percentage Democrats of a
Sample of New Haven Voters, by Ethnic Groups, 1959

Number in Sample	Manual Workers		Democratic	
	Per-cent	Rank	Per-cent	Rank
47 Negroes	76	1	57	2
157 Italian Catholics	61	2	37	5
53 European Catholics	58	3	48	4
56 European Protestants	35	4	16	6
34 American Protestants[a]	27	5	9	7
53 Irish Catholics	20	6	64	1
74 European Jews	15	7	52	3

[a] "American" here means parents and grandparents born in the U. S.
Source: The table is based on 474 persons (of an original sample of 525 voters) who could be identified by religion and by place of birth of themselves, parents, or grandparents. The percentages Democratic are those who identified themselves as Democrats in response to the question: "Generally speaking, do you usually think of yourself as a Republican, a Democrat, or what?"

percentage of foreign-born residents and percentage of the vote for Democratic mayoralty candidates has been *negative* for most elections since 1937.[28]

While Italian Republicanism is a product of local politics, it is also expressed in state and national elections. The ethnic voting that resulted from Italian solidarity in New Haven is now manifested in elections where "recognition" of Italians is not an issue. As Table 20.3 shows, the 10th Ward (for example) has been considerably more Republican than the city as a whole in elections where neither candidate was Irish or Italian. For instance, ex-Governor Ribicoff barely carried the Tenth in 1958, while in the Irish 17th Ward, where the median family income was more than $600 higher, he won by a three-to-one ratio.

Most Italians not only vote for Republican candidates, but consider themselves Republicans. Their party identification was changed and fixed by Celentano's several campaigns. Table 20.4 shows the percentages of blue-collar workers and of Democrats in various ethnic groups. Little more than a third of the Italians are Democrats, although they are second only to Negroes in proportion of manual workers.

These tables show why New Haven politicians customarily explain the outcome of elections in terms of nationality groups rather than social classes: the most important lines of division in the electorate are ethnic rather than economic. In fact, ethnic cleavages wash out the usual relationships between socioeconomic status and partisan preference. When New Haven wards are correlated by median income and Republican vote in the 1959 mayoralty election, the coefficient is —.02.[29] Similarly, there is no relationship between the proportion of manual workers in an ethnic group and the percentage of the group's members who consider themselves Democrats, as Table 20.4 shows. The salience of ethnicity explains the apparent anomaly that the Republican party's stronghold is in the poorest parts of town, while the Democrats draw their strongest support from middle-class Jews and Irishmen, as well as low-income Negroes.[30] Since the two best examples of ethnic voting are the Republican inclinations of working-class Italians and the Democratic affiliation of middle-class Irishmen, the political correlates of ethnicity do not merely represent underlying economic differences.

Plainly, the assimilation theory does not fit the development of Italian bloc voting in New Haven. The New Haven case can be explained by a different view of ethnic voting that I will call a "mobilization theory." I will introduce it by reexamining in greater detail the assumptions of the assimilation theory.

The Mobilization of Ethnic Political Resources

The assimilation theory is based on the assumption that the strength of ethnic voting depends on the intensity of the individual's identification with his ethnic group.[31] The theory supposes that this identification is never stronger than in the early years of residence in this country[32] and declines thereafter as the immigrants gain some measure of well being. There is another prerequisite to ethnic voting that the assimilation theory overlooks: no matter how salient an individual's ethnic identification may be, it will not influence his voting behavior unless he sees a connection between this identity and the choice he makes on election day.[33] How does the Irishman know which candidate (if any) is friendlier to the Irish? The implications of this problem are worth further exploration.

Established politicians appealed to immigrants with tangible rewards and recognition. While one party may have been more vigorous in its efforts, both parties usually made some attempt to win their votes. These campaign efforts posed a twofold communication problem of pervasiveness and persuasion: how could the party get its message to every ethnic voter, and how could it make the message credible? Only some ethnics would get a job or favor, and only some would know of the recognition given by one party or the other; or, confusingly, by both. How did the ethnic know which party was friendlier to his people?

Precinct workers who talk directly to the individual voter are the most effective means of electioneering.[34] There are no systematic data on precinct workers' activity at the peak of the immigrant era. Contemporary accounts indicate that, in at least some cities, few prospective voters could escape the attention of the political organizations.[35] At present the level of precinct work is much lower. In northern cities with over 100,000 population less than 20 percent of the adults reported contact with a party worker in a single presidential election.[36] In New Haven, where both parties have very strong and active campaign organizations, 40 percent of the registered voters have *never* been reached by a precinct worker.[37]

Let us assume that precinct organizations were able to contact almost every potential voter fifty years ago. What if both parties sent workers around? What if both parties had won — or bought — the support of some ethnic leaders?[38] No matter how fervently the ethnic might identify with his group, the appropriate political expression of this identification might not be clear to him.

First-generation ethnic groups seldom had many political resources aside from their votes. Many of their members were illiterate; except for the Irish, many could not speak English. At this stage it was easiest for the parties to compete for ethnic votes, for the enticements least in demand by party activists were most suitable for the immigrants. As time passed children went to school, men prospered, and the ethnic group produced representatives with the organizational and communications skills necessary for political leadership. There were greater demands on both parties for recognition and the men making the demands were more skilled at pressing their claims. Such demands raised the level of bidding between the parties, for now the ethnics were asking for rewards that were both scarcer and more highly prized by the people already established in the party organizations. The ethnics' ambitions were resisted by those who would be displaced. Because of this resistance and the time it took to develop political skills, a generation or more went by before members of the new nationality group found their way into positions of any visibility and influence.[39]

Sooner or later some ethnics will occupy party positions. One party will nominate an ethnic for a minor office. Such positions are unimportant, and if the bid seems to pull votes the other party will soon match the offer.[40] Most ethnic voters still have the problem of figuring out the "right" ticket to vote for, since it is still not evident which party is friendlier. The ethnic group may be given some unity if it has an unquestioned leader who can deliver its vote to the party with which he has made a deal, but this does not appear to have been a common phenomenon. Customarily, ethnic groups were fragmented, with several leaders, each telling his constituents about his exclusive inside track to the political bigwigs.[41]

The day will come when an ethnic will win a party nomination for a major elective office.[12] When this happens the problems of pervasiveness and persuasion will be solved for many of his fellow ethnics. They will all see his name on the ballot, and many will take this as proof that the party that nominated him is the right party for them because it has given the most recognition to their group. The bigotry that often accompanies a "first" candidacy is likely to enhance the political relevance of ethnicity for the members of the candidate's group.

It seems plausible that an ethnic group will get such a major nomination when adversity forces one party or the other to appeal to new sources of support. This seems to have been the case with Celentano's nomination. In the late 1930s the New Haven Republicans were in dire straits. Some of the state party's leading figures had been implicated in the spectacular "Waterbury scandals." In 1937 the local party had suffered its most crushing loss in any mayoralty election in a century. Coming on the heels of Roosevelt's overwhelming reelection victory, Murphy's 1937 landslide must have suggested the need for a new campaign strategy to the city's Republicans; they had little more to lose. It was in this desperate situation that a member of New Haven's most numerous voting bloc was first nominated for mayor.

Celentano was chosen for the 1939 nomination by leaders of the Republican organization. In 1941 and 1943 the party had come close to beating Murphy with non-Italian candidates and by the summer of 1945 the city administration had suffered such a decline in popularity that Republican leaders were confident of winning the election that fall. They did not then want to give the nomination to Celentano, preferring a non-Italian who would be more dependent on their support. Celentano had to wage a hard fight in ward primaries to win the nomination.

The Democrats had nominated Driscoll, their first Irish mayoralty candidate, under similar circumstances a half century earlier. The great controversy over free coinage of silver had split the party and given the 1897 mayoralty election to the Republicans. The defection of Gold Democrats may well have driven the Democratic leaders of that day to adopt a strategy of maximizing their party's appeal to the Irish.[43]

The mobilization theory of ethnic voting states that: *The strength of ethnic voting depends on both the intensity of ethnic identification and the level of ethnic relevance in the election. The most powerful and visible sign of ethnic political relevance is a fellow-ethnic's name at the head of the ticket, evident to everyone who enters the voting booth. Middle-class status is a virtual prerequisite for candidacy for major office; an ethnic group's development of sufficient political skill and influence to secure such a nomination also requires the development of a middle class. Therefore ethnic voting will be greatest when the ethnic group has produced a middle class, i.e., in the second and third generations, not in the first. Furthermore, the shifts in party identification resulting from this first major candidacy will persist beyond the election in which they occurred.*

This is not to say that the growth of a middle class past the point of mobilization will necessarily produce increasing ethnic voting. Nor does the theory state that the resulting alignment is impervious to other political and social developments, or that more than one such shift cannot take place. But it does say that, in a given political arena and for a given nationality group, the development of voting solidarity is a product of leadership; that such leadership requires a middle class; and that such alignments are more durable than the political candidacies that produce them.

The mobilization theory seems to be more useful than the assimilation theory in explaining ethnic voting at the national level. Most members of ethnic groups in big cities are, by and large, strongly Democratic. It is often forgotten that this is a rather recent development. In the early part of the twentieth century, when the foreign population of many big cities was predominantly first and second generation, these cities were carried by Republican presidential candidates as often as not. In 1920, shortly after the ending of unrestricted immigration, the Republicans carried most cities with big immigrant populations. Harding swept New York, Cleveland, Boston, Chicago, Philadelphia, Pittsburgh, and Detroit by an aggregate plurality of 1,330,000 votes. The Republicans did almost as well in 1924. But in 1928 the aggregate Democratic margin in these seven cities was 307,000, and since then they have gone Democratic in every election, usually by substantial margins.[44]

Smith's candidacy seems to have been particularly important in its impact on partisan alignments in Southern New England. Connecticut, Massachusetts, and Rhode Island, with the highest ethnic populations in the country, were also, until 1928, stoutly Republican in state and national elections. Since then they have been in the Democratic column as often as not. Key's article on critical elections demonstrates this point more precisely. Cities which underwent a sharp and durable pro-Democratic change in 1928 had large Catholic, foreign-born populations; cities which reacted in the opposite way were largely Protestant and native-born. In short, the ethnic population of Southern New England has become more Democratic as the duration of its residence in this country has increased.

The Persistence of Ethnic Voting

I have argued that the importance of ethnicity in voting decisions does not steadily diminish from an initial peak, but instead increases during at least the first two generations. What next? While the assimilation theory may be inadequate for the first development of ethnic voting, what about succeeding generations? Does the importance of ethnicity diminish rapidly with more general acculturation and occupational differentiation?[45] Or does it persist as a major independent variable, although perhaps declining somewhat in importance? It is commonly thought that the first alternative is more correct. I shall argue here for the second proposition and suggest some factors that seem to be associated with the persistence of ethnic voting.

Useful trend data on this subject are scarce. Data on Catholic voting patterns are suggestive since Catholicism is analogous to ethnicity as a variable in voting behavior. Catholics, too, tend to be more Democratic then Protestants, and this difference persists when income, occupation, or education is controlled — it is not simply an artifact of Protestants' higher status.[46]

The passage of time by itself does not reduce ethnic salience: witness Quebec. Nationality groups seem to vary in their rates of assimilation. Few Irishmen have ancestors who came to the United States after the turn of the century, yet from all indications there are many places where Irish self-consciousness is still very strong — notably in New York City, for instance. But the Germans, who immigrated there in considerable numbers at about the same time as the Irish, no longer seem to be a self-conscious nationality group.[47] Catholic preference for the Democratic party does not seem to be a result of the disproportionately heavy representation of Catholics among more recent arrivals to this country. When generation of American residence is controlled, Catholic–Protestant differences do not disappear nor even diminish significantly.[48]

The passage of time is thought to be associated with weakening ethnic consciousness not just through attenuation of immigrant memories, but because members of any given ethnic group will get better jobs and, after two or three generations, be represented among all occupational levels, more or less in proportion to their numbers.[49] Occupational mobility is believed to reduce the importance of ethnicity in voting decisions for two reasons: (1) it will produce economic interests inconsistent with ethnic voting; and (2) the mobile individuals will come into contact with a broader, socially heterogeneous environment that will dilute ethnic salience.[50]

The extent to which social mobility alters the political expression of ethnic feelings undoubtedly varies with a number of other circumstances. The voting behavior of the New Haven Irish seems to have been relatively impervious to their changed social status. Although they are almost all in the middle class, their support of the Democratic party is so pronounced that it could not have declined very much as they went from manual labor to white-collar jobs. Even when mobility does produce changes in political perspectives, these changes do not obliterate all hitherto existing predispositions. Social change begins from a "base point" of previous habits. Occupational mobility will change the politics of many of the immigrants' children, but it will do the same for old Americans. The net political difference between the two groups may be as great in the middle class as in the working class. This proposition is supported by the Elmira study, which found that differences between Catholics and Protestants in their support of the Republican presidential candidate were actually greater in the middle and upper than in the lower class.[51] If anything, social mobility had heightened the importance of religion as an independent variable.

Upward-mobile members of the middle class have political characteristics intermediate between those typical of their old and their new status positions. While more Republican than their parents, they are considerably more likely to be Democrats than are status-stable members of their class.[52] The voting behavior studies have established that as many as four-fifths of all voters identify with the same party as their parents.[53] This is not just a reflection of similar life conditions; the authors of *Voting* report that most of their respondents whose vote was "inconsistent" with their social class were following parental political preferences.[54]

The data in Table 20.2 indicate that ethnic voting has not declined in New Haven in the postwar period. Deviation from the citywide vote by Italian and Irish wards was as great in 1959 as in the 1940s. The smaller Italian deviation in 1961 may be a sign of declining ethnic salience, but it may also reflect Italian coolness to a Yankee Republican candidate, or the first wave of population changes resulting from the Wooster Square Renewal Project. At least in New Haven, all the social changes of the 1940s and 1950s do not seem to have reduced the political importance of national origins.

One contemporary trend that may be relevant to ethnic voting has not been mentioned. Most of the data in this paper describe only those ethnics who have chosen to remain in the old core cities. Their neighborhoods tend to be ethnically homogeneous but economically diverse, with working-class and middle-class families intermingled. It is plausible that those ethnics who have decided to stay in such neighborhoods despite their financial ability to move to the suburbs have stronger ethnic identifications, whether as a consequence or as a cause of continued proximity. What about the ethnics who have moved to the suburbs? They should be less ethnically conscious. Suburbs tend to be economically homogeneous and ethnically diverse; in these respects they are the reverse of the old city neighborhoods. It seems likely that these new suburbanites break off the interpersonal and institutional relationships that sustain and transmit ethnic consciousness. Since group solidarity is maintained by personal contact,[55] it is probable that geographical dispersion will dilute ethnic salience. At the same time, however, it will help to maintain the solidarity of the urban survivors by draining off those with the weakest ethnic identifications.[56]

There are not many data relevant to these speculations. *The American Voter*'s discussion of suburbanization is tentative and inconclusive, while an earlier analysis of some of the same data produced findings consistent with the line of argument in the preceding paragraph.[57] The most useful evidence comes from Scott Greer's study of Catholic voting behavior in and around St. Louis. He found that, with education and generation of American residence-controlled, suburban Catholics were more likely than urban Catholics to defect to the Republicans.[58]

Several political circumstances are also associated with the strength of ethnic voting. In general, it appears that ethnicity will be more important in the absence of other plain cues to guide voters' decisions. It is likely to play a greater role in non-partisan elections, where voters cannot rely on the party label.[59] But, while party identification may impede the free play of ethnic salience, it also stabilizes and prolongs ethnic voting by providing a vehicle for continuing perception of ethnic relevance. Celentano's candidacy won Italian support not only for him, but also for the Republican party in subsequent elections because his association with the party led Italians to think that it gave them more recognition. Ethnic voting also seems to be less important when some great issue dominates political perspectives, as the depression did in the 1930s.[60] This may explain the unusually pro-Democratic voting of New Haven Italians in the 1932 and 1936 presidential elections.

The major proposition of this section is that ethnicity is still an important factor in voting behavior and is not eliminated by changes in the economic characteristics of the individuals affected. This is not to say that perspectives formed in the first generations of American residence will persist forever. Ethnic consciousness is fading; it is already faint in some parts of the country and for some ethnic groups. Continuing increases in education, geographical dispersion, intermarriage and intergroup contacts are all likely to reduce ethnic consciousness.

Even when ethnic salience has faded, however, its political effects will remain. One of the most remarkable tendencies in political behavior is the persistence of partisan affiliations for generations after the reasons for their formation have become irrelevant to contemporary society. Key and Munger's article on county voting patterns in Indiana is one of the best-known demonstrations of this proposition. Some Indiana counties were consistently Democratic while others, apparently identical in demographic characteristics, were consistently Republican. The roots of these variations seemed to be the origins of the counties' first settlers — New England or the South: "If one plots on the map of Indiana clusters of underground railroad stations and points at which Union authorities had difficulties in drafting troops, he separates, on the whole, Republican and Democratic counties."[61] Key and Munger conclude that for many voters elections are merely "a reaffirmation of past decisions." It seems plausible that this will be the legacy of ethnic politics: when national origins are forgotten, the political allegiances formed in the old days of ethnic salience will be reflected in the partisan choices of totally assimilated descendants of the old immigrants.

NOTES

[1] This article is part of a paper delivered at the 1964 annual meeting of the American Association for Public Opinion Research, Excelsior Springs, Missouri. I am indebted to Martha Derthick, Heinz Eulau, Joan Heifetz, and my wife, Barbara Kaye Wolfinger, for help in formulating my argument, and to more friends than I can mention for many helpful comments on an earlier draft of the paper.

[2] For a recent statement of this theme see Nathan Glazer and Daniel Patrick Moynihan, *Beyond the Melting Pot* (Cambridge, Mass.: MIT Press and Harvard University Press, 1963). "Ethnic consciousness" or "ethnic salience" exists when: (1) many people think of themselves, and are regarded by others, as members of a particular nationality group; and (2) such classification is salient. The two aspects of ethnic consciousness reinforce each other.

[3] Conflict among ethnic groups is a central topic in descriptions of politics in the Northeast; see, for example, Duane Lockard, *New England State Politics* (Princeton: Princeton University Press, 1959). For treatments of ethnicity in personnel appointments see Theodore J. Lowi, *At the Pleasure of the Mayor* (New York, 1964); and Daniel Patrick Moynihan and James Q. Wilson, "Patronage in New York State, 1955–1959," [*American Political Science Review*], vol. 58 (June 1964), pp. 296–301. For a discussion of the social and political consequences of ethnic politics see Raymond E. Wolfinger, "Some Consequences of Ethnic Politics," in Harmon Zeigler and Kent Jennings, eds., *The Electoral Process* (Englewood Cliffs, N. J., 1966).

[4] A good deal of data to support these propositions will be found in this article. For additional evidence see Angus Campbell, Gerald Gurin and Warren E. Miller, *The Voter Decides* (Evanston, 1954), pp. 77–79; Edward C. Banfield and James Q. Wilson, *City Politics* (Cambridge, Mass.: Harvard University Press, 1963), pp. 230–231; and Lucy S. Davidowicz and Leon J. Goldstein, *Politics in a Pluralist Democracy* (New York: Institute of Human Relations Press, 1963). Ethnicity is only one variable in voting behavior. This article concerns secular trends in its importance. Many short-term influences on voting decisions that also affect its importance are not discussed here; this omission should not be interpreted as an implicit assertion that these short-range factors are not relevant.

[5] I will use the terms "ethnic group" and "nationality group" interchangeably to refer to individuals whose national origins set them apart from the predominantly Protestant old American society.

[6] The assimilation theory is most clearly and explicitly stated in Robert A. Dahl, *Who Governs?* (New Haven: Yale University Press, 1961), pp. 34–36.

[7] Data on New Haven are from an intensive study of that city's politics conducted primarily by Dahl, William H. Flanigan, Nelson W. Polsby, and Raymond E. Wolfinger. It is reported *ibid.*; and in Polsby, *Community Power and Political Theory* (New Haven: Yale University Press, 1963), chap. 4; and Wolfinger, *The Politics of Progress* (New Haven: Yale University Press, forthcoming).

[8] The sample was randomly chosen from voting lists. Sampling procedures are described in greater detail in Dahl, pp. 338–339. The survey was directed by William H. Flanigan.

[9] This figure undoubtedly underrepresents the number of Irish in New Haven, since 83 percent of all Irish immigrants came to the United States before 1900; see U. S. Bureau of the Census, *Statistical Abstract of the United States: 1955* (Washington, 1955), p. 95.

[10] August B. Hollingshead and Frederick C. Redlich, *Social Class and Mental Illness* (New York,

1958), pp. 64–65. These authors report that ethnic identification divides New Haven's social structure "horizontally" just as economic distinctions organize it "vertically."

[11] This table, taken from Banfield and Wilson, *op. cit.*, p. 39, shows the proportion of first- and second-generation Americans in cities with more than 500,000 population in 1960:

Rank	City	%	Rank	City	%
1	New York	48.6	12	Philadelphia	29.1
2	Boston	45.5	13	San Antonio	24.0
3	San Francisco	43.5	14	San Diego	21.5
4	Chicago	35.9	15	Baltimore	14.8
5	Buffalo	35.4	16	St. Louis	14.1
6	Los Angeles	32.6	17	Washington	12.6
7	Detroit	32.2	18	Cincinnati	12.0
8	Seattle	31.4	19	Houston	9.7
9	Cleveland	30.9	20	New Orleans	8.6
10	Pittsburgh	30.3	21	Dallas	6.9
11	Milwaukee	30.0			

There are some regional differences in the national origins of these ethnic populations; the western cities tend to have more Scandinavians, for example. On the other hand, San Francisco, for one, has sizable Irish and Italian groups.

[12] For similar observations about regional differences see Glazer and Moynihan, *op. cit.*, pp. 10, 250. They mention an alternate explanation: residents of western cities moved there after living in the East, hence they are less conscious of their European origins.

This point about regional differences applies only to concern about national origins among whites and does not deal with racial prejudice.

[13] Louis Berg, "Peddlers in Eldorado," *Commentary*, July 1965, p. 64.

[14] This shared experience is thought to be the reason for the inclusion of Jews in San Francisco high society: "the early Jews in the West could boast that they were pioneers among pioneers" (*ibid.*, p. 65).

[15] For a description of these social patterns see Oscar Handlin, *The Uprooted* (Boston, 1952), chaps. 7, 8.

[16] An excellent description of ethnic politics that expresses the style and flavor of these negotiations may be found in William F. Whyte, *Street Corner Society*, enlarged edition (Chicago: University of Chicago Press, 1955).

[17] Lowi suggests that, unlike success in other fields, political eminence has a strong impact on ethnic perspectives: "Success in economic fields is highly individualized; . . . there is relatively little group symbolization of success. In contrast, political success, particularly in the big cities, is symbolized very highly in group terms" (*op. cit.*, p. 46).

[18] The present mayor of New Haven was one of the first politicians to make use of professional sample surveys of the electorate. Data from the surveys he commissions are analyzed by ethnic group, rather than income, occupation, or education.

[19] John W. McConnell, *The Evolution of Social Class* (Washington: American Council on Public Affairs, 1942), p. 214. The data are from the Sample Family Survey conducted by the Yale Institute of Human Relations in 1931–1933.

[20] Jerome K. Myers, "Assimilation in the Political Community," *Sociology and Social Research*, vol. 35 (1951), pp. 175–182. Myers estimated the number of Italians in various categories of municipal jobs from the names in city directories and manuals. The Republicans lost control of City Hall in 1932 to John W. Murphy, a Democrat of the old school. Murphy, who stayed in office until 1946, usually carried the Italian wards, but by somewhat smaller margins than he received in other working-class neighborhoods.

As these findings suggest, there are impediments to a rational strategy of ethnic politics. (1) Party leaders may refrain from cultivating ethnic groups out of prejudice. In much of the East Coast the exclusiveness of Yankee Republican politicians aided the Democrats' proselytizing of immigrants. (2) Party leaders may be reluctant to share political spoils with "outsiders." This seems to have been true of many Irish Democrats. Until a very few years ago, one Democratic ward organization in a New Haven Irish neighborhood would not let Italians participate in any form of campaign activity. (3) There may be principled objections to making appointments on the basis of ethnicity rather than other forms of merit. For examples of this attitude see James Q. Wilson, *The Amateur Democrat* (Chicago: University of Chicago Press, 1962), pp. 283–288. It is quite possible, however, that such scruples are forgotten when the men who hold them actually attain power. Moynihan and Wilson describe the appointment policy followed by the young, liberal, intellectual staff of the newly elected New York Governor Averell Harriman: " . . . great efforts were extended to 'recognize' certain groups and careful records were kept of the racial and religious identity of the appointees" (*op. cit.*, p. 296).

[21] See Myers; and Dahl, *op. cit.*, pp. 43–44. In the 1950s, during a period of Democratic success, Italians held slightly more than their share of municipal elective offices.

[22] For other data casting doubt on the notion of Italian Republicanism see Lockard, *op. cit.*, pp. 210, 305–319; Samuel Lubell, *The Future of American Politics* (Garden City, N. Y., 1956), pp. 225–226; Davidowicz and Goldstein, pp. 11–12, 30–32; Bernard R. Berelson et al., *Voting* (Chicago: University of Chicago Press, 1954), p. 62; and J. Joseph Huthmacher, *Massachusetts People and Politics 1919–1932* (Cambridge, Mass.: Harvard University Press, 1959), pp. 173, 179–184, 252, 260–261.

[23] Jews in New Haven, like those elsewhere, tended to vote Republican until the New Deal; see, e.g., Glazer and Moynihan, *op. cit.*, pp. 168–169.

[24] Except for the 1928 election, when the 10th was 18 percent ahead of the city in its support of Al Smith, and the 1932 and 1936 elections, when Roosevelt ran about 10 percent ahead of the citywide vote there. In other mayoralty and presidential elections prior to 1939, differences were generally minor; see Dahl, *op. cit.*, pp. 48–50.

[25] President Roosevelt's 1940 "stab-in-the-back" speech and World War II are supposed to have cost him some Italian votes in 1940 and 1944. Whatever the extent of this loss, it seems to have been recouped in the 1948 election; see Lubell, *op. cit.*, 225–226. For differing assessments of the impact of Roosevelt's speech, see Whyte, *op. cit.*, pp. 230–231; and V. O. Key, *Public Opinion and American Democracy* (New York, 1961), pp. 271–272.

[26] The success of the Socialist party in nearby Bridgeport was due to different causes. Capitalizing on public revulsion at corrupt "double machine" collusion between the two major parties, the Socialist leader, Jasper McLevy, won the mayoralty there in 1933 and stayed in office for twenty-four years.

[27] V. O. Key, Jr. "A Theory of Critical Elections," *Journal of Politics*, vol. 17 (February 1955), p. 4.

[28] Except for the 1941 and 1943 elections, when Celentano was not a candidate, and 1947, when both candidates were Italians.

[29] The 1st Ward was excluded because most of its residents are Yale students.

[30] Dahl has an interesting table comparing the Negro 19th Ward to the Italian 11th. The two wards have similarly low occupational, income and educational levels, yet the 19th is overwhelmingly Democratic and the 11th is very Republican. This is the reverse of their partisan affinities in 1930 (Dahl, *op. cit.*, p. 57).

[31] Cf. Berelson et al., *op. cit.*, pp. 67–72; and Angus Campbell et al., *The American Voter* (New York, 1960), chap. 12.

[32] This may be a dubious assumption, although it is not crucial to my argument. There are indications that the previous identification of many immigrants was not with the old nation, but the old village or old province. In this view, it was not until the immigrants saw that Americans classified them by nationality that they themselves developed some sense of belonging to a nationality group.

One could also argue that, whatever the locale of his previous identity, the immigrant's first impulse was to forget this old identity and become an American, but that he was forced back into ethnic consciousness by old-settler prejudice. Recurring nativist phenomena like Know-Nothingism, the Ku Klux Klan, Prohibition, and the end of mass immigration probably increased many ethnics' self-consciousness. See, e.g., Richard Hofstadter, *The Age of Reform* (New York, 1955), p. 297.

[33] Cf. the discussion of "political proximity" in Campbell et al.: "Groups as perceived objects may be located according to their proximity to the world of politics . . . at the individual level: *as perception of proximity between the group and the world of politics becomes clearer, the susceptibility of the individual member to group influence in political affairs increases*" (*op. cit.*, p. 311; emphasis in original).

[34] Cf. Handlin, "The immigrant might sometimes read an article on such a matter in his newspaper but was less likely to be persuaded by any intrinsic ideas on the subject than by the character of the persuader" (*op. cit.*, p. 211). Such persuaders included, in addition to overt party workers, priests and the types of immigrant leaders discussed earlier.

[35] See, e.g., Robert A. Woods, *Americans in Process* (Boston, 1903), pp. 155–156.

[36] Source: data from the 1956 SRC study reported in Fred I. Greenstein, "The Changing Pattern of Urban Party Politics," *The Annals*, vol. 353 (May 1964), pp. 8–9.

[37] Raymond E. Wolfinger, "The Influence of Precinct Work on Voting Behavior," *Public Opinion Quarterly*, vol. 27 (Fall 1963), pp. 387–398.

[38] Whyte's discussion of bribery indicates that cash can have a powerful, if temporary, distracting effect on ethnic loyalties.

[39] Cf. Lowi, "The representation of a new minority in places of power occurs long after it has reached considerable size in the population and electorate" (*op. cit.*, p. 39). Elmer E. Cornwell, Jr. reports that in Providence, Rhode Island, "Members of a new group are not likely to appear as ward committeemen at all until some three decades after their first arrival in substantial numbers"; see his "Party Absorption of Ethnic Groups: The Case of Providence, Rhode Island," *Social Forces*, vol. 38 (March 1960), p. 208.

See also Lubell: "The key to the political progress of any minority element in this country would seem to lie in just this success in developing its own middle class" (*op. cit.*, p. 79). Lubell does not discuss specifically the importance of candidacy for major office, which is the key point in any group's mobilization.

[40] Huthmacher has an interesting description of this competitive bidding process in Massachusetts (*op. cit.*, pp. 119–126). His discussion makes clear the dangers of such strategies because of the jealousies aroused when newer groups are recognized.

[41] Prior to Celentano's nomination the Italian community in New Haven was reported to be fragmented; see McConnell, *op. cit.*, pp. 159–160.

[42] For present purposes "major office" may be loosely but serviceably defined as any public elective office which is the central prize in a political system: mayor, governor, perhaps U.S. senator, and, of course, the presidency. Candidacy for minor office does not seem to produce so much ethnic impact, at least where candidates for such positions appear on the ballot below more important ones. This is particularly true in states like Connecticut where one can vote for an entire party slate with one choice. Such arrangements discourage split-ticket voting; see Campbell et al., *op. cit.*, pp. 275–276.

[43] Lowi, who has analyzed top-level mayoral appointments in New York City from 1898 to 1958, reports similar findings: "It has been the role of the minority party in New York to provide a channel of mobility for new ethnic groups.... The dominant Democratic organizations of the twentieth century have made efforts to attract the immigrants, but the minority Republicans made greater use of top patronage for these purposes" (*op. cit.*, pp. 37–39).

[44] Samuel J. Eldersveld, "The Influence of Metropolitan Party Pluralities in Presidential Elections Since 1920: A Study of Twelve Cities," [*American Political Science Review*], vol. 43 (December 1949), p. 1196.

[45] For a statement of this point of view see Dahl, *op. cit.*, pp. 34–36, 59–62.

[46] Berelson et al., *op. cit.*, pp. 61–71; Campbell, Gurin, and Miller, *op. cit.*, p. 71; Campbell et al., *op. cit.*, Chapter 12; and Scott Greer, "Catholic Voters and the Democratic Party," *Public Opinion Quarterly*, vol. 25 (Winter 1961), pp. 611–625. Berelson's study found that Catholicism was a stronger independent variable than socioeconomic status in voting behavior. Like ethnicity, its importance is subject to much short-term variation. For example, Catholicism was much more important in the 1960 presidential election than in 1956; see Philip E. Converse et al., "Stability and Change in 1960; a Reinstating Election" [*American Political Science Review*], vol. 55 (June 1961), pp. 269–280.

[47] On the "disappearance" of the Germans see Glazer and Moynihan, *op. cit.*, p. 311; and Moynihan and Wilson, *op. cit.*, pp. 299–300.

[48] Greer, *op. cit.*, p. 621; and Campbell, Gurin, and Miller, *op. cit.*, p. 79. The latter study found that the partisan difference between Catholics and Protestants was as great in the fourth generation as in the first.

[49] All ethnic groups are not, of course, equally represented in various occupations; see e.g., Glazer and Moynihan, *op. cit.*, pp. 317–324.

[50] This assumes that the direction of ethnic influences will favor the Democratic party. When ethnic pressures are pro-Republican, as in the case of New Haven Italians, the problem of predicting the political consequences of social mobility becomes more complicated.

[51] Berelson et al., *op. cit.*, p. 65.

[52] James A. Barber, Jr., "Social Mobility and Political Behavior," unpublished dissertation, Stanford University, 1965. See also Berelson et al., *op. cit.*, p. 91.

[53] *Ibid.*, p. 89; Campbell et al., *op. cit.*, p. 147.

[54] Berelson et al., *op. cit.*, p. 90. For discussion of the varying strength and characteristics of the relationship between social class and voting behavior, see Campbell et al., *op. cit.*, chap. 13; and Heinz Eulau, *Class and Party in the Eisenhower Years* (New York, 1962). As these books make clear, associations between class and party are mediated by a number of other personal and historical variables. One such is the difference between social class as measured by

objective indicators like income, and subjective class, i.e., what the individual considers his class position to be. When middle-class people identify with the working class their political attitudes and behavior tend to resemble those of members of the working class. Possibly middle-class ethnics are more likely to consider themselves working class than are middle-class Yankees. This suggests one mechanism that would modify the political impact of social mobility.

[55] This proposition is stated in Berelson et al., *op. cit.*, p. 74; and is supported by data in their chap. 6.

Ethnic groups may differ in their willingness to move from old urban habitats. Glazer and Moynihan report that Italians in New York, unlike some other groups, seem to remain, generation after generation, in the same areas where they first settled. The areas of Italian concentration in 1920 and 1960 are substantially the same except where land clearance has displaced people (*op. cit.*, pp. 186–187).

[56] Immigration continues to provide a diminished but by no means negligible fresh supply of ethnics. Most of the 2,500,000 people who entered the United States as immigrants from 1950 to 1959 probably settled in neighborhoods inhabited by earlier arrivals from their respective countries.

[57] Campbell et al., *op. cit.*, pp. 457–460; Fred I. Greenstein and Raymond E. Wolfinger, "The Suburbs and Shifting Party Loyalties," *Public Opinion Quarterly*, vol. 22 (Winter 1958), pp. 473–482).

[58] Greer, *op. cit.*, p. 621. Even in the suburbs, however, Catholicism is a potent independent variable in voting behavior.

[59] Cf. James Q. Wilson, *Negro Politics* (New York, 1960), p. 43.

[60] See Dahl, *op. cit.*, pp. 49–51.

[61] V. O. Key, Jr., and Frank Munger, "Social Determinism and Electoral Decision: the Case of Indiana," in Eugene Burdick and Arthur J. Brodbeck, eds., *American Voting Behavior* (Glencoe, Ill., 1959), pp. 281–299, at p. 457 n. Similar findings for Ohio are reported in V. O. Key, Jr., "Partisanship and County Office: The Case of Ohio," [*American Political Science Review*], vol. 47 (June 1953), pp. 529–531; and Thomas A. Flinn, "The Outline of Ohio Politics," *Western Political Quarterly*, vol. 13 (September 1960), pp. 702–721.

Surge and Decline: A Study
of Electoral Change

Angus Campbell

21

Angus Campbell's examination of popular voting during the 1950s sheds light on the unusual patterns of mass political behavior that contributed to Republican strength in presidential election years and weakness in midterm election years during the Eisenhower period. Campbell characterizes the elections of 1952 and 1956 as "surge" elections, in which Democrats, Independents, and irregular voters temporarily swelled the Republican vote but then returned to their normal political habits of partisanship or abstention when the positive stimulus of Dwight Eisenhower's candidacy disappeared. "Surge" elections are a relatively new phenomenon in American politics. In the period from the 1840s through the 1890s, when most eligibles identified with a political party and normally voted, major changes in the percentage distribution of the vote involved either temporary abstentions by identifiers with one party or lasting shifts by voters from one major party to the other. Professor Campbell is professor of sociology and director of the Institute for Social Research at the University of Michigan.

The study of election statistics has revealed certain impressive regularities in the voting behavior of the American electorate. It has been pointed out by Key[1] that in presidential elections since 1890 sharp upsurges in turnout have invariably been associated with a strong increase in the vote for one party with little change in the vote for the other. Key also documents the well-known fact that since the development of the two-party system in 1860 the party which has won the presidency has, with a single exception, always lost seats in the House of Representatives in the off-year election which followed.

The establishment of regularities of this kind through the use of aggregative data typically leaves unanswered the question as to why the regularity exists. We propose in this article to demonstrate the manner in which survey data can be used to illuminate the nature of aggregative regularities and to present a theory of political motivation and electoral change which will comprehend both of these seemingly unrelated characteristics of the national vote.

SOURCE: Reprinted with permission from *Public Opinion Quarterly*, vol. 24 (Fall 1960), pp. 397–418.

The Nature of Electoral Change

Fluctuations in the turnout and partisanship of the vote in the national elections are primarily determined by short-term political forces which become important for the electorate in an election situation. These forces move the turnout by adding their stimulation to the underlying level of political interest held by the electorate and they move the partisanship of the vote from a baseline provided by the "standing commitments" of the electorate to one or the other of the two parties. In the following pages we will first review a series of propositions which elaborate this general statement and then turn to certain national surveys conducted by the Survey Research Center for relevant empirical evidence.

- *Short-Term Political Stimulation*   Political stimulation in an election situation derives from three sources: the candidates, particularly those leading the ticket; the issues, foreign and domestic; and the recent performance of the parties. The intensity and character of this stimulation vary from one election to the next. There are occasions when none of these components of the world of politics seems important to the electorate, resulting in what we will refer to as a *low-stimulus* election. In other years dramatic issues or events may stir a great deal of interest; popular candidates may stimulate widespread enthusiasm. Such an election, in which the electorate feels the combined impact of these various pressures, we will speak of as a *high-stimulus* election.

The essential difference between a low-stimulus and a high-stimulus election lies in the importance the electorate attaches to the choice between the various party-candidate alternatives which it is offered. If the alternatives are generally seen as implying no important differences resulting from the election of one or the other, the stimulation to vote will be relatively weak. If the alternatives are seen as implying significantly different consequences, the stimulation to vote will be relatively high.[2] It may be assumed that in every election a certain air of excitement is created by the sheer noise level achieved by the mass media and the party apparatus. This type of direct stimulation undoubtedly has some impact that is independent of the particular alternatives which confront the voter and accounts for some of the variation in turnout from one election to another, but for the most part we may assume that the effectiveness of such stimulation varies in a dependent way with the significance the electorate attaches to the particular election decision at issue.

- *Underlying Political Interest*   The individual members of the electorate differ substantially in their level of concern with political matters, in their responsiveness to political stimulation, and in the salience of politics in their psychological environment. This level of interest is an enduring personal characteristic. We assume that it typically develops during the process of early socialization and, having reached its ultimate level, persists as a relatively stable attribute of the adult interest pattern. It is not simply a function of social or economic background; people of high and low political interest are found at all levels of the electorate.

- *Party Identification*   Political partisanship in the United States derives in large part from a basic psychological attachment to one of the two major political parties.[3] A large majority of the electorate identify themselves with greater or less intensity as Republicans or Democrats and this identification is impressively resistant to change. To the extent that they so identify, their political perceptions, attitudes, and acts are influenced in a partisan direction and tend to remain consistently partisan over time. Those members of the electorate without party attachment are free of this influence and are consequently less stable in their partisan positions from year to year.

● *Turnout* Differences in turnout from election to election are brought about by one or both of two causes, either by changes in the other-than-political circumstances which face the electorate on election day, or by variations in the level of political stimulation to which the electorate is subjected from one election to the next. The former factor can have only limited influence. We may assume that bad weather or an epidemic may affect the vote in restricted areas or even nationally on occasion, but such external considerations cannot reasonably be associated with the kind of fluctuation which we know to exist. It is, for example, quite untenable to suppose that the weather or the health of the electorate is always worse in off-year elections than in presidential years. The explanation of these and other fluctuations must lie in the changing motivation of the electorate.

A large proportion of the turnout in any national election consists of people whose level of political interest is sufficiently high to take them to the polls in all national elections, even those in which the level of political stimulation is relatively weak. These "core voters" are joined in a high-stimulus election by additional "peripheral voters" whose level of political interest is lower but whose motivation to vote has been sufficiently increased by the stimulation of the election situation to carry them to the polls. There remains a sizable fraction of the electorate which does not vote even in a high-stimulus election; some of these people are prevented from voting by poor health, failure to meet eligibility requirements, or conflicts of one sort or another. Others do not vote because their level of political interest is so low that no amount of political stimulation will bring their motivation to vote up to the necessary level.

The turnout in any specific election is largely a question of how many of the less interested, less responsive people are sufficiently stimulated by the political circumstances of the moment that they will make the effort to vote. An excited election situation in which a stirring issue or an attractive candidate makes the party-candidate choice seem unusually important may bring these peripheral voters to the polls in large numbers. In an election of lesser apparent importance and weaker total stimulation the participation of these peripheral voters declines, leaving the electoral decision largely to the high-interest core voters. A low-stimulus election is thus not simply a smaller version of a high-stimulus election; in the extent to which the peripheral voters differ from the core voters the two elections may have quite different characteristics.

● *Partisanship* The partisan division of the vote in any particular election is the consequence of the summation of partisan forces on the voters. In every election there are superimposed on the underlying orientations the electorate has toward the two parties (party identifications) the contemporary elements of politics which tend to swing voters one way or the other. In a particular election these elements may be relatively weak and have little impact on the electorate. Despite the best efforts of the party publicists, the candidates may have little appeal and the issues little apparent relevance to the basic interests of the electorate. In such a case the turnout would of course be low and the division of the vote would approximate the underlying distribution of party identifications. In the absence of strong pressures associated with persons or issues prominent at the moment, party loyalty holds the adherents of the two parties to their respective tickets and the independent voters divide their vote between the two. In other words, a low-stimulus election tends to follow party lines.

Contemporary events and personalities occasionally assume great importance for the public and exert a strong influence on the vote. The general increase in the motivation to vote in such an election will, as we have said, bring a surge of peripheral voters to the polls. It will also swing the partisan division of the vote toward the party which happens to be advantaged by the circumstances of the moment. It is very unlikely that a political situation which heightens the public's sense of the importance of choosing one party-candidate alternative rather than the other will favor these alternatives equally. The circumstances which create a high-stimulus election may be expected to create simultaneously a strong differential in the attractiveness of the vote alternatives perceived by the electorate. Increases in turnout will consequently be accompanied by shifts in the partisanship of the vote.[1]

The partisan surge which characterizes a high-stimulus election consists of two components: (1) those peripheral voters for whom the stimulus of highly differentiated party-candidate alternatives provides the needed impetus to move them to the polls and who, depending on the strength of their party identification, are swung toward the ticket of the advantaged party, and (2) those core voters who are drawn from their normal position as Independents or identifiers with the disadvantaged party to the candidate of the party which is advantaged by the political circumstances of the moment. The number of voters who consistently turn out in presidential elections in support of their party's candidates is now sufficiently close to an equal balance between the two parties that the movement of these two components of the partisan surge will almost certainly determine the outcome of any high-stimulus election.

If a high-stimulus election is followed by a low-stimulus election, the reduction in the general level of political stimulation will result in a decline in the total vote. There will also be a decline in the proportion of the vote received by the party advantaged by the political circumstances of the preceding high-stimulus year. This decline also consists of two components: (1) the dropout of those peripheral voters who had gone to the polls in the previous election and who had given the advantaged party a majority of their votes, and (2) the return to their usual voting position of those core voters who had moved in the surge year from their normal position to support the advantaged party, the identifiers with the disadvantaged party moving back to the support of that party and the Independents back to a position between the parties. Those voters whose normal identification was with the advantaged party would of course support it in the high-stimulus election; of these, the less-involved peripheral voters would drop out in the subsequent low-stimulus election and the core voters would continue to support their party.

• *The Cycle of Surge and Decline* In the normal flow of events in American politics, fluctuations in turnout and partisanship follow the "natural" cycle which we have described. The long-run stability of the system depends on the underlying division of party loyalties. Short-term circumstances may swing large numbers of voters away from their usual partisanship or from a position of independence, but when the smoke has settled these people tend strongly to return to their former position, thus restoring the party balance to its former level. Only in the most extraordinary national crises has this cycle been broken and a new balance of party strength created. Such elections, in which a basic realignment of party loyalties occurs, are rare in American electoral history.[5] For the most part, fluctuations in the vote reflect the passing impact of contemporary events and the subsequent decline toward the underlying division of partisanship after these events have lost their salience.

The Evidence

The study of individual change requires data from the same persons at different points in time. Such information can best be provided by a panel study covering the period in which the change took place. It can be obtained somewhat less satisfactorily by asking survey respondents to recall their attitudes or behavior at earlier points in time. Two surveys conducted by the Survey Research Center make available data regarding voting patterns which are relevant to our present concerns. The first of these was a study of the presidential election of 1952 in which a national sample of adults living in private households were asked to report their vote for President in 1952 and to recall their vote for President in 1948.[6] The second was a panel study of a similar national sample, interviewed first in 1956 and again in 1958, being asked on each occasion to report their vote in that year.[7]

1948–1956: A Case of Electoral Surge

The presidential election of 1952 presents a unique opportunity for the study of electoral surge. The election of 1948 had seen one of the lowest turnouts of presidential voters in recent history; with only 48.4 million voters, the proportion of eligible voters who turned out lagged far behind the record of peacetime presidential elections prior to the Second World War. In 1952, 61.6 million voters went to the polls, an increase of more than 25 percent above the total of the previous election. This great surge in turnout was associated, of course, with a tremendous increase in the vote received by the Republican presidential nominee which far exceeded the increment in the Democratic vote.

● *The Increase in Turnout*   The movement in the turnout of the vote from 1948 to 1952 was made up of four components. Of our sample interviewed in November 1952, 58 percent said they had voted in both 1948 and 1952, 6 percent said they had voted in 1948 but not in 1952, 15 percent said they had voted in 1952 but not in 1948, and 21 percent said they had not voted in either election.[8] When we examine the characteristics of these four segments of the electorate we find that the core voters who had voted in both elections and the peripheral voters who had voted in one election but not the other differed very little in respect to those variables which are usually found to be associated with turnout. In education, income, occupation, and sex the two kinds of voter were very similar, although they differed significantly from the persistent nonvoters in all these respects. The characteristic which does discriminate sharply between the core voters and the peripheral voters is their level of political interest.

Several indicators of political interest are available to us from our interviews;

the one which is most free of contamination from the impact of the specific election we are studying is the respondent's report on his previous voting history. In the 1952 interview, our respondents were asked, "In the elections for President since you have been old enough to vote, would you say that you have voted in all of them, most of them, some of them, or none of them?" We assume that people who vote in all elections, regardless of the highs and lows of political stimulation, must be relatively responsive to political matters and those who have never voted must be relatively lacking in political interest.

We may also use the respondent's direct statement of his degree of interest in the campaign currently in progress. In October 1952 we asked the question, "Some people don't pay much attention to the political campaigns. How about you? Would you say that you have been very much interested, somewhat interested, or not much interested in following the political campaigns so far this year?" This question does not give us as clean a measure of long-term interest in political activities as we would like, since it related to the 1952 campaign specifically. The effect of this specific reference almost certainly reduces the range of response we would expect from a more general question, because the impact of current political activities might be expected to raise the interest level of those at the bottom of the range more than those near the top. In other words, the differences we find between the different types of voter would probably be larger if this question were more general in its reference.

When we now compare the levels of interest shown by the four components of the 1956 electorate we find a very consistent pattern. That part of the electorate which reported voting in both the 1948 and 1952 elections was far more responsive to the stimuli of politics than any of the other groups. This is especially impressive in the report of previous voting: 90 percent of those who voted in both elections said they had voted in all or most previous presidential elections, as compared to 66 percent of those who voted in 1948 but not in 1952, 23 percent of those who voted in 1952 but not 1948, and 6 percent of those who did not vote in either election. The interest of the 1948–1952 voters in the campaign then current, as expressed by their subjective report, was also higher than that of any of the other groups: 48 percent of those who voted in both elections said they were "very much interested in the campaign," as compared to 26 percent of those who voted in 1948 but not 1952, 31 percent of those who voted in 1952 but not 1948, and 14 percent of those who did not vote in either election.

On both these measures those people who were responsible for the major part of the difference in turnout between the two elections, the 1952 voters who had not voted in 1948, gave substantially less evidence of high political interest. Although they appear to come from the same strata of society as the more persistent voters, they apparently are drawn from the less concerned and less attentive levels of the stratum to which they belong.

It is clear that the persistent nonvoters, those people whom even the high stimulation of the 1952 campaign could not move to the polls, are not prevented from voting by adventitious considerations of health or weather. For the most part, these people do not vote because their sensitivity to the world of politics is so low that political stimulation does not reach them. As one might expect, they come very heavily from the low-income and low-educational groups. Two-thirds of them are women.

- *The Swing in Partisanship* The 1948 election may be taken as the prototype of a low-stimulus presidential election. In the absence of candidates or issues that might have aroused strong public interest in the choice of alternatives, the turnout was low and the partisanship of the vote was determined largely by the established party loyalties of the voters. Each candidate drew the bulk of his vote from people who shared his party identification; the Independent voters split about equally between the two parties; there was relatively little crossing of party lines and what there was did not favor either candidate.

Of the total Democratic vote for President in 1948,[9] 74 percent came from Democratic party identifiers,[10] 20 percent came from Independents, 6 percent came from Republican party identifiers. Of the total Republican vote for President in 1948, 71 percent came from Republican party identifiers, 23 percent came from Independents, 6 percent came from Democratic party identifiers.

The high-stimulus election in 1952 brought to the polls millions of voters who had not voted in 1948 and shifted the partisanship of the vote of a sizable proportion of those who had. We see in Table 21.1 that the two parties received almost equal support among those people who voted for the same party in both years. Although these consistent core voters made up well over half the voters in 1952, the decisive margin for Mr. Eisenhower was provided by two other groups, those who switched from a 1948 vote for Mr. Truman and those who

Table 21.1   Presidential Votes in 1948 and 1952 as Reported by Survey Research Center Sample in 1952 ($N = 1,614$)

Vote for President in 1948	Vote for President in 1952	Percent
Democratic	Democratic	23
Republican	Republican	24
Democratic	Democratic	11
Republican	Republican	1
Democratic	Did not vote	4
Republican	Did not vote	2
Did not vote	Democratic	6
Did not vote	Republican	8
Did not vote	Did not vote	21
		100

had failed to vote in 1948. The former group appears to have been considerably larger than the latter, although it is likely that the overstatement of the 1948 vote to which we have referred makes our estimate of the number of new voters in 1952 somewhat lower than it actually was. The Democratic party also appears to have lost a little ground among the small proportion of 1948 voters who did not vote in 1952, but this figure is subject to the same overreport and we may assume that this component of the total shift of votes between 1948 and 1952 was not very significant.

We can illuminate the character of these movements considerably if we examine the degree and quality of the customary party identifications of the people in these groups of 1952 voters (Table 21.2). The greatest polarity of party attachment is found among those voters who supported the presidential candidates of the same party in both elections. The fact that the consistent Democratic voters are comprised so heavily of people of Democratic party identification conforms to our supposition regarding the high-stimulus surge. When the political tide is running against a political party it reduces that party to its loyal partisans; the party will lose most of the support it may have received at other times from Independent voters or from defectors from the other party. The advantaged party benefits from this partisan movement, particularly among the Independents and weak adherents of the opposite party who are not strongly held by feelings of party loyalty. This gain is apparent in the Democratic-Republican column of Table 21.2.

Table 21.2   Party Identification of Components of the 1948 and 1952 Vote for President (in percent)

Party Identification	1948: Democratic 1952: Democratic (N = 372)	1948: Republican 1952: Republican (N = 385)	1948: Democratic 1952: Republican (N = 172)	1948: Republican 1952: Democratic (N = 17)	Did Not Vote Democratic (N = 105)	Did Not Vote Republican (N = 130)
Strong Democrat	48	*	19	(4)	36	5
Weak Democrat	33	4	36	(2)	43	23
Independent	17	23	31	(7)	20	29
Weak Republican	2	28	11	(3)	1	26
Strong Republican	*	45	3	(1)	−	15
Apolitical, other	*	*	−	−	−	2
	100	100	100	−	100	100

*Less than one half of 1 percent.
—No cases.
Note: Figures in parentheses are number of persons rather than percent; number of cases is too small to support reliable estimates.

The party affiliations of the two groups of 1952 voters who had failed to vote in 1948 provide additional evidence of the interaction of party identification and the partisan pressures of a surge year. Those previous nonvoters who came to the support of Stevenson in 1952 were largely Democratic party identifiers. The high stimulation of the 1952 campaign brought them out of their nonvoting status, but their party loyalty was sufficiently strong to resist the pro-Republican drift of the times. In contrast, the nonvoters who were inspired to vote for Eisenhower came from all party groups. Some of them were indifferent Republicans who had sat out the Dewey campaign; a large number were Independents; there was a sizable number of Democrats, although few of them called themselves "strong" Democrats. None of these people had voted in 1948, but they contributed significantly to the increase in turnout and the Republican surge in 1952.

The fact that only 1 percent of the electorate in 1952 moved against the Republican tide, from a Republican to a Democratic vote, provides an effective illustration of the nature of a partisan surge. Although the high level of stimulation in 1952 brought some peripheral Democrats to the defense of their party, there was no countervailing Democratic force beyond that of party loyalty to offset the powerful impact of candidates and issues which advantaged the Republican party. This we believe to be the basic characteristic of a surge election; the conditions which give rise to a sharp increase in turnout invariably greatly favor one party over the other. The political circumstances which create the surge in turnout also produce the shift in partisanship.

1956–1958: A Case of Electoral Decline

One of the most dependable regularities of American politics is the decline in the vote in the off-year congressional elections. The turnout in the off-year elections is invariably smaller than in the presidential elections which they follow, usually by a margin of over 25 percent of the presidential vote. Almost as dependable is the loss which the party which has won the White House in the presidential year suffers in the midyear election which follows. As we have observed, in every off-year election since the Civil War, with the exception of 1934, the presidential party has lost seats in the House of Representatives.

The vote for President in 1956 totaled 62 million; the vote for congressional candidates in 1958 was 45.7 million, a decline of slightly less than 25 percent from the vote cast two years earlier. President Eisenhower received nearly 58 percent of the popular vote in 1956. The Republican candidates for Congress in 1958 received 44 percent of the two-party vote, and the Republican party lost 47 of the 200 seats it had held in the House of Representatives.

● *The Decline in Turnout* The off-year election of 1958 was a low-stimulus election. Within the framework of the American electoral system the off-year congressional contests must always present the electorate with a less intensely charged situation than they meet in the presidential elections which precede and follow. The election of a congressman cannot have the importance to the average citizen that the election of a President has; the differential in the expected consequences of the election of one or the other congressional candidate cannot seem as great. Associated with this lesser significance is the fact that party activities are less intense and the mass media somewhat quieter in off-year elections. The impact of the typical congressional election is considerably more muted than that of even the less excited presidential elections.

When we examine the components of the electorate in 1956 and 1958 we find the counterparts of the four segments of the electorate we identified in our survey in 1952. Of our panel interviewed in both 1956 and 1958, 56 percent said they had voted in both elections, 19 percent said they had voted in 1956 but not in 1958, 4 percent said they had voted in 1958 but not in 1956, and 21 percent said they had not voted in either election.[11]

Comparison of the core voters in 1956–1958 with those who voted only in 1956 reveals differences similar to those we observed in the core and peripheral components of the 1952 electorate. Those 1956 voters who dropped out in 1958 were somewhat more distinctive in their socioeconomic characteristics than the 1948 nonvoters who went to the polls in 1952. As compared to those who voted in both 1956 and 1958 they were of somewhat lower status in occupation, income, and education. They were also younger. But these differences were small and very much less impressive than the differences in political interest which distinguished these groups: 92 percent of those who voted in both elections said they had voted in all or most previous presidential elections, as compared to 60 percent of those who voted in 1956 but not in 1958, 59 percent of those who voted in 1958 but not in 1956, and 17 percent of those who did not vote in either election.[12]

Involvement in the 1956 campaign, as expressed in the interviews in that year, was also much lower among those parts of the electorate which did not vote in either or both elections: 40 percent of those who voted in both elections said they were "very much interested" in the campaign, as compared to 21 percent of those who voted in 1956 but not in 1958, 33 percent of those who voted in 1958 but not in 1956, and 12 percent of those who did not vote in either election.

Thus it appears that the people who accounted for the decline in the vote in 1958 were politically similar to the people who contributed the increase in the vote in 1952. They were in-and-out voters, with a very irregular history of previous voting performance and a low level of sensitivity to political affairs. They appear to form a rather inert reservoir of voters, available for service under conditions of high stimulation but not highly motivated by an intrinsic interest in politics. Activated to vote by the highly charged circumstances of the 1956 campaign, they were not sufficiently moved by the lesser impact of the congressional election to go to the polls. Without them, the core voters who had made up 75 percent of the vote in 1956 contributed virtually the entire vote (93 percent) in 1958.

● *The Swing in Partisanship* Like the presidential election of 1948, the congressional election of 1958 attracted a relatively low turnout. Without strong national candidates or issues to give the choice of party alternatives importance in the public mind, the voting decision was determined largely by the standing party loyalties of those voters sufficiently concerned with politics to go to the polls. The sources of the vote which the two parties commanded in 1958 resemble those from which they drew their vote in 1948, although there was apparently more crossing of party lines in the latter election than there had been in the former.[13] Of the total vote for Democratic congressmen in 1958, 69 percent came from Democratic party identifiers, 20 percent came from Independents, and 11 percent came from Republican party identifiers. Of the total vote for Republican congressmen in 1958, 65 percent came from Republican party identifiers, 26 percent came from Independents, and 9 percent came from Democratic party identifiers.

The substantial shift from the comfortable majority which Mr. Eisenhower received in 1956 to the Republican congressional defeat in 1958 was almost wholly accounted for by two segments of the electorate, those Eisenhower supporters in 1956 who switched to a Democratic vote in 1958 and the considerable number of people who voted for President in 1956 but failed to vote in 1958. The number of 1958 voters who had not voted in 1956 and of voters moving against the tide (Democratic to Republican) was much smaller than these larger groups (Table 21.3).

The similarities between Table 21.1 and Table 21.3 are striking, despite the fact that Table 21.1 compares succeeding presidential elections and Table 21.3 compares a presidential election with a congressional election. We now find that when we distribute the party identifications of the people making up the major components of the 1956–1958 electorate, a table results which closely

Table 21.3 Partisanship of the Vote in 1956 and 1958 (N = 1354)

Vote for President in 1956	Vote for Congressman in 1958	Percent
Democratic	Democratic	22
Republican	Republican	22
Democratic	Republican	2
Republican	Democratic	11
Democratic	Did not vote	6
Republican	Did not vote	12
Did not vote	Democratic	3
Did not vote	Republican	1
Did not vote	Did not vote	21
		100

resembles Table 21.2 (see Table 21.4). We find again that those voters who support the same party through both low-turnout and high-turnout elections consist largely of people who identify themselves with that party. These are the core voters upon whom each party relies. They were joined in 1956–1958 by a sizable number of Independent voters but by very few people who identified with the opposite party.

Those people who fail to vote in a low-stimulus election after having been brought to the polls in a preceding high-stimulus election provide a counterpart to those peripheral voters in Table 21.2 who did not vote in 1948 but did turn out in 1952. We see that they have comparable partisan characteristics. The smaller group, people who had voted for Stevenson in 1956 but did not vote in 1958, were heavily Democratic in their party attachments, closely resembling the 1948 nonvoters who went to the polls in 1952 to vote for Stevenson. Those 1956 Eisenhower voters who failed to vote in 1958 by contrast were distinguished by having very few strong identifiers with either party. They include a high proportion of Independents and weak identifiers from each party, just as did the group of people who did not vote in 1948 but turned out for Eisenhower in 1952. In all likelihood these two groups in 1958 consisted largely of individuals who had also failed to vote in the congressional election of 1954, who had been brought to the polls as peripheral voters by the stimulation of the 1956 election, and who dropped out again in response to the weaker stimulus of the 1958 election. They contribute the major part of the surge and decline in turnout in these successive elections; since they tend to come to the polls more favorably disposed to one party than the other, they contribute to the partisan shift in a surge election and their failure to vote in the succeeding election tends to reduce the proportion of the vote the previously advantaged party receives.

The other component of the shift in partisanship in both the 1952 and 1958 elections is the core voters who move from support of one party to the other. We saw in Table 21.2 that in 1952 the bulk of these people, moving then from a Democratic to a Republican vote, were Independents and weak partisans and we see in Table 21.4 that the comparable group, moving in the opposite political direction, had the same characteristics. We assume that the large number of Democrats in the 1958 group were moving back to their "normal" party position

Table 21.4   Party Identification of Components of the Vote for President in 1956 and Vote for Congressman in 1958 (in percent)

Party Identification	1956: Democratic 1958: Democratic (N = 303)	1956: Republican 1958: Republican (N = 294)	1956: Democratic 1958: Republican (N = 21)	1956: Republican 1958: Democratic (N = 144)	1956: Democratic 1958: Did Not Vote (N = 89)	1956: Republican 1958: Did Not Vote (N = 159)
Strong Democrat	50	1	(4)	13	41	6
Weak Democrat	31	4	(9)	27	37	17
Independent	15	26	(6)	30	17	36
Weak Republican	3	25	(2)	20	5	27
Strong Republican	*	44	—	8	—	14
Apolitical, other	1	—	—	2	—	—
	100	100	—	100	100	100

*Less than one half of 1 percent.
—No cases.
Note: Figures in parentheses are number of persons rather than percent; number of cases is too small to support reliable estimates.

after having supported Mr. Eisenhower in the 1956 election. The number of Republican identifiers in this group is larger than we would have anticipated and suggests that the partisan movement in 1958 cannot be entirely attributed to a normal decline toward standing party loyalties after the displacement of the vote in a surge year.[14]

Ticket Splitting and the Congressional Vote

A comparison of the vote for President and the vote for congressman in the ensuing off-year election does not fully describe the movement of voters in this two-year election sequence. Because of the option which the American voter has of splitting his ticket, the relationship of the presidential vote to the subsequent congressional vote may be very different from that of the vote for congressman in a presidential year to the vote for congressman in the subsequent off year. If we examine the consistency with which the 1956–1958 voting groups supported the ticket of the presidential candidate they preferred in 1956, we find convincing support for our earlier observations regarding the characteristics of these groups and we discover a pattern of change in the congressional votes in the two elections quite different from what we found in the comparison of successive presidential and congressional votes.

Table 21.5 presents the 1956 voting patterns of the core and peripheral voters in the 1956 and 1958 elections. We see again that those voters who withstood the Republican surge in the 1956 election were strongly committed to the support of the Democratic party, as indicated by their high level of straight-ticket voting. Fewer than one in ten of the voters in the two major Democratic groups, those who voted for Stevenson in 1956 and a Democratic congressman in 1958 and those who voted for Stevenson in 1956 but did not vote in 1958, split their 1956 vote at the national level. The consistent Republican voters also had a high record of straight-ticket voting, not quite as high as the consistent Democrats because of the large number of Independents included among them. The other Republican group, the Eisenhower voters who did not go to the polls in 1958, had a notably lower proportion of straight-ticket voters and a much larger proportion who split their tickets at the national level. We have seen that this group of peripheral voters who came to the polls in 1956 to vote for Mr. Eisenhower was made up of people of heterogeneous party background, including many Independents and a not inconsiderable number of weakly identified Democrats. Many of these latter people obviously did not go all the way to the Republican position. Thirteen percent of this group (not shown specifically in Table 21.5) voted for Mr. Eisenhower but otherwise supported a straight Democratic ticket.

Table 21.5 1956 Voting Patterns of Major Voting Groups in the Vote for President in 1956 and Vote for Congressman in 1958 (in percent)

1956 Voting Pattern	1956: Democratic 1958: Democratic (N = 289)	Republican Republican (N = 286)	Democratic Republican (N = 21)	Republican Democratic (N = 140)	Democratic Did Not Vote (N = 77)	Republican Did Not Vote (N = 143)
Voted straight ticket at national and local levels	68	60	(10)	26	66	46
Voted straight ticket at national level only	20	20	(5)	15	8	17
Split ticket at the national level	7	15	(6)	49	8	24
Did not vote complete ticket	3	1	—	3	13	8
Other	2	4	—	7	5	5
	100	100	—	100	100	100

—No cases.
Note: Figures in parentheses are number of persons rather than percent; number of cases is too small to support reliable estimates.

The 1956 Eisenhower voters who voted for a Democratic congressman in 1958 present an especially interesting picture of ballot splitting. As we have seen, these core voters consist very largely of Democrats and Independents. Only a quarter of this group voted a straight Republican ticket in 1956, although they all voted for Mr. Eisenhower. A fifth of them voted a straight Democratic ticket with the exception of their vote for President, and an additional quarter or more failed to vote a consistent Republican ticket at the national level. They responded to the personal appeal of Mr. Eisenhower as the Republican candidate in 1956 but they did not accept his party. When Mr. Eisenhower was not on the ballot in 1958, these people moved back toward their usual party positions.

It is significant that both groups of peripheral voters, those who voted for either Eisenhower or Stevenson in 1956 but did not vote in 1958, contain a number of people who reported that they failed to vote a complete ticket when marking their presidential ballot. These are the only groups in which such voters appear in any significant frequency. This evidence of limited involvement in the vote is consistent with our earlier picture of the peripheral voter. Having less intrinsic interest in political matters and coming to the polls only when there is strong stimulation to do so, their concern with the act of voting is inherently weak, in contrast to that of those voters who go to the polls whatever the circumstances.

The decline from the Republican party's proportion of the presidential vote in 1956 to its proportion of the congressional vote in 1958 was associated with a considerably smaller decline from its 1956 congressional vote to its 1958 congressional vote. As our data on ticket splitting make clear, the Republican congressional candidates in 1956 received far fewer votes than their standard bearer, Mr. Eisenhower; they did not in fact achieve a majority of the popular vote. The decline of their congressional vote in 1958 from their congressional vote in 1956 was much smaller than the decline from the high mark of Mr. Eisenhower's vote, and the components of this decline differ somewhat from those of the decline from the presidential vote (Table 21.6).

Table 21.6 Partisanship in the Congressional Vote in 1956 and 1958
($N = 1301$)

Vote for Congressman in 1956	Vote for Congressman in 1958	Percent
Democratic	Democratic	25
Republican	Republican	19
Democratic	Republican	3
Republican	Democratic	6
Democratic	Did not vote	9
Republican	Did not vote	8
Did not vote	Democratic	4
Did not vote	Republican	2
Did not vote	Did not vote	24
		100

It is clear that the dropout of the peripheral voters in 1958 had very little effect on the distribution of congressional votes in that year, since at the same time they were giving Mr. Eisenhower a 2 to 1 margin of their votes in 1956, they were dividing their votes for congressman about equally between the two parties. We would ordinarily expect this component of the vote to have greater importance than it had in 1958. In most elections in which the electorate is strongly motivated to vote we would expect the congressional vote for the advantaged party to swing along with the presidential vote. It was precisely the failure of this joint movement to occur, however, which made the 1956 election remarkable and resulted, for the first time in over a hundred years, in the election of a president of one party and both houses of Congress of the other. The Republican surge in 1956 was largely an Eisenhower surge.

In the absence of any influence from the dropout of 1956 voters, the major contribution to the rather small decline in the vote received by Republican congressional candidates in the two elections was made by party switchers. There were movements in both directions from one election to the next but there were twice as many changes from Republican to Democratic candidates as from Democratic to Republican. It is probable that part of the 3-percentage-point Democratic advantage in this shift reflects the "coattail" effect which Mr. Eisenhower exerted on the 1956 election.[15] Some of these people were Democrats who had gone over to Mr. Eisenhower in 1956 and had voted his party ticket. But when Mr. Eisenhower was no longer on the ballot in 1958 they returned to their usual party choice.

The fact that the off-year elections typically reduce the congressional strength of the party which has won the presidency two years earlier is readily understandable within the terms of our description of surge and decline. As long as there is no significant shift in the distribution of standing party attachments within the electorate, the decline in turnout in an off-year election will almost certainly be associated with a decline in the proportion of the vote received by the presidential party. If the partisan pressures of the presidential election have induced any movement toward the winning candidate among the Independents and members of the opposing party, this movement will recede in the following congressional election, partly through the dropout of voters who have supported the ticket of the winning presidential candidate and partly through the return to their usual voting positions of those Independents and opposing partisans who had been moved during the presidential year.

The one clear reversal of this pattern which has occurred in the last hundred years is instructive. The House of Representatives that was elected with Mr. Roosevelt in 1932 had 310 Democratic members; in the 1934 elections this majority was extended to 319 members, although the turnout in 1934 was approximately 18 percent lower than it had been in 1932. According to our understanding of the nature of electoral decline this could not have happened if the basic division of party loyalties was holding constant during this period. There is substantial reason to believe, however, that the distinguishing feature of American politics in the early 1930s was a realignment in the basic strength of the two parties.[16] The economic collapse associated with the Hoover administration brought millions of Independents and Republicans into the Democratic party, not as temporary supporters but as long-term committed adherents. The Democratic gain in the 1934 election reflected a period of political conversion which gradually changed the Democratic party from the minority party which it had been since at least 1896 into the majority party which it remains today. Such mass realignments of party identification are very infrequent in American politics, however; more commonly the distribution of party loyalties remains stable despite the ups and downs of individual elections. Swings away from the basic division of party loyalties in high-turnout elections tend to swing back in the low-turnout elections which follow.

Conclusion

We have presented a theory of the nature of electoral change, specifically intended to comprehend and explain two well-established regularities of American voting behavior, the highly partisan character of upsurges in turnout in presidential elections and the characteristic loss which the party winning the presidency suffers in the ensuing off-year elections. We have proposed that fluctuations in turnout and partisanship derive from a combination of short-term political forces, superimposed on the underlying level of political interest and on the long-standing psychological attachments of the electorate to the two parties. We have been able to present data from two election sequences, one illustrating electoral surge and the other decline. Additional evidence from other electoral situations would obviously be desirable, but the data in hand give convincing support to our understanding of the dynamics of voting change.

Our discussion has dealt entirely with electoral change within the American political system. We think it likely that the basic concepts which we have relied on in this analysis — political stimulation, political interest, party identification, core voters and peripheral voters, and high- and low-stimulus elections — are equally applicable to the understanding of political behavior in other democratic systems. But it is apparent that political behavior in other societies takes place within different institutional forms than those in the United States and that they would have to be taken into account if we were to attempt in those societies an analysis comparable to the one presented here.

NOTES

[1] V. O. Key, *Politics, Parties, and Pressure Groups,* 4th ed. (New York: Crowell, 1958), p. 638.

[2] Anthony Downs uses the term "expected party differential" to express the degree of importance the voter attaches to the difference between the various party-candidate alternatives offered. See his *Economic Theory of Democracy* (New York: Harper, 1957), chap. 3.

[3] The nature of party identification as a basic orientation toward politics has been examined in a series of publications from the Survey Research Center, the first of which appeared in this journal in 1952. See George Belknap and Angus Campbell, "Political Party Identification and Attitudes toward Foreign Policy," *Public Opinion Quarterly,* vol. 15 (1951), pp. 601–623.

[4] We omit from consideration in this article shifts in the partisanship of the vote which occur in periods of stable turnout. Substantial shifts of this kind can be found in the history of American elections, as for example in the presidential elections of 1928 and 1932, and they pose interesting questions as to how shift in the absence of a surge in turnout differs from shift which accompanies a voting surge. We will be concerned exclusively with the latter type of partisan change in the present discussion.

[5] A discussion of maintaining, deviating, and realigning elections may be found in A. Campbell, P. E. Converse, W. E. Miller, and D. E. Stokes, *The American Voter* (New York: Wiley, 1960), chap. 19.

[6] The 1952 election study was supported by a grant from the Carnegie Corporation of New York. A detailed report of this study appears in A. Campbell, G. Gurin, and W. E. Miller, *The Voter Decides* (Evanston, Ill.: Row, Peterson, 1954).

[7] The panel study of the 1956, 1958, and 1960 elections is being supported by a grant from the Rockefeller Foundation. A full report of this study will appear at a later date.

[8] There is a clear discrepancy between these reports and the election statistics for 1948 and 1952. Survey reports of turnout are always higher than the proportion the total vote is of the total adult population, partly because surveys do not cover the institutional, military, and "floating" populations and partly because some respondents report a vote they did not cast. In the present case, the report of the 1952 vote does not appear to be greatly overstated but the recall of the 1948 vote is more seriously inflated. The proportions saying they voted in both elections or in 1948 but not 1952 are probably both somewhat high. This introduces some distortion in the relative size of the different components of the vote and some restraints on the uses we can make of the data.

[9] All references to voting in 1948 are based on the respondent's recall of this event when interviewed in 1952. Those few individuals who reported having voted for Thurmond or Wallace in 1948 are included in the Democratic vote.

10 Party identification is determined in Survey Research Center surveys by the following questions: "Do you usually think of yourself as a Republican, a Democrat, an Independent, or what? (If a Republican or Democrat): Would you call yourself a strong (Republican-Democrat) or a not very strong (Republican-Democrat)?"

11 We again have some problem of overreport of voting in the low-turnout election. This has the effect of understating the size and importance of the group of 1956 voters who dropped out in 1958. However, since the 19 percent of our sample who place themselves in this category are very unlikely to include individuals who actually voted in 1958, we may regard this as a relatively pure group for analytical purposes, remembering that it is somewhat smaller in size than it should be.

12 The differences in these data from those obtained in 1952 derive in large part from the fact that in this case we are grouping voters according to their performance in a presidential and a congressional election and in the previous case we were grouping voters according to their performance in two successive presidential elections. The 1952 data are further influenced by the fact that about one-fourth of those 1952 voters who had not voted in 1948 were too young to vote in that year. Since the 1956–1958 sample is a panel, there is no comparable group in the 1958 data.

13 A number of factors might be expected to contribute to party crossing in the congressional elections. The personal impact of the congressman in his district is not likely to equal that of a highly publicized presidential candidate, but it may be rather intense within a more limited range of individual voters. Over time a congressman may establish sufficient personal contacts to have a visible effect on the vote. The repeated reelection of congressmen in some districts tends to give them the character of nonpartisan fixtures: they attract cross-party votes which a less well-established candidate on the same ticket would not get. Of course, in those districts where a candidate runs without opposition, members of the minority party must cross party lines if they are to vote at all.

14 Losses going beyond the normal decline have occurred in other off-year elections and may be taken to reflect the development of circumstances unfavorable to the presidential party in the first two years of its term.

15 Additional coattail influence was undoubtedly felt among those people who voted for Eisenhower and a Republican Congressmen in 1956 but did not vote in 1958. For a discussion of the nature of coattail voting, see W. E. Miller, "Presidential Coattails," *Public Opinion Quarterly*, vol. 19 (1955), pp. 353–368.

16 See Campbell, Converse, Miller, and Stokes, *op. cit.*, chap. 7.

Stability and Change in 1960: A Reinstating Election

Philip E. Converse / Angus Campbell
Warren E. Miller / Donald E. Stokes

22

Three factors that influenced the outcome of the presidential election of 1960 are treated in this study by the University of Michigan's Survey Research Center. Two of these — the success of the Democrats in creating a majority coalition during the 1930s and the failure of the Republicans to undermine that coalition despite their presidential victories during the 1950s — made possible the election of John F. Kennedy. On the other hand, the third factor, the powerful impact of the religious issue on established voting patterns, specifically some Democrats' antagonism to Kennedy's Catholicism, reduced his margin to the near vanishing point. All of the authors are members of the Survey Research Center of the University of Michigan.

John F. Kennedy's narrow popular vote margin in 1960 has already insured this presidential election a classic position in the roll call of close American elections. Whatever more substantial judgments historical perspective may bring, we can be sure that the 1960 election will do heavy duty in demonstrations to a reluctant public that after all is said and done, every vote does count. And the margin translated into "votes per precinct" will become standard fare in exhortations to party workers that no stone be left unturned.

The 1960 election is a classic as well in the license it allows for "explanations" of the final outcome. Any event or campaign stratagem that might plausibly have changed the thinnest sprinkling of votes across the nation may, more persuasively than is usual, be called "critical." Viewed in this manner, the 1960 presidential election hung on such a manifold of factors that reasonable men might despair of cataloguing them.

Nevertheless, it is possible to put together an account of the election in terms of the broadest currents influencing the American electorate in 1960. We speak of the gross lines of motivation which gave the election its unique shape, motivations involving millions rather than thousands of votes. Analysis of these

SOURCE: Reprinted with permission from *The American Political Science Review*, vol. 55 (June 1961), pp. 269–280.

broad currents is not intended to explain the hairline differences in popular vote, state by state, which edged the balance in favor of Kennedy rather than Nixon. But can indicate quite clearly the broad forces which reduced the popular vote to a virtual stalemate, rather than any of the other reasonable outcomes between a 60–40 or a 40–60 vote division. And it can thereby help us to understand in parsimonious terms why a last feather thrown on the scales in November 1960 could have spelled victory or defeat for either candidate.

Surface Characteristics of the Election

Any account of the election should not only be consistent with its obvious characteristics as they filtered clear from raw vote tallies in the days after the election, but should organize them into a coherent pattern of meaning as well. These characteristics are, of course, the ones that have nourished postelection speculation. In addition to the close partisan division of the popular vote, the following items deserve mention:

1. *The remarkably high level of turnout.* About 62.7 percent of estimated adults over 21 voted in the 1952 election, a figure which had stood as the high-water mark of vote turnout in recent presidential elections. The comparable turnout proportion for the 1960 presidential election appears to have been 64.3 percent.[1]

2. *Upswing in turnout in the South.*[2] The South appears to have contributed disproportionately to the high level in turnout. Outside the South, the increase in total presidential votes cast in 1960 relative to the 1956 election was about 7 percent, a figure scarcely exceeding estimated population growth in this period. In the South, however, presidential ballots in 1960 increased by more than 25 percent relative to 1956, an increase far outstripping population growth in this region.[3]

3. *Stronger Republican voting at the presidential level.* On balance across the nation Nixon led Republican tickets, while Kennedy trailed behind many other Democratic candidates, especially outside of the Northeast. These discrepancies in the partisanship of presidential voting and ballots at other levels were not, of course, as striking as those in 1956. Nevertheless, their political significance has an obvious bearing on the future expectations of the two youthful candidates, and therefore occasions special interest.

4. *The stamp of the religious factor in 1960 voting patterns.* While the Kennedy victory was initially taken as proof that religion had not been important in the election, all serious students of election statistics have since been impressed by the religious axis visible in the returns. Fenton, Scammon, Bean, Harris and others have commented upon the substantial correlation between aggregate voting patterns and the relative concentration of Catholics and Protestants from district to district.

Of these surface characteristics, probably the last has drawn most attention. Once it became clear that religion had not only played some part but, as these things go, a rather impressive part in presidential voting across the nation, discussions came to hinge on the nature of its role. It could safely be assumed that Kennedy as a Catholic had attracted some unusual Catholic votes, and had lost some normally Democratic Protestant votes. A clear question remained, however, as to the *net* effect. The *New York Times*, summarizing the discussion late in November, spoke of a "narrow consensus" among the experts that Kennedy had won more than he lost as a result of his Catholicism.[4] These are questions, however, which aggregate vote statistics can but dimly illuminate, as the disputed history of Al Smith's 1928 defeat makes clear. Fortunately in 1960 the election was studied extensively by sample surveys, permitting more exact inferences to be drawn.

The national sample survey conducted by the Survey Research Center of The University of Michigan in the fall of 1960 had features which give an unparalleled opportunity to comment on the recent evolution of the American electorate. The fall surveys were part of a long-term "panel" study, in which respondents first interviewed at the time of the 1956 presidential election were reinterviewed.[5] In the fall of 1956 a sample of 1763 adults, chosen by strict probability methods from all the adults living in private households in the United States, had been questioned just before and just after the presidential election. This initial sample was constituted as a panel of respondents and was interviewed again in 1958 and twice in connection with the 1960 presidential election.[6] These materials permit the linking of 1960 and 1956 voting behavior with unusual reliability.[7]

The Evolution of the Electorate, 1956–1960

The difference in presidential election outcome between 1956 and 1960 might depend upon either or both of two broad types of change in the electorate. The first includes shifts in the physical composition of the electorate over time due to nonpolitical factors, i.e., vital processes. Some adult citizens who voted in 1956 were no longer part of the eligible electorate in 1960, primarily because of death or institutionalization. On the other hand, a new cohort of voters who had been too young to vote in 1956 were eligible to participate in the 1960 election. Even in a four-year period, vital processes alone could account for shifts in the vote. In addition, changes in the electoral vote, though not in the nationwide popular vote margin, might result from voters changing their residences without changing their minds.

Secondly, there are obviously genuine changes in the political choice of individuals eligible to vote in both elections. Such citizens may enter or leave the active electorate by choice, or may decide to change the partisanship of their presidential vote.

The contribution of these two types of change to the shift in votes from a 1956 Eisenhower landslide to a narrow 1960 Kennedy margin — a net shift toward the Democrats of almost 8 percent — may be analyzed. Somewhat less than 10 percent of the eligible 1956 electorate had become effectively ineligible by 1960, with death as the principal cause.[8] Older people naturally bulk large in this category. The felt party affiliation or "party identification" expressed in 1956 by these "departing" respondents was somewhat Republican relative to the remainder of the sample.[9] Nonetheless, these people cast a vote for President which was about 48 percent Democratic, or 6 percent *more Democratic* than the vote of the 1956 electorate as a whole. Although this appears to be a contradiction, it is actually nothing more than a logical consequence of existing theory. The high Republican vote in 1956 depended on a massive defection to

Eisenhower by many people identified with the Democratic party. Since the strength of party attachments increases as a function of age, and since defections are inversely related to strength of party identification, it follows that 1956 defection rates were much higher among younger citizens than among older.[10] The data make it clear that the group of older people voting for the last time in 1956 had cast a much straighter "party vote" than their juniors. Only about 5 percent of these older Democrats had defected to Eisenhower, as opposed to about a quarter of all Democrats in the electorate as a whole. So both things are true: this departing cohort was more Republican than average in party identification but had voted more Democratic than average in 1956. If we remove them from the 1956 electorate, then, we arrive at a presidential vote of about 60 percent for Eisenhower among those voters who were to have the option of voting again in 1960. Hence the elimination of this older group from consideration increases the amount of partisan change to be accounted for between 1956 and 1960, rather than decreasing it.

Comparable isolation of the new cohort of young voters in 1960 does very little to change the picture. Little more than one half of this new group of voters normally votes in the first election of eligibility;[11] furthermore, in 1960 its two-party vote division differed only negligibly from that of the nation as a whole. As a result, its analytic removal leaves the vote among the remainder of the electorate nearly unchanged. By way of summary, then, differences in the 1956 and 1960 electorates arising from vital processes do not explain the 1956–1960 vote change; if anything, they extend the amount of change to be otherwise explained.

We may further narrow our focus by considering those people eligible in both 1956 and 1960, who failed to join the active electorate in 1960. A very large majority of these 1960 nonvoters had not voted in 1956, and represent Negroes in the South as well as persistent nonvoters of other types. Among those who *had* voted in 1956, however, the vote had been rather evenly divided between Eisenhower and Stevenson. As with the older voters, removal of this group leaves an active 1956–1960 electorate whose vote for Eisenhower now surpasses 60 percent, broadening again the discrepancy between the two-party divisions in the 1956 and 1960 votes. The final fringe group which we may set aside analytically is constituted of those citizens eligible to have voted in 1956 who did not then participate, yet who joined the electorate in 1960. The fact that young voters often "sit out" their first presidential election or two indicates part of the composition of such a group. Once again, however, these newly ac-

Table 22.1   1956-1960 Vote Change Within the Active Core of the Electorate

| 1960 Vote for | 1956 Vote for | | Total Percent |
	Stevenson Percent	Eisenhower Percent	
Kennedy	33	17	50
Nixon	6	44	50
	39	61	100

Note: Since we usually think of vote shifts in terms of proportions of the total electorate, percentages in this table use the total vote as a base, rather than row or column totals.

tive citizens divided their ballots in 1960 almost equally between the two major candidates, and the residual portion of the 1960 electorate changes little with their removal.

By this point we have eliminated all the fringe groupings whose entry or departure from the active electorate might have contributed to change in the national vote division between 1956 and 1960. We come to focus directly, then, on the individuals who cast a vote for Kennedy or Nixon in 1960 *and had voted for president in 1956* (Table 22.1). As we see, paring away the fringe groupings has had the total effect of increasing the net shift in the vote division between the two years from 8 percent to 11 percent. If we can explain this shift it will be clear that we have dealt with those broad currents in the electorate which brought the 1960 election to a virtual stalemate.

Naturally, the most interesting features of Table 22.1 are the cells involving vote changers. In a sequence of elections such as the 1956–1960 series it is a temptation to assume that about 8 percent of the Eisenhower voters of 1956 shifted to Kennedy in 1960, since this was the net observable change between the two years. Much analysis of aggregate election statistics is forced to proceed on this assumption within any given voting unit. However, we see that the net shift of 11 percent in the vote of the active 1956–1960 electorate in fact derived from a gross shift of 23 percent, over half of which was rendered invisible in the national totals because countermovements canceled themselves out.

A traditional analysis of these vote changers would specify their membership in various population groupings such as age and occupation category, union membership, race and the like. However, results of this sort in 1960 are so uniform across most of these population groupings that they seem to reflect little more than national trends, and change seems at best loosely connected with location in various of these specific categories. If we took the fact in isolation, for example, we might be struck to note that union members voted almost 8 percent more Democratic in 1960 than in 1956. However, such a figure loses much of its interest when we remind ourselves that people who are not labor union members also shifted their votes in the same direction and in about the same degree between 1956 and 1960. Such uniform changes characterize most of the standard sociological categories.

There is, of course, one dramatic exception. Vote change between 1956 and 1960 follows religious lines very closely. Within the 6 percent of the active 1956–1960 electorate who followed a Stevenson-Nixon path (Table 22.1), 90 percent are Protestant and only 8 percent are Catholic. Among the larger group of Eisenhower-Kennedy changers, however, only 40 percent are Protestant and close to 60 percent are Catholic. In the total vote in 1956 and 1960, Protestants show almost no net partisan change. Eisenhower had won 64 percent of the "Protestant vote" in 1956; Nixon won 63 percent. Meanwhile, the Democratic proportion of the two-party vote among Catholics across the nation skyrocketed from a rough 50 percent in the two Eisenhower elections to a vote of 80 percent for Kennedy. These gross totals appear to substantiate the early claims of Kennedy backers that a Catholic candidate would draw back to the Democratic party sufficient Catholics to carry the 1960 election. Furthermore, it appears that Kennedy must have gained more votes than he lost by virtue of his religious affiliation, for relative to Stevenson in 1956, he lost no Protestant votes and attracted a very substantial bloc of Catholic votes.

The question of net gains or losses as a result of the Catholic issue is not, however, so simply laid to rest. The data cited above make a very strong case, as have the aggregate national statistics, that religion played a powerful role in the 1960 outcome. The vote polarized along religious lines in a degree which we have not seen in the course of previous sample survey studies. Moreover, the few interesting deviations in the 1960 vote of other population groupings, to the degree that they are visible at all, seem with minor exceptions to reflect the central religious polarization. That is, where a group exceeded or fell below the magnitude of the national shift to the Democrats, it is usually true that the group is incidentally a more or less Catholic group. The central phenomenon therefore was religious; the question as to its net effect favoring or disfavoring Kennedy remains open.

In a strict sense, of course, the answers to this question can only be estimated. We know how the election came out, with Kennedy a Catholic. We cannot, without major additional assumptions, know what the election returns might have been if Kennedy were a Protestant and all other conditions remained unchanged. We can make an estimate, however, if we can assume some baseline, some vote that would have occurred under "normal" circumstances. A number of such baselines suggest themselves. We might work from the 1956 presidential vote, as we have done above (42 percent Democratic); or from the more recent congressional vote in 1958 (56 percent Democratic); or from some general average of recent nationwide votes. But it is obvious that the simple choice of baseline will go a long way toward determining the answer we propose to the question of net religious effect. If we choose the 1958 vote as a baseline, it is hard to argue that Kennedy could have made any net gains from his religion; if we choose the 1956 presidential vote, it is equally hard to argue that he lost ground on balance.

Indeed, the most cogent arguments documenting a net gain for Kennedy — those accounts which appear to express the majority opinion of election observers — use the 1956 presidential vote quite explicitly as a baseline. Yet the second Eisenhower vote seems the most bizarre choice for a baseline of any which might be suggested. The vote Eisenhower achieved in 1956 stands out as the most disproportionately Republican vote in the total series of nationwide presidential and congressional elections stretching back to 1928. In what sense, then, is this extreme Republican swing plausible as a "normal vote?" Its sole claim seems to lie in the fact that it is the most recent presidential election. Yet other recent elections attest dramatically to the extreme abnormality of the 1956 Eisenhower vote. In the 1954 congressional elections the nation's Democrats, although they turned out less well than Republicans in minor elections, still fashioned a solid majority of votes cast. The fall of 1958 witnessed a Democratic landslide. Even in 1956, "underneath" Eisenhower's towering personal margin, a Democratic popular vote majority exceeding that which Kennedy won in 1960 appeared at other levels of the ticket. Finally, if 1956 is taken as a normal baseline and if it is true that Kennedy did score some relative personal success in 1960, how can we possibly explain the fact that other diverse Democrats on state tickets around the nation tended to win a greater proportion of popular votes than he attracted?

It seems more reasonable to suggest that Kennedy did not in any sense *exceed* the "normal" vote expectations of the generalized and anonymous Democratic candidate; rather, he fell visibly below these expectations, although nowhere nearly as far below them as Adlai Stevenson had fallen. This proposition is congruent not only with the general contours of election returns in the recent period, but with the great mass of sample survey data collected in the past decade as well. With this proposition we can draw into a coherent pattern the several surface characteristics which seemed intriguing from the simple 1960 vote totals. With it, we can locate the 1960 election more generally in the stream of American political history.

The Basic Voting Strength of the Two Parties

We have found it of great explanatory value to think of election results as reflecting the interplay of two sets of forces: stable, long-term partisan dispositions and short-term forces specific to the immediate election situation. The long-term partisan dispositions are very adequately represented by our measures of party identification. The stability of these dispositions over time is a matter of empirical record.[12] Their partisan division over any period, as it may favor one party or the other, provides the point from which one must start to understand any specific election. This underlying division of loyalties lends itself admirably to the goal of indicating what a "normal" vote would be, aside from specific forces associated with the immediate election.

In these terms, the basic Democratic majority in the nation is scarcely subject to dispute. Year in and year out since 1952, national samples of the American electorate have indicated a preference for the Democratic party by a margin approaching 60–40. However, since no election in recent years has shown a Democratic margin of this magnitude, it would be as absurd to take a 60–40 Democratic majority for a baseline as it would be to work from the 1956 presidential vote. Actually there is little temptation to do so. Over the years large amounts of information have been accumulated on the behavior of people identifying with the two major parties, and it is clear that the realistic voting strength of the Democrats — and this is the sort of baseline which interests us — falls well short of a 60–40 majority. The fact that heavy Democratic majorities in the South are concealed by low voting turnout is but one factor which reduces realistic Democratic strength. Outside the South, as well, Democrats under the same conditions of short-term stimulation are less likely to vote than Republicans.

It is possible to manipulate the data in such a fashion as to take into account all of the significant discrepancies between nominal party identification and realistic voting strength. We thereby arrive at a picture of the vote division which could be expected in the normal presidential election, if short-term forces associated with the election favored neither party in particular, but stood at an equilibrium. In such circumstances, we would expect a Democratic proportion of the two-party popular vote to fall in the vicinity of 53–54 percent.[13] Outside of the South, such a vote would fall short of a 50–50 split with the Republicans; within the South there would be a strong Democratic majority exceeding a 2-to-1 division.

Short-term forces associated with a specific election may, according to their net partisan strength, send the actual vote in that election deviating to one side or the other of the equilibrium point. In 1952 and 1956 the popularity of Eisenhower constitutued one such force, and this force was strongly pro-Republican. The distortions produced in the behaviors of party identifiers of different types have now become familiar. If the net partisan force is strong, as in 1956, identifiers of the favored party vote almost *en bloc*, without defection. The small group of "independents" who do not commit themselves to either party divide very disproportionately in favor of the advantaged party, instead of dividing their vote equally as in the equilibrium case. And members of the disfavored party defect in relatively large numbers, as Democrats did in 1956. A useful description of any specific election then is an account of the short-term forces which have introduced these strains across the distribution of party identification.

In such a description, the existing division of deeper party loyalties is taken for granted. Its current character is not to be explained by the immediate political situation. The point is made most clearly by the 1960 election. The fact that the Democrats enjoyed a standing majority was in no way a consequence of the personal duel between Kennedy and Nixon, for it was a majority created long before either candidate became salient as a national political figure, and long before most of the campaign "issues" of 1960 had taken shape. In this perspective, then, we can consider some of the forces which drew the 1960 vote away from its equilibrium state.

Short-Term Forces in the 1960 Election

Popular vote tallies show that Kennedy received 49.8 percent of the two-party vote outside of the South, and 51.2 percent of the popular vote cast in the South. The vote outside the South is almost 1 percent more Democratic than our equilibrium estimates for this part of the nation. In the South, however, the Democratic deficit relative to the same baseline approaches 17 percent. Naturally, some short-term forces may balance out so that no net advantage accrues to either party. But the comparisons between our baselines and the 1960 vote suggest that we should find some short-term forces which gave a very slight net advantage to Kennedy outside of the South, and yet which penalized him heavily within the South.

As in all elections that attract a wide degree of public attention, a number of short-term forces were certainly at work in 1960. A comprehensive assessment of these forces must await further analysis. However, there can be little doubt that the religious issue was the strongest single factor overlaid on basic partisan loyalties in the 1960 election, and we have focused most of our initial analyses in this area. Fortunately we know a great deal about the "normal" voting behavior within different religious categories, and can use this knowledge to provide baselines which aid in estimating the net effect of Kennedy's Catholicism upon his candidacy.

The Catholic Vote

As we have observed, the vote division among Catholics soared from a 50–50 split in the two Eisenhower contests to an 80–20 majority in the 1960 presidential vote. However, it is hard to attribute all of this increment simply to the Kennedy candidacy. In the 1958 election, when there were mild short-term economic forces favoring the Democratic party, the vote among Catholics went well over 70 percent in that direction. Ever since our measurements of party identification began in 1952, only a small minority — less than 20 percent — of Catholics in the nation have considered themselves as Republicans, although a fair portion have typically styled themselves as "Independents." Most of what attracted attention as a Republican trend among Catholics during the 1950s finds little support in our data, at least as a trend peculiar to Catholics. To be sure, many Democratic Catholics defected to vote for Eisenhower in 1952 and 1956. So did many Democratic Protestants. As a matter of fact, the defection rate among Democratic Catholics in 1952 was very slightly less than among Democratic Protestants, and in 1956 was very slightly more. In neither case do the differences exceed sampling error. There is some long-term evidence of a faint and slow erosion in the Catholic Democratic vote; but this has been proceeding at such a glacial pace that the 1956–1960 vote trends which we are treating here dwarf it completely. There is no reason to believe that the short-term personal "pull" exerted on Democrats generally by Eisenhower had a different strength for Catholics than for Protestants. The myths that have arisen to this effect seem to be primarily illusions stemming from the large proportion of Democrats who are Catholics. Their loss was painful in the two Eisenhower votes. But they were at the outset, and remained up to the first glimmer of the Kennedy candidacy, a strongly Democratic group.

We may specify this "normal" Democratic strength among Catholics by applying the same operations for Catholics alone that we have employed for the electorate as a whole. In the equilibrium case, it turns out that one would expect at least a 63 percent Democratic margin among Catholics. The difference between 63 percent and the 80 percent which Kennedy achieved can provisionally be taken as an estimate of the increment in Democratic votes among Catholics above that which the normal, Protestant Democratic presidential candidate could have expected.

We can readily translate this 17 percent vote gain into proportions of the total 1960 vote, taking into account levels of Catholic turnout and the like. On such grounds, it appears that Kennedy won a vote bonus from Catholics amounting to about 4 percent of the national two-party popular vote. This increment is, of course, very unequally divided between the South and the rest of the nation, owing simply to the sparse Catholic population in the South. Within the 1960 non-southern electorate, Kennedy's net gain from the Catholic increment amounts to better than 5 percent of the two-party vote. The same rate of gain represents less than 1 percent of the southern popular vote.

The Anti-Catholic Vote

Respondents talked to our interviewers with remarkable freedom about the Catholic factor during the fall of 1960. This is not to say that all respondents referred to it as a problem. There were even signs that some Protestant respondents were struggling to avoid mention of it although it was a matter of concern. Nonetheless, nearly 40 percent of the sample voluntarily introduced the subject before any direct probing on our part in the early stages of the preelection questionnaire. Since this figure certainly understates the proportion of the population for whom religion was a salient concern in 1960, it testifies rather eloquently to the importance of the factor in conscious political motivations during the fall campaign.

These discussions of the Catholic question, volunteered by our respondents, will, in time, provide more incisive descriptions of the short-term anti-Catholic forces important in the election. Our interest here, however, is to estimate the magnitude of anti-Catholic voting in terms of otherwise Democratic votes which Kennedy lost. In such an enterprise, our material on the political backgrounds of our respondents is most useful.

We focus, therefore, upon the simple rates of defection to Nixon among Protestants who were identified in 1960 with the Democratic party. As Figure 22.1 shows, this defection rate is strongly correlated with regularity of attendance at a Protestant church. Protestant Democrats who, by self-description, never attend church, and hence are not likely to have much identification with it, defected to Nixon only at a rate of 6 percent. This rate, incidentally, is just about the "normal" defection rate which we would predict for both parties in the equilibrium case: it represents the scattered defections which occur for entirely idiosyncratic reasons in any election. Therefore, for Democrats who were nominal Protestants but outside the psychological orbit of their church, the short-term religious force set up by a Catholic candidacy had no visible impact. However, as soon as there is some evidence of identification with a Protestant church, the defection rate rises rapidly.

Although Protestant Independents are not included in Figure 22.1, they show the same gradient at a different level of the two-party vote division. The few Protestant Independents not attending church split close to the theoretically-expected 50-50 point. Then the Nixon vote rises to 61 percent in the "seldom" category; to 72 percent for the "often" category; and to 83 percent for the Protestant Independents attending church regularly. This increment of Republican votes above the "normal" 50–50 division for Independents matches remarkably the increment of Republican votes above the "normal" figure of 6 percent in the case of the Democrats.

We customarily find in our data certain substantial correlations between church attendance and political behavior. The correlation between church attendance and vote among Protestant Democrats and Independents is not, however, one of these.[14] The strong associations seem linked in an obvious way to the 1960 election. We need not assume, of course, that each defection pictured here represents a sermon from the pulpit and an obedient member of the congregation. Social science theory assures us that whether through sermons, informal communication or a private sense of reserve toward Catholicism, the faithful Protestant would react more negatively to the presidential candidacy of a Catholic than would more indifferent Protestants.[15] It remains notable, however, that Democrats who were at the same time regular Protestants defected to Nixon at rates far exceeding those which Eisenhower had attracted in 1952 or 1956.

We may use Figure 22.1, then, as a tool to estimate the magnitude of the anti-Catholic vote. It is easily argued that the area below the dotted line in Figure 22.1 represents "normal" defections within each category of church attendance, and that the votes represented by the triangle above the dotted line are votes which Kennedy lost on religious grounds. It is then a simple mechanical matter to convert this triangle into proportions of the popular vote for South and non-South.

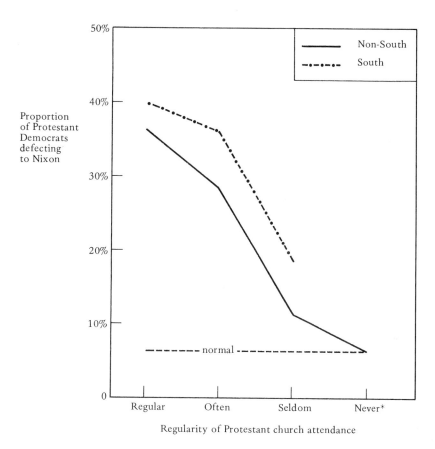

Figure 22.1 *Defections to Nixon Among Protestant Democrats as a Function of Church Attendance.*

*The number of Protestant Democrats who "never" attend church in the South is too small for inclusion.

On the surface, Figure 22.1 seems to say that the impact of the religious factor was very nearly the same, North and South, for the southern gradient of defections is only slightly higher than the non-southern gradient. If we think of the impact of short-term forces *on individuals* as a function of their party and religious loyalties, this conclusion is proper. Indeed, as we consider in later analyses the impact by different types of Protestantism, it may well be that the character of the impact will show no remaining regional difference whatever. However, to construe Figure 22.1 as suggesting that the *magnitude* of the anti-Catholic effect was about the same in votes cast in North and South, is quite improper. The differences between the regions turn out to be substantial.

We must consider first that less than two-thirds of the active non-southern electorate is Protestant, whereas within the South the electorate is almost completely (95 percent) Protestant. Secondly, Protestants are more faithful churchgoers in the South than outside it. Quite specifically, we find that over half of the southern presidential vote is cast by Protestants who go to church regularly, whereas less than 20 percent of the vote outside the South comes from regular, churchgoing Protestants. Finally, of the minority outside the South who are Protestant and attend church regularly, only a small proportion are Democratic identifiers: Republicans clearly predominate in this category. In the South, the situation is reversed, with regular Protestants being far more often than not Democratic identifiers.

This conjunction of regional differences means that the defecting votes represented in Figure 22.1 are of vastly different sizes, South and non-South. It turns out that outside the South regular, churchgoing Protestants who are Democrats cast only about 5 percent of the total non-southern vote. Within the South, however, regular churchgoing Protestants who are Democrats contributed over 35 percent of the total southern vote. Thus it is that the anti-Catholic impact in the South turns out to involve a much larger share of the votes than elsewhere. The anti-Catholic vote in the South fulfills our search for a short-term force of strong net Republican strength in that region.

Table 22.2   Offsetting Effects of the Catholic Issue, 1960 Democratic Presidential Vote

Area		% of 2-Party Vote in Area
Outside the South, Kennedy's "unexpected" . . .		
Gains from Catholics		5.2%
Losses from Protestant Democrats and Independents		− 3.6
	Net	+ 1.6%
Inside the South, Kennedy's "unexpected" . . .		
Gains from Catholics		0.7%
Losses from Protestant Democrats and Independents		−17.2
	Net	−16.5%
For the nation as a whole, Kennedy's "unexpected" . . .		
Gains from Catholics		4.3%
Losses from Protestant Democrats and Independents		− 6.5%
	Net	− 2.2%

Summing up these apparent anti-Catholic votes as proportions of the total vote in the South, the non-South, and the nation as a whole, we can compare them with our estimations of the bonuses received by Kennedy from Catholics. Table 22.2 shows the balance sheet.

There is every reason to believe that these preliminary estimates underestimate the importance of religion in the 1960 vote and, in particular, underestimate the magnitude of the anti-Catholic vote. We have at no point taken account, for example, of the possibility that certain Republican identifiers, exposed to short-term forces which would normally have produced defections to the Democrats, may have been inhibited from such defection by Kennedy's Catholicism. In the Midwest there were signs of a "farm revolt" favoring the Democrats which failed to materialize in the presidential balloting. At lower levels on farm belt tickets one finds that major Democratic candidates consistently surpassed "normal" Democratic expectations. Yet Kennedy seems to have been peculiarly insulated from any of this profit-taking: in these areas he lagged behind other major Democrats by a rather consistent 5 percent. It is difficult not to believe that at lower levels of office net short-term forces were favoring the Democrats, and Republican identifiers were defecting at unusual rates. Analyses may show that religion was a primary force inhibiting such defections at the presidential level.

Other early glimpses of our data also suggest the estimates of anti-Catholicism in Table 22.2 are conservative. It is likely that a number of nonreligious short-term forces generated by the campaign itself were favorable to Kennedy on balance. As a number of other surveys reported, Nixon held a substantial lead over Kennedy in the early stages. At the outset, Kennedy was little known to the public: he stood primarily as the Democratic candidate and a Catholic. As the campaign went on, other and nonreligious aspects of the Kennedy image filled in, and the public impression was usually positive. In this crucial shift in sentiment during the campaign, the television debates probably played an important role. Although there were Democrats who reacted warmly to Nixon's performance, our materials show quite strikingly that the net response to the debates favored Kennedy, as has been commonly supposed. In case studies, a reading of interviews has already turned up numerous Protestants of varying partisanship who were much more impressed by Kennedy as a candidate than by Nixon, yet who could not bring themselves to vote for a Catholic. In the measure that Kennedy's attractiveness as a candidate exceeded Nixon's and other short-term forces apart from religion were favoring the Democrats, the total popular vote should have been drawn to the Democratic side of the equilibrium point. The fact that it stayed instead on the Republican side may represent further damaging effects of religion for Kennedy.[16]

Refined analyses at a later date will permit us to estimate more adequately the role which all the major motivational factors, including religion, played in the 1960 outcome. For the moment, however, it is impressive the degree to which the surface characteristics of the 1960 election become intelligible even when viewed simply as the result of an "ancient" and enduring division of partisan loyalties overlaid by a short-term crosscurrent of religious motivation.

Normally we would expect a national vote falling as close to its equilibrium point as the 1960 case to be a relatively low-turnout election. That is, a vote near the equilibrium point suggests either weak short-term forces or else a balance of stronger forces creating conflict in individuals and thereby lowering their motivation to vote. It is rare that forces strong enough to compel indifferent citizens to come out and vote do not also favor one party over the other quite categorically.

In 1960, however, the motivational picture underlying the vote was somewhat different, and can best be understood by separating the Protestant South from the rest of the nation. In the South, of course, a strong and unidirectional short-term force was reflected in a sharp departure from equilibrium and a surge in turnout, as fits normal expectations. What is abnormal is that this strong Republican short-term force raised motivation in a Democratic preserve, rather than diluting it through conflict. It is likely that conflict *was* created, especially where Democratic partisanship was strong. "Strong" Democrats in our sample made virtually no contribution to the 1960 rise in southern turnout. The increase came from weaker Democrats, whose participation increased so radically over 1952 and 1956 that their turnout even surpassed that of strong Democrats in very exceptional fashion. For these voters, it seems likely that such forces as anti-Catholic feelings rapidly overcame relatively weak party loyalties and left strong motivation to turn out.

While turnout elsewhere did not show the same remarkable surge which appeared in the South, it remained at the fairly high level characteristic of the 1952 and 1956 elections, despite a partisan division of the vote near the regional equilibrium point. Strong balancing forces appear to have been in operation which did not create much conflict within individuals. The reason is clear: to the degree that religious motivations were engaged, forces were conflicting between groups rather than within individuals. Non-southern Catholics, predominantly Democratic, were exposed to strong unidirectional short-term forces motivating them to get out and vote for Kennedy. Non-southern Protestants, predominantly Republican, were exposed to contrary forces, at least where Protestant religious fidelity was strong. Thus the vote fell near the equilibrium point, but there was rather high turnout as well.

The other surface characteristics of the election are equally intelligible in these terms. Despite his position as majority candidate, Kennedy very nearly lost and tended to run behind his ticket. In the Northeast, where concentrations of Catholics are greatest, his relation to the rest of the ticket was not generally unfavorable. The penalty he suffered becomes visible and consistent in the Midwest, where Catholics are fewer and Protestant church attendance is more regular. In the South, and for the same reasons, the differences between the Kennedy vote and that of other Democrats become large indeed. Everywhere, if one compares 1956 vote statistics with 1960 statistics, the course of political change is closely associated with the religious composition of voting units.

There was some relief even outside the more committed Democratic circles when the Kennedy victory, slight though it was, demonstrated that a Catholic was not in practice barred from the White House. Yet it would be naive to suppose that a Catholic candidate no longer suffers any initial disadvantage before the American electorate as a result of his creed. Not only did Kennedy possess a type of personal appeal which the television debates permitted him to exploit in unusual measure, but he was also the candidate of a party enjoying a fundamental majority in the land. Even the combination of these circumstances was barely sufficient to give him a popular vote victory. Lacking such a strong underlying majority, which Al Smith most certainly lacked in 1928, it is doubtful that the most attractive of Catholic presidential candidates in 1960 would have had much chance of success. It remains to be seen how far the experience of a Catholic president may diminish the disadvantage another time.

The 1960 Election in Historical Perspective

In a publication which appeared a few months prior to the 1960 elections[17] we posed the question of "how long a party can hope to hold the White House if it does not have a majority of the party-identified electorate." We had identified the two Eisenhower victories as "deviating elections," in which short-term forces had brought about the defeat of the majority party. We had not found any evidence in our 1952 or 1956 studies that these short-term forces were producing any significant realignment in the basic partisan commitments of the electorate. We felt that unless such a realignment did occur, "the minority party [could] not hope to continue its tenure in office over a very extended period."

We now know that the eight-year Eisenhower period ended with no basic change in the proportions of the public who identify themselves as Republican, Democrat, or Independent. If there had been an opportunity in 1952 for the Republican party to rewin the majority status it had held prior to 1932, it failed to capitalize on it. The Democratic party remained the majority party and the 1960 election returned it to the presidency. It was, to extend the nomenclature of our earlier publication, a "reinstating" election, one in which the party enjoying a majority of party identifiers returns to power. The 1960 election was remarkable not in the fact that the majority party was reinstated but that its return to power was accomplished by such a narrow margin. We had recognized the possibility that "the unfolding of national and international events and the appearance of new political figures" might swing the vote away from its natural equilibrium. We now see that such a deflection did occur and that it very nearly cost the majority party the election.

It may be argued that the deficit the Democratic presidential candidate suffered from his normal expectation did not derive from damaging circumstances which were specific to the 1960 election but from a progressive weakening in the willingness of some Democratic partisans to support their ticket at the presidential level. It has been suggested that some voters who consider themselves to be Democrats and customarily favor Democratic candidates at the lower levels of office may have come during the Eisenhower period to have a perverse interest in favoring Republican candidates for President, either because of notions of party balance in government, because of local considerations in their states, or simply out of admiration for Eisenhower.

Important differences no doubt exist between voting at the presidential level and voting for congressman. Our sutdies have shown, for example, that the popular vote for lesser offices is a more party-determined vote than the vote for President and varies around the normal equilibrium vote figure within a much narrower range than does the presidential vote.[18] However, the supposition that Kennedy failed to win a normal Democratic majority because of a cadre of Democrats who are covertly Republican in their presidential voting is not supported by our data.

Table 22.1 has already demonstrated that the overall shift in partisanship of the vote between 1956 and 1960 cannot be explained as a simple unilateral movement of erstwhile Eisenhower Democrats. The election did not depend, as was often supposed, upon the number of Eisenhower Democrats whom Nixon could retain as "covert Republicans." Our panel materials show that if Nixon had been forced to depend only upon the Eisenhower Democrats whom he retained, he would have suffered a convincing 54–46 defeat, assuming that other Democrats had continued to vote for Kennedy. He did not suffer such a defeat because he drew a new stream of Democratic defections nearly sufficient to put him in the White House.

The patterns of short-term forces in the 1960 election were independent of those shaping the 1956 election, then, in the sense that they affected a new set of people, on new grounds. There were Democrats susceptible to Eisenhower in 1956; there were Democrats sensitive to religion in 1960: the two sets of people do not intersect much more than one would expect by chance. In short, there is little evidence that the two Eisenhower elections had created a set of Democrats peculiarly disposed to vote for a Republican presidential candidate.

Analysis of our 1960 data is not sufficiently complete to enable us to describe the entire pattern of forces to which the electorate was reacting on election day. We do not know, for example, what the partisan impact of international affairs, which had favored the Republican candidate so strongly in the preceding two elections, was in the 1960 election. We do not know the effect of the Negro discrimination issues. We do not know in detail as yet how the personal attributes of the major candidates, other than their religious affiliations, were evaluated by the public. We feel confident, however, that we will not find any short-term force which moved as large a fraction of the 1960 electorate as did the issue of a Catholic President. This was the major cause of the net departure of the vote totals from the division which the comparative underlying strength of the two parties in 1960 would have led us to expect. After two consecutive "deviating" elections won at a presidential level by the minority party, the 1960 election reinstated the Democratic party. But short-term forces generated by the immediate 1960 situation once again favored the Republicans on balance, and the difference in votes which separated this "reinstating election" from a third "deviating election" was slight indeed.

NOTES

[1] Estimates of turnout lack much meaning except as raw vote totals are stated as a proportion of the potential electorate. Whereas the number of adults over 21 in the nation is known with reasonable precision, the number of adult citizens over 21 who are "eligible" according to any of several possible definitions depends on cruder estimates, which can be quite diverse. For the 1952 figure we employ here Table No. 446 for the "Civilian Population 21 Years and Older," *Statistical Abstract of the United States* (1958 edition). The 1960 figure rests on an estimated 107 million adults over 21.

[2] The South is defined throughout this article to include fifteen border and deep southern states. Texas, Oklahoma, Arkansas, Kentucky, West Virginia, and Maryland (but not Delaware) are included and form the western and northern boundaries of the region.

[3] Population growth in areas such as Texas and Florida includes the immigration of American citizens from outside the South who are more accustomed to voting in every election than are Southerners. It seems almost certain, however, that there was a real increase in motivation among long-term southern residents as well. The factor of population change was quite insufficient to account for the 1960 increase in southern turnout.

[4] *New York Times*, November 20, 1960, Section 4, p. E5.

[5] Results of the 1956 survey, considered as a simple cross-section sample of the nation, are reported in Campbell, Converse, Miller, and Stokes, *The American Voter* (New York, 1960). There are natural difficulties in any attempt to retain contact with a farflung national sample over periods of two and four years, especially in a population as geographically mobile as that of the current United States. Of the original 1763 respondents interviewed twice in 1956, nearly 100 had died before the 1960 interview. Others had been effectively removed from the electorate by advanced senility or institutionalization. Of the remaining possible interviews, numbering somewhat over 1600 people, more than 1100 were successfully reinterviewed in the fall of 1960. The 1956 social, economic and political characteristics of the 1960 survivors show almost no sign of deviation from the characteristics of the larger pool of original 1956 respondents. Therefore, although attrition may seem substantial, there is no evidence of alarming bias.

[6] The sequence of interviews in 1956, 1958, and 1960 was carried out under grants from the Rockefeller Foundation. The 1960 sample design provided not only contact with the 1956 panel which, due to aging, no longer gave an adequate representation of the 1960 electorate, but also a set of additional interviews filling out an up-to-date cross-section sample of all adult citizens living in private households in 1960. Analysis of the additional interview material is being carried out under a grant from the Social Science Research Council. Both the

panel and cross-section bodies of data contribute, where appropriate, to materials in this article.

[7] The longitudinal analysis of political change permitted by a panel design can only be poorly approximated in simple cross-section surveys, where deductions must rest on the respondent's recollection of his behavior in time past. Most analysts have justly felt uncomfortable with recall materials of this sort, since it has been clear that the accuracy of a vote report declines rapidly as time passes. In both 1958 and 1960, we asked our respondents to recall their 1956 vote. The results, as compared with actual reports collected just after the 1956 election, demonstrate forcefully the inaccuracies which accumulate with time.

[8] Throughout this article, the "eligible electorate" is taken to consist of those noninstitution-alized citizens over 21. Negroes disqualified in many parts of the South, for example, are included in this bounding of the electorate, as well as those who had moved too recently to have established new voting residences in 1960.

[9] The concept of party identification is treated in detail, Campbell et al., *op. cit.*, p. 120 ff.

[10] Our theoretical understanding of this net of relationships is suggested *ibid.*, pp. 161–167.

[11] Participation rates by age in 1960 follow rather nicely the rates indicated *ibid.*, Fig. 17–1, p. 494.

[12] The absence of any significant change in the distribution of party loyalties throughout the Eisenhower period is best illustrated by Table 6-1, *ibid.*, p. 124. Distributions drawn in 1959 and 1960 continue the same pattern. Furthermore, there is no evidence that this surface stability of party identification is concealing a great flux of compensating changes beneath the surface. There have indeed been one or two slow, modest evolutions since 1952 which do involve compensating changes and hence are not visible in simple distributions. Nevertheless, our panel data show strikingly that among all the political orientations which we measure, partisan identification is by far the most stable for individuals over the periods which our data cover.

[13] This figure should be taken to indicate a rough range. It would vary upward or downward slightly according to the assumptions made concerning the overall proportion of the electorate turning out. While the computations underlying this estimate are tedious, their rationale is entirely straightforward. Turnout rates and the two-party vote division within each of seven categories of party identifiers have shown remarkable regularities over the range of elections which we have studied. These rates are not constant from election to election, but do vary for each type of identifier quite dependably as a function of the net balance of short-term partisan forces characterizing the specific election. While we have observed no election which registered a perfect equilibrium of these forces, we have observed situations in which net forces were Democratic (e.g., 1958) as well as Republican (e.g., 1952 or 1956). It is therefore possible to compute the turnout rate and two-party vote division which could be expected for each type of party identifier in the intermediate case in which short-term forces are balanced. The estimate employed above derives from a summation of these computations across categories of identifiers, weighted in a fashion appropriate to represent the entire electorate.

[14] Reexamination of earlier data shows a faint residual relationship between Republican voting and church attendance among Democratic Protestants which is not statistically significant. In 1956, the rank-order correlations involved were about .05 both within and outside the South. On the other hand, the comparable coefficient for Independents in 1956 was negative, −.04. The text ignores these variations as probably inconsequential.

[15] This is simply a special case of propositions concerning group identifications more generally discussed in Campbell et al., *op. cit.*, chap. 12.

[16] Two other motivational patterns associated with religion in 1960 deserve note. There were undoubtedly broadminded Protestants who were drawn to a Kennedy vote out of a desire to see the religious precedent broken and hence buried; and there were undoubtedly Catholics who were drawn away from a Kennedy vote out of fear that the fact of a Catholic President would keep the religious issue uncomfortably prominent. It is hard to find instances of these viewpoints in our sample, however, and it is to be assumed that their incidence was slight.

[17] Campbell et al., *op. cit.*, chap. 19.

[18] Angus Campbell, "Surge and Decline: A Study of Electoral Change," *Public Opinion Quarterly*, vol. 24 (Fall 1960), pp. 397–418.

American Voting Behavior and the 1964 Election

Walter Dean Burnham

23

Walter Dean Burnham's analysis of national and northeastern survey research and aggregate data from the presidential election of 1964 points to a strong sectional component in the vote against Barry Goldwater in the Northeast. His comparison of aggregate data from that election with similar election data from earlier periods leads him to conclude that in the Northeast, the Goldwater–Johnson campaign reactivated long dormant alignments. Burnham's article underscores the value of analyses of aggregate data in understanding recent electoral behavior as well as the great potential in combining analyses of survey and aggregate data in historically oriented treatments of contemporary political behavior.

An assumption which underlies much of the study of American electoral politics is that the mass base of our major political coalitions has a high degree of stability over time. As V. O. Key, Jr. and Frank Munger have observed, most voting behavior most of the time is a continuing affirmation of preexisting political commitments which were forged under the pressure of a major social trauma. Looked at in terms of the party system as a whole, this profound linkage with the past often amounts to a "standing decision" which is only very infrequently subject to review by any decisively large part of the electorate.[1] Even in the contemporary period the findings of survey research, while documenting the significance of short-term factors in voting outcomes, emphasize that the most important single variable which influences the voter is still his party identification.

A tautology which emerges from this view is that an aggregate system of voting behavior will act like a system over time, i.e., that the system will be more coherently related to itself — especially in the short run — than to any extrapartisan social variables. Key demonstrated the plausibility of this argument by use of the standard correlation coefficient in his book, *A Primer of Statistics for*

SOURCE: Reprinted with permission from *Midwest Journal of Political Science*, vol. 12 (February 1968), pp. 1–40.

Political Scientists.[2] The autocorrelation of pairs of contiguous elections tends to produce coefficients which are among the highest to be found anywhere in the social sciences, such as the 1944–1948 r of $+0.98$ for the ten counties of New Hampshire. Such autocorrelations, which amount to saying that A_{1944} substantially equals A_{1948}, have hitherto been pretty well limited to such methodological inquiries as Key undertook, since reiterations of such statements are not of very great substantive interest once the equation is established.

Yet, paradoxically, the results of recent presidential elections — especially the 1964 election — point in an entirely different direction. As we shall see, two major and "unexpected" characteristics of these elections stand out with particular clarity. First, according to this mode of analysis and using states as components of the national voting system, presidential elections have resembled their immediate predecessors less and less closely since 1948. Second, the 1964 data provide clear geographical traces of alignment patterns more usually associated with the 1896–1932 or even the Civil War alignment systems than with the alignment patterns of contemporary American politics. Since they cast penetrating light into an unexplored corner of American voting behavior, these peculiarities of present-day elections repay study in some detail.

I

It is desirable at the outset to specify the research focus of this study with some clarity. This focus is essentially geographical, involving an examination both of regional biases in the Survey Research Center's 1964 study and aggregate-data analysis of relationships among state components of the national voting system, and county components of certain state voting systems. Aggregate-data analysis, of course, has a number of limitations which have been thoroughly discussed in the literature.[3] In particular, the statewide correlations employed here are designed solely to make inferences concerning the interrelationships of aggregates at that level, and that level alone. It hardly needs saying that macroanalytic study cannot be successfully employed to make direct causal inferences concerning microanalytic units, e.g., concerning the motivations of individual actors in the larger voting system. At the same time, if an irreducible X factor emerges from analysis at this level — a factor whose presence has not yet been adequately recognized by the mainstream of microanalytic research — it cannot but have implications for the future direction of this research, as well as for our knowledge of the social context in which individual voting decisions are made. Moreover, examination of electoral behavior in terms of geographical components need not be defended so far as the 1964 election is concerned. As we shall see, this election was more heavily influenced by sectional factors than any other in the past generation.

If one turns, then, to the statewide correlation arrays by paired elections, he might expect to find both a "normal" pattern of close relationship and a deviation from this norm for 1964. Table 23.1 reveals not only a confirmation of this expectation, but something else besides.[4] It is clear enough that these correlations describe a relative positioning of states along a continuum, and the degree of congruence between that positioning in one election and its immediate successor. The extreme importance of the realignment of 1896 is not captured in the data presented, for example, since nationally it tended to reinforce a sectional alignment which was already partially in existence. Correlation analysis tends to reflect the influence of extreme values only too well, and the "Solid South's" lopsidedly Democratic percentages were in evidence as early as 1880. Thus, it is hardly surprising that the lowest contiguous correlations yielded by the data before World War II were found in the 1924–1928 and 1928–1932 pairs. This reflected the partial disruption of the "normal" array which resulted, especially in the South, from Al Smith's candidacy in 1928.

Even with these limitations in mind, the pattern of postwar statewide alignments is strikingly deviant from the historical norm. In the first place there is clearly a downward progression in each pair of contiguous elections from the 1948–1952 pair down to the present, with each election resembling its predecessor less and less closely. Prior to that time the assumption of congruence between two contiguous elections with which this study began was confirmed: in only three of seventeen pairs between 1880 and 1948 did r fall below $+0.80$, and all three of these were above $+0.70$. There is much evidence from other sources to support the proposition that short-term influences in presidential voting alignments have been growing in relative importance at the expense of long-term continuities and "standing decisions."[5] The evidence here, while hardly amounting to a definitive confirmation of this hypothesis, is entirely consistent with it.

Table 23.1 Correlations of Contiguous Pairs of Presidential Elections by States, 1880/1884-1960/1964

Election Pair	$r =$	$r^2 \times 100 =$
1880-1884	+0.88	77.44
1884-1888	+0.94	88.36
1888-1892	+0.81	65.61
1892-1896	+0.78	60.84
1896-1900	+0.84	70.56
1900-1904	+0.89	79.21
1904-1908	+0.94	88.36
1908-1912	+0.95	90.25
1912-1916	+0.91	82.81
1916-1920	+0.90	81.00
1920-1924	+0.98	96.04
1924-1928	+0.75	56.25
1928-1932	+0.78	60.84
1932-1936	+0.94	88.36
1936-1940	+0.90	81.00
1940-1944	+0.98	96.04
1944-1948	+0.96	92.16
1948-1952	+0.74	54.76
1952-1956	+0.60	36.00
1956-1960	+0.54	29.16
1960-1964	−0.11	1.21

The second point for reflection which arises from Table 23.1 is the extraordinary result of pairing the 1960 and 1964 elections: the production if an *r* which is not only so low as to indicate a virtually random relationship between the statewide percentages in these two elections, but which is actually slightly *negative*. Were such low correlations to become the norm in the present and immediate future, we should be led to suspect that at this level presidential elections would be well on the way to becoming "happenings," discrete phenomena in which long-term continuities play a vanishing role and short-term influences become overwhelming. Nevertheless, it is a major thesis of this study that the system does not in fact operate at random, even when short-term influences are at a maximum. More precisely, it is possible to demonstrate that at least some extraordinarily massive short-term displacements are not random fluctuations, but invoke clear reflections of political alignments which had been widely thought to be dead and buried since the realignments of the 1930s.

The peculiarities of the campaign and election of 1964 need not be recounted in detail here. It is enough to note that the Goldwater campaign was manifestly archaic in substance and tactics, to the extent that discussion of its antique qualities tended to dominate contemporary writing on the subject. This campaign, moreover, broke many of the unwritten rules of modern-day American party politics, particularly those involving coalition-building aimed at winning elections.[6] Goldwater's supporters rose in revolt against the substantive policies of the post-1932 "moving consensus," and in doing so raised significant questions about the mobility of that consensus which were only partially answered by the outcome of the election. Geographically concentrated in the interior, South and West, they constructed an explicitly sectional electoral strategy which was aimed at isolating the Northeast in general and the "eastern establishment" in particular.[7] If they did not produce a critical realignment in the process, it was not for want of trying to do so.

As it was, 1964 displayed many of the behavioral properties which have been associated with major realignments in the past.[8] More precisely, both the tone of the Goldwater campaign and the extraordinary and geographically concentrated voter shifts in November evoke striking impressions of similarity with such sectionally polarized elections as the McKinley-Bryan contest of 1896. This parallelism between 1896 and 1964 is especially marked if similarities in both the nomination and election patterns are viewed together. Of course, one never steps twice into the same river; what appears is thus not a precisely inverse correspondence but a visible though blurred similarity. It nevertheless seems accurate to say, first, that the shape of the 1964 outcome more closely resembles earlier elections marked by a "colonial" revolt of South and West against a northeastern metropole than it resembles any others; and, second, that the alignment era which was inaugurated by the epic struggle of 1896 produced more such elections than any other era before or since.

If such parallelism exists, it should be possible to measure it in quantitative terms, beginning with the nominating convention. In the period from 1896 to 1964, there have been five national party conventions which have been marked by exceptional internal tension: the Democratic conventions of 1896 and 1924, and the Republican conventions of 1912, 1952, and 1964. In each of them, major factional disputes were central to the decisions made; all of them constituted significant turning points in the histories of the respective parties; and all of them except the 1912 Republican convention were marked by sharp sectional cleavages. A study of key votes on procedural questions and platform amendments [Table 23.2] produces the following regional profiles for each convention.[9]

Table 23.2   Similarities and Dissimilarities in Regional Bases of Intraparty Cleavage, 1896-1964

Region	1896 D Gold Plank % Yea	1912 R Rules % Nay	1924 D Klan % Yea	1952 R Brown Am. % Nay	1964 R Civil Rights % Yea
Northeast	90.5	50.3	86.3	82.8	87.0
Midwest	14.2	70.9	54.1	39.5	17.7
West	10.0	32.5	26.2	62.9	10.5
South	1.1	23.7	15.6	24.9	0.3
Total:	32.6	47.2	50.0—	54.6	31.3

As is evident, the 1896 Democratic and 1964 Republican convention voting profiles are virtually identical on the regional level. Indeed, the 1964 Republican pattern has more in common even with the 1924 Democratic convention vote on the Ku Klux Klan than with either of the two other Republican conventions. A correlation of state percentages [Table 23.3] yields similar results.

Table 23.3   Correlations Between Key Votes in Five Party Conventions, by State, 1896-1964

	1896 D	1912 R	1924 D	1952 R	1964 R
1896 D	—	+.07	+.68	+.50	+.78
1912 R	+.07	—	+.09	+.15	−.02
1924 D	+.68	+.09	—	+.29	+.71
1952 R	+.50	+.15	+.29	—	+.51
1964 R	+.78	−.02	+.71	+.51	—

A cluster relationship seems to emerge from this set of coefficients. There are high correlations among 1896 D, 1924 D and 1964 R, with the highest being that between 1896 D and 1964 R; 1952 R "explains" nearly 35 percent less of the 1964 R variance than does 1896 D. There is little or no correlation among the other elements in the matrix; in particular, the 1912 R cleavage seems quite unrelated to anything else.

A reasonable explanation of this set of relationships may be that the 1964 Republican convention involved, beneath differences in overt issues, many of the same latencies of regional antagonism which afflicted the Democratic party during the 1896–1932 alignment era.

The functional parallels between the two conventions are indeed striking: the prior existence of northeastern "establishment" control of presidential nominations, in uneasy balance with a quite different regional center of the party's gravity in Congress; the development of interest and value antagonisms which provided the fuel for a successful effort to overthrow the northeastern President-makers; the effort by the new masters of the convention to construct a coalitional strategy which excluded the vote-rich Northeast; and the massive dislocations in voting behavior, particularly in the Northeast, which contributed

Table 23.4 Correlations of the Election of 1964 with All Earlier Presidential Elections, by States, 1880-1960

Election Pair 1964 and:	r =	r² X 100 =
1880	−0.60	36.00
1884	−0.54	29.16
1888	−0.67	44.89
1892	−0.64	40.96
1896	−0.69	47.61
1900	−0.76	57.76
1904	−0.64	40.96
1908	−0.71	50.41
1912	−0.71	50.41
1916	−0.75	56.25
1920	−0.67	44.89
1924	−0.63	39.69
1928	−0.55	30.25
1932	−0.72	51.84
1936	−0.72	51.84
1940	−0.67	44.89
1944	−0.64	40.96
1948	−0.61	38.44
1952	−0.39	15.21
1956	−0.64	40.96
1960	−0.11	1.21

heavily to a defeat for those who sought a new winning coalition. The gold standard and a civil rights plank may have little enough in common on the overt level but they may share a partial common identity as stalking-horses for a major confrontation between regional power interests and political subcultures.

But the foregoing merely describes some aspects of elite behavior. Assuming that symbolic appeals based on regional and other subcultural antagonisms are of continuing importance in elections, we should expect to find analogous, if less clearly etched, relationships in an analysis of mass voting behavior. General-election results involving 1964 should thus point toward a quite different pattern of relationships among the state components of the national voting system than those assumed at the outset. Such correlations should be uniformly negative rather than positive, and should show some signs of becoming higher as one moves back toward the beginning of the twentieth century. These statewide comparisons, of course, suggest less dramatic differences between elections in the 1930s and their predecessors than do other, more refined modes of analysis, since relative positioning among states during the New Deal was shifted less significantly than within-state alignments. The increasing spans of time between 1964 and the election with which it is paired could also be expected to produce a flattening of the ascending negative curve. Even so, a pattern of the expected type seems to emerge.

Excluding the 1960–1964 pair, a moderately-sloped regression line can be traced back to the 1896–1964 pair. On this line a −0.57 for the 1956–1964 pair would become approximately —0.73 for the 1896–1964 pair. There are reasons — associated with immense short-term appeal of the Bryan campaign to the silver-mining states — for a somewhat lower correlation between that election itself and 1964 than between 1900 or 1916 and 1964. Even so, it seems reasonably clear that the negative relationship between 1964 and the period of elections extending from 1896 through 1916 is significantly stronger than for any other comparable period of time before or after. Assuming with Schattschneider, Key, and others that critical realignments bring a kind of alignment system of some durability into being, this tends to support the thesis that the events of 1964 activated a rough but visible mirror-image of the alignment "system of 1896–1932" as a whole.[10]

A somewhat different type of analysis brings into sharper focus the peculiar relationship of 1964 with earlier elections which possessed similar geographically-concentrated components. Two procedures have been followed in this analysis. In the first place, the eleven ex-Confederate states have been excluded, both because they formed a separate subsystem which did not undergo realignment along national lines until the 1950s, and because the extreme values which they generate in correlations significantly reduce the sharpness of comparisons involving 1964. Secondly, correlations were made between the percentages Republican of the two-party vote in the non-southern states, 1880–1960, and the 1964 Z-score displacement by state.

The standard or Z score is a useful device for measuring the relative magnitude of deviation of a data point from an "expected" norm based on past observation. It is derived by dividing the standard deviation of a mean into the deviation from that mean registered by the data point under investigation. In this case, the standard deviation of a 1932–1960 mean for each state is divided into the 1964 deviation from the 1932–1960 mean percentage Democratic of the two-party vote.[11] Each of two given geographical areas may, for example, show a displacement of 12 percent toward the Democratic nominee between 1960 and 1964. But if one of these areas has shown a tight clustering of percentages around the mean in the 1932–1960 period, while the other has displayed considerable amplitude of partisan swing during that period, two quite different relative electoral movements will be reflected in the same absolute movement. In this instance, the greater the positive or negative score, the greater the pro-Democratic or pro-Republican 1964 deviation from "normal," as defined by the 1932–1960 mean.[12] Measurement of partisan percentages against the 1964 Z score over the period 1880–1960 appears more precisely to identify elections in the past with which 1964 has the most in common.

Of the twenty-one election pairs in Table 23.5, only five realize correlations in excess of ±0.50. In descending order they are 1932, 1936, 1896, 1916 and 1900. It is notable that no election since 1936 produces a coefficient as high even as the rather mediocre correlation between 1908 and 1964 Z. Indeed, each of the high-scoring elections, with the exception of 1936, is to be found in the 1896–1932 alignment era, and each is prominently associated with a strong sectional component, arraying South and West against Northeast, in the aggregate vote.[13]

It may be possible to regard 1936, the most recent election with a high correlation, as a transitional phase between the old alignment and the stable phase of the New Deal alignment. There was undoubtedly a heavy and novel increment of class-related realignment in this election. But while working-class areas mas-

Table 23.5 Relationship Between 1964 Z Scores and Percentages Republican by State,
Non-Southern States, 1880-1960*

Election Pair 1964 Z and:	r =	r² X 100 =
1880	+0.17	2.89
1884	+0.16	2.56
1888	+0.21	4.41
1892	−0.33	10.89
1896	+0.74	54.76
1900	+0.59	34.81
1904	−0.21	4.41
1908	+0.48	23.04
1912	+0.38	14.44
1916	+0.69	47.61
1920	+0.19	3.61
1924	−0.22	4.84
1928	+0.09	0.81
1932	+0.84	70.56
1936	+0.77	59.29
1940	+0.29	8.41
1944	+0.01	0.00+
1948	+0.34	11.56
1952	−0.18	3.24
1956	+0.23	5.29
1960	−0.44	19.36

*The same general procedure which was outlined in note 4 applies here also. For 1880-1888, $N = 27$;
for 1892, $N = 33$; for 1896-1904, $N = 34$; for 1908, $N = 35$; for 1912-1960, $N = 37$. Because it is not
possible to derive a 1932-1960 Z score for Alaska and Hawaii, they are omitted in the 1960-1964 Z
pair. $r_{1964, 1964\ Z} = -0.995$.

sively increased both their total vote and the Democratic share of it between
1932 and 1936, Democratic support tended to remain abnormally heavy among
middle-class and white-collar elements in 1936. This maintenance of Democratic support among these groups — a support which was to be severely diminished in 1940 — was also paralleled by Democratic percentages in the West
which far exceeded even the landslide margins of 1932. While the antics of the
Liberty League and the fate of the *Literary Digest* poll might lead us to think
otherwise, it nevertheless seems that there was a lower index of class voting in
1936 than in any subsequent elections except those of 1956 and 1960.[14] In any
event, the data indicate pretty clearly that, on balance, the 1964 election more
closely resembled elections held during the era of the fourth-party system (1896–
1932) than those of the fifth (1934–1936?).[15]

II

The word *sectionalism* may mean a variety of things. On the level of voting
behavior, sectional influences may be defined as involving differentials in voting alignments along geographical lines which are not to be confused with urbanization levels or other demographic or social variables which may also be
skewed geographically. In extreme cases, a sectional alignment may produce a

sharp reduction or even obliteration of within-area voting cleavages, replacing them with a relatively homogeneous structure of voting behavior among most or all politically active social strata. The implication may be further drawn that this homogeneity arises from a clear voter consciousness of external threat to regional interests or cultural values, though no definitive showing of any such phenomenon can be made from the use of aggregate data alone.

The concept of sectionalism has also been employed systemically to describe an interrelated pattern of elite and nonelite behavior, legislation affecting the size and composition of the regional electorate, and so on, which is aimed at stabilizing and perpetuating a dominant regional interest, as in the case of the formerly "Solid South." In this broader systematic sense, sectional politics is a major variant of nonclass politics. Dominant political cleavages formed around persistent conflicts among regions of uneven socioeconomic development are, indeed, virtually incompatible by definition with a stable division of the electorate along lines of socioeconomic status. So are such alternative variants of nonclass politics as the conflict between French-speaking and English-speaking Canadians, or that between Nationalist and Unionist in Ireland prior to its independence. Such a politics is analogous to politics among nation-states which, even in the Communist world, effectively prevents the emergence of transnational "working-class solidarity." Sectional politics within a given political system tends to be reactionary, since it greatly facilitates control of politics by those who are already economically dominant.[16] It is hardly accidental that the most sectionally polarized alignment system in American political history, that of 1896–1932, was closely associated with a transcendant dominance by corporate business over public policy.[17] Nor is it accidental that the policy deadlock which has existed with few interruptions since 1938 owes much of its existence to the survival of one-partyism in the South into the contemporary period.

For the purposes of this study, however, such larger meanings of sectionalism may be noted and then laid aside. For our purposes it is necessary to demonstrate only that there was a heavy, regionally-structured voter response, a response which, in reaction to the archaisms of the 1964 campaign, produced measurable echoes of archaic electoral alignments. Whether or not individual voters were motivated by regional self-defense, or whether or not permanent policy consequences come to be associated with the aftermath of 1964, the most salient question for the analyst of American voting behavior is this: why was it possible for such an atavism to occur at all as late as the mid-1960s?

The Survey Research Center's 1964 election study reveals the existence of this sectionalism in two ways. It captures the sharp differentiation between voting response in the Northeast and in the rest of the country.[18] Curiously, it also radically overreports the Democratic vote in the South, an anomaly to be discussed later.

As is clear from the data above, the 1964 election in the Northeast largely obliterated the traditional post–New Deal political stratification along class, educational and occupational lines, while — according to this sample — it did nothing of the sort in other regions of the country. This result was brought about by an extraordinarily heavy Democratic vote in the better-educated and higher-status elements of the Northeast's electorate, a swing which evidently brought up the Democratic percentage of the vote among such groups nearly to 1960 working-class levels.[19] Thus, the Northeast produced an index of class voting of only

Table 23.6 Selected Social Characteristics and the 1964 Vote:
The Northeast as Deviant Region*

Social Characteristic	Northeast (N)	% D	% R	Rest of U.S. (N)	% D	% R	Difference % D
Occupation:							
Professional-managerial	(55)	62	38	(143)	52	48	+10
Clerical-sales	(36)	81	18	(100)	63	37	+18
Skilled workers	(29)	72	28	(66)	74	26	− 2
Semi- and unskilled	(49)	76	24	(137)	87	13	−11
Retired	(25)	72	28	(79)	62	38	+10
Housewives, etc.	(105)	79	21	(228)	60	40	+19
Education Level:							
College graduate	(43)	77	23	(99)	38	62	+39
Some college	(38)	66	34	(115)	56	44	+10
High school graduate	(126)	73	27	(244)	64	36	+ 9
Some high school	(45)	71	29	(161)	74	26	− 3
Grade school, none	(56)	84	16	(178)	79	21	+ 5
Perceived Social Class:							
Self-identified:							
Middle class	(88)	69	31	(198)	49	51	+20
Working class	(98)	82	18	(294)	77	23	+ 5
Not self-identified:							
Middle class	(54)	67	33	(143)	53	47	+14
Working class	(55)	80	20	(132)	79	21	+ 1
Rejection of classes	(8)	50	50	(19)	44	56	+ 6
All Sample Responses:	(309)	74	26	(802)	65	35	+ 9

*Data computed from the 1964 election study of the Survey Research Center, University of Michigan; courtesy of the Inter-University Consortium for Political Research. The Northeast is here defined as New England and Middle Atlantic census regions, plus Delaware, Maryland, the District of Columbia, and West Virginia.

4 in 1964, compared with 27 in the rest of the country and 18 in the United States as a whole.[20]

Further exploration by aggregate-data analysis must perforce take us below the gross levels of regions or states and thus, because of a plethora of available data, to a selective study of certain extreme deviations from the norm, primarily in the northeastern states. There are a variety of measures which can be developed to study sectional voting alignments. In the case of the Northeast, they all seem to say the same thing, with variations in emphasis and implication. The first of such measures is the party defection ratio — in this case the Republican defection ratio — which was developed by Key in his study of the 1960 election.[21] Analysis of the 1960–1964 defection ratio by states and counties reveals the epicenter of anti-Goldwater reaction to be in eastern New England. Here, especially in Maine, Massachusetts, and Rhode Island, the movement was so great and widely spread as to be nearly uniform. Of the thirty-five counties in these three states, only seven showed Republican defection ratios of less than 40, while four had defection ratios in excess of 50 — among the highest for white jurisdictions in the nation.[22]

As one moves westward in this region, however, considerable internal variations begin to emerge. In New York State, for example, there is a very clearcut internal differentiation as between the New York City metropolitan area — especially in predominantly white parts of the city's four residential boroughs and the suburban counties — and upstate New York. Thus, predominantly white assembly districts of the city showed a 1960–1964 defection ratio of 24.7; in the suburban counties it was 29.2; while for the state north of the Westchester county line it reached 41.2[23] (The Negro assembly districts of the city, with a defection ratio of 74.6, were in a class by themselves, as were similar areas in other cities.) As measured by this yardstick, the upstate displacements were more or less uniformly massive, with urban centers showing nearly as substantial a Republican defection as the rural areas.

If one explores within-state county variances from a statewide mean over time, a similar pattern emerges.[24] It can be supposed a priori that the greater the within-state variance, the greater the relative weight of components of voting behavior which divided the electorate of a state internally. Conversely, the smaller the variance, the more likely it is that some nationwide political factor or factors suppressing these internal cleavages are at work. Such analysis, of course, does not tell us directly what the focus of these internal cleavages is, and certainly does not imply that this focus remains the same over long periods of time. *Ceteris paribus*, however, a sudden drop in within-state variances would seem to point toward the emergence of a major sectional component in the collective voting decision. A comparison of four northeastern states with three mountain states for the period 1920–1964 vividly illustrates both temporal and regional differentiations of this sort.

Table 23.7   Sectionalism and Within-State Variances, 1920-1964 (Selected States)

Year	Maine	N.J.	Pa.	Vt.	N.M.	Utah	Wyo.
1920	33.42	48.28	81.06	45.98	138.01	37.34	18.97
1924	17.79	56.30	115.10	48.85	173.75	46.84	23.05
1928	48.29	97.56	110.78	152.40	41.98	80.29	45.35
1932	31.40	54.63	81.44	85.09	121.15	74.79	22.75
1936	85.89	66.37	86.54	97.40	108.72	55.89	61.13
1940	81.55	72.94	101.48	81.55	84.25	58.87	76.94
1944	99.95	79.06	94.64	99.95	61.33	71.41	66.55
1948	111.55	87.62	103.63	102.00	104.51	73.27	54.01
1952	75.13	87.62	103.26	74.88	37.06	83.62	95.11
1956	63.45	76.05	73.46	69.93	30.28	65.36	74.68
1960	101.09	87.21	104.48	104.26	74.13	87.21	90.93
1964	39.77	30.57	60.44	25.55	62.46	80.82	90.71

Several features of Table 23.7 stand out with particular clarity. In the first place, five of the seven states displayed markedly lower county variances before 1928 than they have since. Secondly, both 1928 and — to a lesser degree — 1948 and 1960 emerge in most of these states as years of exceptional internal polarization, a finding which is also confirmed by other evidence. Finally, and most important, the 1964 variances show major differences between the four states of the Northeast and the three mountain states. In New Jersey,

Pennsylvania, and Vermont, indeed, the magnitude of the 1964 variance was the smallest on record for the period under consideration, while Maine's variance fell to the lowest level since 1932. In the three mountain states, on the other hand, the differences between the 1960 and 1964 variances were insignificant. It seems clear that the 1964 configuration of issues and candidates' images produced a virtually unprecedented compression of traditional within-state cleavages in the Northeast, and that no such effect was visible in the parts of the West examined here. A vast regional differential in the effect of the Goldwater candidacy on voting behavior almost certainly underlies these movements.

Table 23.8 Sectionalism and the 1964 Election: Z Scores by Quartile and Region*

| Region | Z-Score Quartiles (USA: $Z = +1.27$) | | | | |
	1st (+2.35 to +4.36)	2nd (+1.02 to +2.24)	3rd (+0.03 to +0.99)	4th (−5.45 to −0.35)	Total (+4.36 to −5.45)
Northeast	11	1	—	—	12
Midwest	1	8	3	—	12
West	—	2	8	1	11
South	—	1	1	11	13
Total	12	12	12	12	48

*Alaska and Hawaii excluded. Regions: East—New England, Middle Atlantic, Delaware, Maryland, and West Virginia. Midwest—East and West North Central. West—Mountain and Pacific. South—the eleven ex-Confederate states plus Kentucky and Oklahoma.

Under certain circumstances, a partial liquidation of internal cleavages within given jurisdictions may be associated with differentials which evoke far older, often virtually forgotten cleavage patterns. In the study of this problem, the Republican defection ratio has the limitation that it measures only the movement between two contiguous elections. Similarly, the measurement of within-state variances over time may prove illuminating in dealing with the relative importance of internal and exogenous factors in political cleavage, but it can hardly provide direct information of the sort that would be useful in studying the relevance of the 1964 displacement to pre-1932 alignments. For this purpose, some measure of deviation from "expected" two-party balance in a given area, based on its behavior in the recent past, is more revealing. The Z-score measure discussed above seems well suited to this task. As Tables 23.8 and 23.9 indicate, a Z-score calculation of the 1964 displacements in the national system reveals marked regional differentials which are not simply masks for such social variables as the extent of urbanization.[25]

III

Two states have been selected for detailed county-level analysis by this method: New York and Pennsylvania. The criteria for their selection include their northeastern location, the historical existence of large and well-documented differentials in original settlement patterns, and the presence of large numbers of counties which are not in metropolitan areas and are "off the beaten path," so far as recent population change is concerned. Other things being equal, we

Table 23.9 Urbanism and the 1964 Election: Z Scores and Percentage Urban (1960), by Quartile

Urbanism Quartiles (USA: 69.9%)	Z-Score Quartiles (USA: $Z = +1.27$)				
	1st (+2.35 to +4.36)	2nd (+1.02 to +2.24)	3rd (+0.03 to +0.99)	4th (−5.45 to −0.35)	Total (+4.36 to −5.45)
1st (73.7-88.6%)	5	2	2	3	12
2nd (62.9-73.4%)	3	4	4	1	12
3rd (52.3-62.4%)	1	5	2	4	12
4th (35.2-51.3%)	3	1	4	4	12
Total	12	12	12	12	48

would expect that a county which has shown small variations from a mean will frequently be such an out-of-the-way area, probably rural or semi-rural and largely insulated in its partisan balance from short-term influences — in short, the sort of community most likely to be dominated by an unusually stable "standing decision."[26] Finally, the hypothesis underlying this part of the study can be set forth briefly in propositional terms. If the Goldwater candidacy was structured around a nostalgic sectional appeal historically associated with Democratic rather than Republican campaigns, and if it succeeded in triggering old and deep-rooted cultural hostilities which were latent but not extinct, it should follow that the greatest pro-Democratic deviations from the norm should be associated precisely with the areas having the longest, most durable "standing decision" favoring the Republicans. In such circumstances, in other words, the Z scores should be highest in areas originally settled by New England Yankees, and proportionately lower in areas of different settlement but equally heavy 1932–1960 Republicanism. As Table 23.10 indicates, just such a pattern emerges in New York, a state fortunately blessed with early census data necessary for the comparison.[27]

Table 23.10 The 1964 Election and the Influence of Original Settlement Patterns: The Case of New York State

Type of County	Z Scores, 1964					N	Mean Z by Type of County
	0 to +1.99	+2.00 to +2.99	+3.00 to +3.99	+4.00 to +4.99	+5.00 & Over		
New York City	4	1	—	—	—	(5)	1.36
New York suburban	—	—	4	—	—	(4)	3.47
Upstate metropolitan	—	1	5	4	—	(10)	3.71
Upstate non-metropolitan:							
"Yorker" & mixed (1845)	—	2	9	2	2	(15)	3.94
"Yankee" & Pa. (1845)	—	—	—	4	24	(28)	7.00
Total	4	4	18	10	26	(62)	2.71

As is evident from this array, New York City showed a pro-Democratic displacement in 1964 which was by far the lowest in the state; indeed, it corresponded almost exactly to the national figure. The suburban, upstate metropolitan and nonmetropolitan, non-Yankee counties occupied roughly the same intermediate position, with means in all these categories falling below +4.00. The counties of original New England and Pennsylvania–New England settlement, on the other hand, showed an extraordinarily high and uniform 1964 Z-score displacement. Of the twenty-four counties in the nineteenth-century "Burned-over district," for example, fourteen had 1964 Z scores of over +6.00, compared with +1.27 for the country as a whole and +4.36 for the two most "Yankee" of the New England states, Maine and Vermont. Eight of the remaining thirty-eight counties in New York also had displacements of more than +6.00. Of these, all but one were known areas of transplanted New England settlement, and two of them — Madison and St. Lawrence — played unusually prominent roles in the social-reform politics of a century ago.[28] It thus seems reasonable to suppose, especially when the nonmetropolitan counties are compared, that the New York voting outcome in 1964 was heavily influenced by factors associated with local political subcultures which have not yet evaporated after more than a century.

The ethnocultural cleavages arising out of original settlement patterns in New York and their influences on the state's politics have been so prominent that they have given rise to a substantial literature.[29] Broadly speaking, the most significant original cleavage was between "Yankees" and "Yorkers," that is, between those of New England ancestry who mostly settled in western New York and descendants of the Dutch who were concentrated in the Hudson and Mohawk valleys. As is well known, the Yankees in time developed an extreme social and political activism which reached its culmination during the political realignments of the 1850s. The area west of a line drawn from Binghamton to Watertown, for example, became known throughout the country as the "Burned-over district" because of the endless succession of religious, social and political reform movements which flourished there.[30] Politically, the areas of Yankee settlement were prominent in their support for anti-Masonry, abolitionism and eventually Republicanism. Other major groups, such as the Yorker Dutch and the Irish-German immigrants concentrated in the cities, not only had

Table 23.11   Relationships Between 1856 and 1964: The Case of New York

% R of 3-Party Vote, 1856	County Z Scores, 1964*				Total N
	0 to +2.99	+3.00 to +3.99	+4.00 to +5.99	+6.00 & Over	
20.0–29.9	4	3	1	—	8
30.0–39.9	1	7	1	—	9
40.0–49.9	1	6	2	1	10
50.0–59.9	1	—	7	8	16
60.0 and Over	—	1	3	13	17
Total	7	17	14	22	60

*Based on mean derived from the Democratic percentage of the two-party vote, 1932-1960.

no such urge to reform but were profoundly antagonized by the Yankees who did.[31] It was in this period, more than a century ago, that the foundations were laid for a cleavage which was destined to rival and then supplant the primordial Yankee-Yorker antagonism: the cleavage between New York City and the upstate counties.

Thus the relative 1964 displacements seem to have a visible relationship to a still earlier alignment era than that of the "system of 1896," that is, to the era in which the Republican party itself was born out of these antagonisms and the larger rivalries between North and South. For purposes of analysis, the 1856 election in the Middle Atlantic states seems a particularly useful point of departure. In this election old-line Whigs, for whom the slavery-containment issue was not salient and who were probably not predominantly of New England rural origin, voted in large numbers for a third party, the American or Know-Nothing party. The Democratic following established during the earlier second-party system remained largely intact, except in some areas of the New England diaspora; it was, indeed, later to be augmented considerably by former Whigs who had voted for Fillmore in 1856. The original Republican groupings, which were evidently heavily concentrated in the New England diaspora, carried the state in 1856 with 46.3 percent of the total vote.

As is evident from Table 23.11, there is considerable positive relationship between the original distribution of Republican support in New York and the relative magnitude of the pro-Democratic displacements which occurred in 1964. While many far more contemporarily-grounded factors were doubtless at work in 1964, a significant subcultural differentiating factor also existed. A comparison of the 1860 referendum proposal to enfranchise Negroes — a major symbolic point of early political cleavage with contemporary overtones — with early percentages Republican and 1964 Z scores underlines the point. The r of county percentages in favor of the proposed enfranchisement and percentages Republican was +0.85 for 1856 and +0.90 for 1860.[32] A rank ordering of the 1856 Republican percentage of the three-party vote and 1964 Z scores by counties yields an r_s of +0.73; the corresponding r_s for the 1860 enfranchisement amendment and 1964 Z yields an almost identical result, +0.74.

It should not be inferred from this discussion that the 1856 election is regarded here as *uniquely* close in relationship to 1964 displacements in New York, any more than that 1896 is regarded as *uniquely* close in national voter response to the 1964 outcome.

In all probability, the relationship is closer between 1964 Z and 1856 than between it and any other election down to the emergence of modern alignments in the 1930s. But it is also very likely that there is a stronger relationship between most or all elections in the 1928–1948 period and 1964 Z than between any earlier elections and that measure. Once again, the question arises of what is being measured here.

Leaving aside the possibility that some inflation of post-1932 relationships with 1964 Z may arise from autocorrelation, the 1940 result in Table 23.12 can be explained as the product of peculiar systemic factors which have been a conspicuous aspect of recent New York political life. In large part, it is probably an artifact of the standing political antagonism between New York City and upstate New York. As a recent study of New York politics has pointed out, there has been a clear long-term tendency for massive increases in city Democratic majorities to be met by equally massive increases in upstate Republican majorities, thus preserving close statewide competition while modifying the bases of party support.[33] One consequence of this has been that post-1932 upstate New York has remained quite abnormally Republican, considering the

Table 23.12   Relationships Between County Z Scores, 1964, and Republican Percentages of the Vote in Selected Elections: The Case of New York State

Election Pair 1964 Z and	r =	$r^2 \times 100 =$
1856	+0.73	53.29
1860	+0.72	51.84
1880	+0.60	36.00
1900	+0.46	21.16
1920	+0.58	33.87
1940	+0.86	73.96
1960	+0.69	47.61

high levels of urbanization found in many parts of this region.[34] It can be implied from this latter observation that the city–upstate polarization has tended to reinforce many original voting alignments, and that class politics has probably been less salient in upstate New York than in most other parts of the North since the 1930s. If this explanation is correct, one would in fact anticipate that the net effect of the realignments of the 1920s and 1930s, as measured in terms of the 1964 Z score, would be to produce correspondences as high as or higher than those associated with the mid-nineteenth century. All things considered, the point remains that the electoral displacements of 1964 are remarkably associated in New York with intrastate political divisions which can be traced back to the first instance in which New England subculture became a solidary

Table 23.13   Urbanization, 1856 Republican Support, and 1964 Z Score Displacements: The Case of New York State

% Urban, 1960	1856 Republican Percentage of 3-Party Vote			
	Below State Mean		Above State Mean	
	Mean 1964 Z	N	Mean 1964 Z	N
100.00 (New York City)	1.52	4	None	—
80.00-99.9	3.62	4	3.62	2
50.0-79.9	3.43	4	5.10	9
40.0-49.9	3.40	3	5.79	11
30.0-39.9	4.37	2	8.09	9
0-29.9	3.68	6	7.25	6
Average of county means:	3.27	23	6.30	37

force in the state's politics. As Table 23.13 shows, this relationship also holds up when such variables as levels of urbanization are held constant.

The same analysis produces quite similar, though somewhat less sharply defined, results when it is applied to Pennsylvania. An arraying of the Keystone

State's counties by the magnitude of their 1964 Z-score displacements produces a sharp geographical cleavage within the state. The top quartile (range: +4.21 to +9.43) is overwhelmingly concentrated in the extreme northern and northwestern counties. The bottom quartile (range: +1.02 to +2.09) is, with the major exception of Allegheny County (Pittsburgh), predominantly located in south-central Pennsylvania. The two middle quartiles are broadly distributed in the regions situated between these extremes, and in the Philadelphia metropolitan area.

Those familiar with the historical geography of Pennsylvania can easily recognize this as the most recent manifestation of a very old cleavage pattern within the state. The quartile of counties with the highest 1964 Z scores generally forms a compact area which has been closely identified with two major patterns of settlement and culture for more than a century: the New England–Yankee subculture and the Scots-Irish Presbyterians who settled west of the mountains. It was in this area that the strength of political anti-slaveryism was concentrated; for example, the congressional district represented by the author of the Wilmot Proviso was located here. Since the 1850s this region has remained a Republican bastion, except in the very few areas — such as Erie County — in which heavy industry has subsequently developed. Similarly, with the major exception of the area around Pittsburgh, the quartile of counties showing the greatest relative resistance to the anti-Republican swing of 1964 is largely coterminous with the Pennsylvania Dutch country.

Table 23.14 The 1964 Election and the Influence of Original Settlement Patterns: The Case of Pennsylvania

| | Z Scores, 1964 | | | | | |
Type of County	0 to + 1.99	+ 2.00 to + 2.99	+ 3.00 to + 3.99	+ 4.00 & Over	N	Mean Z by Type of County
Philadelphia metropolitan	—	3	—	2	(5)	3.21
Pittsburgh metropolitan	1	1	2	—	(4)	2.83
Other metropolitan	3	5	2	3	(13)	2.78
Non-metropolitan:						
Less than 32% R, 1856	6	10	4	2	(22)	2.63
More than 32% R, 1856	1	1	8	11	(21)	4.66
Total	11	20	16	18	((65)	3.61

The antagonism between these regions and the subcultures which have dominated them goes back in history about as far as similar divisions in New York. Wherever they settled, the Yankees tended to be strongly reformist and socially activist a century ago, particularly where such issues as free public education and slavery were concerned.[35] The Pennsylvania Germans, like their Dutch and Irish counterparts in New York, were well known for their insularity and their hostility to positive state action in such areas. Unfortunately, we do not possess early census data for this state, or such referenda as the New York proposals of 1846, 1860, and 1869 to grant full suffrage to Negroes. But the historical record leaves little doubt that these Germans a century ago were far more likely to be anti-Negro, on the whole, than anti-southern or anti-slavery in their attitudes. The Democratic gubernatorial candidate of 1863 probably spoke for many of them when he said that if ever the country were to be divided, he wanted the line of division to run north of Pennsylvania. If one examines the county array in a mode similar to that employed in Table 23.10, but with non-metropolitan counties dichotomized relative to their location above or below the state mean percentage Republican in 1856 (32.0 percent of the three-party vote), the following pattern emerges.

Table 23.15 Urbanization, 1856 Republican Support and 1964 Z-Score Displacements: The Case of Pennsylvania

| | 1856 Percentage Republican of 3-Party Vote | | | |
| | Below State Mean | | Above State Mean | |
% Urban, 1960	Mean 1964 Z	N	Mean 1964 Z	N
75.0-100.0	2.16	2	3.22	6
60.0-74.9	2.90	8	3.47	2
45.0-59.9	2.26	5	4.01	5
30.0-44.9	2.63	6	4.00	8
0-29.9	2.75	12	4.87	10
Average of County Means	2.65	33	3.94	31

*Intervals in percentage urban differ somewhat from those in Table 23.13 in order to provide adequate numbers of counties in each category.

As is evident, there are marked differences between New York and Pennsylvania which have the net effect of producing a more diffuse 1964 displacement in the latter state than in the former. In particular, there is far less evidence of sharp difference between major metropolitan and outstate displacements in Pennsylvania than in New York. Several of the suburban Philadelphia counties, in fact, had higher 1964 Z scores than any upstate New York metropolitan area. Conversely, very few Pennsylvania counties had displacements of +6.00: four out of sixty-seven in this state, compared with twenty-two out of sixty-two in New York. Even so, the differential pattern of response in the nonmetropolitan counties tends to indicate a considerable similarity with that of like counties in New York. It seems considerably more than by chance that, of the thirty-one counties showing a Z score of less than +3.00 in 1964, twenty-two had given less than 30 percent of their vote to the first Republican presidential candidate, or that twelve of the eighteen counties with 1964 Z scores in excess of +4.00 gave 48 percent or more of their total vote to Fremont. The same general point is made — analogous but more diffuse displacement patterns — by the derivation of a rank-order correlation of +0.61 between 1856 percentage R and 1964 Z. It also emerges when current levels of urbanization are controlled.

Thus in Pennsylvania as in New York, counties with the oldest Republican "standing decisions" tended to be the most massive 1964 defectors from the Republican candidate. In Pennsylvania as in New York, such counties tended to be historically associated with original settlement by people of New England culture.

It is also of interest to compare the rank-ordering of county percentages Republican with 1964 Z for the two states. Quite dissimilar patterns emerge. While the initial correspondence of 1856 and 1964 Z was lower in Pennsylva-

Table 23.16 Spearman Rank-Order Correlations of County Percentages Republican and 1964 Z Scores: A Comparison of Pennsylvania and New York

Pennsylvania		New York	
Election Pair 1964 Z and	$r_S =$	Election Pair 1964 Z and	$r_S =$
1856	+ 0.61	1856	+ 0.73
1866 (gov.)	+ 0.39	1860	+ 0.72
1892	+ 0.35	1880	+ 0.61
1908	+ 0.30	1900	+ 0.54
1920	+ 0.49	1920	+ 0.57
1928	+ 0.13	1928	+ 0.81
1936	+ 0.43	1936	+ 0.85
1940	+ 0.44	1940	+ 0.80
1952	+ 0.16	1952	+ 0.62
1960	− 0.09	1960	+ 0.76

nia than in New York, it remained higher within this state than for any subsequent election in this array, including post-1932 elections. The New York pattern, on the other hand, tends to display a markedly higher correspondence between 1964 Z and *all* preceding elections than is the case in Pennsylvania. Again, it seems reasonable to suppose that the most significant differentiating factor between the two states is the existence of city-upstate antagonism as an intervening and reinforcing variable in New York and its relative absence in Pennsylvania. They share in common a strong relationship between 1964 Z and the distribution of partisan preferences in the remote past.

IV

In their study of the 1948 campaign in Elmira, the authors of *Voting* mention the existence of a "Republican atmosphere" that contributes significantly to voting outcomes in this community.[36] Much work urgently needs to be done to develop this concept further and fully to operationalize it. If such an atmosphere exists as a major determinant variable in voting, this of course does not presuppose absolute stability in the ethnocultural composition of a given community over time. But if the concept has any meaning — and the findings of this study suggest that it has a great deal — it would imply that the persistence of the cultural norms on which the atmosphere rests probably requires broad long-term continuities in local ethnocultural distributions. In any case, short-term population shifts ought not to be so massive or heterogeneous as to destroy the capacity of the existing norm structure to socialize newcomers, whether migrants or the young of the community. Moreover, it would seem a logical inference from this argument, and one which this study tends to support, that there will be various *kinds* of "Republican atmospheres" in predominantly Republican areas, depending on the nuances of the local political subcultures involved.

The evidence developed here supports the view that the 1964 election was to a striking degree a conflict, laden with political symbolism, between regional political subcultures whose recurrent antagonisms form so much of the stuff of

American political history. The symbolism developed by the Republican campaign was archaic: many of the themes of sectional and subcultural conflict on which the Goldwater campaign played had not been seen in explicit form in a national campaign for many decades. Moreover, there is good reason to believe, both on qualitative and quantitative grounds, that the internal convulsions within the Republican party in 1964 had more in common with those afflicting the pre-1932 Democrats than with those which have occurred in the course of the GOP's own historical development. It is worth recalling again that the alignment pattern in a typical county with a high and positive 1964 Z score had survived two national party realignments and several major crises in the larger society such as the economic crises of 1893 and 1929, and both world wars — with very little change, and that in a Republican direction.

At least two preliminary conclusions arise from this. First, the data suggest both the existence, and occasionally the extreme salience, of durable community political norms which have their historical origins in the values of the original settlers and their descendants. Secondly, the evidence clearly indicates that mass political alignments may fluctuate very widely in response to electoral stimuli, but that they do not fluctuate at random. Put another way, it appears that at any given time there is a dominant or overt cleavage or set of cleavages, but that there are also latent or suppressed cleavages which may endure for decades without losing their capacity to influence voting outcomes. Such cleavages can suddenly be brought into clear view long after they were thought to have become extinct or only of antiquarian interest, and with little regard to intervening, even long-standing, partisan balances in the communities in question.

Whether this phenomenon of multiple latent voting cleavages has always been a feature of American political life, or has come into view only during the past generation or so, is an open question to which no definitive answer can be given at our current level of knowledge. It does seem clear that there has been a series of sharp, if not radical, changes in the salience of major factors involved in political coalition-building since World War II. As *The American Voter* demonstrates, for example, status polarization was quite sharp in 1948, but severely declined in 1952 and 1956.[37] In 1960, in turn, the activation of religious-group antagonisms was of great importance to the outcome. Among other things, it reactivated a Catholic group-involvement frame of reference which was quite unexpected in terms of survey work done during the 1950s. As Philip Converse points out,[38]

> We note immediately that in 1958 the gradients of party preference as a function of both involvement measures were entirely degenerate: either there was no relationship at all or a nonmonotonic progression which summed to a weak positive relationship. On the basis of 1956 data we had once surmised that such seedy patterns as were present at that time in the Catholic instance must reflect the late stages of a decline in group political relevance. . . . [t]he events of 1960 dramatically resuscitated the correlation between involvement terms and at least momentary partisan choice.

In 1964, as both survey and aggregate data abundantly demonstrate, powerful regional or sectional frames of reference produced a similarly dramatic, unexpected result.

In all probability, the phenomenon which Converse describes applies far more generally than has been commonly supposed. If the argument to this point has validity, there appears to be virtually no time limit between a point in political history marked by any given "correlation between involvement terms and ... partisan choice," and a subsequent election whose specific stimuli reactivate that correlation positively or negatively. This, perhaps, may be argued to assume too close an assimilation between the findings of aggregate analysis and survey research. In point of fact, however, it is not easy to see how the community displacements examined above — and reflected, for that matter, in the 1964 SRC sample — can be adequately conceptualized or even tentatively explained without reference to activated group-related involvements among large parts of the community electorate. Part of the problem rests with attempting *any* temporal analysis which takes us back before the beginning of systematic survey analysis. We cannot even be *absolutely* sure, for example, that the Catholic group relevance described by Converse for 1960 was present at all in the 1928 election.[39] A second part of the problem involves the paucity of survey-research literature dealing with community "political atmospheres" and their influences in presidential elections, and a corresponding shortage of interview questions designed to trap regional or subregional attitudes derived from local political subcultures.

What still remains to be explained persuasively is the mechanism which produced such massive displacements as those which have been identified here. In the absence of any direct cross-sectional isolation of that mechanism or measurement of its force, we are left only with probabilistic inferences which may or may not be verified by subsequent, more intensive analysis. Among these is the strong likelihood that American voting behavior in the present era is cross-cut with a far richer mixture of overt and latent cleavages, cleavages of "ancient" and "modern" vintage, than has hitherto been supposed. This behavior appears to have a major and still largely unexplored dimension which, for want of a better term, may be called "political geology."[40]

V

Major implications, both for the understanding and for the substantive dynamics of American voting behavior, arise from such an hypothesis. While some of them are clearly speculative, they may prove useful as points of departure for further work in this area — if only to stimulate the asking of different questions than those raised here, and the giving of more satisfactory answers.

● *1. The Study of Voting Behavior*   It follows from the argument thus far that any theory of American voting behavior with explanatory power extending beyond an election or a decade must be firmly grounded in comparative analysis across both space and time. Moreover, a comprehensively satisfactory behavioral theory of voting in the United States will probably have to be constructed out of empirical research as a set of interrelated, conditional problem statements: if condition A exists, behavior pattern X will emerge; if condition B, pattern Y, and so on. The extraordinary variety in political stimuli and resultant mass voting behavior over the past twenty years suggests rather forcefully that the tentative model of nineteenth-century voting behavior developed by Lee Benson is probably still highly relevant for the study of such behavior in the last half of the twentieth.[41] That is, in the absence of any permanent, systematically-organized conflict within the society over the nature of the political regime or over the legitimacy of the capitalist economic system and the structure of social rewards and status derived from it, an extremely broad range of political conflicts on other dimensions can exist. Of these, ethnocultural and sectional conflicts, emerging from the clash of subcultures with sharply differing values and reference symbols, have historically been the most important. Such conflicts, as the 1964 experience reveals, are still quite capable of moving into at least temporary ascendancy.

Much contemporary research on American voting behavior begins from tacitly uniformitarian assumptions about the American voter. Yet it now seems that any such assumptions are problematical at best. It is very likely that generalizations about voting behavior at any level of analysis which are based on a limited span of observations in any dimension — across time, geographically, or by type of election situation — may prove to be partly or wholly invalid under circumstances other than those in which the generalizations were made. Researchers might well also study the possibility that current cross-sectional methods, including questionnaire construction, were developed without adequate reference to the kinds of deviant situations discussed here. This would hardly be either surprising or blameworthy, but it might lead to a poor fit between the sample and reality in the exceptional situation. Thus, in the 1964 Survey Research Center study, 67.5 percent of its panel said after the election that they had voted for Johnson. The discrepancy between this and the true figure for the electorate, 61.3 percent, is greater than the allowable margin of error for samples of this size.

Aage R. Clausen of the Center has recently reported a validation study which was made to identify the sources of error.[42] Clausen concludes that the most reasonable explanation for the overreporting was that the interview situation itself stimulated marginal nonvoters in the sample to vote.[43] But there is reason to believe that this explanation does not entirely account for the discrepancy. In particular, it takes no account at all of the fact that there was a marked geographic differential in the overreporting of the Democratic vote. To take the extreme regional case, the overreporting of the Democratic vote in the South was 11.5 percent, nearly twice the national average. Moreover, while there was nearly perfect correspondence between survey and aggregate outcomes in the southern metropolitan areas, the overreporting of the Johnson vote was over 20 percent in the nonmetropolitan areas of this section.[44] Thus, so far as Clausen's hypothesis is concerned, it requires still to be explained why the interview stimulus should have had such different gross effects within the South or between the South and the rest of the country.

Moreover, another possible source of error, not mentioned in the validation-study report, may be the geographical incompleteness of the probability-sample grid itself, *under the special circumstances* of *the 1964 election.* Necessarily, the most economical probability sample will be constructed on the tacit assumption that no extreme, geographically-concentrated discrepancies will develop in voter response to short-term campaign stimuli, a perfectly reasonable assumption in light of 1936–1960 experience. In 1964, however, such discrepancies suddenly appeared as major elements in voting behavior, and there is reason to believe that they were not picked up accurately within the existing grid. In particular, there were notable differentiations in southern voting patterns between the deep southern states which Goldwater carried (plus some adjacent areas in other states such as Florida) and the rest of the southern region. A detailed study of the grid in this region reveals, first, that a disproportionate portion of the sample was drawn in metropolitan areas or counties immediately adjacent to them, and, second, that the Deep South subregion was heavily underrepresented in the total regional sample. As to the latter, the Deep South contributed 25.6 percent of the total southern vote, but only 10 percent of the sample.[45]

There is no reason to believe — as there probably is with Clausen's hypothesis — that any long-term error factors of significance are necessarily associated with the geographical basis of this national sample. But it is clear that they were present in 1964 because of the heavy geographical partitioning involved in the election outcome, and probable that they would recur if a similar election were to occur. Had the Deep South been proportionately represented, for example, the response error in the southern region might well have been cut in half.

None of the foregoing discussion should be understood as in any way disparaging the great contribution of survey research to our knowledge of American voting behavior. It does suggest that many complexities and difficulties still exist which preclude any early claim that the study of this behavior has achieved the status of an exact science, whatever the method of study may be.

Table 23.17   Regional Differentials in Overreporting the Democratic Vote: 1964 SRC Study

Region	% D of 2-Party Vote (Aggregate)	% D of 2-Party Vote (SRC)		Pro-D Over-reporting		N
Northwest	68.4	74	(74.1)	6	(5.7)	(309)
Midwest	61.4	66	(65.6)	4	(4.2)	(358)
West	59.6	65	(65.2)	6	(5.6)	(181)
South	52.5*	64	(63.9)	11.5	(11.4)	(263)
Total	61.5*	67.5		6	(6.0)	(1111)

*These percentages assume that the vote for Alabama unpledged Democratic electors is credited to Johnson; the Clausen report evidently does also. Excluding these votes, the correct national percentage is 61.3, and in the South 51.8.

In any event, it would be most desirable now to take up the lead suggested by Peter H. Rossi nearly a decade ago and redirect our resources toward much more thorough examination of the influence of local subcultural variables on nationwide election outcomes.[46] It might even be possible to develop a series of intensive local surveys, with overall coordination at Michigan or elsewhere, which could parallel the nationwide studies and provide invaluable comparative frames of reference in the study of the same event.

The importance of aggregate data in further work on the American electorate need not be stressed here. Aggregate data, of course, give us an indispensable, "hard" set of universe boundaries against which the accuracy of all probability samples can be checked. More than that, however, all past aggregate data may be at least potentially relevant for the study of current voting behavior, granted the peculiar properties of the American voting system. While this may appear to place an enormous burden on scholarship, the recent construction of computerized aggregate-data archives should help to overcome it and result in a proliferation in the near future of long-needed longitudinal studies of electoral phenomena.

● *2. Continuity and Change in American Voting Behavior*   What are the substantive implications of this study? There are two lines of speculation which seem of particular relevance in light of the analysis attempted here. In the first place, it seems very likely that the intensity of the movements described above is associated with a quite exceptional penetration into the mass electorate of some form of political consciousness specifically related to the issues and candidates. Of course, there is no way to ascertain directly from aggregate materials what the nature of that consciousness is, but it is possible to construct a reasonable hypothesis involving it. Assuming that the massive deviations from the norm in 1964 were more than randomly related to the relative awareness of candidates and issues — especially among the older-stock, Protestant electorate in the Northeast — it follows that major short-term differentials in candidate and issue perceptions probably exist among mass electorates. In other words, it is probably useful to think of political consciousness or awareness in any given electorate in terms of its specific context.[47]

The degree of conscious self- or group-defense in the voting act is probably directly dependent upon the larger structure of partisan politics at any given time. If most Americans, most of the time, have tended to vote in accordance with a "standing decision," such behavior would inevitably appear to the observer to be traditionalist, ritualistic and probably indicative of a very low level of voter attention to the issues, candidates, or campaign styles of any specific election. The ritualized or routinized defense of group solidarity or family tradition reflects the peripheral role which politics and elections play in the lives of most Americans most of the time. It also reflects the nonideological, low-pressure political styles which normally dominate major-party organizations and election campaigns in the United States.

But there are at least two kinds of cases in which this norm does not apply. One involves the discrete and insular minority, such as the American Negro, which operates in the political arena under extreme conditions of adverse social pressure. In a multiparty system, Negroes would probably have constructed a *Verzuiling*-type of party some time ago; under such conditions their voting patterns would have tended to display the kind of extreme long-term stability associated with nationality or confessional parties in Europe. Lacking that option, this group is quite capable of moving with astonishing speed and uniformity from one of the major parties to the other, depending on the perceived existence and partisan locus of racist campaigning by one of the major-party candidates. Thus, for example, Negro wards in Baltimore showed an enormous pro-Republican displacement between the presidential election of 1964 and the gubernatorial election of 1966. The Democratic percentage of the two-party vote in these wards fell from 92.6 percent to 13.4 percent in the space of two years, producing a defection ratio of 85.5 compared with a ratio of 20.0 for the city's white wards. There is little question that the specific contexts of each of these elections — particularly the issue of race relations which surfaced in both — were decisive in producing such an extraordinary Negro swing between the parties.[48]

Movements such as these virtually presuppose a high order of issue consciousness among the group's members when the interests and values of the group itself appear at stake, and a very close relating of that consciousness and the voting act. It is particularly suggestive that such clear traces of perceived self- and group-related interest are to be found among a stratum of the population universally conceded to be among the most socially deprived in the nation. But group consciousness and its linkage to political behavior are not inexorably linked to superior education or affluence. It is a function of the structure of politics itself, and ultimately of the social context in which members of the group are formed. If that larger context is one of massive deprivation and constraint, and if the usual influence of cross-pressuring and overlapping memberships is weak or nonexistent, the group will have a far different set of political characteristics from the American norm and its members will have an exceptionally well-developed sense of political consciousness wherever group-related issues appear, as they do so frequently for Negroes.

Rather similar contextual dynamics may well underlie the large electoral movements associated with eras of critical realignment. Certainly there are fundamental differences in voting behavior between such transitional periods and the much longer, more "typical" stable phases of electoral alignments. It is not argued here that 1964 was a realigning election in the classic sense, such as the elections of the 1850s, the 1890s, and the 1930s. It did, however — as we have seen in detail — produce massive deviations from "standing decisions" in many parts of the country, and was otherwise associated with much the same kind of complex value and policy polarization which has been conspicuous in such elections. The areas of maximum displacement from the norm in 1964, as in earlier elections marked by similarly massive electoral shifts, were in all probability areas which were marked by an abnormally high level of public consciousness about issues, related in some way to the defense of threatened local values against external attack.

This would make sense in terms of a pluralistic contextual theory of political consciousness in the electorate. As Donald E. Stokes suggests, critical realignments are probably associated with a tendency for "position issues," those involving apparently clear alternative policy choices, to be much more visible to the mass electorate than usual. Conversely, "valence issues," those about which there are often no "sides," may be the more usual currency of American politics.[49] It is not surprising that when fundamental policy dissensus comes to the surface and is united with value dissensus among well-defined political subcultures, the result is political conflict which has an abnormal tendency to appear as "total" or zero-sum in character. The point is worth making here that such conflicts are just as integral a part of the evolutionary dynamics of American electoral politics as are the more usual, lower-pressure party contests. A working empirical theory of American voting behavior must include both and recognize that there are major differences between them. It is quite possible that a critical election — or one with many characteristics similar to such an election, such as 1964 — may involve the electorate at large in somewhat the same kinds of contextual dynamics for the short term which affect the contemporary Negro electorate on a more or less permanent basis.

The second set of speculative implications arising from this study involves the broader patterns of political development in the United States. The 1964 Republican campaign, with its many archaisms, seems to fit with difficulty into the hypothesis of American electoral development to which the late V. O. Key,

Jr., gave the name "dualism in a moving consensus."[50] The operational word in this phrase is the adjective "moving." It involves the proposition that issues which were once highly controversial receive some kind of resolution through the policy process over time, and that the resolution is confirmed and reconfirmed by successive elections won by the dominant coalition responsible for it. Eventually, after the opposition has come to accept this resolution — and especially after it has administered programs once associated with the heart of the controversy — the whole question becomes a matter of historical interest. New ranges of controversy develop elsewhere in this evolving policy continuum.

This view would thus seem to imply some form of stability and sequential development in electoral coalitions themselves. At the very least, throwbacks to earlier coalitional alignments, granted the growing nationalization of American politics, ought to be as far removed from the politically possible as a major-party campaign against the substance of domestic programs which have been in operation for more than thirty years. Yet just such a throwback did occur in 1964, and at both levels. This is not to say, of course, that there was no consensus emergent from the election concerning the broad issues associated with welfare-state policies. The lopsided election outcome involved a reaffirmation of it, in fact. But can it be said that the case for movement or progression has been as solidly made?

It seems much more likely that the phenomena which have been studied here represent not movement but a curious timelessness. They constitute one more range of data which suggest a remarkably static party system, one which lacks the patterns of sequential evolution or development which are to be found in the life cycles of other western democratic systems.[51] It would seem, among other things, that the contemporary American party system has found as yet no single organizing dimension for its cleavages which can definitely retire earlier cleavages to the history texts. In particular, it seems very likely that the realignments of the 1930s permitted the entry of class-based alignments into the mainstream of American voting behavior, but only to the extent of permitting them to compete with other and often older alignments.

We can so easily discover measurable parallels between discrete elections so far apart in time because American political history shows so few evidences of cumulative development. Such a history, and such a party system, could be expected to exist in a polity which has had a monolithic Lockean–liberal value consensus, but which has been preoccupied from its foundation with problems involving the national integration of diverse and often antagonistic subcultures. While it would be grossly misleading to assume that only a kind of stasis exists in American electoral politics, or to ignore the clear evidences of nationalization of political alignments in recent decades, cases such as 1964 suggest that we are still far from a completion of the national integration phase of political development. Until such time as this phase is completed, the rich and historically-textured diversity of campaign stimuli and voter response which has been described here will continue, in all probability, to be a major factor in the study and practice of American electoral politics.

NOTES

1 V. O. Key, Jr., and Frank Munger, "Social Determinism and Electoral Decision: the Case of Indiana," in Eugene Burdick and Arthur J. Brodbeck (eds.), *American Voting Behavior* (Glencoe, Ill.: The Free Press, 1959), pp. 281–299.

2 New York: Crowell, 1954, pp. 120–123.

3 See in particular the illuminating discussion by Erwin K. Scheuch, "Cross-National Comparisons Using Aggregate Data: Some Substantive and Methodological Problems," in Richard L. Merritt and Stein Rokkan, eds., *Comparing Nations* (New Haven: Yale University Press, 1966), pp. 131–167; Austin Ranney, "The Utility and Limitations of Aggregate Data in the Study of Electoral Behavior," in A. Ranney, ed., *Essays in the Behavioral Study of Politics* (Urbana: University of Illinois Press, 1962), pp. 91–102; and Nils Diederich, *Empirische Wahlforschung* (Köln: Westdeutscher Verlag, 1965), especially pp. 16–60.

4 These computations are based on the Republican percentage of the two-party vote by state, with some exceptions. For analytical purposes the combined Republican-Progressive percentage of the three-party vote is used for 1912, and the Republican percentage of the four-party vote for 1948. The 1892 election presents perplexing choices; here the Republican percentage of the two-party vote was used, except in Alabama, Florida and Mississippi, where the local political situation made a combined Republican-Populist percentage of the three-party vote the most reasonable selection. For the first three pairs, $N = 38$; for the fourth, $N = 44$; for the fifth to seventh, $N = 45$; for the eighth, $N = 46$; for the ninth to twentieth, $N = 48$; for the twenty-first, $N = 50$.

5 See, e.g., Walter Dean Burnham, "The Changing Shape of the American Political Universe," *American Political Science Review*, vol. 59 (1965), pp. 7–28.

6 Stanley Kelley, Jr., "The Presidential Campaign," in Milton C. Cummings, ed., *The National Election of 1964* (Washington, D.C.: Brookings, 1966), pp. 42–81. In a more journalistic vein, see Theodore H. White, *The Making of the President: 1964* (New York: Atheneum, 1965), pp. 325–345; Robert D. Novak, *The Agony of the GOP 1964* (New York: Macmillan, 1965), pp. 439–464.

7 Kelley, *op. cit.*, pp. 47–58; White, *op. cit.*, p. 346.

8 For discussions of these properties, see V. O. Key, Jr., "A Theory of Critical Elections," *Journal of Politics*, vol. 17 (1955), pp. 3–18; Walter Dean Burnham, "The Alabama Senatorial Election of 1962: Return of Interparty Competition," *Journal of Politics*, vol. 24 (1964), pp. 798–824.

9 The convention data for 1896–1952 are found in Richard Bain, *Convention Decisions and Voting Records* (Washington, D.C.: Brookings, 1960), and for 1964 in *Congressional Quarterly Weekly Report*, July 17, 1964, p. 1482.

10 E. E. Schattschneider, *The Semi-Sovereign People* (New York: Holt, Rinehart and Winston, 1960), pp. 78–85.

11 For a useful discussion of this statistical method, see Murray B. Spiegel, *Theory and Problems of Statistics* (New York: Schaum, 1961), pp. 73, 85–86. For this particular case, the formula is

$$Z = \frac{\text{percent deviation (1964) from mean (1932–1960)}}{\text{standard deviation (1932–1960)}}$$

12 For purposes of correlation, the raw Z scores have been converted here into points on a scale ranging from 0 to 100 (maximum negative to maximum positive).

13 Thus we find very low and sometimes negative correlations between 1964 Z and such sectionally-structured elections as 1904, 1920, and 1924, since the sectional ordering among the states (especially as between the Far West and the Northeast) was wholly different from that found in such elections as 1896, 1916, or 1932.

14 For a discussion of this measure, see Robert R. Alford, *Party and Society* (Chicago: Rand McNally, 1963), pp. 79–86. The data supporting the statement in the text are found on p. 352. Averaging the index of class voting in elections for which there are more than one sample, it is as follows: 1936, 15.5; 1940, 25; 1944, 18; 1948, 30; 1952, 20; 1956, 14.5; 1960, 14.5.

15 For a preliminary discussion of the five party systems which have existed in American history at the national level, see my Chapter 10 in William N. Chambers and Walter Dean Burnham, eds., *The American Party Systems: Stages of Political Development* (New York: Oxford University Press, 1967).

16 The *locus classicus* for this observation in the American context is V. O. Key, Jr., *Southern Politics in State and Nation* (New York: Knopf, 1949), pp. 298–311.

17 Schattschneider, *op. cit.*; see also his article, "United States: the Functional Approach to Party Government," in Sigmund Neumann, ed., *Modern Political Parties* (Chicago: University of Chicago Press, 1956), pp. 194–215.

[18] It should be noted that the stratification differentials in the three regions lumped together under "Rest of U. S." — Midwest, West, and South — were, in terms of this sample, extremely small.

[19] This radical pro-Democratic movement among higher-status voters in the Northeast was not matched by a corresponding shift among lower-status voters, except for Negroes. There is good reason to suppose that Goldwater's *relatively* good showing among lower-status whites in the cities, as compared with Nixon's 1960 appeal among the same strata, was at least partly influenced by "backlash" factors. On the whole, however, the net effect of this was not a Republican gain but a near duplication of the already lopsidedly pro-Democratic 1960 percentages.

[20] See Alford, *op. cit.,* pp. 79–86. Because the SRC study for 1964 was seriously far off the mark, especially in the South, it is probable that the "real" index of class voting in 1964 was considerably less than 18 for the nation as a whole.

[21] V. O. Key, Jr., "Interpreting the Election Results," in Paul T. David, ed., *The Presidential Election and Transition 1960–1961* (Washington, D.C.: Brookings, 1961), pp. 150–175. The formula may be expressed as $DR = [(x - y)/x]\ 100$, where x represents a given party's percentage of the two-party vote in one election, and y represents its vote in the following election. Obviously, if y is greater than x, the resultant figure represents accretion rather than defection. While in some parts of the country the 1960–1964 defection ratio may be somewhat inflated because of the special religious-group factors in 1960, this appears not to be a major factor either in New England or New York.

[22] Negro jurisdictions throughout the country showed a very distinctively heavy Republican defection ratio. In St. Louis, for example, eight predominantly Negro wards swung from 19.9 percent Republican in 1960 to 3.3 percent in 1964, with a Republican defection ratio of 83.4. Among the remaining twenty wards, on the other hand, the Republican percentage declined from 38.2 percent to 29.6 percent, a defection ratio of only 22.5.

[23] The defection ratio for the state as a whole was 34.0. It is perhaps worth noting in passing that, of the four residential boroughs of New York City, only one (Queens) had as large an absolute Democratic percentage of the two-party vote in 1964 as in 1936, despite the much higher statewide Democratic percentage in 1964. Twenty-six of the sixty-five assembly districts in the city (40.0 percent) had defection ratios below the national average of 22.4, while forty of the sixty-five (61.5 percent) fell below the state ratio.

[24] These are computed on a wholly geographical basis, i.e., without any attempt to weight the county units in terms of population proportions. The variances in Table 23.7 are based on Republican percentage of the two-party vote by county.

[25] While there is no easily derived set of quantitative scales for correlating regionalism with 1964 Z scores, a correlation between state percentage urban in 1960 and 1964 Z scores yields an r of $+0.30$, "explaining" 9 percent of the variance. Comparison of Tables 23.8 and 23.9 indicates that the positive relationship between region and 1964 Z is far higher than this. For the formula for Z, see note 11.

[26] In New York, for example, fourteen upstate counties had a variation from the 1932–1960 mean of less than one-half the national variation. All of them are heavily Republican, and have been so since 1856. Of the 217 counties in the Middle Atlantic and New England states — most of them also traditionally Republican — Goldwater won just five.

[27] The basic data for the 1845 New York census are taken from Q. L. Holley, ed., *The New-York State Register for 1845–1846* (New York: Disturnell, 1846), 1846 Supplement, p. 123. See also *Census of the State of New York for 1855* (Albany, N. Y.: Van Benthuysen, 1857), especially pp. 168–177. Counties with more than 10 percent of their 1845 native-stock population born in New England were included in the "Yankee" and Pa. column in Table 23.10, except for counties (Clinton and Franklin) in which the foreign-stock population was more than 20 percent of the total. To this group were added seven counties in Western New York which had less than 10 percent New England stock, but were also at least as heavily populated by other out-state elements, mostly from the northern tier of Pennsylvania. The remaining nonmetropolitan counties were classified as "Yorker and mixed."

[28] Madison County was the home of the prominent Abolitionist leader, Gerritt Smith. See Lee Benson, *The Concept of Jacksonian Democracy* (Princeton: Princeton University Press, 1961), p. 113. St. Lawrence County, known in the nineteenth century as "little Vermont," had originally been a Democratic bulwark before 1854, and was the home of Silas Wright, a leader of the more "radical," free-soil wing of the state Democratic party in the 1840s. In 1852 the Democrats won 48.4 percent of the total vote in the county, but only 15.0 percent in 1856. Thereafter its partisan alignments closely resembled Vermont's, as did its 1964 displacement.

[29] See, e.g., Dixon R. Fox, *The Decline of Aristocracy in the Politics of New York* (New York: Columbia University Press, 1919); Benson, *op. cit.,* for the period culminating in the 1844

election; and H. D. A. Donovan, *The Barnburners* (New York: New York University Press, 1925), for a study of the political forces leading to the 1848 Democratic schism and eventually to the realignments of the 1850s.

[30] The definitive account of this unique area and its movements is Whitney R. Cross, *The Burned-Over District* (Ithaca: Cornell University Press, 1950).

[31] A document which is particularly revealing of these antagonistic attitudes of New York City leaders to upstate rule after 1854 is Mayor Fernando Wood's proposal of 1861 for the secession of New York City from the state and the union. See Henry S. Commager, ed., *Documents of American History*, 5th ed. (New York: Appleton-Century-Crofts, 1949), pp. 374–376. New York County gave Lincoln 34.8 percent of the vote in 1860, contrasting with 61.8 percent in the dominantly "Yankee" counties north and west of Albany.

[32] County data for the 1860 referendum are found in *Tribune Almanac for 1861*, p. 41. One of the counties (Orange) failed to make a return in this referendum, so that for all computations involving it, $N = 59$.

[33] Ralph A. Straetz and Frank Munger, *New York Politics* (New York: New York University Press, 1960), pp. 55–67.

[34] *Ibid.*, pp. 39–41.

[35] See, e.g., Charles M. Snyder, *The Jacksonian Heritage: Pennsylvania Politics, 1833–1848* (Harrisburg, Pa., 1958). German antagonism to the free school law of 1834 was so intense that it materially contributed to a split in the Democratic party which caused Governor Wolf's defeat in 1835. See pp. 50–67.

[36] Bernard Berelson, et al., *Voting* (Chicago: University of Chicago Press, 1954), pp. 100–101. In the absence of systematic comparative community studies involving survey methods, of course, speculations involving this "atmosphere" can only be highly suggestive rather than definitive. See Peter H. Rossi, "Four Landmarks in Voting Research," reprinted in Frank Munger and Douglass Price, eds., *Reading in Political Parties and Pressure Groups* (New York: Crowell, 1964), pp. 343–344.

[37] Angus Campbell et al., *The American Voter* (New York: Wiley, 1960), pp. 346–350.

[38] Angus Campbell et al., *Elections and the Political Order* (New York: Wiley, 1966), pp. 109–111.

[39] See Ruth C. Silva, *Rum, Religion and Votes: 1928 Re-Examined* (University Park: Pennsylvania State University Press, 1962). In this study which is based on aggregate data at the state level only, Professor Silva argues forcefully — though not, in my opinion, persuasively — that neither religion nor attitudes toward prohibition were significant correlates of Al Smith's strength in 1928. The difficulty here seems to involve a level-of-analysis problem of the sort discussed by Scheuch (see note 3). Such a view of 1928 seems difficult to square with the reactivation mechanisms discussed by Converse for 1960.

[40] See, e.g., Daniel J. Elazar, *American Federalism: A View from the States* (New York: Crowell, 1966), pp. 79–140, for a good preliminary discussion of this concept.

[41] Benson, *op. cit.*, pp. 270–328.

[42] Aage R. Clausen, "Response Validity: Vote Report," unpublished Survey Research Center paper (January 1967).

[43] *Ibid.*, pp. 36–37. This explanation, which has considerable plausibility, raises the intriguing possibility that a considerable autogenerated error, concentrated among the most marginal, "know-nothing" parts of the electorate, infects not only the 1964 study but others as well. What effect, if any, this discovery may have on the substantive conclusions drawn from these studies about the properties of the American electorate remains unclear.

[44] It is sometimes considered bad form to attempt regional partitions of a nationwide probability sample. Leaving aside the fact that this was done in Angus Campbell et al., *The Voter Decides* (Evanston, Ill.: Row, Peterson, 1954), the justification for making the attempt here is the existence of major discrepancies involving one major region of the country: the Northeast so far as the distribution of the vote is concerned, and the South so far as overreporting of the Democratic proportion of the vote is concerned.

[45] The regions are the same as in the note for Table 23.8, except that Alaska and Hawaii are included in the aggregate totals for the West. Exclusion of them from the aggregate western vote would yield a Democratic percentage of 59.2 and a regional overreporting of 6.0 percent.

[46] It is difficult to disagree with Rossi's conclusion in light of the findings of this study:

> As research findings accumulate from sample surveys, knowledge about the major correlates of the phenomenon grows at the same time that the problems from research become more specific. In short, as more is learned the questions to be put to empirical test tend to become more pointed. Enough is learned about the topic to identify both the crucial problems to be studied and the crucial populations most suitable for settling such problems. The representative sample survey at this stage often becomes an inefficient design. What may be needed most at such stages in the history of research on

a given problem are a number of small, pointedly designed studies of crucial populations, rather than "shotgun" designs.

Munger and Price, op. cit., p. 339

[47] Indeed, this precise point emerges from Survey Research Center work which undertakes to compare political perceptions in one congressional district dominated by the visceral race issue and perceptions in the country as a whole during the 1958 election. See Warren E. Miller and Donald E. Stokes, "Constituency Influence in Congress," *American Political Science Review,* vol. 57 (1963), pp. 45–56.

[48] The Democratic candidate for governor in 1966 campaigned far more explicitly for the "white backlash vote" than Goldwater himself had done in 1964, and with some success. In Baltimore City the Democratic defection ratio, measured between the 1962 and 1966 gubernatorial elections, was 4.2 in white wards with a median 1960 income of $4000-5999, 27.5 in white wards with median income above $6000, and 79.1 in Negro wards. The citywide ratio was 32.0.

[49] Donald E. Stokes, "Spatial Models of Party Competition," reprinted in Angus Campbell et al., *Elections and the Political Order, op. cit.,* pp. 161–179.

[50] V. O. Key, Jr., *Politics, Parties and Pressure Groups,* 5th ed. (New York: Crowell, 1964), pp. 222–227.

[51] See, e.g., Robert A. Dahl's discussion of this point in R. A. Dahl, ed., *Political Oppositions in Western Democracies* (New Haven: Yale University Press, 1966), pp. 34–69.

Continuity and Change in American Politics:

Parties and Issues in the 1968 Election

Philip E. Converse / Warren E. Miller
Jerrold G. Rusk / Arthur C. Wolfe

24

In this article, the Survey Research Center team interprets public opinion survey data, as well as voting data, to bring into focus the three-party presidential campaign and election of 1968. Voters are seen as having responded to the candidacy of George Wallace as an "issue" candidacy — and to the candidacies of Richard Nixon and Hubert Humphrey largely as "party" candidacies. The authors note Wallace's appeal to young voters and point out that older voters — similarly discontented over the drive of blacks for racial equality, the inconclusive war in Vietnam, and crime and civil disorder — were less likely to vote for Wallace because their identification with one or the other major party was stronger than that of their younger counterparts. Thus the article draws attention to the stabilizing influence of a functioning two-party system even during a period of domestic conflict and political agitation outside the party system.

Without much question, the third-party movement of George C. Wallace constituted the most unusual feature of the 1968 presidential election. While this movement failed by a substantial margin in its audacious attempt to throw the presidential contest into the House of Representatives, in any other terms it was a striking success. It represented the first noteworthy intrusion on a two-party election in twenty years. The Wallace ticket drew a larger proportion of the popular vote than any third presidential slate since 1924, and a greater proportion of electoral votes than any such movement for more than a century, back to the curiously divided election of 1860. Indeed, the spectre of an electoral college stalemate loomed sufficiently large that serious efforts at reform have since taken root.

At the same time, the Wallace candidacy was but one more dramatic addition to an unusually crowded rostrum of contenders, who throughout the spring season of primary elections were entering and leaving the lists under circumstances that ranged from the comic through the astonishing to the starkly tragic.

SOURCE: Reprinted with permission from *The American Political Science Review*, vol. 63 (December 1969), pp. 1083–1105.

Six months before the nominating conventions, Lyndon Johnson and Richard Nixon had been the expected 1968 protagonists, with some greater degree of uncertainty, as usual, within the ranks of the party out of power. The nominating process for the Republicans followed the most probable script rather closely, with the only excitement being provided by the spectacle of Governors Romney and Rockefeller proceeding as through revolving doors in an ineffectual set of moves aimed at providing a Republican alternative to the Nixon candidacy. Where things were supposed to be most routine on the Democratic side, however, surprises were legion, including the early enthusiasm for Eugene McCarthy, President Johnson's shocking announcement that he would not run, the assassination of Robert Kennedy in the flush of his first electoral successes, and the dark turmoil in and around the Chicago nominating convention, with new figures like Senators George McGovern and Edward Kennedy coming into focus as challengers to the heir apparent, Vice President Hubert Humphrey.

No recent presidential election has had such a lengthy cast of central characters, nor one that was kept for so long in flux. And under such circumstances, there is an inevitable proliferation of "what ifs." What if Lyndon Johnson had decided to run again? What if Robert Kennedy had not been shot? What if George Wallace had been dissuaded from running, or had remained simply a regional states-rights candidate? What if Eugene McCarthy had accepted party discipline and closed ranks with Humphrey at the Chicago convention? What if Hubert Humphrey had handled the interaction with Mayor Daley and the Chicago demonstrators differently?

Strictly speaking, of course, there is no sure answer to questions of this type. If the attempt on Kennedy's life had failed, for example, an enormous complex of parameters and event sequences would have been different over the course of the campaign. One can never be entirely confident about what would have happened without the opportunity to live that particular sequence out in all its complexity. Nonetheless, given sufficient information as to the state of mind of the electorate during the period in question, plausible reconstructions can be developed which do not even assume that all other things remained constant, but only that they remained *sufficiently* constant that other processes might stay within predictable bounds. And answers of this sort, if not sacrosanct, carry substantial satisfaction.

One of our purposes in this paper will be to address some of these questions, as illuminated by preliminary analyses from the sixth national presidential election survey, carried out by the Survey Research Center of the University of Michigan.[1] An effort to develop answers gives a vehicle for what is frankly descriptive coverage of the 1968 election as seen by the electorate. At the same time, we would hope not to miss along the way some of the more theoretical insights which the peculiar circumstances of the 1968 election help to reveal. In particular, we shall pay close attention to the Wallace campaign, and to the more generic lessons that may be drawn from this example of interplay between a pair of traditional parties, potent new issues, and a protest movement.

The Setting of the Election

The simplest expectation for the 1968 election, and one held widely until March of that year, was that President Johnson would exercise his option to run for a second full term, and that with the advantages of incumbency and the support of the majority party in the land, he would stand a very good chance of winning, although with a margin visibly reduced from his landslide victory over Barry Goldwater in 1964.

We will probably never know what role public opinion may have actually played in his decision to retire. But there is ample evidence that the mood of the electorate had become increasingly surly toward his administration in the months preceding his announcement. When queried in September and October of 1968, barely 40 percent of the electorate thought that he had handled his job well, the rest adjudging the performance to have been fair to poor. A majority of Democratic and independent voters, asked if they would have favored President Johnson as the Democratic nominee had he decided to run, said they would not have. Affective ratings elicited just after the election for all the prominent political figures of the campaign showed Johnson trailing Robert Kennedy in average popularity by a wide margin, and lagging somewhat behind Humphrey and Muskie as well, among other Democrats (see Table 24.2). Given the normal head start that a sitting President usually enjoys in such assays of opinion, Johnson completed his term amid a public bad humor matched only in recent elections by the cloud under which Harry Truman retired from the presidency in 1952. It is correspondingly dubious that Lyndon Johnson could have avoided the embarrassment of defeat had he set his sails for another term.

Indeed, the pattern of concerns exercising the voters and turnover in the players on the presidential stage combined to produce a shift in popular preferences between 1964 and 1968 which was truly massive. It is likely that the proportion of voters casting presidential ballots for the same party in these two successive elections was lower than at any time in recent American history. Among whites who voted in both elections, a full third switched their party. Almost one Goldwater voter out of every five turned either to Humphrey or to Wallace four years later (dividing almost 3 to 1 for Wallace over Humphrey); at the same time, three in every ten white Johnson voters switched to Nixon or Wallace, with Nixon the favorite by a 4-to-1 ratio. A full 40 percent of Nixon's votes came from citizens who had supported Lyndon Johnson in 1964! Much of this flood, of course, came from Republicans who were returning home after their desertions from Goldwater.

Nevertheless, Democrats and Independents who had voted for Johnson and then turned to Nixon four years later made up nearly half of *all* the remaining vote switches, more than matching the combined flow of Johnson and Goldwater voters who supported Wallace, and almost equaling the total Wallace vote. The Johnson-Nixon switchers easily outweighed the flow away from Goldwater to Humphrey and Wallace, and the Republican presidential vote rose from 39 percent to 43 percent in 1968 as a consequence. At the same time, the loss of more than a quarter of the total Johnson vote to Wallace and Nixon was scarcely offset by the trickle of votes from Goldwater to Humphrey, and the Democratic proportion of the vote across the land dropped a shattering 19 percentage points from more than 61 percent to less than 43 percent.

Such a massive drain from the Democratic ranks establishes a broader parallel with 1952, for in both cases an electorate professing to be of Democratic allegiance by a considerable majority, had arrived at a sufficient accumulation of grievances with a Democratic administration as to wish it out of office, thereby producing what we have labeled elsewhere a "deviating election."[2] Indeed, the frantic motion of the electorate in its presidential votes between 1964 and 1968 may be ironically juxtaposed against the serene stability of party identifications in the country, for the overall proportions of self-proclaimed Democrats, Independents and Republicans have scarcely changed over the past twenty years, much less in the past four. Of course this juxtaposition calls into question the predictive value of party identification, relative to other kinds of determinants of the vote, and we shall undertake a more intensive discussion of this matter presently. For now, however, let us simply point out that while the inert distribution of party loyalties cannot by definition explain the complex flows of the presidential vote between 1964 and 1968, it was handsomely reflected in the 1968 congressional elections, as it has been in virtually all of the biennial congressional contests of the current era. Despite widespread dissatisfaction with Democratic performance, the Republican proportion of seats in the House rose only a minute 1 percent, from 43 in 1966 to 44 percent on the strength of the Nixon victory. Even at more local levels, the continuing dominance of Democratic partisanship across the nation is documented by the results of thousands of races for state legislative seats. Prior to the election, Democrats controlled 57.7 percent of all legislative seats. After the election, which saw contests for some or all seats in forty-three states, Democratic control had dropped from 4269 seats (or 57.7 percent) to 4250 seats (57.5 percent).[3]

In view of such continued stability of partisanship, it is clear we must turn elsewhere to account for the remarkable changes in voting at the presidential level between 1964 and 1968. The classic assumption is, of course, that such change must spring from some flux in "short-term forces" — the impact of the most salient current issues, and the way in which these issues interlock with the leadership options, or the cast of potential presidential figures in the specific year of 1968. These terms obviously best define the setting of the 1968 election.

When asked on the eve of the presidential election to identify the most important problem facing the government in Washington, over 40 percent of the electorate cited the war in Vietnam. The salience of this issue provided another striking parallel with 1952. In both presidential elections, widespread public discouragement with the progress of a "bleeding war" in the Far East, seen as initiated by a Democratic administration, was a major source of indignation.

But the Vietnam issue did not, of course, stand alone. Offering vivid testimony to another bitter current of controversy was a simple, though little-noted, pattern in the popular presidential vote itself: while some 97 percent of black voters in the nation cast their ballots for Hubert Humphrey, less than 35 percent of white voters did so. Thus the presidential vote must have been as sharply polarized along racial lines as at any time during American history.[1] One major irony surrounding this cleavage was the fact that it was the comfortable white majority that was agitating to overturn control of the White House, while the aggrieved black minority was casting its vote as one in an effort to preserve the partisan status quo.

Indeed, this irony is compounded when the role of the Vietnam issue is jointly taken into account. We have indicated above that the public was deeply impatient with the Johnson administration, in part because of the handling of the war. Blacks stood out as the major demographic grouping most exercised about the entanglement in Vietnam. They were more likely than whites to opine that the government should never have undertaken the military commitment there. They also were more likely to feel that American troops should be brought home immediately, a position not generally associated with the Johnson administration. Nonetheless, as Table 24.2 will document, Negro enthusiasm not only for Hubert Humphrey but for Lyndon Johnson as well remained high to the very end. It seems quite evident that when black citizens were making decisions about their vote, Vietnam attitudes paled into relative insignificance by contrast with attitudes toward progress on civil rights within the country; and that where such progress was concerned, the Johnson–Humphrey administration was seen as much more friendly than the other 1968 alternatives.

Because of the near-unanimity of the black vote, many of our analyses below have been focused on differences within the white vote taken alone.[5] At the same time, this treatment must not be allowed to obscure in any way the deep imprint of racial cleavage on the election outcome. The additional "between-race" variance in the vote, concealed when data are presented only for whites, remains extreme, and is a faithful reflection of the crescendo to which civil rights tumult had risen over the four preceding years. It should be kept in mind.

To say that Vietnam and civil rights were dominant issues for the public in 1968 is not equivalent, however, to saying that voter positions on these issues can account for the large-scale voting change we have observed for whites between 1964 and 1968. As the comparisons provided by Table 24.1 suggest, changes in public thinking about strategic alternatives in Vietnam or civil rights outcomes over this period were rather limited. Where Vietnam was concerned, opinion was somewhat more crystallized in 1968 than in 1964 but there had been no sweeping shift of sentiment from hawk to dove in mass feeling. On civil rights, the drift of white opinion had been if anything toward a more liberal stance, and hence can hardly explain a vote which seemed to vibrate with "blacklash." Thus public positioning on these two central issues taken alone seems no more capable of illuminating vote change from 1964 to 1968 than the inert partisan identifications.

What *had* changed, of course, was the public view of the success of Administration performance in these areas. As we have discussed elsewhere, throughout the 1950s citizens who felt the Republicans were better at keeping the country out of war outnumbered those who had more confidence in Democrats by a consistently wide margin, much as the Democratic party tended to be seen as better at keeping the country out of economic depression. In 1964, however, the pleas of Barry Goldwater for an escalation of the Vietnam War in order to produce a military victory served to frighten the public, and rapidly reversed the standing perception: by the time of the November election more people felt the Democrats were better able to avert a large war.[6] But this novel perception was transient. President Johnson himself saw fit to authorize an escalation of bombing in Vietnam almost immediately after the 1964 election. By the time of the 1966 congressional election, the balance in popular assessments had already shifted back to the point where a slight majority chose the Republicans as more adept in avoiding war. By 1968, exasperation at the handling of the war had increased sufficiently that among people who felt there was a difference in the capacity of the two parties to avoid a larger war, the Republicans were favored once again by a margin of two to one.

To the bungled war in Vietnam, the white majority could readily add a sense

Table 24.1 Comparison of Attitudes on Current Vietnam Policy and Racial Desegregation, 1964 and 1968, for Whites Only

"Which of the following do you think we should do *now* in Vietnam?
1. Pull out of Vietnam entirely.
2. Keep our soldiers in Vietnam but try to end the fighting.
3. Take a stronger stand even if it means invading North Vietnam."

	Pull Out	Status Quo	Stronger Stand	Don't Know, Other	Total
		Northern Democrats			
1964	8%	25	29	38	100%
1968	20%	39	35	6	100%
		Northern Republicans			
1964	8%	19	38	35	100%
1968	20%	39	36	5	100%
		Southern Democrats			
1964	8%	25	23	39	100%
1968	17%	36	38	9	100%
		Southern Republicans			
1964	10%	18	42	30	100%
1968	15%	29	48	8	100%

"What about you? Are you in favor of desegregation, strict segregation, or something in between?" (This was the fourth question in a series asking about others' attitudes toward racial desegregation.)

	Desegregation	Mixed Feelings	Strict Segregation	Other	Total
		Northern Democrats			
1964	31%	50	17	2	100%
1968	38%	45	14	3	100%
		Northern Republicans			
1964	32%	51	13	4	100%
1968	35%	50	10	5	100%
		Southern Democrats			
1964	12%	35	52	1	100%
1968	18%	45	30	7	100%
		Southern Republicans			
1964	15%	44	40	1	100%
1968	15%	60	20	5	100%

of frustration at a racial confrontation that had taken on increasingly ugly dimensions between 1964 and 1968. Although national opinion had evolved in a direction somewhat more favorable to desegregation, largely through the swelling proportions of college-educated young, some persistently grim facts had been underscored by the Kerner Commission report in the spring of the year: forbidding proportions of the white citizenry outside of the South as well as within it had little enthusiasm for the redress of Negro grievances to begin with. And even among whites with some genuine sympathy for the plight of blacks, the spectacle of city centers aflame had scarcely contributed to a sense of confidence in the Administration handling of the problem.

From Vietnam and the racial crisis a corollary discontent crystallized that might be treated as a third towering issue of the 1968 campaign, or as nothing more than a restatement of the other two issues. This was the cry for "law and order" and against "crime in the streets." While Goldwater had talked in these terms somewhat in 1964, events had conspired to raise their salience very considerably for the public by 1968. For some, these slogans may have had no connotations involving either the black race or Vietnam, signifying instead a concern over rising crime rates and the alleged "coddling" of criminal offenders by the courts. More commonly by 1968, however, the connection was very close: they were rallying cries for more severe police suppression of black rioting in the urban ghettos, and of public political dissent of the type represented by the Vietnam peace demonstrations at Chicago during the Democratic convention.

In view of these latter connotations, it is not surprising that people responsive to the "law and order" theme tended, like George Wallace, to be upset at the same time by civil rights gains and the lack of a more aggressive policy in Vietnam. Therefore it might seem redundant to treat "law and order" as a third major issue in its own right. Nevertheless, we have found it important to do so, even where the "order" being imposed is on black militants or peace demonstrators, for the simple reason that many members of the electorate reacted as though the control of dissent was quite an independent issue. This becomes very clear where support for blacks and opposition to the war are accompanied with a strong revulsion against street protest and other forms of active dissent. And this combination occurs more frequently than an academic audience may believe.

One would expect, for example, to find support for peace demonstrations among the set of people in the sample who said (a) that we made a mistake in getting involved in the Vietnam War; and (b) that the preferable course of action at the moment would be to "pull out" of that country entirely. Such expectations are clearly fulfilled among the numerous blacks matching these specifications. Among whites, however, the picture is different. First, a smaller proportion of whites — about one in six or seven — expressed this combination of feelings about Vietnam. Among those who expressed such feelings it remains true that there is relatively less disfavor vented about some of the active forms of peace dissent that had become customary by 1968. What is striking, however, is the absolute division of evaluative attitudes toward peace dissenters among those who were themselves relative "doves," and this is probably the more politically significant fact as well. Asked to rate "Vietnam war protestors" on the same kind of scale as used in Table 24.2, for example, a clear majority of these whites who themselves were opposed to the Administration's Vietnam policy located their reactions on the negative side of the scale, and nearly one-quarter (23 percent) placed them at the point of most extreme hostility.

Even more telling, perhaps, are the attitudes of these same whites toward the peace demonstrations surrounding the Democratic convention at Chicago, for in this case the protestors were given undeniably sympathetic coverage by the television networks. Keeping in mind that we are dealing here with only those whites who took clear "dove" positions on Vietnam policy, it is noteworthy indeed that almost 70 percent of those giving an opinion rejected the suggestion that "too much force" was used by Chicago police against the peace demonstrators, and the *modal* opinion (almost 40 percent) was that "not enough force" had been used to suppress the demonstration.[7]

Table 24.2 Average Ratings of Major 1968 Political Figures by a National Sample, November-December, 1968

	Total Sample	Non-South		South	
		White (N's of 785-843)	Black (N's of 54-64)	White (N's of 315-340)	Black (N's of 55-66)
Robert Kennedy	70.1	70.4	94.1	60.5	91.2
Richard Nixon	66.5	67.7	53.0	67.8	56.6
Hubert Humphrey	61.7	61.2	86.1	53.4	85.8
Lyndon Johnson	58.4	56.6	81.9	53.7	82.7
Eugene McCarthy	54.8	56.5	59.1	49.8	54.0
Nelson Rockfeller	53.8	54.4	61.6	50.7	53.5
Ronald Reagan	49.1	49.6	42.9	50.0	41.8
George Romney	49.0	50.4	48.3	45.6	50.2
George Wallace	31.4	27.7	9.4	48.2	13.2
Edmund Muskie	61.4	62.7	71.0	54.7	68.9
Spiro Agnew	50.4	50.9	37.7	52.9	42.4
Curtis LeMay	35.2	33.6	21.1	43.9	22.9

It should be abundantly clear from this description that the white minority who by the autumn of 1968 felt our intervention in Vietnam was a mistake and was opting for a withdrawal of troops turns out to fit the campus image of peace sentiment rather poorly. Such a disjuncture between stereotypes developed from the mass media and cross-section survey data are not at all uncommon. However, as certain other aspects of the election may be quite unintelligible unless this fact has been absorbed by the reader, it is worth underscoring here. This is not to say that the more familiar Vietnam dissent cannot be detected in a national sample. Among whites resenting Vietnam and wishing to get out, for example, a unique and telltale bulge of 12 percent gave ratings of the most extreme sympathy to the stimulus "Vietnam war protestors." Now this fragment of the electorate shows all of the characteristics expected of McCarthy workers or the New Left: its members are very young, are disproportionately college-educated, Jewish, and metropolitan in background, and register extreme sympathy with civil rights and the Chicago convention demonstrations. The problem is that this group represents such a small component (one eighth) of the 1968 dove sentiment on Vietnam being singled out here that its attitudes on other issues are very nearly obscured by rather different viewpoints held by the other 88 percent of the dove contingent. On the larger national scene, in turn, those who opposed Vietnam policy and were sympathetic to Vietnam war protestors make up less than 3 percent of the electorate — even if we add comparable blacks to the group — and law and order were not unpopular with the 97 percent.

In the broad American public, then, there was a widespread sense of breakdown in authority and discipline that fed as readily on militant political dissent as on race riots and more conventional crime. This disenchantment registered

maybe, the key concern was the "order"

even among citizens who apparently were sympathetic to the goals of the dissent on pure policy grounds, and everywhere added to a sense of cumulative grievance with the party in possession of the White House. Thus the "law and order" phrase, ambiguous though it might be, had considerable resonance among the voters, and deserves to be catalogued along with Vietnam and the racial crisis among major issue influences on the election.

While the 1968 situation bore a number of resemblances to the basic ingredients and outcome of the 1952 election, the analogy is far from perfect. In 1952, the public turned out to vote in proportions that were quite unusual for the immediate period, a phenomenon generally taken to reflect the intensity of frustrations over the trends of government. It is easy to argue that aggravations were fully as intense in 1968 as they had been in 1952, and more intense than for any of the elections in between. Yet the proportion turning out to vote in 1968 fell off somewhat from its 1964 level.[8]

Of course any equation between indignation and turning out to vote does presuppose the offering of satisfactory alternatives, and there was somewhat greater talk than usual in 1968 that the candidate options in November were inadequate. Certainly the array of potential candidates was lengthy, whatever the actual nominees, and our account of the short-term forces affecting the electorate would be quite incomplete without consideration of the emotions with which the public regarded the dramatis personae in 1968. Just after the election, respondents in our national sample were asked to locate each of twelve political figures on a "feeling thermometer" running from zero (cold) to 100° (warm), with a response of 50° representing the indifference point. Table 24.2 summarizes the mean values for the total sample, as well as those within relevant regional and racial partitions.

Numerous well-chronicled features of the campaign are raised into quantitative relief by this tabulation, including Wallace's sharply regional and racial appeal, Muskie's instant popularity and near upstaging of Humphrey, and the limited interest that McCarthy seemed to hold for Negroes compared to other Democratic candidates. At the same time, other less evident comparisons can be culled from these materials, although the reader is cautioned to keep in mind that these scores refer to the period just after the election, and not necessarily to the period of the spring primaries or the summer conventions.[9] This may be of particular importance in the case of the ratings of Eugene McCarthy. When respondents were asked before the election which candidate from the spring they had hoped would win nomination, over 20 percent of Democrats and Independents recalling some preference mentioned McCarthy. However, many of these citizens gave quite negative ratings to McCarthy by November, so it appears that some disenchantment set in between the primaries and the election.

The question of timing poses itself acutely as well where Robert Kennedy is concerned.

Taken at face value, the data of Table 24.2 imply that aside from the tragedy at Los Angeles, Kennedy should have been given the Democratic nomination and would have won the presidential election rather handily. Yet how much of this massive popularity is due to some posthumous halo of martyrdom? It seems almost certain that at least some small increment is of this sort, and that the harsh realities of a tough campaign would have eroded the bright edges of Kennedy appeal. Nevertheless, both in contested primaries and poll data of the spring period,[10] as well as in the retrospective glances of our autumn respondents, one cannot fail to be impressed by the reverberations of Kennedy charisma even in the least likely quarters, such as among southern whites or among Republicans elsewhere. And rank-and-file Democrats outside the South reported themselves to have favored Kennedy for the nomination over Humphrey by two-to-one margins, and over McCarthy by nearly three-to-one. Clearly a Kennedy candidacy could not have drawn a much greater proportion of the black vote than Humphrey received, although it might have encouraged higher turnout there. But there is evidence of enough edge elsewhere to suggest that Robert Kennedy might have won an election over Richard Nixon, and perhaps even with greater ease than he would have won his own party's nomination.

As it was, Humphrey received the mantle of party power from Lyndon Johnson and, with Robert Kennedy missing, captured the Democratic nomination without serious challenge. At that point he faced much the same dilemma as Adlai Stevenson had suffered in 1952: without gracelessly biting the hand that fed him, how could he dissociate himself from the unpopular record of the preceding administration? In 1952, Stevenson did not escape public disgust with the Truman administration, and was punished for its shortcomings. The 1968 data make clear in a similar manner that Humphrey was closely linked to Lyndon Johnson in the public eye through the period of the election. For example, the matrix of intercorrelations of the candidate ratings presented in Table 24.2 shows, as one would expect, rather high associations in attitudes toward presidential and vice presidential candidates on the same ticket. Thus the Humphrey-Muskie intercorrelation is .58, the Nixon-Agnew figure is .59, and the Wallace-LeMay figure is .69. But the highest intercorrelation in the whole matrix, a coefficient of .70, links public attitudes toward Lyndon Johnson and those toward Hubert Humphrey. Humphrey was highly assimilated to the Johnson image, and his support came largely from sectors of the population for which the administration had not "worn thin."

When we consider the relative strength of Kennedy enthusiasts as opposed to loyal Humphrey-Johnson supporters among identifiers with the Democratic party within the mass public, the line of differentiation that most quickly strikes the eye is the noteworthy generation gap. As we have seen above, Kennedy supporters enjoy a marked overall plurality. However, this margin comes entirely from the young. For Democrats under thirty, only about one in five giving a preconvention nomination preference picks Humphrey or Johnson, and Kennedy partisans outnumber them by nearly three to one. Among Democrats over fifty, however, Humphrey-Johnson supporters can claim a clear plurality.[11] The "wings" of the Democratic party that emerged in the struggle for the nomination had an "old guard" and "young Turk" flavor, even as reflected in a cross-section sample of party sympathizers.[12]

This completes our summary of the setting in which the 1968 election took place. We have seen that despite great continuity in party loyalties and a surprising constancy in policy positions of the public, there was an unusual degree of change in partisan preference at the presidential level by comparison with 1964. This change occurred in part as a response to increased salience of some issues, such as the question of "law and order," and in part because of the way in which contending leadership cadres had come to be identified with certain policies or past performance. The Democratic party lost, as quickly as it had won, its perceived capacity to cope with international affairs and the exacerbating war in Vietnam. Hubert Humphrey, long a major figure in his own right, could not move swiftly enough to escape his links with a discredited regime.

Let us now pursue some of the more obvious analytic questions posed by the general discontent among voters in 1968, and by the Wallace movement in particular. We shall first consider influences on the actual partitioning of the vote on election day, and then examine some of the attitudinal and social bases underlying the outcome.

Hypothetical Variations on the Vote Outcome

Impact of the Wallace Ticket

There were signs of some concern in both the Nixon and Humphrey camps that the success of George Wallace in getting his name on the ballot might divert votes and lower their respective chances of success. Nixon was more alarmed by the prospective loss of the electoral votes in the Deep South that Goldwater had won in 1964, while Humphrey was alarmed in turn by intelligence that Wallace was making inroads outside the South among unionized labor that had been customarily Democratic since the New Deal. At the very least, the Wallace ticket was responsible for the injection of unusual uncertainty in a game already replete with unknowns. Now that the dust has settled, we can ask more systematically how the election might have been affected if Wallace had been dissuaded from running.

Numerous polls made clear at the time of the election that Wallace voters tended to be quite disproportionately nominal Democrats, and data from our sample are congruent with this conclusion, although the differences were more notable in the South than elsewhere. For the South, 68 percent of Wallace voters considered themselves Democrats, and 20 percent Republicans.

Outside the South, proportions were 46 percent Democratic and 34 percent Republican. Yet these proportions taken alone do not address in any satisfying fashion what might have happened if Wallace had not run. In the first place, these partisan proportions among Wallace voters do not differ very markedly from those which characterize the regional electorates taken as a whole. Indeed, as we shall see, the overall association between partisanship and attitudes toward Wallace (the rating scale) shows Republicans slightly more favorable across the nation as a whole, although this fact is faintly reversed with blacks set aside, and the main lesson seems to be that the "true" correlation is of utterly trivial magnitude (.05 or less). More important still, however, is the obvious fact that Democrats voting for Wallace were repudiating the standard national ticket, as many as a third of them for the second time in a row. If Wallace had not run, we can have little confidence that they would have faithfully supported Humphrey and Muskie.

It is clear that the crucial datum involves the relative preferences of the Wallace voters for either Nixon or Humphrey, assuming that these preferences would have been the same without Wallace and that these citizens would have gone to the polls in any event. This information is available in the leader ratings used for Table 24.2. In Table 24.3 we have arrayed the total sample according to whether Humphrey or Nixon was given the higher rating, or the two were tied, as well as by the respondent's party identification. Within each cell so defined,

Table 24.3 Distribution of the Wallace Vote, by Traditional Parties and Candidates*

		Party Identification		
		Democratic	Independent	Republican
Rating of Two Major Candidates	Humphrey over Nixon	4% (347)	26% (23)	21% (24)
	Tied	24% (79)	9% (11)	6% (17)
	Nixon over Humphrey	26% (132)	15% (53)	7% (314)

*The percentage figure indicates the proportion of all voters in the cell who reported casting a ballot for Wallace. The number of voters is indicated between parentheses.

we indicate the proportion of the vote won by Wallace, and the number of voters on which the proportion is based. The latter figures show familiar patterns. Of voters with both a party and a candidate preference, more than four-fifths prefer the nominee of their party. And while Democrats are in a majority, it is clear that the tides are running against them since they are suffering the bulk of defections.

It is interesting how the Wallace vote is drawn from across this surface. While the numbers of cases are too small to yield very reliable estimates in some of the internal cells, it is obvious that Wallace made least inroads among partisans satisfied with their party's nominee, and showed major strength where such partisans were sufficiently disgusted with their own party nominee actually to prefer that of the opposing party. Conceptually, it is significant that these protestors included Republicans unenthusiastic about Nixon as well as the more expected Democrats cool to Humphrey. Practically, however, Nixon Democrats so far outnumbered Humphrey Republicans that while Wallace drew at nearly equal rates from both groups, the majority of his votes were from Democrats who otherwise preferred Nixon rather than from Republicans who might have given their favors to Humphrey.

This in turn provides much of the answer to one of our primary questions. While the data underlying Table 24.3 can be manipulated in a variety of ways, all reasonable reconstructions of the popular vote as it might have stood without the Wallace candidacy leave Nixon either enjoying about the same proportion of the two-party vote that he actually won or a slightly greater share, depending on the region and the detailed assumptions made. In short, unless one makes some entirely extravagant assumptions about the mediating electoral college, it is very difficult to maintain any suspicion that the Wallace intrusion by itself changed the major outcome of the election.

Impact of the McCarthy Movement

If he was ever tempted at all, Eugene McCarthy decided against mounting a fourth-party campaign for the presidency. At the same time, he withheld anything resembling enthusiastic personal support for Hubert Humphrey. In view of his devoted following, some observers felt that McCarthy's refusal to close party ranks after Chicago cost the Democratic nominee precious votes, and conceivably even the presidency.

In order to understand the basis of McCarthy support at the time of the election, it is useful to trace what is known of the evolution of McCarthy strength from the time of the first primary in the spring. It will be recalled that McCarthy was the sole Democrat to challenge the Johnson administration in the New Hampshire primary. With the aid of many student volunteer campaign workers, he polled a surprising 42 percent of the vote among Democrats, as opposed to 48 percent drawn by an organized write-in campaign for President Johnson. Although he failed to upset the President in the vote, most observers saw his performance as remarkably strong, and a clear harbinger of discontent which could unseat Lyndon Johnson in the fall election. This reading was plainly shared by Robert Kennedy, who announced his own candidacy for the nomination four days later, and probably by Johnson himself, who withdrew from any contention less than three weeks later.

Sample survey data from New Hampshire at the time of the primary show some expected patterns underlying that first McCarthy vote, but also some rather unexpected ones as well. First, the vote among Democrats split toward Johnson or McCarthy in obvious ways according to expressions of satisfaction or dissatisfaction with administration performance in general and its Vietnam policy in particular. The McCarthy vote in New Hampshire certainly reflected a groundswell of anger at the Johnson administration, and an expression of desire for a change which was simply reiterated in November. Surprisingly, however, in view of McCarthy's clear and dissenting "dove" position on Vietnam, the vote he drew in New Hampshire could scarcely be labeled a "peace vote," despite the fact that such a conclusion was frequently drawn. There was, of course, some hard-core peace sentiment among New Hampshire Democrats that was drawn quite naturally to McCarthy. Among his supporters in the primary, however, those who were unhappy with the Johnson administration for not pursuing a *harder* line against Hanoi outnumbered those advocating a withdrawal from Vietnam by nearly a three to two margin! Thus the McCarthy tide in New Hampshire was, to say the least, quite heterogeneous in its policy preferences: the only common denominator seems to have been a deep dissatisfaction with the Johnson administration.[13] McCarthy simply represented the only formal alternative available to registered Democrats. This desire for an alternative was underlined by the fact that most of the 10 percent of the Democratic vote that did not go to Johnson or McCarthy went to Nixon as a write-in candidate on the Democratic ballot.

The entry of Robert Kennedy into the race did provide another alternative and, as we have seen, a very popular one as well. He made major inroads into the potential McCarthy strength, and by the time our autumn sample was asked what candidate of the spring would have been preferred for the Democratic nomination, 46 percent of those Democrats with some preference cited Kennedy first while only 18 percent mentioned McCarthy. Nevertheless, even this 18 percent cannot be thought of as constituting hard-core McCarthy support at the time of the actual election, since almost two-thirds of this group had turned their attention elsewhere, giving at least one of the other presidential hopefuls a higher rating than they gave McCarthy in the responses underlying Table 24.2. The remainder who reported McCarthy as their preconvention favorite and awarded him their highest ratings just after the election, make up some 6 percent of Democrats having some clear candidate preference, or 3 percent of all Democrats. Along with a handful of Independents and Republicans showing the same reiterated McCarthy preference, these people can be considered the McCarthy "hard core."

While it is this hard core whose voting decisions interest us most, it is instructive to note where the other two-thirds of the preconvention McCarthy support among Democrats went, over the course of the campaign. If these migrations are judged according to which presidential aspirant among the nine hopefuls of Table 24.2 was given the highest rating in November, one discovers that a slight plurality of these erstwhile McCarthy backers found George Wallace their preferred candidate in the fall. Slightly smaller groups favored Kennedy and Nixon, and a scatter picked other Republicans like Reagan and Rockefeller, despite their own Democratic partisanship. Very few of these McCarthy Democrats — about one in seven — migrated to a preference for Hubert Humphrey. Where the actual presidential vote was concerned, the choice was of course more constrained.

Since the McCarthy movement was commonly thought of as somewhat to the left of Humphrey and the administration, while Wallace was located rather markedly to the right, a major McCarthy-to-Wallace transfer of preferences may seem ideologically perplexing. Were McCarthy supporters so furious with the Humphrey nomination that pure spite overcame issue feelings and led to a protest vote for Wallace? Although there were rumors of such a reaction at the time, our data suggest a somewhat simpler interpretation. We have already noted the attitudinal heterogeneity of McCarthy voters in New Hampshire. Those in our autumn sample who recall a preconvention preference for McCarthy are similarly heterogeneous. Indeed, on some issues of social welfare and civil rights, preconvention McCarthy supporters are actually more conservative than backers of either Humphrey or Kennedy.

This heterogeneity declined markedly, however, as the size of the McCarthy group eroded over the summer to what we have defined as the hard core. If we compare the attitudes of that hard core on major issues with those of the professed early backers of McCarthy who subsequently supported Wallace, the differences are usually extreme. The McCarthy-Wallace group was against desegregation, in favor of an increased military effort in Vietnam, and was highly indignant with the situation in the nation where "law and order" was concerned (see Table 24.4). People supporting McCarthy to the bitter end took opposite positions on all of these major issues. Similarly, the winnowing down of the McCarthy support operated very sharply along demographic lines. Among nonsouthern white Democrats who reported a preconvention McCarthy preference, for example, the hard core that remained enthusiastic about McCarthy through to the actual election were 60 percent of college background, whereas, of those whose ardor cooled, only 18 percent had had any connection with college.

In short, then, it is evident again that among Democrats particularly, McCarthy was an initial rallying point for voters of all policy persuasions who were thoroughly displeased with the Johnson administration. When the Wallace candidacy crystallized and his issue advocacies became more broadly known,

Table 24.4 Issue Differences Among Whites Preferring McCarthy as the Democratic Nominee, According to November Preferences for McCarthy or Wallace

		McCarthy "Hard Core"*	Voted Wallace†
"Are you in favor of desegregation, strict segregation, or something in between?"	Desegregation	79%	7%
	In Between	21	50
	Segregation	0	43
		100%	100%
		(24)	(14)
"Do you think the [Chicago] police [at the Democratic Convention] used too much force, or not enough force with the demonstrators?"	Too Much Force	91%	0%
	Right Amount	9	50
	Not Enough	0	50
		100%	100%
		(23)	(12)
"Which of the following do you think we should do now in Vietnam: pull out of Vietnam entirely, keep our soldiers in Vietnam but try to end the fighting, or take a stronger stand even if it means invading North Vietnam?"	Pull Out	50%	7%
	Status Quo	50	7
	Stronger Stand	9	86
		100%	100%
		(24)	(13)

*This column is limited to whites whose preconvention favorite was Eugene McCarthy and who continued to give him their top rating after the November election.
†It is to be emphasized that this column includes *only* those Wallace voters who said that in the spring of 1968 they had hoped Eugene McCarthy would win the Democratic nomination. This fact explains the small case numbers. However, in view of the relative homogeneity of respondents in the table—all are whites who reported a preconvention McCarthy preference and most happen in addition to be nominal identifiers of the Democratic party—the disparities in issue position are the more impressive.

that portion of the discontented to whom he spoke most directly flocked to him. Hence it seems very doubtful that Humphrey would have won many votes from this group even if McCarthy had lent the Vice President his personal support in a wholehearted fashion. The main motivation of this group was to register its disgust with incumbent leaders concerning civil rights advances, timidity in Vietnam, and outbreaks of social disorder. It may well be that by September, with the far more congenial candidacy of Wallace available, Senator McCarthy would already have become a relatively negative reference point for this two-thirds of his early support, especially if he had joined forces with Humphrey. Therefore if we are to search for votes withheld from Humphrey because of the kinds of discontent McCarthy helped to crystallize, they are much more likely to be found among the McCarthy hard core.

We persist in looking for such withheld votes, not simply because of rumors they existed, but also because there are rather tangible signs in the data that they were present in 1968. Such votes could take any one of four major alternative forms: they could be located among citizens who went to the polls but did not vote for President; they could be reflected in votes for minor party candidates; they could involve staying at home on election day; or they could take the form of votes spitefully transferred to Humphrey's chief rival, Mr. Nixon. Easiest to establish as "withheld votes" are the first two categories. Although their incidence is naturally very limited, both types can be discerned in the sample and do occur in conjunction with strong enthusiasm for McCarthy. Projected back to the nation's electorate, perhaps as much as a half-million votes are represented here, lying primarily outside the South. This is only a faint trace when sprinkled across the political map of the nation, however, and taken alone would probably have made little or no difference in the distribution of votes from the electoral college.

It is more difficult to say that specific instances of abstinence from any voting in 1968, or "defection" to Richard Nixon, reflect an abiding loyalty to McCarthy that Humphrey could not replace, and would not have occurred but for the McCarthy intrusion. There is a faint edge of nonvoting that looks suspiciously of this sort, but it is again very limited: most ardent McCarthy fans were too politically involved to have thrown away a chance to vote at other levels of office. Far more numerous are the defections to Nixon on the part of voters of liberal and Democratic predispositions, who reported sympathy toward McCarthy. Here, however, it is difficult to be confident that McCarthy made any necessary contribution to the decision equation: the situation itself might have soured these people sufficiently, McCarthy or no. Nevertheless, when one begins to add together putative "withheld votes" from the preceding three categories one does not need to factor in any very large proportion of these defectors to arrive at a total large enough to have provided Humphrey with a tiny majority in the electoral college, without requiring any gross maldistribution of these newfound popular votes outside the South.

We should reiterate, of course, that any such hypothetical reconstructions must be taken with a grain of salt. If McCarthy had embraced Humphrey on the final night in Chicago, not all of his most fervent supporters would necessarily have followed suit, and Humphrey would have needed most of them for a victory. Or if Humphrey had catered more dramatically to the McCarthy wing in terms of Vietnam policy after the election, he might have suffered losses of much greater proportion to Wallace on his right, for there is simply no question but that Democrats sharing the circle of ideas espoused by Wallace outnumbered the Democrats attuned to McCarthy by a very wide margin — perhaps as great as ten to one. Moreover, it is appropriate to keep in mind our earlier suggestion that the Wallace intrusion hurt Nixon's vote more than Humphrey's: if we now remove Wallace as well as McCarthy from the scene, the net result might remain a Nixon victory.

However all this may be, it seems probable that the entire roster of prominent Democratic candidates — McCarthy, Wallace, Kennedy, McGovern — who were in their various ways opposing the administration, must have contributed cumulatively to Humphrey's problem of retaining the loyalty of fellow Democrats in the electorate. Certainly the failure of liberal Republican leaders to rally around the Goldwater candidacy in 1964, itself an unusual departure from tradition, had contributed to the Republican disaster of that year. 1968 provided something of a mirror image, and the result was an inordinate movement of the electorate between the two consultations.

The "Responsible Electorate" of 1968

In describing the current of discontent that swirled around the Democratic party and the White House in 1968, we indicated that disgruntled Democrats rather indiscriminately supported McCarthy in the earliest primaries, but soon began to sort themselves into those staying with McCarthy versus those shifting to Nixon or Wallace, according to their more precise policy grievances on the major issues of Vietnam, civil rights, and the problem of "law and order." By the time of the election, the sorting had become remarkably clean: in particular, differences in issue position between Wallace supporters and what we have called the McCarthy hard core are impressive in magnitude.

Even more generally, 1968 seems to be a prototypical case of the election that does not produce many changes of policy preferences but does permit electors to sort themselves and the candidates into groups of substantial homogeneity on matters of public policy. This trend over the course of the campaign calls to mind the posthumous contention of V. O. Key, in *The Responsible Electorate*, that the mass electorate is a good deal less irrational, ill-informed or sheeplike than it had become fashionable to suppose. He presented empirical materials to develop a counterimage of "an electorate moved by concern about central and relevant questions of public policy, of governmental performance, and of executive personality."[14] He argued that in a general way voters behaved rationally and responsibly, or at least as rationally and responsibly as could be expected in view of the pap they were frequently fed by contending politicians, while recognizing in the same breath that contentions of this unequivocal nature were necessarily overstatements.

To our point of view, Key's general thesis represented a welcome corrective on some earlier emphases, but his findings were hardly as discontinuous with earlier work as was often presumed, and the "corrective" nature of his argument has itself become badly exaggerated at numerous points. We cannot begin to examine here the many facets of his thesis that deserve comment. However, several features of the 1968 campaign seem to us to demonstrate admirably the importance of the Key corrective, while at the very same time illustrating vividly the perspective in which that corrective must be kept.

It is obvious, as Key himself recognized, that flat assertions about the electorate being rational or not are of scant value. In New Hampshire, as we have observed earlier, Democrats exasperated at Johnson's lack of success with the Vietnam War voted for Eugene McCarthy as an alternative. The relationship between this disapproval and the vote decision is exactly the type of empirical finding that Key musters in profusion from a sequence of seven presidential elections as his main proof of voter rationality and responsibility. In the New Hampshire case, however, we might probe the data a little farther to discover that more often than not, McCarthy voters were upset that Johnson had failed to scourge Vietnam a good deal more vigorously with American military might, which is to say they took a position diametrically opposed to that of their chosen candidate. This realization might shake our confidence somewhat in the preceding "proof" of voter rationality. But then we push our analysis still another step and find that many of the New Hampshire people fuming about Vietnam in a hawkish mood voted for McCarthy without having any idea of where he stood on the matter. Hence while they may have voted directly counter to their own policy preferences, they at least did not know this was what they were doing, so the charge of irrationality may be a bit ungenerous. In the most anemic sense of "rationality," one that merely implies people have perceived reasons for their behavior, these votes perhaps remain "rational."

However, when we reflect on the rather intensive coverage given by the national mass media to Eugene McCarthy's dissenting position on Vietnam for many months before the New Hampshire primary, and consider how difficult it must have been to avoid knowledge of the fact, particularly if one had more than the most casual interest in the Vietnam question, we might continue to wonder how lavishly we should praise the electorate as "responsible." Here, as at so many other points, pushing beyond the expression of narrow and superficial attitudes in the mass public to the cognitive texture which underlies the attitudes is a rather disillusioning experience. It is regrettable that none of the data presented in *The Responsible Electorate* can be probed in this fashion.

Key was interested in showing that the public reacted in a vital way to central policy concerns, at least as selected by the contending political factions, and was not driven mainly by dark Freudian urges, flock instinct, or worse still, the toss of a coin. With much of this we agree wholeheartedly. In addition, to put the discussion in a slightly different light, let us imagine, in a vein not unfamiliar from the literature of the 1950s, that voting decisions in the American electorate might be seen as a function of reactions to party, issue, and candidate personality factors. Let us imagine furthermore that research suggests that these determinants typically have relative weights in our presidential elections of 60 for the party factor, and 40 divided between the issue and candidate determinants. The exact figures are, of course, quite fanciful but the rough magnitudes continue to be familiar. Since classical assumptions about voting behavior have attributed overweening weight to the issue factor, it is scarcely surprising that investigative attention shifts heavily away from that factor to the less expected party and candidate influences. If the issue factor draws comment at all, the finding of greatest interest is its surprisingly diluted role.

It is at this point that the Key volume exerts its most useful influence. Key points out that there *is*, after all, an issue factor, and he develops an analytic format which dramatizes the role that issue reactions do play. This dramatic heightening is achieved by focusing attention on voters who are shifting their vote from one party to the other over a pair of elections. If we set for ourselves the explanatory chore of understanding why the change which occurs moves in the direction it did, it is patently evident that the party factor — which merely explains the abiding finding that "standpatters" persistently outnumber "changers" by factors usually greater than four — is to be set aside as irrelevant. If this in turn leaves candidate and issue factors sharing the explanatory burden, our sense of the relative importance of the issue factor is, of course, radically increased, even though it is our question that has changed, rather than anything about the empirical lay of the land. Key was quite explicit in his desire to explain movement and change in the electorate, rather than voting behavior in a more general sense, and there is no gainsaying the fact that from many points of view it is indeed the change — marginal gains and losses — which forms the critical part of the story of elections.

In our analyses of such changes in the national vote over the course of presidential elections in the 1950s and 1960s we have been impressed with the magnitude of the effects introduced as new candidates focus on different issues of public policy, and as external events give particular candidate-issue intersections greater salience for the nation.[15] However, 1968 provides an opportunity to examine relative weights of party, candidate, and issue factors under more varied circumstances than United States presidential elections usually proffer. We have talked above for illustrative purposes as though there were "standard" relative weights that would pertain for these three factors in some situation-free way. This is of course not the case: we can imagine many kinds of elections which would vastly shift the weights of such factors, if indeed they can be defined at all.

The Wallace movement is a good case in point. By Key's definition nobody who voted for Wallace could have been a "standpatter": all must be classed as "changers." Therefore party identification as a motivating factor accounting for attraction to Wallace is forced back to zero, and any variance to be understood must have its roots distributed between Wallace's attraction as a personality and the appeal of the issue positions that he advocated.[16]

In point of fact, the Wallace candidacy was reacted to by the public as an *issue* candidacy, a matter which our data make clear in several ways. For example, about half of the reasons volunteered by our respondents for favorable feelings toward Wallace had to do with positions he was taking on current issues; only a little more than a quarter of the reactions supporting either of the two conventional candidates were cast in this mode. Still more noteworthy is the relative purity of the issue feelings among the Wallace clientele where the major controversies of 1968 were concerned. Among the *whites* who voted for one of the two major candidates, only 10 percent favored continued segregation rather than desegregation or "something in between"; among Wallace voters, all of whom were white, almost 40 percent wanted segregation. Where the issue of "law and order" was concerned, a substantial portion of the voters felt that Mayor Daley's police had used about the right amount of force in quelling the Chicago demonstrations. However, among white voters for Nixon or Humphrey, the remainder of the opinion was fairly evenly split between criticizing the police for using too much force or too little, with a small majority (55 percent) favoring the latter "tough line." Among Wallace voters, the comparable ratio was 87–13 favoring a tougher policy. Or again, 36 percent of white voters for the conventional parties felt we should "take a stronger stand (in Vietnam) even if it means invading North Vietnam." Among Wallace voters, the figure was 67 percent. Much more generally speaking, it may be observed that all Wallace voters were exercised by strong discontents in at least one of these three primary domains, and most were angry about more than one. Wallace was a "backlash" candidate, and there is no question but that the positions communicated to the public and accounted for his electoral support in a very primary sense. The pattern of correlations betweeen issue positions and the vote for these "changers" would support Key's thesis of a "rational" and "responsible" electorate even more impressively than most of the data he found for earlier elections.

Another way of organizing these preference materials helps to illuminate even more sharply the contrast between the bases of Wallace support and those of the conventional candidates. It will be recalled that all respondents were asked to give an affective evaluation of each of the three candidates taken separately, along with other aspirants. If we examine the pattern of correlations between issue positions and the ratings of Humphrey, Nixon, and Wallace, we capture gradations of enthusiasm, indifference, and hostility felt toward each man instead of the mere vote threshold, and we can explore the antecedents or correlates of the variations in sentiment toward the individual candidates.

Where the ratings of Wallace given by whites are concerned, patterns vary somewhat South and non-South, but substantial correlations with issue positions appear everywhere. In the South, the most generic question of civil rights policy shows a relation of .49 (gamma) with Wallace reactions; the most generic question on "law and order" shows a .39; and the central Vietnam policy question shows a relationship of .30. Party identification, however, shows a relation of only .04. Other ancillary questions probing more specific aspects of policy feelings in these areas vary around the most generic items somewhat, but tend to show fairly similar magnitudes of relationship. Outside the South, patterns are a little less sharp but remain unequivocal. Instead of the above correlations of .49, .39 and .30 in the main issue domains, the figures are .25 (civil rights), .27 (law and order), and .25 (Vietnam). The relationship of party identification to Wallace ratings among whites, however, is .01. Thus it is true in both regions that party identification is entirely dwarfed by any of several issue positions in predicting reactions to Wallace among whites, and in terms of "variance ac-

Table 24.5   Correlations Between Issue Positions, Partisanship and Affective Ratings of the Major Candidates (Whites Only)*

Issue Domain:	Non-South			South		
	Humphrey	Nixon	Wallace	Humphrey	Nixon	Wallace
A. Civil rights (6 or 7 items)†	.17	.09	.27	.24	.08	.41
B. Law and order (2 items)	.25	.05	.27	.19	.01	.35
C. Vietnam (2 items)	.05	.03	.23	.14	.02	.26
D. Cold war (4 items)	.12	.11	.15	.16	.05	.28
E. Social welfare (2 or 3 items)†	.22	.20	.09	.26	.13	.10
F. Federal gov't too powerful? (1 item)	.37	.18	.17	.49	.13	.15
Sum: 18 issue items	.19	.10	.20	.22	.07	.31
Sum: Three major 1968 issue domains (A, B, C)	.16	.07	.26	.22	.07	.37
Partisanship: (3 items)	.47	.47	.04	.39	.36	.03

*Cell entries are average absolute values of gamma ordinal correlations between items of the types listed in the rows and affective ratings of the candidates noted in the columns.
†An item having to do with the role of the federal government in aid to local education was considered a social welfare item outside the South, but a civil rights issue within that region.

counted for" the differences between issues and party would best be expressed in terms of *orders of magnitude.*

Differences that are almost as sharp turn up in the relationships surrounding the ratings of Nixon and Humphrey. Here, however, everything is exactly reversed: it is *party* that towers over all other predictors, and the central 1968 issues tend to give rather diminutive relationships. Thus comparable correlations (gammas) between partisanship and candidate ratings all run between .36 and .44, varying only slightly by region and man. Where Nixon is concerned, the average correlation values for issue items in the three main domains emphasized in the 1968 election never get as high as .10, and fall as low as .01, with the central tendency about .05. Where Humphrey is concerned, somewhat higher issue values are observed, varying between .05 and .25 according to the region and the domain. Moreover, there is another issue domain not hitherto cited in which average values over three items for Humphrey considerably outstrip the Wallace correlation in both North and South. Significantly, this is the domain of items concerning governmental social welfare activities that one might associate with the period running from the New Deal through the 1950s.[17] Nevertheless, averaging correlations across all of these issue domains (the obsolescing as well as the three most salient in 1968) suggests that party identification still accounts for three to five times as much variance in Humphrey ratings as does the average issue among the eighteen issues posed in the study. These correlation patterns are summarized by region in Table 24.5.

Such dramatic comparisons between types of support for Wallace on one hand and the conventional candidates on the other may be perplexing to the casual reader who is keeping the thesis of V. O. Key in mind. After all, it is the pattern of Wallace support that shows the kind of strong issue orientation Key sought to demonstrate, whereas evaluations of both Humphrey and Nixon seem to show a strong factor of traditional party allegiance suffocating most issue concerns into relative obscurity. Yet the span of time Key's data covered limited him almost completely to observation of races of the routine Humphrey-Nixon type. Did these earlier two-party races look more like the Wallace patterns for some unknown reason?

The answer, of course, is very probably not. However, if we set the Wallace phenomenon in 1968 aside and limit our attention in the Key fashion to two contrasting groups of "changers" between the 1964 and 1968 election (Johnson to Nixon; Goldwater to Humphrey) we can show correlations with issue differences which look very much like those presented in cross-tabulations by Key for earlier elections: some strong, some weak, but nearly always "in the right direction." There are, to be sure, other problems of interpretation surrounding such correlations that one would need to thrash out before accepting the Key evidence fully.[18] But our principal point here is the simple one that even with Wallace analytically discarded from the 1968 scene, the rest of the 1968 data seem perfectly compatible with the data Key used. The only reason there may seem to be a discontinuity, then, is due to the different nature of the question being asked by Key which, by focusing on marginal change from election to election, effectively defines party loyalty out of the explanation and correspondingly opens the way for greater orienting weight for issues.

It is because the change in vote division from election to election is so critical that V. O. Key's contribution is a welcome corrective. On the other hand, the configurations of 1968 data we have summarized here help to put that contribution into perspective. The patterns of Wallace support show how empirical data *can* look when issues play a strongly orienting role. The contrasts between these patterns and those generated by routine two-party politics may help to suggest why investigators have tended to be more impressed by the feeble role of issues than by their strength.

The lessons to be drawn are several. One is a simple point of methodology. It has been suggested upon occasion in the past that relationships between issue positions and voting choice turn out to be as pallid as they usually are because investigators fail to ask the right questions or word them in confusing ways. We feel that improvement in these matters is always possible. However, we have seen that exactly the same issue items which continue to look pallid in accounting for assessments of Humphrey and Nixon blaze forth into rather robust correlations where Wallace is concerned. Hence we conclude that poor item choice scarcely accounts for past findings.

Another lesson is more substantive. Some past findings have been to our mind "overinterpreted" as implying that issues are poorly linked to voting preferences because of innate and hence incorrigible cognitive deficiencies suffered by the mass electorate in the United States.[19] Merely the Wallace data taken alone would suffice to show, exactly as Key argued, that the public can relate policy controversies to its own estimates of the world and vote accordingly. The fact that it does not display this propensity on any large scale very often invites more careful spelling out of the conditions under which it will or will not.

It seems clear from the 1968 data that one of the cardinal limiting conditions is the "drag" or inertia represented by habitual party loyalties: as soon as features of the situation limit or neutralize the relevance of such a factor, issue evaluations play a more vital role. Much research has shown that partisanship is fixed early in life and tends to endure. As the individual moves through the life cycle, old political controversies die away and new ones arise toward which at least some individuals crystallize opinions. While the parties try to lead this new opinion formation among their faithful, and probably succeed on a modest scale, there are many independent sources of such opinion for the citizen. The average citizen either does not know his party's position well enough to be influenced on many matters, or if he knows, frequently resists the influence. As a result, policy opinions are very loosely or anachronistically linked to party preference at any point in time. But in the moment of truth in the polling booth, party allegiance seems the most relevant cue for many voters *if conditions permit it to be used.*

Another type of condition which mediates the links between citizen position on issues and voting choice is the "objective" degree of difference between parties or candidates with respect to policy controversy, or the clarity with which any objective difference gets communicated to the populace. In every United States election there are accusations from one quarter or another that the two conventional parties provide no more than "tweedledee" and "tweedledum" candidates. However, these accusations as aired in the public media rose to something of a crescendo in 1968 from both the Wallace and the McCarthy perspectives. And even as measured a source as the *New York Times* noted wryly that it would take no more than the deletion of two or three codicils to make the official 1968 campaign platforms of the Democratic and Republican parties into utterly undistinguishable documents. If the main discriminable difference between Humphrey and Nixon began and ended with the party label then it would certainly not be surprising that the public sorted itself into voting camps by party allegiance and little more, save where Wallace was concerned. In this case, the public would be limited to exactly that "echo chamber" role which Key ascribed to it.

As a matter of pure logic, nobody can deny that policy differentiation between parties is likely to be a precondition for meaningful relationships between policy feelings and partisan voting decisions. Our only problem here is to evaluate whether the party/issue data configurations surrounding Humphrey and Nixon are the obvious result of some lack of policy difference peculiar to 1968, or represent instead some more abiding feature of presidential voting in the United States. Unfortunately, there is no obvious way to arrive at an objective measurement of "degree of party difference." Perhaps the closest approximation is to ask the public how clear the differences appear to be. Nevertheless, since some people invariably feel party differences are big and others feel they are nonexistent, even this approach leaves one without reference points as to "how big is big" where reports of this kind are concerned, except inasmuch as trends in such reports can be observed over periods of time. In this light, it can be said while reports of "important differences" between the Democrats and the Republicans were slightly fewer in 1968 than in 1964 (the year of Goldwater's "choice, not an echo"), they show a reasonable parity with such reports for 1952 and 1960. Hence in the public eye, at least, differences between what the major parties stand for were not lacking in unusual degree in 1968.

It may be useful to note that whereas we have labeled the Wallace effort in 1968 an "issue candidacy" from the point of view of the electorate, we have not said that it was an ideological candidacy from that same point of view. From other viewpoints of political analysis, it was of course just that: a movement of the "radical right." Moreover, with occasional exceptions, data on issue positions show Wallace voters to differ from Humphrey voters in the same "conservative" direction that Nixon voters do, only much more so. Therefore by customary definitions, not only the leadership of the radical right, but the rank and file espoused clearly "rightist" positions of a sort which were frequently extreme, on highly specific questions of public policy.[20]

Yet there was an element of ideological self-recognition present among Goldwater voters in 1964 that was simply lacking among Wallace voters in 1968. One measure of ideological location which we use involves the respondent in rating the terms "liberal" and "conservative." If the respondent gives the highest possible score to the stimulus "liberal" and the lowest possible score to "conservative," he is rated as the most extreme liberal, with a score of 100. In the reverse case, the extreme conservative receives a score of zero. At 50 are clustered individuals who either do not recognize these terms, or give the same affective rating to both.[21] In 1964 there was a rather considerable relationship between such a measure and response to Goldwater, in the expected direction. In 1968, the same scale showed only a very limited correlation with reactions toward Wallace (gammas of .13 and .09 among whites within the South and outside, respectively). Indeed, as Table 24.6 shows, in both political regions of the country Wallace voters were more favorable to the "liberal" label than Nixon voters!

Thus while Wallace supporters were entirely distinctive in their "backlash" feelings on public policy, they were much less ideologically attuned to a left-right spectrum than their Goldwater predecessors.

Although Wallace supporters did not seem anywhere nearly as distinctive in terms of ideological measures as they did on specific issues, they did show some moderate trends in terms of other more generic political attitudes. In particular, various measures bearing on discontent with the responsiveness and probity of government show correlations with ratings given by whites to Wallace, and are related but with opposite signs to ratings of the "establishment" candidates, Humphrey and Nixon. Since Wallace was more of a mainstream candidate in the South than in the rest of the country, it might be thought that his appeal in that region might depend less strictly on this syndrome of political alienation than it would elsewhere. However, these relationships are stronger and more pervasive in the South, and seem only weakly mirrored in other parts of the nation. Within the South, white attitudes toward Wallace are quite sharply associated with our scales of political efficacy and cynicism about government. People drawn to Wallace tended to feel they had little capacity to influence government, and expressed distrust of the morality and efficiency of political leadership. These correlations reach a peak on items where the referent is most explicitly "the federal government in Washington," and it is plain that southern voters felt more or less attracted to Wallace in the degree that they responded to his complaints that Washington bureaucrats had been persistently and unjustly bullying the South with particular respect to civil rights. Since there is no methodological need for it to be true, it is of particular interest that ratings of Humphrey show as substantial correlations in the opposing direction, in the South and other regions as well: people responding warmly to Humphrey had quite sanguine views of government.

Table 24.6 Ideological Responses of White Voters for Different Presidential Candidates in 1964 and 1968*

	1964		1968		
	Johnson	Goldwater	Humphrey	Nixon	Wallace
Non-South	51.8	39.9	51.8	43.4	44.9
South	49.6	35.9	49.5	40.7	41.9

*The cell entry registers the mean value shown on the ideological scale described in the text for white voters for each of the candidates listed. A high value indicates that liberalism is held in relative favor; a low value means that conservatism is preferred.

All told, then, a sense of political alienation was a rather visible correlate of a sorting of the citizenry away from the conventional candidates toward Wallace, as was certainly to be expected and necessary if terms such as "backlash" are relevant. At the same time, it is worth keeping the apparent temporal sequences clear. The data suggest that southern whites have become alienated with government because prior attitudes, particularly racial ones, have been contradictory to national policy for nearly twenty years. Thus there is a readiness to condemn government on a much broader front, and Wallace appealed in obvious ways to this readiness in the South. Outside the South Wallace also articulated the same array of specific grievances and received a clear response.

However, the evidence suggests that any resonance he might have achieved in terms of a more generic condemnation of government, while present, was relatively limited.

The Social Bases of Wallace Support

A variety of facts already cited about the Wallace movement of 1968 makes clear that while there was some modest overlap in support for Goldwater in 1964 and Wallace in 1968, it was at best a weak correlation and the Wallace clientele differed quite notably from Goldwater's. Thus, for example, almost exactly half of our 1968 Wallace voters who had participated in the 1964 election reported that they had voted for Johnson. Or again, we have seen that the majority of Wallace voters, like the electorate as a whole, was identified with the Democratic party, while it is obvious that most Goldwater voters were Republican identifiers. Similarly, we have just noted that the Wallace movement had a much less clear ideological focus among its sympathizers than marked Goldwater supporters in 1964.

This discrepancy in clientele may seem perplexing. After all, in the terms of conventional analysis in political sociology both candidates were "darlings of the radical right." Yet the limited degree of overlap between Goldwater and Wallace voters is confirmed in equally impressive fashion when one compares their social backgrounds or even their simplest demographic characteristics. Among Goldwater voters, for example, women both South and non-South showed the same slight majority they enjoy in the electorate; Wallace voters in the South showed a similar balance, but elsewhere were rather markedly (almost 60–40) male. The Goldwater vote had been much more urban, while the Wallace vote was relatively rural and small-town, particularly in the South. Outside the South, the age distribution of Wallace voters departed markedly from that shown by Goldwater in 1964, with the proportion under 35 being about twice as great and that over 65 only half as large.

The well-publicized appeal of Wallace to the unionized laboring man is clearly reflected in our data: outside the South, the proportion of white union members preferring Wallace over the other major candidates was more than three times as great as it was within households having no unionized members (19 percent to 6 percent); even in the South, where other appeals were present and the unionization of labor is more limited, the contrast between the preferences of union members and nonunion households remains dramatic (52 percent to 28 percent giving top preference to Wallace over the conventional candidates). Indeed, in both regions the occupational center of gravity of Wallace popularity was clearly among white skilled workers. Nationwide, only about 10 percent of the Wallace vote was contributed by the professional and managerial strata, whereas persons of these occupations had given Goldwater almost half of his vote (46 percent). Needless to say, the proportion of unionized labor supporting Goldwater was very low. Along with these class differences, marked discrepancies in educational background can be taken for granted. In the South, one-third of Wallace's support came from whites with no more than grade school education, while the national figure for Goldwater was 13 percent. The proportion of voters of college experience backing Goldwater was about double that found voting for Wallace either in the South or elsewhere.

All of these comparisons help to underscore the major disparities in the so-cial bases of support for Goldwater and Wallace, despite the apparent common policy ground of the relatively extreme right. While one should not lose track of the fact that there was a small and systematic overlap in clientele, it is abun-dantly clear that neither candidate exhausted the potential support for a severely conservative program in matters of civil rights, law and order, or Vietnam. In a very real sense, it can be seen that Wallace was a poor man's Goldwater. As we suggested at the time, Goldwater pitched his campaign on an ideolog-ical plane which rather escaped some members of the electorate who might oth-erwise have found his positions congenial.[22] Wallace's perfectly direct appeal to citizens of this latter description, along with the undercurrent of populism alien to the Goldwater conservatism, apparently sufficed to put off some of the Arizona senator's more well-to-do supporters.[23] The Goldwater support was drawn from a relatively urbane and sophisticated conservatism; Wallace ap-pealed to many similar instincts, but the style was folksy and tailored to the common man.

In a significant way, too, Wallace remained a regional candidate despite his discovery that he could win more than scattered votes in the North and his consequent presence on every state's ballot. Over half of his popular votes came from the states of the Confederacy. Everything, from his lack of political experi-ence at a federal level to his marked southern accent, suggested a parochial relevance that had rarely been salient where Goldwater was concerned. While electoral maps leave no doubt as to the regional nature of the response, sample survey data show that even these visible effects have been diluted by interre-gional migration. Thus, for example, while much has been written about the Wallace appeal in various European ethnic communities of northern cities, little has been said about the "American ethnic group" of southern white migrants, most of whom are blue collar and frequently in a position to take special plea-sure in the spectacle of a southern compatriot coming north to give the Yankees what-for. Our data indicate that Wallace drew over 14 percent of the vote from these migrants, and less than 7 percent otherwise outside the South. On the other hand, the significant stream of migration of Yankees into the South, the political implications of which we have described elsewhere,[24] provided some-

Table 24.7   Reactions of Whites to Wallace by Region of Socialization and Residence

		Respondent Now Resides . . .		
		Outside the South	Within the South	Total
Respondent	Outside the South:	26.2* (757)	26.5 (51)	26.2 (808)
Grew up	Within the South:	34.7 (53)	50.0 (281)	48.5 (334)
	Total:	26.7 (810)	46.3 (332)	

*Cell entries are mean values of ratings on a scale from 0 (hostility) to 100 (sympathy) accorded to George Wallace by white respondents of the types indicated.

thing of a barrier to further Wallace successes. Heavily Republican in a non-Southern sense and now constituting better than one-seventh of white voters in the region, these migrants were even less interested in voting for Wallace than were southern whites in the North, and gave the former Alabama governor only 10 percent of their vote while their native southern white colleagues were casting almost one vote in every three for him.

Table 24.7 summarizes the affective ratings given Wallace by our respondents according to the region in which they grew up as well as their current region of residence. It is rather clear that the region of socialization is a more critical determinant of these assessments of Wallace than is the region of current residence. Moreover, it is easy to show that regional differences in correlates of Wallace preference also follow lines of socialization rather than those of current residence. For example, we have noted that Wallace's appeal to women outside the South was rather limited. For white women of southern background living outside the South, the response was much as it was in the South. Setting the migrants aside, the sex ratio among white Wallace enthusiasts outside the South is even more sharply masculine.

It is not our purpose here to do more than briefly summarize the social and demographic correlates of Wallace preferences, for numerous other essays are being prepared to treat the subject in detail. However, one correlate which has frequently surprised observers deserves more extended discussion, both because of its practical significance and because of its high relevance to some of the theoretical issues uniquely illuminated by the 1968 election. We speak of the relationship between the Wallace movement and the generational cleavages so evident at other points in data from the presidential campaign.

It would seem self-evident that Wallace's primary appeal to traditional and even obsolescing American values, as well as his caustic treatment of the rebels of the younger generation, would have brought him votes that were even more heavily clustered among the elderly than those drawn by Goldwater in 1964. We have already noted that Wallace took issue positions that were communicated with unusual clarity, and that these positions determined in unusual degree the nature of his clientele. On almost every issue of nearly a score surveyed, the position characteristic of Wallace voters in our sample is also the position associated with older citizens, where there is any age correlation at all. Hence it is somewhat surprising to discover that among white southerners there is actually a faint *negative* correlation between age and a Wallace vote. And it is perplexing indeed to discover that outside the South voting for Wallace occurred very disproportionately among the young. For example, Wallace captured less than 3 percent of the vote among people over 70 outside the South, but 13 percent of those under 30, with a regular gradient connecting these two extremes. One of the major ironies of the election, then, was that Wallace made his appeal to the old but mainly received the vote of the young.

However, a whole cluster of empirical theory has grown up in recent years which, without any particular knowledge of the Wallace platform, would predict that such a third-party candidate would draw votes primarily from the young in just this way. It is established, for example, that repeated commitments of votes to a political party tend to increase the strength of psychological identification with that party, and it is an immediate corollary that voters of the older generation are more fixed in their party loyalties than are relatively new voters.[25] It follows with equal logic that when some new candidate or *ad hoc* party arises to challenge the conventional parties of a system, it should have relative difficulty making headway among the older generation, even though it might have natural appeals to such voters.

We have never had a chance to test this somewhat nonobvious expectation, although reconstructions of the fall of the Weimar Republic have always suggested that voters for the Nazi party in its culminating surge were very disproportionately drawn from the youngest cohorts of the German electorate. Therefore the age distribution of Wallace support has been of uncommon interest to us. When issue appeals of a rather vital sort conflict with long-established party loyalties, as they must have in Wallace's case for many older voters, which factor is likely to exert most influence on the voting decision? The apparent difficulties older people had in voting for Wallace, particularly outside the South where he was a less "legitimate" Democrat and hence a less conventional candidate, seem to provide a rather clear answer.

However, if this interpretation is correct, a variety of ancillary effects should be discernible in the 1968 data. For example, if prior party identification is truly the critical source of resistance to a Wallace vote simply because of the disloyalty implied, the prediction that the young would vote more heavily for him need not mean the young have any monopoly on admiration for him. Indeed, one could almost predict that the older generation should have shown more warmth of feeling toward Wallace per vote allotted him than would be true of the younger generation, simply because of the "artificial" inhibition on the vote represented by greater loyalty to a conventional party. Moreover, since strength of identification is measured explicitly in this study, it is of importance to show that it does indeed vary positively as in times past with age; that such identification with a conventional party is indeed negatively associated with voting for Wallace; and that the tendency of young persons to vote for Wallace did co-occur with weak conventional loyalties.

All of these empirical expectations are borne out, and usually in rather handsome fashion. First, while the young voted more heavily for Wallace, the correlation between age and effective rating of him as a political figure is nonexistent. Second, the old in 1968 were, as always, much more strongly identified with one of the two conventional parties than the young. Third, defection from a conventional party to vote for Wallace was indeed strongly related to degree of party identification, particularly outside the South:[26] the probability of a Wallace vote doubles there as one moves each step from strong through weak to "independent" or leaning identifiers. And finally, when strength of partisanship is controlled, the sharp inverse correlation between age and a Wallace vote outside the South is very nearly wiped out; within the South where it was a somewhat ragged relationship to begin with, it completely disappears or if anything, shows a slight reversal as though Wallace might in fact have had some extra drawing power for the older voter, aside from the complications posed by other allegiances.

This nest of relationships holds more than detached clinical interest in several directions. The reader concerned about the future of the Wallace movement as an electoral force on the American scene is likely to be interested in the fact that the clientele was young rather than aging. In one sense this is a pertinent datum and in another it is not. It is unquestionable that a Wallace candidacy in 1972 has a brighter future than it would have if its 1968 legions were dying out of the population. Nonetheless, the whole thrust of our argument above is that the Wallace movement is not in any special good fortune to have drawn young voters: this will be true of virtually any new party entering the lists in an old party system, and but for the habits which kept older voters with the conventional parties, the initial Wallace vote would probably have been significantly larger. Still more to the point, we would hazard that the future of the Wallace movement as a third party will be determined more by Wallace's personal plans and the organizational aspirations of his entourage on one hand, and by the evolution of events affecting national frustrations on the other, than by the age level of its 1968 voters.

Nevertheless, the youthful nature of Wallace's clientele provides a further irony to the backdrop of generational cleavage reflected in the 1968 campaign. For while such a cleavage was genuine and intense, as some of our earlier data have witnessed, one of the most important yet hidden lines of cleavage split the younger generation itself. Although privileged young college students angry at Vietnam and the shabby treatment of the Negro saw themselves as sallying forth to do battle against a corrupted and cynical older generation, a more head-on confrontation at the polls, if a less apparent one, was with their own age mates who had gone from high school off to the factory instead of college, and who were appalled by the collapse of patriotism and respect for the law that they saw about them. Outside of the election period, when verbal articulateness and leisure for political activism count most heavily, it was the college share of the younger generation — or at least its politicized vanguard — that was most prominent as a political force. At the polls, however, the game shifts to "one man, one vote," and this vanguard is numerically swamped even within its own generation.

This lack of numerical strength is no intrinsic handicap: any cadre of opinion leadership is small in number. However, it must successfully appeal to some potential rank and file, and it certainly cannot risk becoming a negative reference point for large numbers of people if it expects to operate in a medium involving popular elections. In part because of collegiate naiveté concerning forms of dissent that maintain sympathy,[27] and in part because the public image of constructive efforts by the many can be so rapidly colored by a few whose needs are mainly to antagonize as much of society as possible, this vanguard became a negative reference point for most Americans. The result at the election thus had a different coloration from what went before: McCarthy did not run and Wallace captured a proportion of the vote which was historically amazing. Indeed, it was probably the political stodginess of the older generation so decried by campus activists which kept the vote of "people over 30" within the channels of the conventional parties and prevented the Wallace vote from rising still higher. Certainly it is true that in several major metropolises of the United States where party loyalty has been nullified in primary election settings in the spring of 1969, candidates of relative Wallace coloration have surprised observers with their mounting popularity.

There can be no question but that dramatic and persistent displays of dissent on the campuses between 1964 and 1968 helped to place question marks around "consensual" national policies which might otherwise have continued to be taken for granted by most of the citizenry. At the same time, disregard for the occasional junctures of electoral decision when the mass public has some say in the political process may mean that a battle was won but a war was lost. For some few, this *politique de pire* is quite intentional, being thought to help "radicalize" the electorate in ways that can be controlled and manipulated. For most student activists, however, success in raising questions is of little value if one is helping in the same stroke to elect "wrong people" to answer them. And quite apart from the nature of the leadership elected in 1968, it is obvious to any "rational" politician hoping to maximize votes in 1970 or 1972 that there are several times more votes to be gained by leaning toward Wallace than by leaning toward McCarthy.

If these facts were inevitable consequences of "raising the issues" from the campuses, the dilemma would be severe indeed. It is not clear to us, however, that any intrinsic dilemma is involved. Much of the backlash expressed in the 1968 voting received its impetus less from irreconcilable policy disagreement — although on civil rights there is more than a modicum of that — than from resentment at the frequency with which the message of dissent from the campuses was clothed to "bait" conventional opinion. In the degree that the feelings and opinion reflexes of the common man, including age peers of lower circumstances, were comprehended at all by campus activists, they tended to be a subject for derision or disdain. Strange to say, such hostile postures communicate with great speed even across social gulfs, and are reciprocated with uncommon reliability. Fully as often, of course, there was simply no comprehension of the dynamics of public opinion at all.

Whether one likes it or not, the United States does retain some occasional elements of participatory democracy. A young and well-educated elite-to-be that is too impatient to cope with this bit of reality by undertaking the tedium of positive persuasion may find its political efforts worse than wasted.

NOTES

[1] The 1968 national sample survey ($N = 1559$) was made possible by a grant from the Ford Foundation, whose support we gratefully acknowledge. A total of 1559 citizens of voting age were interviewed, most of them both before and after election day. The preliminary nature of this report is to be emphasized, since the data on which it is based had not been fully cleaned at the time of writing. When the study is released through the Inter-University Consortium for Political Research, interested analysts may discover small discrepancies from the statistics reported here. Readers should also remember that all sample statistics are subject to varying amounts of sampling error in relation to the number of cases on which they are based.

[2] A deviating election is one in which the party commanding the identifications of a majority of the electorate is nonetheless voted out of power temporarily. See A. Campbell, P. Converse, W. Miller, and D. Stokes, *The American Voter* (New York: John Wiley, 1960), chap. 19.

[3] *Congressional Quarterly*, November 22, 1968, p. 3177.

[4] The percentage difference of 62 percent in candidate preference between blacks and whites is substantially larger than class differentiation or other social cleavages and partisanship within the United States in recent history or for democracies of Western Europe.

[5] Such segregation is indicated simply because of the fact that within the black vote in 1968 there is next to no meaningful "variance" to be "accounted for." When categories of "Nixon voters" and "Wallace voters" are presented, they are necessarily "lily-white" in composition. Therefore when "Humphrey voters" are contrasted with them, it is confusing if differences may be totally a function of the large admixtures of blacks in the Humphrey support, as opposed to differences which would stand up even with comparisons limited to whites.

[6] See "Voting and Foreign Policy," by Warren E. Miller, chap. 7 in James N. Rosenau, ed., *Domestic Sources of Foreign Policy* (New York: The Free Press, 1967).

[7] A separate analysis, carried out by a colleague in the Survey Research Center Political Be-

havior Program and using the same body of data from the SRC 1968 election study, suggests, moreover, that many voters who thought the police used too little force deserted Humphrey in the course of the campaign while the minority who objected that too much force was used voted more heavily for the Democratic nominee. See John P. Robinson, "Voter Reaction to Chicago 1968," Survey Research Center (1969), mimeo.

[8] The decline was only on the order of 1½ percent nationally, but the overall figures are somewhat misleading. Enormous efforts devoted to voter registration projects among southern blacks between 1964 and 1968 appear to have paid off by increasing voter participation in that sector from 44 percent to 51 percent. Perhaps in counterpoint, southern whites increased their turnout by 2 percent, thereby inching ever closer to the national norm. Thus the decline in turnout was concentrated outside the South, and there approached the more substantial drop of 4 percent. Even this figure is misleading, since whites outside the South showed a 3 percent loss in percentage points of turnout, while nonwhites declined by almost 11 percentage points! See *Current Population Reports*, "Voter Participation in November 1968," Series P-20, No. 177, December 27, 1968. Although such turnout figures, apart from the more general mobilizing of southern blacks, are consistent with a proposition that whites were more eager to "throw the rascals out" than blacks, and that among whites, southerners had the fiercest grievances of all, there is no hiding the fact of anemic turnout in most of the country in 1968. Interestingly enough, the decline from 1964 was uniformly distributed across the entire spectrum of party allegiances from loyal Democrats to strong Republicans.

[9] The reader should also keep in mind several other things about Table 24.2. The "South" here refers, as it will throughout this paper, to the Census Bureau definition of the region that includes fifteen states and the District of Columbia. Hence such border states as Maryland or West Virginia are included along with the deeper southern states of the old confederacy. Presumably, for example, George Wallace's rating among whites of a more hard-core South would be correspondingly higher. Secondly, it should be remembered for some of the lesser candidates that respondents knowing so little about a candidate as to be indifferent to him would end up rating him "50°." Thus it would be questionable to conclude from Table 24.2 that LeMay was more popular than George Wallace, except in a very limited sense. Actually, three times as many respondents (nearly one third) left LeMay at the indifference point as did so for Wallace. Thus lack of visibility helped to make him *less unpopular*. But among those who reacted to both men, LeMay was less popular than Wallace. Similarly, Wallace's low rating must be understood as a compound of an admiring minority and a hostile majority. The variance of Wallace ratings is much greater than those for other candidates, even in the South.

[10] Just after the decision of Robert Kennedy to run and before Lyndon Johnson's withdrawal, the Gallup poll showed Democrats favoring Kennedy as the party's nominee by a 44–41 margin.

[11] Interestingly enough, the same generational cleavages among southern white Democrats occur at an earlier age than those elsewhere. In that region, Humphrey–Johnson preferences hold a plurality in all age cohorts over 30, despite the fact that Kennedy support has an edge of better than three to one among those under 30 (N of 34), perhaps because the latter group has less of a memory of the fury in the Deep South at the Kennedy family prior to the assassination of President John Kennedy in Dallas in 1963.

[12] Although there is some slight tendency for preconvention supporters of McCarthy to be relatively young, the distribution by age is more homogeneous than expected, and much more so than is the case for Kennedy. It is possible that young people supporting McCarthy as the only alternative to the Administration switched more heavily than the middle-aged to Kennedy when he announced his candidacy.

[13] See also the accounts for New Hampshire by Louis Harris, "How Voters See the Issues," *Newsweek* (March 25, 1968), p. 26.

[14] V. O. Key, Jr., *The Responsible Electorate: Rationality in Presidential Voting, 1936–1960* (Cambridge, Mass.: Belknap Press, 1966), pp. 7–8.

[15] Donald E. Stokes, "Some Dynamic Elements of Contests for the Presidency," [*American Political Science Review*], vol. 60 (March 1966), pp. 19–28.

[16] This is not to say that it would be inconceivable for identification with one of the two traditional parties to correlate with preference for some third-party candidate. For example, it is possible that most of the voters for Henry Wallace's Progressive party in 1948 were identified with the Democratic party. However, it is clear that in such an instance "party loyalty" would have been a rather spurious name for the motivating factor. In the case of George Wallace, even this kind of spurious correlation is absent, except insofar as his Democratic origins and the invisibility of his American Independent party label made it easy for Democrats to support him. Indeed, in the context of this argument it will be fascinating to discover whether Republicans and Democrats invoked different images of Wallace's party location in order

to satisfy their need for consonance while voting for a man who reflects their own issue commitments.

[17] Another domain of issues surrounding the "cold war" as it confronted the nation in the 1950s with controversies over foreign aid and trade with communist countries shows only modest correlations with the candidate rankings, and Nixon and Humphrey ratings show more of a parity with the Wallace correlations, although in an absolute sense the latter continue to outrun the former sharply in the South and mildly elsewhere. See Table 24.5.

[18] These include such considerations as that of the causal direction underlying the observed relationships; or known and systematic biases in recollection of a presidential vote four years later; or the superficiality of the issues that show such patterns, as opposed to issues thought basic by sophisticated observers; or blatant misinformation supporting the issue positions registered; or a tendency for the less informed to "shift" more quickly than the better informed, with position on any given issue held constant, etc.

[19] We much prefer an interpretation which hinges on a general inattention which is endemic because information costs are relatively high where little information is already in hand, and the stakes are rarely seen as being very large. While such a "condition" is likely to persist in mass electorates, there is nothing about it which is immutable given the proper convergence of circumstances.

[20] This was not true across every issue domain. The most notable exception was in the area of social welfare issues such as medicare and full employment guarantees, on which issues Wallace voters were significantly more "liberal" than Nixon voters, and almost matched the liberalism of Humphrey voters. This admixture was of course familiar in Wallace's frequent appeals to the underdog and the workingman, in the tradition of southern populism.

[21] For reasons discussed elsewhere, a rather large proportion of the American electorate — nearly half — is found at this point of ideological neutrality.

[22] P. Converse, A. Clausen, and W. Miller, "Electoral Myth and Reality: The 1964 Election," [American Political Science Review], vol. 59 (June 1965), pp. 321–336.

[23] It is quite possible, however, that some of this support might have moved to Wallace had the Republican party nominated anybody but Nixon or Reagan, among the main contenders.

[24] A. Campbell, P. Converse, W. Miller, and D. Stokes, Elections and the Political Order (New York: John Wiley, 1965), chap. 12.

[25] Philip E. Converse, "Of Time and Partisan Stability," Journal of Comparative Politics (issue to be announced).

[26] The South shows somewhat diluted patterns here, compatible with the likelihood that for at least some southern Democrats, a vote for Wallace was not conceived as a defection.

[27] The American public seems to have a very low tolerance for unusual or "showy" forms of political dissent. Responses to an extended set of items in the 1968 study on the subject are appalling from a civil libertarian point of view. At the most acceptable end of the continuum of "ways for people to show their disapproval or disagreement with governmental policies and actions" we asked about "taking part in protest meetings or marches that are permitted by the local authorities" (italics not in original question). Less than 20 percent of all respondents, and scarcely more than 20 percent of those giving an opinion, would approve of such subversive behavior, and more than half would disapprove (the remainder accepted the alternative presented that their reaction "would depend on the circumstances"). In view of such assumptions, the overwhelmingly negative reaction to the Chicago demonstrations despite sympathetic media treatment (cited earlier) is hardly surprising.

Bibliography

Part One

The notes in the selections included in this book are the best introduction to current work in the history of American popular voting behavior. Therefore we will note here only those books and articles we consider especially important for further development of the themes underscored. The best introduction to the present state of research on American popular voting behavior can be found in the two major reports of the University of Michigan's Survey Research Center, which has had more impact on the systematic study of popular voting than any other institution. See Angus Campbell, Philip E. Converse, Warren E. Miller, and Donald E. Stokes, *The American Voter* (New York, 1960); and, by the same authors, *Elections and the Political Order* (New York, 1966). In addition, Donald E. Stokes, "The Nature of Belief Systems in Mass Publics," in *Ideology and Discontent*, ed. David Apter (New York, 1964), brilliantly expands and develops those findings. A useful summary and critique of the conclusions of the Michigan group is by Peter M. Natchez, "Images of Voting: The Social Psychologists," *Public Policy*, vol. 18 (Summer 1970), pp. 553–588. Robert Lane, *Political Life, Why and How People Get Involved in Politics* (New York, paperback edition, 1964), and his *Political Ideology, Why The American Common Man Believes What He Does* (New York, 1962) are classic summaries of our knowledge about individual motivation and belief in politics. V. O. Key, Jr., *Public Opinion and American Democracy* (New York, 1961), relates the findings of survey research about individuals and politics to a wide range of formal and informal governmental processes.

The historical perspective in popular voting behavior studies, emphasizing the use of time series of aggregate election data, is well introduced in Lee Benson, "Research Problems in American Political Historiography," in *Common Frontiers of the Social Sciences*, ed. Mirra Komarovsky (Glencoe, 1957), pp. 113–183. Some of the results of his challenge to traditional political historiography are reported in Allan G. Bogue, "United States: The New Political History," in *The New History, Trends in Historical Research and Writing Since World War II*, eds. Walter Lacqueur and George Mosse (New York, 1967), pp. 185–207; Robert Swierenga, ed., *Quantification in American History: Theory and Research* (New York, 1970); Morton Rothstein et al., "Quantification in American History:

An Assessment," in *The State of American History*, ed. Herbert Bass (Chicago, 1970), pp. 298–329; Samuel P. Hays, "New Possibilities in American Political History," in *Sociology and History: Methods*, eds. Seymour Martin Lipset and Richard Hofstadter (New York, 1968), pp. 181–227; and, finally, Robert P. Swierenga, "Clio and Computers: A Survey of Computerized Research in History," *Computers and the Humanities*, vol. 5 (September 1970), pp. 1–22. All of these take up some of the methodological problems involved. For further insight into such problems generally, see William O. Aydelotte, "Quantification in History," *American Historical Review*, vol. 71 (April 1966), pp. 803–825; and more specifically on popular voting behavior, Lee Benson, "An Approach to the Scientific Study of Past Public Opinion," *Public Opinion Quarterly*, vol. 31 (Winter 1967–1968), pp. 522–567.

The cyclical pattern of American voting behavior is presented in Benson, "Research Problems," referred to above, and, more formally in Charles G. Sellers, Jr., "The Equilibrium Cycle in Two Party Politics," *Public Opinion Quarterly*, vol. 29 (Spring 1965), pp. 16–38. In addition see the two seminal articles by V. O. Key, Jr., "A Theory of Critical Elections," *Journal of Politics*, vol. 17 (February 1955), pp. 3–18; and "Secular Realignment and the Party System," *Journal of Politics*, vol. 21 (May 1959), pp. 198–210 and Thomas P. Jahnige, "Critical Elections and Social Change: Towards a Dynamic Explanation of National Party Competition in the United States," *Polity*, vol. 3 (Summer 1971), pp. 465–500. These cycles are employed to help describe specific eras of political party history in *The American Party Systems*, eds. Walter Dean Burnham and William Nisbet Chambers (New York, 1968). This book is also an excellent introduction to the roles parties play in structuring voting behavior.

There are a number of general studies of the underlying motivation of voting behavior in the American past — particularly of the ethnic factor. An intelligent summary of our knowledge in this area can be found in Robert Swierenga, "Ethnocultural Political Analysis: A New Approach to American Ethnic Studies," *Journal of American Studies*, vol. 5 (April 1971), pp. 59–79. Earlier studies that remain useful include Seymour Martin Lipset, "Religion and Politics in the American Past and Present" in *Religion and Social Conflict*, eds. Robert Lee and Martin Marty (New York, 1964), pp. 69–126; and Lawrence Fuchs, ed., *American Ethnic Politics* (New York, 1968), which contains a number of articles of particular interest to the historian as well as a quite good introductory bibliography. Edgar Litt's new book, *Beyond Pluralism: Ethnic Politics in America* (Glenview, Ill., 1970), focuses on current politics but does provide a good general introduction to the subject. No survey of the literature on voting behavior would be complete without noting Robert Merton's interpretation of reference group attitudes in his *Social Theory and Social Structure* (New York, rev. ed., 1957), pp. 225–386, which seeks to provide a theoretical underpinning for the understanding of the psychology of voting. See also Lee Benson's chapter, "Outline for a Theory of American Voting Behavior," in *The Concept of Jacksonian Democracy: New York as a Test Case* (Princeton, 1961), pp. 270–328, for a sensitive use of Merton as well as a more general analysis of the nature of American popular voting behavior.

Part Two

J. R. Pole has published a number of quantitative articles dealing with the extent of suffrage and voting participation in the early national period. See, for example, "Constitutional Reform and Election Statistics in Maryland, 1790–1812," *Maryland Historical Magazine*, vol. 55 (December 1960), pp. 275–292. Richard McCormick has provided the most thorough analysis of popular turnout throughout the pre-1860 period in "New Perspectives on Jacksonian Politics," *American Historical Review*, vol. 65 (January 1960), pp. 288–301.

Lee Benson in *The Concept of Jacksonian Democracy*, noted previously, presents the most complete case study based on quantitative analysis on the nature of electoral patterns and the forces affecting voting behavior in the early nineteenth century. His study has implications far beyond a single state. There are a number of other articles that usefully focus on particular aspects of voting behavior in different periods and places. See especially Lynn L. Marshall, "The Genesis of Grass Roots Democracy in Kentucky," *Mid-America*, vol. 47 (October 1965), pp. 269–287; and John L. Stanley, "Majority Tyranny in Tocqueville's America: The Failure of Negro Suffrage in 1846," *Political Science Quarterly*, vol. 84 (September 1969), pp. 412–435.

Most of the current quantitative work on this period remains unpublished. Ronald Formisano's manuscript "Egalitarians and Evangelicals, Parties and Voters, Michigan, 1835–1861," will appear in 1971. Roger Petersen, "The Reaction to a Heterogeneous Society: A Behavioral and Quantitative Analysis of Northern Voting Behavior, 1845–1870, Pennsylvania a Test Case," a recently completed doctoral dissertation at the University of Pittsburgh, is also forthcoming. In addition, Thomas P. Alexander and his students are completing a number of studies investigating voting patterns in the South and elsewhere before the Civil War.

The major analysis of the realignment of the 1850s is Michael Holt, *Forging a Majority: The Formation of the Republican Party in Pittsburgh, 1848–1860* (New Haven, 1969), portions of which are included in this book. Aida DiPace Donald, "The Decline of Whiggery and the Formation of The Republican Party in Rochester, 1848–1856," *Rochester History*, vol. 20 (July 1958), pp. 1–19, employs quantitative analysis in a single locality. The Formisano and Petersen studies referred to above also ably cover the period of realignment in their respective states. Finally, Lee Benson and Joel Silbey are investigating the realignment period in New York State in a study tentatively entitled, "New York Public Opinion and the Coming of the Civil War."

Part Three

Paul Kleppner, *The Cross of Culture: A Social Analysis of Midwestern Politics, 1850–1900* (New York, 1970), provides a seminal overview of political behavior during this period. Among important articles on the presidential election of 1860 (in addition to that by George Daniels, included above) are: Robert P. Swierenga, "The Ethnic Voter and the First Lincoln Election," *Civil War History*, vol. 11 (March 1965), pp. 27–43, which deals with Dutch voters in Iowa; and Paul Kleppner, "Lincoln and the Immigrant Vote: A Case of Religious Polarization," *Mid-America*, vol. 48 (July 1966), pp. 176–195, an analysis of Protestant-Catholic cleavages within the German and Irish communities of Pittsburgh. Phyllis Field of Cornell University is currently completing a doctoral dissertation analyzing the black suffrage referenda of 1846, 1860, and 1869 in New York State.

Frederick Luebke ably treats the political behavior of subgroups within the

German population of one state in *Immigrants and Politics: The Germans of Nebraska, 1880–1900* (Lincoln, 1969). Lee Benson places the presidential election of 1884 in historical perspective in "Research Problems in American Political Historiography," in *Common Frontiers of the Social Sciences*, ed. Mirra Komarovsky (Glencoe, 1957), pp. 155–171. Roger E. Wyman, "Wisconsin Ethnic Groups and the Election of 1890," *Wisconsin Magazine of History*, vol. 51 (Summer 1968), pp. 269–294, is substantively and methodologically important.

Recent quantitative analyses of the popular bases of the People's party include: Stanley B. Parsons, Jr., "Who Were the Nebraska Populists?" *Nebraska History*, vol. 44 (June 1963), pp. 83–99; Walter T. K. Nugent, "Some Parameters of Populism," *Agricultural History*, vol. 40 (October 1966), pp. 255–270; Sheldon Hackney, *Populism to Progressivism in Alabama* (Princeton, 1969); Michael P. Rogin and John L. Shover, *Political Change in California: Critical Elections and Social Movements, 1890–1966* (Westport, Conn., 1970), chap. i; and Michael P. Rogin, *The Intellectuals and McCarthy: The Radical Specter* (Cambridge, Mass., 1967). Stanley Parsons's extended study of the Nebraska Populists is forthcoming.

In addition to the full-length studies by Richard Jensen, Paul Kleppner, and Samuel McSeveney cited in notes in Part Three, the following essays deal with the political realignment of the 1890s: V. O. Key, Jr., "A Theory of Critical Elections," *Journal of Politics*, vol. 17 (February 1955), pp. 3–18; Duncan MacRae, Jr., and James A. Meldrum, "Critical Elections in Illinois, 1888–1958," *American Political Science Review*, vol. 54 (September 1960), pp. 669–683; Walter Dean Burnham, *Critical Elections and the Mainsprings of American Politics* (New York, 1970), chaps. iii, iv; Michael Rogin and John Shover, *Political Change in California: Critical Elections and Social Movements, 1890–1966* (Westport, Conn., 1970) chap. i; and Elmer E. Cornwell, Jr., "A Note on Providence Politics in the Age of Bryan," *Rhode Island History*, vol. 19 (April 1960), pp. 33–40.

Part Four

Among studies treating popular voting behavior over extended periods of the twentieth century are two by the late V. O. Key, Jr.: *Southern Politics in State and Nation* (New York, 1949); and "Secular Realignment and the Party System," *Journal of Politics*, vol. 21 (May 1959), pp. 198–210. Also see Walter Dean Burnham, *Critical Elections and the Mainsprings of American Politics* (New York, 1970); Perry H. Howard, *Political Tendencies in Louisiana* (Baton Rouge, rev. ed., 1970); Michael P. Rogin and John L. Shover, *Political Change in California: Critical Elections and Social Movements, 1890–1966* (Westport, Conn., 1970); and Michael P. Rogin, *The Intellectuals and McCarthy: The Radical Specter* (Cambridge, Mass., 1967), whose quantitative focus is on North Dakota, South Dakota, and Wisconsin.

Sheldon Hackney, *Populism to Progressivism in Alabama* (Princeton, 1969); Michael P. Rogin, "Progressivism and the California Electorate," *Journal of American History*, vol. 55 (September 1968), pp. 297–314; and Melvyn Dubofsky, "Success and Failure of Socialism in New York City, 1900–1918: A Case Study," *Labor History*, vol. 9 (Fall 1968), pp. 361–375, are among the limited number of studies that deal with popular voting behavior during the first two decades of the twentieth century. See, too, the works covering broader periods cited above.

On the 1920s, David Burner, *The Politics of Provincialism: The Democratic Party in Transition, 1918–1932* (New York, 1968); J. Joseph Huthmacher, *Massachusetts People and Politics, 1919–1933* (Cambridge, Mass., 1959); and John Allswang, *A House for All Peoples: Ethnic Politics in Chicago, 1890–1936* (Lexington, Ky., 1971) are important.

The presidential election of 1928 has received more attention from political scientists and historians than any other national contest during the present century. Studies that place the election in historical perspective include: V. O. Key, Jr., "A Theory of Critical Elections," *Journal of Politics*, vol. 17 (February 1955), pp. 3–18; Duncan MacRae, Jr., and James A. Meldrum, "Critical Elections in Illinois, 1888–1958," *American Political Science Review*, vol. 54 (September 1960), pp. 669–683; John Shover, "Was 1928 a Critical Election in California?" *Pacific Northwest Quarterly*, vol. 58 (October 1967), pp. 196–204; and Ruth C. Silva, *Rum, Religion, and Votes: 1928 Re-Examined* (University Park, Pa., 1962).

Part Five

The works by V. O. Key, Walter Dean Burnham, Perry Howard, Michael Rogin, and John Shover cited in Part Four cover American popular voting behavior since 1932. V. O. Key, Jr.'s posthumously-published *The Responsible Electorate: Rationality in Presidential Voting, 1936–1960* (Cambridge, Mass., 1966) emphasizes voters' issue-awareness in explaining political shifts during the period. Samuel Lubell utilizes selected election data to interpret the New Deal and post–New Deal eras in *The Future of American Politics* (New York, 3rd ed., 1965); and (less successfully) *Revolt of the Moderates* (New York, 1956).

On the New Deal period, see John Allswang, *A House for All Peoples: Ethnic Politics in Chicago, 1890–1936* (Lexington, Ky., 1971); and Bruce M. Stave, *The New Deal and the Last Hurrah: Pittsburgh Machine Politics* (Pittsburgh, 1970). Arthur Mann deals with the ethnocultural and socioeconomic dimensions of a municipal reform election in New York City in *La Guardia Comes to Power: 1933* (Philadelphia and New York, 1965). Samuel T. McSeveney, "The Michigan Gubernatorial Campaign of 1938," *Michigan History*, vol. 45 (June 1961), pp. 97–127, analyzes the reversal of Democratic fortunes during the late 1930s. Howard W. Allen, "Isolationism and German–Americans," *Journal of the Illinois State Historical Society*, vol. 57 (Summer 1964), pp. 143–149, covers 1932–1960 in Hamilton County, Illinois.

Paul Lazarsfeld, Bernard Berelson, and Hazel Gaudet pioneered the survey study of popular voting behavior in *The People's Choice* (New York, 1944), a work on Erie County, Pennsylvania, in the presidential election of 1940. Berelson, Lazarsfeld, and William N. McPhee, *Voting: A Study of Opinion Formation in a Presidential Campaign* (Chicago, 1954), deals with Elmira, N.Y., in 1948. Important studies by the Survey Research Center of the University of Michigan include: Angus Campbell and Robert L. Kahn, *The People Elect a President* (Ann Arbor, 1952), on 1948; Campbell, Gerald Gurin, and Warren E. Miller, *The Voter Decides* (Chicago, 1954), on 1952; and the two seminal books by Campbell, Philip E. Converse, Miller, and Donald E. Stokes, *The American Voter* (New York, 1960); and *Elections and the Political Order* (New York, 1966), which carry their analysis into the 1960s. Also see V. O. Key, Jr., "Interpreting the Election Results," in *The Presidential Election and Transition, 1960–1961,* ed. Paul T. David (Washington, D.C., 1961), pp. 150–175; and Angus Campbell, "Interpreting the Presidential Victory," in *The National Election of 1964,* ed. Milton Cummings (Washington, D.C., 1966), pp. 256–281. Michael Rogin analyzes the sources of popular support for Senator Joseph McCarthy and Governor George Wallace (in the 1964 Democratic presidential primary) in Wisconsin in *The Intellectuals and McCarthy: The Radical Specter* (Cambridge, Mass., 1967), chapter 3; and "Wallace and the Middle Class: The White Backlash in Wisconsin," *Public Opinion Quarterly,* vol. 30 (Spring 1966), pp. 98–108.

Among studies that base opinions regarding the likely shape of American politics during the 1970s on a reading of American politics over the recent past, see in particular, Richard M. Scammon and Ben J. Wattenberg, *The Real Majority* (New York, 1970); Kevin Phillips, *The Emerging Republican Majority* (New Rochelle, 1969); and Walter Dean Burnham, "The End of American Party Politics," *Trans-action,* vol. 7 (December 1969), pp. 12–22.

A B C D E F G H I J   9 8 7 6 5 4 3 2